FOR THE
IB DIPL
PROGRA

Computer Science

Paul Baumgarten
Ioana Ganea
Carl Turland

hachette
LEARNING

To order, please visit www.HachetteLearning.com or contact Customer Service at education@hachette.co.uk / +44 (0)1235 827827.

ISBN: 978 1 0360 0900 7

© Paul Baumgarten, Ioana Ganea, Carl Turland 2025

First published in 2025 by Hachette Learning,
An Hachette UK Company
Carmelite House
50 Victoria Embankment
London EC4Y 0DZ

www.HachetteLearning.com

Impression number   10 9 8 7 6 5 4 3 2 1

Year   2029 2028 2027 2026 2025

Cover photo © sdecoret - stock.adobe.com

Typeset in ITC Berkeley Oldstyle Std 10/14pt by DC Graphic Design Limited, Hextable, Kent

Printed and Bound in Great Britain by Bell & Bain Ltd, Glasgow

A catalogue record for this title is available from the British Library.

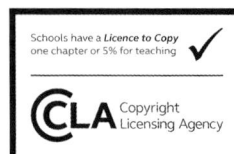

MIX
Paper | Supporting responsible forestry
FSC
www.fsc.org   FSC™ C104740

Schools have a *Licence to Copy* one chapter or 5% for teaching ✓
CLA Copyright Licensing Agency

Contents

Introduction v

How to use this book vi

About the authors viii

A CONCEPTS OF COMPUTER SCIENCE 1

A1 Computer fundamentals 1
    A1.1 Computer hardware and operation 2
    A1.2 Data representation and computer logic 24
    A1.3 Operating systems and control systems 67
    A1.4 Translation 103

A2 Networks 111
    A2.1 Network fundamentals 112
    A2.2 Network architecture 127
    A2.3 Data transmissions 136
    A2.4 Network security 144

A3 Databases 167
    A3.1 Database fundamentals 168
    A3.2 Database design 174
    A3.3 Database programming 186
    A3.4 Alternative databases and data warehouses 195

A4 Machine learning 205
    A4.1 Machine learning fundamentals 206
    A4.2 Data preprocessing 215
    A4.3 Machine learning approaches 223
    A4.4 Ethical considerations 274

B COMPUTATIONAL THINKING AND PROBLEM SOLVING 281

B1 Computational thinking 281
   B1.1 Approaches to computational thinking 282

B2 Programming 295
   B2.1 Programming fundamentals (part 1) 296
   B2.3 Programming constructs 311
   B2.1 Programming fundamentals (part 2) 333
   B2.2 Data structures 342
   B2.4 Programming algorithms 358
   B2.5 File processing 378

B3 Object-oriented programming (OOP) 393
   B3.1 Fundamentals of OOP for a single class 394
   B3.2 Fundamentals of OOP for multiple classes 417

B4 Abstract data types (ADTs) 453
   B4.1 Fundamentals of abstract data types 454

CASE STUDY 481

INTERNAL ASSESSMENT 493

Acknowledgements 537

Glossary 538

Index 547

Introduction

Welcome to *Computer Science for the IB Diploma*, written to meet the criteria of the new *International Baccalaureate (IB) Diploma Programme Computer science guide* (published 2025, first exams May 2027). This text addresses the full scope of the syllabus, both the Standard Level and Higher Level components, and caters for both the Python and Java programming language options.

It has been said that computer science is a modern-day superpower, and rightly so. It has a profound impact on society and has driven much of the transformational change we have experienced in recent years. It has advanced fields as diverse as agriculture, finance, manufacturing, health and medicine, transportation, education and global communications. Contemporary living has been forever altered thanks to changes enabled by advances in computing. This impact will only continue to grow exponentially in the years ahead, and the opportunities are limited only by your imagination.

We hope you are excited about the journey ahead and ready to embrace the challenges and opportunities it brings!

The "In collaboration with IB" logo signifies that the content of this book has been reviewed by the IB to ensure it fully aligns with the current IB curriculum and offers high-quality guidance and support for IB teaching and learning.

How to use this book

The following features of this book will help you consolidate and develop your understanding of Computer Science, through concept-based learning:

These are key prompts from the IBDP Computer science guide that frame each section with the purpose of promoting inquiry.

SYLLABUS CONTENT

▶ This coursebook follows the order of the contents of the IB Computer Science Diploma syllabus, with two exceptions.
  ▷ B2.3 is inserted between B2.1 part 1 and B2.1 part 2. This allows us to introduce the programming fundamentals of selection, loops and functions before B2.2, which introduces data structures. B2.2 would have been far more theoretical and abstract if we sought to introduce data structures prior to concepts such as if-statements and loops.
  ▷ B3.1.3 appears after B3.1.5. This allows us to introduce the idea of static methods and properties after learning how to write code that implements objects.
  In both cases, we felt a small reordering created a better flow and provided for a more practical teaching and learning sequence. The alternative would have resulted in attempting to teach programming ideas before introducing the concepts on which they depend.
▶ At the beginning of each chapter is a list of the content to be covered, with all subsections clearly linked to the content statements, and showing the breadth and depth of understanding required.

Key information

These boxes highlight essential knowledge needed for the examination.

◆ Definitions appear throughout in the margin to provide context and help you understand the language of Computer Science. There is also a glossary of all the key terms at the end of the book.

ACTIVITY

Approaches to learning (ATL), including learning through inquiry, are integral to IB pedagogy. These activities are designed to get you to think about real-world applications of Computer Science.

Common mistake

These boxes detail some common misunderstandings and typical errors made by students, so that you can avoid making the same mistakes yourself.

Top tip!

This feature includes advice relating to the content being discussed and tips to help you retain the knowledge you need. These boxes also include advice on how to approach various common programming scenarios – whether in programming code or in written form, such as in the exams.

TOK

Links to Theory of Knowledge allow you to develop your critical-thinking skills and deepen your understanding of Computer Science by bringing in discussions about the subject beyond the scope of the content of the curriculum.

● Linking questions

Each section has a set of linking questions that connect to other parts of the syllabus or TOK. They are designed to facilitate connections and promote conceptual understanding. The list in this coursebook is not exhaustive; you may encounter other connections between concepts, leading you to create your own linking questions.

REVIEW QUESTIONS

Self-assessment questions appear throughout the chapters, phrased to assist comprehension and recall.

PROGRAMMING EXERCISES

Programming exercises appear at the end of chapters. Their purpose is to provide practical, hands-on experience in applying the concepts and principles of Computer Science to a programmed solution. Being able to solve exercises so they work on the computer will be essential to gaining the confidence needed to solve similar problems in exam settings, when you only have paper and pen to work with.

Finally, these programming exercises will help build your expertise for the internal assessment.

Sample answers to the programming exercises in Sections B2 and B3 can be found at www.hachettelearning.com/answers-and-extras

EXAM PRACTICE QUESTIONS

Author-written exam-style questions appear at the end of each section. These simulate scenario-based questions of the breadth and depth that can be anticipated in your examinations. They are intended to serve as a revision and preparation tool to assist you in identifying areas of strength and weakness, as well as to refine your problem-solving skills.

It is recommended that you use these practice questions under exam conditions to make the most of them. Each question has a marks allocation, which also approximates the number of minutes it should take for you to complete. Once you have completed a batch, check the answers while the material is fresh (answers can be found at www.hachettelearning.com/answers-and-extras). Create a log of recurring mistakes for you to review and practise further.

For the programming questions, do make sure you take the time to practise hand-writing your responses. Typing code on the computer is very different from hand-writing it, so you want to have plenty of practice at hand-writing code before your IB examinations. Pay particular attention to consistency of spelling; use of upper and lowercase; and clear lines of indentation.

International mindedness is indicated by this icon. It explores how the exchange of information and ideas across national boundaries has been essential to the progress of Computer Science and illustrates the international aspects of the subject.

The IB learner profile icon indicates material that is particularly useful to help you towards developing the following attributes: to be inquirers, knowledgeable, thinkers, communicators, principled, open-minded, caring, risk-takers, balanced and reflective. When you see the icon, think about what learner profile attribute you might be demonstrating – it could be more than one.

About the authors

Paul Baumgarten

Paul is a Computer Science teacher who has had a life-long fascination with all things geeky. He started tinkering with electronics at age 8 and has been programming since 13, when he taught himself BASIC. Holding a BSc (Computer Science) from Edith Cowan University and a Graduate Diploma in Education from University of Western Australia, he has been teaching Computing since 2006. He moved to Switzerland in 2015, where he began teaching the International Baccalaureate Diploma programme, and is currently teaching in Hong Kong. Passionate about promoting diversity in the tech field, he is committed to increasing representation of women and minorities in Computer Science, believing that societal advances through technology are only truly possible when the contributions and perspectives of everyone are included. Beyond teaching, he is an avid science-fiction reader and enthusiast, particularly relating to space and time travel. He is also the founder of CodingQuest.io, an annual online programming competition for secondary Computer Science students globally.

Ioana Ganea

Ioana Ganea is an experienced educator, having taught Computer Science for over 15 years in different international environments, such as Romania, Germany, the United Kingdom, Egypt and Luxembourg. Her passion for Computer Science started at the age of 11 when her father purchased her very first device and encouraged her to explore both hardware and software concepts without thinking that something can go wrong, as a computer can always be replaced. She graduated from the Academy of Economic Studies in Bucharest, Romania, with a bachelor's degree in Economic Cybernetics, Statistics and Informatics, specializing in Economic Informatics, and she obtained a master's degree in Civil Engineering from the Technical University of Civil Engineering of Bucharest (Computer Assisted Technologies – Department of Teacher Training). She is an experienced examiner, moderator and team leader for various exam boards, and she has collaborated with Oxford Study Courses, offering Computer Science revision courses for IB DP Computer Science, both Standard Level and Higher Level. As an educator, she strives to raise each student's potential and encourage them to believe in themselves. She enjoys teaching students to apply their knowledge, so they can face the challenges of life with confidence, integrity, compassion, creativity and love of peace.

Carl Turland

Originally from Chessington in the United Kingdom, Carl has spent much of his career abroad, teaching in Indonesia, Thailand and Switzerland. He began his professional journey as a programmer for Sky Television in the UK, and now serves as the Head of Design and Computer Science at the International School of Lausanne. Carl holds an HND in Computer Science from Nottingham Trent University, and earned a BA (Hons) in Information Communication Technology with QTS from Brighton University. He was one of the pioneering teachers of the reintroduced Computer Science curriculum in the UK in 2016 and, during that time, helped establish his school as a UK lead in the subject, while contributing to the Compute-IT series (Hodder Education). He later moved abroad to help establish Computer Science programmes at several schools, before joining the International School of Lausanne, where he is now in his sixth year. Carl continues to innovate within the curriculum, expanding into robotics. Outside of the classroom, he is passionate about running, travelling, spending quality time with his wife and young daughter, and cheering on his beloved Crystal Palace football team from the comfort of his sofa.

A1 Computer fundamentals

Computer hardware and operation

What principles underpin the operation of a computer, from low-level hardware functionality to operating systems' interaction?

SYLLABUS CONTENT

By the end of this chapter, you should be able to:
▶ A1.1.1 Describe the function and interaction of the main central processing unit (CPU) components
▶ A1.1.2 Describe the role of a graphics processing unit (GPU)
▶ A1.1.3 Explain the difference between the CPU and the GPU (HL)
▶ A1.1.4 Explain the purposes of different primary memory types
▶ A1.1.5 Describe the fetch, decode and execute cycle
▶ A1.1.6 Describe the process of pipelining in multi-core architectures (HL)
▶ A1.1.7 Describe the internal and external types of secondary memory storage
▶ A1.1.8 Describe the concept of compression
▶ A1.1.9 Describe the different types of services in cloud implementation

A1.1.1 Function and interaction of the main central processing unit components

■ A central processing unit (CPU) from above and underneath

■ What is the central processing unit?

The central processing unit (CPU) is often referred to as the "brain" of the computer. It is a critical component that carries out the majority of the processing inside a device.

The CPU is made up of two main units: the control unit (CU) and the arithmetic logic unit (ALU).

Control unit (CU)

The control unit directs the operations of the processor. It is responsible for the fetch–decode–execute cycle, managing all three operations and directing the computer's memory, ALU and input/output devices to respond appropriately.

Arithmetic logic lnit (ALU)

This unit is responsible for performing arithmetic and logic operations. These include basic arithmetic operations such as addition, subtraction, multiplication and division, as well as logic operations including AND, OR, XOR and NOT.

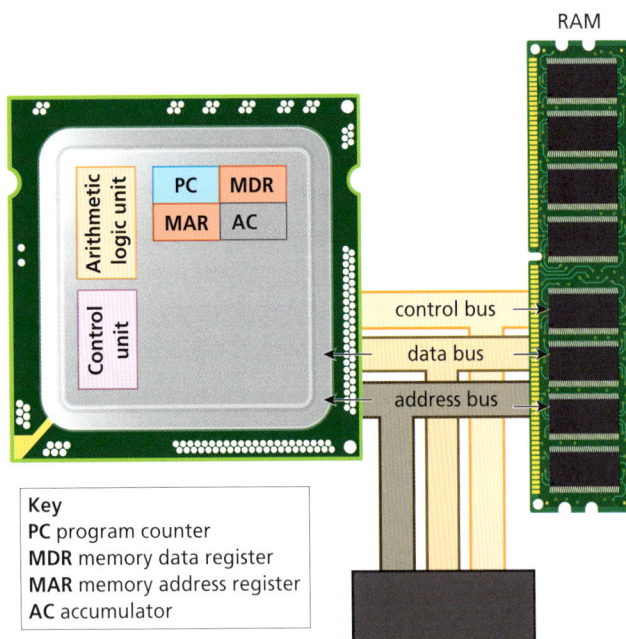

Key
PC program counter
MDR memory data register
MAR memory address register
AC accumulator

■ A model of the CPU

■ What are registers?

Registers are very small amounts of storage that are available directly on the CPU to hold temporary data that the CPU may be working on. The registers are instruction register (IR), program counter (PC), memory address register (MAR), memory data register (MDR) and accumulator (AC).

Instruction register

When an instruction is fetched from memory, it is held in the IR within the CPU. This register holds the instruction that is currently being executed by the CPU.

Program counter

The PC holds the address of the next instruction that is to be fetched from memory. Once the instruction has been fetched, the PC updates to point to the next instruction that will be needed.

Memory address register

The MAR holds the memory address that is currently being fetched. The content from the PC is copied to the MAR, and the MAR provides this address to the memory unit, so that data and instructions can be read from or copied to that location.

Memory data register

This holds the data that has been fetched or is about to be written to the memory address currently in the MAR.

Accumulator (AC)

This stores the intermediate arithmetic or logical results produced by the ALU.

■ What are buses?

Buses are a critical component of the computer system, as they transfer data between various devices, including the CPU, memory, storage and peripherals. Buses have *widths* that are measured in bits. The bigger the width of the bus, the more data it can transmit at one time. There are three main types of buses: control bus, data bus and address bus.

Control bus

The control bus is used to transmit command and control signals from the CPU to other components of the system, and vice versa. Due to the need for signals to be sent and received, this bus is **bidirectional**. Some of the signals that would be transmitted via the control bus are read / write operations, interrupt requests, clock signals for synchronization and status signals from hardware components.

◆ **Bidirectional bus:** a bus that can transfer data in both directions.

Data bus

The data bus carries the data being processed between the CPU, memory and other peripherals. The width of the data bus is important for determining the amount of data it can transfer at one time. Common data bus widths are 8, 16, 32 and 64 bits. As data needs to be read from and written to memory, data buses are usually bidirectional.

Address bus

The address bus is used to transmit the address that is to be read from or written to in memory. The width of this bus determines the memory capacity of the system. For example, a 32-bit address bus can address 2^{32} memory locations.

■ What are cores?

CPUs come in a number of different configurations. These include single-core processors, multi-core processors and co-processors.

Single-core processors

This CPU has a single processing unit, meaning it can only handle one task at a time. These are more often found in low-end computers or older machines. They are adequate for simple tasks that do not require heavy multitasking. Single-core processors are able to run more than a single application at a time, but the CPU has to be shared between these applications, which can impact performance.

Multi-core processors

A CPU with multi-core processors has two or more cores that can run multiple instructions simultaneously. These are often referred to as dual-core (two processors), quad-core (four processors), hexa-core (six) or octa-core (eight). Their performance is significantly faster than single-core processors and they are ideal for multitasking, gaming and servers. However, software has to be written to take advantage of these extra cores. Older software that does not do this would likely run at a similar speed as on a single-core processor.

Co-processors

A co-processor is a special type of processor that has a specific job to support the main CPU. These are built with a distinct purpose to achieve optimal performance compared to a general-purpose CPU. Tasks are offloaded by the CPU to the co-processor so they can run in parallel, enhancing the system's performance. Examples of co-processors are graphics processing units (covered in Section A1.1.2), audio processors and digital signal processors (DSPs), which are used in telecommunications and image compression.

●Common mistake

A common mistake is thinking that adding more cores to a CPU always makes it faster in a straightforward way – like assuming a dual-core CPU is twice as fast as a single-core, or a quad-core is four times faster. This isn't always true, because the speed increase depends on how well the software can use multiple cores at the same time. Many programs aren't designed to take full advantage of multiple cores, so the extra cores may not make a noticeable difference. Other factors, such as memory speed and how the CPU is designed, also affect how fast it can run. So, just having more cores doesn't automatically mean much faster processing.

REVIEW QUESTIONS

1 What is the primary function of the arithmetic logic unit (ALU) in a computer's CPU?
2 How does the control unit (CU) direct the operations of the CPU?
3 Why is the program counter (PC) important for executing a sequence of instructions?
4 What roles do the data bus and address bus play in the functioning of the CPU?
5 How does the memory address register (MAR) work in conjunction with other CPU components to access memory?
6 How do multi-core processors differ from single-core processors in handling tasks?

A1 Computer fundamentals

A1.1.2 Role of a graphics processing unit

A graphics processing unit (GPU) is a specialized electronic circuit designed to accelerate the rendering of images, videos and animations by performing rapid mathematical calculations. Initially developed to handle the demanding graphics workloads of video games and visual applications, GPUs have evolved to play a crucial role in various fields beyond graphics rendering. Their structure, consisting of thousands of small, efficient cores, allows them to process multiple tasks simultaneously, making them exceptionally well-suited for computationally intensive applications. This capability has led to their widespread adoption in scientific research, machine learning, artificial intelligence and cryptocurrency mining. By offloading these intensive tasks from the CPU, GPUs enhance overall system performance, enabling faster and more efficient data processing and visualization.

■ A graphics processing unit (GPU)

■ Graphics processing

■ Video game graphics

GPUs are designed with a highly parallel structure, enabling them to perform many calculations simultaneously. This makes them exceptionally well-suited for rendering the complex and resource-intensive graphics seen in modern video games and applications. They also handle the application of **shaders and textures** to 3D models, which includes lighting, shading and texture mapping, enhancing the realism of the scene.

■ Video processing

GPUs assist in the decoding and encoding of video files, making processes such as playback, streaming and editing more efficient and faster. This is particularly helpful for those working with high-resolution video files of 4k or higher.

■ Artificial intelligence and machine learning

GPUs were originally created for graphical processing; however, in the early 2000s, researchers and engineers began to recognize their potential for handling general-purpose calculations, including those required for machine learning and AI. The shift towards using GPUs for this was largely due to their ability to perform many simple calculations simultaneously, and because many GPUs can be run in **parallel**. Many AI models rely heavily on **matrix and vector multiplications**, and GPUs far outperform a CPU when trying to process these quickly.

◆ **Shaders and textures:** techniques used in 3D rendering to apply effects, lighting and details to models.

◆ **Parallel processing:** the ability of the GPU to perform many calculations simultaneously due to its highly parallel structure.

◆ **Matrix and vector multiplications:** fundamental operations in machine learning and graphics that involve complex mathematical calculations.

◆ **Deep learning:**
a subset of machine learning that uses an artificial neural network to imitate the design of the human brain to find generalizations in complex data that can be used for decision-making.

◆ **Proof of work:** a consensus mechanism requiring cryptominers to solve complex problems to add a new block to the blockchain.

This realization gained momentum as machine learning models, especially **deep learning** models, became more complex and required significant computational power for training. By the mid-2000s, GPUs had become essential tools in the field of AI and machine learning, transforming how data scientists and researchers approached problems, significantly reducing the time it took to train complex models.

■ Blockchain and cryptocurrency mining

■ The cryptocurrency boom – at its peak in November 2021, the total market capitalization of cryptocurrencies reached approximately $3 trillion

In 2010, the use of GPUs for Bitcoin mining surged as miners discovered that GPUs significantly outperformed CPUs in solving cryptographic puzzles, such as finding the nonce in the hashing algorithm for the **proof-of-work** system. This realization led to a dramatic shift towards GPU mining. The cryptocurrency boom between 2017 and 2021 further escalated the demand for GPUs, resulting in skyrocketing prices and global shortages.

As of 2023, this demand had reduced somewhat and prices of GPUs were becoming more stable. This was for a number of reasons:

■ The volatility and reduced profitability of cryptocurrency mining had led to less demand for GPUs, specifically for mining purposes.

■ Big manufacturers had increased production to meet the demands.

■ Application-Specific Integrated Circuits (ASICs), which are specifically designed for mining, had largely replaced the use of GPUs in many mining operations.

REVIEW QUESTIONS

1 What is the role of a graphics processing unit (GPU) in a computer?
2 How do GPUs enhance the performance of video games and video processing tasks?
3 Why have GPUs become essential in fields such as artificial intelligence, machine learning and cryptocurrency mining?

A1.1.3 Differences between the CPU and the GPU (HL)

The central processing unit (CPU) and the graphical processing unit (GPU) are both core components of modern computers. They are designed differently, which is why they are used for different kinds of tasks. The CPU is great for handling various jobs, but the GPU is better for doing the same job many times on a lot of data at once.

A1 Computer fundamentals

■ Design philosophies

CPUs are generally called "general-purpose processors" because they can handle many types of tasks. They are designed to run the operating system, process user input and manage programs. CPUs are good at tasks where decisions need to be made quickly, and where different types of work are being done at the same time.

GPUs are specialized processors because they focus on specific types of tasks. They are made for processing large amounts of data in parallel. This means they can work on many calculations at the same time. For example, GPUs are used to process images and videos because they can work on thousands of pixels at once.

■ Core architecture

The CPU has only a few cores, but these cores are very powerful. Each core can handle many different instructions, but it works best when doing one task at a time. This makes the CPU very good for such tasks as running the operating system, where quick responses are needed. CPUs also have features including branch prediction (where the CPU tries to guess what will happen next) and out-of-order execution (where the CPU can work on tasks that are ready before others).

The GPU has many smaller cores. These cores are not as powerful as the CPU cores, but there are thousands of them, and they all work at the same time. This is why the GPU is very good for tasks such as rendering 3D images, where many similar calculations need to happen at once. The GPU's architecture is designed to work on large sets of data all at the same time.

■ Memory access and power efficiency

The CPU and GPU access memory differently. The CPU uses a smaller, high-speed memory cache to get data quickly. This is useful when the CPU needs to access small amounts of data many times, such as when running programs or handling user inputs.

The GPU uses its own special memory called VRAM (video RAM). VRAM has a very high bandwidth, meaning it can move large amounts of data at once, such as images and videos. However, the GPU uses more power because it must process a lot of data at the same time, especially when rendering videos or running complex simulations.

■ Comparison of central processing units (CPUs) and graphics processing units (GPUs)

Processor	Processing	Architecture	Functionality
CPU	It is a **general** purpose processor, capable of handling many different tasks. It executes the instructions of computer programs, involving operations such as arithmetic, logic and controlling input / output (I/O) operations, as directed by the operating system.	CPUs generally have fewer cores. General user devices tend to have between 4 and 8 cores; however, there are some advanced CPUs that now have 64 cores or more. Each core is very versatile, making it capable of handling complex computations that require sequential processing.	Allows the user to switch between multiple tasks and applications. This makes it ideal for running the operating system and general software applications.
GPU	It is a **specialized** processor, with a focus on handling graphics, **rendering** images, video and animations.	Composed of hundreds or thousands of small cores that are well-suited for tasks that can be run in parallel. While each core is not as powerful as a standard CPU core, the high number of cores allows them to perform a large number of calculations simultaneously, making them perfect for graphical processing.	Suited for tasks that require simultaneous processing of large blocks of data, such as rendering images, video processing and deep learning applications.

◆ **Rendering:** the process of generating an image from a model by means of computer programs.

Key information

To summarize, CPUs are better for tasks that require high-speed, complex decision-making and versatility. GPUs are better when the same operation needs to be performed on many data points simultaneously. This means that for tasks such as gaming, video editing and computational research (AI and machine learning), GPUs often significantly outperform CPUs.

■ How the CPU and GPU work together to increase video-game performance

When playing video games, the CPU and GPU work together to deliver a seamless and immersive experience. The CPU handles the game's core logic, including rules, physical calculations and AI behaviour. It processes the inputs from the player (processing the outcomes of their actions and updating the game state accordingly). The GPU's primary role is to render the game's visuals. It processes **vertex and pixel data** to draw images on to the screen, including 3D objects, textures and effects such as lighting and shadows.

◆ **Vertex and pixel data:** data used by the GPU to render 3D objects and images.

◆ **Frame:** a single image in a sequence of images that makes up a video or animation.

PROGRAMMING EXERCISE

Run benchmark software on your device to see your overall system performance. There are many options out there that you can search for; **https://novabench.com** and **www.userbenchmark.com** have free versions.

Typical scenario

1 **Player input:** The player presses a key to move a character. The CPU processes this input, updates the character's position based on game physics and determines the new game state.
2 **Data preparation:** The CPU prepares the new position and state data and sends it to the GPU.
3 **Rendering:** The GPU updates the **frame** with the character's new position, applies lighting and shading and renders the scene.
4 **Display:** The rendered frame is displayed on the screen, providing immediate feedback to the player.

REVIEW QUESTIONS

1 How do the CPU and GPU work together to enhance video-game performance?
2 Why is a GPU better suited than a CPU for tasks such as video rendering or AI computations?
3 What are shaders and textures, and how do they contribute to the rendering process handled by the GPU?

A1.1.4 Purposes of different primary memory types

■ Memory types

The primary memory of the computer stores data and instructions that the CPU needs in order to process tasks. Primary memory includes several different types: RAM (random access memory), ROM (read-only memory), caches and registers (covered in Section A1.1.1). These are all types of primary memory, meaning they are used directly by the CPU.

A1 Computer fundamentals

■ Sticks of random access memory (RAM)

■ Read-only memory (ROM) attached to a motherboard

◆ **Volatile:** a type of memory or storage that loses its data when the power is turned off.

RAM

RAM (random access memory) holds instructions and data for programs that are currently running. For example, when you open an app on your phone or computer, it loads into RAM so that is can be accessed quickly by the CPU.

RAM is **volatile**, meaning that it loses its contents when the power to the computer is turned off. This is why, when playing a game, you lose your progress unless you save the game (which is then stored in secondary memory).

One real-world example of using RAM is in smartphones, which use RAM to switch quickly between apps. When you leave an app, it stays in the RAM, so you can return to it quickly without reloading it from scratch.

ROM

ROM (read-only memory) is used for storing instructions that are very rarely modified. ROM is used for the BIOS (basic input / output system) of the computer, which is located on the motherboard. The BIOS' main role is to initialize and test the system hardware components on startup, and to load the operating system (OS) software from the secondary memory storage into the RAM, ready for the CPU to fetch, decode and execute the instructions.

ROM is non-volatile memory, meaning it does not lose its contents when the computer does not have power. While ROM is "read only", meaning it cannot easily change its data, most modern computers use flash memory, which allows for updates and reprogramming. This allows motherboard companies to update their software when required.

A real-world example of using ROM is in smartphones, where ROM stores the operating system and core applications, which do not change unless you perform an update. This ensures that your phone can boot up reliably every time.

Cache (L1, L2 and L3)

| CPU | Cache memory | Main memory | Secondary memory |

■ The order a CPU goes through when trying to retrieve data

Cache memory is small, but provides high-speed access to the CPU compared to the RAM. It acts as a buffer between the CPU and the slower RAM, storing frequently used data and instructions.

There are three types of cache: L1, L2 and L3, each with different sizes and speeds. The closer to the CPU, the faster it is.

- **L1 cache** is located directly on the CPU, making it the fastest type of cache. It can be accessed almost instantly due to its location. However, it is also the smallest, often only a few kilobytes in size (32KB to 128KB per core). Each CPU core usually has its own L1 cache, which is typically split into two sections: L1i to store instructions and L1d to store data.

- **L2 cache** can either be on the CPU, like L1, or situated very close to the CPU. L2 cache is larger than L1 and can be up to several megabytes in size (256KB to 2MB per core), providing more storage for frequently used instructions. It is faster than L3, but slightly slower than L1, though it still significantly speeds up processing by reducing the need to fetch data from the slower RAM.

- **L3 cache** is often located the furthest from the CPU chip. L3 cache may be shared on multiple-core CPUs, whereas L1 and L2 are usually exclusive to a single core. It is the largest of the three, and can be up to tens of megabytes in size (2MB to 64MB shared across all cores). It is the slowest of the three types of caches, but is still significantly faster than RAM.

The terms **cache hit** and **cache miss** are used to describe the efficiency of the CPU's cache memory when retrieving data. A cache hit is the ideal scenario, where the CPU requests data and it is found in the cache memory. A cache miss means it was not found, necessitating retrieval from the slower main memory (RAM) or even slower storage (SSD / HDD).

The percentage of hit rate determines the efficiency and effectiveness of the cache. A low percentage means the system would suffer more from latency, where the data has to be fetched from elsewhere, hindering performance speed. Systems with a larger cache size will generally perform better, as well as systems with more intelligent prefetching techniques that can predict which data will be needed soon and load it into cache ahead of time.

● Top tip!

Imagine an onion with its layers representing the levels of cache:
- **L1 cache** is the smallest and fastest, like the very centre of the onion, where everything is tightly packed and closest to the core of the CPU.
- **L2 cache** is slightly larger and slower, like the next layer out – still close to the centre, but not as quick to access as the very core.
- **L3 cache** is the largest and slowest, like the outer layers of the onion. It's still important, but it takes a bit longer to get to, just like how the CPU takes a bit more time to access data in L3 cache compared to L1 and L2.

Optimizing CPU performance with cache

The cache plays a critical role in ensuring that the CPU can access data as quickly as possible. When the CPU finds the searched-for data in the cache (a cache hit), the data can be processed very quickly. However, when there is a cache miss, the CPU has to look for the data in the slower memory, which causes a delay.

Imagine you are playing a video game on a computer. The CPU frequently checks the L1, L2 and L3 cache to find the data it needs to run the game smoothly. The game's core functions, such as player controls and game logic, might be stored in the L1 cache, while the less frequently accessed data, such as background textures, may be in the L3 cache. The layering system helps to ensure that the game runs smoothly, without interruptions.

A CPU with a larger cache or more advanced prefetching (a technique where the CPU predicts what data it will need and loads it into cache ahead of time) has fewer cache misses and performs better overall.

A1.1.5 The fetch–decode–execute cycle

The fetch–decode–execute cycle, also known as the "instruction cycle", is the fundamental process that a CPU uses to execute instructions. The cycle consists of three main stages:

1   **Fetch:** The CPU fetches an instruction from the memory.
2   **Decode:** The CPU interprets the instruction and prepares the necessary operations to execute it.
3   **Execute:** The CPU performs the actions required by the instruction.

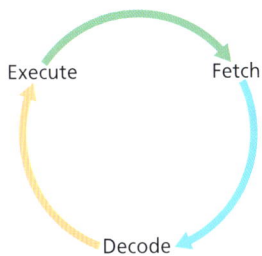

■ The fetch–decode–execute cycle

■ Little Man Computer

An easier way to see these stages carried out in more detail is to use an educational CPU model known as Little Man Computer, which you can search for online or use the one available here: **https://peterhigginson.co.uk/lmc**. This model uses assembly language – a simple set of instructions, each represented by three letters, which is stored as a three-digit code in the memory. The full set of instructions is:

Instruction	Code	Description
INP	901	Input a value and store it in the accumulator
OUT	902	Output the value from the accumulator
DAT	N/A	Used to define data values directly in memory at the point of declaration, often for constants or variables.
LDA	5XX	Load the value from the specified memory address into the accumulator
STA	3XX	Store the value in the accumulator at the specified memory address
ADD	1XX	Add the value from the specified memory address to the accumulator
SUB	2XX	Subtract the value from the specified memory address from the accumulator
HLT	000	Halt the program
BRA	6XX	Branch (jump) to the specified memory address
BRZ	7XX	Branch to the specified memory address if the accumulator is zero
BRP	8XX	Branch to the specified memory address if the accumulator is positive

Enter the following program into the left-hand column and assemble into RAM. You will see the three-digit representation for each instruction stored at a memory address on the right. For example, LDA 4 has been stored as 504 in memory address 0.

```
LDA 4
ADD 5
STA 5
HLT
DAT 23
DAT 12
```

Your LMC should look like this:

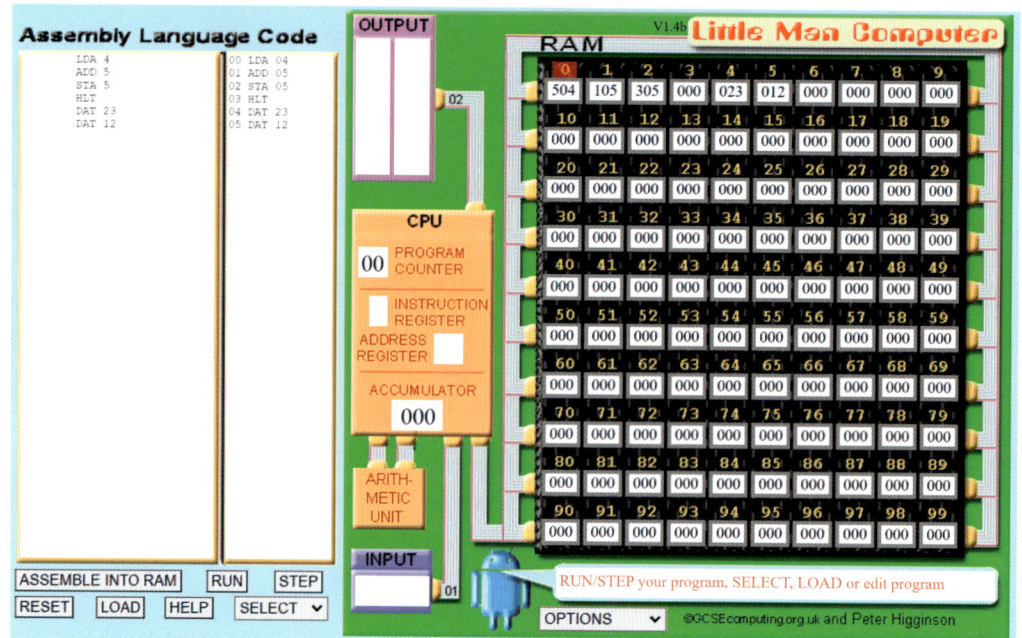

Assembly Language Code:
```
LDA 4        00 LDA 04
ADD 5        01 ADD 05
STA 5        02 STA 05
HLT          03 HLT
DAT 23       04 DAT 23
DAT 12       05 DAT 12
```

■ Peter Higginson's LMC model

First cycle

Click **step**.

1 **Fetch:** The PC (program counter) is currently set to 0, so the instruction at memory location 0 is fetched (504) by opening the 0 address in RAM using the address bus and fetching the instruction on the data bus. The control bus sends a read signal to initiate this process. 5 is stored in the instruction register and 04 in the address register.
   While this happens, you will see the PC gets incremented to 1 via the ALU, ready for the next instruction.

2 **Decode:** Once the instruction is fetched, the CPU decodes the instruction. The control unit uses the control bus to co-ordinate this process. The instruction stored in the instruction register is 5, which decodes as "load into the accumulator". The address register 04 indicates the address of the data to load.

3 **Execute:** The command is then carried out. Address 4 is opened on the address bus, and the control bus sends the appropriate signals to retrieve the data (23) from that location on the data bus and store it into the accumulator.

Second cycle

Click **step**.

1 **Fetch:** The CPU now uses the PC to know which instruction to fetch next: 1 is currently stored. Address 1 is opened, and the instruction 105 is fetched. The control bus sends a read signal to initiate this. 1 is stored in the instruction register and 05 in the address register.
   The PC is incremented to 2 by the ALU.

2 **Decode:** The instruction 1 is decoded as "add to accumulator"; the address register is the address of the data to add (5). The control unit uses the control bus to co-ordinate this.

3 **Execute:** Address 5 is opened, the data 12 is fetched and both the accumulator (currently 23) and the fetched data (12) are passed to the ALU. The result of 23 + 12 is stored in the accumulator (35).

Third cycle

Click **step**.

1 **Fetch:** The PC is currently 2, so the instruction at memory address 2 is fetched (305). The control bus sends a read signal to initiate this. 3 is stored in the instruction register, and 05 is stored in the address register.

   The PC is incremented to 3 via the ALU.

2 **Decode:** The instruction 3 decodes as "store accumulator to address" and the address register gives the location of where to store the data (05). The control unit uses the control bus to co-ordinate this.

3 **Execute:** Memory address 5 is opened via the address bus, and the control bus sends the appropriate signals to send the accumulator contents down the data bus and store them at address 5 (overwriting the current data).

Fourth cycle

Click **step**.

1 **Fetch:** The PC is currently 3, so the instruction at memory address 3 is fetched (000). The control bus sends a read signal to initiate this. 0 is stored in the instruction register, and 00 is stored in the address register.

   The PC is incremented to 4 via the ALU.

2 **Decode:** The instruction 0 decodes as "halt". The control unit uses the control bus to signal this operation.

3 **Execute:** The computer halts all operations and ends the program.

● Common mistake

A common mistake is assuming that the program counter (PC) gets updated after the execute stage of the fetch–decode–execute cycle. The PC is usually updated during or immediately after the fetch stage, so it points to the next instruction in memory before the current instruction is even decoded or executed. This ensures that the CPU always knows where to find the next instruction in the sequence.

PROGRAMMING EXERCISES

Write an LMC program to:

1 input two numbers, add them, and output the result

2 input a number and output whether it is positive or zero

3 calculate the sum of the first five natural numbers

4 input two numbers and output the larger one

5 input three numbers and output them in ascending order.

REVIEW QUESTIONS

1 What are the main steps in the fetch–decode–execute cycle, and why is this cycle fundamental to CPU operations?

2 How does the CPU use the address, data and control buses during the fetch–decode–execute cycle?

3 Why is the interaction between memory and registers crucial during the fetch phase of the CPU cycle?

A1.1.6 The process of pipelining in multi-core architectures (HL)

Pipelining is a powerful technique used in **multi-core architectures** to enhance CPU performance by overlapping the execution of multiple instructions. To understand this concept, imagine a carwash service that processes cars through several stages: initial wash, detailed cleaning, rinse and drying. Each stage takes five minutes.

■ A carwash team operating in parallel execution to get the job done faster

In a non-pipelined operation, each car must complete all stages before the next car begins:

Car								
A	initial wash	detailed cleaning	rinse	drying				
B					initial wash	detailed cleaning	rinse	drying

The total time it takes to process two cars is 5 × 8 = 40 minutes. So the time to clean one car is 40 / 2 = **20 minutes**.

The problem with this system is that, once car A has had the initial wash, that stage is then left idle, waiting for car A to complete, before car B enters. This is not efficient and, if we continue with this system, the only way we can improve the operation is to increase the speed of each stage.

It is the same situation with the performance of a CPU, where we are limited by the speed of the hardware, and improving this can be very expensive. Being more efficient with what we have is more beneficial.

In a pipelined solution, as soon as car A finishes a stage, car B enters that stage:

Car					
A	initial wash	detailed cleaning	rinse	drying	
B		initial wash	detailed cleaning	rinse	drying

The total time it takes to process two cars is 5 × 5 = 25 minutes. So the time to clean one car is 25 / 2 = **12.5 minutes**.

In this pipelined solution, rather than one stage sitting idle until the cycle is complete, the moment it is finished with car A, car B enters that stage.

■ Design of a basic pipeline

In a pipelined processor, the pipeline consists of multiple stages or segments situated between an input end and an output end. Each stage performs a specific operation, and the output of one stage becomes the input for the next. Intermediate outputs are held in interface registers, also known as "latches" or "buffers". All stages and interface registers are synchronized by a common clock, ensuring co-ordinated operation across the entire pipeline.

In the CPU, the fetch–decode–execute cycle is divided into distinct stages:

1 **Fetch:** The instruction is retrieved from memory.
2 **Decode:** The instruction is interpreted to understand the required operation.
3 **Execute:** The operation is carried out.
4 **Memory access:** Any necessary data is read from or written to memory.
5 **Write back:** The result is written back to the CPU register.

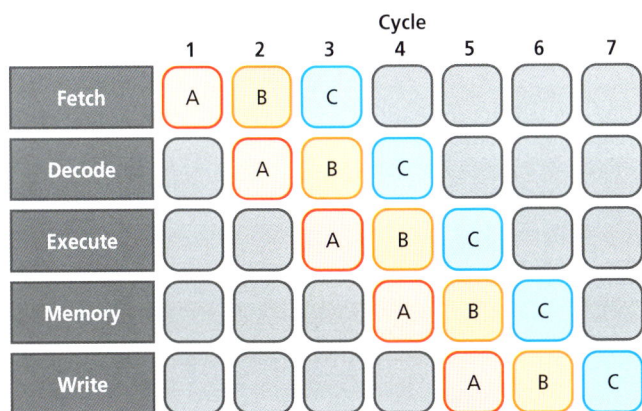
■ Example of a pipeline cycle

Rather than measuring performance in minutes, as in the carwash example, pipeline performance in CPUs is measured in cycles. To manage the five stages mentioned, the CPU is constructed with a five-stage instruction pipeline, ensuring continuous and efficient processing of instructions. A well-optimized pipeline can achieve close to one instruction per cycle, maximizing the CPU's performance by reducing idle times and ensuring continuous instruction processing.

■ How cores in multi-core processors work independently and in parallel

In multi-core architectures, each core can independently execute its own pipeline of instructions. This is similar to having multiple carwash teams, each capable of processing cars simultaneously but independently. They are also capable of parallel execution when dealing with larger, more complex tasks, where each team completes a part of a larger task to improve execution time. This combination of pipelining and parallelism significantly boosts computational efficiency, enabling modern processors to handle complex and resource-intensive tasks more effectively.

Independent execution

Each core in a multi-core processor has its own set of pipelines, allowing it to fetch, decode, execute and write back instructions independently of the other cores. This independence means that, even if one core is handling a computationally intensive task, other cores can continue to execute their tasks without waiting for the first core to finish. This increases overall efficiency and utilization of the CPU resources.

Consider our carwash with multiple bays:

Team 1 (Core 1): Car A undergoes initial wash – detailed cleaning – rinse – drying

Team 2 (Core 2): Car B undergoes initial wash – detailed cleaning – rinse – drying

While Team 1 is drying car A, Team 2 might be rinsing car B. Both bays operate independently.

Parallel execution

Parallel execution takes the concept further, by allowing multiple cores to work on different parts of a single large task or multiple tasks simultaneously. For instance, in a multi-threaded application, different threads can be scheduled on different cores, with each core processing its thread in parallel. This drastically reduces the time needed to complete complex computations.

Imagine a large car that needs washing, detailing and interior cleaning. Multiple teams (cores) can work on different sections of the car at the same time:

Team 1 (Core 1): Washes the exterior

Team 2 (Core 2): Details the interior

Team 3 (Core 3): Cleans the wheels and undercarriage.

Each team works in parallel on different parts of the same car, drastically reducing the overall time required to complete the job.

⬤ Top tip!

Think of pipelining like an assembly line in a factory. Each stage in the pipeline handles a different part of the process and, once a stage finishes its task, it passes the work to the next stage and immediately starts on a new task. This way, multiple instructions are being processed simultaneously, just at different stages. In a multi-core architecture, imagine multiple assembly lines (cores) working in parallel, each running its own pipeline. This set-up greatly increases efficiency because more tasks are completed in less time, and the CPU can handle multiple instructions or even different programs at one time.

REVIEW QUESTIONS

1 What is pipelining and how does it improve performance?

2 How does a non-pipelined CPU differ from a pipelined CPU in terms of instruction execution?

3 What are the stages of a basic instruction pipeline, and how do they function together in a CPU?

4 How do multi-core processors use pipelining and parallel execution to improve computational efficiency?

A1.1.7 Internal and external types of secondary memory storage

◼ Internal storage

Hard disk drive (HDD) and solid state drive (SSD)

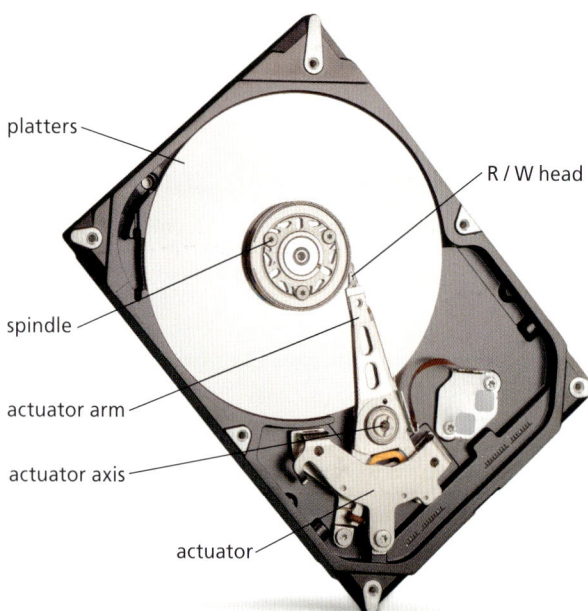

platters

R / W head

spindle

actuator arm

actuator axis

actuator

cache

controller

NAND flash memory

◼ The internals of an HDD and an SSD

A1 Computer fundamentals

Hard disk drives (HDD) and solid state drives (SSD) are the most typical storage solutions for personal computers. HDDs are older technology but are still often used, especially in non-mobile devices, as they are relatively cheap compared to the amount of storage they offer. HDDs utilize a spinning magnetic disk to read / write data. They are suitable for storing large volumes of data, such as media files, backups and documents, where speed is not so critical.

SSDs have no moving parts. They use flash memory to store data, offering high-speed data access and durability. This makes them very popular in portable devices such as laptops and tablets. They are ideal for operating systems, software applications and games due to their fast read / write speed, which enhances the overall system performance.

■ HDD vs SSD

Feature	HDD (hard disk drive)	SSD (solid state drive)
Storage technology	Magnetic storage with spinning disks and read / write heads	Flash memory with no moving parts
Speed	Slower read / write speeds (generally 50–150 MB/s)	Faster read / write speeds (generally 200–500 MB/s)
Durability	More prone to physical damage due to moving parts	More durable; resistant to physical shock
Noise	Produces noise due to moving parts	Silent operation
Power consumption	Higher power usage due to mechanical parts	Lower power consumption
Cost	Generally cheaper per GB	More expensive per GB
Capacity	Available in larger capacities (up to several TB)	Typically available in smaller capacities (up to several TB, but at a higher cost)
Weight	Heavier due to mechanical components	Lighter
Heat generation	Generates more heat due to moving parts	Generates less heat

There is another form factor for SSDs that is currently popular and offers various advantages. M.2 SSDs look like a stick of chewing gum. They are very small and thin, and take up a lot less space than a standard SSD. M.2 NVMe SSDs are also faster than 2.5" SATA SSDs and are considered easier to install – you just slot them into the motherboard and use a single screw to keep them in place.

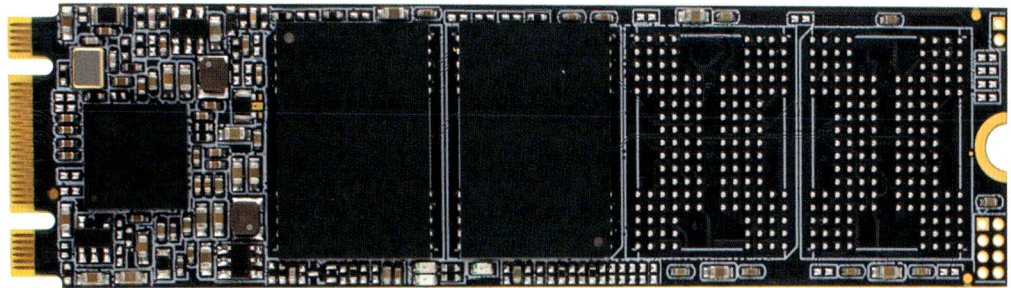

■ M.2 SSD

eMMC (Embedded MultiMediaCard)

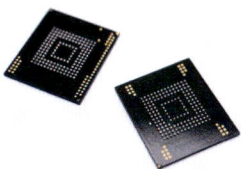

■ Two eMMCs

In low-cost devices, such as entry-level smartphones and budget laptops, where all the benefits of SSDs are not essential, eMMCs are a popular choice. They are also a type of flash storage that utilizes NAND flash memory. They are soldered directly on to the motherboard of the device. While the capacity and speed do not match a standard SSD, their performance is adequate for basic computing needs and simple applications.

■ External storage

Hard disk drive (HDD) and solid state drive (SSD)

As external storage solutions, both HDD and SSD are popular choices. Their performance and comparison are identical to the internal versions. Which is used depends on the requirements of the user. If you require quick file transfers, backups and a portable solution that is less likely to be impacted by being carried around, SSDs are the best choice. If you need to do extensive backups, store media files or transport large files, but speed is less critical, you may decide an HDD is the better option.

Optical discs and optical drives

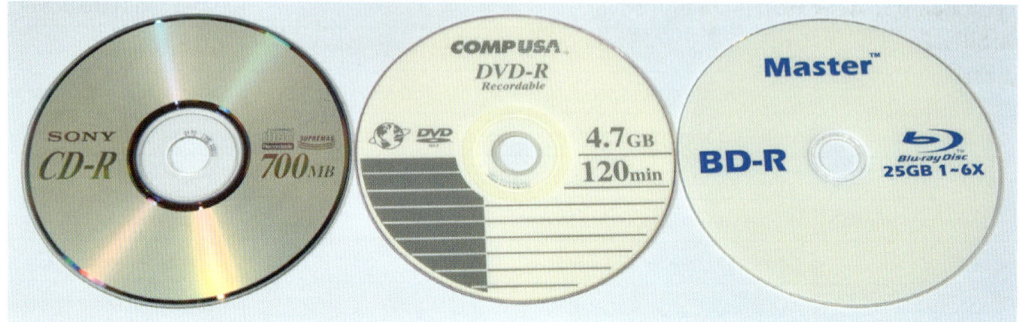

■ From left to right: CD, DVD and Blu-Ray

Optical drives that read / write optical discs, such as CDs, DVDs or Blu-Rays, are becoming less popular, but are still a consideration for external media storage. The cost of an optical disc is low compared to an HDD or SSD and, while their read / write speeds may be slower, they are sufficient for data archiving and playback. However, the discs are prone to scratches, especially if they are not stored correctly, and they require an optical drive to read and write to them, and these are becoming less common in devices these days.

Memory cards

Memory cards are compact storage devices often used in cameras, smartphones and other portable devices. They are ideal for expanding storage in mobile devices and for storing photos and videos in cameras, using NAND flash memory. They come in multiple sizes, such as SD, microSD and CompactFlash, catering to different devices and space requirements. They are known for their durability – they are resistant to physical shocks, extreme temperatures and water, making them ideal for portable devices. Their read / write times are generally slower than SSDs, but outperform those of optical discs.

Network Attached Storage (NAS)

◆ **RAID (Redundant Array of Independent Disks):** a data storage technology that combines multiple physical drives into a single logical unit to improve performance, provide redundancy and ensure data protection.

NAS is a dedicated file storage connected to a network that allows multiple users to access data. It is often used in homes or businesses for centralizing data storage, file storage and data backup. NAS is usually made up of multiple HDDs or SSDs configured in **RAID (Redundant Array of Independent Disks)** configuration. It is normally connected to the network via Ethernet, and runs a lightweight operating system designed for file storage, and the management and sharing of files. As it uses multiple HDDs or SSDs, its capacity is usually high, and it is possible to expand the system further by adding additional drives.

A1 Computer fundamentals

■ Memory cards

■ NAS storage solution

A1.1.8 Describe the concept of compression

Compression is the process of encoding information using fewer bits than the original representation. Making file sizes smaller has two main advantages: it takes less room on secondary storage and it is faster to transfer across a network. There are two main types of compression: lossless and lossy.

■ Lossless vs lossy compression

Lossless compression is when data is compressed to a smaller size, but can be restored back to the original without any loss of information. This is important for files such as text files and databases, where a loss of information would be critical. This technique works by identifying and eliminating **statistical redundancy** within the data, and this process can be reversed when needed.

Lossy compression generally outperforms lossless compression when it comes to file sizes; however, it reduces files by permanently eliminating certain information. This information is redundant or less critical data, resulting in a compressed version that is not identical to the original but is, ideally, indistinguishable from the original to human senses. Lossy compression is commonly used for compressing multimedia files such as images, audio and video, where some loss of quality is acceptable in exchange for significantly reduced file sizes.

◆ **Statistical redundancy:** the repetition of information within a data set that does not contribute to its uniqueness.

This can be seen in the images below. While it may be pretty difficult to visually distinguish the difference in quality, the lossy version uses 50 per cent less data than the original.

Original	Lossless	Saved	Lossy	Saved
1.73 MB	1.58 MB	9%	886 KB	50%

■ Run-length encoding (RLE)

Run-length encoding is an effective lossless data-compression technique used to reduce the size of files containing many consecutive repeated characters.

For example, take this string:

AAAAABBBCCDAA

RLE looks for "runs" where a character is repeated. In the example above, we have five runs:

AAAAA BBB CC D AA

Once RLE has identified these, it encodes the run by replacing it with a pair: the character that repeats and the number of repetitions. So, the runs above become:

5A 3B 2C 1D 2A

The encoded string is then stored as:

5A3B2C1D2A

If we assume each letter stores 8 bits of information, the initial data is $13 \times 8 = 104$ bits, or 13 bytes.

After compressing with RLE, the data is $10 \times 8 = 80$ bits or 10 bytes: a 23 per cent reduction in size.

RLE is straightforward to implement and it is very effective for data with lots of repetitions, such as simple graphics and certain types of text files. RLE was often used on fax machines, which would send text documents via the telephone line. This was because they contained a lot of white space, which meant RLE could achieve compression ratios of up to 8:1. However, for data that does not contain many repeated characters, like a portrait photograph, RLE may not be very effective and, in some cases, may even increase the file size.

PROGRAMMING EXERCISE

Create an RLE application that has two options: compress or decompress.

The compress option should receive a string and output the encoded version using the RLE algorithm.

The decompress option should do the opposite.

■ Transform coding

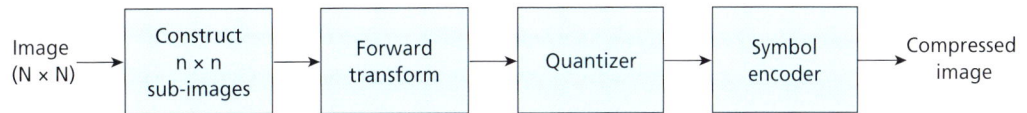

Image (N × N) → [Construct n × n sub-images] → [Forward transform] → [Quantizer] → [Symbol encoder] → Compressed image

■ The stages of transform coding

Transform coding is a form of lossy compression often used in JPEG image compression or MP3 audio compression.

Using JPEG compression as an example:

■ Transform coding takes an image of N × N size and sections it into smaller sub-images of size n × n.

■ Then the *forward transform* is carried out on each of the sub-images. The forward transform can use different algorithms, depending on the type of file compression, but for JPEGs DCT (discrete cosine transform) is used. This takes the image data from the spatial domain (pixel values) to the frequency domain. The output breaks the sub-image down into **low-** and **high-frequency** coefficients.

■ These frequency coefficients are then passed to the *quantizer*. This step significantly reduces file size by simplifying the frequency coefficients obtained from the DCT. The purpose of quantization is to reduce the precision of high-frequency components (the fine details) rather than low-frequency components. This is because the human eye is less sensitive to high-frequency data loss compared to low-frequency detail. The extent of the quantization determines the compression level and the quality of the final image.

■ The final step of transform coding is the *symbol encoder*. This is where the quantized coefficients are further compressed using entropy coding techniques. This runs through three further algorithms to reduce the file size by efficiently representing the frequency of occurrence of each symbol. The algorithms used at this stage are (in this order):

1 Zigzag scan
2 Run-length encoding (RLE)
3 Huffman coding.

Once this stage has finished, the final compressed image is complete.

> ♦ **Low-frequency data:** correspond to slow changes in pixel values, such as broad areas.
>
> ♦ **High-frequency data:** correspond to rapid changes in pixel values, representing fine details, edges and textures.

REVIEW QUESTIONS

1 What are the two main advantages of compressing files?
2 Explain the difference between lossless and lossy compression.
3 How does run-length encoding (RLE) work, and in what types of files is it most effective?
4 Describe the process of transform coding in JPEG image compression and explain why it is considered a lossy compression method.

A1.1.9 Types of services in cloud implementation

Cloud computing has revolutionized how organizations manage and deploy IT resources, offering flexible and scalable solutions to meet diverse business needs. There are three primary cloud service models: Software as a Service (SaaS), Platform as a Service (PaaS) and Infrastructure as a Service (IaaS). Each one provides distinct levels of control, flexibility and management solutions.

◼ Software as a Solution (SaaS)

SaaS delivers software applications over the internet. Users can access these applications through web browsers without needing to install, maintain or update the software locally. SaaS provides a cost-effective and convenient solution for businesses and individuals, offering a wide range of applications from productivity tools to customer-relationship management systems.

SaaS allows users to access their software from anywhere, on any device, as long as they have an internet connection. This eliminates the need for complex software installations. Many SaaS providers charge a subscription fee, which is often less than the cost of purchasing software licences. Additionally, updates and new features are automatically added by the provider, ensuring that users always have the most up-to-date version of the software.

However, SaaS software relies on the user having an internet connection; without it, they cannot run the software, unlike locally installed software. Data security is also a concern, as users rely on the provider's security measures to protect sensitive data.

Example

Google Workspace is an example of SaaS. This suite provides productivity tools, including Gmail, Google Docs and Google Drive, used by businesses and educational institutions for communication, collaboration and storage.

◼ Platform as a Service (PaaS)

PaaS provides a cloud-based platform that allows developers to build, test and deploy applications without managing the underlying infrastructure. PaaS includes tools and services to facilitate application development, such as databases, **middleware** and development frameworks.

◆ **Middleware:** software that connects different applications, allowing them to communicate and share data. It helps different parts of a computer system work together smoothly.

PaaS accelerates software development by allowing developers to focus on coding rather than infrastructure management. It also makes it easier and cheaper to scale hardware as the user base increases. However, this solution can lead to vendor lock-in, making it difficult to move applications to different platforms and offering less control over the hosting environment.

Example

Microsoft Azure App Service is an example of PaaS. It is a platform for building, deploying and scaling web apps and APIs, used by developers to create scalable and reliable applications without managing the underlying servers.

◼ Infrastructure as a Service (IaaS)

IaaS provides virtualized computing resources over the internet, such as virtual machines, storage and networks. This allows businesses to rent IT infrastructure instead of buying and managing physical servers.

Unlike PaaS, IaaS gives users full control over their virtual machines and networks. This reduces the need for upfront investment in hardware and allows businesses to rent solutions at a lower initial cost using a subscription model. IaaS is also scalable, making it easy to adjust resources as the user base grows. However, IaaS requires more technical knowledge than PaaS, as users must manage their own devices and secure their own data and applications.

Example

Amazon Web Services (AWS) EC2 is an example of IaaS. Businesses use AWS EC2 to create and manage virtual servers, providing the flexibility to run applications without owning physical hardware.

1 What is Software as a Service (SaaS) and how does it differ from traditional software installation?

2 Explain how Platform as a Service (PaaS) benefits software developers.

3 Why might a business choose Infrastructure as a Service (IaaS) over purchasing physical hardware?

EXAM PRACTICE QUESTIONS

Note: All the exam practice questions are representative of those that will be found on Paper 1 for the International Baccalaureate Diploma in Computer Science.

1 Describe the function of the arithmetic logic unit (ALU). [2]

2 Outline the role of the program counter (PC). [2]

3 Explain the advantages of multi-core processors compared to single-core processors. [3]

4 Describe how the architecture of a GPU differs from a CPU, and why it is better suited for tasks such as video rendering. [3]

5 Compare the processing power of a CPU and a GPU in handling complex computations. [4]

6 Explain the role of L1 cache in a computer system. [2]

7 Describe the fetch–decode–execute cycle that a CPU uses to process instructions. [4]

8 Explain the concept of pipelining in multi-core processors. [3]

9 Describe the differences between solid state drives (SSD) and hard disk drives (HDD). [4]

10 Describe the method of lossy compression and give an example of its use. [3]

Data representation and computer logic

A1.2.1 Principal methods of representing data

■ The Analytical Engine, conceived by Charles Babbage in the 19th century

■ The Setun computer, developed in 1958

Binary (base-2) is the language for modern-day computers; however, this was not always the case. When developing early computers, several number systems were trialled. Charles Babbage, the inventor of the Analytical Engine, used decimal for his inventions. This seemed a logical choice as people already commonly used base-10.

The ternary system (base-3) was also explored. The Setun computer, developed in the Soviet Union in 1958, used this system. Over 50 of these were produced for educational and scientific institutions to help explore the benefits of ternary logic in computing. Despite its innovative approach, the practical challenges and the widespread adoption of binary logic eventually led to its replacement.

Other scientists and inventors also explored quaternary (base-4) and other number systems. However, practical implementations of these systems were rare due to the increased complexity in hardware design and the limited benefits compared to binary.

Modern computing ultimately settled on binary (base-2) as the primary number system. The base-2 system represents two possible states: 1 or 0. This is in contrast to the number system we are all comfortable with, the decimal system (base-10), which has ten possible states: 0 to 9. The binary system is particularly well-suited to represent the state of electrical switches within a computer system: on (1) and off (0). This simplicity reduces hardware complexity and enhances reliability.

Binary reduces the complexity in hardware design because digital electronics, such as transistors, naturally operate in binary mode. Transistors act as switches that can be turned on or off, aligning perfectly with the binary system's two-state logic. Additionally, Boolean algebra, the mathematical framework for logical circuit design and operation, enables straightforward implementation of complex operations using simple logic gates with binary inputs: 1 (on / true) or 0 (off / false).

The increased reliability of binary systems stems from their use of only two states. Small variations in signal strength do not affect data integrity as much as in systems using larger bases, making binary more robust in **noisy** environments.

As all data on a computer system is stored in binary, we need systems to represent numerous types of data, such as integers, strings, characters, images, audio and video, in binary form.

■ Representation of integers in binary

To represent numbers in binary, it is useful to remember the basics of our decimal system (base-10).

In the decimal system, as we count, we start with a single digit and increment it by 1 until we reach 9. After 9, we introduce a new digit to the front to represent larger numbers. Let's break down the decimal number 1024:

1000s	100s	10s	1s
1	0	2	4

This can be expressed as:

$(1 \times 1000) + (0 \times 100) + (2 \times 10) + (4 \times 1) = 1024$

Each decimal place value increases by a multiple of 10 as we move to the left because we are working in base-10.

Binary, and other base systems, work in a similar way but, instead of 10 possible states per digit, binary has only two (0 and 1). Consequently, each digit increases by a multiple of 2. Let's break down the binary number 0110:

8s	4s	2s	1s
0	1	1	0

This can be expressed as:

$(0 \times 8) + (1 \times 4) + (1 \times 2) + (0 \times 1) = 6$

In this example, we have no 8s, one 4, one 2 and no 1s. Adding 4 + 2 gives us the decimal (base-10) equivalent of the binary (base-2) number 0110. To clearly denote whether we are showing a binary or decimal number, we usually put the base as a subscript, to avoid confusion:

$0110_2 = 6_{10}$

When working with computer systems, we usually deal with **8-bit binary numbers**. A **bit** can be defined as a "binary digit", and 8 bits is equivalent to 1 **byte**. If the number does not require 8 bits to represent it, we usually pad out the extras with 0s. For example, the decimal number 33 would be represented as:

128s	64s	32s	16s	8s	4s	2s	1s
0	0	1	0	0	0	0	1

This means that with 8 bits, we can represent **256 different numbers**, from **0 to 255**. If we want to represent larger numbers, we need more bits to represent this.

◆ **Noise:** unwanted electrical disturbances that can affect the integrity of signals being processed by a computer; this noise is not related to sound, but to variations in voltage or current that can disrupt the accurate transmission and processing of digital data.

◆ **Bit:** binary digit; a single digit, either 1 or 0.

◆ **Byte:** 8 bits.

●Common mistake

When seeing the number 11111111_2, a common mistake is to say this is 256. However, remember that while there are 256 number possibilities, 255 is the largest number we can represent in 1 byte (as 0 can also be represented).

When referring to bits and bytes, a lowercase "b" is used to represent bits and an uppercase "B" is used to represent bytes. We then use a prefix system as the numbers increase.

There are two types of prefixes when referring to bits and bytes: one for base-10 (e.g. kilo, mega, giga) and another for base-2. There was a time when base-10 prefixes were also used for base-2 quantities due to their similarity (e.g. 1024 is close to 1000). However, the confusion this generated led to calls for change. To address this, in 1999 the IEC introduced new prefixes (e.g. kibi, mebi, gibi) specifically for base-2 multiples (1024, 1,048,576, 1,073,741,824).

Kibibyte KiB	Mebibyte MiB	Gibibyte GiB	Tebibyte TiB	Pebibyte PiB	Exbibyte EiB	Zebibyte ZiB
1 KiB = 1024 bytes	1 MiB = 1024 KiB	1 GiB = 1024 MiB	1 TiB = 1024 GiB	1 PiB = 1024 TiB	1EiB = 1024 PiB	1 ZiB = 1024 EiB
Kilobyte KB	Megabyte MB	Gigabyte GB	Terabyte TB	Petabyte PB	Exabyte EB	Zettabyte ZB
1 KB = 1000 bytes	1 MB = 1000 KB	1 GB = 1000 MB	1 TB = 1000 GB	1 PB = 1000 TB	1 EB = 1000 PB	1 ZB = 1000 EB

REVIEW QUESTION

Bits and byte notation are worth knowing when dealing with mobile-phone and internet companies.

Download speeds of up to 100Mb/s!

or

Download speeds of up to 100MB/s!

If the two advertisements above were from two different internet companies, assuming the cost is the same, which one offers faster speeds and by how much?

Converting binary numbers to decimal

There are two main methods for converting a binary number to decimal: the positional notation method and the doubling method.

Positional notation method:

This is possibly the most straightforward method, where you assign the place values and sum.

1 Starting from the right, assign the place values for each binary bit.
2 Sum each of the place values that has a 1 underneath it.

For example, to convert 10111011_2 to decimal:

128	64	32	16	8	4	2	1
1	0	1	1	1	0	1	1

$128 + 32 + 16 + 8 + 2 + 1 = 187$

Doubling method:

1 Start with the leftmost bit (the most significant bit).
2 Double the current total and add the next bit.
3 Repeat until all bits are processed.

Top tip!

When converting to and from binary, it is always a good idea to write the digit place values down first. Trying to remember these in your head can lead to silly mistakes.

128	64	32
16	8	4
2	1	

A1 Computer fundamentals

For example, to convert 10111011_2 to decimal:

Step	Binary digit	Current total	Calculation
1	1	1	Initial value
2	0	2	$1 \times 2 + 0 = 2$
3	1	5	$2 \times 2 + 1 = 5$
4	1	11	$5 \times 2 + 1 = 11$
5	1	23	$11 \times 2 + 1 = 23$
6	0	46	$23 \times 2 + 0 = 46$
7	1	93	$46 \times 2 + 1 = 93$
8	1	187	$93 \times 2 + 1 = 187$

● Common mistake

If you use this method, remember to start with the most significant bit (MSB), not the **least significant bit** (LSB).

◆ **Least significant bit (LSB):** the rightmost bit in a binary number, representing the smallest value position (0 or 1).

◆ **Quotient:** the result obtained when one number is divided by another, e.g. in the division of 15 by 3, the quotient is 5.

REVIEW QUESTIONS

Convert the following binary (base-2) numbers to decimal (base-10):

1 11001010_2
2 01101101_2
3 10110011_2
4 00011110_2
5 11100001_2

Converting decimal numbers to binary

There are two main methods for converting a decimal number to binary: the division method and the subtraction method.

Division method:

1 Divide the decimal number by 2.
2 Write down the **quotient** and the remainder.
   The remainder will be either 0 or 1. This represents a digit of the binary number (the LSB on the first division).
3 Update the quotient.
4 Repeat until the quotient is 0.
5 Construct the binary number (this is read from the remainders from the first to the last).

For example, to convert 42_{10} to binary:

Division step	Quotient	Remainder
42 / 2	21	0
21 / 2	10	1
10 / 2	5	0
5 / 2	2	1
2 / 2	1	0
1 / 2	0	1

● Common mistake

Remember to construct the remainders in the correct order to format your binary number. The first remainder is the least significant bit (LSB).

Construct the binary number from the remainders and pad to 8-bits: 00101010_2

Subtraction method:

Write down the place values for an 8-bit binary number:

128   64   32   16   8   4   2   1

Starting with the largest place value (128):

1 Try and subtract it from the number you are converting.
- ☐ If the place value is larger than the number, write a 0 below it.
- ☐ If it is smaller or equal to it, write a 1 and calculate the remainder of the subtraction, carrying the result to the next place value.

2 Repeat.

For example, to convert 42_{10} to binary:

128_{10} and 64_{10} are larger than 42_{10}, so we write 0 below these.

128	64	32	16	8	4	2	1
0	0						

32_{10} is smaller, so we write a 1 below it and calculate the remainder from the subtraction, the result of which will carry to the next place value:

$42_{10} - 32_{10} = 10_{10}$

128	64	32	16	8	4	2	1
0	0	1	0				

16 is larger than 10, so write a 0

8 is smaller, so write a 1 and calculate the remainder:

$10_{10} - 8_{10} = 2_{10}$

4_{10} is larger than 2_{10}, so write a 0

2_{10} is equal, so calculate the remainder (0) and write a 1

128	64	32	16	8	4	2	1
0	0	1	0	1	0	1	0

REVIEW QUESTIONS

Convert the following decimal (base-10) numbers to binary (base-2):

1 20_{10}

2 87_{10}

3 123_{10}

4 199_{10}

5 250_{10}

PROGRAMMING EXERCISE

Write a binary-to-decimal and decimal-to-binary application in either Python or Java.

■ Representation of integers in hexadecimal

Hexadecimal (often abbreviated as hex) is a base-16 number system that uses 16 distinct symbols to represent values, rather than the 10 of decimal or 2 of binary. The symbols include the digits 0 to 9 and then the letters A to F, where A represents 10, B represents 11, C represents 12, D represents 13, E represents 14 and F represents 15.

Hexadecimal is used with computers for several reasons. The ease of conversion between binary and hexadecimal is straightforward because each hex digit maps directly to a 4-bit binary sequence. For example, the binary number 1111 can be represented as F in hex. Another reason is that it provides a more compact way to represent a binary value. This makes it much easier for us to read and communicate large binary numbers. This is why you often see hex used in **debugging tools**, **memory dumps** and assembly language programming.

Converting binary numbers to hexadecimal

Converting binary to hexadecimal is a straightforward calculation.

1 Split the binary byte (8 bits) into two **nibbles** (2×4 bits).
2 Calculate the decimal value of these 4 bits.
3 Convert the decimal values into their hexadecimal equivalents and rejoin them.

For example, to convert 01101011_2 to hexadecimal:

1 Split the byte into 2 nibbles:

0110_2 1011_2

2 Calculate the decimal value:

6_{10} 11_{10}

3 Convert both decimal values to their hexadecimal equivalents and rejoin them:

$6B_{16}$

> ### REVIEW QUESTIONS
>
> Convert the following binary (base-2) numbers to hexadecimal (base-16):
>
> 1 10101100_2 4 00111010_2
>
> 2 11010110_2 5 10011101_2
>
> 3 11010001_2

Converting hexadecimal numbers to binary

Moving from hex to binary is just a reverse of the binary-to-hexadecimal process:

1 Split the two hexadecimal digits.
2 Convert each of them to a 4-bit binary number using the same integer-to-binary method.
3 Join the two 4-bit numbers together to form 1 byte.

For example, to convert $F2_{16}$ to binary:

1 Split the two hexadecimal digits:

F_{16} 2_{16}

2 Convert each of them to a 4-bit binary number using the same integer-to-binary method:

1111_2 0010_2

3 Join the two 4-bit numbers together to form 1 byte:

11110010_2

Convert the following hexadecimal (base-16) numbers to binary (base-2):

1 $3F_{16}$

2 $A9_{16}$

3 10_{16}

4 $7C_{16}$

5 $E2_{16}$

Converting decimal numbers to hexadecimal

To move between decimal and hexadecimal is one of the trickier calculations to perform, as you need to be comfortable with your 16 times table. To convert a decimal number to hex:

1 Divide the decimal number by 16 and record the remainder.

2 Repeat the process with the quotient until the quotient is 0.

3 Form the hex number from the remainders, with the last remainder obtained being the most significant bit (the number on the left).

For example, to convert 254_{10} to hexadecimal:

1 Divide the decimal number by 16 and record the remainder:

$254_{10} / 16_{10} = 15_{10}$ remainder 14_{10}

quotient = 15_{10}

remainder $14_{10} = E_{16}$

2 Repeat the process with the quotient until the quotient is 0:

$15_{10} / 16_{10} = 0_{10}$ remainder 15_{10}

quotient = 0_{10}

remainder $15_{10} = F_{16}$

3 Form the hex number from the remainders, with the last remainder obtained being the most significant bit (the number on the left):

FE_{16}

REVIEW QUESTIONS

Convert the following decimal (base-10) numbers to hexadecimal (base-16):

1 42_{10}

2 157_{10}

3 89_{10}

4 200_{10}

5 123_{10}

Converting hexadecimal numbers to decimal

To convert from hexadecimal to decimal:

1 Convert hex digits to their decimal equivalents.

2 Multiply them by 16 raised to the power of its position index, starting from 0 on the right.

3 Sum the results.

For example, to convert $2F_{16}$ to decimal:

1 Convert hex digits to their decimal equivalents:

$2_{16} = 2_{10}$

$F_{16} = 15_{10}$

2 Multiply them by 16 raised to the power of its position index, starting from 0 on the right:

$2 \times 16^1 = 2 \times 16 = 32_{10}$

$15 \times 16^0 = 15 \times 1 = 15_{10}$

3 Sum the results:

$32 + 15 = 47_{10}$

PROGRAMMING EXERCISE

Add hexadecimal conversion functionality to the binary converter app you created before.

A1.2.2 How binary is used to store data

The binary system underpins everything from numerical values and textual information to complex multimedia files, ensuring efficient and reliable data processing. In this section, we are going to discover the mechanisms that are used to store such data as characters, strings, images, audio and video in binary form.

■ Characters and strings

Characters and strings are stored using standardized binary encoding schemes, enabling consistent storage, retrieval and processing across different systems and applications. The most common encoding standards are ASCII (American Standard Code for Information Interchange) and Unicode.

ASCII encoding

The development of ASCII began in 1960 and was officially standardized in 1963. It was developed because there was no standardized way to encode text characters, which led to compatibility issues between devices and systems. Each manufacturer used its own proprietary encoding system, which made it very difficult for devices to communicate with each other. ASCII was designed to provide a common standard for the interchange of text data.

ASCII initially started out as a 7-bit encoding system, which gave it the ability to represent 128 (2^7) different characters, which was considered sufficient for most basic text data (letters, numbers, punctuation and control characters). However, as computing became more global and applications required support for additional characters, an 8-bit extension to ASCII was developed, giving it the ability to represent 256 (2^8) characters. This was referred to as extended ASCII, and the new characters were mainly used for Western European languages.

ASCII uses a simple but clever system to represent characters in binary (as long as we are only considering the Latin (English) alphabet). The first five bits from the right are used to represent the letter by its numerical place in the alphabet.

For example:

01100001_2	=	1_{10}	=	a
01100010_2	=	2_{10}	=	b
01100011_2	=	3_{10}	=	c

If the first five bits from the right are 00000 (five zeros), it is almost certainly a space (00100000).

If the first three bits from the left are not 011 or 010, it is likely to be a punctuation mark.

The first three bits from the left represent whether it is an uppercase or lowercase letter. 011 = lowercase; 010 = uppercase:

01100001_2 =   a

01000001_2 =   A

REVIEW QUESTION

Convert the following binary back into text to reveal the hidden message.

01000110 01101111 01101100 01101100 01101111 01110111 00100000 01110100 01101000 01100101 00100000 01110111 01101000 01101001 01110100 01100101 00100000 01110010 01100001 01100010 01100010 01101001 01110100

PROGRAMMING EXERCISE

Create an application so that you can send secret messages to your friends.

Write an application that accepts either a string of characters or a stream of binary. It should either encode the characters using ASCII and binary or convert the binary back into text.

To make the binary less easy to decode by hand, you could remove all spacing between the 8-bit characters.

Unicode encoding

In the 1960s, the United States and the majority of English-speaking countries had a system in 7-bit ASCII that worked for the English alphabet. Other non-English speaking countries had their own unique encoding systems to work with their own languages. When the ASCII system was increased to 8 bits (extended ASCII), allowing for 256 characters for use in modern computers, countries did not agree on the same standard. Nordic countries started using the extra space to encode characters for their own languages, and Japan used four different systems that were not even compatible with each other. This was not a huge issue as communication between these systems was rare, but then the internet was launched and compatibility became very important as more and more information was being shared between systems in different countries.

In 1991, the Unicode Consortium was created to try and solve this problem. The organization was established to develop, maintain and promote the Unicode Standard, which provides a unique number for every character, regardless of platform, program or language. It needed to create a system that was capable of storing all the characters and punctuation marks from all the languages in the world, but also wanted it to be backwards compatible with ASCII. At the time of writing, the current Unicode Standard version 15.0, released in September 2022, encodes 149,186 different characters. Unicode includes the Latin, Cyrillic, Greek and Arabic alphabets, and Chinese characters, as well as many others, and also includes emojis and mathematical and other technical symbols. In Unicode, each letter or symbol is assigned a unique number, for example:

- A = 65
- 汉 = 27721
- 💩 = 128169

You can find the numerical representation for any character or symbol using the code below:

Python

```python
# Python examples
char_a = 'A'
char_han = '汉'
char_poo = '💩'
# Get Unicode code points as integers
code_point_a = ord(char_a)  # 65
code_point_han = ord(char_han)  # 27721
code_point_poo = ord(char_poo)  # 128169
# Print integer representations
print(code_point_a)  # Output: 65
print(code_point_han)  # Output: 27721
print(code_point_poo)  # Output: 128169
```

Java

```java
public class UnicodeExample {
    public static void main(String[] args) {
        // Define characters
        char charA = 'A';
        char charHan = '汉';
        String charPoo = "💩"; // Note: Java uses UTF-16 and
        // the emoji is usually a surrogate pair
        // Get Unicode code points as integers
        int codePointA = (int) charA; // 65
        int codePointHan = (int) charHan; // 27721
        int codePointPoo = charPoo.codePointAt(0); // 128169
        // Print integer representations
        System.out.println("Unicode code point of 'A': " +
        codePointA); // Output: 65
        System.out.println("Unicode code point of '汉': " +
        codePointHan); // Output: 27721
        System.out.println("Unicode code point of '💩': " +
        codePointPoo); // Output: 128169
    }
}
```

How did they manage this? The story is that it was conceived in a café on the back of a napkin when Joe Becker (Xerox), Lee Collins (Apple) and Mark Davis (Apple and later Google) met and designed the encoding scheme in 1987. There are a few different versions of Unicode: UTF-8, UTF-16 and UTF-32. Each has its own uses:

	UTF-8	UTF-16	UTF-32
Variable length encoding	1–4 bytes per character	2 or 4 bytes per character	4 bytes per character
Note	Compatibility: backward compatible with ASCII	Surrogate pairs: for characters outside the **Basic Multilingual Plane (BMP)**, two 16-bit code units are used	Simplicity: easier to process because each character is exactly 4 bytes
Usage	Most commonly used encoding on the web and in many applications	Often used in Windows and Java environments	Less common due to higher storage requirements

◆ **Basic Multilingual Plane (BMP):** the most commonly used characters and symbols for almost all modern languages.

Let's examine UTF-8, the most commonly used encoding system, and understand its functionality.

Instead of merely expanding the size to accommodate over 100,000 characters, which would have adversely impacted most online content, a more efficient solution was devised. Had all characters been standardized to use 32 bits, each letter in the ASCII system would have quadrupled in size. This would have resulted in significantly larger documents and web pages, leading to increased storage requirements and slower transfer times. The system also needed never to send eight zeros (00000000) in a row, as many older systems would see this as the end of communication and would stop listening.

So the UTF-8 system kept the ASCII system the same. The letter "A" is encoded as:

01000001 = A

However, if the character needed went beyond the standard ASCII system, "é" for example, more than one byte would be required:

11000011 **10**101001 = é

The bits in bold are important. The first three significant bits "110" on the first byte represent that this character is made up of two bytes in total (a 0 is needed at the end to show when this information is finished). The second byte starts "10", which means this is a continuation. If you remove those 5 bits and then put both bytes together:

000 1110 1001 = 233 = é

Another example is:

11110000 **10**011111 **10**011000 **10**000100 = 😄

This emoji requires four bytes using the UTF-8 system. The first byte communicates that this character is made up of four bytes ("11110") and the next three bytes start with "10", showing they are continuation bytes. If we remove that information:

0001 1111 0110 0000 0100 = 128516 = 😄

UTF-8 has been adopted by the internet as the main character encoding system; however, it doesn't come without some issues. Due to the variable length, some characters (especially those from Asian languages or emojis) take more space compared to single-byte encodings. This can lead to larger file sizes in certain contexts. The processing required to handle variable-length encoding also requires more complex processing compared to fixed-length systems such as UTF-32.

Despite these issues, UTF-8 has proved to be a versatile and effective encoding standard that meets the needs of the modern internet. Its backward compatibility, efficiency and broad support make it an enduring choice for encoding text. While it does have some challenges, particularly with handling non-ASCII characters and variable-length encoding, these are not significant enough ever to warrant a wholesale replacement. Therefore, it's likely that UTF-8 will continue to be the dominant text encoding standard for the foreseeable future.

PROGRAMMING EXERCISES

The code below uses a Caesar cipher to encrypt the string that is input using a key. A Caesar cipher is a simple **shift cipher**, where each letter is considered to be an integer (a = 1, b = 2, c = 3, and so on) and the key is added to this to find the encrypted letter, for example:

String input: "Hello"

Key input: 1

Output: Ifmmp

Python

```python
def caesar_cipher_encrypt(message, key):
    encrypted_message = ""
    for char in message:
        if char.isalpha():  # Check whether the character is a letter
            shift = ord("A") if char.isupper() else ord("a")  # Determine the
            # ASCII offset
            # Shift the character and wrap around the alphabet if necessary
            encrypted_char = chr((ord(char) - shift + key) % 26 + shift)
            encrypted_message += encrypted_char
        else:
            encrypted_message += char  # Non-letter characters remain unchanged
    return encrypted_message
# User input
message = input("Enter the message to encrypt: ")
key = int(input("Enter the key (an integer): "))
# Encrypt the message
encrypted_message = caesar_cipher_encrypt(message, key)
print(f"Encrypted message: {encrypted_message}")
```

Java

```java
import java.util.Scanner;
public class CaesarCipher {
    public static String caesarCipherEncrypt(String message, int key) {
        StringBuilder encryptedMessage = new StringBuilder();
        for (char ch : message.toCharArray()) {
            if (Character.isLetter(ch)) {  // Check whether the character is
            // a letter
                char shift;
                if (Character.isUpperCase(ch)) {
                    shift = 'A';  // Determine the ASCII offset for uppercase
                    // letters
                } else {
                    shift = 'a';  // Determine the ASCII offset for lowercase
                    // letters
                }
                // Shift the character and wrap around the alphabet if
                // necessary
                char encryptedChar = (char) ((ch - shift + key) % 26 + shift);
                encryptedMessage.append(encryptedChar);
            } else {
                encryptedMessage.append(ch);  // Non-letter characters remain
                // unchanged
            }
        }
        return encryptedMessage.toString();
    }
    public static void main(String[] args) {
        Scanner scanner = new Scanner(System.in);
        // User input
        System.out.print("Enter the message to encrypt: ");
        String message = scanner.nextLine();
        System.out.print("Enter the key (an integer): ");
        int key = scanner.nextInt();
        // Encrypt the message
        String encryptedMessage = caesarCipherEncrypt(message, key);
        System.out.println("Encrypted message: " + encryptedMessage);
    }
}
```

1   After studying how this code works, write the decrypt function for someone who receives an encrypted message.

2   Write a function that is able to **brute force** an encrypted message so you can identify the key used.

◆ **Brute force:** a method of breaking a cipher by systematically trying every possible key until the correct one is found.

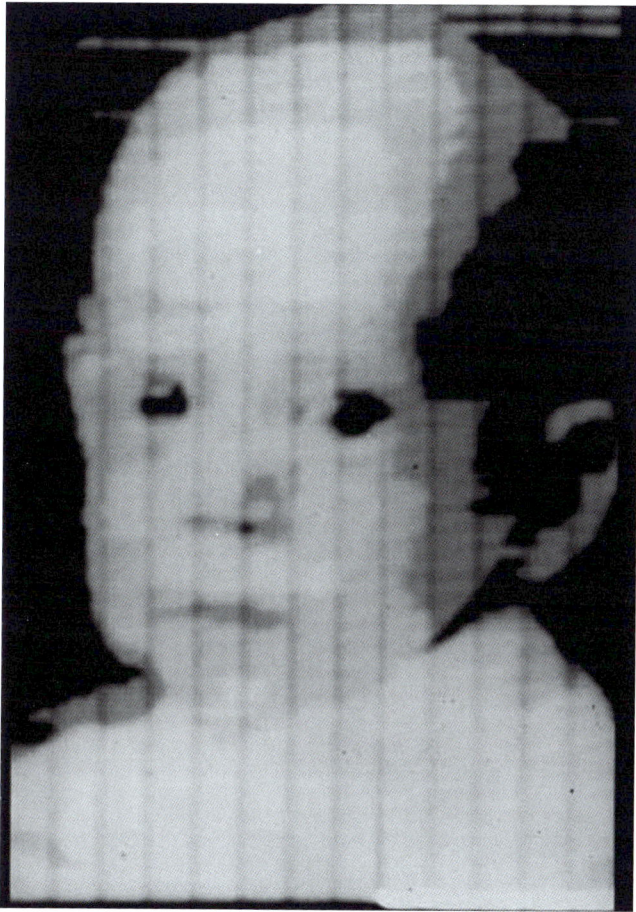

The first ever digital image: Russel Kirch's son, Walden, in 1957

Images

In 1957, Russel Kirch scanned an **analogue** photo of his son Walden, converting the picture into a digital file. This was the first ever digital image created. It was a significant milestone in the evolution of visual technology, revolutionizing the way we capture, store and manipulate pictures. The development of early digital cameras and scanners, which enabled devices to convert light into digital data, started the trend that has now become commonplace, and the transition from film to digital has transformed numerous industries, from photography and medical imaging to telecommunications and entertainment.

Bitmap images

Bitmap images, also known as "raster" images, are one of the most fundamental forms of digital graphics. They reproduce images by using a grid of **pixels**, with each pixel assigned a specific colour and intensity.

At the bottom of the page is a bitmap image with an **image resolution** dimension of 13×10 (13 pixels wide by 10 pixels high). Each pixel is "described" using 1 bit of data: either 1 or 0. In this case, 1 = black and 0 = white (a monochrome image), and the amount of bits used to describe the colour is known as the "bit depth" or **colour depth**. So, we have a 13×10 image with a 1-bit colour depth in this example.

◆ **Analogue:** a continuous signal that represents varying physical quantities, such as sound waves, which varies smoothly over a range; digital represents data in discrete binary values (0s and 1s), enabling precise and error-resistant processing.

◆ **Bitmap:** a type of digital image composed of a grid of pixels, each holding a specific colour value, representing the image in a rasterized format.

◆ **Pixel:** short for "picture element"; the smallest unit of a digital image or display, representing a single point in the image with a specific colour and intensity.

To calculate the size of this image, the formula is:

image size = width (pixels) × height (pixels) × colour depth (bits per pixel)

$13 \times 10 \times 1 = 130$ bits (or $130 / 8 = 16.25$ bytes)

However, in reality, this calculation is not completely accurate, as the image would require more data to store **metadata** and other header information. This could include information such as dimensions, colour depth and other attributes that allow the CPU to read the image data accurately so it displays the image correctly to the screen.

0	0	0	0	0	0	0	0	0	0	0	0	0
0	0	1	0	0	0	0	0	0	1	0	0	0
0	0	0	1	0	0	0	0	1	0	0	0	0
0	0	1	1	1	1	1	1	1	1	1	0	0
0	0	1	1	0	1	1	1	0	1	1	0	0
0	1	1	1	1	1	1	1	1	1	1	1	0
0	1	0	1	0	0	0	0	0	1	0	1	0
0	1	0	1	0	0	0	0	0	1	0	1	0
0	0	0	0	1	1	0	1	1	0	0	0	0
0	0	0	0	0	0	0	0	0	0	0	0	0

◆ Image resolution: the number of pixels contained within a digital image, typically expressed as the dimensions (width × height) in pixels, and sometimes as the pixel density (PPI / DPI) for print quality.

◆ Colour depth: also known as "bit depth"; the number of bits used to represent the colour of each pixel in a digital image, determining the range and precision of colours that can be displayed.

◆ Metadata: information that describes other data, providing context and details about the data's content, structure and attributes. In the context of digital images, metadata includes such information as the image's dimensions, colour depth, creation date, author, camera settings and other properties that help with managing, understanding and using the image effectively.

To improve the quality of a bitmap image, we have two options: We can increase the number of pixels (resolution) or we can increase the colour depth.

Resolution – increasing the number of pixels:

Increasing the number of pixels in a bitmap image increases the image quality. A higher resolution allows for greater detail and clarity, and images with lower resolutions can lead to a loss of detail and a pixelated appearance. However, the quantity of pixels is not the only consideration: the size of the screen they are displayed on is also important. Images with a higher PPI (pixels per inch) look clearer than those with a lower PPI. Imagine having an image with a resolution of 1024×768 shown on your phone compared to on a cinema screen. The higher PPI on the phone will give a clearer image due to the increased pixel density. The trade-off for a higher resolution image is larger file size, which can impact storage and transfer efficiency.

■ Common image resolutions

Resolution name	Pixel dimensions	Common usage
VGA	640 × 480	Early computer screens, basic web graphics
SVGA	800 × 600	Standard computer monitors, web graphics
HD (720p)	1280 × 760	HD video, basic HD television
Full HD (1080p)	1920 × 1080	Full HD video, modern monitors and televisions
2K	2048 × 1080	Digital cinema, some monitors
Quad HD (1440p)	2560 × 1440	High-resolution monitors, gaming, professional use
4K (Ultra HD)	3840 × 2160	Ultra HD televisions, high-end monitors, video
8K	7680 × 4320	Cutting-edge televisions, professional video

Colour depth – increasing the amount of colours:

When we increase the colour depth, it allows for a wider range of colours to be represented, resulting in more vibrant and accurate images. If an image's colour depth is low, this can lead to banding, where gradients appear as distinct steps rather than smooth transitions. However, just like image resolution, we must also consider the impact of file size for storage and transfer times. The higher the colour depth, the larger the file size.

To work out the number of colours available, we calculate 2 to the power of the colour depth of the image; for example, for an image with an 8-bit colour depth:

$2^8 = 256$

■ Common colour depths

Colour depth (bits per pixel)	Number of colours	Common usage
1 bit	2	Simple graphics, monochrome displays
4 bit	16	Early computer graphics, icons
8 bit	256	GIF images, simple web graphics
16 bit	65,536	High-colour images, some video formats
24 bit (true colour)	16.8 million	Standard for most images and video, digital photography
30 bit (deep colour)	Over 1 billion	Professional photography, high-end monitors and televisions
36 bit	Over 68 billion	Medical imaging, professional graphics
48 bit	Trillions	High-end personal applications, detailed scientific imaging

A1 Computer fundamentals

The majority of modern-day screens are 24 bit, allowing for 16.8 million colours. They have three lights per pixel: a red, a green and a blue light, otherwise known as "RGB", and have a value range from 0 to 255 (1 byte per colour channel). This is sufficient for most applications, as most human eyes can only distinguish between around 10 million distinct colours. Monitors that go beyond 24 bit are normally only necessary in professional fields where precision is crucial.

On the left is a high-resolution image. If we zoom in to the dress on this image, we can see the breakdown of the individual pixels and the values of the distinct colour channels. When working with graphics, these values are often shown in hexadecimal. If we take the top left pixel of the dress as an example:

R: 216, G: 190, B: 199 = #d8bec7

■ A high-resolution image with a resolution of 2268 × 4032, a 24-bit colour depth and a file size of 1.77 MB

■ A zoomed-in area of the image above, showing the value of each pixel – created using www.csfieldguide.org.nz/en/interactives/pixel-viewer

RGB Calculator

```
rgb(216, 190, 199)

#d8bec7

hsl(339, 25%, 80%)
```

R: 216

G: 190

B: 199

■ The colour values for the top left pixel of the dress in the photo – created using www.w3schools.com/colors/colors_rgb.asp

We can also see the impact of lower colour depths on the same image:

The same image using multiple colour depths: 24 bits to 0 bits – created using **www.csfieldguide.org.nz/en/interactives/image-bit-comparer**

REVIEW QUESTIONS

1   A bitmap image uses a colour depth of 3 bits, allowing for eight distinct colours.

    How many bits are needed to represent the colours if the bitmap image uses 32 distinct colours?

2   Raj is creating a bitmap graphic for a game. The image dimensions are 10 pixels wide and 12 pixels tall.

    How many pixels are there in total in the image?

3   Alice is organizing her digital artwork collection that she has created over the years.

    While transferring her artwork files to a new cloud storage service, she notices that each file is larger than she anticipated. This is because, aside from the actual image data, the file includes extra information necessary for accurate reproduction of the image. What is this additional information, which contains details about the pixel data, called?

4   Determine the storage capacity needed for a bitmap image with dimensions of 800 × 600 pixels that supports 512 different colours.

    Then, calculate the file size in kilobytes (kB) if the file metadata occupies an additional 25 per cent of the space. Present your answer as a real number, including the decimal values.

PROGRAMMING EXERCISES

Here are some fun ways to explore images in more depth using Python or Java.

1 Extract and print RGB values.

Java

```java
import java.awt.Color;
import java.awt.image.BufferedImage;
import java.io.File;
import java.io.IOException;
import javax.imageio.ImageIO;
public class ImageToRGB {
    public static void main(String[] args) {
        try {
            // Load the image
            BufferedImage image = ImageIO.read(new File("sample_image.jpg"));
            // Get image dimensions
            int width = image.getWidth();
            int height = image.getHeight();
            // Loop through each pixel
            for (int y = 0; y < height; y++) {
                for (int x = 0; x < width; x++) {
                    // Get the RGB value of the pixel
                    int pixel = image.getRGB(x, y);
                    Color color = new Color(pixel);
                    // Extract the red, green and blue components
                    int red = color.getRed();
                    int green = color.getGreen();
                    int blue = color.getBlue();
                    // Print the RGB values
                    System.out.println("Pixel at (" + x + ", " + y + "): R=" +
                    red + ", G=" + green + ", B=" + blue);
                }
            }
        } catch (IOException e) {
            e.printStackTrace();
        }
    }
}
```

For Python, you need to install the Pillow library first. Run this command in your terminal to install the necessary libraries:

```
pip install pillow
```

Python

```
pip install pillow
Use this code to access the RGB values for each pixel
from PIL import Image
# Load the image
image = Image.open("sample_image.jpg")
# Convert the image to RGB mode
image = image.convert("RGB")
# Get the image dimensions
width, height = image.size
# Extract and print RGB values
for y in range(height):
    for x in range(width):
        pixel = image.getpixel((x, y))
        red, green, blue = pixel
        print(f"Pixel at ({x}, {y}): R={red}, G={green}, B={blue}")
```

2   Apply a grayscale filter.

Warning:

This code processes the image pixel by pixel, which means it iterates through every pixel in the image to apply the grayscale filter. For very large images (e.g. high-resolution photos), this process can be computationally intensive and take a significant amount of time to complete. Consider testing this code on smaller images first (e.g. 100x100 pixels) to observe its behaviour before applying it to larger files.

Python

```
from PIL import Image
# Load the image
image = Image.open("sample_image.jpg")
# Convert the image to RGB mode
image = image.convert('RGB')
# Get the image dimensions
width, height = image.size
# Create a new image to store the grayscale result
grayscale_image = Image.new("RGB", (width, height))
# Apply a grayscale filter
for y in range(height):
    for x in range(width):
        pixel = image.getpixel((x, y))
        red, green, blue = pixel
        grayscale = int(0.3 * red + 0.59 * green + 0.11 * blue)
        grayscale_image.putpixel((x, y), (grayscale, grayscale, grayscale))
# Save the grayscale image
grayscale_image.save("grayscale_image.jpg")
```

A1 Computer fundamentals

Java

```java
import java.awt.Color;
import java.awt.image.BufferedImage;
import java.io.File;
import java.io.IOException;
import javax.imageio.ImageIO;
public class ImageToGrayScale {
    public static void main(String[] args) {
        try {
            // Load the image
            BufferedImage image = ImageIO.read(new File("sample_image.jpg"));
            // Get image dimensions
            int width = image.getWidth();
            int height = image.getHeight();
            // Create a new image to store the grayscale result
            BufferedImage grayscaleImage = new BufferedImage(width, height,
            BufferedImage.TYPE_INT_RGB);
            // Apply a grayscale filter
            for (int y = 0; y < height; y++) {
                for (int x = 0; x < width; x++) {
                    // Get the RGB value of the pixel
                    int pixel = image.getRGB(x, y);
                    Color color = new Color(pixel);
                    // Extract the red, green and blue components
                    int red = color.getRed();
                    int green = color.getGreen();
                    int blue = color.getBlue();
                    // Compute the grayscale value
                    int grayscale = (int) (0.3 * red + 0.59 * green + 0.11 *
                    blue);
                    // Create a new Color object with the grayscale value
                    Color grayColor = new Color(grayscale, grayscale, grayscale);
                    // Set the new pixel value in the grayscale image
                    grayscaleImage.setRGB(x, y, grayColor.getRGB());
                }
            }
            // Save the grayscale image
            ImageIO.write(grayscaleImage, "jpg", new File("grayscale_image_
            java.jpg"));
        } catch (IOException e) {
            e.printStackTrace();
        }
    }
}
```

3   After studying how the grayscale filter works, are you now able to create your own unique filters?

◼ Audio

Audio in its analogue form is a continuous signal that represents sound waves through variations of air pressure. These sound waves can be captured through input devices, such as microphones, which convert the sound waves into a digital signal, which is stored as binary. This process involves several steps:

Analogue-to-digital conversion (ADC)

Sound is a continuous analogue signal. An ADC samples the **amplitude** (loudness) of the sound at discrete intervals in a process known as **sampling**. The rate at which this happens is measured in Hertz (Hz) – the higher the Hertz, the more samples are recorded per second. CD-quality audio uses 44.1 **kHz**, but professional quality audio is sampled at 48 kHz.

This sample is then stored and represented as a numerical value in binary. The precision is determined by the bit depth. The larger the bit depth, the more possible values that can be used to describe the sample. For example, the bit depth of CD-quality sound is 16 bit, which gives 2^{16}, or 65,536, values. Professional audio, which uses 24 bit, has 2^{24}, or 16,777,216, values.

A single second of a 44.1 kHz, 16-bit **stereo** (meaning two channels) audio has:

- 44,100 samples per second

- each sample represented by 16 bits

- a total storage need per second of 44,100 samples / second × 16 bits / sample × 2 channels = 1,411,200 bits per second, or 176,400 bytes per second.

Analogue vs digital sound

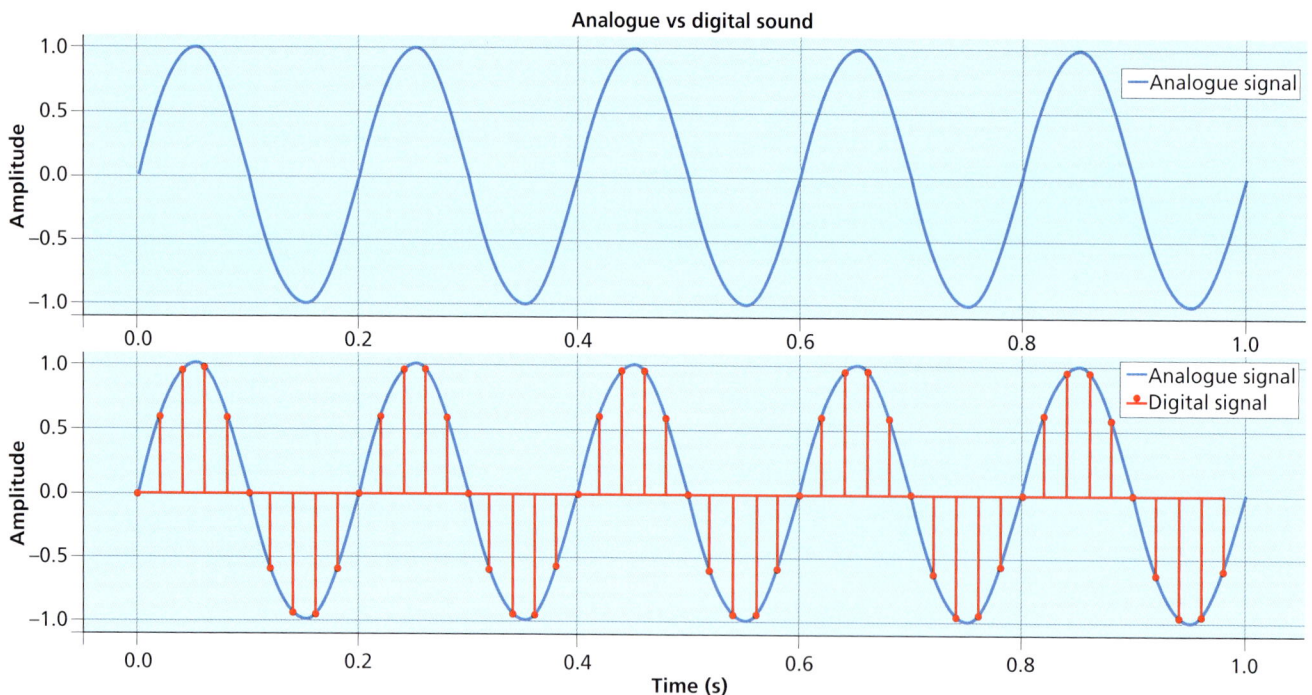

◼ The blue continuous waveform represents an analogue signal, which is a smooth and continuous representation of sound. The digital signal consists of discrete samples taken at regular intervals (sampling rate), illustrating how the continuous analogue signal is converted into a series of discrete points in digital form.

Storage formats

There are many different types of file formats for storing audio. The most common are WAV, AIFF, MP3 and FLAC. They mainly differ by whether they are compressed or uncompressed. Uncompressed formats store the raw binary data, whereas compressed formats use algorithms to reduce the file size for storage or transmission. Just like with image compression, audio compression attempts to reduce the file size by removing parts of the audio signal that are less noticeable to human senses, in this case the ears. There are both lossy and lossless types of compression used with audio. Lossless algorithms compress the data without any loss of quality, whereas lossy algorithms permanently remove audio that is less noticeable to the human ear on the recording.

- **WAV** (Waveform Audio File Format): uncompressed
- **AIFF** (Audio Interchange File Format): uncompressed
- **MP3** (MPEG Audio Layer III): compressed (lossy)
- **FLAC** (Free Lossless Audio Codec): compressed (lossless)

REVIEW QUESTIONS

1   What is the main difference between an analogue signal and a digital signal in the context of audio?
2   What is the process of converting an analogue audio signal into a digital signal called, and what does it involve?
3   Calculate the storage needed per minute for a 44.1 kHz, 16-bit stereo audio file.
4   Explain the difference between lossy and lossless audio compression and give an example of each type of format.

PROGRAMMING EXERCISE

Explore audio files further using the code below. This will allow you to analyse the amplitude of any MP3 file.
You will need to install the following libraries:
- soundfile
- numpy
- matplotlib
- scipy.

Run this command in your terminal:

```
pip install soundfile numpy matplotlib scipy
```

Python

```python
import soundfile as sf
import numpy as np
import matplotlib.pyplot as plt
from scipy.fftpack import fft
# Load the audio file
samples, sample_rate = sf.read("name_of_file.mp3")
# If stereo, select one channel
if samples.ndim > 1:
    samples = samples[:, 0]
# Visualize the waveform
plt.figure(figsize=(12, 6))
plt.plot(samples)
plt.title("Audio Waveform")
```

```
plt.xlabel("Sample Index")
plt.ylabel("Amplitude")
plt.show()
# Perform FFT
spectrum = fft(samples)
frequencies = np.fft.fftfreq(len(spectrum), 1 / sample_rate)
plt.figure(figsize=(12, 6))
plt.plot(frequencies[:len(frequencies)//2],
np.abs(spectrum[:len(spectrum)//2]))
plt.title("Audio Spectrum")
plt.xlabel("Frequency (Hz)")
plt.ylabel("Magnitude")
plt.show()
```

■ Video

Videos are made up of various components that are all contained within an encapsulated container format such as MP4, MKV or AVI. The components are:

- frames (visual data)
- audio tracks
- metadata
- subtitles and closed captions.

Audio is stored as described in the Audio section above, and metadata and subtitles are stored as text, so this section will focus only on how the video data is stored.

Video is essentially stored as a sequence of still images, otherwise known as "frames". When played in quick succession (usually 24 to 60 frames per second), these frames create the illusion of motion. This is very similar to the technique you may have used to create a flipbook. The frames are stored and encoded in binary format, utilizing various techniques to optimize space and ensure efficient playback.

■ Digital video playback is similar to a flipbook: a number of images that are shown quickly, creating the illusion of motion

Frames

In their raw form, frames are stored the same as images, with each pixel having a value that can be represented using a colour model such as RGB. To improve colour efficiency, frames are often converted from the RGB colour model to a different one such as YUV. This helps with compression, as this colour model emphasizes luminance (brightness), which the human eye is more sensitive to than changes in colour detail.

However, we cannot store frames in the same way as we store photos because, in this format, they would be too large. They need to be compressed, and there are two main techniques used for this: spatial (intraframe) and temporal (interframe).

Compression techniques

Spatial compression is particularly effective and commonly used for video that has significant detail variation in each frame. It reduces file size by eliminating redundant information within each frame, such as colour depth or detail levels. This approach is important for videos with a lot of detail that may change significantly between frames, such as animations, nature documentaries and live news broadcasts.

Temporal compression is particularly effective and commonly used for video that has consistent motion across frames. It reduces file size by eliminating redundant information between consecutive frames, capturing only the changes or movements from one frame to the next. As a predictive compression technique, it predicts frame content based on the preceding and sometimes following frames, only storing the differences. This approach is important for videos with a lot of detail that may change significantly between frames, such as animations, nature documentaries and live news broadcasts.

REVIEW QUESTIONS

1 What is the role of frames in a video, and how do they create the illusion of motion?
2 Explain the difference between spatial compression and temporal compression in video storage.
3 Describe how converting video frames from the RGB colour model to the YUV colour model can improve compression efficiency.
4 Calculate the total storage needed for a 10-minute video with a frame rate of 30 frames per second, using 24-bit colour depth and a resolution of 1920×1080 pixels. Assume no compression.

■ Different binary methods for storing integers

Unsigned binary

This is the system we covered in Section A1.2.1. This system only represents positive integers using straightforward binary digits (0s and 1s).

Signed binary

This includes methods for representing both positive and negative integers.

Two's complement:

Two's complement is a method for representing signed integers in binary, where the most significant bit (MSB) indicates the sign (0 for positive, 1 for negative). To convert a positive binary number to its negative counterpart in two's complement, you first invert all the bits (change 0s to 1s and 1s to 0s) and then add 1 to the least significant bit (LSB).

For example:

00000101 = +5

Invert the bits

11111010

Add 1

11111011 = −5

However, a limitation of two's complement is that, in an 8-bit system, it reduces the range of representable numbers. Instead of being able to represent 0 to 255, as with unsigned binary, two's complement allows for numbers ranging from –128 to +127, effectively halving the number of positive values that can be represented.

One's complement:

One's complement is a binary representation method for signed integers, where the most significant bit (MSB) indicates the sign (0 for positive, 1 for negative). To obtain the one's complement of a positive number, you simply invert all the bits (change 0s to 1s and 1s to 0s).

For example:

00000101 = +5

11111010 = –5

Unlike two's complement, one's complement has two representations of the number zero: positive zero (00000000) and negative zero (11111111). This is one of its main limitations and can cause confusion when using arithmetic and logical operations. This means two's complement is normally the preferred system to use. Similarly to two's complement, one's complement also has a limited range, representing numbers from –127 to +127.

Sign-magnitude:

Sign-magnitude is a binary representation method for signed integers where the most significant bit (MSB) serves as the sign indicator, with 0 representing positive numbers and 1 representing negative numbers. The remaining bits represent the magnitude of the number, like how unsigned binary numbers work.

For example:

00000101 = +5

10000101 = –5

This system also has two representations for zero: positive zero (00000000) and negative zero (10000000). It also has the same range as one's complement, from –127 to +127. It is a simple system but, like one's complement, is less efficient compared to two's complement.

Binary-coded decimal

Binary-coded decimal (BCD) is a method of representing decimal numbers where each digit of the decimal number is encoded separately into its own binary form. Unlike pure binary representation, which converts the entire decimal number into a single binary sequence, BCD assigns a 4-bit binary code to each decimal digit (0–9).

For example:

0100 0101 = 45

as 0100 represents 4, and 0101 represents 5

This system is useful where exact decimal representation is crucial, such as financial applications or digital clocks, as it avoids the rounding errors that can occur in other systems. However, due to using four bits per digit, more bits are required to store numbers, making it less space efficient than pure binary representations. Calculations using BCD are also more complex as they require additional steps to handle carry and overflow, so they are not good choices for general-purpose computing.

Gray code (reflected binary code)

Gray code is a binary system where two successive values are only allowed to differ by one bit. That makes this system particularly useful in situations where data integrity during transitions is important. An example system is a robotic arm where we want to monitor its position. As the arm rotates, the rotary encoder generates a sequence of binary outputs corresponding to the arm's angle. If the encoder used standard binary code, small mechanical vibrations or inaccuracies could cause multiple bits to change simultaneously, leading to incorrect readings. However, by using Gray code, the risk of these transition errors is minimized.

■ Comparison of Gray code to standard binary for the numbers 0–7

Numbers	Standard binary	Gray code
0	000	000
1	001	001
2	010	011
3	011	010
4	100	110
5	101	111
6	110	101
7	111	100

Excess-N (biased representation)

Excess-N is a system where a fixed bias (N) is added to the actual value to form an encoded value, and you subtract this bias to decode it. This is used to make all signed integers appear as non-negative binary numbers to allow for easier comparisons and arithmetic operations.

For example, with Excess-3:

The decimal number 2 would be encoded as:

2 + 3 = 5

0101

The decimal number –2 would be encoded as:

–2 + 3 = 1

0001

In an 8-bit system, Excess-127 is often used, which adds 127 to encode an 8-bit number and subtracts 127 to decode it. If you consider trying to order a set of signed binary numbers, this can be difficult as the negative numbers are larger binary numbers than the positive.

For example, take 127 and –127 (using sign-magnitude):

Pre-encoded numbers:

01111111 = 127

10000001 = –127

When we encode these numbers with Excess-127, the positive numbers now appear larger than the negative numbers, making them easier to put in order:

Encoded numbers (Excess-127):

127 + 127 = 254

11111110

–127 + 127 = 0

00000000

After this process has been completed, we decode the numbers again to return them to their original form:

Decoded numbers (Excess-127):

254 – 127 = 127

11111110

0 – 127 = –127

00000000

Fixed-point representation

Fixed-point representation is a method used to store real numbers (numbers with fractional parts) in binary by fixing the position of the binary point. In a fixed-point system, the binary point is placed at a predetermined position, either between certain bits or at a specific location in the binary sequence. This allows for a straightforward representation of fractional numbers, though with some trade-offs in terms of precision and range.

For example, if we want to represent 5.25 in an 8-bit system where four bits represent the integer and four bits represent the fractional part:

Integer part (four bits): 0101 = 5

Fractional part (four bits): 0100 = 0.25

Combined: 0101.0100

Note: Binary fractions are used for the fractional part, where the first bit to the right represents $\frac{1}{2}$, the second bit represents $\frac{1}{4}$, the third $\frac{1}{8}$ and the fourth $\frac{1}{16}$. So, in the example above, we have $0\frac{1}{2}$, $1\frac{1}{4}$, $0\frac{1}{8}$ and $0\frac{1}{16}$.

The number of bits assigned in this system limits the range and precision. In this example, with a 4-bit signed integer, we only have the range of –8 to 7.9375, with the smallest representable value being 0.0625 ($\frac{1}{16}$). This means this system is unable to handle very large or very small numbers effectively. However, it is a simpler and faster system compared to floating-point arithmetic (see below), and does not require any complex operations to adjust the position of the binary point.

Floating-point representation

Floating-point representation is a method used to represent real numbers that can have a very large range or fractional parts. It does this by storing numbers in a format that includes a sign, an exponent and a mantissa (or significand). This format allows computers to efficiently handle very large numbers, very small numbers and numbers with fractional parts, all with a reasonable degree of precision.

Using the IEEE 754 standard for single-precision floating-point numbers (which uses 32 bits):

1 Sign bit (one bit):

The sign bit determines whether the number is positive or negative.

2 Exponent (eight bits):

This is used to scale the number by a power of two and is stored using the Excess-127 system in its "biased" form; in other words, 127 is added to the actual exponent value.

3 Mantissa (23 bits):

This represents the significant digits of the number. The mantissa does not store leading ones (in normalized form).

For example, this is how we could represent the decimal number −5.75:

Convert the number to binary:

101.11

Normalize this number to the form of $1.xxxxx \times 2^n$:

1.0111×2^2

Determine the components:

Sign bit: 1 (as it is a negative number)

Exponent: 2 + 127 (Excess-127) = 129 = 10000001

Mantissa: 01110000000000000000000 (ignoring the leading 1)

So, the IEEE 754 single-precision binary representation of −5.75 is:

1 (sign) 10000001 (exponent) 01110000000000000000000 (mantissa)

This system allows for the representation of both very large and very small numbers, which is essential in scientific computing, engineering and graphics, and is more precise than fixed-point representation.

However, it is still not precise enough to represent all decimal numbers, and this can lead to rounding errors. The complexity of the system also makes it slower than others, often requiring special handling in hardware.

A1.2.3 Purpose and use of logic gates

■ The history of logic gates

In the mid-19th century, a British mathematician named George Boole developed an algebraic system known as "Boolean algebra". This provided a mathematical framework for representing logical statements and operations that laid the foundations for modern digital logic.

In the early 20th century, an American mathematician and electrical engineer named Claude Shannon was the first person to recognize the potential of Boolean algebra for electrical circuit design. He demonstrated how the design of electrical relay circuits could be optimized using Boolean algebra, and then the development of semiconductor technology further propelled the evolution of logic gates.

The transistor was then invented in 1947 at Bell Labs, which made it possible to build compact and efficient logic gates. By the 1960s to 1970s, integrated circuits were incorporating multiple transistors on a single chip, which led to the development of microprocessors. Logic gates are the building blocks of modern digital systems, from the basic calculator to advanced supercomputers.

■ George Boole, the British mathematician who developed Boolean algebra, laying the groundwork for digital logic and modern computer science

◼ Basic gates

Logic gates are fundamental components in digital electronics, crucial for building various types of circuits within computers and other digital devices. The basic types of logic gates include AND, OR and NOT gates, each performing a specific logical function. These gates take one or more binary inputs and produce a binary output based on the logical operation they perform. To understand and verify the behaviour of these gates, we use truth tables, which systematically list all possible input combinations and their corresponding outputs, providing a clear representation of the gate's function. Additionally, each gate has a corresponding Boolean algebra representation that simplifies complex logical expressions.

Logic gates are made up of transistors, which act as electronic switches, allowing or blocking the flow of electrical current. In a transistor, the control wire (or "gate") regulates the current between the two electrodes, known as the "source" and the "drain". When voltage is applied to the gate, it allows current to flow from the source to the drain, enabling the transistor to switch states and perform logical operations.

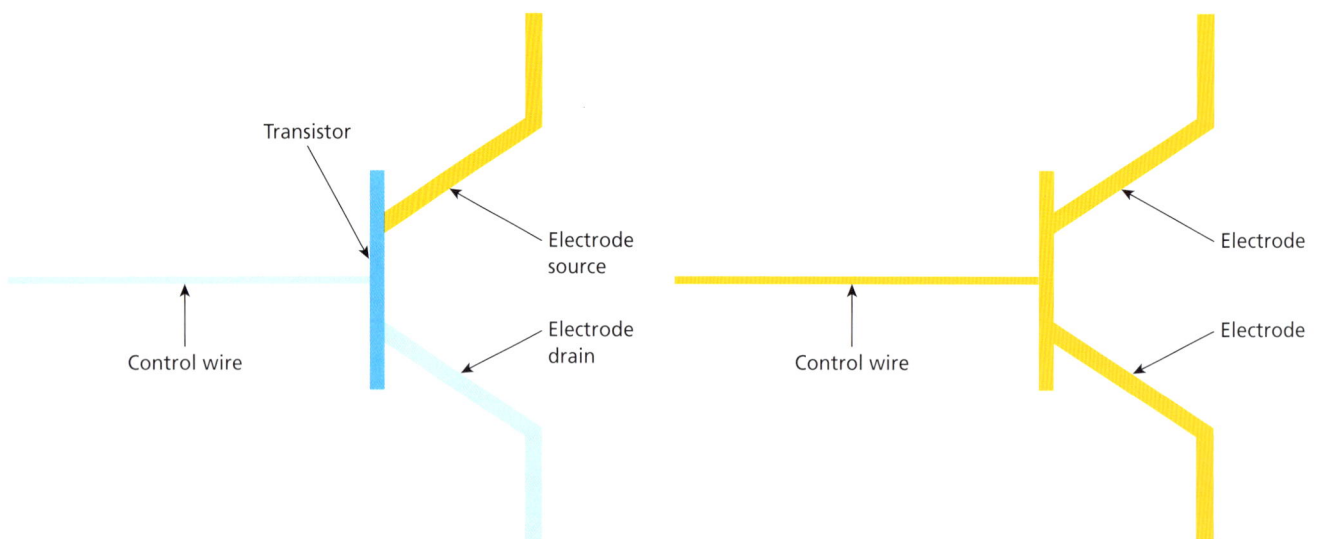

Transistor

Electrode source

Electrode drain

Control wire

Electrode

Electrode

Control wire

◼ A Buffer gate that shows the inner workings of the gate – when the control wire is off, no electricity can flow between the electrodes

◼ When electricity flows down the control wire, the transistor allows for the flow of electricity between electrodes

Above is a simple Buffer gate, where we can consider the control wire as the input and the electrode drain as the output. If the input is on, the output is on; and if the input is off, the output is off. We can show this using a truth table:

Buffer gate truth table	
Input A	**Output X**
1	1
0	0

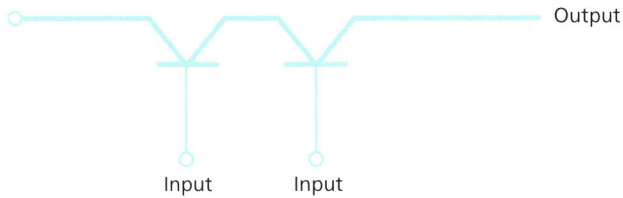

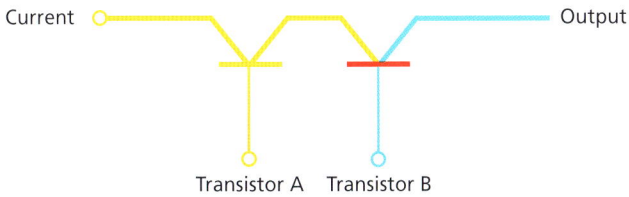

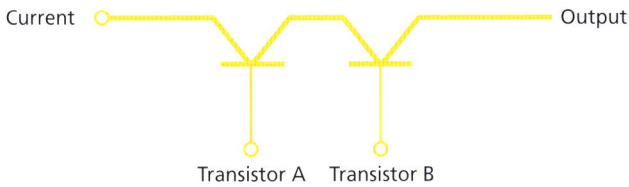

Transistor-level schematic of an AND gate

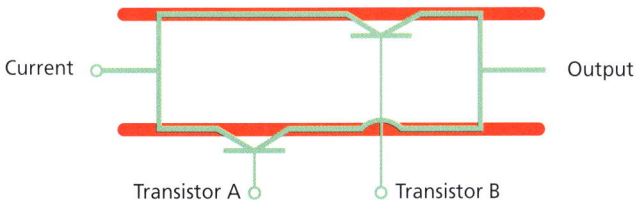

Transistor-level schematic of an OR gate

AND gate

The diagram on the left shows an AND gate implemented using transistors. The gate has two inputs and one output. If only one of the inputs is on, one of the transistors without an input would stop the current passing through. It is only when both inputs are high (1) that the transistors allow current to pass through, resulting in a high output (1).

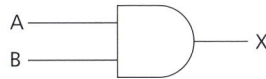

■ AND gate

■ **Input and output rules:** The AND gate outputs 1 only if both inputs are 1

AND gate truth table		
Input A	**Input B**	**Output X**
0	0	0
0	1	0
1	0	0
1	1	1

Boolean algebra: $X = A \cdot B$

OR gate

The diagram on the left shows an OR gate implemented using transistors. The gate has two inputs – A and B – and one output. When either input A or B is high (1), the corresponding transistor turns on, allowing current to flow through the circuit and resulting in a high output (1). When both inputs are low (0), neither transistor conducts and the output remains low (0).

■ OR gate

■ **Input and output rules:** The OR gate outputs 1 if at least one input is 1

OR gate truth table		
Input A	**Input B**	**Output X**
0	0	0
0	1	1
1	0	1
1	1	1

Boolean algebra: $X = A + B$

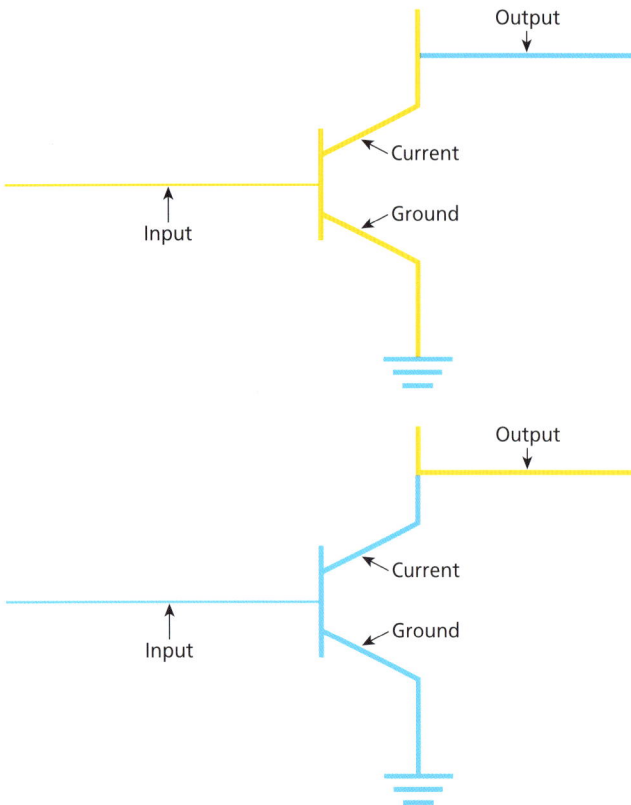

Transistor-level schematic of a NOT gate

NOT gate

The diagram below illustrates a NOT gate (inverter) using a transistor. In this configuration, the input line is connected to the gate of the transistor, the output line is connected to the source and the drain is connected to ground.

■ NOT gate

When the input is high (1), the transistor turns on, allowing current to flow from the source to the drain, effectively grounding the output and resulting in a low voltage at the output (0). When the input is low (0), the transistor turns off, preventing current from flowing to the ground. In this state, the output then outputs a high voltage (1).

■ **Input and output rules:** The NOT gate outputs the opposite value of the input

NOT gate truth table	
Input A	**Output X**
0	1
1	0

Boolean algebra: $X = \overline{A}$

■ Derived (complex) gates

The following gates – NAND, NOR, XOR and XNOR – are examples of derived gates. Derived gates are combinations of the basic gates and provide more complex logic functions. To show these, we will move up a level of abstraction and, rather than examine the transistor schematic, we will look at how the basic gates are combined to create them.

NAND gate (NOT AND)

A NAND gate is constructed with an AND gate followed by a NOT gate. Due to this, it gives the opposite output to an AND gate. If both inputs are high (1), the output is low (0). In all other cases, the output is high (1).

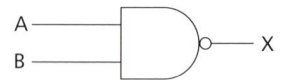

■ How a NAND gate is constructed: an AND gate followed by a NOT gate

■ NAND gate

■ **Input and output rules:** The NAND gate outputs 1 unless both inputs are 1

NAND gate truth table		
Input A	**Input B**	**Output X**
0	0	1
0	1	1
1	0	1
1	1	0

Boolean algebra: $X = \overline{A \cdot B}$

NOR gate (NOT OR)

An NOR gate gives the opposite output to an OR gate as it is constructed using an OR gate followed by a NOT gate. This means that it is only when both inputs are low (0) that the output is high (1). In all other cases, the output is low (0).

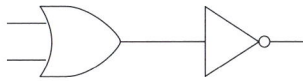

■ How a NOR gate is constructed: an OR gate followed by a NOT gate   ■ A NOR gate

■ **Input and output rules:** The NOR gate outputs 1 only if both inputs are 0

NOR gate truth table		
Input A	**Input B**	**Output X**
0	0	1
0	1	0
1	0	0
1	1	0

Boolean algebra: $X = \overline{A + B}$

XOR gate (exclusive OR)

The XOR (exclusive OR) gate differs from the OR gate in one key way: its output is true only when the inputs are different. This means the XOR gate outputs true when exactly one of the inputs is true, but false when both inputs are the same. For example, if both inputs are high (1), the XOR gate's output is low (0). This is unlike the OR gate, which would output high (1) in this case.

■ How an XOR gate is constructed   ■ An XOR gate

■ **Input and output rules:** The XOR gate outputs 1 if the inputs are different

XOR gate truth table		
Input A	**Input B**	**Output X**
0	0	0
0	1	1
1	0	1
1	1	0

Boolean algebra: $X = A \oplus B$

XNOR gate (exclusive NOT OR)

The XNOR gate is constructed using an XOR gate followed by a NOT gate. This means the output is the opposite to an XOR gate, only outputting high (1) when both inputs are the same (either high or low).

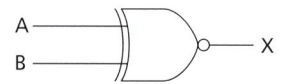

■ How an XNOR gate is constructed: an XOR gate followed by a NOT gate ■ An XNOR gate

■ **Input and output rules:** The XNOR gate outputs 1 if the inputs are the same

XNOR gate truth table		
Input A	**Input B**	**Output X**
0	0	1
0	1	0
1	0	0
1	1	1

Boolean algebra: $X = \overline{A \oplus B}$

A1.2.4 Constructing and analysing truth tables

■ Truth tables to predict the output of simple logic circuits

The following diagram shows a logic circuit, where a number of logic gates are connected together. In this scenario, you need to be able to handle circuits with up to three inputs.

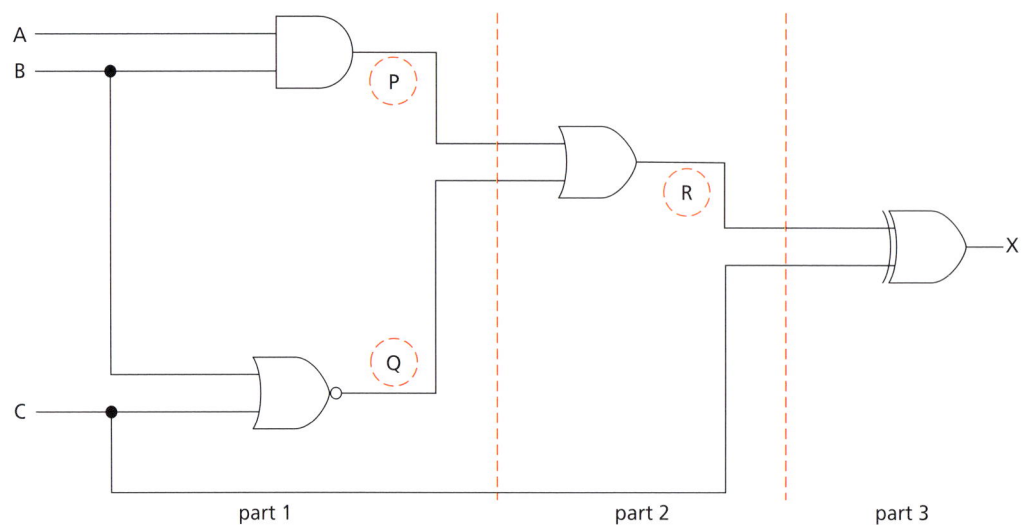

When creating a truth table, first enter the three inputs and their possible input states; in this case, A, B and C. As there are three inputs, you can calculate the number of rows you will need by 2^n, where n represents the number of inputs. In this example:

$2^3 = 8$

Populate the furthest right column, alternating between 0 and 1.

Populate the middle column by alternating, every two rows, between 0 and 1.

Populate the left-hand column by alternating, every four rows, between 0 and 1.

Following this pattern will give you every possible input state.

A	B	C
0	0	0
0	0	1
0	1	0
0	1	1
1	0	0
1	0	1
1	1	0
1	1	1

Once this is complete, we then add the intermediate values to make it easier to remember the state at each stage of the circuit. In this example, we have three intermediate values: P, Q and R. Finally, we add the output column, X.

A	B	C	P	Q	R	X
0	0	0				
0	0	1				
0	1	0				
0	1	1				
1	0	0				
1	0	1				
1	1	0				
1	1	1				

Now, starting with the intermediate values, work through the logic circuit.

A	B	C	P (A AND B)	Q (B NOR C)	R (P OR Q)	X (C XOR R)
0	0	0	0	1	1	1
0	0	1	0	0	0	1
0	1	0	0	0	0	0
0	1	1	0	0	0	1
1	0	0	0	1	1	1
1	0	1	0	0	0	1
1	1	0	1	0	1	1
1	1	1	1	0	1	0

Produce the truth tables for the following logic circuits.

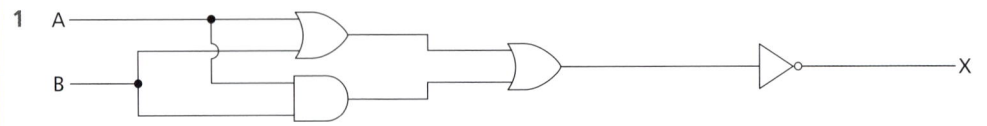

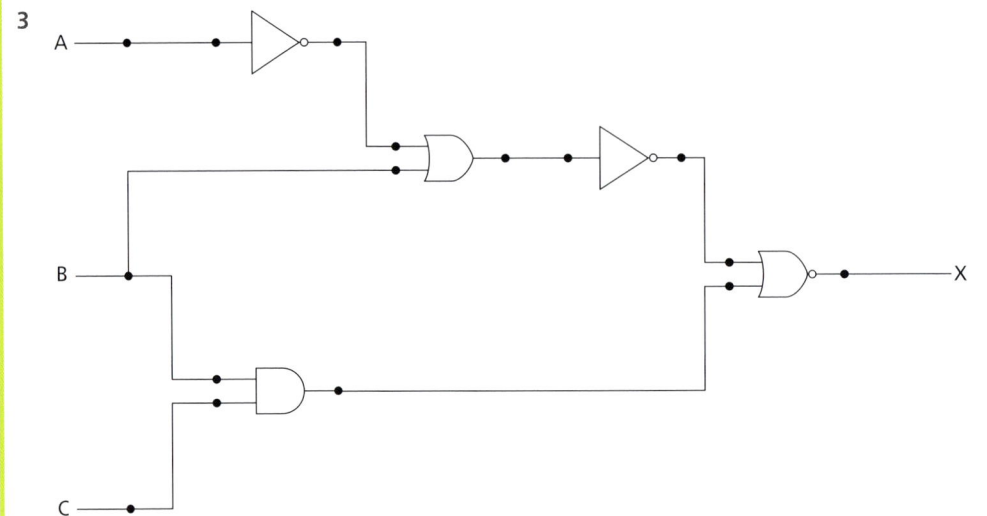

1

2

3

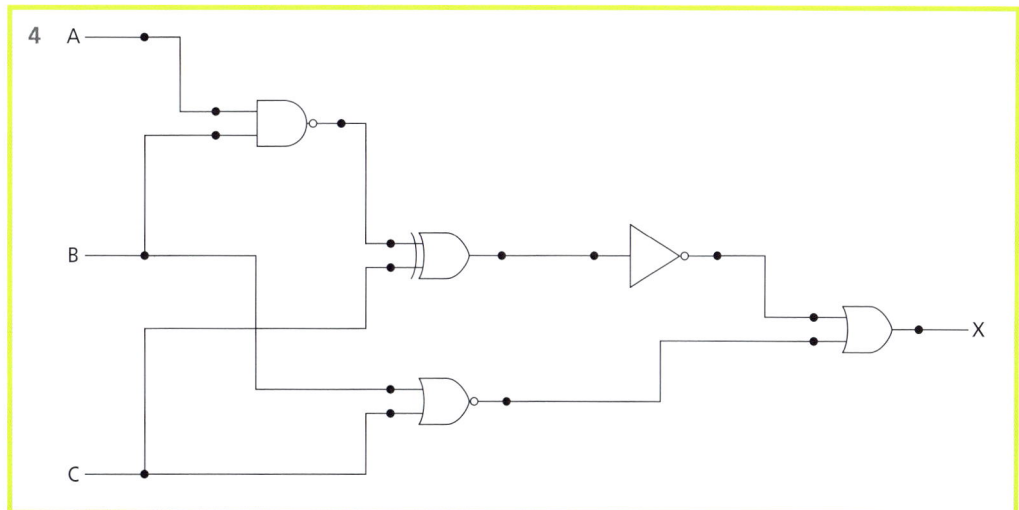

■ Truth tables to determine outputs from inputs for a problem description

Problem description: *A baby alarm that goes off when the alarm is switched on and the baby is crying or the room is too cold.*

With a problem description, we first need to identify the inputs. Here we have three: alarm switch, baby crying and room temperature, which we can represent as A, B and C and set up our truth table.

We know the alarm goes off if the device is switched on AND the baby is crying OR the room is too cold. From here, we can identify the logic gates in the description. We can determine from this that the device must be switched on before the alarm can go off, so if the switch is off, all outputs would be 0. If the device is switched on, at least one of the other two inputs must be on for the alarm to trigger. We have one intermediate value (baby crying OR room is cold), represented with P.

A (switch)	B (crying)	C (cold)	P (B or C)	X (A and P)
0	0	0	0	0
0	0	1	1	0
0	1	0	1	0
0	1	1	1	0
1	0	0	0	0
1	0	1	1	1
1	1	0	1	1
1	1	1	1	1

REVIEW QUESTIONS

Complete the truth tables for the following problem descriptions:

1 A traffic light control system that changes to green only if the pedestrian button is not pressed and the road sensor detects no cars waiting on the side road.
2 A water irrigation system that activates if the soil is dry or the temperature is high, provided the system is manually enabled.
3 A nuclear missile launcher: the missile should only launch if the president and two of his three cabinet ministers flip the switch.

Logical expressions

We can represent logic circuits using Boolean algebra. If we use the baby alarm scenario again, we can represent this as:

$X = A \cdot (B + C)$

In Boolean algebra, parentheses are often used to indicate which operations should be performed first. However, there is a standard order of operations, similar to PEMDAS (or BODMAS) in mathematics. If no parentheses are present, follow this sequence:

- NOT
- AND (including NAND)
- OR (including NOR and XOR)

This ensures that operations are executed in the correct order for accurate results.

REVIEW QUESTIONS

Using the Boolean algebra from the gates in Section A1.2.3, write the Boolean algebra for the three logic circuits created in the previous problem descriptions:

1 Traffic light control system
2 Water irrigation system
3 Nuclear missile launcher

Karnaugh maps and algebraic simplification

Karnaugh maps (K-maps) are a tool that helps simplify Boolean expressions, making it easier to create simpler and more efficient digital circuits. Instead of using complicated algebraic methods, K-maps allow you to visually group terms from a truth table, which makes it faster to find a simplified expression. This process is useful because it reduces the number of logic gates needed in a circuit, saving time, space, cost and power consumption.

Two inputs

This two-input K-map is used for expressions with two variables. In this map, variable A is placed along the side and variable B across the top. However, the order of the variables doesn't matter – B could be along the side and A across the top. Both possible states (0 and 1) for each variable are shown in the map, representing all combinations of their values.

Expression: A + B

A \ B		B 0	B 1
A	0		
A	1		

We split the expression at the OR operator and focus first on the term involving A. We populate the K-map where A is 1, which, in this case, corresponds to the entire bottom row. At this stage, we ignore B and only fill in the cells where A is 1.

A \ B		B 0	B 1
A	0		
A	1	1	1

We now do the same for the second part of the expression: B.

A \ B		B 0	B 1
A	0		1
A	1	1	1

This completed K-map now shows the expression A + B.

This is another example of a completed map for the expression $\overline{A} + B$:

A \ B		B 0	B 1
A	0	1	1
A	1		1

Expression: $A \cdot B + A \cdot \overline{B}$

This is a more complicated expression, but still has only two inputs. Using this expression, the circuit would look like this:

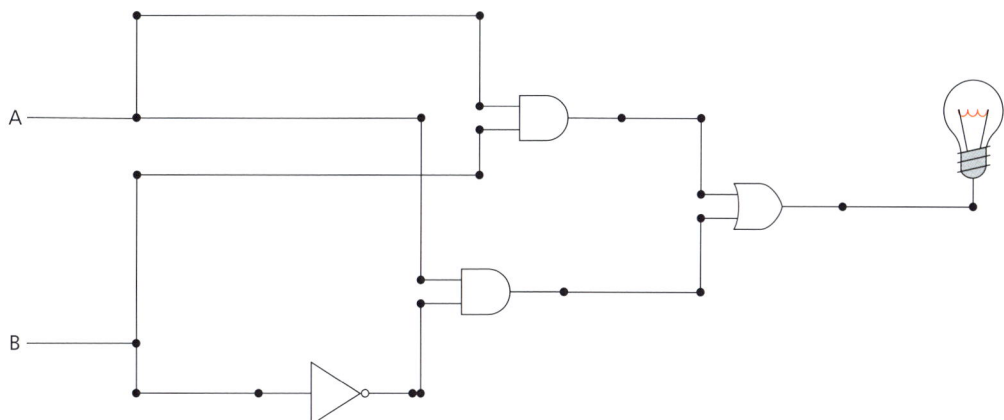

The table map structure is still the same:

A \ B		B 0	B 1
A	0		
A	1		

We again split the expression at the OR symbol, focusing initially on A · B. In this case, we insert a 1 into only one cell, where both A and B are 1.

A \ B		B 0	B 1
A	0		
A	1		1

Next, we focus on the second part of the expression, $A \cdot \overline{B}$. In this case, we insert a 1 into the cell where A is 1 and B is 0.

A \ B		B 0	B 1
A	0		
A	1	1	1

The K-map is now complete and shows that the value of B has no impact on the outcome, allowing us to simplify the expression to just A. If we create the circuit using this simplified expression, we can see that the circuit is significantly more efficient, while still performing the same function.

A ———————————————————————

Three inputs
Expression: $\overline{A} \cdot B \cdot C + A \cdot \overline{B} \cdot C + A \cdot B \cdot C$

With three inputs, we use a similar K-map but, this time, we place two of the inputs across the top. The digits across the top may seem out of order compared to standard binary counting (00, 01, 10, 11). Instead, they follow the Gray code convention (see Section A1.2.2 for more information), where only one digit changes at a time. It is important to set the map up this way to ensure correct grouping and simplification.

C \ AB		AB 00	AB 01	AB 11	AB 10
C	0				
C	1				

We now follow similar steps as with the two-input K-map. We separate the expression by the OR operator and focus on the first term: $\overline{A} \cdot B \cdot C$. In this step, we populate the K-map by inserting a 1 into the cells where A is 0, B is 1 and C is 1.

C \ AB		AB 00	AB 01	AB 11	AB 10
C	0				
C	1		1		

Followed by: $A \cdot \overline{B} \cdot C$

C \ AB		AB 00	AB 01	AB 11	AB 10
C	0				
C	1		1		1

And finally: $A \cdot B \cdot C$

C \ AB		AB 00	AB 01	AB 11	AB 10
C	0				
C	1		1	1	1

Grouping the 1s and simplifying the expression

Although it wasn't explicitly stated before, you may have noticed the boxes drawn around groups of 1s in the K-maps. These boxes help simplify the Boolean expression, but there are some important rules that must be followed when grouping 1s:

- **Groups must contain powers of 2:** One, two, four, eight or sixteen 1s can be grouped together.

- **Groups must be rectangular or square:** Each group should form a rectangle or square shape.

- **Groups cannot be diagonal:** Adjacent 1s can only be grouped horizontally or vertically, not diagonally.

- **Groups must be as large as possible:** Always aim to make the largest groups to simplify the expression further.

- **Groups can overlap:** Some 1s may be included in more than one group if it helps form larger groups.

- **Minimize the total number of groups:** The goal is to use the smallest number of groups to cover all the 1s.

To determine the expression from the groups, we look at each group of cells and refer to the variables. If a variable's value stays the same across all the cells in the group, we keep that variable in the simplified expression. However, if the variable's value changes across the group, we discard it from the expression.

C \ AB		AB 00	AB 01	AB 11	AB 10
C	0				
C	1		1	1	1

The first group is entirely along the bottom row, meaning C stays the same (C = 1), so we keep it in the expression. A changes from 0 to 1 between the cells in the group, so we discard A. B remains 1 in both cells, so we keep B. Therefore, the first part of our final expression is:

$B \cdot C$

C \ AB		AB	AB	AB	AB
		00	01	11	10
C	0				
C	1		1	1	1

The second group, like the first, is located along the bottom row, meaning that C stays as 1 because it does not change across the group. In this case, A remains 1 in both cells, while B changes from 0 to 1. Since B changes, we discard B from this part of the expression. As a result, we keep A and C, giving us the second part of our expression:

$A \cdot C$

We then combine these expressions with an OR operator, giving us the final expression:

$B \cdot C + A \cdot C$

● Common mistake

When setting up your K-map for three inputs, make sure to use Gray code for the headings, not standard binary. Gray code ensures that only one bit changes between adjacent cells, which helps when grouping 1s and simplifies the expression more effectively.

Wrapping around edges in K-maps

Here is the K-map for the expression:

$\bar{B} + A \cdot B \cdot C$

C \ AB		AB	AB	AB	AB
		00	01	11	10
C	0	1			1
C	1	1		1	1

To group these 1s, you may assume this is the answer:

C \ AB		AB	AB	AB	AB
		00	01	11	10
C	0	1			1
C	1	1		1	1

However, K-maps are considered three-dimensional, and groups can be formed from left to right and top to bottom (although only left to right is possible with three inputs). In this example, it is possible to build a larger group by combining the two groups on the edges, forming a square group of four 1s.

C \ AB		AB	AB	AB	AB
		00	01	11	10
C	0	1			1
C	1	1		1	1

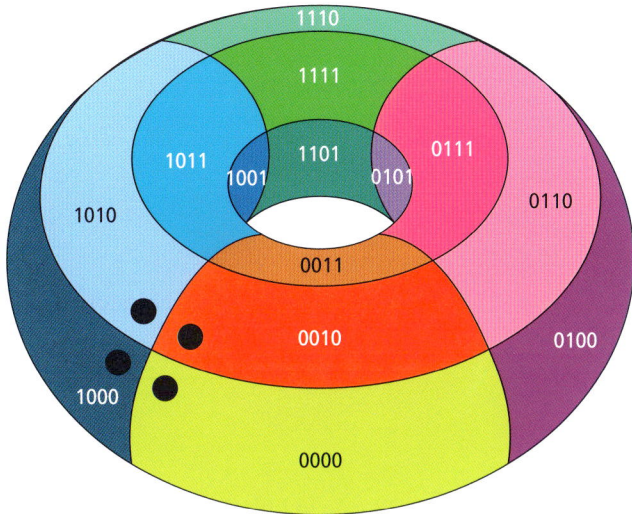

Using these groups, we can form the simplified expression:

$A \cdot C + \overline{B}$

REVIEW QUESTIONS

$\overline{A} \cdot B + A \cdot B$

1 Draw the truth table for the above expression.
2 Draw the Karnaugh map for the expression and write the simplified expression.

$\overline{A} \cdot B \cdot C + A \cdot B \cdot C + \overline{A} \cdot B \cdot \overline{C}$

3 Draw the truth table for the above expression.
4 Draw the Karnaugh map for the expression and write the simplified expression.

$\overline{A} \cdot \overline{B} \cdot C + \overline{A} \cdot B \cdot C + A \cdot \overline{B} \cdot C$

5 Draw the truth table for the above expression.
6 Draw the Karnaugh map for the expression and write the simplified expression.

■ K-map drawn on a torus and in a plane – the dot-marked cells are adjacent

A1.2.5 Constructing logic diagrams

■ Designing digital circuits from Boolean algebra expressions

By understanding the principles of Boolean algebra, we can simplify complex logic expressions and translate them into circuit diagrams. This journey from abstract mathematical notation to circuit design is essential for creating efficient and reliable digital systems. We will start by creating the digital circuit from the expression below:

$Y = (A \cdot B) + (\overline{A} \cdot \overline{B})$

1 Start with two inputs: A and B.
2 Work on the first parenthesis by introducing an AND gate and joining both A and B to it.

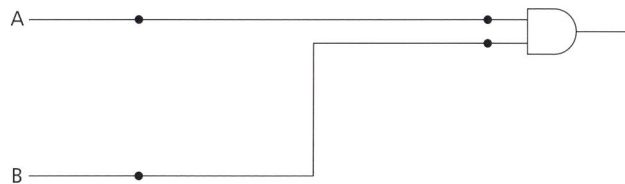

3 Work on the second parenthesis, connecting A to a NOT gate and B to a NOT gate.

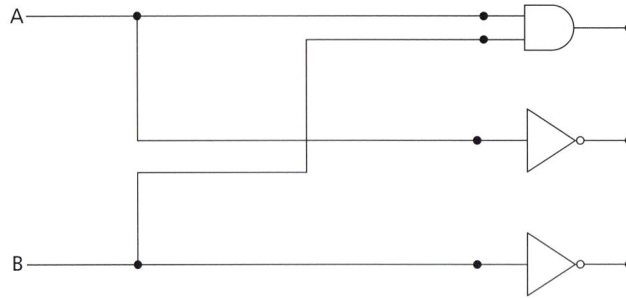

4 Connect both the outputs to an AND gate.

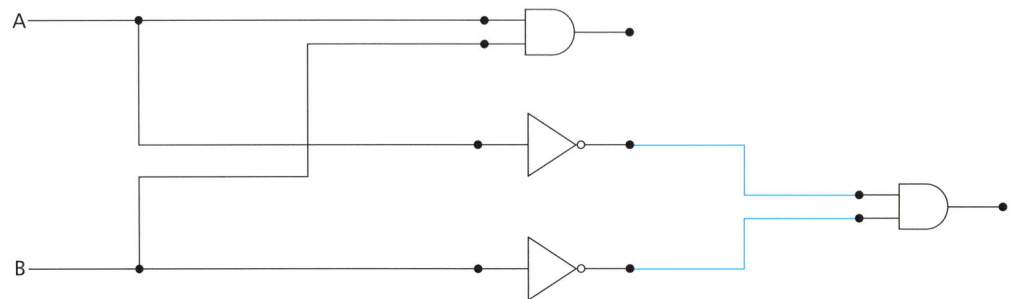

5 Now work outside the parentheses and introduce the OR gate to link them together.

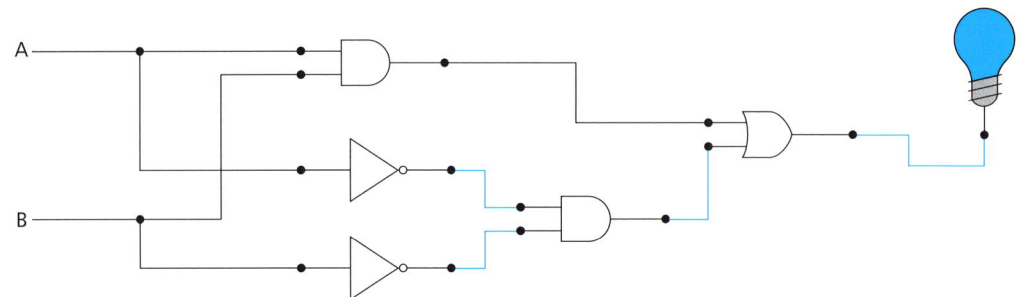

REVIEW QUESTIONS

Create the digital circuits from the following Boolean expressions.

1 $Y = (A \cdot B) \oplus \overline{A}$

2 $Y = (A + B) \cdot \overline{A \cdot B}$

3 $Y = A \cdot \overline{(B + C)}$

4 $Y = (A \oplus B) \cdot (B \oplus C)$

5 $Y = (A \cdot B) \cdot \overline{C} + \overline{(A + B)}$

Operating systems and control systems

A1.3.1 The role of operating systems

An operating system (OS) is the fundamental software that manages computer hardware and software resources and provides common services for computer programs. It acts as an intermediary between the user and the computer hardware, ensuring efficient and secure operation of the system.

Operating systems simplify user interactions with computer hardware by abstracting the underlying complexities. This means users and applications do not need to understand the detailed workings of hardware components such as CPUs, memory and input / output devices. Instead, the OS provides a set of high-level services and interfaces that hide these complexities, making the system easier to use and program.

The primary role of an operating system is to manage the computer's resources effectively. This includes:

- **CPU management:** allocating CPU time to various processes and ensuring efficient execution

- **memory management:** handling the allocation and de-allocation of memory to applications, and managing virtual memory to extend physical memory capacity

- **storage management:** organizing and managing data on storage devices, ensuring reliable data storage and retrieval

- **device management:** controlling and co-ordinating hardware devices, providing drivers and interfaces for seamless operation.

Some of the most famous modern operating systems are Microsoft Windows, Apple macOS and Linux on larger computers and laptops, with Android and iOS being more popular for smaller portable devices such as smartphones.

A1.3.2 Functions of an operating system

Operating system functions are multifaceted, ensuring that the system runs smoothly, efficiently and securely. Here, we will delve into the various critical functions of an operating system, illustrating how it maintains system integrity while running background operations and managing resources.

■ Memory management

Memory management is a fundamental function of an operating system (OS), involving the control and co-ordination of a computer's primary memory (RAM). The OS ensures that memory is allocated efficiently to processes and applications, maintains system stability and protects memory areas from unauthorized access.

When you open / run an application, the OS will load it into RAM. First, it will locate the application on the storage device (likely a hard disk drive or solid state drive) and read the executable file (.exe on Windows or .app on Mac). This file contains all the application's code and initial data.

The OS then allocates the necessary memory space for the application. This includes space for the code, data and any other required resources. The OS ensures that the application has enough space to execute without interfering with other processes.

> ◆ **Virtual memory:** a memory-management technique that allows a computer to use more memory than is physically available by temporarily transferring data from RAM to disk storage, enabling the execution of larger programs and multitasking.

Once the application is loaded into RAM, the OS continuously manages memory to ensure efficient operation and system stability. While the application is running, the OS can dynamically allocate and de-allocate memory as needed by the application. The OS also ensures that each process operates within its own memory space. This prevents processes from interfering with each other, which enhances the security and stability of the system.

If the applications require more memory than is available in the RAM, the OS can use **virtual memory** to keep the system running smoothly. Virtual memory is when the OS allocates some space on the hard disk drive (HDD) or solid state drive (SSD) to use as RAM. This is not an ideal situation, as reading from a storage device is much slower than accessing RAM but, by switching processes with a higher priority into RAM, and those with lower priority into virtual memory, the OS is able to continue to run the system at an optimal level.

Virtual memory (per process)

Physical memory

Another process's memory

RAM

Disk

■ Relationship between virtual memory and physical memory

●Top tip!

Think of memory management as organizing books on a bookshelf. The operating system allocates each book (process) its own space on the shelf (memory). Just as you wouldn't let books overlap or mix up, the OS ensures that each process has its own protected area in memory.

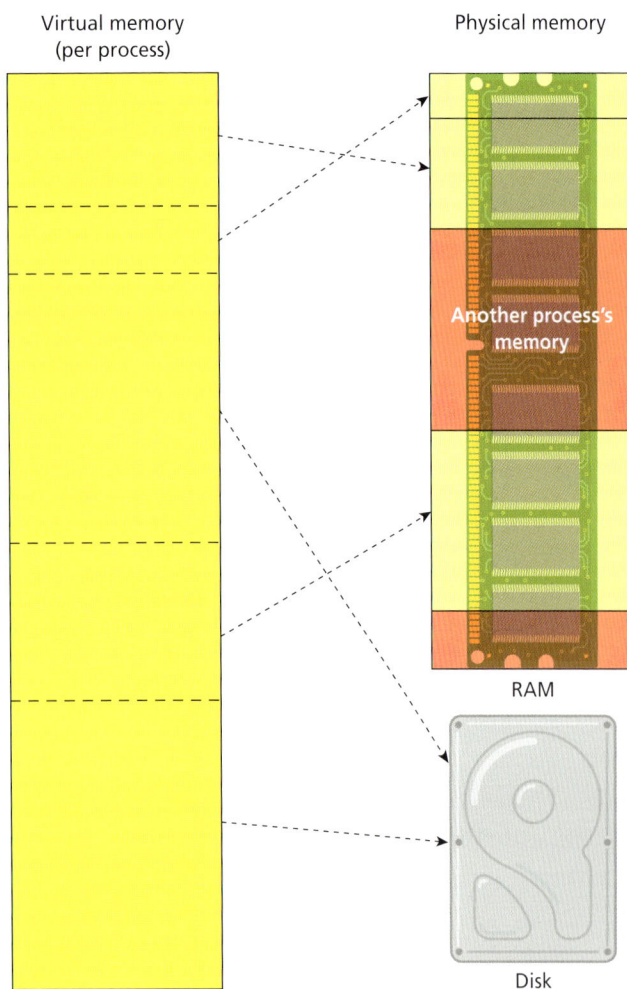

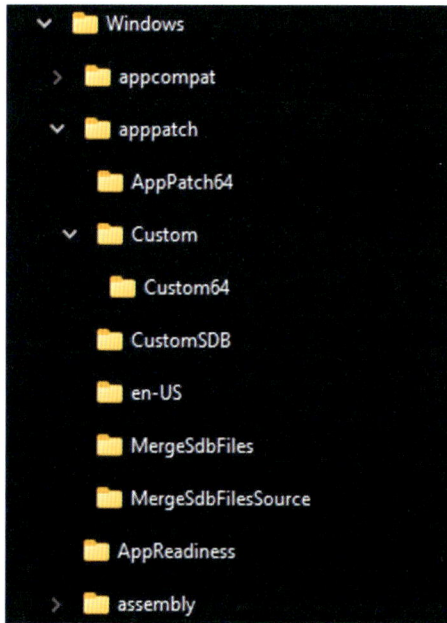

Windows File Explorer view displaying a hierarchical directory structure

▪ File management

File management is a crucial function of an OS, involving the storage, retrieval, organization and manipulation of data on storage devices. The OS provides a structured way to manage files and directories, ensuring system stability and security.

The OS employs a hierarchical file system to organize files in a logical and structured manner. Files are organized into directories (or folders), which can contain further directories, creating a tree-like structure. This organization makes it easier for users and applications to locate and manage data.

The OS allows a number of set file operations that users and applications can perform on the files and directories, including creating new files and directories; reading and writing data to files; deleting files; renaming files; and moving or copying files and directories to different locations.

To ensure consistency and avoid conflicts, the OS enforces rules for naming files, ensuring no two files in the same directory have the same name. Files often have **extensions**, like .jpg or .exe, to indicate the file type and associated application although, depending on the OS settings, these may be hidden from the user.

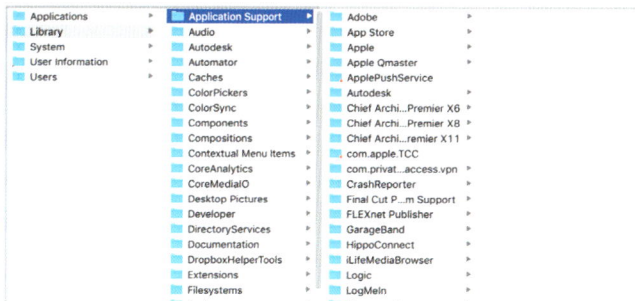

▪ MacOS finder view displaying a hierarchical directory structure

▪ Some of the most commonly used file extensions

◆ **File extension:** a suffix at the end of a filename that indicates the file type and the program associated with opening or processing that file (e.g. .docx for Word documents, .jpg for images).

◆ **Defragmentation:** the process of reorganizing the data on a hard drive so that files are stored in contiguous blocks, reducing fragmentation and improving access speed and overall system performance.

When managing the storage of files, the OS uses various methods to improve performance; this includes how it allocates files on the physical storage medium, manages free space and performs maintenance on the saved data. One important maintenance task is **defragmentation**, which reorganizes fragmented data on a hard disk drive (HDD). Fragmentation occurs over time as files are created, modified and deleted, causing them to be scattered across different sectors of the disk. Defragmentation aims to rearrange these file fragments into contiguous sequences, so improving system performance.

◆ **Device drivers:**
specialized software programs that allow the operating system to communicate with and control hardware devices, e.g. printers, graphics cards or network adapters, by providing the necessary instructions and protocols.

◆ **Buffering:** the process of temporarily storing data in a memory area (buffer) while it is being transferred between two devices or processes, helping to manage differences in data-flow rates and ensuring smooth, uninterrupted operation.

◆ **Caching:** the process of temporarily storing frequently accessed data in a high-speed storage area (cache) to reduce access time and improve system performance by enabling quicker retrieval of the data.

◆ **Spooling:** the process of queuing data or tasks in a buffer, typically for input / output devices such as printers, so that they can be processed sequentially and at their own pace, allowing the system to continue working on other tasks in the meantime.

◆ **Plug and Play (PnP):**
a technology that allows the operating system to detect, configure and install drivers automatically for new hardware devices when they are connected to the computer, enabling them to work without requiring manual set-up by the user.

■ Device management

Operating system device management ensures that hardware devices operate efficiently and interact seamlessly with software applications. The OS controls and co-ordinates the use of hardware components such as printers, disk drives, display screens, keyboards and network interfaces through specialized software called **device drivers**. Device drivers are essential programs that enable the OS to communicate with connected hardware. Each piece of hardware requires a specific driver to function correctly and efficiently. The OS uses these drivers to provide a uniform interface, allowing applications to interact with the hardware without needing to understand the hardware's specifics.

The OS also handles input/output (I/O) management to co-ordinate data transfer between the computer and peripheral devices. It employs techniques such as **buffering**, **caching** and **spooling** to optimize performance and reliability. Buffering involves using temporary storage areas to hold data while it is being transferred between devices, accommodating speed differences between the CPU and peripheral devices. Caching stores frequently accessed data to reduce access times, improving overall system efficiency. Spooling queues data and sends it in a manageable order to devices such as printers that cannot handle interleaved data streams.

Modern operating systems have introduced user-friendly ways of connecting devices, such as **Plug and Play (PnP)** technology. With PnP, the OS can automatically identify a device that has been attached and install the necessary drivers and configure settings without the need for user interaction. The OS is also capable of detecting errors and taking action to recover from them, by resetting the device, reinitializing drivers or notifying the user of the issue. Additionally, the OS provides security and access control to ensure that only authorized users and processes can access certain devices, maintaining system integrity and security.

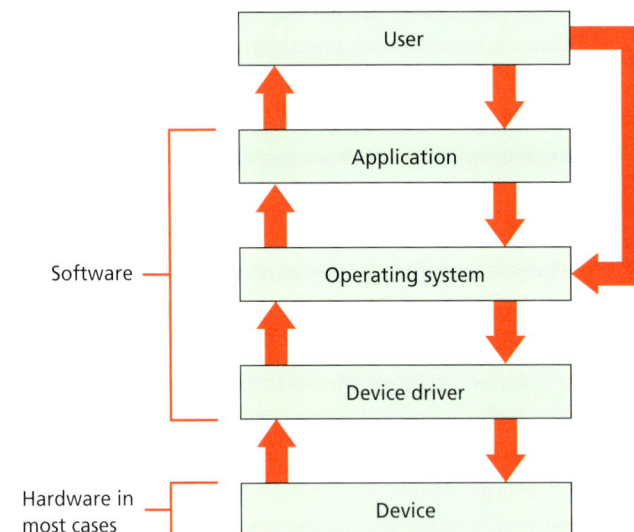

■ Device drivers act as intermediaries between the operating system and hardware devices, enabling software to communicate effectively with hardware components

■ Scheduling

The OS schedules the process of managing the execution of multiple processes by determining which process runs at any given time. The scheduler is responsible for allocating CPU time to processes, ensuring efficient and fair use of system resources. This function is crucial for multitasking environments, where multiple applications and background processes run concurrently. By implementing various scheduling algorithms, the OS aims to optimize performance, reduce wait times and maintain system stability.

In Section A1.3.3, we will delve deeper into specific scheduling approaches, including first come first served, round robin, multilevel queue scheduling and priority scheduling. Each method has its own advantages and trade-offs, and its suitability depends on the specific requirements and goals of the system.

■ Security

The OS security is designed to protect the integrity, confidentiality and availability of information and resources within the computer system. It has mechanisms to safeguard against threats, prevent unauthorized access and ensure that users and applications can operate securely.

User authentication

User authentication can be used in multiple ways. Initially, the OS may require the user to authenticate themselves to log in to the system. It would require the user to provide credentials such as a username and password, biometric data or **security tokens**. Once logged on, based on the user settings, the OS can then grant or prevent access to certain files, folders or applications on the system. This allows systems to have multiple users with different access credentials, such as an administrator and a standard user.

◆ **Security tokens:** physical or digital devices that generate or store authentication credentials, such as one-time passwords or cryptographic keys, used to verify a user's identity and secure access to systems, networks or online services.

Encryption

The OS can provide tools and frameworks for encrypting files, communication channels and devices. The encryption ensures that the data, even if it is intercepted or accessed by unauthorized individuals, cannot be read without the decryption key.

Auditing and monitoring

All system activities, such as users logging in, file access, system errors and administrator actions, are tracked by the OS in a log. These logs are used for auditing and monitoring purposes and can help administrators detect suspicious activities and potential security breaches. They can also be used to help identify issues and areas for improving the system performance.

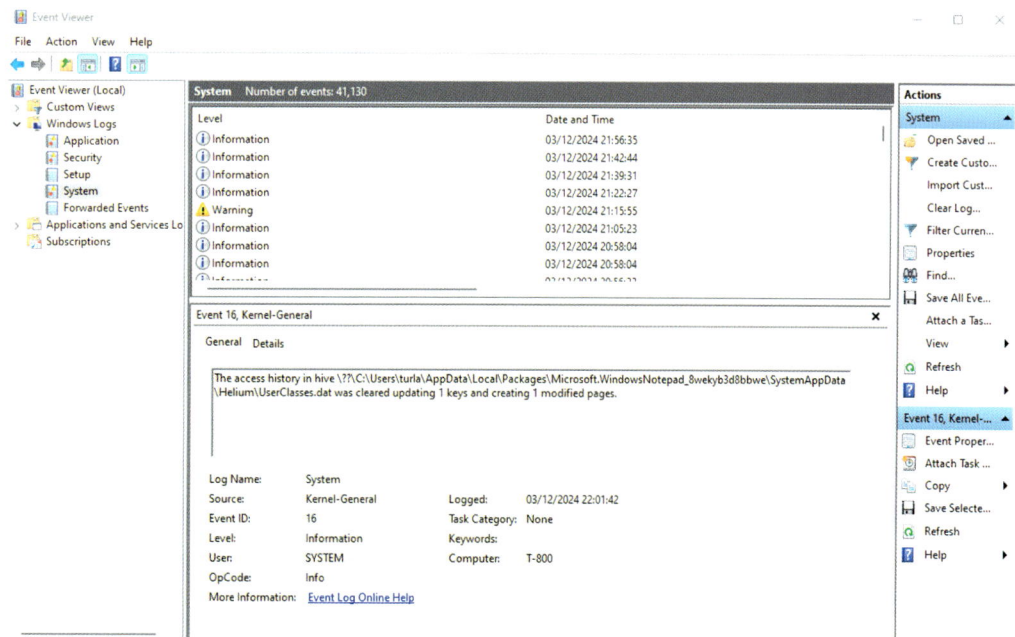

■ Windows Event Viewer

Malware protection

The OS includes mechanisms to detect and prevent **malware** infections and intruders. These include antivirus software, firewalls and intrusion detection systems (IDS). These tools scan for malicious software, monitor network traffic and block unauthorized access attempts, protecting the system from **viruses**, **worms**, **trojans** and other malicious threats.

■ Accounting

Operating system accounting functions are essential for monitoring and managing the usage of system resources. These functions track resource consumption by users and processes, providing valuable data for system administrators to analyse performance, allocate costs and optimize resource utilization. The key aspects of OS accounting functions include:

■ **Resource usage tracking**

The OS continuously monitors the consumption of various resources by users and processes; this includes tracking:

☐ **CPU usage:** the amount of CPU time consumed by each process or user

☐ **memory usage:** the amount of RAM allocated and used by each process

☐ **disk usage:** the amount of storage space occupied by files and directories owned by each user

☐ **network usage:** the volume of data sent and received over the network by each process or user.

■ **Process accounting**

Process accounting involves maintaining detailed records of each process that runs on the system; this includes information such as:

☐ **process ID:** a unique identifier for each process

☐ **user ID:** the identifier of the user who initiated the process

☐ **execution time:** the total CPU time used by the process

☐ **start and end times:** the timestamps indicating when the process started and finished

☐ **resource consumption:** details on the amount of memory, disk I/O and other resources used by the process.

■ **User accounting**

User accounting tracks the resource usage by individual users or user groups; this information is crucial for:

☐ **cost allocation:** in multi-user environments, such as universities or enterprises, resource usage data can be used to allocate costs to different departments or projects based on their consumption

☐ **quota management:** enforcing resource usage limits for users to prevent any single user from monopolizing system resources; this can include disk quotas, limiting the amount of storage a user can use and memory quotas.

■ **Performance monitoring**

The OS accounting functions are integral to performance monitoring; by analysing resource usage data, system administrators can identify:

☐ **bottlenecks:** areas where resources are being overutilized, causing performance degradation

☐ **underutilization:** resources that are underused, indicating potential areas for optimization

☐ **trends:** patterns in resource usage over time, which can inform capacity planning and system upgrades.

- **Auditing and reporting**

  The OS generates detailed reports based on the collected accounting data; these reports can be used for:

  - **auditing:** ensuring compliance with organizational policies and regulatory requirements by reviewing resource usage and access patterns
  - **security analysis:** detecting unusual or suspicious activity by analysing resource usage anomalies
  - **resource management:** making informed decisions about resource allocation, system configuration and future investments.

- **Billing and chargeback**

  In environments where resource usage needs to be billed to individual users or departments, such as cloud-computing services or academic institutions, OS accounting functions enable:

  - **usage-based billing:** charging users based on their actual resource consumption, such as CPU hours, memory usage and network bandwidth
  - **chargeback:** allocating costs to different departments or projects based on their resource usage, promoting accountability and efficient resource use.

◼ Graphical user interface

By offering visual elements such as windows, icons, menus and pointers, the OS provides a user-friendly environment for interacting with the computer and allows the user to execute commands, manage files and run applications.

◼ The Ubuntu GUI

User interface elements

The user interface elements provided by the OS allow the user to interact with the system intuitively. These elements include windows, which display the contents of applications, documents or system information. Icons give graphical representation to applications, files and system functions, providing quick access to frequently used items. Menus offer lists of commands or options to access various functions, making navigation and operation straightforward. Pointers, usually represented by an arrow or cursor, can be controlled with an input device like a mouse, enabling users to select, drag and interact with GUI elements seamlessly.

Application management

The GUI facilitates the management of and interaction with multiple applications, enhancing user productivity and experience. Task switching allows users to move quickly between open applications, with features like the taskbar or application switcher (Alt + tab) enabling efficient navigation. Window management helps users organize their workspace by arranging, overlapping and tiling windows. Features such as snapping windows to edges or corners create a split-screen effect for multitasking. The desktop environment, where users can place icons, shortcuts and widgets, allows for a personalized and organized workspace, catering to individual preferences.

File and system management

The GUI simplifies file and system management tasks through visual tools and interfaces. A GUI-based file management tool, like the File Explorer, allows users to navigate directories, view file properties and perform operations such as copying, moving, deleting and renaming files and folders. This tool often includes features such as search, sort and filter to facilitate file management. The GUI also provides access to system settings and control panels, enabling users to configure hardware, software and system preferences through intuitive graphical interfaces. Drag-and-drop functionality offers a user-friendly method for transferring files and data between applications and directories.

Accessibility

The GUI includes features that enhance accessibility for users with disabilities, ensuring that the system is usable by everyone. Screen readers convert text and GUI elements into speech or Braille, helping visually impaired users to navigate the system. High-contrast themes and screen magnifiers improve readability for users with low vision. Keyboard shortcuts allow users to perform actions quickly without relying on a mouse or touchpad, benefiting users with limited mobility.

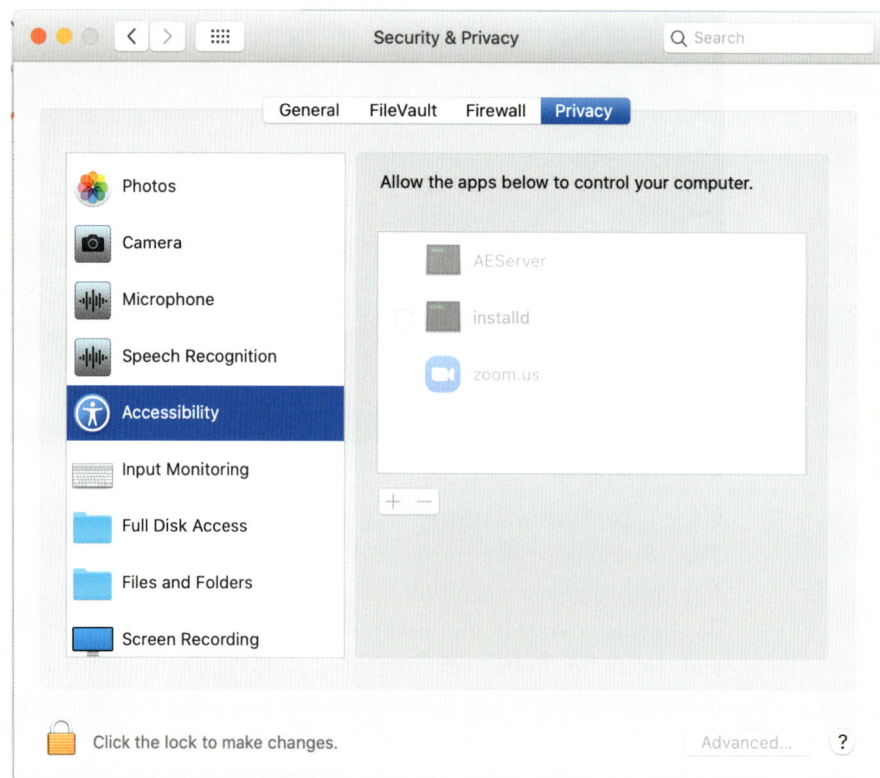

■ MacOS accessibility features

Visual feedback

The GUI provides immediate visual feedback to user actions, enhancing the overall user experience. Progress indicators, including progress bars and loading animations, inform users about the status of ongoing operations such as file transfers or software installations. Notifications, in the form of pop-up messages and alerts, keep users informed about important events, updates or errors. Tooltips – small informative text boxes that appear when users hover over icons or interface elements – provide additional information or guidance.

Customization and personalization

The GUI allows users to personalize their computing environment to suit their preferences, making the system more enjoyable and efficient to use. Users can change the appearance of the GUI by selecting different themes, wallpapers and window styles, creating a more customized experience. Widgets and gadgets – small applications that provide quick access to information and tools such as weather updates, calendars and system monitors – enhance the functionality and aesthetics of the desktop. These customization options enable users to tailor their workspace to their needs and preferences, improving overall satisfaction and productivity.

■ Virtualization

Virtualization is a key feature of modern operating systems that allows multiple virtual machines (VMs) to run on a single physical machine. Each VM operates independently, with its own OS and applications. The operating system manages this through a **hypervisor**, which allocates CPU time, memory and storage to each VM, ensuring efficient use of resources and allowing each VM to function as if it were on a separate physical machine.

Virtualization enhances security and stability by isolating VMs from each other, preventing issues in one VM from affecting others. It also allows for snapshots and backups, enabling administrators to save the current state of a VM and revert to it if necessary. Live migrations, which move VMs from one physical host to another without interrupting services, are another crucial feature, aiding in **load balancing** and hardware maintenance.

Additionally, virtualization supports disaster recovery and cloud services. By allowing VMs to be easily backed up and restored, the OS ensures that critical applications and data can be quickly recovered in case of failure. Virtualization also enables dynamic scaling of IT infrastructure in cloud environments, allowing businesses to adapt quickly to changing demands.

■ Networking

Operating systems manage and facilitate network communication. One of the primary functions of an OS in networking is to establish and maintain network connections. The OS manages network interfaces and protocols, enabling devices to connect to local area networks (LANs), wide area networks (WANs) and the internet. It configures network settings, assigns IP addresses through DHCP (Dynamic Host Configuration Protocol) and handles the underlying hardware, such as network interface cards (NICs), ensuring that devices can communicate effectively.

The OS also provides essential services for data transmission and communication between devices. It implements various networking protocols, such as TCP/IP (Transmission Control Protocol/Internet Protocol), which govern how data is packetized, addressed, transmitted, routed and received. The OS ensures data integrity and efficient transmission by handling error checking, flow control and congestion avoidance. Additionally, the OS supports higher-level protocols and services, such as HTTP for web browsing, FTP for file transfers and

◆ **Hypervisor:** software that creates and manages virtual machines by allowing multiple operating systems to run simultaneously on a single physical machine, sharing the underlying hardware resources.

◆ **Load balancing:** the process of distributing network or application traffic across multiple servers or resources to ensure optimal performance, reliability and availability, preventing any single server from becoming overwhelmed.

SMTP for email communication, facilitating seamless interaction between applications and network resources.

Security and access control are critical network functions managed by the OS. The OS employs firewalls, encryption and authentication mechanisms to protect data as it travels across networks. Firewalls monitor and control incoming and outgoing network traffic based on predetermined security rules, helping to prevent unauthorized access and attacks. The OS also supports virtual private networks (VPNs), which encrypt data and create secure connections over public networks, ensuring privacy and security for remote users. These security features safeguard network communication and ensure that only authorized users and devices can access network resources.

REVIEW QUESTIONS

1   What is the primary role of an operating system in a computer?

2   How does the operating system abstract hardware complexities for users? Provide an example.

3   Explain how the operating system manages multitasking and resource allocation. Why is this important?

4   What are some of the key challenges the operating system faces in resource management?

5   What is memory management, and how does the operating system ensure efficient use of memory?

6   Describe the role of device drivers in operating system device management.

7   How does the operating system manage files and directories? Give examples of file-management operations.

8   What is the importance of process scheduling, and what are some common scheduling algorithms used by operating systems?

9   Explain how the operating system handles security and access control. Why are these functions critical?

ACTIVITY

Risk-taker: Research and information literacy

In this task, you will improve your research and information literacy skills by installing Ubuntu, a popular Linux distribution, and comparing it with another operating system of your choice.

1   Install Ubuntu on to a device (this could be a spare PC, a Raspberry Pi, a virtual machine or even a USB drive). Document the installation process, noting how the OS manages hardware and interacts with the user.

2   Research and compare:
   a   Choose another OS you are familiar with (for example Windows or macOS).
   b   Research the difference in how Ubuntu and your chosen OS handle key aspects such as:
      i   user interface (including accessibility features)
      ii   file management
      iii memory management
      iv   software installation and updates.

3   Present your findings:
   a   Create a comparison table or chart to visually present the differences.
   b   Include a reflection on what you learned.

PROGRAMMING EXERCISES

1   Run the simple Python "Memory Hog" program below, which continuously allocates memory until the system runs out.

   Important note: Running this script may cause your system to become unresponsive, as it will use up all available memory. It's recommended to run this in a controlled environment, such as a virtual machine. You can use Ctrl + C (Windows) or Cmd + C (Mac) to stop the program running.

Python

```python
memory_hog = []
try:
    while True:
        # Allocate a large list and append it to the
        # memory_hog list
        memory_hog.append([0] * 10**6)  # Each list has
        # 1 million zeros
        print(f"Allocated {len(memory_hog)} million items")
except MemoryError:
    print("Memory allocation failed! The system has run out
    of memory.")
```

This script creates a large list and appends a million zeros each time it loops. When the system can no longer allocate memory (due to running out of available RAM), a "MemoryError" exception is raised and will be output. You can monitor your system memory using Task Manager on Windows or Activity Monitor on macOS.

Name	Status	9% CPU	52% Memory	0% Disk	0% Network
> 🌐 Google Chrome (81)	🍃	1.5%	9,330.3 MB	0.3 MB/s	0.1 Mbps
> 🔷 Steam Client WebHelper (8)		1.5%	321.4 MB	0 MB/s	0 Mbps
> ☒ Search (9)	🍃	0%	226.6 MB	0.1 MB/s	0 Mbps
📁 Windows Explorer		1.2%	201.4 MB	0.1 MB/s	0 Mbps

Name	Status	23% CPU	96%	4% Disk	0% Network
> 🐍 Python (2)		14.4%	15,956.8 ...	0.1 MB/s	0 Mbps
> 🌐 Google Chrome (77)	🍃	0.5%	8,984.2 MB	4.6 MB/s	0.1 Mbps
> 🔷 Steam Client WebHelper (8)		1.8%	316.7 MB	0 MB/s	0 Mbps
📁 Windows Explorer		0%	199.2 MB	0 MB/s	0 Mbps

■ Windows Task Manager showing the memory usage of the program above as it runs

2 File-management tasks

  a Creating directories and files:

  Step 1: Open the File Explorer (Windows) or Finder (macOS) on your computer.

  Step 2: Navigate to a location where you can create a new directory (for example your desktop or documents folder).
  - Windows: Right-click > New > Folder
  - MacOS: Right-click or Ctrl-click > New Folder

  Step 3: Inside "ProjectFiles", create three subfolders named "Reports", "Data" and "Images".

  Step 4: Within the "Reports" folder, create three text files named "Report1.txt", "Report2.txt" and "Summary.txt". Use a text editor (for example Notepad or TextEdit) to create these files, and include a few lines of sample text in each file.

  b Moving files:

  Step 1: Move "Report2.txt" from the "Reports" folder to the "Data" folder.
  - Windows: Drag and drop the file to the new location or right-click > Cut, then right-click in the destination folder and select Paste
  - MacOS: Drag and drop the file or use Cmd + C (copy) and Cmd + V (paste).

  Step 2: Move "Summary.txt" from the "Reports" folder to the "Images" folder using the same methods.

  c Renaming files:

  Step 1: Rename "Report1.txt" to "FinalReport.txt".
  - Windows: Right-click the file > Rename
  - MacOS: Click the file name once to select, then click again to edit.

  Step 2: Rename the "Data" folder "ProjectData".

  d Deleting files and directories:

  Step 1: Delete the "Images" folder along with its contents.
  - Windows: Right-click the folder > Delete
  - MacOS: Drag the folder to the Trash or right-click > Move to Trash.

  Step 2: Recover the deleted "Images" folder from the Recycle Bin (Windows) or Trash (macOS).
  - Windows: Open the Recycle Bin, right-click on the "Images" folder, and choose "Restore"
  - MacOS: Open the Trash, locate the "Images" folder, right-click it, and choose "Put Back" to restore it to its original location.

3 Research how to complete the same tasks away from the GUI using the OS terminal (Command Prompt / cmd on Windows or Terminal on macOS).

4 Accessibility features

  Complete one of the following tasks on your chosen OS.

  a Explore accessibility features on Windows:

  Step 1: Open the Control Panel by pressing Windows + R, typing control, and pressing Enter.

  Step 2: Navigate to Ease of Access Center.

  Step 3: Explore various accessibility features, such as Narrator (screen reader), Magnifier, High Contrast Mode, Speech Recognition and On-Screen Keyboard.

  Step 4: Activate and interact with at least two of these features, for example turn on Narrator and Magnifier, and navigate through the desktop or a web page to understand how these features assist users.

  b Explore accessibility features on macOS:

  Step 1: Open System Preferences by clicking on the Apple menu and selecting System Preferences.

  Step 2: Go to the Accessibility section.

  Step 3: Explore various features, such as VoiceOver (screen reader), Zoom, Display (for colour filters, invert colours), Speak Selection and Dictation.

  Step 4: Activate and interact with at least two of these features, for example enable VoiceOver and Zoom and use them to navigate the system or read through a document.

A1.3.3 Approaches for scheduling

An operating system needs scheduling methods to efficiently manage the execution of multiple processes, ensuring optimal use of the CPU and other resources. Scheduling determines the order in which processes are granted access to the CPU and their duration, balancing the needs of various applications and maintaining system responsiveness. Without effective scheduling, processes could experience significant delays or **monopolize resources**, leading to poor performance and user frustration. In the following section, we will examine several different scheduling methods, including first come first served, round robin, priority scheduling and multilevel queue scheduling, each with its own advantages and trade-offs.

■ First come first served

First come first served (FCFS) is one of the simplest scheduling algorithms used by operating systems to manage the execution of processes. In FCFS scheduling, the processes are executed in the order they arrive in the ready queue. When a process arrives, it is added to the end of the queue. The CPU scheduler selects the process at the front of the queue and assigns it to the CPU until it completes its execution or moves to an I/O wait state. Once the current process is finished, the next process in the queue is selected, and this continues until all processes have been executed.

The simplicity of FCFS makes it easy to implement and understand. However, it has some drawbacks, such as the "convoy effect", where short processes may be delayed by long-running processes, leading to increased waiting time and lower system throughput. This method is non-pre-emptive, meaning that once a process is assigned to the CPU, it cannot be interrupted until it completes, which can cause inefficiency in certain scenarios.

■ FCFS: waiting in line to be served

Advantages	Disadvantages
Simple and easy to implement	Convoy effect can cause significant delays
Fair, as it processes requests in the order they arrive	Non-pre-emptive nature can lead to inefficiency and longer than average waiting times

In this example, P1 arrives first and is executed immediately, followed by P2 and P3 in the order they arrive. Each process runs to completion before the next process begins.

Process	Queue
P1 arrives	P1
P2 arrives	P1, P2
P3 arrives	P1, P2, P3

Process	Time									
	0	1	2	3	4	5	6	7	8	9
P1										
P2										
P3										

■ Round robin

Round robin (RR) is a pre-emptive scheduling algorithm designed to provide fair time-sharing among processes. Each process is assigned a fixed time slice, known as a "quantum", during which it can execute. When a process's quantum expires, the CPU scheduler pre-empts the process and places it at the end of the ready queue, then selects the next process in line for execution. This cycle continues until all processes are completed.

The primary advantage of round robin scheduling is that it ensures a high level of responsiveness, as no process can monopolize the CPU for an extended period. This approach is especially effective in time-sharing systems where multiple users or applications need to interact with the CPU frequently. The length of the time quantum is critical: if it is too short, the system spends too much time switching between processes; if it is too long, it resembles FCFS scheduling.

Advantages	Disadvantages
Fair allocation of CPU time between processes	Time quantum selection is crucial for performance
High responsiveness and improved system interactivity	High context-switching overhead if the time quantum is too short
Prevents any single process from monopolizing the CPU	Potential inefficiency if processes frequently complete their tasks within a single quantum

In this example, process P1 runs from time 0 to 2, then is pre-empted. Process P2 runs from time 2 to 4, then is pre-empted. Then, process P3 runs from time 4 to 6 and is pre-empted. The cycle repeats, with P1 running again from time 6 to 8, P2 from 8 to 10 and P3 from 10 to 12.

Process	Queue
P1 arrives	P1
P2 arrives	P1, P2
P3 arrives	P1, P2, P3

Process	Time											
	0	1	2	3	4	5	6	7	8	9	10	11
P1												
P2												
P3												

■ Priority scheduling

■ An example of a priority lane at an airport, where passengers with higher priority (such as first class ticketholders or those with a disability) are given faster service

Priority scheduling is a method where each process is assigned a priority level, and the CPU is allocated to the process with the highest priority. Processes with higher priority levels are executed before those with lower priority levels. If two processes have the same priority, they are scheduled according to their arrival order, typically using FCFS. Priority can be either static (meaning it is assigned when the process is created and does not change) or dynamic (meaning it can change over time based on various factors such as ageing).

The main goal of priority scheduling is to ensure that critical tasks are executed as soon as possible, enhancing the responsiveness of high-priority processes. However, a significant drawback is the potential for low-priority processes to suffer from starvation if high-priority processes continually dominate CPU time. To mitigate this, some systems implement ageing, which gradually increases the priority of waiting processes to ensure they eventually receive CPU time.

Advantages	Disadvantages
Prioritizes important tasks, improving system responsiveness for critical applications	Risk of starvation for low-priority processes
Flexible, as priorities can be adjusted dynamically based on system needs	More complex to implement and manage than simpler scheduling methods
	Priority inversion, where a lower-priority process holds a resource needed by a higher-priority process, can be an issue if not handled properly

In this example, P1 and P4, both high-priority processes, are executed first. After the high-priority processes are completed, the medium-priority process P2 is executed, followed by the low-priority process P3.

Process	Arrival time	Priority level
P1	0	High
P2	1	Medium
P3	2	Low
P4	3	High

Process	Time							
	0	1	2	3	4	5	6	7
P1 (High)								
P2 (Medium)								
P3 (Low)								
P4 (High)								

Multilevel queue scheduling

Multilevel queue scheduling is a scheduling algorithm that partitions the ready queue into several separate queues, each with its own scheduling algorithm and priority level. Processes are permanently assigned to one of these queues based on certain characteristics, such as process type, priority or memory requirements. Each queue may use a different scheduling algorithm, such as FCFS or round robin, and the queues themselves are scheduled in a specific order, often based on priority.

In this approach, higher-priority queues are given more CPU time compared to lower-priority queues. For example, interactive processes might be placed in a high-priority queue scheduled with round robin, while batch processes are placed in a lower-priority queue scheduled with FCFS. The CPU scheduler selects processes from the highest-priority queue first, moving to lower-priority queues only when the higher-priority queues are empty.

Advantages	Disadvantages
Flexibility in handling different types of processes	Starvation of lower-priority processes if higher-priority queues are frequently occupied
Prioritizes critical and interactive processes, improving responsiveness for important tasks	Complex implementation and management
Different scheduling algorithms can be tailored to the needs of each queue	Processes are permanently assigned to queues, which might not be optimal if their behaviour changes over time

In this example, processes in the high-priority queue (P1 and P2) are scheduled first using round robin. Both P1 and P2 complete. The scheduler then moves to the medium-priority queue (P3), and then to the low-priority queue (P4) only when the high-priority queue does not have processes ready to run. However, it frequently checks back to the high-priority queue, which is why P2 (high) runs again after P4 (low).

Queue priority	Process type	Scheduling algorithm	Process queue
Q1 – High	Interactive	Round robin (time quantum = 2)	P1, P2
Q2 – Medium	Batch	FCFS	P3
Q3 – Low	Background / idle	FCFS	P4

Process	Time												
	0	1	2	3	4	5	6	7	8	9	10	11	12
P1 (High)	▓				▓								
P2 (High)			▓							▓			
P3 (Medium)							▓					▓	
P4 (Low)									▓				

⦿ Common mistake

Don't forget that context switching – when the CPU switches from one task to another – can slow things down. Even though it allows for multitasking, too much switching can reduce how efficiently the system runs because the CPU spends time saving and restoring tasks.

REVIEW QUESTIONS

1 Explain the difference between first come first served (FCFS) scheduling and round robin scheduling. How does the choice of time quantum in round robin affect process performance?

2 What is the purpose of priority scheduling, and how does it differ from multilevel queue scheduling? Provide an example of where each might be preferred.

3 In the context of operating systems, what is meant by context switching, and why is it important in process scheduling?

4 Describe how multilevel queue scheduling works and discuss its advantages and disadvantages.

5 How does the operating system ensure fairness in scheduling while also optimizing performance? Discuss this in the context of round robin and priority scheduling.

6 What are the potential drawbacks of using a first come first served scheduling algorithm in a multi-user environment?

7 Why might an operating system choose to implement a hybrid scheduling approach, and what benefits does this provide?

PROGRAMMING EXERCISE

Write a program to simulate different CPU scheduling algorithms and analyse their performance on process execution. Here is an example of how you could implement FCFS scheduling in Python.

Python

```python
# Define a class to represent a process in the system
class Process:
    def __init__(self, pid, arrival_time, burst_time):
        self.pid = pid  # Process ID
        self.arrival_time = arrival_time  # The time at which the process
        # arrives in the system
        self.burst_time = burst_time  # The total time required by the
        # process to complete execution
        self.waiting_time = 0  # Time the process has to wait before it
        # starts execution
        self.turnaround_time = 0  # Total time taken from arrival to
        # completion (waiting_time + burst_time)
# Define a function to simulate FCFS scheduling
def calculate_fcfs(processes):
    start_time = 0  # Variable to track the current time at which a process
    # starts execution
    # Iterate over each process in the list
    for process in processes:
        # If the current time is less than the process's arrival time,
        # the CPU remains idle until the process arrives
        if start_time < process.arrival_time:
            start_time = process.arrival_time
        # Calculate the waiting time for the process
```

```python
        process.waiting_time = start_time - process.arrival_time
        # Calculate the turnaround time for the process
        process.turnaround_time = process.waiting_time + process.burst_time
        # Update the current time to reflect the process's execution
        start_time += process.burst_time
    # After all processes are scheduled, calculate the total and average
    # waiting / turnaround times
    total_waiting_time = sum([p.waiting_time for p in processes])   # Sum of
    # all waiting times
    total_turnaround_time = sum([p.turnaround_time for p in processes]) # Sum
    # of all turnaround times
    avg_waiting_time = total_waiting_time / len(processes)   # Average waiting
    # time
    avg_turnaround_time = total_turnaround_time / len(processes) # Average
    # turnaround time
    # Display the results in a table format
    print("Process\tArrival Time\tBurst Time\tWaiting Time\tTurnaround Time")
    for process in processes:
        print(f"{process.pid}\t{process.arrival_time}\t\t{process.burst_time}\
        t\t{process.waiting_time}\t\t{process.turnaround_time}")
    # Print the calculated average times
    print(f"\nAverage Waiting Time: {avg_waiting_time:.2f}")
    print(f"Average Turnaround Time: {avg_turnaround_time:.2f}")
# Example process list to simulate FCFS scheduling
processes = [
    Process(1, 0, 5),   # Process 1 arrives at time 0 and requires 5 time
    # units to complete
    Process(2, 2, 3),   # Process 2 arrives at time 2 and requires 3 time
    # units to complete
    Process(3, 4, 1),   # Process 3 arrives at time 4 and requires 1 time unit
    # to complete
    Process(4, 6, 7)    # Process 4 arrives at time 6 and requires 7 time
    # units to complete
]
# Sort the processes by their arrival time before running the FCFS algorithm
processes.sort(key=lambda x: x.arrival_time)
# Run the FCFS scheduling simulation
calculate_fcfs(processes)
```

A1.3.4 Interrupt handling and polling

Interrupt handling and polling are two fundamental techniques used by operating systems to manage communication between the CPU and peripheral devices. Each method has its own advantages and drawbacks that can affect system performance and efficiency, depending on the context in which they are used.

■ Interrupt handling

Interrupt handling is a mechanism where peripheral devices signal the CPU to gain its attention and request service. When an event occurs, such as an input from a keyboard or data from a network interface, the device sends an interrupt signal to the CPU. The CPU then pauses its current operations, saves its state and executes an **interrupt service routine (ISR)** to address the event. This method allows the CPU to remain idle or perform other tasks until an event actually occurs, making it highly efficient in environments where events happen sporadically or unpredictably. Interrupt handling ensures that the CPU only deals with events when necessary, reducing unnecessary CPU cycles spent on checking for events.

However, the frequent occurrence of interrupts can introduce processing overheads due to the context switching involved. Each time an interrupt is handled, the CPU must save its current state and later restore it, which can be time-consuming and resource-intensive if interrupts are too frequent. Additionally, handling a high volume of interrupts can lead to increased power consumption, which is particularly critical for battery-powered devices. Despite these potential drawbacks, the efficiency of interrupt handling in managing sporadic events and minimizing CPU idle time makes it a preferred method in many real-time and interactive systems where immediate response to events is crucial.

● Top tip!

An interrupt is like a doorbell ringing while you're busy working. You stop what you're doing (pause the current process), answer the door (handle the interrupt) and then return to your task. The operating system manages these interruptions efficiently so that your work (the main process) isn't significantly delayed.

■ Polling

Polling, on the other hand, involves the CPU periodically checking each peripheral device to see whether it requires attention. This method is straightforward and can be efficient in systems where events occur at regular, predictable intervals. Polling ensures controlled **latency**, as the CPU checks devices at predetermined times, making it suitable for real-time applications where timely response is crucial. Polling can be implemented easily and provides a simple mechanism to ensure that devices are checked regularly.

However, polling can lead to significant CPU processing overheads, as the CPU spends a considerable amount of time repeatedly checking devices instead of performing useful work. This continuous checking is resource-intensive and can detract from the system's overall efficiency. Additionally, polling is less power-efficient compared to interrupt handling, as the CPU remains active even when there are no events to process. This constant activity can drain the battery in portable devices more quickly than systems that utilize interrupt handling. In environments where event frequency is low or unpredictable, polling can be highly inefficient and wasteful, consuming CPU cycles without necessarily detecting any new events.

■ Interrupts vs polling

Criteria	Interrupts	Polling
Event frequency	Efficient for infrequent or unpredictable events, as the CPU only responds when an event occurs	More effective for regular, predictable events, as the CPU checks devices at set intervals regardless of event occurrence
CPU processing overheads	Lower overhead for infrequent events but can increase with high-frequency interrupts due to context switching	Higher overhead due to constant checking of devices, consuming CPU cycles even when no events occur
Power source	More power-efficient, especially for battery-powered devices, as the CPU remains idle until an event occurs	Less power-efficient, as the CPU remains active and continuously checks devices, leading to higher power consumption
Event predictability	Best for unpredictable events, as the system responds immediately to any event occurrence	Suitable for predictable events, ensuring regular checks at set intervals
Controlled latency	Can provide quick response times but, if interrupts are too frequent, it can lead to variability in response times	Provides controlled latency with predictable response times, as checks occur at regular intervals
Security concerns	Potentially more secure as the system can quickly respond to critical events, reducing the window for malicious activity	Less secure if polling intervals are too long, as it may delay the detection of critical events

The choice between interrupt handling and polling depends on the specific requirements and constraints of the system. Interrupt handling is generally more efficient for sporadic events and battery-powered devices, but can introduce overheads with high-frequency events. Polling offers predictable latency and is straightforward to implement, but can lead to inefficiencies and higher power consumption. Understanding the trade-offs between these methods is crucial for designing effective and efficient systems.

● Common mistake

Remember that specific context is very important when deciding whether polling or interrupt handling is a better system solution. It is not a simple choice of one being better than the other. Interrupts are great for events that happen unpredictably, while polling is better for regular, predictable events. Make sure you understand the difference so you can choose the right method for each situation.

■ Real-world scenarios

Mouse and keyboard

When a user moves the mouse or presses a key, these devices generate interrupt signals that prompt the CPU to immediately pause its current tasks and execute the appropriate interrupt service routine (ISR). This ensures that user inputs are processed in real-time, providing instant feedback and seamless interaction. For example, as a user types, each keystroke generates an interrupt that the OS handles promptly, ensuring that characters appear on the screen without delay. Conversely, using polling for these devices would require the CPU to continuously check the status of the mouse and keyboard, leading to unnecessary processing overheads and increased power consumption, especially in battery-powered devices like laptops. Polling could also result in delayed responses if the CPU is busy with other tasks when a user input occurs.

For basic embedded systems like simple data-entry terminals or kiosks, where user interaction is infrequent and the system is primarily idle, polling might be sufficient. Polling at regular intervals to check for user input can simplify the system design and avoid the overhead of setting up and handling interrupts. This is acceptable in low-activity environments where immediate response is not critical.

Network communications

When data packets arrive at a network interface card (NIC), they generate interrupt signals that alert the CPU to process the incoming data immediately. This prompt handling ensures that data is quickly received, processed and passed to the appropriate application, maintaining smooth and efficient network performance. For instance, during a video conference, interrupts enable real-time processing of audio and video data, ensuring minimal latency and high-quality communication. Conversely, using polling for network communications would require the CPU to continually check the NIC for new data, leading to increased processing overheads and potentially missing incoming packets if the CPU is occupied with other tasks. This could result in delays, reduced network performance and higher power consumption, especially in devices like smartphones or tablets.

In scenarios where network traffic is minimal and predictable, such as a remote monitoring system that periodically sends small data packets, polling can be more efficient. Polling at regular intervals to check for network activity reduces the complexity of interrupt handling and is sufficient to handle the infrequent, predictable communication needs.

Disk input / output operations

When a disk drive completes a read or write operation, it generates an interrupt signal that alerts the CPU to handle the data transfer immediately. This approach allows the CPU to execute other tasks while waiting for the disk operation to complete, enhancing overall system efficiency. For example, when a file is saved, the CPU can continue processing other applications until the disk signals that the write operation is finished, at which point the CPU promptly transfers the data to the appropriate location. Conversely, using polling for disk I/O operations would require the CPU to continuously check the status of the disk drive, leading to significant processing overheads and reduced efficiency. The CPU would waste valuable cycles repeatedly checking for completion, especially during lengthy disk operations, resulting in slower system performance and increased power consumption.

In a system where disk access is predictable and infrequent, such as a data logger that writes to a disk at fixed intervals, polling can be appropriate. Polling the disk for readiness before scheduled writes can simplify the implementation and eliminate the need for interrupt-driven complexity, making the system easier to manage.

Embedded systems

Embedded systems, such as those in automotive control units or industrial machinery, often need to respond quickly to sensor inputs and external signals. For example, in an automotive airbag system, sensors detecting a collision generate interrupt signals that prompt the CPU to immediately deploy the airbags. This rapid response is crucial for the safety and effectiveness of the system. Conversely, using polling in this scenario would require the CPU to continuously check sensor statuses, leading to increased processing overheads and potentially missing critical events if the CPU is occupied with other tasks. This delay in response could be catastrophic in time-sensitive applications.

In situations where events occur at regular, predictable intervals and the overhead of handling interrupts is not justified, polling can be a better approach. For example, in a climate-control system for a building, the temperature sensors might need to be checked at regular intervals to maintain a constant environment. Here, polling would be advantageous.

Real-time systems

In real-time systems, the choice between polling and interrupt handling depends on the specific requirements of the application. While interrupts are typically preferred for their quick response times, there are scenarios where polling can be more suitable.

For instance, in a real-time system that controls an industrial robot performing repetitive tasks at fixed intervals, polling can be more predictable and easier to manage. The robot might perform sensor checks and actuator adjustments at precise, regular intervals, ensuring that the tasks are executed in a controlled manner. This use of polling can simplify the design and avoid the overhead associated with frequent context switching that comes with interrupts, ensuring that the system meets its timing requirements consistently. In this scenario, the predictability and regularity of the events make polling a viable option, as it ensures that the system performs checks and adjustments at the exact required intervals without the complexity of handling numerous interrupts.

In a real-time system like an automotive airbag deployment system, interrupt handling is crucial. The system must respond immediately to sensor inputs indicating a collision. When sensors detect a rapid deceleration or impact, they generate interrupts that prompt the CPU to execute the airbag deployment routine instantly. This immediate response is essential to ensure the airbags deploy in time to protect the occupants. In such critical applications, the ability of interrupts to provide an immediate and high-priority response to specific events makes them the preferred choice, as any delay in processing could result in catastrophic consequences.

REVIEW QUESTIONS

1   Explain the fundamental difference between interrupt handling and polling in terms of how they manage CPU attention for peripheral devices.

2   In what scenarios might polling be more efficient than interrupt handling, and why?

3   Describe a situation in which interrupt handling could be preferred over polling, considering factors such as power consumption and response time.

4   How does the frequency of events affect the choice between interrupt handling and polling?

5   What are the potential drawbacks of using interrupt handling in a system with high event frequency?

6   Discuss how power source (battery vs mains power) can influence the choice between using interrupts or polling in a system.

7   How does the need for controlled latency impact the decision between using interrupt handling and polling? Provide an example of a system where controlled latency is critical.

8   Explain how security concerns could affect the choice between interrupt handling and polling in a networked system.

A1.3.5 The role of the operating system in managing multitasking and resource allocation (HL)

The operating system (OS) plays a critical role in managing multitasking and resource allocation, ensuring that multiple processes can run concurrently and efficiently on a computer system. Multitasking allows a system to perform multiple tasks seemingly simultaneously by quickly switching between them, while resource allocation ensures that each task receives the necessary resources (CPU time, memory, I/O devices) to execute properly. This involves several key functions and faces numerous challenges.

■ Task scheduling

Task scheduling is one of the primary responsibilities of the OS in a multitasking environment. The scheduler decides the order in which processes are executed, aiming to maximize CPU utilization and system responsiveness. As discussed in Section A1.3.3, there are various scheduling algorithms, such as first come first served (FCFS), round robin, priority scheduling and multilevel queue scheduling, each with advantages and drawbacks. The scheduler must balance the need to provide quick response times for interactive processes with the efficient processing of background tasks. This balancing act is crucial for maintaining system performance and user satisfaction.

■ Resource contention

Resource contention occurs when multiple processes compete for the same resources, such as CPU time, memory or I/O devices. The OS must manage this contention to prevent conflicts and ensure fair and efficient resource usage. Techniques like mutual exclusion are used to manage access to shared resources. Mutual exclusion is a key concept used in concurrent programming to prevent multiple processes from accessing a shared resource or critical section simultaneously. This ensures that only one process can use the resource at a time, preventing data corruption and ensuring consistency. Techniques for achieving mutual exclusion include using semaphores, locks and monitors.

Improper management can lead to such issues as resource starvation, where a process is constantly denied necessary resources, or priority inversion, where a lower-priority process holds a resource needed by a higher-priority process. The OS must implement strategies to handle these conflicts effectively to maintain system stability and performance.

Semaphores

Semaphores are synchronization tools used to control access to shared resources in a concurrent system. A semaphore is an integer variable that can be incremented (signal) or decremented (wait) atomically. There are two types of semaphores:

- **Binary semaphores (mutex):** Can only be 0 or 1, effectively acting as a lock to ensure mutual exclusion.

  For example: There are two processes that need to write to the same log file. To prevent both processes from writing to the file at the same time (which could cause data corruption):

  1 The semaphore is initially set to 1, indicating that the log file is available.
  2 When Process A wants to write to the log file, it checks the semaphore. If the semaphore is 1, Process A sets it to 0 (locking the resource) and proceeds to write to the log file.

3   If Process B tries to write to the log file while Process A is still writing, it will find the semaphore set to 0 and will be blocked until Process A is finished.

4   Once Process A finishes writing, it sets the semaphore back to 1, allowing Process B to proceed.

5   Process B then sets the semaphore to 0, writes to the log file, and finally sets the semaphore back to 1 when done.

- **Counting semaphores:** Can take any non-negative value, allowing multiple instances of a resource to be managed.

  For example: There is a limited number of database connections (e.g. three connections) available to a group of processes:

  1   The semaphore is initialized with a value of 3, representing the three available connections.

  2   When Process A needs a connection, it checks the semaphore. If the value is greater than 0, Process A decrements the semaphore by 1 and gains access to a connection.

  3   Process B and Process C do the same, decrementing the semaphore by 1 each time they gain access, leaving the semaphore value at 0 once all three connections are in use.

  4   If Process D then requests a connection, it finds the semaphore at 0 and must wait until one of the other processes releases a connection.

  5   When Process A finishes using its connection, it increments the semaphore by 1, signalling that a connection is now available. Process D can then proceed to use the connection.

Locks

Locks are tools used to make sure that only one process can use a shared resource at a time. For example, if two programs want to write to the same file, the first one must "lock" the file before it can start writing. If the file is already locked by another program, the second program has to wait until the lock is released. There are different types of locks, such as binary locks (also called "mutexes"), which allow only one process at a time, and readers-writer locks, which let multiple processes read a resource but only one process write to it.

Monitors

Monitors are tools used in programming to help manage access to shared resources safely. They ensure that only one process can use certain variables or methods at a time, preventing conflicts. A monitor acts like a container that holds shared variables and the code (methods) that works with them. When a process uses a monitors method, it automatically locks the monitor, so no other process can use it until the first one is done. Monitors also have condition variables that let processes wait for certain events to happen and notify others when those events occur. This makes it easier to manage and co-ordinate tasks between different processes safely.

■ Deadlock

Deadlock is a problem in multitasking systems where processes get stuck because each one is waiting for a resource that another process has, creating a cycle with no way to move forward. To handle deadlocks, the OS can use different strategies:

- **Deadlock prevention** involves designing the system so that deadlocks can't happen.
- **Deadlock avoidance,** such as using the Banker's algorithm, ensures a system only allocates resources if it can guarantee that all processes can eventually complete without entering an unsafe state.
- **Deadlock detection** means regularly checking for stuck processes and then taking steps to fix the problem.

- **Deadlock recovery** might involve stopping one or more processes to break the cycle or reallocating resources differently.

Multitasking challenges

The challenges of multitasking extend beyond task scheduling and resource contention. The OS must also manage context-switching efficiently, where the state of a currently running process is saved so that another process can be executed. Frequent context switches can introduce overheads, reducing overall system performance. The OS must also ensure data consistency and integrity, particularly when multiple processes access shared data. This involves implementing robust synchronization mechanisms to prevent data corruption and ensure that processes do not interfere with each other.

REVIEW QUESTIONS

1 Explain how the operating system uses task scheduling to manage multitasking. Why is it important for maintaining system performance?

2 What is resource contention, and how does the operating system resolve it to prevent issues such as resource starvation and priority inversion?

3 Describe the role of semaphores in managing resource allocation in a multitasking environment. How do binary and counting semaphores differ?

4 How does the operating system handle deadlock in multitasking systems, and what strategies can be used to prevent, avoid or resolve deadlocks?

5 What challenges does the operating system face in managing context-switching, and how does this impact overall system performance?

A1.3.6 The use of the control system components (HL)

Control systems are fundamental in automating and regulating processes across a wide range of industries, from manufacturing to robotics and environmental control. At the core of any control system are various components that work together to achieve desired outcomes by managing inputs, processing data and generating outputs. These systems rely on a precise feedback mechanism to ensure that the process remains stable and meets the set objectives.

This section explores the key elements of control systems, including the roles of the input, process, output and feedback mechanisms, as well as the critical components such as controllers, sensors, actuators and transducers, and the control algorithms that drive them. Understanding these components and their interactions is essential for designing effective and efficient control systems.

Input, process, output and feedback mechanism

Input

In a control system, the input is the initial signal or data received by the system, representing the desired condition or target that the system aims to achieve. This input could be anything from a set temperature in a heating system to the desired speed in a motor-control application. The input is typically generated by a user, another system or an environmental condition, and serves as the reference point for the system's operation.

Output

The output is the result produced by the control system after processing the input. It represents the actual state or action of the system, such as turning on a heater to reach a set temperature or adjusting the speed of a motor. The output is directly influenced by the input and the control process, and it is typically the element that can be observed or measured to determine the effectiveness of the system in achieving its desired goals.

Feedback mechanism (open-loop and closed-loop)

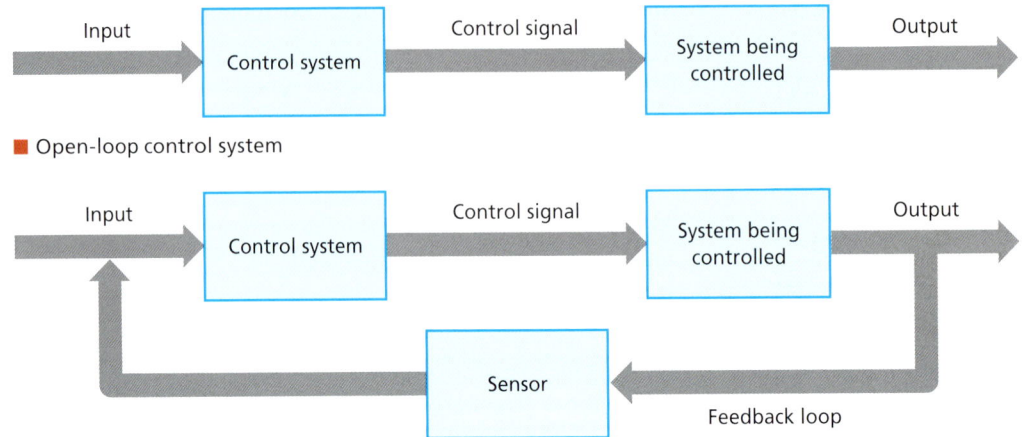

■ Open-loop control system

■ Closed-loop control system

The feedback mechanism is a critical component in determining how a control system operates and adjusts itself to maintain desired performance.

■ **Open-loop control:** In an open-loop system, there is no feedback from the output back to the input or process. The system operates solely based on the initial input without any correction or adjustment based on the actual output. This type of control is simple and used in situations where the relationship between input and output is straightforward and predictable, such as in basic timers or simple heating systems.

■ **Closed-loop control:** A closed-loop system, also known as a "feedback control system", continuously monitors the output and feeds this information back into the system to adjust the process accordingly. If the output deviates from the desired input, the system makes corrections in real time to bring the output back in line with the target. This type of control is essential in applications requiring high accuracy and adaptability, such as temperature control in HVAC systems, where the system must adjust heating or cooling based on actual temperature readings.

■ Key components

Controller

The controller is the central component of a control system that governs the operation by processing inputs and generating appropriate outputs. It acts as the "brain" of the system, implementing the control algorithm to make decisions based on the input data and feedback. The controller compares the input (desired value) with the feedback from the output (actual value) and determines the necessary actions to minimize the difference, or error, between them. This decision-making process can involve complex calculations, adjustments or commands that are sent to actuators or other system components to achieve the desired outcome. Controllers can range from simple devices such as thermostats to complex microprocessors used in industrial automation.

A1 Computer fundamentals

Sensors

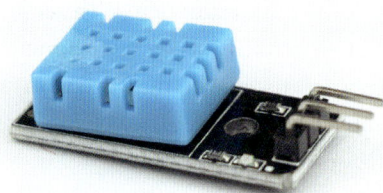
Temperature and humidity sensor

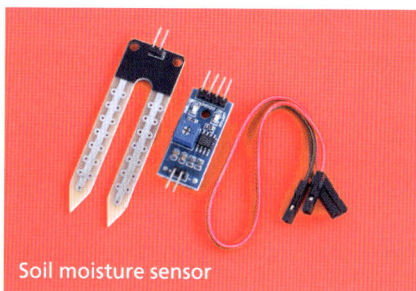
Soil moisture sensor

Water / rain sensor

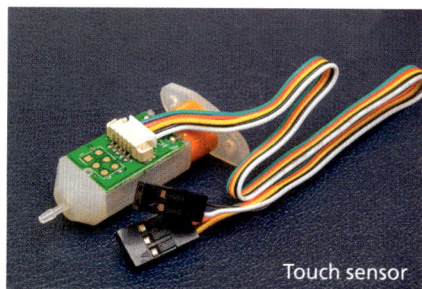
Touch sensor

Proximity sensor

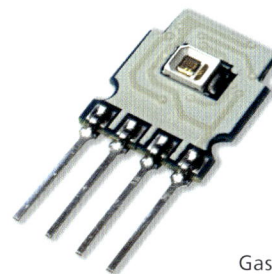
Gas sensor

■ Different types of sensors

Sensors are devices that detect and measure physical quantities from the environment or the system itself, such as temperature, pressure, speed or light. These measurements are then converted into electrical signals that can be interpreted by the controller. Sensors serve as the "eyes and ears" of the control system, providing the necessary data for the controller to make informed decisions. The accuracy and reliability of the sensors directly impact the performance of the control system, as they provide the critical feedback needed to adjust the system's operations. For example, a temperature sensor in a climate-control system constantly monitors the room temperature, allowing the controller to adjust heating or cooling to maintain the desired setpoint.

Actuators

Actuators are the components in a control system that carry out the physical actions or adjustments in response to commands from the controller. They are responsible for converting the controller's electrical signals into mechanical motion or other forms of energy, such as turning a valve, moving a robotic arm or adjusting a motor's speed. Actuators are the "muscles" of the control system, executing the tasks that directly impact the system's output. The performance and precision of actuators are critical in applications where exact control of movements or processes is required, such as in manufacturing equipment or robotics.

Transducers

Transducers are devices that convert one form of energy into another, typically used to bridge the gap between sensors and actuators and the control system. In many cases, a sensor or actuator may not directly provide the type of signal that the controller can process or that is needed to drive the actuator. A transducer converts these signals into a compatible form. For example, a pressure sensor might detect mechanical pressure and convert it into an electrical signal that the controller can interpret. Similarly, an actuator might require a specific voltage or current that is supplied by a transducer. Transducers play a crucial role in ensuring that all parts of the control system can communicate effectively, enabling accurate and efficient operation.

Control algorithm

The control algorithm is the set of rules or mathematical procedures that the controller uses to determine the appropriate output based on the input and feedback it receives. It is the logic that drives the decision-making process within the controller. Control algorithms can vary in complexity, from simple proportional control, where the output is adjusted in direct proportion to the error, to more advanced methods like Proportional-Integral-Derivative (PID) control, which considers past, present and future errors to make precise adjustments. The choice of control algorithm depends on the specific requirements of the system, such as the desired accuracy, speed of response and stability. A well-designed control algorithm is essential for achieving optimal performance and ensuring that the system meets its objectives efficiently and reliably.

REVIEW QUESTIONS

1   Explain the role of the controller in a control system. How does it interact with sensors and actuators to maintain system stability?

2   Describe how a feedback mechanism works in a closed-loop control system. Why is feedback essential for maintaining accuracy and stability?

3   Differentiate between open-loop and closed-loop control systems with examples. Which type is more suitable for complex, dynamic environments?

4   What is the function of a transducer in a control system? Provide an example of a transducer used in industrial automation.

5   Explain the importance of the control algorithm in a control system. How does it impact the performance and reliability of the system?

A1.3.7 Uses of control systems (HL)

■ Home thermostat

A home thermostat controls the room temperature by processing data from a temperature sensor that continuously monitors the environment. This sensor provides input to the thermostat, which compares the current temperature to the desired set point. If the temperature deviates from the set value, the thermostat's controller processes this information and decides whether to activate the heating or cooling system to bring the temperature back to the desired level.

The system uses a closed-loop feedback mechanism, where the temperature sensor continually feeds updated data back to the controller. As the heating or cooling system adjusts the temperature, the sensor monitors the changes and provides real-time feedback to the thermostat.

■ Automatic elevator control

An automatic elevator control system manages the movement of an elevator by processing input from various sensors, such as those detecting the elevator's current position, floor requests and door status. These inputs are fed into the controller, which processes the data to determine the elevator's next action, such as moving up or down, stopping at a requested floor or opening and closing the doors.

The system operates using a closed-loop feedback mechanism. As the elevator moves, sensors continuously provide real-time updates to the controller about the elevator's position and speed. If the elevator needs to stop at a specific floor, the controller adjusts the motor's operation to slow down and halt the elevator precisely at the correct floor.

■ Autonomous vehicles

Autonomous vehicles rely on a sophisticated control system that integrates key components such as sensors, controllers, actuators and transducers to navigate and operate safely without human input. The system begins with various sensors, including cameras, LiDAR, radar and GPS, which gather critical data about the vehicle's environment, such as obstacles, road conditions and traffic signals. This data serves as the input for the vehicle's control system. The controller, often powered by advanced AI algorithms, processes this input using control algorithms to make real-time decisions about the vehicle's speed, direction and braking. The controller then sends commands to the actuators, which carry out these decisions by controlling the steering, acceleration and braking systems.

The control system operates within a closed-loop feedback mechanism, where sensors continuously monitor the vehicle's actions and environment, feeding updated data back to the controller. This allows the system to adjust its actions in real time, ensuring the vehicle can adapt to changes such as sudden obstacles or shifting traffic conditions. Transducers play a crucial role in converting sensor data into signals that the controller can process and in translating controller commands into the appropriate actions by the actuators.

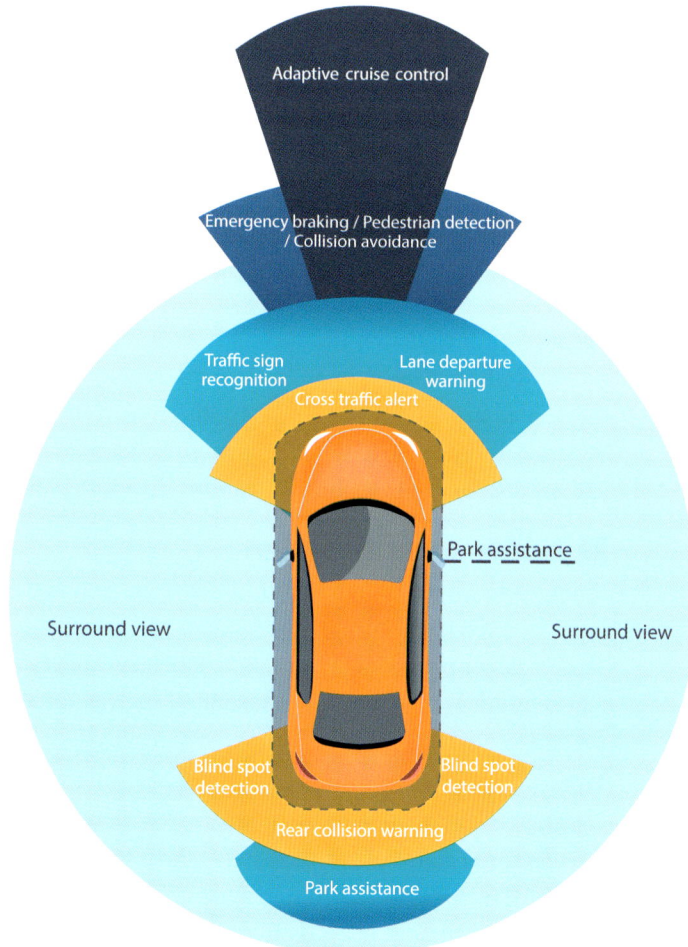

■ The sensors used for input and output by an autonomous vehicle

■ Automatic washing machine

An automatic washing machine uses a control system to manage the washing process by processing input from sensors that monitor water levels, load size and cycle progress. These inputs are sent to the controller, which determines the appropriate actions, such as filling the drum with water, agitating the clothes (the motion used by the washing machine to move the clothes around in the water) or draining the water after the wash cycle.

The system operates with a closed-loop feedback mechanism, where sensors continuously update the controller on the current state of the washing process. For instance, when the water reaches the required level, the sensor signals the controller to stop filling and begin the washing cycle. Similarly, the controller adjusts the duration and intensity of the spin cycle based on the load size detected by the sensors.

■ Traffic signal control system

A traffic signal control system manages the flow of vehicles at intersections by processing input from sensors that detect the presence of vehicles and pedestrians and sometimes traffic conditions. These inputs are fed into the controller, which processes the data to determine the timing and sequence of the traffic lights – when to turn red, amber or green for each direction.

The system operates using a closed-loop feedback mechanism. As vehicles approach the intersection, sensors detect their presence and provide real-time updates to the controller. The controller then adjusts the signal timing based on current traffic conditions, such as extending the green light for a congested lane or triggering a pedestrian crossing light when needed. By continuously adapting to real-time data, the system optimizes traffic flow and reduces congestion, contributing to smoother and safer movement through intersections.

■ Irrigation control system

An irrigation control system automates the watering of agricultural fields or gardens by processing input from sensors that monitor soil moisture levels, weather conditions and sometimes the time of day. These inputs are sent to the controller, which determines when and how much water should be delivered to the plants.

The system utilizes a closed-loop feedback mechanism, where the sensors continuously update the controller on the current moisture levels in the soil. If the soil becomes too dry, the controller activates the irrigation system to deliver the appropriate amount of water. Once the desired moisture level is reached, the system shuts off the water supply. By responding dynamically to the actual needs of the soil and plants, the irrigation system conserves water and ensures optimal growing conditions, avoiding both under- and over-watering.

■ Home-security system

A home-security system uses a control system to monitor and protect a property by processing input from various sensors, such as door and window sensors, motion detectors and cameras. These sensors provide real-time data to the controller, which assesses potential security threats and determines the appropriate response, such as sounding an alarm, sending notifications to the homeowner or contacting emergency services.

The system operates within a closed-loop feedback mechanism, where the sensors continuously send updates to the controller about the status of the home. If a sensor detects an intrusion, the controller immediately triggers the security protocols, such as locking doors or activating cameras to record the event.

■ Automatic doors

An automatic-door system uses a control system to manage the opening and closing of doors by processing input from sensors that detect the presence of people or objects near the entrance. These sensors, such as infrared motion detectors or pressure mats, send signals to the controller, which then decides when to open or close the doors.

The system operates using a closed-loop feedback mechanism. As soon as the sensors detect movement or pressure, they trigger the controller to open the doors. Once the person or object has passed through and the sensors no longer detect any presence, the controller signals the doors to close.

REVIEW QUESTIONS

1 Describe how a control system operates in an autonomous vehicle. What components are involved, and how do they interact to ensure safe and efficient operation?

2 Compare the control system used in a home thermostat with that of an irrigation control system. What are the similarities and differences in how these systems maintain the desired environmental conditions?

3 Explain the importance of a closed-loop feedback mechanism in the operation of an automatic elevator control system. How does it ensure accurate and safe operation?

4 In the context of a traffic-signal control system, discuss how the control system adapts to changing traffic conditions. How does the use of sensors and feedback help in optimizing traffic flow?

5 Describe how a smart home-lighting system operates as a control system. Identify the key components, including the controller, sensors, actuators and feedback mechanism, and explain how they interact to automatically adjust the lighting in the home based on the time of day and occupancy.

PROGRAMMING EXERCISES 1

1 Simulate a traffic-light control system. If you have access to an Arduino and the components, you can build this for real. Otherwise, you can use simulation software such as Tinkercad.

Tinkercad instructions:

Step 1: Click on Circuits from the dashboard, and then click on Create new Circuit.

Step 2: From the component library, search for and add the following components to your workspace:
- [ ] One Arduino Uno R3 with breadboard
- [ ] Three LEDs (Red, Yellow, Green) for one traffic light
- [ ] Three resistors (220 ohms each)
- [ ] Breadboard (optional, for better organization)
- [ ] Pushbutton (optional, for triggering sensors)

Step 3:
- [ ] Red LED:
  - Connect the longer leg (anode – the bent leg) of the red LED to pin 13 on the Arduino.
  - Connect the other end of the resistor to the ground (GND) on the Arduino.

- [ ] Yellow LED:
  - Connect the anode of the yellow LED to pin 12.
  - Connect the cathode to one end of a 220-ohm resistor.
  - Connect the other end of the resistor to GND.
- [ ] Green LED:
  - Connect the anode of the green LED to pin 11.
  - Connect the cathode to one end of a 220-ohm resistor.
  - Connect the other end of the resistor to GND.

Step 4 (optional):
- [ ] Place a pushbutton on the breadboard.
- [ ] Connect one side of the pushbutton to 5V.
- [ ] Connect the other side to a digital pin on the Arduino (e.g. pin 7).
- [ ] Add a 10k-ohm resistor connecting the same side of the pushbutton to GND (which acts as a pull-down resistor).

Set-up 1:

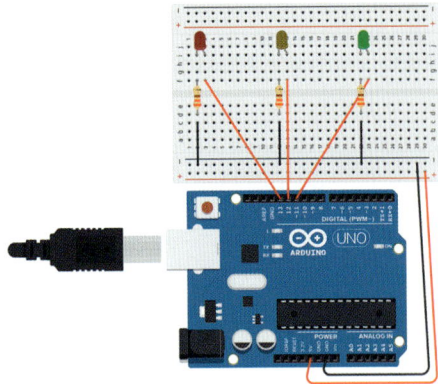

C++

```cpp
// Pin assignments for LEDs
int redLED = 13;
int yellowLED = 12;
int greenLED = 11;
void setup() {
    // Set up the LED pins as outputs
    pinMode(redLED, OUTPUT);
    pinMode(yellowLED, OUTPUT);
    pinMode(greenLED, OUTPUT);
}
void loop() {
    // Turn on the green light for 5 seconds
    digitalWrite(greenLED, HIGH);
    delay(5000); // wait 5 seconds
    // Turn off green, turn on yellow for 2 seconds
    digitalWrite(greenLED, LOW);
    digitalWrite(yellowLED, HIGH);
    delay(2000); // wait 2 seconds
    // Turn off yellow, turn on red for 5 seconds
    digitalWrite(yellowLED, LOW);
    digitalWrite(redLED, HIGH);
    delay(5000); // wait 5 seconds
    // Turn off red, and repeat the cycle
    digitalWrite(redLED, LOW);
}
```

A1 Computer fundamentals

Set-up 2 (with optional pushbutton):

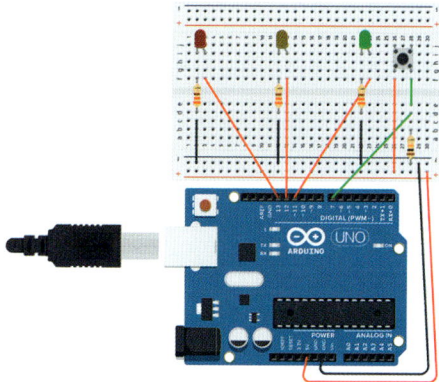

C++

```cpp
int buttonPin = 7; // Pin for the sensor (pushbutton)
int buttonState = 0;
int greenLED = 11; // Pin for green light
int yellowLED = 12; // Pin for yellow light
int redLED = 13; // Pin for red light
unsigned long previousMillis = 0; // Variable to store the last time the light
// changed
const long greenInterval = 5000; // Duration the green light stays on
// (in milliseconds)
const long yellowInterval = 2000; // Duration the yellow light stays on
// (in milliseconds)
const long redInterval = 5000; // Duration the red light stays on
// (in milliseconds)
// Define possible states for the traffic light
enum LightState {GREEN, YELLOW, RED};
LightState currentState = GREEN; // Start with the green light on
void setup() {
    pinMode(buttonPin, INPUT); // Set the pushbutton pin as an input
    pinMode(greenLED, OUTPUT); // Set the green LED pin as an output
    pinMode(yellowLED, OUTPUT); // Set the yellow LED pin as an output
    pinMode(redLED, OUTPUT); // Set the red LED pin as an output
    digitalWrite(greenLED, HIGH); // Initially turn on the green light
}
void loop() {
    unsigned long currentMillis = millis(); // Get the current time in milliseconds
    buttonState = digitalRead(buttonPin); // Read the state of the pushbutton
    switch(currentState) {
        case GREEN:
            // If the button is pressed or the green light has been on for the
            // full interval
            if (buttonState == HIGH || currentMillis - previousMillis >=
            greenInterval) {
```

```
                    digitalWrite(greenLED, LOW); // Turn off the green light
                    digitalWrite(yellowLED, HIGH); // Turn on the yellow light
                    currentState = YELLOW; // Change the state to YELLOW
                    previousMillis = currentMillis; // Reset the timer to the
                    // current time
            }
            break;
        // The YELLOW and RED cases follow similar logic
        case YELLOW:
            if (currentMillis - previousMillis >= yellowInterval) {
                    digitalWrite(yellowLED, LOW);
                    digitalWrite(redLED, HIGH);
                    currentState = RED;
                    previousMillis = currentMillis; // Reset the timer to the
                    // current time
            }
            break;
        case RED:
            if (currentMillis - previousMillis >= redInterval) {
                    digitalWrite(redLED, LOW);
                    digitalWrite(greenLED, HIGH);
                    currentState = GREEN;
                    previousMillis = currentMillis; // Reset the timer to the
                    // current time
            }
            break;
    }
}
```

2   Observe how the control system manages the traffic-light sequence and adapts to changes (if a sensor is used).

3   Discuss how the components (LEDs, controller, optional sensor) work together as part of the control system.

4   Discuss the effectiveness of your traffic-light control system and how it could be improved or extended.

PROGRAMMING EXERCISES 2

1   Simulate a motor control system where the speed of the motor is adjusted based on feedback from a sensor. It also has a maximum speed that is set in code and should not be exceeded by the motor. If you have access to an Arduino and the components, you can build this for real. Otherwise, you can use simulation software such as Tinkercad.

Tinkercad instructions:

Step 1: Click on Circuits from the dashboard, and then click on Create new Circuit.

Step 2: From the component library, search for and add the following components to your workspace:
- ☐   One Arduino Uno R3 with breadboard
- ☐   One potentiometer
- ☐   H-Bridge motor driver (L293D)
- ☐   One DC motor
- ☐   One 9V battery

Step 3:

☐ Arduino:
- Connect 5V to the bottom positive (red) power rail on the breadboard.
- Connect GND to the bottom negative (black) ground rail on the breadboard.
- Connect the bottom negative (black) ground rail on the breadboard to the top negative (black) ground rail on the breadboard.

☐ Potentiometer:
- Connect Terminal 1 to the ground (GND) on the Arduino.
- Connect Terminal 2 to the 5V on the Arduino.
- Connect Wiper to A0.

☐ 9V battery:
- Connect the positive terminal of the battery to the top positive (red) power rail on the breadboard.
- Connect the negative terminal of the battery to the top negative (black) ground rail on the breadboard.

☐ H-Bridge motor driver (L293D):
- Place it, ensuring that it straddles the centre gap between the two sides of the breadboard.
- Connect "Enable 1 & 2" to the 5V on the Arduino.
- Connect Power 1 to the 9V on the battery.
- Connect all four ground pins to the GND.
- Connect Power 2 to the top positive (red) rail on the breadboard.
- Connect Input 1 to pin 5 on the Arduino.
- Connect Input 2 to pin 6 on the Arduino.

☐ DC motor:
- Connect Terminal 1 to Output 2 on the L293D.
- Connect Terminal 2 to Output 1 on the L293D.

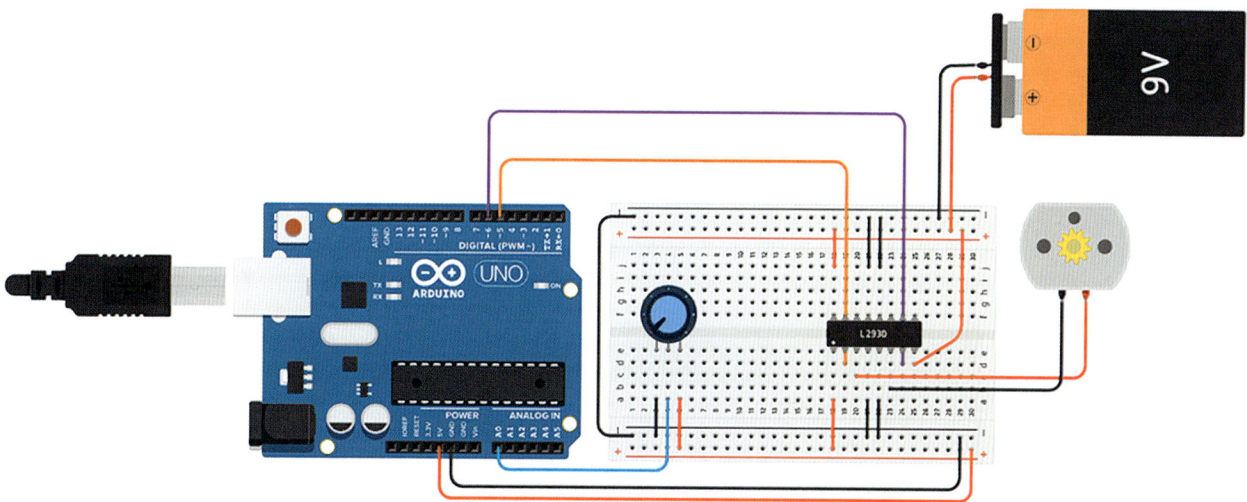

C++

```
int potValue; // Variable to store the potentiometer input value
int maximumSpeed = 128; // Maximum motor speed (should not be exceeded)
int forwardPin = 5; // Pin connected to the forward control input on the
// motor driver
int reversePin = 6; // Pin connected to the reverse control input on the
// motor driver
```

```
void setup() {
    pinMode(forwardPin, OUTPUT); // Set the forward pin as an output
    pinMode(reversePin, OUTPUT); // Set the reverse pin as an output
    Serial.begin(9600); // Initialize serial communication at 9600 baud for
    // debugging
}
void loop() {
    potValue = analogRead(A0); // Read the analog value from the potentiometer
    // (0-1023)
    int motorSpeed = map(potValue, 0, 1023, 0, 255); // Scale the potentiometer
    // value to match PWM range (0-255)
    // Ensure the motor speed does not exceed the desired value
    if (motorSpeed > maximumSpeed) {
        motorSpeed = maximumSpeed;
    }
    // Write the PWM value to the forward pin
    analogWrite(forwardPin, motorSpeed);
    analogWrite(reversePin, 0); // Ensure reverse pin is off
    // Print the motor speed value and desired speed to the serial monitor
    Serial.print("Motor Speed: ");
    Serial.print(motorSpeed);
    Serial.print(" | Desired Speed: ");
    Serial.println(maximumSpeed);
    delay(100); // Short delay to make the serial output readable
}
```

2 Observe how the motor speed changes as the sensor value changes. For example, turning the potentiometer should increase or decrease the motor speed, depending on the direction.

3 Modify the `maximumSpeed` in the code to see how the system responds to different target speeds or positions.

EXAM PRACTICE QUESTIONS

1 Describe the role of an operating system in organizing files within a directory structure. [2]
2 Outline the steps an operating system takes to load an application into memory. [3]
3 Describe the function of memory management within an operating system. [3]
4 Describe the function of process scheduling in an operating system. [3]
5 Describe how an operating system ensures security through user authentication. [2]
6 Compare the advantages and disadvantages of using first come first served (FCFS) and round robin (RR) scheduling algorithms in operating systems. [4]
7 Explain how priority scheduling can cause some processes to be ignored or delayed in an operating system. Describe a way to prevent this problem. [4]
8 Discuss how event frequency and CPU processing overheads influence the choice between interrupt handling and polling. [4]
9 Describe the role of the operating system in preventing deadlock during multitasking. [3]
10 Describe how an irrigation control system operates as a control system. What components are involved, and how do they interact to ensure optimal watering conditions? [4]

Translation

SYLLABUS CONTENT

By the end of this chapter, you should be able to:
▶ A1.4.1 Evaluate the translation processes of interpreters and compilers

A1.4.1 Translation processes of interpreters and compilers

Understanding the translation processes of interpreters and compilers is essential for grasping how programming languages are executed by computers. Interpreters and compilers both transform high-level code into machine-readable instructions, yet they do so through different methods, each with unique implications for performance, error handling and development efficiency. This section delves into the specifics of how interpreters and compilers function, examining their respective strengths and weaknesses and how these impact the choice of translation method for different programming scenarios.

■ Interpreters

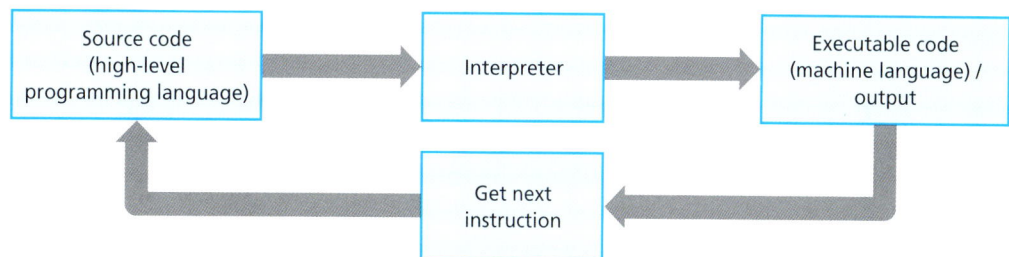

■ The interpreter process

Mechanics

Interpreters translate high-level programming code into machine code line-by-line or statement-by-statement, executing each line as it is translated. Unlike compilers, interpreters do not generate an intermediate machine-code file; instead, they directly execute the source code on the fly. This means that the interpreter reads the code, translates it and runs it immediately, repeating this process for each line or block of code until the entire program has been executed.

One key characteristic of interpreters is their ability to start executing a program without needing to process the entire codebase upfront. This allows for immediate feedback, which is particularly useful during the development and debugging phases. However, this line-by-line execution can result in slower overall performance compared to compiled code, as the interpreter must repeatedly translate and execute code during each run of the program.

Use cases

Interpreters are commonly used in scenarios where quick testing and debugging are essential. Languages including Python, JavaScript and Ruby are often interpreted, making them popular choices for web development, scripting and rapid application development. The ability to execute code immediately without a lengthy compilation process allows developers to experiment and iterate quickly. Additionally, interpreters are ideal for educational purposes, as they enable beginners to see the results of their code in real time, making it easier to understand programming concepts.

Interpreters are also favoured in environments where portability is important. Since the interpreter itself handles the execution, the same source code can be run on different platforms without modification, provided the appropriate interpreter is available on each platform.

■ Compilers

Source code (high-level language) → Compiler → Object code (machine language)

■ The compiler process

Mechanics

Compilers, in contrast to interpreters, translate the entire high-level source code into machine code in a single, comprehensive process before the program is executed. This process involves several stages, including lexical analysis, syntax analysis, semantic analysis, optimization and code generation. The final output is a standalone executable file, typically in machine code or an intermediate form like bytecode, which can be run directly on the target machine.

Once compiled, the machine code does not need further translation, allowing the program to execute much faster than interpreted code. However, the initial compilation process can be time-consuming, especially for large and complex programs. Additionally, because the entire code must be compiled before execution, any errors in the source code need to be addressed before the program can run, which can slow down the development cycle.

Use cases

Compilers are typically used in scenarios where performance is a critical concern. Languages including C, C++ and Java (which compiles to bytecode for the JVM) are compiled, making them well suited for system software, application development and situations requiring high-performance execution, such as video games or real-time processing systems.

Compiled code is also advantageous in environments where security and resource control are important. Since the machine code is pre-generated and optimized, it can be more difficult for malicious actors to reverse-engineer, and the execution is less dependent on external environments compared to interpreted code.

Compilers are often chosen when the software needs to be deployed across various environments with different hardware specifications. The compilation process can be tailored to optimize the executable for specific architectures, resulting in better performance and resource usage on the target system.

● Top tip!

An **interpreter** is like someone who translates each sentence of a book for you as you read, providing immediate understanding but requiring them to translate each line every time you revisit it.

In contrast, a **compiler** is like a translator who first converts the entire book into your native language, allowing you to read it smoothly without needing further translation, but requiring you to wait until the whole book is translated before you can start reading.

A1 Computer fundamentals

■ Advanced compilers and interpreters

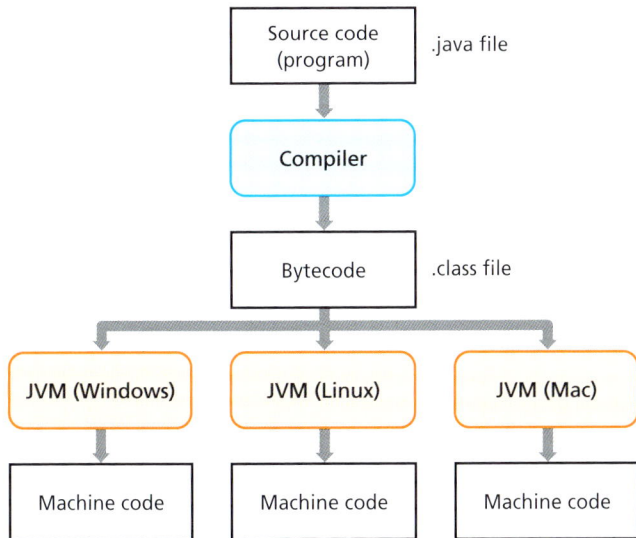

■ The Java Bytecode interpretation process

Bytecode interpreters

Mechanics:

Bytecode interpreters operate by first translating high-level source code into an intermediate form known as "bytecode". This bytecode is not directly executed by the machine's hardware, but is instead run on a virtual machine (VM) or an interpreter that understands the bytecode's instructions. The bytecode serves as a compact, platform-independent representation of the program, which allows it to be executed on any system that has the appropriate VM or interpreter. The bytecode interpreter reads and executes the bytecode instructions, often with some optimization, though it typically does so at a slower pace than fully compiled machine code because each instruction is interpreted at runtime.

Use cases:

Bytecode interpreters are widely used in scenarios where portability and cross-platform compatibility are important. Java is a prime example, where code is compiled into bytecode that runs on the Java Virtual Machine (JVM). This allows Java applications to run on any platform with a JVM, making it ideal for enterprise applications, web services and mobile apps that need to operate across diverse environments. Python also uses a similar approach, where the source code is compiled into bytecode (with the .pyc extension) and then executed by the Python interpreter. This makes bytecode interpreters useful in educational settings, web development and scripting, where flexibility and ease of deployment are more critical than raw performance.

Just-in-time (JIT) compilation

Mechanics:

Just-in-time (JIT) compilation is a dynamic approach that combines elements of both interpretation and compilation. Initially, the source code is compiled into bytecode, which is then interpreted by a virtual machine. As the program runs, the JIT compiler identifies frequently executed sections of the bytecode – often called "hot spots" – and compiles them into machine code on the fly. This machine code is then cached, so the next time the same code is executed, the system uses the compiled version instead of interpreting it again. This process allows JIT-compiled code to execute much faster than interpreted code, while still offering the flexibility and platform independence of bytecode.

Use cases:

JIT compilation is particularly beneficial in environments where performance is critical, but where the application also needs to be portable and dynamically optimized. The Java Virtual Machine (JVM) and the .NET runtime both use JIT compilation to improve the performance of applications. This approach is especially valuable in long-running applications, such as servers, where the overhead of JIT compilation is outweighed by the performance gains in subsequent executions of the same code paths. JIT is also used in web browsers for JavaScript execution, where it optimizes frequently used scripts to improve page load times and responsiveness. In general, JIT compilation is well suited for scenarios where applications need to balance the need for speed with the ability to run on multiple platforms.

■ Evaluation of different translation processes

Error detection

Error detection varies significantly across these translation processes. Compilers offer the most robust error detection because they analyse the entire source code before producing an executable. This analysis ensures that all syntax and some semantic errors are caught and must be resolved before the program can run, resulting in fewer runtime errors and a more stable final product.

Interpreters detect errors at runtime, as they execute code line by line. This approach allows developers to quickly identify and correct errors during development, which is especially useful for testing and debugging. However, because errors are only discovered when the specific problematic code is executed, there is a risk of encountering runtime errors that could disrupt program execution unexpectedly.

Bytecode interpreters provide a middle ground. While they do compile source code into bytecode before execution, allowing for some upfront error detection, errors may still occur at runtime as the bytecode is interpreted. This combination of pre-runtime error-checking with runtime interpretation can reduce the frequency of runtime errors compared to traditional interpreters, but it does not offer the exhaustive error-checking of full compilation.

JIT compilation combines elements of both interpretation and compilation. While some errors may still be detected at runtime, the JIT compiler's ability to dynamically compile frequently executed bytecode into machine code during execution can catch and optimize issues in repeated executions, improving the reliability of long-running programs.

● Common mistake

Be careful not to underestimate the differences in error detection between interpreters and compilers.

With interpreters, errors are caught as the code runs, which means they can occur unexpectedly during execution.

Compilers catch all syntax and some semantic errors before the program runs, preventing the program from executing until these errors are fixed.

PROGRAMMING EXERCISES

In these exercises, you will explore the differences in error detection between an interpreted language (Python) and a compiled language (Java). By running and compiling short programs in both languages, you will observe how and when errors are detected, providing insight into the advantages and challenges of each approach.

1   Run the Python script below and observe what happens when the interpreter encounters the error. What is the last line of output before the program crashes? What error message is displayed?

Python

```python
def greet(name):
    print("Hello, " + name + "!")
greet("Alice")
# Intentional error: Trying to use an undefined variable
print("The length of the name is " + str(len(name)))
```

A1 Computer fundamentals

2　Attempt to compile the program below and observe what happens when the compiler encounters the error. Does the program compile successfully? What error message is displayed?

```java
Java
public class SimpleProgram {
    public static void main(String[] args) {
        System.out.println("Hello, World!");
        // Intentional error: Missing semicolon
        System.out.println("This line has a syntax error")
    }
}
```

Compare the outcomes of running the Python script and compiling the Java program.

3　At what point is the error detected in each language?

4　How does the error-detection process affect the development workflow in each language?

5　What are the advantages and disadvantages of detecting errors at runtime vs at compile time?

Translation time

Compilers require a considerable amount of time initially to convert the entire source code into machine code before it can be executed. While this process may take longer, especially with large projects, the payoff is that the compiled program runs significantly faster once the translation is completed.

Interpreters, by contrast, execute code directly by translating it line by line. This allows the program to run almost immediately, which is advantageous for quickly testing and iterating code. However, because the code is translated during execution, programs with larger codebases may experience slower overall performance.

Bytecode interpreters provide a balance between these approaches. The initial step of compiling source code into bytecode is quicker than fully compiling it into machine code. The bytecode is then executed more efficiently than direct interpretation of source code, resulting in a compromise between start-up speed and execution efficiency.

JIT compilation goes a step further by converting bytecode into machine code dynamically as the program runs. Although this introduces some runtime overhead, it enables the system to optimize performance on the fly, particularly for code paths that are executed frequently. This dynamic approach allows JIT to reduce initial translation time while improving execution speed as the program continues to run.

Portability

Portability is a significant advantage of interpreters and bytecode interpreters. Since interpreters execute source code directly, the same code can run on any platform with the appropriate interpreter, making it ideal for cross-platform applications. Bytecode interpreters extend this portability by compiling source code into a platform-independent bytecode, which can be executed on any system with the appropriate virtual machine (for example Java's JVM). This makes bytecode interpreters particularly valuable in environments where applications must operate across diverse platforms without modification.

Compilers, however, produce machine code tailored to specific hardware architectures, resulting in highly efficient but less portable executables. Each target platform may require separate compilation, limiting the flexibility of deploying the same code across multiple environments.

JIT compilation preserves the portability of bytecode while enhancing performance. The bytecode can be distributed across different platforms, and the JIT compiler dynamically optimizes the execution for the specific hardware at runtime. This combination ensures that applications remain portable while still benefiting from platform-specific optimizations.

● Common mistake

It is easy to overlook the importance of portability. Interpreters and bytecode interpreters allow the same code to run on different platforms without modification, as long as the appropriate interpreter or virtual machine is available. Compiled code is optimized for specific hardware, making it less portable.

Applicability

The applicability of these translation processes varies depending on the requirements of the project. Compilers are best suited for applications where performance is critical, such as system software, high-performance computing and real-time systems. The upfront time investment in compilation is justified by the high execution speed of the compiled code.

Interpreters are ideal for scenarios where rapid development, testing and iteration are essential, such as in scripting, web development and educational environments. Their immediate execution and ease of use make them suitable for applications where flexibility and quick feedback are more important than raw performance.

Bytecode interpreters are commonly used in enterprise applications, web services and mobile apps where cross-platform compatibility is crucial. They offer a flexible solution that balances the need for portability with efficient execution, making them suitable for environments that demand both.

JIT compilation is particularly valuable in long-running applications and complex systems where performance needs to improve over time. It is well suited for server environments, dynamic web applications and platforms such as Java and .NET, where the balance of portability, performance and dynamic optimization is critical.

Criteria	Compilers	Interpreters	Bytecode interpreters	JIT compilation
Error detection	Comprehensive, with all errors caught before execution	Runtime errors detected as code is executed line by line	Some errors are caught before execution, but others at runtime	Combines runtime error detection with dynamic optimization
Translation time	High initial translation time, but results in fast execution	Immediate execution, low initial translation time, but slower overall execution	Moderate initial translation time, with moderately fast execution	Balances initial translation with dynamic compilation for optimized execution
Portability	Low; requires separate compilation for each platform	High; code runs on any platform with the appropriate interpreter	High; bytecode is platform-independent and runs on any system with the appropriate VM	High; maintains portability with platform-specific optimizations at runtime
Applicability	Best for performance-critical applications and system software	Ideal for rapid development, testing and cross-platform scripting	Suited for cross-platform applications with moderate performance needs	Well suited for long-running applications requiring dynamic optimization

A1 Computer fundamentals

■ Example scenarios

Scenario	Best translation method	Explanation
Rapid development and testing	Interpreters	• Interpreters allow immediate execution of code, enabling quick iterations, debugging and real-time feedback • Ideal for scripting languages such as Python or JavaScript
Performance-critical applications	Compilers	• Compilers optimize the entire codebase into machine code before execution, resulting in highly efficient and fast-performing applications • Suitable for system software, gaming and real-time systems using languages such as C or C++
Cross-platform development	Bytecode interpreters and JIT compilation	• Bytecode interpreters (e.g. Java's JVM) provide platform independence by compiling code into an intermediate bytecode, which can run on any platform with the appropriate virtual machine • JIT compilation enhances performance by optimizing frequently executed code at runtime, balancing portability with execution speed • Ideal for applications such as enterprise software, mobile apps and web services

Rapid development and testing

Example: A startup developing a prototype web application using Python.

The team needs to quickly test and iterate on their codebase, making adjustments on the fly. An interpreter allows them to run their code immediately and see the results of changes without waiting for compilation.

Performance-critical applications

Example: A company developing a real-time trading system in C++ that requires high-speed data processing with minimal latency.

A compiler is used to translate the entire codebase into optimized machine code, ensuring the system performs at the highest efficiency possible.

Cross-platform development

Example: A software firm creating an enterprise-level application in Java that needs to run on Windows, macOS and Linux environments.

By compiling the code into bytecode, the application can be run on any platform with the Java Virtual Machine (JVM). To enhance performance, the JVM's JIT compiler further optimizes the application's execution on each specific platform.

EXAM PRACTICE QUESTIONS

1 Compare the advantages and disadvantages of using a compiler vs an interpreter in software development. [4]
2 Describe the process of just-in-time (JIT) compilation and explain how it combines elements of both interpretation and compilation. [4]
3 Compare the error-detection capabilities of compilers and interpreters, and discuss the implications for software development. [4]

Linking questions

1 What role does multitasking in an operating system play in machine learning? (A4)
2 How might a conditional statement be constructed by Boolean logic gates in a circuit? (B2)
3 What role does task scheduling in an operating system play in managing network traffic and requests? (A1)
4 How does resource allocation in an operating system impact network performance and stability? (A2)
5 What role do GPUs play in non-graphics computational tasks? (A4)
6 To what extent should computer systems not cause harm? (TOK)

A2 Networks

A2.1

Network fundamentals

What are the principles and concepts that underpin how networks operate?

SYLLABUS CONTENT

By the end of this chapter, you should be able to:
▶ A2.1.1 Describe the purpose and characteristics of networks
▶ A2.1.2 Describe the purpose, benefits and limitations of modern digital infrastructures
▶ A2.1.3 Describe the function of network devices
▶ A2.1.4 Describe the network protocols used for transport and application
▶ A2.1.5 Describe the function of the TCP/IP model (HL)

A2.1.1 The purpose and characteristics of networks

◆ **Computer network:** a system that connects computers and other devices to share resources (digital or physical) and information.

◆ **Local area network:** a system that connects computers and other devices within a small geographical area, such as an office or home.

Welcome to **computer networks**. In recent decades, networks have become an all-pervasive and integral part of our modern lives. We use networks to:

■ instantly communicate and collaborate with people around the world

■ access a wealth of information, entertainment and services at our fingertips

■ conduct business transactions, banking and online shopping with ease

■ learn new skills, attend virtual classes and expand our knowledge

■ remotely control and monitor our homes, cars and other connected devices

■ share photos, videos and stories with family and friends in real time.

The power and ubiquity of computer networks have truly transformed the way we live, work and play. In this chapter, we will delve into the inner workings of these complex systems that have become so ubiquitous that we barely give them a moment's thought – except when things go wrong.

■ Local area networks (LAN)

A **local area network** is a network of computers that are interconnected in a small geographical location, typically limited to a single property such as a home, building or campus. These are the oldest types of networks, though the equipment used in modern versions looks nothing like the historical versions.

The purpose of these networks is to facilitate sharing resources between the different computers, such as files, printers, applications and access to external networks, such as the internet.

LANs typically have a high bandwidth internally, with speeds ranging from 100 Mbps (Megabits per second) to 10 Gbps (Gigabits per second). Their small geographical range means there are typically no issues with latency (the time delay for data to transmit across the network).

Most homes and many corporate LANs now use a mix of wired Ethernet cables and wireless networking technologies. Dedicated wireless LANs may sometimes be referred to as WLANs.

■ Wide area networks (WAN)

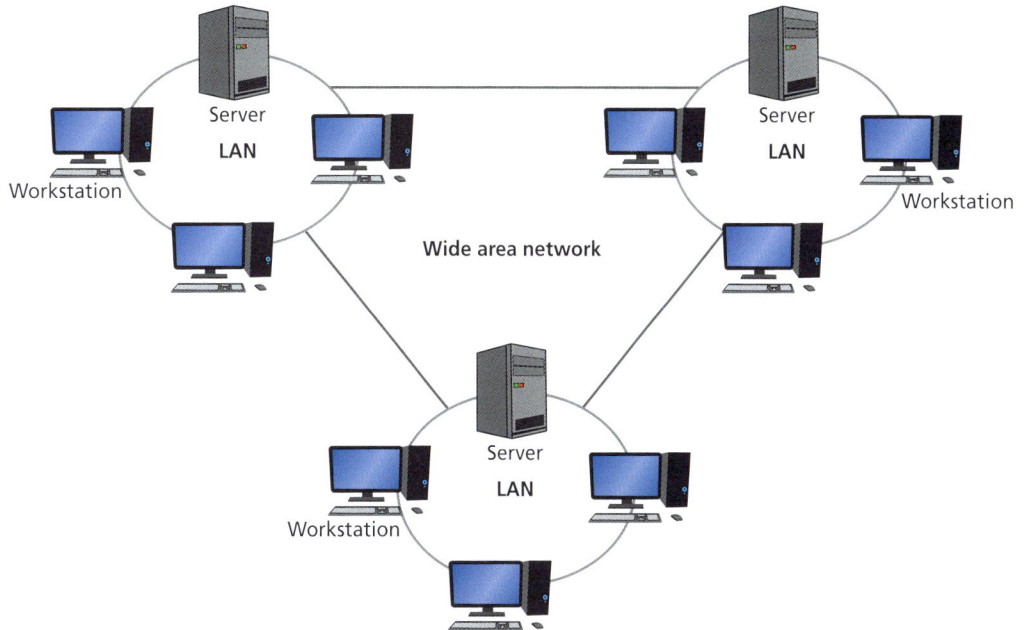

◆ **Wide area network:** a system that connects computers and other devices across a large geographic area, usually connecting multiple LANs together.

◆ **Personal area network:** a network for personal devices within the range of an individual person, usually connected with Bluetooth.

A **wide area network** provides for the interconnection of multiple local area networks over a wider geographical distance. This connection distance may be across town, between different cities or even different continents. For example, this could be for sharing resources across different office branches of a company.

Classically, a WAN does not use the internet for this interconnection; instead it would have its own dedicated networking infrastructure for long-distance connections, such as fibre-optic cabling or point-to-point microwave transmission.

In practice, most modern WANs use the existing infrastructure of high-speed internet and establish a virtualized WAN through the use of virtual private networking technology, discussed below.

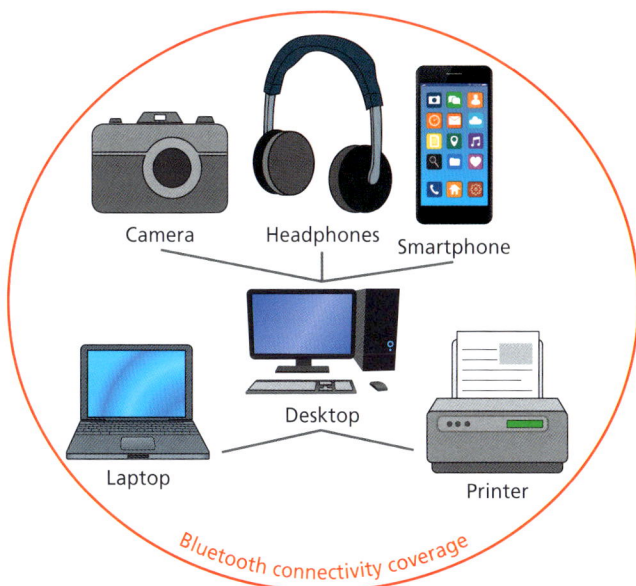

■ Personal area networks (PAN)

A **personal area network** refers to the devices that are interconnected, centred around an individual person. A PAN covers a very small range, and is typically limited to about 10 metres.

While USB cable-connected devices could be said to be part of a person's PAN, Bluetooth is the connectivity technology most commonly associated with PANs. The interconnected nature of your headphones, phone, camera, watch and whatever other devices you may be carrying on your person is what forms your PAN.

Virtual private networks (VPN)

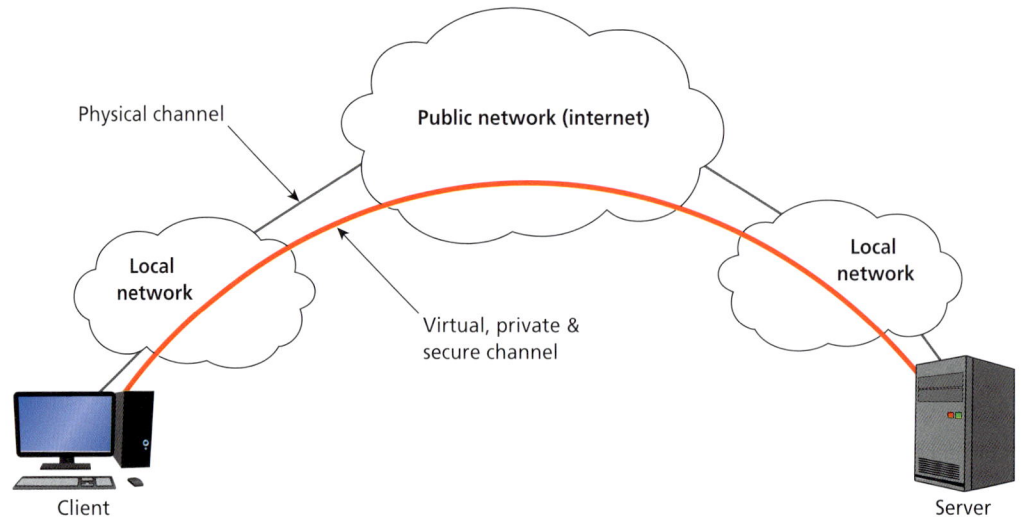

Virtual private networking refers to using public networking infrastructure to establish a secure, private tunnel for your own communication purposes. The encryption enables users to send and receive data across the public internet, as if their computing devices were directly connected on their own private network.

There are many "VPN companies" that advertise their services to retail consumers to make use of technology so that their internet browsing activities can appear to be taking place from a different geographical location from where they truly are. While this is a useful technology for getting around geo-blocks and the like, it is a different use case from the corporate use of VPNs.

Companies use the secure tunnel of a VPN to provide employees with remote access to their corporate networks as if they were physically present at their corporate headquarters.

VPNs help reduce the need for expensive dedicated networking infrastructure over long distances, as would historically have been required for a WAN.

◆ **Virtual private network:** a secure connection that runs across the internet to provide private communication between your network and a remote server.

◆ **Internet:** a global network of computer networks that are interconnected with each other and communicate through standardized protocols.

A2.1.2 The purpose, benefits and limitations of modern digital infrastructures

Internet

To suggest the **internet** is a core component of modern digital infrastructure is a bit like saying water is wet. The internet is *the* global network. It connects millions of private, public, academic, business and government networks to one massive global network. It provides easy access to a vast amount of information and services, as well as facilitating near-instant communications. Commerce, businesses and global marketplaces are now extremely dependent upon it.

That said, the internet is far from perfect. In the 1970s and 80s, as key components of what would become the internet were being developed, there was no master plan, and the sheer scale of the result would have been impossible to imagine or foresee. This means there are vulnerabilities baked into the core technologies on which the internet depends. It is susceptible to hacking, denial of service, phishing and many other threats that we will look at later in this chapter.

■ Cloud computing

The cloud is a mysterious-sounding name for a critical part of modern infrastructure devised by a marketing major somewhere. In essence, it is computing services being made available for rent by large technology companies so that you don't need to purchase your own physical computer systems for servers and other infrastructure. Businesses and individuals can use the internet to access the software and hardware provided by these technology companies in their giant data centres.

There are some benefits to this approach. It means resource utilization can be easily scaled up or down without large financial investment. It also reduces the IT maintenance costs for small companies, as it is all part of the rented service.

Due to communication with cloud-rented systems occurring over the internet, that clearly means reliable, stable, high-speed internet connectivity is a must. Concerns about the security and privacy of data held on these third-party systems can also be a legitimate concern, as these systems are beyond your control.

Amazon Web Services, Google Cloud and Microsoft Azure are three big cloud providers, at the time of writing.

● TOK

Role of experts in consumption or acquisition of knowledge

Computer networks, such as the internet, rely upon the expertise of network engineers to keep the system stable, efficient and effective. How has their contribution shaped the way we consume or acquire knowledge?

● Linking question

How do cloud computing and distributed systems utilize networking to deliver services?

■ Distributed systems

A distributed system connects multiple computers, or networks of computers, together to achieve common goals. They are more fault tolerant than other systems as, if one node fails, there are other paths of connectivity through which the rest of the network can continue to function. This resilience comes at the cost of complexity, meaning they are more difficult to design, manage and maintain. In particular, ensuring data consistency across the various nodes can be a challenge.

Peer-to-peer networking tools, such as BitTorrent, are examples of distributed systems, as are Blockchains. Distributed systems used by some large corporate networks include Content Delivery Networks to help distribute content to users worldwide.

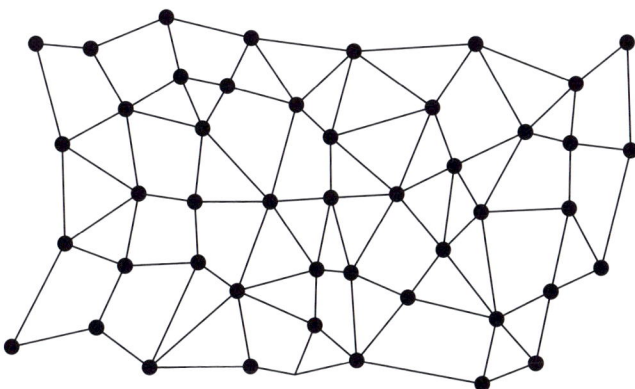

■ With each dot representing a node on the network, a distributed system has many different paths to traverse between any two points

■ Edge computing

Edge computing brings the computational and data storage capacity closer to the physical location where it is needed, to reduce latency and save bandwidth.

Large content delivery companies, such as Netflix, Spotify and the like, may use the edge computing model to deploy clusters of servers in key cities so as to reduce the amount of traffic that must travel back and forth to their main hubs. These servers can cache the most commonly sought-after files for each region, significantly speeding up the service for those customers, while preserving bandwidth for obtaining occasionally requested files that are not in the local cache.

This increase in endpoints to the network presents an increase in attack vectors for an adversary, so it comes with increased security and maintenance complexities.

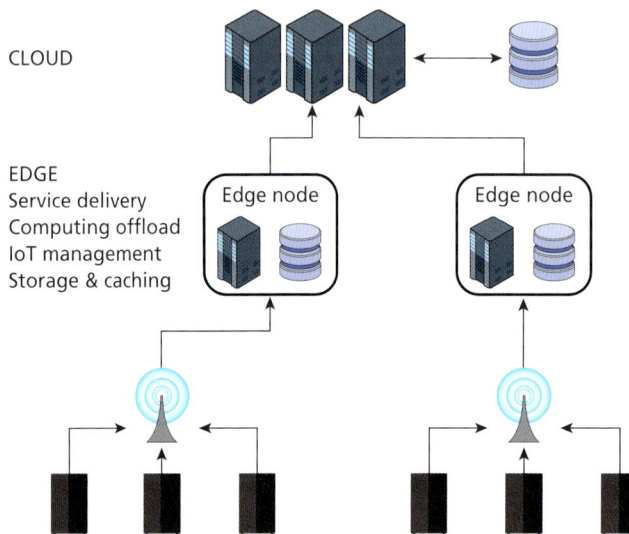

CLOUD

EDGE
Service delivery
Computing offload
IoT management
Storage & caching

Edge node

Edge node

■ Edge computing places computational resources closer to the point of demand, which reduces network load for the core servers in the cloud

■ Mobile networks

Mobile telecommunications networks are now globally ubiquitous. There are many parts of the world where mobile connectivity is the only connectivity available, as mobile networks can be deployed without the cost of digging up the ground for cabling installations.

The mobility that these networks facilitate allows convenient access to information and communication while on the go, and supports vast regions. That said, the necessity to place towers everywhere and the complexities of geography do mean that mobile-phone networks do have *dead zones*, which are areas without network coverage. Signal strength can vary, which affects quality of service and bandwidth throughput.

At the time of writing, many countries are in the process of deploying fifth generation mobile networks (5G), which will increase speeds to up to 10 Gbps for peak data, with an average of 100 Mbps.

■ Mobile
telecommunications tower

A2.1.3 The function of network devices

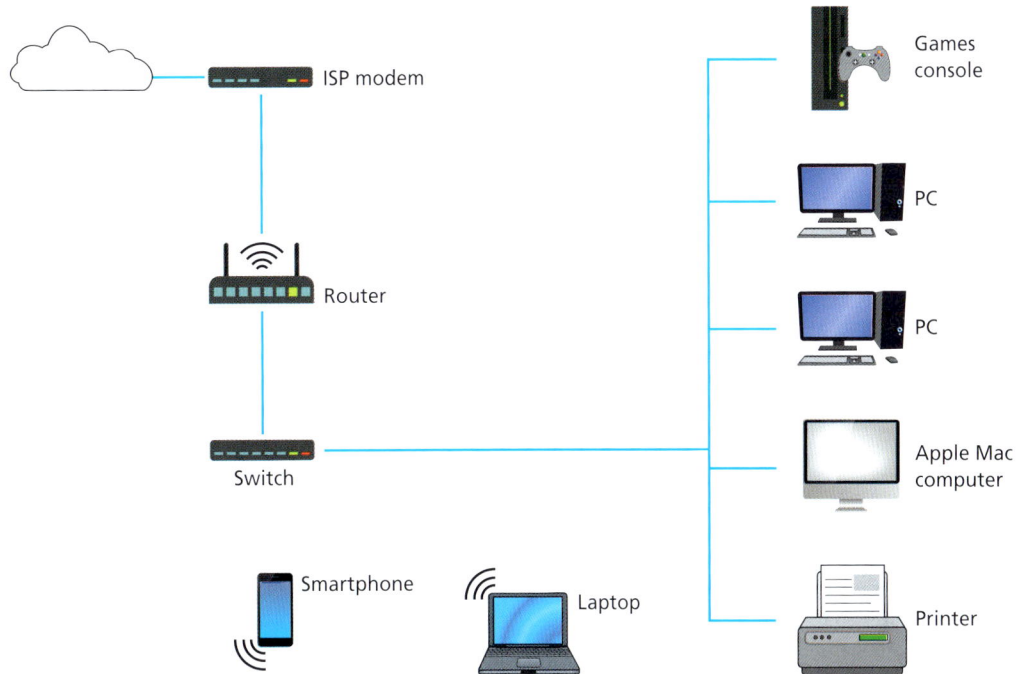

■ Devices in a typical home or small office network

Many home or small office networks might have only a single physical device that connects all their devices to their internet service provider. This single device might be colloquially referred to as the router or modem. The reality is that there are several logical devices at work, even if they are all co-located in a single physical unit. We will examine the roles of these different devices now.

> ### ◯ Top tip!
>
> **Understand the purpose!**
>
> There are a lot of different devices that serve different roles within a computer network. It can be easy to get them confused because most home networks have one physical device that plays many of these roles. Focus on understanding each device type's purpose and functionality. Ask yourself why this device type is needed, and what problems it solves.

■ Gateway

◆ **Gateway:** a device that connects different networks together and manages the traffic flow between them; often used to connect a local network to the internet.

A **gateway** is, as the name implies, the gate or connection between two networks. These networks may be communicating with two different protocols, and the gateway performs the translation task required to convert between the protocols.

For instance, in a typical home environment where the gateway connects to the internet service provider via a fibre-optic cable, it may be translating between EPON (Ethernet passive optical network) and regular Ethernet.

Because it converts from one network to another, it primarily operates at the application layer of the TCP/IP model (see Section A2.1.5).

■ Hardware firewall

The hardware **firewall** monitors and allows or denies incoming and outgoing network traffic based on a predetermined set of security rules. The purpose is to be a safeguarding barrier between the locally trusted network and the untrusted network of the internet.

Firewall rules are typically a list of IP addresses and / or TCP/UDP ports to allow or deny traffic, based on the origin address or port and destination address or port.

The device functions at the transport and internet layers of the TCP/IP model (see Section A2.1.5).

■ Modem

A modem is a modulator–demodulator. It is used to convert between digital and analogue signals. A digital signal is modulated to encode digital data into an analogue form, transmitted across the analogue medium, such as phone lines, and then demodulated at the other end to extract the digital data.

The device functions at the physical, network interface layer of the TCP/IP model (see Section A2.1.5).

■ Network interface card

The network interface card is the hardware component on an individual device, such as a laptop or mobile phone, that allows it to connect to the network. It may be a card that requires connecting a physical cable, such as Ethernet twisted pair or fibre optic, or it could have an antenna attached for connecting to a wireless network.

The device functions at the physical, network interface layer of the TCP/IP model (see Section A2.1.5).

■ Router

The **router** directs the path packets of data take between networks. It inspects the network address information in the packet header to determine the ultimate destination and uses that to send the packet on the optimal route.

The router typically operates at the network interface layer of the TCP/IP model, as it uses TCP/IP addresses to make its routing decisions (see Section A2.1.5).

ACTIVITY

Thinking skills: A network router on a rocket flight has been accidentally reset, so that it is blocking legitimate traffic between the rocket and mission control. The task to fix it falls to you. Search Coding Quest and select "Broken firewall", or go to https://codingquest.io/problem/29, to complete this activity.

■ Switch

A **network switch** connects devices within a single segment of a network. The switch effectively creates a network; it is the central spoke in a star-based network. A switch receives incoming packets of data and sends them on to their destination within the local area network using MAC addresses.

The switch operates at the network interface layer of the TCP/IP model (see Section A2.1.5).

Wireless access point

Wireless access points connect wireless devices together to form a network, in the same way that a switch does for a physical network. They can also act as range extenders for wireless signals.

A wireless access point operates at the network interface layer of the TCP/IP model (see Section A2.1.5).

A2.1.4 Network protocols used for transport and application

> ● **Linking question**
>
> How do the concepts of binary and hexadecimal data structures relate to network communications? (B2)

■ Transmission Control Protocol (TCP) and User Datagram Protocol (UDP)

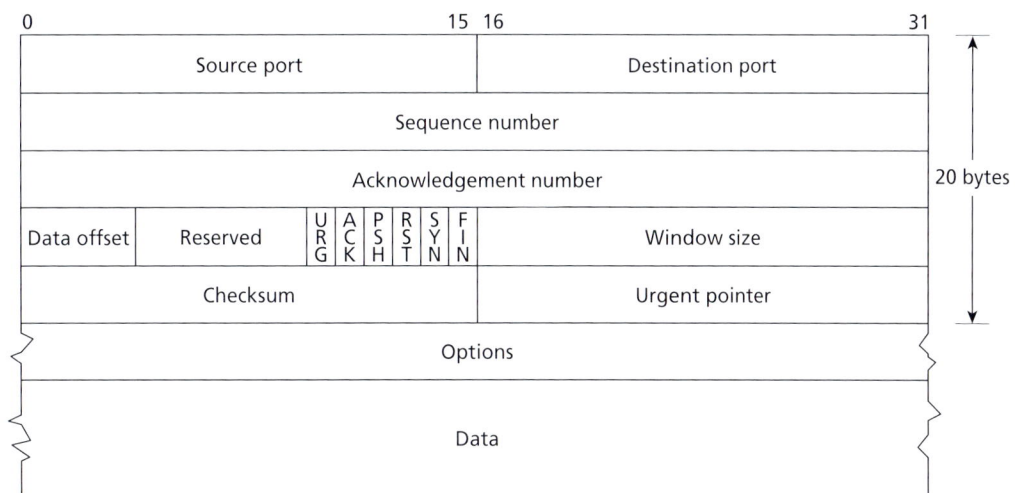

■ TCP protocol

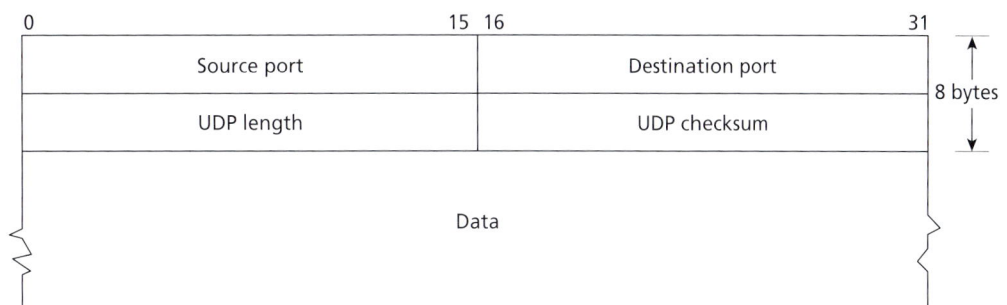

■ UDP protocol

The Transmission Control Protocol (TCP) and User Datagram Protocol (UDP) operate on the transport layer of the TCP/IP model. That is, they are packets that are contained within the data portion of an IP packet. Where IP is responsible for getting a packet from one computer system to another, the TCP or UDP is responsible for getting data from one application to another.

These **protocols** facilitate multiple applications sharing a common network connection at once. For instance, if a server is running both an email-server application and a web-server application, the host operating system needs a means of determining which application to send inbound traffic to for processing. This is where port numbers come in. Think of these as phone extensions, or apartment numbers within a building address. To assist matters even further, the industry has standardized default port numbers for commonly used applications. The Simple Mail Transfer Protocol (SMTP) uses port 587 and Hypertext Transfer Protocol (HTTP) uses port 80, whereas Hypertext Transfer Protocol Secure (HTTPS) uses 443 and the Secure Shell (SSH) uses port 22.

TCP is a connection-oriented protocol. This means it establishes and maintains an active connection with the remote server until the application programs on both ends have finished exchanging messages. TCP ensures that data is delivered in order, without errors, and that data is acknowledged upon receipt. If there is an error in the receipt of a packet (either it doesn't arrive or is corrupted in some way), it is re-sent. The sequence number is used to ensure packets are reassembled into their correct order by the receiving application, and the checksum is used to ensure it is not corrupted during transmission.

UDP is a connectionless protocol. Data is transmitted, but there is no guarantee of reliability or order of delivery. UDP is used for applications such as streaming video, where maintaining speed and staying up to date with the broadcast is more important than the occasional missed frame or subset of pixels.

Sometimes a light-hearted approach can help communicate the difference between two items. Here is an anecdote that does the rounds of the internet comparing TCP and UDP:

> **A TCP joke:**
> Hello, would you like to hear a TCP joke?
> Yes, I'd like to hear a TCP joke.
> OK, I'll tell you a TCP joke.
> OK, I'll hear a TCP joke.
> Are you ready to hear a TCP joke?
> Yes, I am ready to hear a TCP joke.
> OK, I'm about to send the TCP joke. It will last 10 seconds, it has two characters, it does not have a setting, it ends with a punchline.
> OK, I'm ready to hear the TCP joke that will last 10 seconds, has two characters, does not have a setting and will end with a punchline.
> I'm sorry, your connection has timed out … Hello, would you like to hear a TCP joke?

> **A UDP joke:**
> I know a UDP joke, but you might not get it.

You can programmatically experiment with communicating directly over TCP/IP connections with code similar to the following code.

◆ **Protocol:** a set of rules and standards that define how data is transmitted and received across a network for a given application.

For a server that receives requests, processes them and then replies with a response:

Python

```python
import socket
def run_server(host="0.0.0.0", port=65432):
    # Create a socket object using IPv4 (AF_INET) and TCP protocol (SOCK_STREAM)
    with socket.socket(socket.AF_INET, socket.SOCK_STREAM) as s:
        # Bind the socket to the address and port, and start listing
        s.bind((host, port))
        s.listen()
        print(f"Server is running and listening at {host}:{port}")
        # Wait for connection. The code will pause here until connection
        conn, addr = s.accept()
        with conn:
            print(f"Connected by {addr}")
            while True:
                data = conn.recv(1024) # Receive up to 1024 bytes
                if not data:
                    break
                received_message = data.decode() # Decode bytes to string
                print(f"Received message: {received_message}")
                new_message = received_message.upper()
                print(f"Converted message: {new_message}")
                conn.sendall(new_message.encode()) # Encode to send as bytes
if __name__ == "__main__":
    run_server()
```

The following code is for a client that generates a request, sends it and then receives the response. You must ensure the server code (above) is running, and the code below is updated with the IP address of the server. You may need to adjust your firewall settings to allow this demonstration to work.

Python

```python
import socket
def run_client(server_ip_addr, server_port=65432):
    # Create IPv4 and TCP socket
    with socket.socket(socket.AF_INET, socket.SOCK_STREAM) as s:
        s.connect((server_ip_addr, server_port))
        message = "Hello, server!"
        s.sendall(message.encode())
        data = s.recv(1024).decode() # Get response and decode from bytes to string
        print(f"Received {data} from the server")
if __name__ == "__main__":
    server_ip_addr = "127.0.0.1"
    run_client(server_ip_addr)
```

■ Hypertext Transfer Protocol (HTTP)

HTTP is the foundation of the world wide web. It is the protocol used for the transmission of hypermedia documents, such as HTML, as well as associated text files (Javascript, CSS) or binary files (images and so on).

HTTP is a stateless protocol. This means that each command is executed independently of any previous commands, with no recollection or knowledge of them. The client (such as a web browser) sends requests to the web server, which then responds with the requested resource or an error code.

HTTP communication occurs as unicode text strings, so it is human-readable.

An example of an HTTP request from a browser might resemble the following text. The client is sending a GET request for a particular file called index.html from the server hosting www.example.com.

```
GET /index.html HTTP/1.1
Host: www.example.com
```

The associated reply from the web server follows. The server begins by indicating it is replying using the HTTP v1.1 protocol and a status code of 200, which means OK. If there is an error then a different status code would be received. For instance, if the requested file was not found then a status of 404 would be sent.

```
HTTP/1.1 200 OK
Content-Type: text/html
Content-Length: 1456
<!DOCTYPE html>
<html>
<head>
  <title>Example Website</title>
</head>
<body>
  <h1>Welcome to the Example Website!</h1>
  <p>This is the content of the index.html web page.</p>
</body>
</html>
```

This is a simple example; in practice, there is also commonly authentication information, cookies and other data sent as part of the request or response.

You can programmatically experiment with sending your own HTTP requests and receiving the responses with Python by using the `requests` library. For instance, a simple program may look like this:

Python
```python
import requests
response = requests.get("https://www.example.com")
print(response.status_code)
print(response.text)
```

The `requests` library is very powerful and even lets you download or upload text files and binary files.

If you'd like to create your own web server that receives and processes HTTP requests, take a look at Python's `Flask` library. A simple web-server application may resemble the following code:

Python
```python
from flask import Flask, render_template, request, redirect, send_file
app = Flask(__name__)
app.config["SECRET_KEY"] = "code used to secure cookies from tampering"
# Return templates/index.html
@app.route("/")
def index_page():
    return render_template("index.html")
# Return a binary file
@app.route("/promotional_video")
def promotional_video():
    return send_file("promotional_video.mp4")
# Use the URL path to supply a parameter
@app.route("/user/<userid>")
def users(userid):
    return "User page for "+userid
# Get values from an HTML form
@app.route("/page2", methods=["GET","POST"])
def page2():
    # HTML with <input name='person'> will create a request.values['person']
    form = dict(request.values) # Convert all values into a dictionary
    person = form["person"]
    return f"Hello, {person}, welcome to my website"
# Start the web server. These should be the last lines
if __name__ == "__main__":
    app.run(host="0.0.0.0", port=80, debug=True)
```

■ Hypertext Transfer Protocol Secure (HTTPS)

HTTPS is the secure version of Hypertext Transfer Protocol. It is designed to ensure communication is encrypted between the client and server to help protect against man-in-the-middle attacks and eavesdroppers. There are three key features that HTTPS offers over the original HTTP:

■ **Encryption:** typically achieved through the use of either SSL or TLS encryption methods.

■ **Authentication:** a digitally signed certificate is issued by the server so your client application can verify it is connecting to the correct server (i.e. to protect against an imposter posing as your bank website, for instance).

■ **Data integrity:** ensures that the data sent and received is not altered in transit.

These ideas are discussed further in Section A2.4.4.

■ Dynamic Host Configuration Protocol (DHCP)

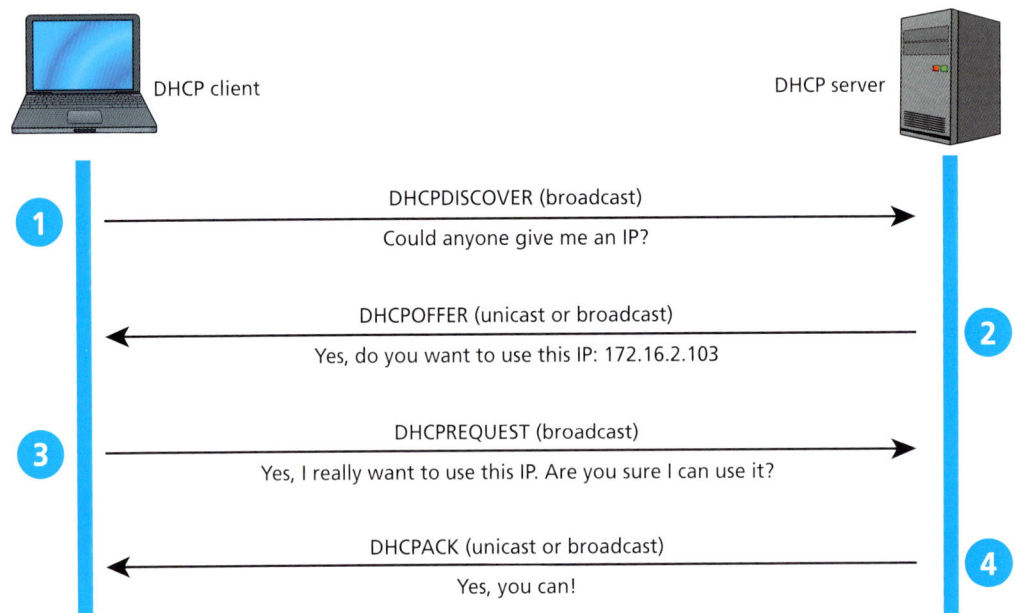

DHCP is a network-management protocol. It is used most commonly when a computer first joins a computer network (for example on system start-up). DHCP is the process by which the computer requests and receives a valid IP address for use on that network. In many home and small office networks, the device commonly known as the "router" also runs a DHCP server on it, providing IP addresses to devices that connect to it within the home.

The client device broadcasts (that is, sends a message for all devices on the network to see) a **DHCP Discover** message in which it provides its hardware MAC address and any preferences regarding subnet, router, DNS server or IP address lease time.

A DHCP server responds with a **DHCP Offer** message to assign an IP address from within a defined pool of addresses available to it. IP addresses are "leased" to devices for a specific period, after which the device must request to renew its lease. This process allows for reconfiguration and reuse of addresses. The offer also includes information about subnet, domain name server and other matters.

In the home or small office space, there are a number of addresses that have been reserved for private internal networks to use. These addresses are not used by valid servers and are not routable on the public internet. These address ranges are:

- 10.0.0.0 to 10.255.255.255
- 172.16.0.0 to 172.31.255.255
- 192.168.0.0 to 192.168.255.255

Networks that use these addresses for their internal devices rely on services such as network address translation to connect to the public internet. See Section A2.3.1 for a discussion about this.

A2.1.5 The function of the TCP/IP model (HL)

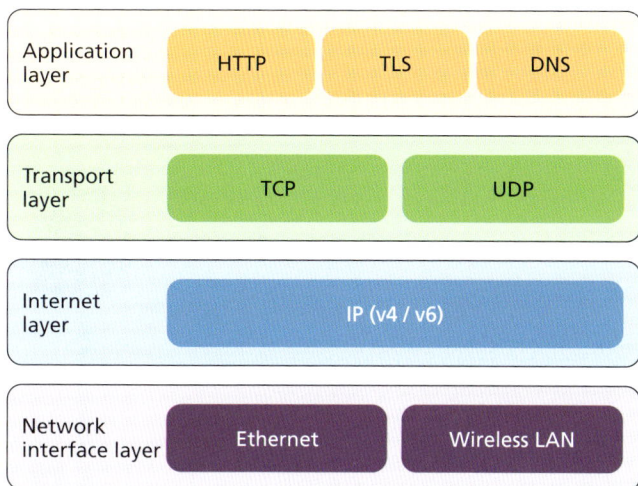

■ The allocation of bits in the TCP and UDP protocols.

The TCP/IP model is a conceptual approach to understanding the different roles and responsibilities of networking communication. It largely supersedes and streamlines the previously used OSI model.

The TCP/IP model is broken down into the four layers: the network interface layer (also known as the "physical layer"), the internet layer, the transport layer and, finally, the application layer.

■ Application

The application layer is the topmost level and is where the protocols used by actual applications reside. They include applications such as HTTP and HTTPS for web browsing; FTP for file transfer; SMTP and POP3 for email; and DNS. The application is responsible for using and correctly forming messages transmitted through these protocols.

■ Transport

On initiation of a communication request from an application, the operating system uses the transport layer to help ensure the data gets from the correct source application to the correct target application at the destination.

The two primary protocols that reside in the transport layer are TCP (Transport Control Protocol) and UDP (User Datagram Protocol).

The transport layer receives data from the application layer, segments it and handles error detection and correction (if using TCP), along with retransmitting lost packets.

These segments or datagrams are then transferred to the internet layer.

■ Internet

The internet layer is responsible for managing the movement of packets across the network, including ensuring they are routed to the correct destination.

■ TCP/IP data as packets

To do this, it receives segmented data from the transport layer, encapsulates it into packets and decides on the best route for the packets to travel across networks. These packets are then forwarded to the network interface layer, which takes care of transmitting the bits to the next physical device in the chain.

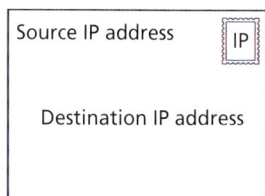

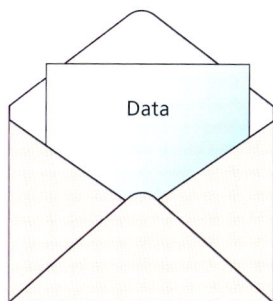

■ Network interface

The network interface layer manages the process of physical transmission of the data across the networking hardware and transmission media. It includes the protocols and hardware necessary to deliver the data across the local media, and aspects such as Ethernet, WiFi and physical network components including routers, cabling and switches.

The network interface layer receives data packets from the internet layer and converts them into a form suitable for transmission over the network, such as over Ethernet cabling or WiFi. Hardware addressing, such as MAC addresses, is managed by this layer.

● Common mistake

It's common to confuse which protocols operate at which layer of the TCP/IP model. Keep a clear map of where TCP, UDP, HTTP, HTTPS and DHCP fit within the layers.

REVIEW QUESTIONS

1 Which network is typically used to cover a geographical area that spans a city or a group of buildings?

   a PAN   b LAN   c WAN   d VPN

2 Which type of modern digital infrastructure would be most suitable for handling real-time data processing close to data sources?

   a Internet

   b Cloud computing

   c Distributed systems

   d Edge computing

3 Which device is responsible for enabling multiple computers to connect to the internet through a shared connection?

   a Modem

   b Switch

   c Router

   d Network interface card (NIC)

4 Which protocol ensures delivery of packets and is used for activities requiring high reliability, such as file transfers?

   a TCP   b UDP   c HTTP   d DHCP

5 In the TCP/IP model, which layer is primarily responsible for routing and forwarding packets?

   a Application

   b Transport

   c Internet

   d Network interface

6 Describe one characteristic that distinguishes a virtual private network (VPN) from other types of networks.

7 Identify one major limitation of using cloud computing in digital infrastructure.

8 Describe the primary function of a wireless access point in a network.

9 Describe three main differences between HTTP and HTTPS.

10 Describe the role of the application layer in the TCP/IP model.

A2.2 Network architecture

A2.2 · Network architecture

Network architecture

By the end of this chapter, you should be able to:
▶ A2.2.1 Describe the function and practical applications of network topologies
▶ A2.2.2 Describe the function of servers (HL)
▶ A2.2.3 Compare and contrast networking models
▶ A2.2.4 Explain the concepts and applications of network segmentation

TOK

Organizing and classifying knowledge

If the sum of human knowledge is being stored on servers accessible through the global interconnected computer network known as the "internet", how does the organization and classification of the internet, and its constituent networks, affect what we know?

● Linking questions

1 How can network types, or transmissions, impact database performance? (A3)
2 How do network topologies influence machine learning algorithms (A4)?

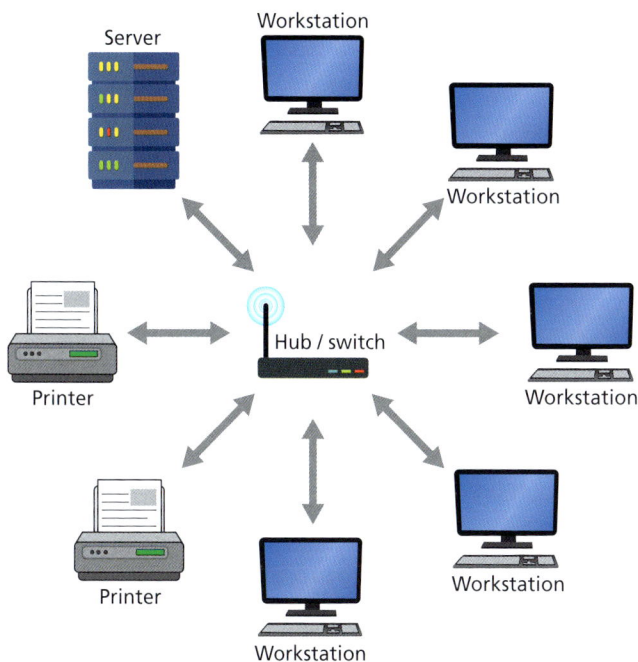

■ Star topology has all the individual nodes emanating from a central point

A2.2.1 The function and practical applications of network topologies

Network topology refers to the physical layout and structure of the nodes and connections within a network.

■ Star topology

In a star topology, all nodes connect to a single central device (such as a network switch). The central switch manages the task of routing messages between the various nodes. This approach is very common in homes and small offices, where a single switch provides all the capacity needed for the various devices that are connecting.

A few factors to consider with the star topology include:

- **Reliability:** If the central device fails, the network fails.
- **Bandwidth speed:** While each device has its own dedicated connection to the hub, the overall throughput speed is dependent on the processing capacity of that central hub.
- **Scalability:** The central switch typically has a limited number of ports or connections that it can handle, possibly limiting expansion to accommodate future needs.
- **Collisions:** There is minimal risk of data collision as every node has its own dedicated connection.
- **Cost:** Quite low if only a few nodes are needed; however, costs can increase if the capacity limits of the central node are exceeded and upgrades are required.

Top tip!

Each topology (star, mesh, hybrid) serves different needs. Be sure to understand why each one is more suitable than another for specific situations. Learn the diagrams of the different topologies to visualize how nodes are connected, as that provides a crucial understanding of how the flow of data is impacted if a node fails.

Mesh topology

In a mesh topology, every node has an immediate, direct connection to every other node. While most often depicted as a full mesh, partial meshes do also exist.

Meshes are suitable for large environments where reliability of individual pathways may be a concern. Critical infrastructure, such as military and aviation environments, is more inclined to use a mesh topology to help ensure robust resilience of the network against any point of failure.

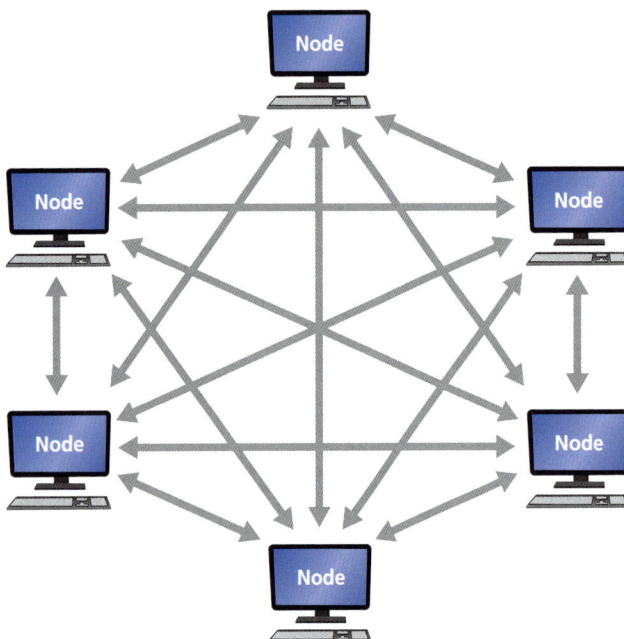

Wireless mesh systems, such as Meshtastic, have also started to gain popularity among tech hobbyists and as a means of providing connectivity in remote and disaster-prone areas.

Factors worth considering in a mesh environment include:

- **Reliability:** Highly reliable and robust against the failure of any individual node or communication path.
- **Bandwidth speed:** High, given that each node can communicate directly with its intended target node.
- **Scalability:** Adding new nodes is expensive as cabling and infrastructure must be run to all other nodes on the network.
- **Collisions:** Minimal risk of collisions due to the direct connections available.
- **Cost:** High due to all the additional cabling and networking infrastructure required for all the redundant connections.

■ In a mesh topology, all nodes are interconnected to all other nodes

A2 Networks

Hybrid topology

The hybrid topology combines a mix of two or more other topologies. It makes maximum use of the advantages of each approach while minimizing the downsides. Hybrid approaches are suitable for large enterprises and telecommunications networks. In the illustration, a mesh approach is used for the interconnection of different base stations to provide reliability and durability between base stations, and then each base station manages a star topology for the individual devices connected to it.

Factors to consider for a hybrid approach include:

- **Reliability:** Generally quite high; if a node fails, it only affects the clients immediately connected to it, but not other parts of the network.
- **Transmission speed:** This is dependent on the exact configuration and mix of topologies deployed; bottlenecks can be an issue if it is not carefully designed.
- **Scalability:** Typically highly scalable and adaptable to changing needs and circumstances; a small addition to a network could start as a spoke on a star, and then later be upgraded to a full node in a mesh if needed.
- **Collisions:** Again, this is dependent on the configuration and mix of topologies.
- **Cost:** Likely to be higher to get started but generally more efficient over the long run.

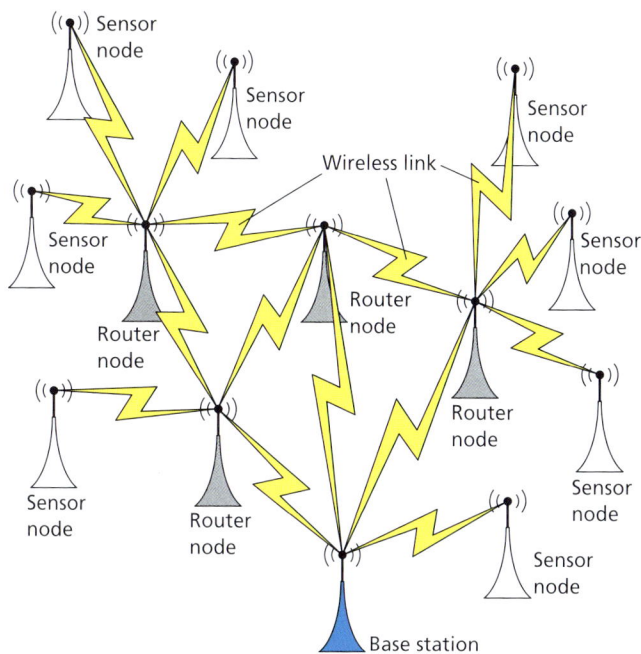

■ The hybrid topology is a mix of the mesh and star topologies; key points in the network are interlinked like a mesh, and then each of those points is the central point for its own star of connected nodes

A2.2.2 The function of servers (HL)

● Top tip!

It is very common for one physical computer acting as a server to have many server-based applications running on it simultaneously. The one computer could have a web server on port 80 and 443; an FTP server on 20 and 21; an SSH server running on port 22; and a DNS server on 53.

In this section, "server" relates more to the separate server software applications rather than separate physical devices.

◆ **Server:** a computer or device on a network that manages and provides various network resources on behalf of other computers (clients) on the network.

◆ **Domain name:** a human-readable name assigned to a specific IP address on the internet, e.g. www.example.com.

A **server** is a computer that provides a service to other computers or devices on a network. Typically, these are dedicated machines housed in a specialized room, centrally located on the network with backup power supplies and other systems.

This section looks at some of the common application servers frequently seen on networks. We will look at each from a perspective of their function, scalability, reliability and security.

■ Domain name server (DNS)

The **domain name** server provides a translation service that converts human-readable domain names into the IP addresses that are required for routing purposes. For example, at the time of writing, hachettelearning.com translates to 78.136.36.226.

The client device sends the DNS request to its configured DNS server. This can either be specified manually in the operating system settings, or it can be provided via DHCP when the device connects to the network. If the DNS server that receives the request does not know the answer to the query, it asks its DNS server, and so on up the chain until a server can provide a response. The DNS server then typically caches that response for a while in case it receives the same query.

On Windows computers, the `nslookup` terminal command allows you to execute DNS queries, and on macOS machines use the `host` command. In Python, there is a built-in `dns.resolver` module that you can use.

Python

```python
import dnspython as dns
import dns.resolver
domain = "www.example.com"
try:
    resolver = dns.resolver.Resolver()
    answer = resolver.resolve(domain, "A")
    for record in answer:
        print(record.to_text())
except dns.resolver.NXDOMAIN:
    print(f"The domain {domain} does not exist.")
except dns.resolver.Timeout:
    print(f"The DNS lookup for {domain} timed out.")
except dns.resolver.NoAnswer:
    print(f"No answer found for {domain}.")
except Exception as e:
    print(f"An error occurred: {e}")
```

- **Scalability:** DNS uses a distributed database and caching. This system allows for the global domain name system to manage with ease the billions of requests made per day.

- **Reliability:** DNS is a mission-critical system for the internet. Any downtime, particularly from the upstream servers, can affect many thousands or millions of client devices. With that in mind, the system is built with a lot of redundancy in place, where each server typically has at least three alternatives to query.

- **Security:** Given the global importance of DNS, it is frequently the subject of malicious behaviour. The key domain name servers around the world require extremely robust security systems including firewalls, intrusion detection systems and other countermeasures.

Dynamic Host Configuration Protocol (DHCP)

As previously discussed in Section A2.1.4, DHCP is responsible for assigning IP addresses and network settings to devices that request them on the network.

File server

A file server provides a centralized location to store, access and manage files. There are several commonly used approaches for this.

FTP (file transfer protocol) or SFTP (secure FTP) are protocols that are commonly used for accessing remote systems for the transfer of files. FTP usually involves opening dedicated FTP transfer utility software to perform the task.

For an office environment, it is usually preferential for the storage of a file server to be present within the file, folder and disk structure of the local computer operating system as a mounted drive letter (Windows) or folder (macOS). To do this, protocols such as Server Message Block (SMB), Network File System (NFS) or Apple Filing Protocol (AFP) are more commonly used.

- **Scalability:** File servers are typically scaled through adding drives to provide additional storage, and upgrading the speed of the network interface cards when they are shared between many client devices.

- **Reliability:** RAID (redundant array of independent disks) is a technology that allows for combining multiple physical disk drives into one logical unit. This can be used to pool the storage together to create one larger drive (for example two 1 TB drives pooled together to present as if they were a 2 TB drive), or to provide backup redundancy in the case of one drive failing. RAID also allows for a hybrid approach to mix both functions together.

- **Security:** Access permissions need to be carefully managed to protect against unauthorized access or alteration of data. These access permissions can typically be set at a file or folder level, and can have either read-only permission or read–write permission.

◼ Mail server

The mail server stores emails for local users on a network, and exchanges them with other mail servers when users send an email. Commonly used protocols include the SMTP (Simple Mail Transfer Protocol) and POP3 (Post Office Protocol).

- **Scalability:** Mail servers need to handle large volumes of emails and attachments efficiently. Many companies contract out their mail systems to third-party providers to help manage the demand.

- **Reliability:** As a critical system, email servers typically employ such mechanisms as queues and redundant systems to help maintain reliability.

- **Security:** Strong security systems for email are essential, given the frequency with which email is used as an attack vector for spam, phishing, pharming, malware attachments and other security threats. Best practice now involves the use of email authentication protocols such as SPF (Sender Policy Framework) and DomainKeys Identified Mail (DKIM). SPF allows domain name owners to specify which email servers are authorized to send emails on their behalf. DKIM allows domain name owners to sign their emails digitally with a cryptographic signature that can be checked by the recipient to ensure the email has not been tampered with en route.

◼ Proxy server

In the business and commercial world of contracts, a proxy is a person you authorize to act on your behalf.

In that vein, a proxy server is traditionally used to act as the client device on your behalf to browse the greater internet. Its caching functionality is useful as it means it can remember content for you from different addresses and return that request immediately without having to generate additional external traffic. Organizations such as schools and offices may use a proxy server for requests coming from their internal network to reduce costs. As the request being received by a server appears to have originated from

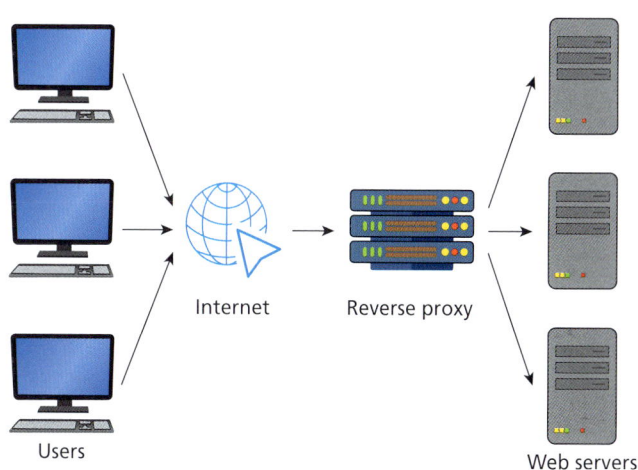

Users   Internet   Reverse proxy   Web servers

■ Reverse proxy server

the proxy and not the actual client, students may also use proxy servers installed on computers at home as a means of getting around school network filters.

Proxy servers can also be configured to act on behalf of the server rather than just client devices. This arrangement is known as a "reverse proxy". This arrangement is typically used to help distribute the load of incoming requests among a range of servers, and also to cache the common responses given to save calculation and processing load on the servers themselves.

- **Scalability:** Reverse proxy configurations can dramatically improve the scalability of a web server to handle significantly more traffic than would otherwise be the case.
- **Reliability:** When used to balance loads, a proxy server provides fault tolerance capacity.
- **Security:** A proxy server provides an additional layer of security by shielding internal client devices from direct exposure to the internet.

■ Web server

A web server hosts web pages and related content, and serves them to client devices across the internet. The web pages can either be static documents (such as HTML) or dynamically produced at runtime from programming code, in which case the web server sends the request to the application in the style of a reverse proxy, and then sends the reply back to the original client.

Nginx is a popular open source web server.

- **Scalability:** Modern web servers are quite efficient but, when demand for their services is high, the load is typically distributed across multiple servers, with a reverse proxy server acting as the public interface.
- **Reliability:** If the web server fails, then all websites it is hosting also fail. As web-based applications become critical infrastructure for some organizations, the importance of reliable web server software grows.
- **Security:** A web server needs to be secured against attacks such as distributed denial of service. Additionally, modern web servers provide encryption and authentication through SSL to run HTTPS, rather than just HTTP traffic, for a safer browsing experience. Let's Encrypt (**https://letsencrypt.org**) provides a free service for obtaining the SSL certificates needed to offer HTTPS browsing through a web server.

A2.2.3 Networking models

■ Client–server

The client–server model is where devices take on the role of either being the client that requests a network service, or the server that provides a network service.

Benefits:

- **Centralized control:** It is easier to manage and update systems from a central point.
- **Scalability:** It is easier to add a more powerful server (for example with increased processing, memory or storage) if it is a central system.
- **Efficiency:** A server can be optimized for a specific task.
- **Security:** It is much easier to manage security risks if everything is run from a central point.

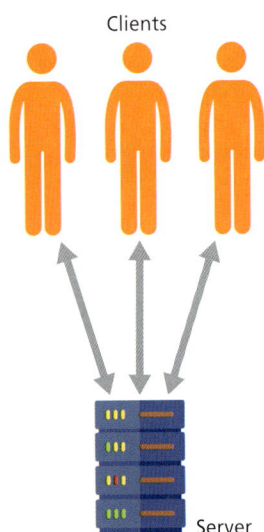

Clients

Server

Drawbacks:

- **Single point of failure:** If the server goes down, all services attached to it fail.
- **Single point of risk:** If the security of the server is compromised, all data and services managed by the central point are also exposed and vulnerable.
- **Cost:** Creating a central point to manage all the requests means a significant investment in expensive hardware and software to cope with that demand.

Real-world applications:

- **Web browsing:** Clients (browsers) request web pages from servers.
- **Email:** Email servers manage the sending and receiving of emails to and from client applications.
- **Online banking:** Central servers handle transactions, authentication and data storage, offering high security and reliability.

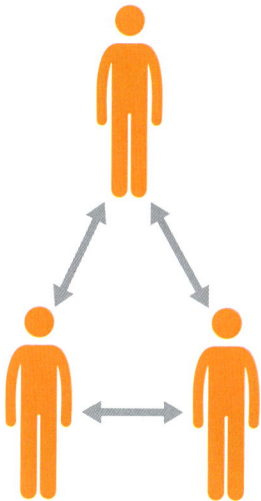

■ Peer-to-peer

In the peer-to-peer model, there is no server that co-ordinates the network services; each device is both a client and a server, and communicates with all other peers. The provision of network services is distributed across the devices.

The challenge with peer-to-peer is co-ordination, since there is no obvious "authoritative" source to query where to find certain services.

Benefits:

- **Decentralization:** There is no single point of failure or risk.
- **Cost effective:** There is no need to spend money on expensive hardware or software, as the load is shared among all the clients themselves.
- **Scalability:** As the size of the network grows, so too does the scale of services it can provide. Each additional peer also adds additional capacity.
- **Direct sharing:** Services can be provided directly from one computer to another, reducing bottlenecks.

Drawbacks:

- **Co-ordination:** Maintaining settings, security patches and synchronization of data across multiple nodes on the network can be very challenging.
- **Reliability:** Since services are being provided by peers, which are just client devices on the network, if someone turns their device off, then it is no longer providing whatever services it was supplying to the network. Availability of systems and resources on the network can vary without much notice.

⦿ Common mistake

Networking models

Don't oversimplify the distinction between client–server and peer-to-peer models. Understand the nuances involved that might make one more suitable than the other for specific scenarios. Failing to consider scalability and maintenance aspects can lead to incomplete understandings.

Real-world applications:

- **BitTorrent:** Files are shared directly between users without a co-ordinated central hub.
- **Voice over IP:** The data for calls and video conferencing are routed directly from client to client, rather than creating massive data bottlenecks for a centralized server.
- **Blockchain:** Bitcoin and other blockchains operate decentralized databases across many nodes to help guard against tampering with the transaction ledger.

A2.2.4 Concepts and applications of network segmentation

◆ **Network segmentation:** dividing a computer network into smaller, distinct subnetworks to improve performance, security and management.

Network segmentation refers to logically splitting a larger network into smaller, more manageable parts. Each of these segments can be isolated from each other to provide better security, performance or management of system resources.

Two commonly used approaches for network segmentation are subnetting and virtual local area networks (VLANs).

Subnetting divides a network into subnetworks based on unique ranges of IP addresses. For instance, a school may place staff devices on 192.168.0.X, and student devices on 192.168.1.X. Each subnet can share the same networking infrastructure, such as wireless access points, switches and cabling, but would not "see" the devices on the alternate subnet. This approach allows devices to be logically grouped based on department, function or geography, and can allow for different security policies to be applied, depending on the organization's needs.

Virtual LANs are another way of separating one physical network into two logical networks without requiring duplication of infrastructure. They create distinct broadcast domains that are mutually isolated unless explicitly allowed to communicate via routing. Traffic is isolated to members of the VLAN only. Where a client device may change its subnet by manually changing its IP address, VLANs are more secure and typically use MAC addresses or login credentials to determine which VLAN a device gets connected to. Because a virtual LAN is a logical construct rather than a physical one, it is worth noting that a VLAN could extend over numerous physical networks (such as over a VPN link).

Whichever method is used, segmentation reduces overall network traffic within each segment, allowing for more efficient data transmission. Network congestion for high bandwidth applications can be contained to an individual network segment, resulting in the other segments within the network being unaffected. Security is also significantly enhanced, as visibility of servers and their services can be restricted to particular VLANs.

⦿ Common mistake

Network segmentation

Mixing up segmentation, subnetting and VLANs is common. Make sure you define and distinguish each clearly.

REVIEW QUESTIONS

1 Which network topology is most beneficial in a large campus setting due to its scalability and robustness?

   a Star

   b Mesh

   c Hybrid

   d Ring

2 Which type of server is responsible for translating domain names into IP addresses?

   a DHCP server

   b DNS server

   c File server

   d Web server

3 Which networking model typically involves one or more central servers that manage data and resources for client devices?

   a Client–server

   b Peer-to-peer

   c Hybrid

   d None of the above

4 What is the primary purpose of implementing network segmentation within a corporate environment?

   a To increase the number of devices on the network

   b To enhance security and performance by reducing congestion

   c To eliminate the need for routers

   d To simplify network management

5 Outline three benefits of using a star topology in a home office setting.

6 Describe one function of a proxy server for each of:

   a a large university campus

   b a personal home.

7 Outline how a reverse proxy functions, in contrast to a normal proxy. What are its benefits?

8 Explain a key disadvantage of using a peer-to-peer network model for online banking.

9 Explain how VLANs contribute to network segmentation.

Data transmissions

By the end of this chapter, you should be able to:
- ▶ A2.3.1 Describe different types of IP addressing
- ▶ A2.3.2 Compare types of media for data transmission
- ▶ A2.3.3 Explain how packet switching is used to send data across a network
- ▶ A2.3.4 Explain how static routing and dynamic routing move data across local area networks (HL)

A2.3.1 Types of IP addressing

■ TCP/IP version 4 and version 6

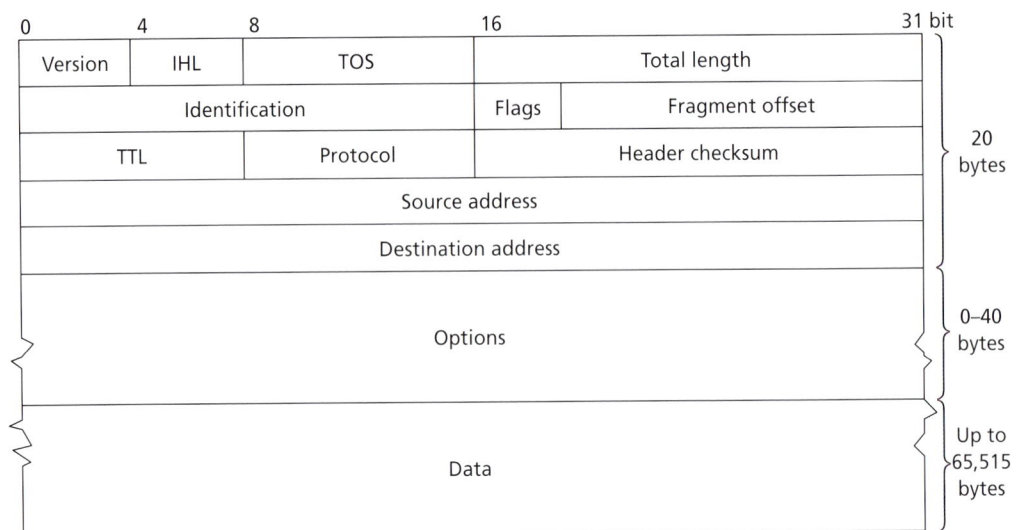

■ Structure of IP version 4

> **Common mistake**
>
> **IP addressing**
>
> Don't mix up the address constructions of IPv4 and IPv6. Be sure to know the length and formatting of each version of IP addresses.

> ◆ **IP address:** a set of numbers that uniquely identifies each computer based on the Internet Protocol (either version 4 or version 6).

> **● Linking question**
>
> Are similar ethical principles needed when transmitting data over a network as when using data in machine learning algorithms? (TOK)

The key difference between **IP** version 4 and version 6 is the size of the **address** space. IPv6 was designed to deal with the long-anticipated problem of IPv4 addresses running out.

IPv4 uses a four-byte or 32-bit address, which is why it is typically displayed as four numbers separated by dots, where each number is in the range of a byte, 0–255, for example `192.168.0.1`. Given there are 2^{32} possible addresses using these numbers, it means IPv4 is limited to approximately 4,300,000,000 nodes on the network.

IPv6, on the other hand, uses 16 bytes or 128 bits for its addresses. These addresses are typically displayed as eight groups of four bytes written in hexadecimal form, such as `2001:0db8:85a3:0000:0000:8a2e:0370:7334`. Having 2^{128} addresses equates to a capacity for a staggering 340,282,370,000,000,000,000,000,000,000,000,000,000 nodes.

◼ Public and private addresses

The key difference between public and private addresses is their visibility on the public internet.

IP addresses that are used on the public internet must be globally unique. They are typically assigned to websites, external-facing servers and routers that connect to the internet. The allocation of these public internet addresses is managed by ICANN (the Internet Corporation for Assigned Names and Numbers).

Private IP addresses used within a private network are not directly routable on the global internet. They are commonly used in home and corporate networks for devices such as computers, tablets and internal servers. Traffic from these devices must be converted to a public address by the router to get on to the public internet.

ICANN has reserved certain ranges of addresses as private, non-routable addresses for organizations to use for their internal networks. These are:

- 10.0.0.0 to 10.255.255.255
- 172.16.0.0 to 172.31.255.255
- 192.168.0.0 to 192.168.255.255
- IPv6 has FC00:0000:0000:0000:0000:0000:0000:0000 to FDFF:FFFF:FFFF:FFFF:FFFF:FFFF:FFFF:FFFF.

◼ Static and dynamic addresses

Static IP addresses are those that are permanently assigned to a device. The device uses the same IP address every time it connects to the network. Static IP addresses are essential for servers so that client devices know where to locate them on a network.

In contrast, a dynamic IP address is one that is assigned to a device when it connects to the network. This process is overseen by a DHCP server that allocates connecting devices an address from a predetermined pool of addresses that it has available to it. Dynamic addresses help reduce overheads by more efficiently utilizing a limited number of IP addresses in environments where devices frequently connect and disconnect.

◼ Network address translation (NAT)

◆ **Network address translation:** modifies the IP addresses of data packets as they pass through a router or firewall; this helps improve security and manages the limited number of IP addresses available through IPv4 by allowing multiple devices to share a single global IP address.

⬤ Top tip!

Network address translation

Make sure you have an appreciation of, and recognize the role of, **network address translation** (NAT). Its capacity to allow multiple devices on a private network to share a single IP address for internet communications has kept the internet as a viable, functioning system. Its role in conserving global IP address space cannot be overstated.

Network address translation is a process whereby networks translate private IP addresses to public IP addresses, and vice versa. The process enables multiple devices on a network to share a single public IP address.

NAT has been crucial for the effective operation of the internet as it still remains highly dependent on IPv4 addresses, which have been all but exhausted. It also helps provide an additional layer of security for home and small office networks by hiding internal IP addresses from the external network.

A2.3.2 Types of media for data transmission

● Top tip!

Side by side

Create a side-by-side comparison table for fibre-optic, twisted-pair and wireless media, with a focus on bandwidth, cost and installation complexity. Consider the roles for each type, such as fibre optic in data centres, twisted pair in offices and wireless for campuses, homes and mobile set-ups. Pay special attention to how security varies across the different media, particularly the susceptibility to eavesdropping or interference.

■ Fibre-optic cabling

Advantages:

- **Bandwidth**: Fibre optic has the highest data-transmission rates of the media under consideration in this section. Active research continues to make it even better, but current technology already allows for terabits per second to be transmitted.

- **Interference susceptibility**: As fibre-optic cabling uses light waves to transmit data, it is not susceptible to electromagnetic interference, making it ideal for environments with electrical noise, such as that generated by motors.

- **Range and attenuation**: Fibre-optic cabling is the medium of choice for the intercontinental submarine cables that run across the ocean floor, due to its very low signal loss over long distances. Commercially available single-mode fibre-optic cables can easily run distances of tens or hundreds of kilometres before a repeater is required.

- **Security**: Fibre-optic cables are very difficult to "tap" without detection, making them an excellent option where security is a concern.

Disadvantages:

- **Cost**: Fibre-optic cables are generally more expensive than other forms of cabling, both with respect to the cabling materials and supporting hardware infrastructure and the installation labour time.

- **Reliability**: Fibre-optic cables are more fragile than metallic cables and are prone to damage if improperly handled. Specifically, they have a limited radius for the maximum bend they can safely operate under.

- **Installation complexity**: The issues regarding supporting infrastructure requirements and proper handling of the cables themselves tend to result in fibre-optic cables requiring more specialized skills and equipment for installation and maintenance operations.

■ Twisted-pair cabling

Advantages:

- **Cost:** Twisted-pair cabling has been a well-known and established technology for decades now. It is widely and cheaply available.

- **Installation complexity:** Installation is considerably less complex than for fibre optic. A do-it-yourself approach is frequently taken for installation of simple home and small office networks, with telephony technicians typically only required for outdoor and other complex environments.

- **Reliability:** The cables are vastly more flexible, meaning they can be safely and reliably installed into tight spaces.

Disadvantages:

- **Bandwidth:** Twisted-pair cabling is typically an order of magnitude slower than the equivalent in fibre optic. That said, it is still quite adequate for most home and small office arrangements, offering Gigabit bandwidth performance. Twisted-pair cabling also significantly outperforms wireless networks. The highest quality twisted-pair cable currently available – Category 7 Ethernet – is rated for speeds of up to 10 Gb/s.

- **Interference susceptibility:** Given it is a cable that uses electrical signals to transmit data, twisted-pair cabling is quite susceptible to electromagnetic interference from the surrounding environment. This is particularly the case where shielding has not been wrapped around the cables.

- **Range and attenuation:** The range of twisted pair is considerably less than fibre optic. Category 6a twisted-pair Ethernet cables typically only have a range of approximately 100 metres.

- **Security:** As it is easier to tap into than fibre-optic cables, twisted pair poses a more significant security risk; however, an attacker must still get in close physical proximity to the cable, unlike with wireless.

■ Wireless transmission

Advantages:

- **Installation complexity:** There are no physical cables, so installation complexity and cost are significantly lower than for physical cable media.

- **Cost:** Wireless networks can be a cost-effective means of covering a large area where cabling is not practical.

- **Reliability:** Wireless networks provide mobility for devices to connect from, whatever the location, provided it is within the signal range. That said, reliability can be impacted through radio interference, discussed below.

Disadvantages:

- **Bandwidth:** In practical scenarios, the total available bandwidth is shared among connected devices, so the individual device throughput varies based on network conditions and the number of devices connected. Typically, a total bandwidth capacity of several Gb/s is available for the devices to share. This is lower than the equivalent twisted pair or fibre optic, and these also come with their own dedicated bandwidth, rather than a shared connection.

- **Interference susceptibility:** Wireless is very susceptible to interference from other wireless or radio signals, and physical obstructions can significantly affect signal quality.

- **Range and attenuation:** Range is typically limited to a maximum of about 90 metres in clear, line-of-sight conditions. Strength and quality of the signal deteriorate with distance and physical obstructions, such as walls.

- **Security:** Wireless technologies have a long and complicated history of being security risks since an attacker does not have to be physically present at a network connection to intercept the signal. Often, attackers can sit in a car outside the home or office and collect all your WiFi signals over the air. A lot of effort has been made to add layers of encryption to modern WiFi to mitigate this problem, but risks still exist.

A2.3.3 Packet switching

◆ **Packet switching:** a method of sending data in small blocks, known as "packets", across a network. Each packet can take a different path to reach its destination.

Common mistake

Confusing routers and switches

Ensure you don't misunderstand the functional differences between routers and switches in network data transmission.

Packet switching is the foundation of most modern networking technologies, including the internet. It involves breaking large pieces of data into smaller, more manageable chunks called "packets". These packets are transmitted across the network independently of each other and reassembled into the original whole at the destination. Packet switching is a highly scalable tool that allows efficient use of network resources, in contrast to older technologies such as circuit switching, where an entire dedicated channel or cable was used for the duration of a communication session (which deprived other devices of being able to use it).

The full process includes:

- **Segmentation:** Data (such as a file or email) that needs to be sent across the network is broken into smaller pieces known as "packets". These packets contain a chunk of the data, plus information known as the "header" that contains source and destination network addresses and other control information. The MTU (maximum transmission unit) size of a packet is typically 1500 bytes, including header information.

- **Packet header:** The header of each packet contains information that helps ensure the efficient and reliable transmission of the packet across the network, such as the source and destination IP addresses. Additionally, each packet contains a sequence number that is used to reorder the packets at the destination into their correct sequence, so that the content of the data file is not jumbled. The header also contains error-checking information such as checksums, which calculate whether the packet has arrived correctly, or whether the source has to be asked to retransmit it.

- **Routing:** Each packet is sent through the computer network independently of any of the other packets associated with it. This means that packets for the same file may travel different paths across the network, based on conditions such as congestion and route availability. This flexibility in routing helps networks optimize usage and provide for a robust environment that is more tolerant of failures within the network.

- **Routers:** These devices determine the optimal path for each packet passing through to reach its destination. They inspect the packet destination address and use routing tables and algorithms to decide the next hop in the network to forward each packet to.

- **Switches:** These devices are typically operated within local area networks and direct packets between devices on the same network. They use the MAC addresses to process and forward packets.

- **Reassembly:** Once the packet has reached its destination, it is checked for sequencing information and then reassembled into the original file in the correct order. Importantly, because no two packets are guaranteed to be transmitted along the same path, it is impossible to assume that packets have arrived in the correct order. Additionally, some packets may have been lost or corrupted in transmission, so the source needs to be requested to retransmit those packets.

A2.3.4 Static routing and dynamic routing in local area networks (HL)

Network **routing** refers to the algorithms that determine the path for traffic in a network, or between and across multiple networks. Within local area networks, routing decisions can be handled by one of two methods: static or dynamic routing.

■ Static routing

◆ **Routing:** the process of selecting paths along a computer network to send network traffic, based on the routing table, network performance and protocols.

Static routing is where the network routes are manually configured and entered into a routing table by the network administrator. These routes do not change except by manual update.

This method is easy to implement in small networks where the routes do not change much, but can be too complex to manage in networks with hundreds or thousands of nodes. Static routing provides predictability in the behaviour of your network, and does not require additional processing or bandwidth due to one router communicating with another for route discovery and optimization.

In addition to the challenge of scale, other issues around static routing include the lack of fault tolerance as, if a connection fails, static routing does not automatically attempt to find a workaround; and the maintenance workload associated with it, as every small change in the network requires manual updating of the routing table.

■ Dynamic routing

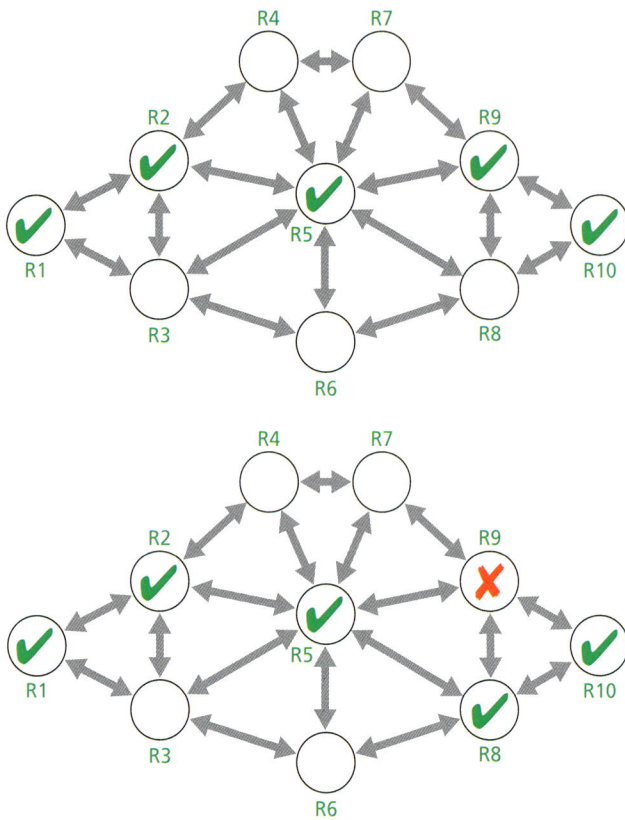

■ Dynamic routing coping with node failure

As can likely be inferred, dynamic routing contrasts with static routing by using an algorithmic approach to automatically adjust routes in the routing table. To do this, routers communicate with each other to share information about their connections, topology and demand on their network resources. This information is used to adjust the routes in runtime, with the goal of ensuring optimal paths for network efficiency.

Dynamic routing scales well for larger networks, as they can automatically adapt as changes occur. This also improves fault tolerance, as network traffic can be automatically re-routed around a failed connection.

Dynamic routing does pose some challenges. Its dynamic nature requires additional computational and bandwidth resources to manage. The combination of the larger networks and the dynamic routing do make for a more complex routing table that needs to be configured and maintained. This necessitates a deeper understanding of network concepts by the staff maintaining such a network. Finally, given each router is maintaining its own copy of a routing table, there can be delays in the convergence of the routing table while the individual routers communicate and negotiate with each other. This can lead to occasional routing inconsistencies in the short term.

REVIEW QUESTIONS

1   Which type of IP addressing is specifically designed to provide a larger address space than its predecessor?

   a   IPv4

   b   IPv6

   c   Static IP

   d   Dynamic IP

2   Which type of data-transmission media is most susceptible to electromagnetic interference?

   a   Fibre optic

   b   Twisted pair

   c   Wireless

3   What role do routers play in the process of packet switching?

   a   They prevent packet collision

   b   They direct packets along the most efficient paths to their destination

   c   They combine packets into a single data stream

   d   They generate the data packets from the user data

4 Which type of routing is better suited for networks that require frequent updates due to topology changes?

    a Static routing

    b Dynamic routing

    c Both are equally suited

    d Neither is suitable

5 Describe the main purpose of network address translation (NAT).

6 Describe one advantage and one disadvantage of using fibre-optic cables for data transmission.

7 Explain why packet switching is considered efficient for data transmission over a network.

8 Explain one main advantage of static routing compared to dynamic routing.

SYLLABUS CONTENT

By the end of this chapter, you should be able to:
▶ A2.4.1 Discuss the effectiveness of firewalls for protecting a network
▶ A2.4.2 Describe common network vulnerabilities (HL)
▶ A2.4.3 Describe common network countermeasures (HL)
▶ A2.4.4 Describe the process of encryption and digital certificates

A2.4.1 Firewalls

Firewalls obviously play a key role in helping protect computer networks, but what exactly do they do?

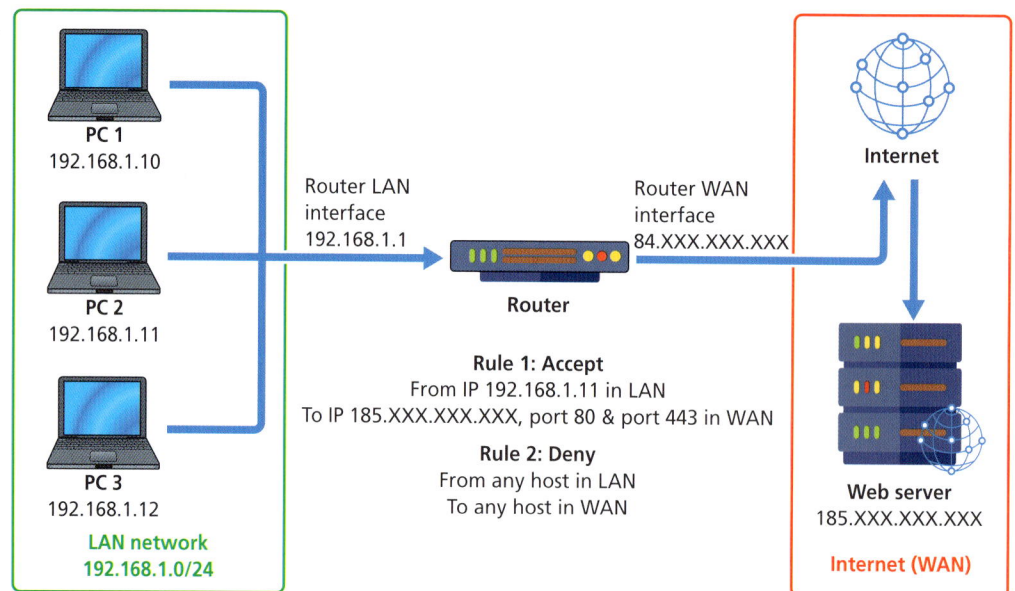

■ Firewall in action

A firewall inspects the IP packets that pass through it, and filters the incoming and outgoing traffic, based on a set of predefined security rules. In the illustration above, Rule 1 is allowing traffic from PC2 on the internal LAN to access any external IP address that begins with 185.?.?.? for destination ports 80 or 443. Rule 2 then denies all other internal requests. Each individual packet is checked against the rules until a rule is encountered that allows or denies passage through the firewall.

Some firewalls are also capable of applying stateful inspection, where the state of active connections is monitored and can be used to determine passage through the firewall, for instance once a connection has been allowed to be established, packets are allowed to continue back and forth through the connection until it closes.

The rules comprise a set of allow lists and deny lists. These lists are IP addresses or ranges of IP addresses, and optionally can also specify application port numbers.

Using the rule lists, firewalls control access to the internal network from external sources, and can also be used to control which external destinations are accessible from internal sources. Additionally, firewalls log traffic requests, which can be useful for detecting and responding to suspicious activity or for identifying a potential breach.

Firewalls are just one tool for securing a network, and are not perfect for protecting against all types of attacks. For instance, firewalls are less effective against threats from within the network such as a malicious insider, or if an external threat has gained local presence on the network via compromised WiFi. Some threats can be quite sophisticated and can mimic legitimate traffic. Finally, a firewall is only as good as its configuration. If a network manager doesn't keep the deny lists updated and the firewall firmware up to date, then vulnerabilities can be exposed.

● Common mistake

Over-reliance on firewalls

Don't assume that a firewall alone is sufficient to protect a computer network. Firewalls are gatekeepers for ranges of addresses and ports. Most firewalls do not inspect the content of the data beyond the source and destination address and port, meaning malicious data can easily still be let through if destined for a legitimate location.

■ Network address translation

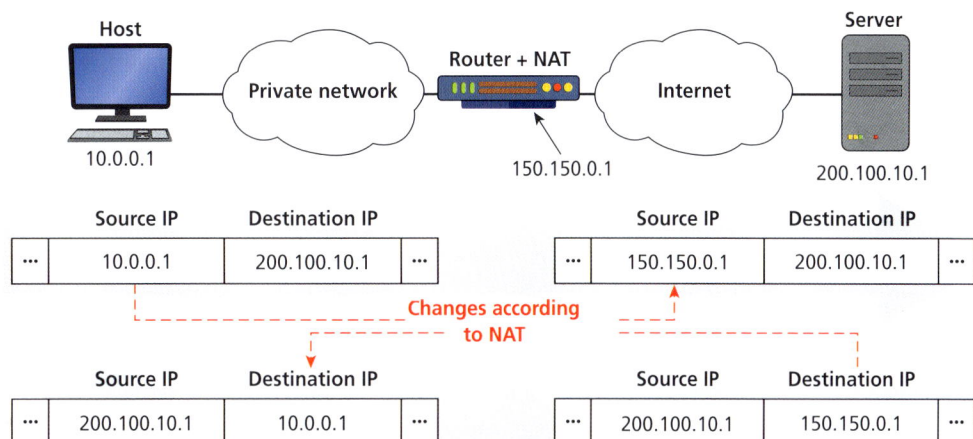

	Source IP	Destination IP	
...	10.0.0.1	200.100.10.1	...

	Source IP	Destination IP	
...	150.150.0.1	200.100.10.1	...

Changes according to NAT

	Source IP	Destination IP	
...	200.100.10.1	10.0.0.1	...

	Source IP	Destination IP	
...	200.100.10.1	150.150.0.1	...

■ Network address translation in action

You were previously introduced to the concept of network address translation in Section A2.3.1.

Beyond the convenience that network address translation has provided through allowing the internet to continue to function despite having exhausted IPv4 addresses years ago, it has also had an additional benefit with respect to network security.

Since NAT modifies the IP address information in packet headers, the process helps to hide internal IP addresses on a network, which makes it more difficult for an external attacker to reach internal systems. Although it is not technically a security feature by design, it does provide an additional layer of difficulty that attackers must overcome, as the internal structure of your network and IP addresses are not directly exposed. In this sense, it could be described as a case of security by obscurity.

A2.4.2 Common network vulnerabilities (HL)

In this section, we briefly consider a range of common attack vectors and vulnerabilities within computer networks. In the subsequent section, we review strategies to mitigate these risks.

● **Linking question**

What are the similarities and differences between network security and database security? (A3)

■ Distributed denial of service (DDoS)

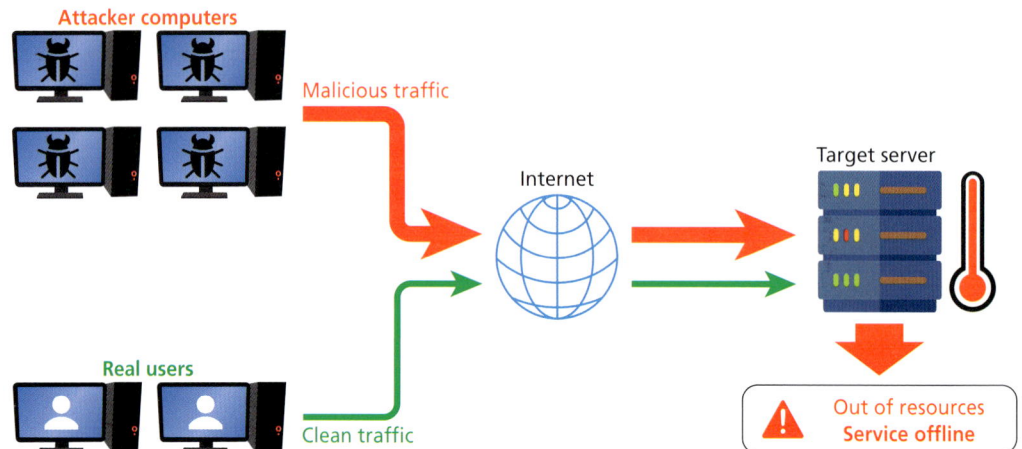

A distributed denial of service (DDoS) attack is one in which multiple systems under the control of the malicious actor generate a massive number of network requests, with the goal of overwhelming the target system. This can cause the target to slow down, so that it becomes unusable or unavailable for legitimate users.

It is important to point out that the computers being used for the attack are typically not even devices directly owned or operated by the attacker. It is more likely that they are devices that have fallen victim to having unwittingly installed malware on their system that the attacker can then use to contribute towards the overall DDoS attack.

■ Insecure network protocols

There are many older or poorly designed network protocols still in widespread use that do not include modern security features. These older protocols allow attackers to intercept, or even alter and manipulate, the content of data in transit on the internet.

Examples of these older protocols are HTTP, FTP and Telnet, all of which transmit their data in the clear without any form of encryption. The modern alternatives are HTTPS, SFTP and SSH.

■ Malware

"Malware", or "malicious software", is the overarching term for a classic range of attacks that have had various names applied to them over the years. If you've come across terms such as "computer viruses", "worms", "trojan horses" and "ransomware", these are all various forms of malware. They are software that is designed to harm or exploit vulnerable devices and to seek out and spread to other vulnerable devices. They can lead to data loss, data theft and loss of full control of the device. Malware can sometimes sit idle for extended periods of time until triggered to activate (such as in the case of a DDoS client).

■ Man-in-the-middle (MitM)

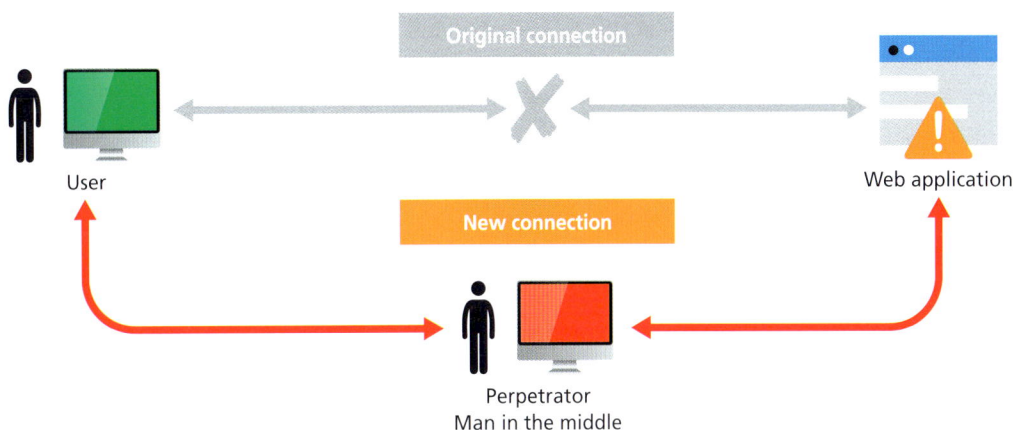

A man-in-the-middle attack (now also sometimes referred to as an on-path attack) is where an attacker eavesdrops on communications between two systems.

This can result in data breaches, or data alteration, without the knowledge of the original parties involved.

■ Phishing

Phishing is when a victim receives, and responds to, a seemingly legitimate message (such as an email) that has the aim of deceiving the victim into providing sensitive information, such as login credentials or bank account details. This can result in unauthorized access to other systems, identity theft and financial crimes.

■ SQL injection

An SQL injection is where an attacker exploits vulnerabilities in the way an application or website has been designed to work with its database. It relies upon the programmers not applying sufficient validation checks to the user inputs, so that the application can make unintended changes to the underlying database. This can result in unauthorized viewing of user lists (and their passwords), deletion of data or granting administrative control of the database to the attacker.

To understand how the SQL injection attack works, consider the impact the following Python would have to the SQL statement if executed on a database:

```
first_name = "Robert'); DROP TABLE Students; --"
family_name = "Doe"
sql = "INSERT INTO Students VALUES ('" + first_name + "', '"
+ family_name + "')";
```

The SQL string now actually contains three different SQL commands:

1 INSERT INTO Students VALUES ('Robert');
2 DROP TABLE Students;
3 -', 'Doe');

Never trust inputs from users or feed them straight into your database without verifying and validating them first!

Cross site scripting (XSS)

Cross site scripting attacks operate on similar principles to the SQL injection attack. Instead of using insufficient validation to send rogue database instructions, a cross site scripting attacker injects their own code to run client-side on pages viewed by other users. This can bypass access controls, deface websites or redirect users to malicious sites.

Any website that loads and executes JavaScript that is being hosted by a third party (a very common practice for many JavaScript libraries) makes itself potentially vulnerable to this scenario, as the website is effectively inviting the third party to run their own code on the website.

Unpatched software

Unpatched software refers to software that has not had all published security updates applied to it. Once security updates are released by software vendors, it is particularly important to apply them as soon as possible as not only do they help address and correct a vulnerability, they also advertise the existence of the vulnerability, making devices lacking the update even more vulnerable to attack.

Weak authentication

Systems that have poorly designed authentication systems make themselves vulnerable to attack by design. Examples of this might be websites that do not properly hash and salt their passwords, or that store their security keys in insecure folders. Multifactor authentication systems, and the use of tools such as OAuth, are industry standard for a reason.

Developers should be discouraged from rolling out their own authentication system for anything other than as a learning tool. Use and rely on the excellent high-quality authentication systems that have been built upon the tears of those who have gone before you.

Zero-day exploits

A zero-day exploit is when an attacker takes advantage of a previously unknown weakness in software or hardware, before its maintainers have had the opportunity to create a patch to fix the vulnerability. These types of exploits are especially dangerous because, by their very nature, there is no known defence against them.

Perhaps the best-known historical example of a zero-day exploit was Stuxnet. It was malware that was used to break into Iran's uranium-enrichment centrifuges in 2006, and is suspected to have been created by the USA's National Security Agency (NSA).

A2.4.3 Common network countermeasures (HL)

⬤ Common mistake

Network security is more than having anti-malware software and using encryption

Many times, when students are asked how to protect a computer or data on a network, they simply revert to saying "install anti-malware software" or "use encryption". These are lazy answers that do not capture the nuance of the approaches outlined in this section. Network security requires a complex, multi-layered approach to protect against attacks. Be sure to understand the different strategies outlined and be prepared to discuss them in assessments.

⬤ Top tip!

Match the threat to the countermeasure

One method of ensuring you master a more detailed understanding of the complexities of securing a computer network is to review the various threats discussed in the previous section, and match each to the appropriate countermeasure discussed in this section. For instance, multifactor authentication can help counter weak authentication issues.

◼ Content security policies

The content security policy header is settings that can be placed into the HTTP header to define which sources are permitted to load content on to a particular website. Properly set, they can help guard against XSS attacks and similar injection exploits.

For more information, search online for Mozilla's content-security-policy documentation (**https://developer.mozilla.org/en-US/docs/Web/HTTP/Headers/Content-Security-Policy**).

◼ Complex password policies

Password policies are continually a vexed and contentious issue.

Some in the industry continue to argue for password rules that enforce the creation of strong, hard-to-brute-force passwords that require minimum lengths and a mix of letters, numbers and special characters.

Others in the industry argue that best practice should be to help users cope with what is described as "password overload". Security experts such as Troy Hunt argue best practice should entail:

- only using passwords where they are really needed
- using technical solutions to reduce the burden on users
- allowing users to securely record and store their passwords
- only asking users to change their passwords on suspicion of compromise
- allowing users to reset passwords easily, quickly and cheaply.

For more on modern understanding of password policies, search online for Troy Hunt's excellent article "Passwords Evolved: Authentication Guidance for the Modern Era" (**www.troyhunt.com/passwords-evolved-authentication-guidance-for-the-modern-era**).

Major companies such as Microsoft and Google are now promoting the use of passwordless authentication as much as possible. As Google states: "Developers and users both hate passwords: they give a poor user experience, they add conversion friction, and they create security liability for both users and developers."

Passkeys are being promoted as a safer and easier alternative. This can take one of a variety of forms, including:

- biometric sensor login (fingerprint or face recognition)
- PIN
- pattern.

Read more about passkeys by searching online for Google Developer's "Passwordless login with passkeys" (**https://developers.google.com/identity/passkeys**).

If you do use a website that still requires a password, be concerned if it imposes a maximum length on the password you set. If a password is properly hashed, it won't matter how long it is, so if you are told by a system that the password has a maximum length, chances are it means they are storing it in unhashed clear text! Run, run far away, and definitely do not reuse a "real" password on that service! (The author has been known to use variations of "thisPasswordIsNotSecure" on such websites 😉)

Distributed denial of service (DDoS) mitigation tools

To help guard a server against a DDoS attack, most firewalls and web servers have settings available that help absorb or deflect traffic overloads. They do this by rate limiting (allowing a maximum number of requests in a given time-period from any individual source), traffic analysis and also subscribing to cloud-based DDoS protection services, such as those provided by the major cloud-hosting companies.

Email filtering solutions

One of the most common attack vectors used for the spread of malicious software remains email. To this end, having modern and up-to-date email-filtering systems to scan incoming emails for malicious attachments, phishing attempts and general marketing spam can go a long way to protect end-users from email-based threats.

Encrypted protocols

To protect against man-in-the-middle and other similar attacks is trivially easy now. Simply do not use unencrypted protocols such as HTTP, FTP or Telnet. Only use systems that accommodate the secure, encrypted modern versions of HTTPS, SFTP or SSH.

Input validation

A maxim in Computer Science is never to trust user inputs: always validate them!

Use a range of input-validation tools, such as presence check, length check, type check and format check to validate that the structure of the incoming data is in the style and format expected. For instance, your software shouldn't be accepting kilobytes of data when the entry box is for a person's name or date of birth!

A few simple checks on the input data being received from the user, prior to accepting and processing it, goes a long way to protecting systems from harmful data.

An example of where lack of input validation caused global security concerns was the Heartbleed vulnerability that was hidden within the important OpenSSL cryptography library, which is a widely used implementation of the transport layer security protocol.

For a simplified look at how the attack worked, search online for "1354: Heartbleed Explanation" (**www.explainxkcd.com/wiki/index.php/1354:_Heartbleed_Explanation**).

■ Intrusion detection systems (IDS) and intrusion prevention systems (IPS)

Intrusion detection and prevention systems are specialized software tools that actively monitor network traffic and the broader state of your system. Their goal is not just to detect potential threats, but proactively to block them before they succeed in compromising your systems.

The intrusion *detection* system focuses on monitoring network and system traffic to spot suspicious activities and potential threats. It sends alerts to network administrators when it identifies such activity. The IDS is a passive system, meaning that it does not interfere with the flow of traffic on the system.

The intrusion *prevention* system is an active system. When it detects a threat, it takes proactive measures to prevent the threat from gaining access to, or harming, the network. It can block traffic, drop malicious packets, close connections and more.

In modern cybersecurity solutions, the IDS and IPS roles are often bundled together into a comprehensive security product, allowing for both detection of threats and active measures to prevent those threats from causing harm. These modern tools have taken on the name of "endpoint protection" to describe their role. Endpoint-protection software typically also bundles other security functions, such as antivirus, anti-malware, firewalls and others, with the goal of integration being to provide a robust protection regime.

Most operating systems come with their own basic endpoint-protection utilities installed (in Windows it is known as Defender), but there are many commercial operators in this space. CrowdStrike is one such operator, which became famous for all the wrong reasons when, on 19 July 2024, it sent out a faulty update for its Falcon Sensor product that resulted in over 8 million Windows computers getting stuck at the infamous Blue Screen of Death (BSOD), affecting critical systems for airlines, banks, hospitals, supermarkets and many other organizations around the globe.

■ Multifactor authentication (MFA)

One-time passcode

Multifactor authentication systems are an easy-to-implement measure that require more than one method of authentication by users to verify their identity.

The commonly stated goal of introducing multiple factors is to require two of the three means by which a user can prove their identity:

- Something they know (e.g. a password).
- Something they have (e.g. their phone – by way of receiving or generating a code).
- Something they are (e.g. a biometric, such as fingerprint or facial recognition).

As a consumer, you should enable two-factor authentication on as many services as possible and use an app such as Authy.

> ## ● Top tip!
>
> **Adding one-time codes to your projects**
>
> As a beginner software developer, there are libraries available that make it very easy to incorporate one-time codes that are compatible with all the major authentication apps. For Python, search online for the PyOPT library (**https://github.com/pyauth/pyotp**).

■ Secure socket layer (SSL) certificate and transport layer security (TLS) certificate

SSL and TLS certificates allow consumers to authenticate the developer or organization that authored a software product. Developers and companies can use these certificates to digitally sign the project as their work, thereby giving trust and confidence to the consumer. These digital certificates are discussed in more detail in Section A2.4.4.

■ Update software

Keeping your software up to date by regularly applying all the latest security patches is an important step for mitigating the risk of falling victim to a security vulnerability.

■ Virtual private networks (VPN)

As previously discussed, VPNs provide a secure means to exchange data with a remote office as if your device was connected directly to the private network. Companies regularly require their employees to make use of VPN technologies whenever they are working remotely away from the office.

■ Testing and training

Regular testing of your security measures, including "white hat" penetration testing and vulnerability assessments, forms a critical part of ensuring systems remain secure. Testing helps ensure your systems still work as you expect, and that no new weaknesses have emerged.

As part of the testing, there should also be regular training for staff within an organization. Many security breaches occur through human error, so training employees in security best practices on an ongoing basis is also a crucial part of any security regime.

■ Wireless security measures

Wireless networks pose a unique vulnerability to any computer network and require special security measures to identify and mitigate risks. One commonly used measure is to restrict access to the network to each device's unique media access control (MAC) address. The MAC address is a unique 48-bit address assigned to each network card by the manufacturer, so these can be used to populate an allow-list of devices permitted to connect to the network.

■ Secured backups

When was the last time you backed up your files?! For data that matters to you, take responsibility for its care and protection. Don't just rely on cloud services either, as they are known to fail occasionally. Purchase a spare portable drive to keep in the back of your sock drawer, and copy your data to it at least once a month.

Top tip!

Data synchronization tool

For students confident with using console commands, rsync is the best tool for copying files for backups. Search online for "manpagez: man pages & more man rsync(1)" for the documentation (**www.manpagez.com/man/1/rsync**).

If you are less confident with the console, search online for "Free File Sync", a free, open-source file synchronization tool (**https://freefilesync.org**).

Finally, if your backups resemble a collection of portable drives, you should consider the security of your backups! An attacker doesn't need to penetrate your network if they can just pinch a USB drive!

Top tip!

File-encryption tool

Consider encrypting your backups with a tool such as gnupg (**https://gnupg.org/download**): just don't forget the password!

- To encrypt:
  ```
  gpg --output encrypted_backup.enc --symmetric --cipher-algo AES256 mybackup.zip
  ```
- To decrypt:
  ```
  gpg --output mybackup.zip --decrypt encrypted_backup.enc
  ```

Linking question

Do networks and databases use the same form of **encryption** algorithms? (A3)

◆ **Encryption:** the conversion of information or data into a mathematically secure format that cannot be easily understood by unauthorized people.

A2.4.4 The process of encryption and digital certificates

Common mistake

Thinking digital signatures and digital certificates are the same thing

Ensure you understand the nuance of the distinction between a digital signature and a digital certificate. They are not the same thing.

■ Symmetric encryption

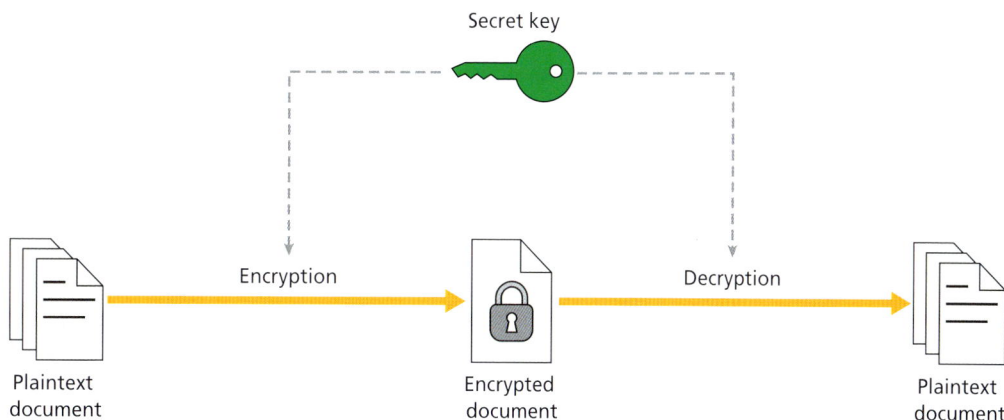

Symmetric encryption is where the same **key** is used for both encrypting and decrypting the data. This means the key must be shared between both the sender and receiver in a secure manner.

Symmetric encryption is generally faster and less computationally intensive than its asymmetric equivalent, so it makes sense to use it for encrypting large files.

When physical distance separates the sender and receiver, it can be difficult to share the encryption key in such a manner as to be protected against eavesdroppers. There are two common solutions to this problem:

- Use asymmetric encryption to establish secure communications. Use this asymmetric method to exchange and agree on a symmetric key, and then switch communications to the faster, more efficient symmetric approach.

- Use a mathematically secure method to exchange keys, such as Diffie Hellman (covered later in this section).

■ Asymmetric encryption

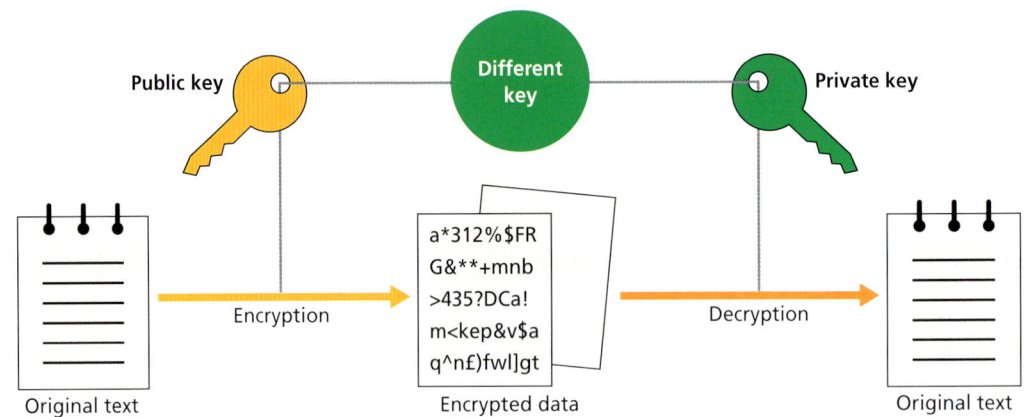

Asymmetric encryption is when the security key used to encrypt data is different from the key used to decrypt it. If it can work successfully, there are significant benefits to be gained, as it means two parties wanting to communicate in encrypted form do not have to meet privately to exchange an agreed-upon encryption key, as is required for symmetric encryption. Instead, the encryption key can be published publicly, and any person wishing to send a message can use it to encrypt the data, so that only the recipient and key-holder can decrypt it to read.

For example: If Alice wants to send a secure message to Bob, she encrypts it using Bob's public key. Only Bob can decrypt this message with his private key.

How does it work? How is it algorithmically possible to use one cipher key to encode the data and a different key to decode it? The answer is mathematics! The following walkthrough, inspired by an example by Henry J. Schmale, is simplified and loosely based on the RSA (Rivest–Shamir–Adleman) encryption algorithm.

Key information

The mathematical walkthrough is provided to demonstrate how such algorithms are possible, as an exercise of intellectual interest. Understanding the mathematics is beyond the scope of the syllabus. You will not be examined on this procedure or asked to do these calculations in the exams.

Step 1: Generate your public and private key

Start by selecting two prime numbers. These are generally very large: up to 2048 bits is typical. We will use 61 and 53 for our walkthrough.

$p = 61$

$q = 53$

Find **n**, the product of the two primes, and $\lambda(n)$ (known as "Carmichael's totient function"). To follow the maths, all you need to appreciate is that it is the least common multiple of $(p - 1)(q - 1)$.

$n = pq = 61 \times 53 = 3233$

and

$\lambda(n) = lcm[(p - 1)(q - 1)] = lcm(60,52) = 780$

Select an integer, **e**, that is a prime number, less than $\lambda(n)$, and not a factor of $\lambda(n)$. A common choice is $2^{16} + 1$, being 65537.

$e = 17$

Solve **d**, where $(d \times e) \bmod \lambda(n) = 1$. This is known as the "modular multiplicative inverse". That is, $(17 \, d) \bmod (780) = 1$. One valid answer in this case is $d = 413$.

The public key will be the two numbers $n = 3233$, $e = 17$, and the private key will be the two numbers $n = 3233$, $d = 413$.

Step 2: Encrypt your secret message

The cipher text, **c**, for a secret message, **m**, is given by the following equation:

$c(m) = m^c \bmod n$

So, if the secret message is **A**, which is ASCII 65:

$c(65) = 65^{17} \bmod 3233 = 2790$

Step 3: Decrypt your secret message

The message, **m**, for cipher text **c** is given by the following equation:

$m(c) = c^d \bmod n$

So, when given cipher text 2790, this would be decrypted as follows:

$m(2790) = 2790^{413} \bmod 3233 = 65^{17}$

The security of the algorithm rests in the size of the prime numbers and that factorizing a number into its two constituent primes is still not possible except by brute force of trying every possible set of values. The original prime number factors are required to be able to calculate $\lambda(n)$. In this case, it would be trivial to find the factors of 3233, but finding the factors of a 4096-bit number would take hundreds or thousands of years.

One area of active computing research that may threaten the security of RSA-encrypted data is quantum computing. Shor's algorithm, specifically, is a quantum algorithm for the factorization of integers that could work very quickly and render modern cryptography obsolete.

■ Role of digital certificates

Digital certificates are used as a way of certifying identity on the internet. For HTTPS traffic, they are issued by a mutually trusted third party known as a "certificate authority (CA)".

When a digital certificate is presented in a network transaction, it helps the recipient verify that the public key belongs to the sender and not an imposter. Digital certificates form a key part of the network of trust on the internet. It's not enough to know that your communication with `yourbank.com` is encrypted, if any ol' person can pose as the legitimate web server for `yourbank.com`. You want to know the web server you are logging in to is the one you want to share your secrets with.

Obtaining a certificate

The process starts by `yourbank.com` requesting that a certificate authority (that is mutually trusted by both parties) issues a certificate that can be used to prove they are, indeed, the legitimate server for `yourbank.com`. The bank will generate a public and private key using a process similar to that previously discussed with the RSA algorithm. The private key is kept secure on the bank's server, while the public key is sent to the certificate authority with the request for certification.

Using the public key provided in the certification request, the CA will verify the identity and legitimacy of the bank. This process varies, and is dependent on the process applied by the certificate authority. In the early days of the internet, it required sending photo ID proof, business ownership certificates and other legal documents to the CA. Modern practice has simplified this significantly to encourage broader adoption of HTTPS, so now certificate authorities such as `letsencrypt.org` offer the service for free and without complex paperwork.

Once the CA is satisfied with the verification, it will use its private key to sign the public key of the bank or other website. This signing process involves creating a hash of the certificate that is then encrypted using the CA's private key. This encrypted hash becomes the electronic signature. It can't be produced without the CA's private key, but it can be validated through using the CA's public key.

Using digital certificates

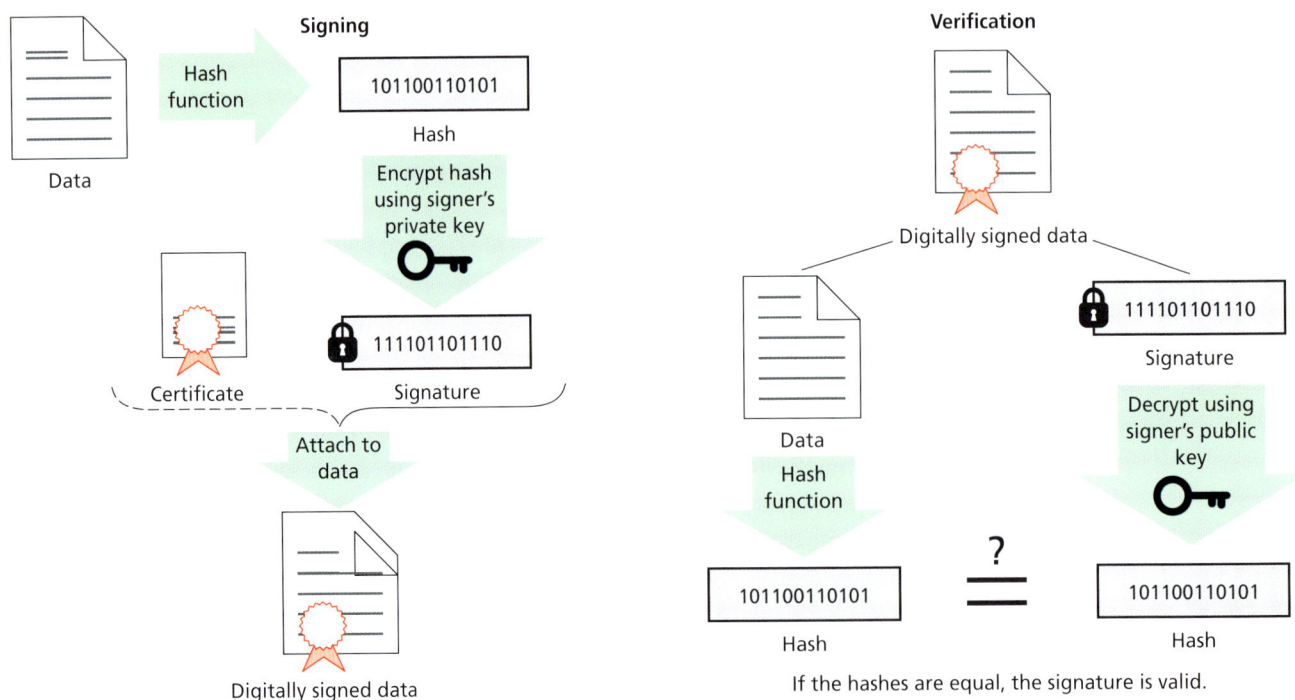

Signing with a digital certificate

Once issued, the digital certificate can be attached to all communications from the bank or other organization, and used to cryptographically sign the communication. This provides a mechanism of allowing recipients to algorithmically verify the authenticity of the origin of the communication.

Digital certificates can also be self-generated to create public and private keys that can be used for secure login to network services, such as via SSH (Secure Shell). In this case, your public key is uploaded to the remote machine you want to authenticate yourself to later and you keep the private key secure on your own local machine. The private key is equivalent to your password. When you want to log in via SSH, the server will generate a challenge to you that is encrypted with the public key. You, as the sole person in possession of the private key, are therefore the only person able to decrypt the challenge and thereby prove your identity.

Given the crucial importance of cryptographic keys in the modern interconnected economy, proper storage of keys is essential. If anyone gains unauthorized access to an organization's private keys, they can act as an imposter of that organization in all electronic transactions for which that key has been set up to be used. The creation, distribution, usage, storage and eventual retirement and deletion of encryption keys is therefore a key task of any effective IT infrastructure.

Digital certificates are a core part of blockchain technologies such as cryptocurrencies. All transactions on a blockchain are both signed and hashed. Senders use their private keys to digitally sign transactions as part of the process of validating themselves as the owner of the cryptocoin that they are spending. This signature serves to authenticate the identity of the sender and ensure the non-repudiation of the transaction. The sender cannot later deny having made the transaction.

ACTIVITY

Thinking skills: Spot the forgery at Coding Quest in the 2022 challenge (**https://codingquest.io/problem/5**).

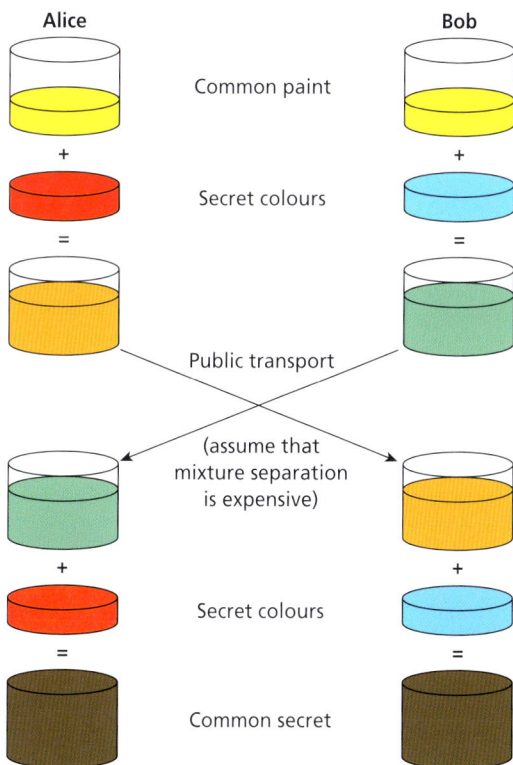

Alice — Common paint — Bob
+ Secret colours +
= =
Public transport
(assume that mixture separation is expensive)
+ Secret colours +
= =
Common secret

◼ Diffie Hellman key exchange

Given that asymmetric encryption algorithms require significantly more processing than symmetric algorithms, it is ideal if lengthy communication sessions can occur using symmetric encryption. The obvious problem that occurs then is to find a secure method of exchanging and agreeing on the symmetric key. While asymmetric encryption could be used to do this, it is slower and more processing intensive. An alternative approach that is commonly used is known as the "Diffie Hellman key exchange".

The analogy used to describe Diffie Hellman is the difficulty of unmixing colours of paint. While we may have a vague idea of which colours might be used to constitute brown, it is almost impossible to unmix the input colours perfectly.

From an algorithmic perspective, Diffie Hellman relies on the same principles of asymmetric encryption with respect to prime numbers and the mathematical difficulty of determining the prime factors of a number once run through a modulus operation.

This is a mathematical walkthrough of the Diffie Hellman algorithm:

Step 1

Agree (in public) on a base and a modulus. The modulus must be a prime number.

Person 1

base = 109, *modulus* = 811

Person 2

base = 109, *modulus* = 811

Step 2

Pick a secret number as your exponent. Calculate the base, raised it to the secret, and then put it through the modulus.

secret = 197

109^{197}% 811 = 679

secret = 312

109^{312}% 811 = 337

Step 3

Exchange the result of step 2 with your friend.

received = 337

received = 679

Step 4

Calculate your common secret by taking the received number, raising it to your original secret and then running the result through the modulus.

337^{197}% 811 = 215

679^{312}% 811 = 215

Key information

Video walkthrough

Search for the YouTube video "Diffie-Hellman Key Exchange: How to Share a Secret" by Spanning Tree.

REVIEW QUESTIONS

1 What is a primary function of a firewall in a network security context?

   a Monitoring network performance

   b Inspecting and filtering traffic based on set rules

   c Increasing the speed of network traffic

   d Providing physical security to network devices

2 Which attack involves overwhelming a service with excessive requests in order to make it unavailable?

   a Phishing

   b SQL injection

   c DDoS

   d MitM

3 What type of attack intercepts and possibly alters the communication between two parties who believe they are directly communicating with each other?

   a DDoS

   b MitM

   c Phishing

   d XSS

4 Which vulnerability arises when software has not been updated to address known security issues?

   a Insecure network protocols

   b Unpatched software

   c Weak authentication

   d Malware

5 Which network countermeasure is specifically designed to prevent unauthorized access by verifying users through multiple methods?

   a Multifactor authentication (MFA)

   b Intrusion detection system (IDS)

   c Virtual private network (VPN)

   d Email filtering

6 Which countermeasure can help protect a network against interception and unauthorized access to data in transit?

   a Multifactor authentication (MFA)

   b Intrusion prevention system (IPS)

   c Transport layer security (TLS) certificate

   d Virtual private networs (VPN)

7 Which security practice involves verifying the legitimacy of a website's connection to ensure it is secure?

   a Applying content security policies

   b Updating software regularly

   c Using secure socket layer (SSL) certificates

   d Email filtering

8 Which type of cryptography uses the same key for encryption and decryption?

   a Symmetric

   b Asymmetric

   c Both A and B

   d Neither A nor B

9 Describe how network address translation (NAT) contributes to enhancing network security.

10 Describe what is meant by "zero-day exploit".

11 Describe SQL injection and how it can affect a database-driven website.

12 Describe how weak authentication can pose a risk to network security.

13 Describe the purpose of using intrusion detection systems (IDS) and how they function.

14 Describe how DDoS mitigation tools work to protect a network.

15 Describe the role of digital certificates in establishing secure network connections.

Thinking skills: Design a network with Raspberry Pi

■ Raspberry Pi network structure

Create a small network using Raspberry Pi to simulate real-world network scenarios, including client–server and peer-to-peer architectures, routing and basic network security implementations.

If you are completing this task as a class, split into small groups, allocating one Raspberry Pi per group. Assign each Raspberry Pi one of the following roles:

■ Firewall and router
■ Proxy server
■ Web server
■ DHCP server
■ Wireless access point server
■ DNS server (optional)

The following instructions suggest utility programs and configuration files that would be useful for achieving your objectives but lack sufficient particularity to complete the instruction without further research by your team. The information provided is mostly to help you know you are on the right track when searching for guides online.

Materials needed:

■ Several Raspberry Pi computers (at least one per group; ideally three or four per group for diverse roles)
■ SD cards with Raspberry Pi OS installed
■ Ethernet cables
■ Network switch (or a router with multiple Ethernet ports)
■ Monitors, keyboards and mice for interfacing with the Raspberry Pi computers
■ Internet connection (for downloading packages and updates)

Initial set-up for all Raspberry Pi computers:

■ Each Raspberry Pi needs the Raspberry Pi OS installed and updated. You can download the latest version from the official Raspberry Pi website and write it to an SD card. Connect the Raspberry Pi to a keyboard, monitor and mouse and power up. The default login credentials are username `pi` and password `raspberry`. When configuring the Raspberry Pi computers, enable `SSH` and `VNC` to ease remote access later.
■ You may need occasionally to temporarily connect the Raspberry Pi computers directly to an internet connection, rather than to your custom network, for the purposes of installing updates and other programs.

For the Raspberry Pi designated as router and firewall:

1   Ensure the Raspberry Pi is obtaining an IP address from the DHCP server. This Pi will need a static IP (so other Pi computers can find it to request internet traffic), so the DHCP server will need the MAC address of this Pi so as to assign it the same IP address each time. To view the IP address from the console, use the command `ip a`.
2   To set a static IP directly (without the DHCP server), edit the file `/etc/dhcpcd.conf` as follows:

```
interface eth0
static ip _ address=192.168.1.1/24
static routers=192.168.1.254
static domain _ name _ servers=192.168.1.254
```

3   Enable IP forwarding by editing `/etc/sysctl.conf`.
4   Set up the WiFi connection to your school WiFi network (or other network providing outbound internet access) by running `sudo raspi-config`.
5   Configure NAT and the firewall with `nftables`. The main configuration file will be `/etc/nftables.conf`. A basic template configuration may resemble:

```
table inet filter {
    chain input {
        type filter hook input priority 0;
        # Accept any localhost traffic
        iif lo accept
        # Accept traffic already established
        ct state established,related accept
        # Enable HTTP and HTTPS
        tcp dport { http, https } accept
        # Drop everything else
        counter drop
    }
}
```

6   To apply change to rules, run this command: `sudo nft -f /etc/nftables.conf`.
7   Reboot the Pi for settings to take effect, and then test.

For the Raspberry Pi designated as wireless access point:

1   Install `hostapd` as your access point host software.
2   The main configuration file will be `/etc/hostapd/hostapd.conf`. Suggested settings include:

```
interface=wlan0                    auth _ algs=1
bridge=br0                         ignore _ broadcast _ ssid=0
driver=nl80211                     wpa=2
ssid=PiNet                         wpa _ passphrase=YourPasswordHere
hw _ mode=g                        wpa _ key _ mgmt=WPA-PSK
channel=7                          wpa _ pairwise=TKIP
wmm _ enabled=0                    rsn _ pairwise=CCMP
macaddr _ acl=0
```

3   Configure `hostapd` to use that configuration file by editing `/etc/default/hostapd`.
4   Prevent the wireless network card from being managed by the default network manager by changing `/etc/dhcpcd.conf` and specifying `denyinterfaces wlan0`.

For the Raspberry Pi designated as DHCP server:
1   Install `isc-dhcp-server` as a DHCP server.
2   The main configuration files will be `/etc/dhcp/dhcpd.conf` and `/etc/default/isc-dhcp-server`.
3   An example template for `/etc/dhcp/dhcpd.conf` is:

```
subnet 192.168.1.0 netmask 255.255.255.0 {
    range 192.168.1.10 192.168.1.100;
    option domain-name-servers 192.168.1.1;
    option routers 192.168.1.1;
    default-lease-time 600;
    max-lease-time 7200;
}
```

4   Ensure the DHCP server is configured to start on boot.
5   Check the logs for errors by using `cat /var/log/syslog | grep dhcp`.

For the Raspberry Pi designated as web server:
1   Ensure the Raspberry Pi is obtaining an IP address from the DHCP server. This Pi will need a static IP (so other Pi computers can find it to request a webpage), so the DHCP server will need the MAC address of this Pi so as to assign it the same IP address each time. To view the IP address from the console, use the command `ip a`.
2   Install `nginx` as the web server software, and set it to start automatically on boot.
3   Create a web page at `/var/www/html`.
4   The main configuration files for `nginx` can be found in `/etc/nginx`.
5   If `nginx` fails to start, you can check for configuration errors by using `sudo nginx -t`.
6   An example HTML file for `/va/www/html/index.html` might resemble:

```
<!DOCTYPE html>
<html lang="en">
<head>
    <meta charset="UTF-8">
    <title>Welcome to Pi Web Server</title>
</head>
<body>
    <h1>Hello, Raspberry Pi Network!</h1>
    <p>This is a simple web page served from the Raspberry Pi web server.</p>
</body>
</html>
```

For the Raspberry Pi designated as proxy server:
1   Ensure the Raspberry Pi is obtaining an IP address from the DHCP server. This Pi will need a static IP (so other Pi computers can find it to request a webpage), so the DHCP server will need the MAC address of this Pi so as to assign it the same IP address each time. To view the IP address from the console, use the command `ip a`.
2   Install `squid` proxy server software, and set it to start automatically on boot.
3   The main configuration file is at `/etc/squid/squid.conf`.

4 In addition to acting as a web cache, because all traffic passes through a proxy it can also be used as a content filter, for example you could block requests for given URLs. This is similar, though functionally different, from the firewall approach. Investigate how to use squid to block certain websites.

For the Raspberry Pi designated as DNS server:

1 Ensure the Raspberry Pi is obtaining an IP address from the DHCP server. This Pi will need a static IP (so other Pi computers can find it to request a webpage), so the DHCP server will need the MAC address of this Pi so as to assign it the same IP address each time. To view the IP address from the console, use the command `ip a`.

2 When the configuration for the DNS server is complete, the DHCP server will need updating so clients know to look to this computer for DNS resolution queries.

3 Install `bind9` as your DNS server software, and ensure that it is set to start on boot.

4 The main configuration files will be in the folder `/etc/bind`.

5 To check the configuration for errors, go to `sudo named-checkconf` and `sudo named-checkzone myhome.local /etc/bind/zones/db.myhome.local`.

6 An example ZONE file `/etc/bind/db.myhome.local` to create your own DNS domain (that would work on your internal network) might resemble:

```
$TTL        604800
@           IN        SOA       ns1.myhome.local.          admin.myhome.local. (
                                3                          ; Serial
                                604800                     ; Refresh
                                86400                      ; Retry
                                2419200                    ; Expire
                                604800  )                  ; Negative Cache TTL
;
@           IN        NS        ns1.myhome.local.
ns1         IN        A         192.168.1.1
@           IN        A         192.168.1.1
www         IN        A         192.168.1.2
```

ATL alignment links

Research skills:
- Finding and selecting appropriate software and hardware resources.
- Understanding documentation to configure each Raspberry Pi for its specific role.
- Comparing solutions and different methods or options to determine what will work best for project requirements.

Thinking skills:
- Problem-solving the numerous challenges that come in setting up a new network, such as IP address conflicts, firewall rules and ensuring all devices can communicate effectively.
- Critical thinking to evaluate the effectiveness of each network component and troubleshoot issues.
- Decision-making the design of the network.

Social skills:
- Collaboration by working together in a group to divide tasks, share findings and support each other.
- Conflict resolution of different opinions on how to configure the network or solve problems.
- Responsibility-sharing and relying on the contributions of others.

Communication skills:
- Technical writing to document the network set-up and configuration steps.
- Oral communication to explain complex concepts such as DNS or DHCP with peers or teachers.

Self-management skills:
- Planning and organization to manage a large, cumulative task.
- Adaptability to deal with unexpected issues.
- Self-motivation and initiative to go beyond a basic set-up, such as implementing additional network services or security measures.

EXAM PRACTICE QUESTIONS

1 **Small business network set-up**

A small business has recently expanded and needs to update its network infrastructure to support more employees and provide secure, efficient access to resources.

a Identify one piece of network hardware that would connect multiple computers within the office to create a local area network (LAN). [1]

b The business has chosen a star topology for its network. Describe one advantage of using a star topology in a small business environment. [2]

c The company uses both HTTP and HTTPS protocols on its internal websites. Describe one key difference between HTTP and HTTPS. [2]

d In the context of the TCP/IP model, describe the function of the transport layer. [3]

e The network architecture includes both client–server and peer-to-peer set-ups. Compare these two types of network architecture in terms of resource management. [3]

f The business plans to use IPv6. Identify one advantage of using IPv6 over IPv4 in a growing business. [1]

g The business is choosing between using fibre-optic cables and wireless transmission for connecting different departments. Discuss two factors that should be considered. [2]

h Describe how routers in the network use dynamic routing to manage data traffic. [3]

i The company is concerned about network security. Describe one common network vulnerability and a corresponding countermeasure. [3]

j Data encryption is crucial for the company's operations. Describe the difference between symmetric and asymmetric encryption in the context of data security. [3]

k Outline how digital certificates contribute to network security. [2]

2 **University campus network**

A large university campus network needs to support thousands of users in a dynamic, high-demand environment.

a State one network device essential for connecting campus buildings spread over a wide area. [1]

b The university uses a hybrid network topology. Describe one benefit of using a hybrid topology in a university setting. [2]

c DNS servers are critical in a university network. Describe the role of DNS in network operations. [2]

d Describe how the internet layer of the TCP/IP model facilitates connectivity between different buildings on campus. [3]

e The campus uses both IPv4 and IPv6 addressing. Outline these two types of IP addressing in terms of address availability. [2]

f Evaluate the use of twisted-pair cables vs fibre-optic cables for data transmission within academic buildings. Consider factors such as cost and speed. [3]

g Explain how packet switching enables efficient data-traffic management on a busy university network. [3]

h Describe one network security measure that should be implemented to protect students' grades and other sensitive data from alteration by the students themselves, while still allowing them access to the campus network. [2]

i The university employs digital signatures for document verification. Describe how digital signatures enhance security. [3]

j Outline the use of certificate authorities in the university's network-security framework. [2]

3 **Airline network infrastructure**

An airline operates a comprehensive network infrastructure to manage its public-facing website for customer bookings, co-ordinate hundreds of staff across multiple locations and handle customer interactions through self-check-in kiosks.

a   i   Identify one network device that is essential for connecting the airline's global offices to its central database. [1]

   ii   Outline one key network-security technique that should be used. [2]

b   The airline's network uses a mesh topology for critical systems. Outline one advantage of using a mesh topology for such applications. [2]

c   HTTPS is mandated for the airline's booking website. Describe the role of SSL/TLS in HTTPS. [2]

d   Describe the role of the application layer in the TCP/IP model, particularly in processing online bookings. [3]

e   The network includes a mix of wired and wireless technologies. Compare these two technologies in terms of reliability and security, specifically for use in high-traffic customer areas such as airports. [3]

f   Describe the importance of using IPv6 for the airline's network, focusing on its ability to handle numerous devices and security features. [1]

g   Describe how network routers ensure data packets find the optimal path across complex networks. [3]

h   Data security is a major concern for the airline, especially with customer data. Describe one potential network threat and a preventative measure that can be implemented. [3]

i   The airline uses VLANs to segment network traffic. Explain how VLANs enhance network security and efficiency. [3]

j   Outline the significance of using a reverse proxy in managing the high traffic on the airline's booking website. [2]

k   Describe the role of firewalls in protecting the network infrastructure of the airline, especially in scenarios involving customer data and payment transactions. [2]

A3 Databases

Database fundamentals

*What are the principles, structures and operations
that form the basis of database systems?*

SYLLABUS CONTENT

By the end of this chapter, you should be able to:
▶ A3.1.1 Explain the features, benefits and limitations of a relational database

A3.1.1 Relational databases

◼ Features

A **database** refers to an organized collection of structured information or data that can be accessed in different ways. Typically, a database is stored electronically for fast retrieval and manipulation of data. There are different types of databases, but your focus will be on relational databases.

Relational databases have been predominantly used since 1980. Data in a relational database is organized as a set of tables made of columns and rows.

Tables

The **table** is used to describe entities. An **entity** refers to a living or non-living thing that can have data stored about it that can be described, such as a person, a chair or an aeroplane.

Each row, also called a **tuple**, will include a **record** or an instance of an entity, for example a specific person, a specific chair or a specific aeroplane. Each column, also called a "field" or an **attribute**, will include a data item or a characteristic of an entity, such as the age or the name of a person, the colour of a chair, the model of an aeroplane, and so on.

Consider the following example:

AEROPLANE

Model	Manufacturer	PhysicalClassEngine	NoOfEngines
Rockwell Commander 112	Rockwell	Piston	1
Airbus A319 Neo	Airbus	Jet	2
Boeing 747-100	Boeing	Jet	4
Boeing 777-8	Boeing	Jet	2
Airbus A400M Atlas	Airbus	Turboprop	4
Boeing 747-100	Boeing	Jet	4

In the example above, the table name is AEROPLANE (this is the entity) and there are six records or tuples (rows in the table, excluding the table heading) and four attributes or fields (columns).

◆ Database: an organized collection of structured information or data that can be accessed in different ways.

◆ Table: a structure of rows and columns for storing a group of similar data.

◆ Entity: a living or non-living thing that can have data stored about it that can be described, e.g. a person, a chair or an aeroplane.

◆ Tuple: one instance of an entity; a row in a table.

◆ Record: one instance of an entity; a row in a table.

◆ Attribute: a data item or a characteristic of an entity; a column in a table.

Primary key

If you are to uniquely identify a record in this table, you should add an extra field. This is required, as all the given fields have repeating values, so they cannot be used to identify a record. It is possible for a company to have two aeroplanes of the same type, manufactured by the same company, with the same type of engine, and so on.

Therefore, by adding an extra field to uniquely identify each record, the table will look like this:

AEROPLANE

PlaneID	Model	Manufacturer	PhysicalClassEngine	NoOfEngines
A01	Rockwell Commander 112	Rockwell	Piston	1
A02	Airbus A319 Neo	Airbus	Jet	2
A03	Boeing 747-100	Boeing	Jet	4
A04	Boeing 777-8	Boeing	Jet	2
A05	Airbus A400M Atlas	Airbus	Turboprop	4
A06	Boeing 747-100	Boeing	Jet	4

◆ **Primary key:** a field that uniquely identifies a record in a table.

◆ **Foreign key:** an attribute in a table that refers to the primary key in another table.

The PlaneID field is unique for each record (it has no duplicates) and this is called a **primary key**.

Foreign key

Consider that you want to record data about specific flights at an airport. The AEROPLANE table only provides information about the planes. Therefore, you will need to create a new table to register the flight details.

FLIGHTS

FlightID	Departure	Destination	PlaneID	FlightDate	DeptTime	ArrivalTime
LG8903	LUX	OTP	A03	01/07/25	17:00	20:20
OS864	CAI	VIE	A04	15/01/25	16:45	19:20
GB961	LHR	ZRH	A03	25/02/25	8:40	11:35

In this table, the FlightID acts as a primary key.

The two tables, FLIGHTS and AEROPLANE, are building a relationship, as the PlaneID from the AEROPLANE table is used in the FLIGHTS table to identify the type of plane being used for a specific flight. However, the PlaneID is no longer a primary key in the FLIGHTS table, as it has repeating values; here it acts as a **foreign key**.

A foreign key is an attribute or a set of attributes in one table that refers to the primary key in another table.

Composite key

If you are to introduce a third table to register pilots on the flight, it might look like this:

PILOTFLIGHT

FlightID	PilotID
LG8903	P500
OS864	P104
GB961	P500

The `FlightID` links to the `FLIGHTS` table and the `PilotID` links to the `PILOTS` table (supposing there is a `PILOTS` table as well that records pilots' details). In the `PILOTFLIGHT` table, there is no primary key. A solution could be to use a **composite key**, formed from the two attributes `FlightID` and `PilotID`.

A composite key is a set of attributes that forms a primary key to provide a unique identifier for a table.

■ Relationships

A **relationship** is created when there is a logical association between two or more database tables, in which one table contains one or more foreign keys that reference the primary keys of the other tables. They enable relational databases to divide and store data in separate tables, while connecting their data items.

To ensure data is always accurate, accessible and consistent, relational databases follow certain integrity rules. For example, the referential integrity rule prevents users or applications from entering inconsistent data. It is a constraint that ensures that no table will contain values of a foreign key that are not matched to the corresponding primary key. In other words, it makes sure that a foreign key always refers to a record that exists in another table. By applying referential integrity constraints, the data stays consistent throughout operations such as insertion, deletion and modification of tuples.

There are several types of relationships:

- one-to-one (1:1)
- one-to-many (1:m)
- many-to-one (m:1)
- many-to-many (m:m).

One-to-one relationships

When there is a one-to-one relationship between two tables, that means that one record in a table is associated with exactly one record in another table: the primary key corresponds to one or no data in another table. For example, each staff member of a school has one single staff ID; each country has exactly one capital city; or a user on a social media platform has a single user profile. Those are very rare types of relationships, which you will not frequently encounter when dealing with databases.

One-to-many relationships

This is a frequently used type of relationship, and it refers to one record in a table being associated with one or more records in another table: the foreign key of one table references the primary key of another table. Examples of one-to-many relationships are where one teacher teaches many subjects; one tourist visits many countries; one person owns many properties; one person has many bank accounts.

Many-to-one relationships

Many-to-one relationships are similar to one-to-many relationships, but they differ in their directionality. The availability of the entity and the side of the relationship it is on determines whether it is a one-to-many or a many-to-one relationship. For example, if one teacher is teaching multiple subjects, the relationship between the teachers and the subjects is one-to-many, while the relationship between subjects and the teachers is many-to-one. Examples of many-to-one relationships are where many students enrol in a single course; many people work for a single company; there are many galaxies in the universe.

Many-to-many relationships

This type of relationship appears when multiple records in a table have a relation with multiple records in another table. Examples of many-to-many relationships are where many customers purchase many products; many actors act in many movies.

The problem with a many-to-many relationship is that a foreign key attribute can hold a single value and so it cannot handle the many references required.

To implement such relationships in relational databases you must introduce a linking entity. This means that two one-to-many relationships will be created: one between the first table and the linking table and another one between the second table and the linking table.

In the example above, when you wanted to connect the FLIGHTS table with the PILOTS table, a third table was introduced called PILOTFLIGHT. As such, a relationship of one-to-many was established between the FLIGHTS and PILOTFLIGHT tables and a relationship of one-to-many was established between the PILOTS and PILOTFLIGHT tables. This is done because a many-to-many relationship cannot be physically represented in a database.

■ Benefits of relational databases

Community support

Relational databases have been around since the 1970s, and this is the most widely accepted model for databases. Therefore, there are lots of online communities able to provide support and guidance in building, maintaining and troubleshooting them.

Concurrency control

Concurrency control is a crucial database management system (DBMS) component. It manages simultaneous operations without them conflicting with each other, and its purpose is to maintain data integrity, consistency and isolation when multiple users or applications access the database at the same time.

Data consistency

Data consistency refers to data remaining in a consistent state from start to finish, reinforcing data integrity. This means that all copies or instances of the data are the same across all systems and databases. In relational databases, each piece of data is stored in only one place, and all related data is stored together in the same table. This ensures all users have access to accurate and up-to-date information.

Data integrity

Data integrity refers to the accuracy, completeness and consistency of data throughout its lifecycle. It ensures the data hasn't been tampered with or altered in any unauthorized way. Data validation techniques can be used to ensure data integrity.

Data retrieval

The process of retrieving data from a relational database is efficient and flexible. SQL allows for complex queries to be written to retrieve exactly the data needed, using SELECT statements, JOINs, WHERE clauses, and more. Users can also create ad hoc queries to retrieve data without needing predefined reports or programs.

Reduced data duplication

Relational databases ensure that you have common fields to be used to link up tables and match records, without having to duplicate all the details several times. Identifying and removing duplicate data reduces the amount of storage needed to store the data.

Reduced redundancy

Data redundancy refers to storing the same data in multiple locations at the same time. This may lead to inconsistencies, partial updates and unnecessary duplications. Relational databases allow you to reduce redundancy by normalizing the database (organizing the data to be stored into several tables, creating relationships between them to avoid repeated groups of attributes, and correctly enforcing their dependencies; non-key attributes being independent).

Reliable transaction processing

A transaction refers to a sequence of actions performed on a database that is considered as a single unit (such as inserting, deleting, updating data in a table). A transaction is a unit of work, or a logical action, that is independent of other transactions and is performed on a database by a database management system. A transaction is either executed in full or it is not executed at all. Transactions ensure data integrity and reliability within relational databases.

Scalability

Database scalability refers to the ability of a database to handle increasing amounts of data, number of users and types of requests without sacrificing performance or availability. Relational databases are vertically scalable, meaning that they support the idea of adding more resources (CPU, RAM, hard drive space) to existing systems, which is a cheaper, easier and faster approach to handling increases.

Security features

Relational databases increase security by controlling access to stored data, ensuring only authorized users can interact with the database. They allow the assignment of unique user accounts with specific permissions based on the users' roles and responsibilities. They allow different views of tables for different access rights.

■ Limitations of relational databases

Big data scalability issues

Relational databases can be more difficult to scale as the size and complexity of the data increases. The performance can drop when manipulating large data sets (horizontal scaling) or dealing with complex queries; joins between tables can be slow and indexing strategies can be difficult to optimize.

Design complexity

Relational databases require a lot of structure and planning to design the tables and the relationships between them in a way that fits correctly to the requirements.

Hierarchical data handling

Storing hierarchical data in relational databases is challenging due to the mismatch between the hierarchical structure and the tabular nature of relational databases. Even if this is done through a strategy such as an adjacency list model (where each record contains a reference to its parent record, forming a tree-like structure, such as an employee table having a field referencing the manager's ID for each employee), it is challenging to retrieve and traverse hierarchies, especially for large sets of data, or to reorder nodes and perform queries on the subtrees created.

Rigid schema

Relational databases have a predefined schema (structure of the data and how it will be stored in the database). Defining the schema can be challenging as it is not easy to predict the data structure of the database beforehand, and changing it later is complicated. When it comes to changing the database structure, updating the schema is time-consuming and complicated.

Object-relational impedance mismatch

Object-relational impedance mismatch refers to the difficulties encountered when relational databases are used by a program written in an object-oriented programming language. A major mismatch between relational databases and OOP languages is the data type differences. Relational models do not allow the use of by-reference attributes (pointers), while OOP languages embrace this behaviour. There is no clear way to translate all OOP concepts into relational databases or vice versa, such as there is no way to translate inheritance to a relational database concept.

Unstructured data handling

Unstructured data refers to a collection of data where one record differs from another record. Not being able to identify common fields or attributes for the records makes it impossible to design a schema for such data (to represent them as relational databases).

● Common mistake

When asked to explain concepts such as benefits and limitations of relational databases within a given scenario, candidates often identify general benefits and limitations without making any connections to the given scenario. To gain full marks, the scenario must be taken into consideration, as well as the number of marks awarded for the respective question.

ACTIVITY

Self-management skills: Create plans to prepare for summative assessments – keep track of topics that have been covered and how well you mastered each of them. Identify what you can do to master any topics you found more challenging.

REVIEW QUESTIONS

1 Define the terms:
   a "primary key"
   b "foreign key".
2 Explain what is meant by referential integrity.
3 Explain the one-to-one, one-to-many and many-to-many types of relationships.
4 Discuss the benefits and limitations of a relational database.
5 Define the term "database".

Database design

SYLLABUS CONTENT

By the end of this chapter, you should be able to:

▶ A3.2.1 Describe database schema
▶ A3.2.2 Construct entity-relationship diagrams (ERDs)
▶ A3.2.3 Outline the different data types used in relational databases
▶ A3.2.4 Construct tables for relational databases
▶ A3.2.5 Explain the difference between normal forms
▶ A3.2.6 Construct a database normalized to 3NF for a range of real-life scenarios
▶ A3.2.7 Evaluate the need for denormalizing databases

A3.2.1 Database schema

◆ **Database schema:**
an architecture
showing how data is
organized and how the
relationship between
data is managed.

◆ **Conceptual
schema:** an abstract
model describing the
structure of the data
without considering
how it will physically be
implemented.

Database schema is an architecture showing how data is organized and how the relationship between data is managed. It provides a logical view of the database.

There are different types of database schemas:

■ **Conceptual schema:** An abstract model describing the structure of the data without considering how it will physically be implemented.

■ **Logical schema:** A detailed design of the structure of the tables (fields and data types), relationships between tables and constraints.

■ **Physical schema:** Represents the implementation of the logical schema into a specific DBMS (database management system), showing how data is stored, indexed or accessed.

The use of database schemas improves:

■ **data organization:** it provides clear structure for storing and organizing the data

■ **data security:** it defines user permissions and views to protect data

■ **data integrity:** it uses rules and constraints to maintain data accuracy and consistency

■ **performance:** through the use of queries

■ **scalability:** it allows for changes to the database without disrupting current applications.

The DBMS controls the creation, maintenance and usage of a database and it mediates between the data-handling applications and the operating system. The DBMS offers features such as database queries, forms, reports and charts to display the data.

■ Conceptual schema

Conceptual schema is a high-level representation of the database, defining its structure and organization. It is an abstract model that hides details such as implementation of the data structures or physical storage. It defines the entities, attributes and relationships between entities.

A common method of implementing conceptual schema is by using entity-relationship diagrams (ERDs).

For example, consider a sales system with the following structure:

- Entities
  - ☐ Products
  - ☐ Orders
  - ☐ Customers
- Attributes
  - ☐ In Products (ProductID, ProductName, Price)
  - ☐ In Orders (OrderID, OrderDate)
  - ☐ In Customers (CustomerID, CustomerName, EmailAddress)
- Relationships
  - ☐ Customer places an order
  - ☐ An order includes one or more products

Conceptual schema is a model with insufficient details to build an actual database.

◼ Logical schema

♦ Logical schema: a detailed design of the structure of tables (fields and data types), relationships between tables and constraints.

Logical schema is a model that defines the structure of the database, including entities, attributes, data types, constraints, keys and relationships. It is a design that doesn't take into consideration the requirements of a specific database management system (DBMS). The logical schema is derived from the conceptual schema by:

- converting the entities into detailed tables
- defining the attributes by specifying the data types and constraints for each field in the table
- establishing primary and foreign keys
- defining relationships between the tables by using the keys
- normalizing the database to minimize data redundancy
- ensuring data integrity.

In the previous example:

Tables:

- Products
  - ☐ ProductID: INTEGER (PRIMARY KEY)
  - ☐ ProductName: VARCHAR
  - ☐ Price: REAL
- Orders
  - ☐ OrderID: INTEGER (PRIMARY KEY)
  - ☐ OrderDate: DATE
  - ☐ CustomerID: INTEGER (FOREIGN KEY)
  - ☐ PRODUCTID: INTEGER (FOREIGN KEY)
- Customers
  - ☐ CustomerID: PRIMARY KEY
  - ☐ CustomerName: VARCHAR
  - ☐ EmailAddress: VARCHAR, UNIQUE

Relationships:

- A customer places one or more orders (one-to-many).
- An order includes one or more products (one-to-many).

◼ Physical schema

Physical schema includes specifics of storage devices, access methods, indexing, partitioning, access methods, views and configuration of the database on the storage media. It translates the logical schema into an implementation that fits the requirements of a specific database management system.

In the previous example:

Tables:

- Products
  - ☐ ProductID: INT PRIMARY KEY AUTO_INCREMENT
  - ☐ ProductName: VARCHAR(100) NOT NULL
  - ☐ Price: REAL NOT NULL

  INDEX on ProductName for faster access based on the product name

- Orders
  - ☐ OrderID: INT PRIMARY KEY AUTO_INCREMENT
  - ☐ OrderDate: DATE NOT NULL
  - ☐ CustomerID: INT FOREIGN KEY NOT NULL
  - ☐ ProductID: INT FOREIGN KEY NOT NULL

  INDEX on CustomerID and ProductID for faster joins

- Customers
  - ☐ CustomerID: INT PRIMARY KEY AUTO_INCREMENT
  - ☐ LastName: VARCHAR(100) NOT NULL
  - ☐ FirstName: VARCHAR(100) NOT NULL
  - ☐ EmailAddress: VARCHAR(100) NOT NULL UNIQUE

  INDEX on LastName for faster access based on the last name

Storage parameters:

- ◼ Use indices described above for fast retrieval of data.

- ◼ Partition large tables like Orders by OrderID to improve query performance.

A3.2.2 Entity-relationship diagrams

An **entity-relationship diagram** (ERD) is a visual representation of the entities in the database and the relationship between them.

Besides providing a clear overview of the database structure, ERDs facilitate communication between stakeholders; act as documentation for the database design; support future development and maintenance of the database; and ensure data integrity and consistency through constraints and well-defined relationships.

For the sales system with Products, Orders and Customers entities, the ERD looks like this:

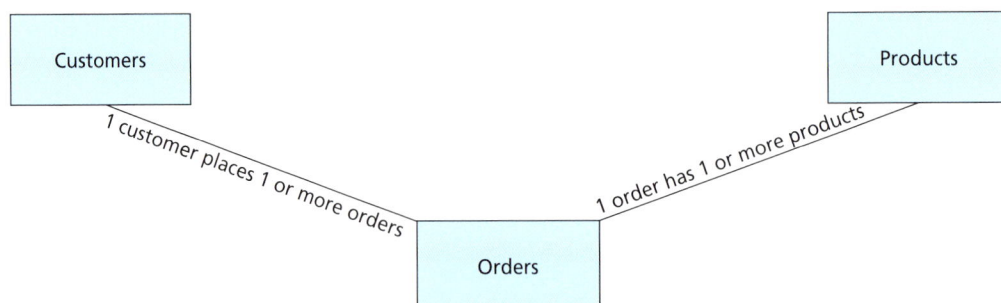

— one

— one and only one

—O+ zero or one

—< many

—K one or many

—O< zero or many

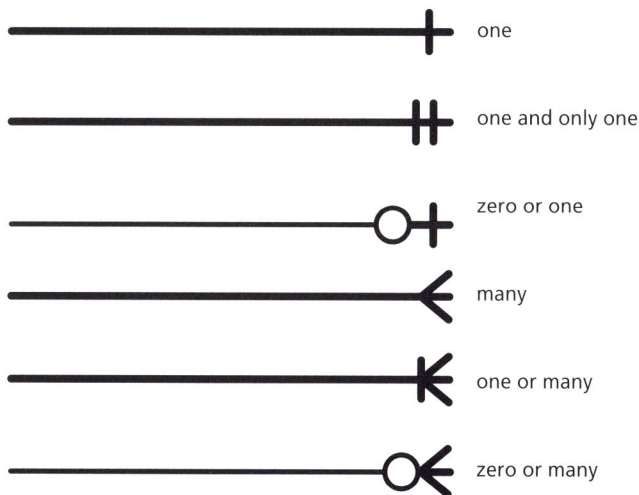

Modality of relationships

◆ **Modality:** the minimum number of instances of one entity that can be associated with an instance of another entity.

◆ **Cardinality:** the maximum number of times an instance in one entity can be associated with instances in the related entity.

Modality in ERDs refers to the minimum number of instances of one entity that can be associated with an instance of another entity. It defines whether the participation of an entity in a relationship is optional (0) or mandatory (1).

Consider an example involving data about patients and their medical records in a medical healthcare system. Most patients will have associated medical records, but new patients or newborn children might not have any medical history, therefore this is a type of optional relationship.

On the other hand, if you are to consider an e-commerce platform, every order must be associated with a customer (you cannot become a customer unless you place an order), so that is a type of mandatory relationship.

The cardinality of relationships refers to the nature and extent of relationships between entities in an ERD. It specifies the number of instances of one entity that can or must be associated with each instance of another entity.

Cardinality refers to the maximum number of times an instance in one entity can be associated with instances in the related entity. It describes the "many" side of the relationship and it can be defined as:

- one-to-one
- one-to-many
- many-to-one
- many-to-many.

For example, consider a school management system that includes students and clubs as entities.

Entity `STUDENT` has `StudentID`, `FirstName`, `LastName`, `Email` as attributes.

Entity `CLUB` has `ClubID`, `Title`, `TeacherID`, `Location` as attributes.

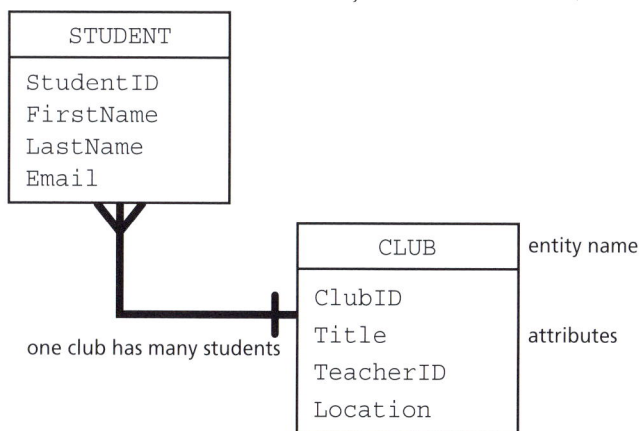

STUDENT

StudentID
FirstName
LastName
Email

CLUB — entity name

ClubID
Title — attributes
TeacherID
Location

one club has many students

The relationship between the two entities can be represented as "a club has many students".

Cardinality: one student can enrol in multiple clubs (one-to-many).

Modality: a club must have at least one student enrolled (mandatory for clubs); a student might not enrol in any clubs (optional for students).

Understanding both cardinality and modality is essential for accurately modelling the relationships and constraints in a database, ensuring it effectively reflects the real-world requirements and business rules.

ACTIVITY

Social skills: Support other students with application skills on practical tasks – help your classmates to analyse different database scenarios, identify entities, establish the appropriate relationships between tables and provide feedback to each other on how appropriate ERDs can be created.

A3.2.3 Data types used in relational databases

Data type for attributes	Description
CHARACTER	Fixed length text
VARCHAR(n)	Variable length text (n indicates the maximum number of characters)
INTEGER	Whole number
REAL	Number with a decimal part
DATE	Date as YYYY-MM-DD
TIME	Time as HH:MM:SS
BOOLEAN	True or False

Choosing the right data type is important for ensuring efficient indexing. For example, using CHARACTER(8) for fixed-length data like UserID is more efficient than using VARCHAR(8), as this can lead to extra time during query execution due to the variable length storage. Also, the data type indicates the type of operations permitted. For example, if you store the quantity and price as fixed-length text, to perform calculations you will need to convert the text to integer or real values in the application, before using the data.

Another aspect of using appropriate data types is being able to store the data in the database into the corresponding field. If the type of data does not match the data type of the attribute in the database, the insertion attempt will throw errors.

Data consistency ensures users have access to up-to-date and accurate information, where all copies or instances are the same across all systems and database tables. Using different data types to refer to the same attribute on different platforms (database and application system) will lead to problems such as not being able to perform operations specific to the required data type, incorrect updates or queries.

A3.2.4 Constructing tables for relational databases

Properly defining the tables in a database supports the design of appropriate ERDs and ensures data integrity.

Considering a school management system, this could include the following tables:

■ STUDENT (StudentID, FirstName, LastName, DateOfBirth, Email)

■ CLUB (StudentID, ClubTitle, TeacherName)

■ TEACHER (TeacherClub, Location)

STUDENT

StudentID	FirstName	LastName	DateOfBirth	Email
101	Fatema	Kada	02/01/2010	f.kada@email.com
105	Alexandru	Buchidau	05/11/2009	a.buchidau@email.com
202	Kada	Hussein	07/25/2011	k.hussein@email.com

In the STUDENT table, the StudentID acts as a primary key to uniquely identify each record in the table.

CLUB

StudentID	ClubTitle	TeacherName
105	Robotics	Bobby Williams
202	Taekwondo	Dima White
101	Robotics	Bobby Williams
105	Arts and Crafts	Jane Doe

In the CLUB table, the StudentID is a foreign key (as it is a primary key in the STUDENT table). However, none of the fields in this table can act as a primary key, as they all have duplicates. But you could set the primary key to be a composite key, formed from the attributes StudentID and ClubTitle. On the other hand, you could add a new attribute ClubID to act as a primary key.

In case there is a need for a single field to act as primary key, it is possible to combine data from several attributes into one to act as a concatenated key.

TEACHER

TeacherClub	Location
Jane Doe Arts and Crafts	L101
Bobby Williams Robotics	H203
Dima White Taekwondo	B353

In the TEACHER table, the primary key is a concatenated key, formed from the attributes TeacherName and ClubTitle.

A3.2.5 Differences between normal forms

◆ **Normalization:** the process of organizing data in a relational database in a way to reduce data redundancy and to improve data integrity.

◆ **First normal form:** the status of a relational database in which entities do not contain repeating groups of attributes.

◆ **Atomic:** each attribute in a table containing indivisible values (values that cannot be broken down into more detailed sub-values).

Data **normalization** represents the process of organizing data in a relational database in a way to reduce data redundancy and to improve data integrity. Data redundancy is reduced as each item of data only occurs in one location in the database. This can reduce the possibility of update anomalies occurring, and it makes more efficient use of memory. Normalization leads to smaller tables with less information in each row, which leads to a reduction of input / output transfers, and so the CPU can work at full capacity since the likelihood of CPU activities being suspended is reduced. Normalization is achieved through a series of stages called "normal forms", where each normal form has specific requirements for the table to be considered normalized at that level.

■ First normal form (1NF)

In **first normal form**, the table:

- has a primary key
- includes no duplicate attributes from the same table
- includes no repeated groups of attributes.

Therefore, you need to create separate tables for each group of related data, identifying each record by using the primary key, which is made of one single attribute or a set of attributes (composite or compound key), and ensure the entities do not contain repeated groups of attributes.

In 1NF, data in each field must be **atomic**. This means that each attribute contains indivisible values (values that cannot be broken down into more detailed sub-values). For example, an attribute called TeacherName in the TEACHER table is not an atomic field as this could be further split into two different attributes called `LastName` and `FirstName`. Once this is achieved, the fields are atomic.

Atomicity ensures that each cell in the table will contain a single value, not complex structures like arrays or lists.

Functional dependency is a relationship that exists between attributes, where one set of attributes (the determinant) determines the value of the other set (the dependent). Typically, this is a relationship between the primary-key attribute and a non-key attribute. For example, in the `STUDENT` table, the `StudentID` (primary key and the determinant) determines the `FirstName`, `LastName`, `DateOfBirth` and `Email` values (the dependent). This means that, given the value of the `StudentID`, you can find the other details, but not vice versa. To ensure functional dependency in 1NF, you need to ensure entity atomicity and to remove repeating groups of attributes.

There are different types of functional dependencies:

- **Full functional dependency**: The dependent attributes are determined by the determinant attributes. For example, the `StudentID` fully determines the student's `FirstName`, `LastName`, `DateOfBirth` and `Email`.

- **Partial functional dependency**: The dependent attributes are partially determined by the determinant attributes. For example, the `StudentID` could partially determine the `FirstName`, `LastName` and `DateOfBirth` of the student, but not their course instructor for a club.

- **Transitive dependency**: The dependent attributes are determined by a set of attributes that are not included in the determinant attributes. For example, in an `EMPLOYEES` table, the `EmployeeID` may determine the `EmployeeDepartment`, which in turns determines their salary.

◼ Second normal form (2NF)

In **second normal form** (2NF):

- entities are in 1NF

- any non-key attributes are fully functionally dependent on the primary key; there are no partial dependencies.

Partial-key dependency occurs in a table that has a composite key as primary key and one or more non-key attributes are dependent on only a subset of the composite primary key, rather than on the entire composite key. For example, in the `CLUB` table, the non-key attribute `TeacherName` is dependent on the `ClubTitle`, but not on the `StudentID`. As the primary key in this table is a composite key formed of both the `ClubTitle` and the `StudentID` fields, the `TeacherName` should have been fully functionally dependent on these two fields.

◼ Third normal form (3NF)

In **third normal form** (3NF):

- entities are in 2NF

- all non-key attributes are independent (remove columns that are not fully functionally dependent on the primary key); the table contains no non-key dependencies.

Non-key or transitive dependency is a type of functional dependency that occurs when a non-prime attribute is dependent on another non-prime attribute, rather than on the primary key.

◆ **Functional dependency:** a relationship that exists between attributes, where one set of attributes (the determinant) determines the value of the other set (the dependent).

◆ **Full functional dependency:** where dependent attributes are determined by the determinant attributes.

◆ **Partial functional dependency:** when dependent attributes are partially determined by the determinant attributes.

◆ **Transitive dependency:** a type of functional dependency that occurs when a non-prime attribute is dependent on another non-prime attribute, rather than on the primary key.

◆ **Second normal form:** the status of a relational database in which entities are in 1NF and any non-key attributes depend upon the primary key.

◆ **Third normal form:** the status of a relational database in which entities are in 2NF and all non-key attributes are independent.

If the CLUB table looked like the one below, the primary key in the table would be ClubID. The ClubTitle is fully functionally dependent on the ClubID; however, the TeacherLastName is dependent on the TeacherID, which is not a primary key in the table.

CLUB

ClubID	ClubTitle	TeacherID	TeacherLastName
105	Robotics	1	Williams
202	Taekwondo	2	White
105	Robotics	1	Williams
106	Arts and Crafts	4	Doe

To resolve this non-key dependency, the table should be split into two: one storing club details (ClubID, ClubTitle and TeacherID) and the other teacher details (TeacherID and TeacherLastName).

CLUBDETAILS

ClubID	ClubTitle	TeacherID
105	Robotics	1
202	Taekwondo	2
106	Arts and Crafts	4

TEACHERDETAILS

TeacherID	TeacherFirstName	TeacherLastName
1	Bobby	Williams
2	Dima	White
4	Jane	Doe

Normalization issues can encompass data duplication, missing data and a range of dependency concerns, including data dependencies, composite key dependencies, transitive dependencies and multi-valued dependencies. For example, a car manufacturer produces two colours (black and grey) of each model every year. The attributes Colour and ManufacturingYear are dependent on the field CarModel, but they are independent of each other. Therefore, they can be called "multi-valued dependencies" on the CarModel.

Multi-valued dependencies occur when two attributes in a table are independent of each other, but both depend on a third attribute. This is important for achieving fourth normal form (4NF), which addresses certain types of redundancy not handled by earlier normal forms.

A3.2.6 Normalized databases (3NF)

Consider a library management system that stores the data in a table called "books":

BOOKS

BookID	AuthorID	Author	Title	Pages	ProofReader
1	101	Boris Brown	History of AI	353	Amanda
2	102	Chris Joe	The Great G	200	Hamilton
3	19	Danny Bill	Big Tonny	190	Juan
5	101	Boris Brown	Amazing Future	399	Amanda

Normalizing this database to 3NF means:

1 Normalize it to 1NF:

☐ Set `BookID` as the primary key.

☐ Split the author into two different attributes: `AuthorFirstName` and `AuthorLastName`.

BookID	AuthorID	AuthorFirstName	AuthorLastName	Title	Pages	ProofReader
1	101	Boris	Brown	History of AI	353	Amanda
2	102	Chris	Joe	The Great G	200	Hamilton
3	19	Danny	Bill	Big Tonny	190	Juan
5	101	Boris	Brown	Amazing Future	399	Amanda

2 Normalize it to 2NF:

☐ Entities are in 1NF.

☐ There are no partial dependencies.

`AuthorFirstName` and `AuthorLastName` are dependent on `AuthorID`, while `Title`, `Pages` and `ProofReader` are dependent on the primary key (`BookID`). Therefore, we need to split this table as follows:

BOOKS

BookID	AuthorID	Title	Pages	ProofReader
1	101	History of AI	353	Amanda
2	102	The Great G	200	Hamilton
3	19	Big Tonny	190	Juan
5	101	Amazing Future	399	Amanda

AUTHOR

AuthorID	AuthorFirstName	AuthorLastName
101	Boris	Brown
102	Chris	Joe
19	Danny	Bill

3 Normalize it to 3NF:

☐ Entities are in 2NF.

☐ There are no transitive dependencies.

The `ProofReader` field has repeating values, and it is not necessarily fully functionally dependent on the `BookID`. Therefore, to remove non-transitive dependencies, you can create a new table for proof readers.

BOOKS

BookID	AuthorID	Title	Pages
1	101	History of AI	353
2	102	The Great G	200
3	19	Big Tonny	190
5	101	Amazing Future	399

AUTHOR

AuthorID	AuthorFirstName	AuthorLastName
101	Boris	Brown
102	Chris	Joe
19	Danny	Bill

PROOFREADERS

ProofReaderID	ProofReader
100	Amanda
222	Hamilton
123	Juan

Now, you need to link the BOOKS table with the PROOFREADERS table, so a new table is created.

BOOKS_PROOFREADERS

BookID	ProofReaderID
1	100
2	222
3	123
5	100

A3.2.7 Denormalizing databases

There are both advantages and disadvantages to normalizing and denormalizing databases.

Overall, normalization plays a crucial role in designing efficient, maintainable and reliable databases that support data integrity and consistency while optimizing performance and scalability.

◼ Normalization

Advantages	Disadvantages
Minimizes data redundancy Data is organized into separate tables for each entity, so it reduces data duplicates, saves storage space and ensures consistency.	**Complexity in database schema** Complex schema with multiple tables and relationships can make it difficult for developers to understand and maintain the database structure, especially in large or evolving systems.
Ensures data integrity Using specific rules regarding relationships and dependencies, normalization ensures insertion, update, delete queries and maintains data integrity.	**Increased query complexity** When needing to join multiple tables to perform queries, performance can drop.
Facilitates efficient data retrieval Well-defined relationships between tables support the development of efficient queries.	**Increased storage requirements** The increased number of tables and relationships may lead to higher storage requirements.
Supports scalability New data can be added without significantly altering the existing structure.	**Not ideal for all use cases** Normalization is based on relational database principles, and it may not fit all applications or types of data.

Advantages	Disadvantages
Promotes data consistency	**Difficulty in balancing normalization**
Eliminating data redundancy and defining clear relationships promotes data consistency.	When normalizing a database, you need to aim for a balance between reducing data redundancy and maintaining performance. Over-normalization (too many tables and relationships) or under-normalization (failing to separate data appropriately) may lead to maintenance issues and low performance.
Simplifies database maintenance	**Overheads in updates**
Changes can be made to a single table without affecting other tables.	Updating records may require changing data in different places, which can reduce performance or increase the complexity of update operations.

■ Denormalization

◆ **Denormalization:** deliberately allowing for data redundancy in a database design to improve the performance of queries.

Denormalization refers to deliberately allowing for data redundancy in a database design to improve the performance of queries.

Advantages	Disadvantages
Improved query performance	**Data redundancy**
There is less need for joins; the simpler structure of the tables improves the performance of read-heavy queries.	There is the possibility of inconsistencies if updates are not properly managed; it is more challenging to synchronize and maintain the data.
Simplified data retrieval	**Increased storage overhead**
Data is stored closer to the way it is accessed by applications so it allows for faster retrieval of data as there are less complex joins between tables.	Redundant data requires additional storage space, which can become significant in large or evolving systems.
Enhanced scalability	**Maintenance challenges**
This reduces the overhead of maintaining complex relationships, so it supports larger data sets and higher transaction volumes without sacrificing performance.	Managing denormalized databases requires careful planning and maintenance to ensure data integrity and consistency.

There are situations where denormalization can enhance performance, especially when read performance is crucial and outweighs concerns about data redundancy and updates complexity. Some specific scenarios are as follows:

Read-intensive applications

Read-intensive applications refer to applications in which the focus is on retrieving data, rather than updating it. By reducing the number of tables, relationships and joins, data can be accessed faster, improving query performance and response time.

Reporting and analytics

Reporting and analytics are used when generating complex reports or analysing large sets of data. Reducing the number of tables, simplifying relationships and decreasing the need for joins speeds up reporting and analytics queries.

Data warehousing

In data warehousing, the focus is on storing and analysing historical data from different sources. Simplifying complex queries across different data sources and using fewer tables to organize related data improves query performance and response time.

Denormalization simplifies query structures by reducing the need for joins between tables. Simpler queries are easier to write, faster to execute, easier to understand and easier to maintain. On the other side, allowing for data redundancy means increased storage requirements, and increased complexity in maintenance and update operations. Therefore, there is a need to find a balance between the two, and this requires:

- analysing the specific requirements of the application (is the focus on reading or retrieving the data or on updating it?)
- identifying whether the benefits of denormalizing the database are higher than the risk of data redundancy and complexity (sometimes a partially denormalized schema might be a solution)
- implementing appropriate strategies to mitigate risks and optimize performance (implement robust data validation, monitor query performance and storage requirements, and so on).

ACTIVITY

Independent learning: Independent reflection and targets for improvement – identify your strongest and weakest points and set short-term goals for achieving success. When analysing your strongest and weakest points, consider: technical skills and soft skills; constructive or positive feedback from peers and teachers; successful projects; formative assessments; and knowledge gaps or technical gaps. Short-term goals will keep you focused; they will allow you to set an action plan that can be monitored and evaluated progressively.

TOK

Utilitarianism, the greatest good for the greatest number. The ends justify the means.

Utilitarianism is an ethical theory that suggests the best action is the one that maximizes overall happiness or well-being. This approach is often summarized by the phrase "the greatest good for the greatest number". According to this view, the moral value of an action is determined by its outcome or consequences, rather than by any intrinsic qualities of the action itself. For example, if sacrificing the well-being of a few individuals leads to a greater overall benefit for society, a utilitarian would argue that such a sacrifice is justified.

When managing databases, particularly those containing personal information, there's often a trade-off between privacy and utility. A utilitarian approach might justify the use of personal data without explicit consent if it leads to a greater good, such as improving public health through data-driven insights. During a pandemic, health authorities might access and analyse large data sets of personal health information to track the spread of the virus. From a utilitarian perspective, the potential benefits to society (for example, controlling the pandemic) might outweigh individual privacy concerns. The utilitarian principle of "the greatest good for the greatest number" provides a framework for making decisions about how databases are managed, used and secured.

Discuss how this approach may be balanced against other ethical considerations, such as individual rights and fairness, which may not always align with a purely utilitarian perspective.

REVIEW QUESTIONS

1 Define the term "schema".
2 Discuss the characteristics of a normalized database.
3 Identify two issues caused by data redundancy.
4 State the characteristics of:
   a 1NF   **b** 2NF   **c** 3NF
5 Distinguish between conceptual and logical schema.

Database programming

By the end of this chapter, you should be able to:
▶ A3.3.1 Outline the difference between data language types within structured query language (SQL)
▶ A3.3.2 Construct queries between two tables in SQL
▶ A3.3.3 Explain how SQL can be used to update data in a database
▶ A3.3.4 Construct calculations within a database using SQL's aggregate functions (HL)
▶ A3.3.5 Describe different database views (HL)
▶ A3.3.6 Describe how transactions maintain data integrity in a database (HL)

A3.3.1 Data language types within SQL

Data language types include data definition language (DDL) and data manipulation language (DML).

■ Data definition language (DDL)

Data definition language (DDL) is used to create, modify and remove data structures from a relational database.

◆ **Data definition language:** language that is used to create, modify and remove data structures from a relational database.

SQL DDL instructions	Explanation
CREATE	Create a new database object (table, view, index)
PRIMARY KEY	Set a field as a primary key
FOREIGN KEY ... REFERENCES ...	Set a field as a foreign key by specifying the field and the table it is associated with
ALTER	Change the structure of an existing database object: alter a table structure, by adding or removing columns or adding constraints
DROP	Delete database objects (tables, indices, views)

CREATE statements

CREATE DATABASE:

```
CREATE DATABASE HOSPITAL
```

CREATE TABLE:

```
CREATE TABLE Employees (
EmployeeID INT,
DepartmentID INT PRIMARY KEY,
LastName VARCHAR(20)
);
```

CREATE VIEW:

```
CREATE VIEW EmployeeDetails AS

SELECT EmployeeID, LastName

FROM Employees

JOIN Departments ON Employees.DepartmentID = Departments.
DepartmentID;
```

CREATE INDEX:

```
CREATE INDEX idx_last_name ON Employees(LastName);
```

ALTER statements

Add primary key:

```
ALTER TABLE Employees

ADD PRIMARY KEY (EmployeeID);
```

Add foreign key:

```
ALTER TABLE Employees

ADD FOREIGN KEY DepartmentID REFERENCES Department(DepartmentID);
```

Add a column:

```
ALTER TABLE Employees

ADD Email VARCHAR(25);
```

Drop a column:

```
ALTER TABLE Employees

DROP COLUMN Email;
```

Add a constraint:

```
ALTER TABLE Employees

ADD CONSTRAINT FK_DepartmentID

FOREIGN KEY (DepartmentID) REFERENCES Departments(DepartmentID);
```

DROP statements

Drop table:

```
DROP TABLE Employees;
```

Drop index:

```
DROP INDEX idx_last_name;
```

Drop view:

```
DROP VIEW EmployeeData;
```

■ Data manipulation language (DML)

Data manipulation languages are used to add, modify, delete and retrieve data stored in relational databases.

SQL DML instructions	Explanation
SELECT	Retrieves data from one or more tables
INSERT	Adds records into a table
DELETE	Removes records from a table
UPDATE	Modifies existing records in a table

♦ **Data manipulation language:** language that is used to add, modify, delete and retrieve data stored in relational databases.

A3.3 Database programming

187

SELECT statements

Retrieve records by displaying specific columns:

```
SELECT field1, field2, field3...
FROM table_name;
```

Retrieve records by displaying attributes that match a given criterion:

```
SELECT field1, field2, ...
FROM table_name
WHERE condition;
```

Retrieve all records:

```
SELECT * FROM table_name;
```

Retrieve records by checking whether specific fields meet specific criteria:

```
SELECT * FROM table_name WHERE condition;
```

A3.3.2 SQL queries between two tables

Including a JOIN in a SELECT statement allows you to aggregate data from multiple tables. For example, considering the employees table and the department table, the script below retrieves the salary expense grouped by department.

■ JOIN in a SELECT statement

```
SELECT Employees.DepartmentName, SUM(Employees.Salary) AS TotalSalary
FROM Employees
JOIN Department ON Employees.DepartmentID = Department.DepartmentID
GROUP BY Department.DepartmentName;
```

■ DISTINCT in a SELECT statement

When you want to retrieve unique records and ignore duplicates, you can use the keyword DISTINCT.

```
SELECT DISTINCT column1, column2, ...
FROM table_name;
```

■ HAVING clause vs WHERE clause

The HAVING clause is used to filter groups of records created by the GROUP BY clause, for example when needing to retrieve the department ID and the average salary per department where the average salary is above 10,000.

The WHERE clause is used to filter records *before* grouping, while the HAVING clause is used to filter groups *after* aggregation.

```
SELECT DepartmentID, Salary
FROM Employees
GROUP BY DepartmentID
HAVING Salary > 10000;
```

RELATIONAL operators

Relational operators can be used to fetch data that meets specific criteria.

Operator	Example
Equals to	`SELECT * FROM Employees WHERE DepartmentID = 1;`
Not equals to	`SELECT * FROM Employees WHERE DepartmentID <> 1;`
Greater than	`SELECT * FROM Employees WHERE Salary > 10000;`
Smaller than	`SELECT * FROM Employees WHERE Salary < 10000;`
Greater than or equals to	`SELECT * FROM Employees WHERE Salary >= 10000;`
Smaller than or equals to	`SELECT * FROM Employees WHERE Salary <= 10000;`

FILTERING

Operator	Example
BETWEEN filters values between a range	`SELECT * FROM Employees` `WHERE Salary BETWEEN 50000 AND 100000;`
IN filters values that match any value in a given list	`SELECT * FROM Employees` `WHERE DepartmentID IN (1, 2, 3);`
IS NULL filters records with null values	`SELECT * FROM Employees` `WHERE ManagerID IS NULL;`
IS NOT NULL filters records with non-null values	`SELECT * FROM Employees` `WHERE ManagerID IS NOT NULL;`

Combining conditions using logic operators	`SELECT * FROM Employees`
	`WHERE (DepartmentID = 5 AND Salary > 50000) OR`
	`(DepartmentID = 1 AND Salary > 10000);`

Pattern matching

- `LIKE` filters values based on a pattern.
- `%` is used for any sequence of characters (zero or more).
- `_` is used for one single character.

This will retrieve records that start with the letter D:

```
SELECT * FROM Employees
WHERE LastName LIKE 'D%';
```

This will retrieve records that end with the letter d:

```
SELECT * FROM Employees
WHERE LastName LIKE '%d';
```

This will retrieve records that match a specific pattern (start with the letter D, followed by a character, followed by the letter m and followed by zero or more characters):

```
SELECT * FROM Employees
WHERE LastName LIKE 'D_m%';
```

This will retrieve records that are made of three characters:

```
SELECT * FROM Employees
WHERE LastName LIKE '_ _ _';
```

■ Ordering data

Ordering by a single field:

```
SELECT * FROM Employees
ORDER BY LastName;
```

Ordering by a single field in ascending order:

```
SELECT * FROM Employees
ORDER BY LastName ASC;
```

Ordering by a single field in descending order:

```
SELECT * FROM Employees
ORDER BY LastName DESC;
```

Ordering by multiple fields:

```
SELECT * FROM Employees
ORDER BY DepartmentID, Salary DESC;
```

A3.3.3 SQL update queries

SQL statement	Explanation	Example
INSERT	Adds new records	INSERT INTO table_name (field1, field2, ...) VALUES (value1, value2, ...);
DELETE	Deletes records	DELETE FROM table_name WHERE condition;
UPDATE	Modifies records	UPDATE table_name SET field1 = value1, field2 = value2, ... WHERE condition;

Indexed columns optimize query performance, but updating data in indexed columns may impact performance. When an update is performed for an indexed column, the index needs to be updated as well, which can slow down the operation. Also, index updates can lead to blocking other transactions that need access to a specific record. To overcome those challenges, you can batch the updates to reduce the number of times the index needs to be changed; frequently rebuild or reorganize indexes to reduce fragmentation; or use partial indexes or filtered indexes to limit the scope of the index only to the most relevant records.

A3.3.4 SQL's aggregate functions (HL)

Aggregate functions are used to perform calculations on multiple records based on a given field. Such functions are AVERAGE, COUNT, MAX, MIN, SUM.

◆ **Aggregate functions:** functions used to perform calculations on multiple records based on a given field, e.g. AVERAGE, COUNT, MAX, MIN, SUM.

Aggregate function	Example
SUM returns the total value of a numerical field	SELECT SUM(Salary) FROM Employees;
COUNT returns the number of records that meet the given criteria	SELECT COUNT(EmployeeID) FROM Employees;
AVERAGE returns the average value of a numerical field	SELECT AVG(Salary) FROM Employees;
MIN returns the smallest value in a field	SELECT MIN(Salary) FROM Employees;
MAX returns the largest value in a field	SELECT MAX(Salary) FROM Employees;

Aggregate functions on grouped data

Using aggregate functions on grouped data aids reporting and decision-making. An example would be to display the number of employees for each department:

```
SELECT Department.DepartmentName, COUNT(Employees.EmployeeID)
AS ECount
FROM Employees
JOIN Department ON Department.DepartmentID = Employees.DepartmentID
GROUP BY Department.DepartmentName;
```

Another example is when you want to display the average salary for each department:

```
SELECT Department.DepartmentName, AVG(Employees.Salary) AS AvgSalary
FROM Employees
JOIN Department ON Employees.DepartmentID = Department.DepartmentID
GROUP BY Department.DepartmentName;
```

And yet another example would be to display the minimum and maximum salary per department:

```
SELECT DepartmentID, MIN(Salary) AS MinSal, MAX(Salary) AS MaxSal
FROM Employees
GROUP BY DepartmentID;
```

A3.3.5 Database views (HL)

◆ **View:** a virtual table based on the result set of a SELECT query. They do not store data themselves but provide a way to present the data from one or more tables in a customized manner.

A **view** is a virtual table based on the result set of a SELECT query. They do not store data themselves, but provide a way to present the data from one or more tables in a customized manner. Multiple views present different subsets of the data to different users, with the data being presented in different ways according to the user's needs.

There are several advantages of using views:

- **Data complexity hiding:** Views can encapsulate complex queries, simplifying the process for users to query data without needing to understand the underlying SQL.
- **Data consistency:** Views can present data in a consistent manner, even if the underlying tables are modified.
- **Data independence:** The database schema can be changed without affecting the user views.
- **Performance:** Views can increase performance by simplifying complex queries, by abstracting join operations into a single reusable object (the view).
- **Query simplification:** Queries can be simplified by breaking them down into smaller parts, hiding unnecessary details, applying filters and calculations and displaying the results in a view.
- **Read-only or updatable views:** When updating a view, the changes are passed through to the underlying tables from which the view was created, only if certain conditions are met. If those conditions are met, the view is updatable; otherwise, it is read-only. There are three conditions for a view to be updatable: it must be a subset of a single table or another updatable view; all base table fields excluded from the view definition should allow NULL values; and the SELECT statement of the view should not contain sub-queries (a DISTINCT predicate, a HAVING clause, aggregate functions, joined tables, user-defined functions or stored procedures).

■ **Security:** Views can limit access to specific attributes or records, providing a way to control which data users have access to. There are different types of database views. Some of those types are simple views, complex views or materialized (snapshot) views.

■ Simple views

Simple views are views based on a single table that do not include complex queries, such as aggregate functions or joins.

An example of a simple view is when displaying some fields from a table. In this case, three fields (EmployeeID, FirstName and LastName) are displayed from the Employees table.

```
CREATE VIEW EmpNames AS

SELECT EmployeeID, FirstName, LastName

FROM Employees;
```

■ Complex views

Complex views are views that include multiple tables and complex queries, such as aggregate functions or joins.

An example of a complex view would be to display data from the Employees and Department tables.

```
CREATE VIEW EmpDepartment AS

SELECT Employees.EmployeeID, Employees.LastName,
  Department.DepartmentName

FROM Employees

JOIN Department ON Employees.DepartmentID = Department.DepartmentID;
```

■ Materialized (snapshot) views

Materialized views are views that can be frequently refreshed that store pre-computed data sets derived from a SELECT query and stored for later use. As it avoids query re-run (which is used in regular views), it often delivers data faster. The code below is an example of a view that displays the employee ID and their salary for each employee in the Employees table.

Creating the snapshot view:

```
CREATE MATERIALIZED VIEW TotalSalaries AS

SELECT EmployeeID, SUM(Salary) AS TotalSal

FROM Employees

GROUP BY EmployeeID;
```

Querying the snapshot view:

```
SELECT * FROM TotalSalaries;
```

A3.3.6 How transactions maintain data integrity in a database (HL)

◼ ACID

Transactions are sequences of SQL operations that are executed as a single unit of work, ensuring data integrity and consistency.

ACID is an acronym that refers to the four properties that define a transaction:

- **Atomicity**

  Transactions are atomic (indivisible and treated as a whole). Either all the actions within a transaction are completed successfully, or none of them is. If any part of the transaction fails, the entire transaction is rolled back, and the database remains unaffected.

- **Consistency**

  Transactions ensure the data follows predefined rules or constraints. The database must be in a valid and expected state after the completion of a transaction.

- **Isolation**

  Transactions are isolated from each other to prevent interference. This ensures that concurrent execution of multiple transactions does not lead to data inconsistencies.

- **Durability**

  Once a transaction is committed and completed successfully, its changes are permanent. Even if the system fails, the changes made by a committed transaction are preserved. Durability is important because transaction data changes must be available even if the database is failing.

● Top tip!

When approaching exam questions, ensure you make efficient use of terminology. Often, candidates seem to understand the concepts, but they provide generic responses, with their answers often lacking precision. Terminology must be used precisely when writing responses to gain full marks.

◼ Transaction control language (TCL) commands

TCL commands in SQL are used to manage the transactions. Some of those commands are:

- `BEGIN TRANSACTION`: Used to start a new transaction in SQL.

- `COMMIT`: Used to save all changes made during the current transaction to the database. Once this operation is performed, the changes are permanent and visible to other users.

  ```
  BEGIN TRANSACTION;
  UPDATE Employees SET Salary = Salary + 100 WHERE EmployeeID = 1;
  UPDATE Employees SET Salary = Salary - 100 WHERE EmployeeID = 5;
  COMMIT;
  ```

  In the example above, the `UPDATE` statements for the two records are written and they are both saved once the `COMMIT` statement is reached.

■ ROLLBACK: Used to undo all changes made during the current transaction. It reverts the database to the state it was in before the transaction began.

In the example below, the two UPDATE statements are reversed, and so the table would reach its state prior to the updates being made.

```
BEGIN TRANSACTION;
UPDATE Employees SET Salary = Salary + 100 WHERE EmployeeID = 1;
UPDATE Employees SET Salary = Salary - 100 WHERE EmployeeID = 5;
ROLLBACK;
```

TOK

How has the development of database technology influenced the way we acquire and process knowledge?

The development of database technology has profoundly influenced the ways in which we acquire and process knowledge, touching on key areas such as the nature of knowledge, how it is shared and the ethical considerations involved.

Databases store vast amounts of data, but this raw data only becomes useful when it is processed into information and then interpreted as knowledge. This raises questions about the nature of knowledge itself. How do we distinguish between data, information and knowledge? How does the structure of a database influence what we consider to be true or valuable knowledge?

Databases rely on structured query languages (SQL) and other forms of data communication. The precision and clarity required in database queries contrast with the ambiguity and richness of natural language. This might lead to a more structured, but potentially limited, way of knowing. How does the structured nature of database queries influence our understanding of complex or ambiguous information?

REVIEW QUESTIONS

1 Discuss whether a view is physically stored in a database.
2 Define the term "database transaction".
3 Identify a reason a transaction may need to be rolled back by giving an example.
4 State the effect of rolling back a transaction.
5 Describe the four properties that describe a transaction.

Alternative databases and data warehouses (HL)

By the end of this chapter, you should be able to:
- ▶ A3.4.1 Outline the different types of databases as approaches to storing data
- ▶ A3.4.2 Explain the primary objectives of data warehouses in data management and business intelligence
- ▶ A3.4.3 Explain the role of online analytical processing (OLAP) and data mining for business
- ▶ A3.4.4 Describe the features of distributed databases

A3.4.1 Types of databases as approaches to storing data

Database models represent frameworks that determine the logical structure of a database and influence how data is stored, organized and manipulated. Different database models cater to different types of applications and requirements.

■ NoSQL databases

◆ **NoSQL database:** a database designed to handle large volumes of data and diverse data types, structured differently from relational databases.

NoSQL databases are designed to handle large volumes of data and diverse data types. They offer flexibility and scalability, making them suitable for modern web applications, such as e-commerce platforms, big data and real-time analytics.

NoSQL databases store data differently from relational databases. There are four main types of NoSQL databases: document databases, key-value databases, wide-column store databases and graph databases.

Document databases

In document databases, data is stored in documents like JSON (JavaScript Object Notation) objects. The documents contain pairs of fields and values, and document databases are used for content management systems and e-commerce platforms. They offer a flexible data model, suitable for semi-structured and unstructured data sets. They provide an easy way to represent hierarchical data, but a disadvantage is that they pose a risk of data redundancy and inconsistency. An example of such a database is MongoDB. Here is an example:

```
{
    "_id": "12345",
    "name": "blabla",
    "email": "blabla@car.com",
    "address": {
        "street": "bloblo street",
        "city": "omega city",
        },
    "services": ["transport", "tourism"]
}
```

Key-value databases

In key-value databases, data is stored as key-value pairs. Key-value databases are used for real-time analytics, caching and session management. They are simple databases that allow for fast read and write operations; however, they have limited querying capabilities. An example of a key-value database is Redis. Here is an example:

```
Key: user:12345
Value: {"name": "blabla", "email": "blabla@car.com", "job": "transporter"}
```

Wide-column store databases

In wide-column store databases, data is stored in tables, rows and dynamic columns. Different rows can have different sets of columns. They enable efficient retrieval of sparse and wide data and are used in big-data applications or real-time analytics. They are proven to be efficient for read and write operations on large data sets and are easy to scale horizontally; however, this is a complex model to implement. An example of a wide-column store database is Cassandra. Here is an example:

name	id	email	dateOfBirth
blabla	12345	blabla@car.com	
nathan	1234		12-12-2000

Graph databases

In graph databases, data is stored as nodes and edges in a graph structure. Nodes usually store data about people, places or things, and edges store data about the relationships between nodes. They are used for social-media platforms or recommendation engines. Graph databases are great for representing and querying complex relationships, but they use a specialized query language, and it is more complex to maintain and optimize them. An example of a graph database is OrientDB. Here are two examples of graph databases:

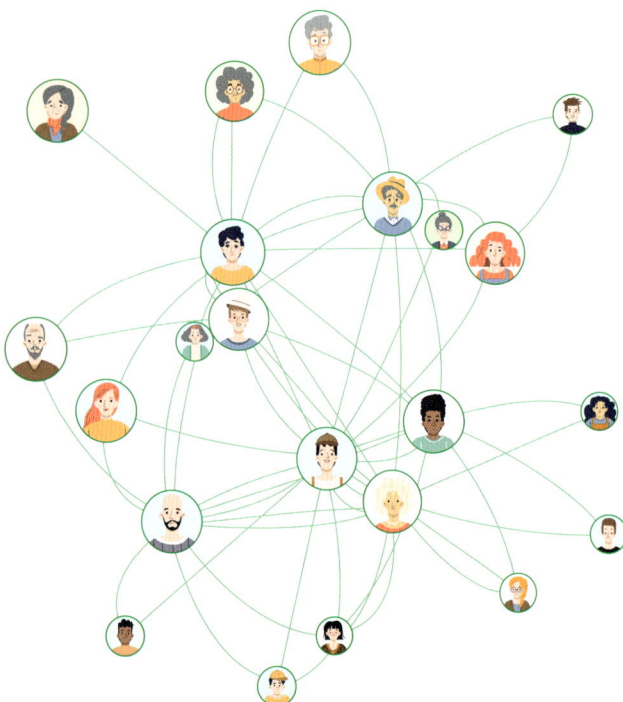

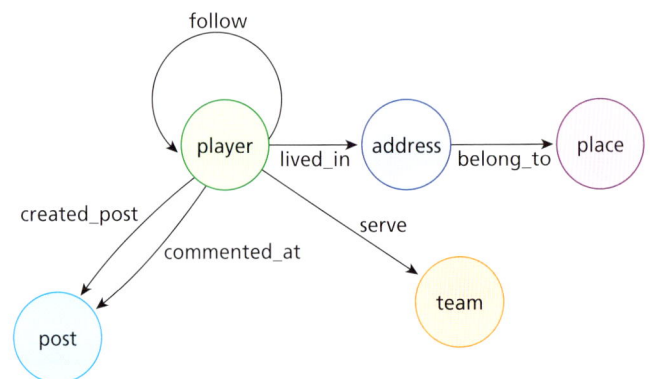

■ Cloud databases

Cloud databases are databases that run on cloud computing platforms, providing scalability, high availability and flexible resource management. They can be NoSQL or SQL databases.

In cloud databases, pricing is based on the use of system resources, which can be provisioned on demand as needed to meet processing workloads. Organizations can choose between two models when they opt for cloud databases:

■ **Self-managed database:** An infrastructure as a service (IaaS) environment, in which the database runs on a virtual machine on a system operated by a cloud provider. The provider manages and supports the cloud infrastructure, including servers, operating systems and storage devices. But the organization is responsible for database deployment, administration and maintenance, so it has full control over the database.

■ **Managed database services:** Fully managed by the vendor, both the system infrastructure and the database platform are managed for the customer; the vendor handles provisioning, backups, scaling, patching, upgrades and other basic database administration functions; organizations monitor the database, and they can collaborate with the vendor on some administrative functions.

Examples of database-as-a-service (DBaaS) are Amazon DynamoDB and Azure Cosmos DB. They are used for startups, IoT or web-scale applications; they are fully managed, offer pay-as-you-go pricing and the organization has limited control over the infrastructure.

Examples of managed databases are Amazon RDS, Google Cloud SQL and Azure SQL database. They are used for web and enterprise applications, and they depend on cloud providers and potentially have higher costs.

■ Spatial databases

Spatial databases are optimized to store and query data related to objects in space, including points, lines, polygons, 3D shapes and coordinates. They support spatial data types and spatial indexes to access the data, and they support geometric functions. They are used for Geographic Information Systems (GIS), location-based services and mapping applications. Examples are: Oracle Spatial, PostGis and MongoDB with Geospatial Indexes. Such models efficiently store and query spatial data, but they use complex data types and queries that require specialized knowledge or experts.

■ In-memory databases

In-memory databases store data entirely in the main memory (RAM) rather than on disk, providing extremely fast read and write operations. They are used for real-time analytics, caching and gaming applications. They allow for extremely fast data access and transaction processing, but they have low latency for read and write operations. Examples are Redis and Oracle TimesTen.

A3.4.2 Primary objectives of data warehouses in data management and business intelligence

A **data warehouse** is a specialized type of database designed for analytical purposes rather than transactional processing. It is used to store and analyse large volumes of historical data from various sources to support decision-making processes within organizations. A data warehouse represents a repository of stored data related to a specific subject. It includes tools to extract, transform and load data into the repository and tools to manage and retrieve the metadata.

◆ Cloud database: a database that runs on cloud computing platforms, providing scalability, high availability and flexible resource management.

◆ Spatial database: a database optimized to store and query data related to objects in space, including points, lines and polygons.

◆ In-memory database: a database that stores data entirely in the main memory (RAM) rather than on disk, providing extremely fast read and write operations.

◆ Data warehouse: a specialized type of database designed for analytical purposes rather than transactional processing.

The characteristics of data warehouses are discussed below:

■ Append-only

This characteristic means that, when data is loaded using append-only, existing records are not updated, but instead are appended to tables as new rows. Therefore, at a later stage, the tables will contain different versions of the records, so that how they changed over time can be analysed.

■ Subject-oriented

Data warehouses are organized around key subjects or themes relevant to the organization, such as sales, marketing or finance. They help with organizing and presenting data in a way that is aligned with the analytical needs and objectives of the organization.

■ Integrated data

Data from multiple operational systems and external sources are integrated into a single repository using ETL (**extract**, **transform**, **load**) processes. This consolidates information from multiple sources into a centralized repository, providing a single source of truth for the organization. When ETL is carried out, certain precautions should be taken, such as:

- ensuring the extraction does not affect the source system
- ensuring the extracted data can be read by the current system
- ensuring the different data formats being extracted can be converted to become readable by the system and can be formatted
- ensuring that the data is relevant to what the user wants to extract and utilize.

■ Time-variant

Data warehouses store historical data to support time-based analysis, enabling comparisons and trend analysis over time. Data warehousing is time-dependent because the content in the data warehouse is only valid for a period, because the data undergoes changes dynamically, and its focus on change over time is time-variant.

■ Non-volatile

Data once loaded into the data warehouse is rarely updated or deleted, ensuring data integrity and consistency for analytical purposes.

■ Optimized for query performance

Data warehouses seek to determine the most efficient way to execute a given query by considering a variety of query execution strategies. It directly impacts the speed and efficiency of data retrieval and analysis processes.

A3.4.3 The role of OLAP and data mining for business intelligence

Business intelligence refers to the technologies, applications and practices for collecting, integrating, analysing and presenting business information. Its aim is to support data-driven decision-making and improve business performance.

Online analytical processing (OLAP) and **data mining** are technologies used for data analysis and business intelligence, enabling organizations to extract valuable insights and make informed decisions from their data.

◆ **Extract:** to gather data from various operational databases, flat files, APIs, etc.

◆ **Transform:** to aggregate and transform data into a consistent format suitable for analysis.

◆ **Load:** to load transformed data into a data warehouse.

◆ **Business intelligence:** technologies, applications and practices for collecting, integrating, analysing and presenting business information.

◆ **Online analytical processing:** the software technology you can use to analyse business data from different points of view.

◆ **Data mining:** the process of sorting through large data sets to identify patterns and relationships that can help solve business problems through data analysis.

■ Role of OLAP in business intelligence

OLAP facilitates interactive analysis of multidimensional data, allowing users to explore data from various dimensions, such as time, product or region. It provides pre-aggregated views of data, which are optimized for querying and reporting, allowing for quick retrieval of summarized information, and supports decision-making processes. OLAP supports complex calculations and analytical functions directly on aggregated data, such as year-over-year comparisons. It supports data visualization techniques, such as charts, graphs and dashboards, and users can create ad hoc queries to explore data dynamically and answer specific business questions without needing to rely on predefined reports.

■ Role of data mining in business intelligence

Data mining involves discovering patterns and relationships within large data sets, using statistical algorithms, machine learning techniques and artificial intelligence to uncover hidden insights. It enables predictive modelling by analysing historical data to forecast future trends and outcomes, which helps with predicting customer behaviour, demand forecasting and risk assessment. As such, it helps in customer segmentation based on attributes and behaviours, by identifying customer segments with similar characteristics for targeted marketing campaigns and personalized customer experiences. It can detect anomalies in data, which may indicate fraud, errors or unusual patterns that require further investigation. Database segmentation can help to increase the profit of the organization, increase its reputation, increase the number of customers and provide better opportunities for growth.

Data mining techniques include the following:

- **Classification:**
  - □ A supervised learning technique that categorizes data into labels based on input features.
  - □ Used in spam email detection, sentiment analysis and credit scoring.

- **Clustering:**
  - □ An unsupervised learning technique that groups similar data points together into clusters based on their characteristics or proximity in feature space.
  - □ Finds patterns in customer behaviour by grouping and analysing variables to connect them; it can find previously unknown links that help in decision-making.
  - □ Used in market segmentation, customer profiling and anomaly detection.

- **Regression:**
  - □ Predicts continuous numerical values based on input variables, aiming to establish relationships between variables.
  - □ Used in sales forecasting, price predictions and risk assessment.

- **Association rule discovery:**
  - □ Identifies relationships or associations between items in large data sets, typically in transactional databases.
  - □ Looks at how entities or events are connected, and finds where one or more events may lead to another.
  - □ Correlates the presence of a set of items with another range of values for another set of variables, breaking up the data sets by variables such as location, age, gender.
  - □ Used in cross-selling recommendations.

- **Sequential pattern discovery:**
  - □ Discovers patterns or sequences in data, where events occur in a specific order, over a specific period of time (temporal patterns).
  - □ Used in web log analysis and clickstream analysis.

- **Anomaly detection:**
  - ☐ Identifies rare or unusual patterns in data that do not conform to expected behaviour.
  - ☐ Used in fraud detection, network security monitoring and equipment failure prediction.

A3.4.4 Features of distributed databases

A **distributed database** is a database made of two or more files located on different sites on the same network or on completely different networks. Although they are stored on different sites or different computer systems, they provide a fully functional, unified view of data to users and applications.

Distributed databases are used in different areas, such as online retailers using them to manage product catalogues, inventory and transactions across distributed warehouses, and telecom companies using them to manage subscriptions, network traffic analysis and service provisioning across different geographical locations.

Maintaining data consistency in a distributed system is crucial for ensuring the reliability, accuracy and trustworthiness of data across all nodes and users. This helps with reliable decision-making; avoiding data corruption; maintaining data integrity; and increasing user satisfaction and trust.

The role of atomicity, consistency, isolation and durability (ACID) to ensure reliable processing of transactions in distributed databases is as follows:

- **Atomicity**

  Atomicity ensures that distributed transactions are either committed across all nodes or rolled back completely if any part of the transaction fails. This prevents partial updates and maintains data consistency across nodes.

- **Consistency**

  Consistency in distributed systems ensures that all nodes have access to the same consistent view of data after a transaction is completed.

- **Isolation**

  Isolation prevents interference between concurrent transactions executing on different nodes. It prevents the modification of the same data item by two different transactions.

- **Durability**

  Durability ensures that committed transactions are reliably stored and replicated across distributed nodes.

The features of distributed databases are described below:

Concurrency control

Concurrency control refers to techniques used to manage simultaneous access and modifications to shared data across multiple nodes in a distributed database. It ensures that transactions execute correctly and maintain consistency, despite potential conflicts that may arise due to concurrent operations. Locking mechanisms can be used to enforce isolation and prevent conflicting operations, or unique timestamps can be assigned to each transaction to determine the order of execution. For example, different systems may attempt to access the same data at the same time, such as two systems attempting to update the same piece of data. If one starts the update and then the second finishes before the first is saved,

♦ **Distributed database:** a database made of two or more files located on different sites on the same network or on completely different networks.

this could potentially lead to inconsistent updates. In such cases, the solution is to isolate the transactions; when one system is accessing the data, that transaction is locked, and it is released only after the transaction is committed.

Data consistency

All copies of data across distributed nodes are synchronized and reflect the most recent, correct state of information. Strong consistency models ensure that all updates to data are visible to all nodes immediately after they occur.

Data partitioning

Data partitioning improves performance, scalability and manageability by distributing data across multiple nodes or servers. It allows databases to handle large volumes of data and high transaction rates efficiently.

Data security

By implementing robust security measures and continuously monitoring for threats and vulnerabilities, organizations can mitigate risks and safeguard sensitive data across distributed environments effectively. To achieve this, organizations can:

- encrypt sensitive data stored on disks or databases to protect against unauthorized access
- define roles and permissions that restrict access to data based on users' roles
- use strong authentication mechanisms (multifactor authentication) to verify user identities before granting access to the database.

Distribution transparency

Distribution transparency refers to the ability to access and manipulate data across multiple nodes or servers in a transparent and seamless manner.

Fault tolerance

Fault tolerance refers to systems' ability to continue operating and providing services even in the presence of hardware failures, software errors or network disruptions, by using data-redundancy systems, monitoring and recovery in case of failure detection.

Global query processing

Global query processing involves the coordination and execution of queries that span multiple distributed nodes or databases.

Location transparency

Location transparency refers to the ability of a system to hide the physical or logical location of resources and services (network address or server details) from users and applications. It ensures that users can access resources or services without being aware of their specific location, simplifying system management.

Replication

Replication addresses the creation and maintenance of copies of data across multiple nodes, servers or locations, which enhances data availability, reliability and performance.

Scalability

Scalability refers to the ability of the database system to handle increasing amounts of data and user requests by efficiently distributing workload across multiple nodes or servers. It ensures the database can grow to meet performance and capacity requirements as demands increase.

ACTIVITY

Social skills: Listen actively to other perspectives and ideas – there are different ways to solve a problem, some better than others; listen to advice and try new techniques and problem-solving strategies. In any collaborative environment, actively listening to the perspectives and ideas of others is crucial for effective problem-solving and decision-making. Different individuals bring diverse experiences, viewpoints and approaches to the table, each offering unique insights into how a problem can be addressed. By carefully listening to others, you not only gain a broader understanding of the problem, but you also become aware of innovative solutions that you might not have considered on your own.

REVIEW QUESTIONS

1   Define the term "data mining".

2   Define the term "data warehouse".

3   Describe how regression is used in data mining.

4   Describe the concurrency control feature in distributed databases. Explain how this can be achieved.

5   Explain the role of integrated data in a data warehouse.

6   Outline two methods to ensure the security of a data warehouse.

7   Compare classification and sequential pattern discovery in data mining.

8   Outline the differences between a database view and a data warehouse.

Linking questions

1   What processes are needed to store data in database structures so that they can be used in machine learning? (A4)

2   How does database programming in SQL differ from programming computationally in a high-level language? (B2)

3   To what extent is the effectiveness of the distributed database determined by the network that connects the various tables? (A2)

4   How could machine learning be applied to databases? (A4)

5   How do programming languages interact with databases to store, retrieve and manipulate data? (B2)

EXAM PRACTICE QUESTIONS

1 A telecommunications company is designing a relational database to store its desk tickets. The database will have the following tables:

`Operator(OperatorID, OperatorName, Location)`
`Engineer(EngineerID, EngFirstName, EngLastName, EngLocation, Salary)`
`Ticket(TicketNo, Location, Status, OperatorID, TicketDate, TicketPriority)`
`Supplier(SupplierID, Email, PhoneNo)`
`Product(ProductID, ProductName, Price, SupplierID)`
`ProductOrder(TicketNo, OrderID, ProductID, Quantity, EngineerID)`

   a Identify the primary key for each of the tables described above. [3]
   b Identify three benefits of a relational database. [3]
   c Construct an ERD for the relational database. [3]
   d Construct the SQL DDL instructions to create the `Ticket` table. [1]
   e Construct the SQL DML statements to return the total product quantity ordered by the engineer with the engineer ID D893. [4]
   f Identify a foreign key in the `Product` table. [1]
   g State whether the database is normalized and whether it is in third normal form (3NF). [1]
   h Describe the characteristics of a database that is in third normal form (3NF). [3]
   i The following table is an example of the `Engineer` table.

EngineerID	EngFirstName	EngLastName	EngLocation	Salary
D893	Daniel	Buchidau	Trier	7000
D894	Constantin	Constantin	Heidelberg	6000
D895	Martin	Bond	Cologne	6500

     Define the term "tuple". Give an example of a tuple from the `Engineer` table. [2]
   j State the number of fields in the `Engineer` table. [1]
   k Construct an SQL statement to increase the salary of the engineer with the ID D894 by 300. [2]
   l Construct SQL statements to update the `Engineer` table to include two more fields: one called `Experience`, to store how many years of experience each engineer has, and one called `IncreaseDate`, which includes the date when the last salary raise occurred. [4]
   m Construct an SQL script to find the average salary in the `Engineer` table. [2]
2 State what a transaction is and identify the four properties that define a transaction. [2]
3 Identify three advantages of using views in a database. [3]
4 Explain three data mining techniques. [6]
5 Compare cloud and spatial databases. [4]
6 Describe two features of distributed databases. [2]
7 Identify and compare a NoSQL database with a relational database. [4]
8 Explain the role of online analytical processing (OLAP) in business intelligence. [3]
9 Explain the COMMIT transaction control language (TCL) command. [1]
10 Other than COMMIT, identify another transaction control language (TCL) command. [1]

A4 Machine learning

Machine learning fundamentals

What principals and approaches should be considered to ensure machine learning models produce accurate results ethically?

By the end of this chapter, you should be able to:
▶ A4.1.1 Describe the types of machine learning and their applications in the real world
▶ A4.1.2 Describe the hardware requirements for various scenarios where machine learning is deployed

---

◆ **Generative AI:** a form of artificial intelligence capable of generating text, images, audio, video and other digital artefacts, usually in response to a prompt. It is a form experiencing rapid advances at the time of writing.

◆ **Machine learning:** a branch of AI where computers learn from data and experiences to perform specific tasks or solve specific problems, without being explicitly programmed to do so.

◆ **Artificial intelligence:** computer technology able to perform tasks and make decisions in a manner that imitates human intelligence. There are two main forms of AI: narrow (or weak) AI is designed to perform specific tasks or solve specific types of problems; general (or strong) AI processes human-level intelligence and can operate across a range of domains. While speculation persists that general AI is "close", at this time only narrow AI technology is available.

A4.1.1 Types of machine learning and their applications

TOK

What counts as knowledge?

Machine learning models "learn" from data, which raises questions about what constitutes knowledge.

Views on knowledge often distinguish between knowledge gained through experience (empirical) and knowledge gained through reasoning (rational). Machine learning models acquire knowledge empirically by processing vast amounts of data. However, unlike humans, machines do not "understand" or reason about this data in the human sense. This raises the question: Can the patterns and predictions that machines generate be considered "knowledge", or are they simply data-processed outputs?

Welcome to the world of machine learning! We live in a time of exciting growth and rapid innovation in machine learning. **Generative AI** is making global headlines and has changed the way we live and work in a very short timeframe. Speculation is rife that "general AI" is not far from becoming reality. Certainly, it is an exciting topic, but what are machine learning and artificial intelligence, and how do they work? Gaining an understanding of what is happening behind the scenes is the goal of this chapter.

This chapter will not seek to dissect the details of the latest, greatest, news-making developments in the field. That would be a fool's errand as it would be obsolete before the book is printed. Instead, the aim is to give you a solid understanding of the core theories and techniques that form the basis of the entire field of machine learning. From these foundations, you will be in a much stronger position to understand the true implications of modern developments occurring in the field.

Before proceeding any further, it is important to clarify and differentiate between the terms **machine learning** (ML) and **artificial intelligence** (AI). Artificial intelligence is a broad field that seeks to create systems capable of performing tasks that typically require human intelligence.

Take the time to appreciate the differences between types of machine learning: supervised, unsupervised, reinforcement, deep learning and transfer learning. Know what scenarios each is best suited for, and the typical algorithms used in each category. In this topic, terms and definitions are foundational for answering theoretical questions accurately. Using terminology in an incorrect context will cost marks.

♦ **Neural network:** a computer algorithm that imitates the design of the human brain by using a set of interconnected nodes for the processing and analysing of data.

This can include, but is not limited to, reasoning, learning, perception, problem-solving, understanding and interaction. Machine learning is a subset of artificial intelligence that focuses on the learning aspect of AI. It seeks to teach computers to learn from data, identify the patterns in that data and make decisions based on what it has learned, with minimal human intervention. Implementing machine learning programmatically is heavily reliant on the mathematics of statistics, linear algebra and calculus.

Machine learning applications are being increasingly used throughout commerce, industry, research and government. They are used for everything from market analysis to robotics; from generative art to diagnosing medical conditions. The applications for machine learning will only grow as the technology continues to develop.

Within machine learning, there are many further subcategories we will consider in A4.3 Machine learning approaches. These can be broadly described as:

- supervised learning: linear regression
- supervised learning: classification
- unsupervised learning: clustering
- unsupervised learning: association rule
- reinforcement learning
- genetic algorithms
- artificial neural networks
- convolutional neural networks.

■ Deep learning

The term "deep learning" is used to imply the use of a **neural network** within a machine learning algorithm. There are a variety of machine learning techniques that work perfectly fine without the need for a neural network, so the "deep learning" term is used to distinguish between those that do and those that do not make use of a neural network. For example, you can refer to "reinforcement learning" and "deep reinforcement learning".

A neural network is where algorithms and data structures have been constructed in such a manner as to replicate biology's understanding of how the brain functions: as an interconnected network of neurons, each of which has various input connections and generates an output on the basis of the combination of inputs.

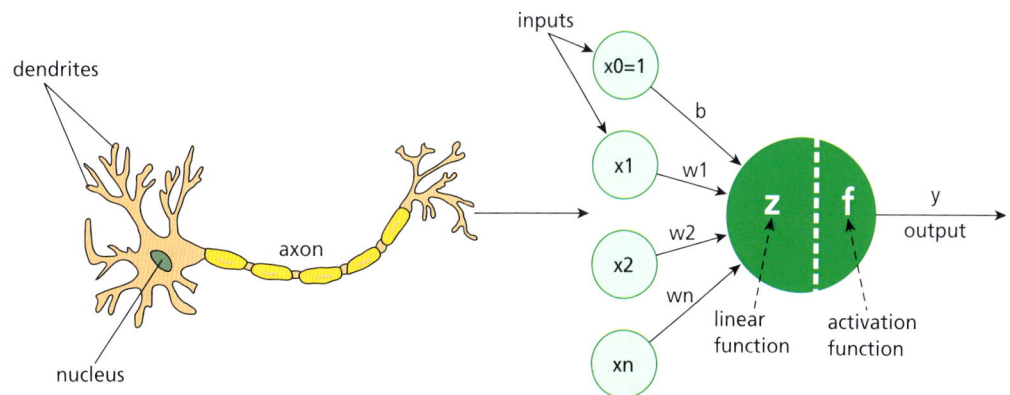

■ Comparison of a biological neuron with that used by artificial neural networks

A more detailed examination of how neural networks function will be provided in A4.3.8 Artificial neural networks.

Common mistake

Deep learning is a subset of machine learning. Deep learning is not separate from machine learning, but rather is a specific approach within it. It utilizes layers of neural networks to extract progressively higher-level features from the input. Machine learning includes many other types of algorithms that do not require neural networks.

■ Supervised learning

◆ **Supervised learning:** when a machine learning algorithm is provided a data set of pairs of items, where the pair comprises a value and what response the network should provide if it sees that value. By learning the answers to the values given, the network will make generalizations to be able to estimate the answer when given a previously unseen value.

◆ **Regression:** machine learning where the output generated should be a numerical value.

◆ **Classification:** machine learning where the output generated should be a category, chosen from among a discrete set of categories available.

Supervised learning refers to an algorithm that is trained on labelled data sets. These data sets comprise example input values, and the correct output response that should be given if the algorithm sees something resembling that input. Generally, the larger and better the data set, the more accurate the results that will be produced by the supervised learning algorithm. Data sets used by the major technology companies contain many millions of records.

Supervised learning can be used for regression and classification tasks.

A **regression** task is where the algorithm is predicting a numerical value for the output within an allocated range, for example:

- A grade-prediction algorithm might take inputs of hours studied, attendance record, class participation, scores on previous tests, hours spent on homework; and output a final predicted grade in the range 0–100.

- A weather-forecasting algorithm might take inputs of historical temperatures for each day over the last week, humidity, wind speed, air pressure; and output a predicted temperature for the coming day in a given range.

A **classification** task is where the algorithm predicts which category the input item belongs to, for example an image recognition algorithm might input an image and seek to classify it as either a dog or a muffin.

Common mistake

Confusing the goals of regression and classification

Be clear about the difference in outputs between regression and classification tasks in supervised learning. Regression models predict a continuous output (numerical values), whereas classification models predict categorical outputs (class labels). For example, predicting the price of a house based on its features (like size and location) is a regression problem because price is a continuous variable. On the other hand, determining whether an email is spam or not spam is a classification problem because there are discrete categories (spam or not spam) to choose from.

A music genre classification algorithm may input song tempo, rhythm, pitch, instruments used; and output the music genre as either pop, rock, hip-hop, classical, and so on.

A handwriting recognition algorithm may input an image of a character and seek to classify it as an individual letter, number or punctuation mark.

Unsupervised learning

Unsupervised learning is where the algorithm is constructed to identify patterns or structures within its data sets without being provided with an explicit label indicating the correct output. This may be because the nature of the data involved doesn't lend itself to having a "correct" response paired with it, or because the algorithm is constantly learning based on user interactions that don't have a fixed right or wrong answer. Examples include:

- An algorithm that seeks to identify a user's social group: The input data may consist of social-media activity such as likes, comments and follows. The algorithm could analyse this data to identify other users with mutual acquaintances or similar interests. Interestingly, this type of social-group analysis can take place without needing any content from the messages or chats between the parties involved. This is why social-media companies such as WhatsApp are perfectly happy to offer end-to-end encrypted messaging as, even without the message content, just knowing how many messages are exchanged between each pair of users is enough to perform social-group analysis.

- Retail stores use unsupervised learning to find associations and correlations between the different products that customers purchase, and identify similarities in purchasing behaviour and preferences. The reason that so many brands run customer loyalty schemes is it allows them to build a profile of data to match against other customers, from which they can tailor marketing strategies.

- Media companies such as Netflix, Spotify and YouTube use unsupervised learning to train recommendation systems to refine their suggestions to users for future watching or listening.

Reinforcement learning

Reinforcement learning is where the algorithm looks at its input data and decides on a particular output, and is then informed how good or bad that decision was after the fact. It uses that information to refine future actions when presented with a similar situation. Reinforcement learning can be thought of as learning from trial and error.

Some common situations where reinforcement learning is used include:

- **Gaming:** Reinforcement learning algorithms can be trained to act as AI players or bots within computer games.

- **Robotics:** Reinforcement learning can be used to teach a robot how to walk, pick up objects or perform other mechanical tasks. As a subtype of robotics, autonomous self-driving cars also make use of reinforcement learning to better and more safely navigate the complexities of roads and traffic.

- **Finance:** Reinforcement learning bots can trade securities on the market and receive feedback based on whether the bot made or lost money on the trade.

- **Recommendation systems:** Reinforcement learning can also be part of a suite of algorithms used in generating user recommendations. The engagement of the user (did they watch or listen to the suggested item?) can be used to provide feedback to the algorithm to refine future recommendations.

◆ **Unsupervised learning:** a method of machine learning where the data set does not include the "answers" or expected outputs for the data provided. The algorithm will attempt to discover the patterns on its own.

◆ **Reinforcement learning:** machine learning by trial and error. Based on what it has learned at any moment in time, the algorithm selects an action to take in a given environment. The environment provides feedback (called a "reward"), which the algorithm will use to learn from and refine its decision-making process moving forward.

■ Transfer learning

Transfer learning is where the knowledge gained from solving one problem can be used to help solve a different but somewhat related problem. The benefit of transfer learning is that it requires less data, as the algorithm is already partially trained and may just require a little fine-tuning for the new task being asked of it.

Consider the following examples:

- **Image recognition:** Given a model that has been trained on a massive data set such as ImageNet (over a million labelled images and 1000 different categories), transfer learning could take that model and fine-tune it to recognize specific types of objects, such as a species of flower or breed of dog. The model would already be adept at processing images and easily able to identify features such as edges and shapes, so it would only need to learn how to distinguish between the new categories.

- **Speech recognition:** Using a generalized model that has been trained on spoken language to transcribe it into text, transfer learning can be used to adapt it to work with particular accents or specialized jargon for use within a particular industry.

- **Customized chatbot:** By using a publicly available pre-trained LLaMA (large language model meta AI), a company might fine-tune it by training it on customer-service logs to create a chatbot that can be added to its website for handling domain-specific queries.

- **Customized image generators:** Pre-trained models for tools such as Stable Diffusion can be further extended and fine-tuned to generate images that mimic a particular artistic style, or be specialized in images for a particular industry or domain. This can be done relatively quickly and easily without the burden of redoing the massive task of original training that went into the underlying model.

A4.1.2 Hardware requirements

The hardware required for machine learning purposes will continue to innovate and evolve throughout the lifetime of this text. Accordingly, this section is not going to make recommendations as to specific model numbers of processors, but will rather discuss the broad categories of hardware technology available and their various use cases.

■ Computing platforms

Standard laptops

The starting point is obviously the standard laptop available on the retail market. At the time of writing, this might be an i7 processor with 16 GB or 32 GB of RAM, or an Apple Silicon equivalent.

These machines are generally limited to small-scale machine learning tasks, such as the development and testing of a simple machine learning model. For educational purposes, there is a lot that can be done with a standard laptop, but you would not want to be training a commercial-grade machine learning model with such equipment as it would be too slow, and lack sufficient memory or storage.

Some recent developments do aim to improve the capacity of standard laptops when it comes to machine learning. One is the introduction of Apple Silicon M processors into Apple MacBooks. Apple integrates the CPU, GPU, neural engine and other components into a single system-on-a-chip (SoC) structure, allowing better performance and energy efficiencies. By integrating the CPU and GPU functions on to a single chip, they pool and share the same memory. This is in contrast to the traditional approach of GPUs having their own dedicated memory, separate from the RAM used by the CPU. This is why those with an Apple Silicon-based computer are often able to perform machine learning tasks that traditional Intel laptop owners are unable to do without access to a dedicated GPU.

Not wanting to allow Windows users to be left behind, Microsoft has launched its Microsoft Copilot AI-supported branding, which requires laptops to have an integrated neural processing unit (NPU), which is discussed further in the section regarding CPUs coming up.

Dedicated workstation

After a standard laptop, the next step would be the purchase of a dedicated desktop workstation with a GPU, such as an NVIDIA RTX.

Having a true GPU can offer an order of magnitude improvement in processing speeds for machine learning calculations and would serve as an excellent platform for some quite sophisticated projects.

The primary advantage of a GPU is its parallel processing capabilities, which come from having thousands of small processing cores that are optimized for parallel processing. Machine learning algorithms often involve performing the same computations on large amounts of data. GPUs can perform these same calculations on different values simultaneously, whereas a CPU has to queue them up for processing one by one.

Edge devices

Edge devices refer to computing systems that perform data processing at or near the location where data is being generated, rather than relying on centralized computing resources such as the cloud.

Processing data locally reduces the need to send data back and forth to a distant data centre. This reduction in data being transmitted has the added benefit of improving privacy and security.

The downside is that you are still committed to investing in the physical hardware infrastructure yourself, along with all the maintenance workload associated with it.

Cloud-based platforms

To perform training on large or complex models generally requires the use of online cloud-based platforms (in lieu of investing in the massive infrastructure yourself). Cloud platforms are accessible over the internet and provide services on demand to users worldwide.

These cloud providers allow you to vary the combination and specifications of CPUs, GPUs and Tensor Processing Units (TPUs) available for your project on demand. They can also scale to provide large quantities of RAM, storage and network connectivity, as required. The cloud-based services are also useful for deployment of your model as an API for other systems to access.

The main downside with cloud-based platforms is the dependency and reliance your project will have on an external provider. You have to trust their data and network security arrangements; you have to transmit your data to their network to have it perform tasks for you; and you are committing yourself to the monthly subscription costs involved. The flexibility of cloud-based systems always comes with a cost, and this should not be treated lightly.

At the time of writing, the major industry leaders that provide cloud-based platforms with machine learning specialist equipment available include AWS, Google Cloud and Microsoft Azure. A good tool for getting started with minimal set-up requirements is Google Colab; it allows you to create a Python Notebook and utilize GPU or TPU technology just by changing the settings in the Runtime menu.

High-performance computing (HPC) centres

In contrast to the publicly available, user-pays approach of cloud-based providers, HPC centres are dedicated facilities designed to support large-scale scientific or academic research objectives. In this way, access to an HPC is more restricted, often requiring membership; affiliation with an academic or research institution; or specific research grants or time allocation processes.

They are data centres that have been designed to be suitable for highly demanding workloads that require sustained high-performance computing resources. They are built around a model of catering to resource-intensive computational tasks, not an as-a-service model.

Many universities have made investments in their own HPCs for use by their research students.

■ Processors for machine learning

Having considered the various platforms available for accessing the computing power necessary for machine learning, it is time to review the electronics within the computers that make machine learning happen.

Central processing units (CPUs)

CPUs are the generalized processors inside all modern computer systems. They are designed to perform a wide range of computing operations, are highly flexible and can process complex tasks. They are not specialized devices designed specifically for machine learning. While it is feasible to perform some introductory machine learning tasks with a CPU, they are generally limited to tasks that do not require intensive parallel processing.

Neural processing units (NPUs) have recently been integrated alongside traditional CPUs in consumer-level laptops. NPUs are specialized processors designed specifically to handle the computations required for neural networks and deep learning, such as matrix and vector operations. By having specialized processors in the computing device, it provides faster processing times and lower power consumption for AI-related tasks, compared to general-purpose CPUs.

As of 2024, laptops marketed as being Microsoft Copilot AI-supported include NPUs with a minimum capability of 40 TOPS (trillion operations per second).

Graphics processing units (GPUs)

GPUs contain hundreds or thousands of small cores designed for highly parallel tasks such as rendering graphics. The GPU allows all the cores to perform the same calculation on different values simultaneously, so if there are large arrays that need processing, where every element requires the same operation performed, GPUs provide significant time savings. GPUs excel at parallel processing of matrix and vector operations, which is the very mathematics that forms the basis of neural networks.

The presence of a dedicated GPU can often produce training speed improvements of up to ten times over using just a CPU.

Tensor Processing Units (TPUs)

Building on the idea of the GPU, the TPU was custom-designed by Google specifically for **tensor** computations. They are optimized for high volume, low precision calculations to increase the efficiency of neural network tasks. Low precision in this context typically means calculations occur at a maximum of 16 bits, in contrast to the 32 bits or 64 bits in a normal GPU. Machine learning generally does not require that level of precision, so 16 bits or even 8 bits will do the job.

> ◆ **Tensor:** a mathematical term for an array with three or more dimensions. A single number (no dimensions) is known as a "scalar". A one-dimensional array of numbers is known as a "vector". A two-dimensional array of numbers is known as a "matrix". Three or more dimensions is known as a "tensor".

At the heart of a TPU is a large matrix multiplication unit. Matrix multiplication is fundamental to neural networks, so having a unit within the processor specifically optimized for this task helps make TPUs well suited for machine learning.

The TensorFlow library is tailored to make use of TPUs when available, and Google Cloud services, such as Google Colab, make TPUs easily available for the general public.

Application-specific integrated circuits (ASICs)

ASICs are custom-designed for a specific use rather than general-purpose computing. They are engineered to perform a particular set of tasks with optimal efficiency. They offer peak performance and efficiency for these tasks, but lack the general-purpose flexibility of a CPU.

If your machine learning workload can be precisely defined and won't change much over time, an ASIC may perform these tasks faster than a GPU or TPU as, while these are optimized for parallelism, they are still generalized processors.

Due to the degree of specialization involved, ASICs tend to be more energy efficient and have lower operating costs over the long term. The downside is that the upfront cost is typically very high as the chips require custom design and development. This means they are really only viable where a machine learning application is going to be deployed on a very large scale, as the per-unit cost of the ASIC will decrease significantly with scale when mass-produced.

Examples of well-known, mass-produced ASICs include the Apple A-series chips used in iPhones and Qualcomm's Snapdragon.

You should conduct some research into the current state-of-the-art ASICs available for machine learning operations at the time of reading, and be familiar with what differentiates them from just using a typical GPU or TPU.

Field-programmable gate arrays (FPGAs)

FPGAs can be programmed and reprogrammed to perform specialized computing tasks, offering a balance between the flexibility of CPUs / GPUs and the efficiency of ASICs.

As such, they are ideal for prototyping machine learning models or applications that require custom hardware acceleration, however that may change over time.

FPGAs are used for high-frequency trading systems where microseconds can make a significant difference in the profitability of trades.

●Common mistake

Confusing the differences between each of the processor types

There are a lot of separate technologies listed in this topic, many of which you will not have had personal hands-on experience with. That makes it harder to have an intuitive understanding of the differences between them.

- **ASICs** are designed for specific tasks and are not reprogrammable.
- **FPGAs** are versatile and can be reprogrammed.
- **GPUs** are great for parallel processing tasks.
- **TPUs** are specialized chips designed by Google, optimized for tensor calculations in deep learning for large-scale models.
- **NPUs** are designed to accelerate neural network computations for consumer-grade devices.

Adapt the following as a guide to help determine which is the best device for a given scenario.

- For large and complete models, does it require real-time processing?
  - ☐ Yes: Consider GPUs for their parallel-processing capabilities
  - ☐ No: TPUs might be a better choice for batch processing with high efficiency in tensor operations
- For real-time inference (using a model for decision-making after training), is the model deployed on edge devices?
  - ☐ Yes: NPUs or ASICs, for optimized power and efficiency
  - ☐ No: Consider FPGAs for flexibility or ASICs for efficiency if the task won't change

- For models requiring future flexibility, are future updates expected?
  - ☐ Yes: FPGAs, due to their reprogrammability
  - ☐ No: ASICs or GPUs, depending on whether the task is more about speed or parallel processing
- Is low cost more important than cutting-edge performance?
  - ☐ Yes: Consider older generation GPUs or cloud-based solutions where hardware costs can be easily absorbed
- Will there be a need to quickly scale processing power?
  - ☐ Yes: Cloud GPUs or TPUs can offer scalable resources as required

REVIEW QUESTIONS

1 A hospital is integrating a system that can automatically diagnose diseases from patient-imaging data.

    a Describe whether this system should be classified as artificial intelligence, machine learning or deep learning.

    b Distinguish between regression-based and classification-based machine learning.

2 An email client uses a program to sort incoming emails into "Primary", "Social", "Promotions" and "Spam" folders.

    a Identify whether this is an example of supervised or unsupervised learning.

    b Describe your reasoning for this choice.

3 An autonomous vehicle company transfers the knowledge from a model trained in one city to a new model designed to navigate another city.

    a Define "transfer learning".

    b Outline how this is an example of transfer learning.

    c Outline one possible limitation to the effectiveness of this approach.

    d The original model was trained from thousands of hours of driving on roads under human supervision to monitor and correct it when required. Describe the form of machine learning used for the original model.

4 A tech start-up is planning to deploy a large-scale machine learning system to predict stock prices in real time.

    a Identify one type of hardware that would be critical for processing large volumes of real-time data in this context.

    b Outline one reason that this type of hardware is suitable for real-time data processing in machine learning applications.

    c Discuss one potential limitation of the identified hardware when used for machine learning.

5 A university plans to implement an AI-driven system to analyse video lectures for enhancing online learning experiences.

    a Identify two types of hardware that could be used for conducting machine learning processing of video data in real time.

    b For the two types of hardware identified, outline one possible reason for selecting each device over the other.

A4.2

Data preprocessing (HL)

SYLLABUS CONTENT

By the end of this chapter, you should be able to:
▶ A4.2.1 Describe the significance of data cleaning
▶ A4.2.2 Describe the role of feature selection
▶ A4.2.3 Describe the importance of dimensionality reduction

A4.2.1 Data cleaning

High-quality data builds high-quality models. If the training data is full of errors or redundant features, the model will learn from these inaccuracies and make poor predictions.

Taking the time to ensure your data is as clean as possible will reap rewards with respect to efficiency and accuracy. There are several steps that may be useful for cleaning your data set.

1   **Handling outliers**: Statistical methods, such as using the interquartile range or Z-scores, can detect outlying data. Once found, depending on the context, outlying data may be capped, transformed or removed as appropriate.

◆ **Outlier:** a data point that deviates from the typical pattern of values in a data set, indicating a possible unusual or erroneous value that should be discounted.

Python

```python
import numpy as np
# Create random array of values between 0 and 100
# Set one extreme value to act as an outlier
data = np.random.randint(0, 100, size=1000)
data[999] = 937
# Calculate outliers via Z-scores
mea = np.mean(data)
std_dev = np.std(data)
z_scores = (data - mean) / std_dev
threshold = 3 # Outliers if 3 stddev from mean
outliers = data[np.abs(z_scored) > threshold]
print("mean", mean, "stddev", std_dev)
print("Outliers:", outliers)
# Calculate outliers via IQR
q1 = np.percentile(data, 25)
q3 = np.percentile(data, 75)
iqr = q3-q1
cutoff = 1.5 * iqr
lower_bound = q1 - cutoff
upper_bound = q3 + cutoff
outliers = data[(data < lower_bound) | (data > upper_bound)]
print("Outliers:", outliers)
```

2 **Removing duplicate data:** Identifying and removing duplicate data will assist in preventing the model from becoming biased towards over-represented values. For data sets where individual records contain a large number of variables, calculating and comparing SHA256 hash values can be a useful mechanism for detecting duplicates (see Section B4.1.6 for more about hash values). Depending on the context of the model, near-duplicate data may also need to be consolidated into a single record.

3 **Identifying incorrect data:** Process your data through validation rules to ensure obviously incorrect data can be found and removed. This may mean checking the ranges given for dates and times, or amounts given for currency values, and so on. Set sensible limits and have your program detect anomalies for possible manual checking.

4 **Filtering irrelevant data:** If there is no measurable correlation between an input variable and the outcome variable, it may be completely irrelevant and contribute nothing to the predictive power of the model. Keeping such data in the training process is only going to make the process less efficient and less accurate.

Additionally, just because data may appear to be correlated doesn't mean it is. As the Spurious Correlations website demonstrates, if you compare enough unrelated data sets, you will find correlations that are, in fact, not.

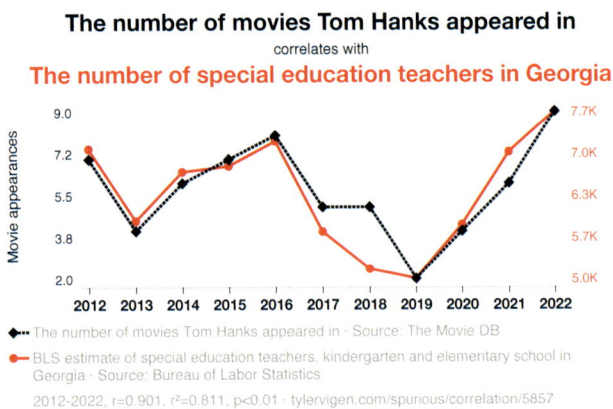

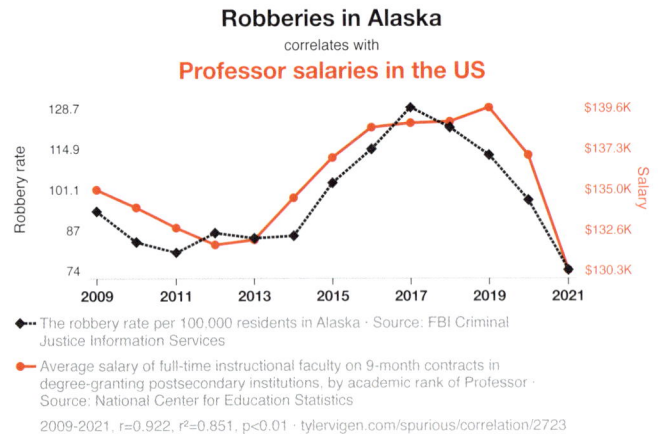

The number of movies Tom Hanks appeared in
correlates with
The number of special education teachers in Georgia

2012-2022, r=0.901, r²=0.811, p<0.01 · tylervigen.com/spurious/correlation/5857

■ Tom Hanks movies vs special education teachers in Georgia

Robberies in Alaska
correlates with
Professor salaries in the US

2009-2021, r=0.922, r²=0.851, p<0.01 · tylervigen.com/spurious/correlation/2723

■ Robberies in Alaska vs professor salaries

5 **Transform improperly formatted data:** Data may be incorrectly formatted but easily correctable to ensure consistency in what is presented to the machine learning model, for example:
   ☐ Ensure all dates are in a consistent style (not having a mix of day / month / year, month / day / year, or ISO yyyy-mm-dd formats).
   ☐ Ensure numerical values are formatted, and to the same level of precision.
   ☐ Ensure images are correctly rotated and oriented, and of matching ratio and size.

6 **Missing data:** Sometimes it may be necessary to use models to predict missing values to ensure full coverage of the data set. Mean / mode imputation, k-nearest neighbours or regression models could be used for this, if required.

7 **Normalization and standardization:** Many machine learning algorithms will benefit from completing preprocessing of data by performing the statistical operations of normalization and standardization to scale data to a standard range or distribution.
   ☐ Normalization can be used to rescale input data to a range of [0,1] or [−1,1], which is useful when various features (input variables) have different scales.
   ☐ Standardization can be used to transform the input data to have a mean score of 0 and standard deviation of 1 (Gaussian distribution). (Note that it is not mathematically possible for the range to be [−1,1] and to have a standard deviation of 1; you need to determine which is required for your model.)

Python

```python
import numpy as np
data = np.array([10, 20, 30, 40, 50])
# Normalize the data to have a mean of 0, and have range [-1, 1]
data_mean_centered = data - np.mean(data)
max_abs_val = np.max(np.abs(data_mean_centered))
normalized_data = data_mean_centered/max_abs_val
print(normalized_data)
# Standardize the data to have a mean of 0, and std dev of 1
standardized_data = (data - np.mean(data))/np.std(data)
print(standardized_data)
```

A4.2.2 Feature selection

● TOK

How does the way that we organize or classify knowledge affect what we know?

The structuring of data sets and the choice of features directly influence the insights gained from machine learning algorithms.

The way data is structured can significantly determine what the machine learning model can learn. For instance, missing values; the inclusion or exclusion of certain data points; or the way categories are defined and labelled can all skew or bias the model's outputs. This structuring determines how the machine "views" and "understands" the world, directly influencing the patterns it recognizes and the predictions it makes.

The features chosen can amplify or suppress certain patterns within the data. For example, in a model predicting creditworthiness, choosing features like income might reflect economic factors, whereas including features like zip code could inadvertently introduce socio-economic biases related to geographical areas.

The decisions made in data structuring and feature selection are not value-neutral. They reflect the biases, perspectives and priorities of those who design the data sets and algorithms.

◆ **Feature:** a numeric property that can be used to contribute a data point for a machine learning algorithm to train on. Think of it as a variable in your data set.

Feature selection refers to taking care to select only the most relevant features for use in your machine learning models. In the context of machine learning, a **feature** is a variable that you wish to use as input values for generating predictions. While it may seem like a lot of additional effort to perform manual feature selection, the process can dramatically impact the overall performance and accuracy of your machine learning model.

Removal of irrelevant detail will result in a more generalized model that is better suited to processing new, previously unseen data.

Three commonly used methods to help determine which features to select are filter methods, wrapper methods and embedded methods.

● See also

For more detail on these approaches, along with example code, search online for scikit-learn's section 1.13 "Feature selection" documentation (**https://scikit-learn.org/stable/modules/feature_selection.html**).

■ Filter methods

So-called as they help "filter out" features, filter methods involve applying a statistical metric to determine which features are best to be retained and which should be removed from the model. Features are ranked by their score, and those that don't meet the threshold can be filtered out.

As a purely statistical measure, using filter methods is less computationally expensive than retaining the feature in the model for full training. The downside is this does not detect interaction between features. That is, if one feature is affecting another, then a filter may suggest deleting a feature that is actually important. This is where manual appreciation of the context of your model is always important.

The most common, and easy-to-use, filter is to calculate the r value of the correlation (Pearson's product moment correlation coefficient). The r value of a data set may be calculated using

$$r = \frac{\sum (x_i - \bar{x})(y_i - \bar{y})}{\sqrt{\sum (x_i - \bar{x})^2 (y_i - \bar{y})^2}}$$

where x_i and y_i are your individual data points and $\bar{x}$ and $\bar{y}$ are the mean of each data series.

Once calculated, records with r values beyond a given threshold can be flagged for deletion.

■ Wrapper methods

Wrapper methods involve iterating over different combinations of the input features and comparing which subset produces optimal performance.

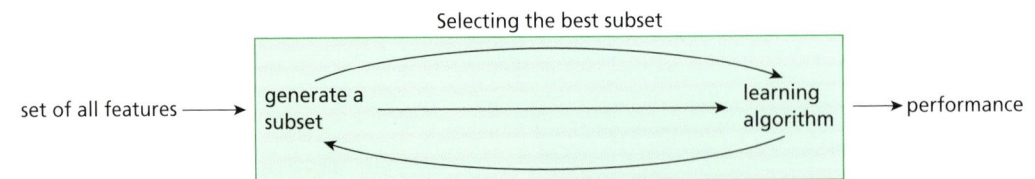

■ Wrapper methods

This can be a time-consuming and computationally expensive process, especially when compared to filter methods. There is also an increased risk of overfitting the model. The benefit, however, can be a very quick and efficient final model at the end of the process.

For further study on suitable techniques, do some research into recursive feature elimination (RFE), and sequential feature selection (forward selection, backward elimination). The scikit-learn library (online) provides functionality for both.

■ Embedded methods

Embedded methods draw on both filter and wrapper methods, but incorporate them directly into the model training algorithm. This means that the feature selection is performed simultaneously with the model training, rather than as a separate step before training.

Embedded methods can be more computationally efficient since they don't require separate iteration of the data prior to training. An embedded method will automatically assess the relevance or importance of features and adjust their weights or inclusion in the model accordingly during the training process.

While embedded methods can save manual labour by eliminating the need for feature selection processes prior to training, they typically require more computational time compared to simpler filter methods. The effectiveness of embedded methods depends on the model's ability to accurately assess feature relevance during the training process.

ACTIVITY

Research skills: Select and analyse an existing open-source data set relevant to a specific machine learning problem. Learn about the data cleaning and feature selection process used by these "professional" projects, and make recommendations for students learning to use data-cleaning methods for the first time.

A4 Machine learning

A4.2.3 Dimensionality reduction

When getting started with machine learning, it is easy to make the mistake of giving too much data to your model. While more quality entries in your data set is usually good, supplying too many features for each entry can easily cause more harm than good.

A typical way of thinking about this as a beginner would be "The more attributes or features I supply, the more detail about my data the model will learn, and perhaps it'll discover a pattern that I hadn't thought of". The problem is that machine learning algorithms are at their best when they are able to make generalizations about the training data. If there is too much detail in each item, and not enough items overall to compensate for that extra detail, then challenges arise.

These challenges are known as the **curse of dimensionality**, and describe the problems that arise in highly dimensional data. The following visualization is a useful way to help understand the problem.

◆ **Curse of dimensionality:** each feature in a machine learning model adds another dimension to the overall model the algorithm is attempting to map and create generalizations about; the curse of dimensionality refers to the problem that occurs when there are too many dimensions relative to the quantity of data available, so that patterns cannot be meaningfully observed.

◆ **Data sparsity:** how "spread out" data points are from each other in a model.

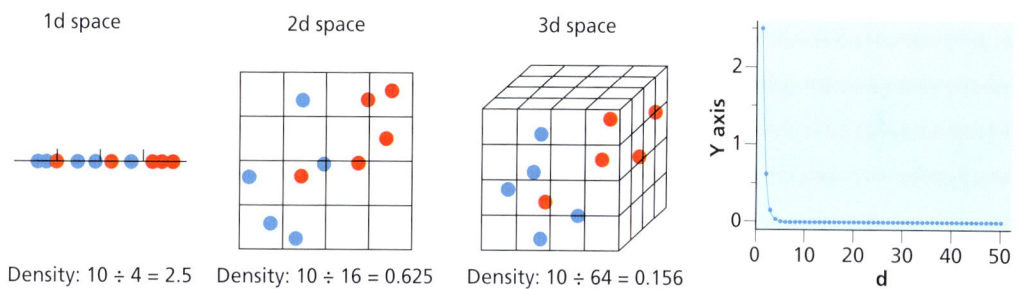

1d space   2d space   3d space

Density: $10 \div 4 = 2.5$ Density: $10 \div 16 = 0.625$ Density: $10 \div 64 = 0.156$

■ Data increases in sparsity as more dimensions are added

In the first panel, there are 10 data points in one dimension, which represents one feature or variable that the model is training with. With 10 points spread across a range of [0,4], there are 2.5 data points per unit. Visually, you can see it is quite crowded, meaning there is a lot of data available to make conclusions and generalizations from.

In the second panel, the same 10 data points are now spread across two dimensions. While both dimensions still have the range [0,4], the effect of the extra dimension is that it squares the space available, so those 10 data points now spread out such that there are only 0.625 data points per unit.

In the third panel, the third dimension is added. With three dimensions, representing three features or variables, there is now only one data point per 0.156 units of space.

The additional detail that comes from adding the extra dimensions acts to spread the data out, making it a lot more difficult for the model to find the generalizations it needs to be useful. To keep the ratio of data points to space consistent, the third panel needs 160 items in its training data instead of just 10. If you don't compensate for additional dimensions with additional quantity of data, the quality of your model will deteriorate.

The empty cells in the diagram above are an example of **data sparsity**, which is where the data points are too far from each other, and the data set contains a high number of empty values. If asked to generate a prediction when given those values that are empty in the training set, the model will have no basis on which to make an accurate estimation.

Sparsity is problematic as it makes it difficult for models to find patterns without overfitting, which is where the model effectively memorizes the individual items in the data set, including the noisy little details.

Distance metrics, such as calculating the Euclidean distance between points, lose meaning as the distances between all pairs of points are similar (a long way away). Without being able to find the patterns needed to make generalizations, the model will not be useful with unseen, untrained data when you need it to be.

An over-abundance of dimensions also poses challenges for you and those on your developer team with respect to data visualization. The mental capacity required to visualize highly dimensional data is very difficult or impossible, and most humans struggle to wrap their mind around more than three dimensions. This lack of intuition will make it difficult to analyse the patterns and relationships within your data.

While increasing the sample size will help compensate for additional dimensions with respect to model accuracy, it does introduce its own issues. Large sample sizes require increased processing time and capacity for training, and increase memory usage requirements. Every additional dimension already adds an extra order of magnitude to the memory required by the model, so the increase in sample size required not to lose model accuracy only exacerbates the memory and processing requirements. This all works to reduce the accessibility of your model for limited hardware environments such as mobile or portable computing, home / office computing and those without specialized infrastructure such as GPUs.

For these reasons, it can often be better to reduce rather than increase the number of dimensions in your machine learning model. Keeping it simple will help the model learn the generalizations it needs and reduce the demands on your limited processing hardware.

● Common mistake

Misunderstanding the goals of dimensionality reduction

It is important to bear in mind that dimensionality reduction does not *always* lead to better model performance. The primary goal of dimensionality reduction is to simplify the model by reducing the number of variables, which can help in some cases but might also lead to loss of critical information. There is a careful balance to be struck with the retention of relevant data aspects, which can take a lot of practice to get right.

■ Reducing dimensions of existing data sets

You can either make decisions about which dimensions to reduce manually, or make use of statistical tools to assist in the process.

Two commonly used statistical techniques to help reduce the number of features are PCA (principal component analysis) and LDA (linear discriminant analysis). PCA and LDA are beyond the scope of your course, but you don't have to know how they work to be able to make use of them in your IA (if you wish or need to), as scikit has the functionality built in.

PCA is used for dimensionality reduction without considering your data set labels. It's good for data compression, visualization and speeding up learning algorithms by reducing the number of input variables.

LDA is supervised in the sense that it uses your training data labels. It reduces a data set to a specified number of dimensions in a manner that best discriminates between the classes, based on their statistical properties. For this reason, it is particularly used to prepare data for classification tasks.

Top tip!

Sklearn, also known as scikit-learn, is a Python module for machine learning built on top of SciPy and distributed under the 4-Clause BSD licence.

To install this module, please refer to the instructions at **https://scikit-learn.org/stable/install.html**

Python

```python
import numpy as np
from sklearn.datasets import make_classification
from sklearn.decomposition import PCA
from sklearn.discriminant_analysis import
LinearDiscriminantAnalysis as LDA
# Generate synthetic data
# x will be 2d array of 1000 rows, 20 columns
# y will be 1d array of integers of values 0, 1 or 2
x, y = make_classification(n_samples=1000, n_features=20,
    n_informative=10, n_redundant=10,
    n_clusters_per_class=1, n_classes=3)
print("Original Data Shape:", x.shape)
# PCA
# Transform sample data from 1000x20 to 1000x2
pca = PCA(n_components=2)
x_reduced_pca = pca.fit_transform(x)
print("PCA Reduced Data Shape:", x_reduced_pca.shape)
# LDA
# Transform sample data from 1000x20 to 1000x2
lda = LDA(n_components=2)
x_reduced_lda = lda.fit_transform(x, y)
print("LDA Reduced Data Shape:", x_reduced_lda.shape)
```

See also

For more about using scikit-learn tools to help reduce dimensions in your data sets, search online for scikit-learn's section 1.2 "Linear and Quadratic Discriminant Analysis" (**https://scikit-learn.org/stable/modules/lda_qda.html**).

Top tip!

For discussing data preprocessing needs in an examination setting, be sure to attain a thorough understanding of the different role and effect of each one.

Some key points to remember for each one:

- **Inputting missing data:** The input of missing data will improve model accuracy through providing a complete data set, but it can introduce bias if the resulting data set does not match actual data distribution.
- **Deleting missing data:** Simplifies the model by removing incomplete cases to reduce overfitting, but this could lead to the loss of valuable data.
- **Removing duplicates:** Enhances reliability and prevents skewing of results.
- **Removing outliers:** The model can become more generalized as it prevents extreme values from disproportionally influencing predictions.

- **Filtering irrelevant features:** By concentrating on what is most relevant, the model will perform better and faster. It reduces the risk of overfitting.
- **Normalization and standardization:** Most algorithms perform better when features are all on a similar scale.
- **Filter methods:** Computationally less expensive, they can be used regardless of model type.
- **Wrapper methods:** Provide better performance as they consider feature interaction and are tailored to the model in question. If the data set is small, it can lead to overfitting.
- **Embedded methods:** A balanced approach between filter and wrapper methods, their effectiveness is dependent on the model they are designed for.

REVIEW QUESTIONS

1   A marketing firm uses machine learning to analyse customer survey data to improve targeting strategies.

   a   Describe one common issue in survey data that would necessitate data cleaning.

   b   Describe how feature selection could impact the performance of a machine learning model in this scenario.

   c   Outline the role of dimensionality reduction in handling high-dimensional data such as survey responses.

2   A financial analytics firm uses machine learning to predict stock-market trends based on historical data.

   a   List one common data-quality issue that might require cleaning in this historical stock data.

   b   Describe the role of feature selection in improving model performance in financial predictions.

   c   Describe the importance of dimensionality reduction on model complexity and performance.

3   A school district analyses standardized test results to predict student performance and identify at-risk students.

   a   List one common data issue that might arise with standardized test-result data.

   b   Describe the possible implications if the school district was to import raw test data for all questions completed by students into the machine learning model.

   c   Outline two commonly used methods of feature selection that could be beneficial in this educational context.

A4.3 Machine learning approaches (HL)

SYLLABUS CONTENT

By the end of this chapter, you should be able to:
- ▶ A4.3.1 Explain how linear regression is used to predict continuous outcomes
- ▶ A4.3.2 Explain how classification techniques in supervised learning are used to predict discrete categorical outcomes
- ▶ A4.3.3 Explain the role of hyperparameter tuning when evaluating supervised learning algorithms
- ▶ A4.3.4 Describe how clustering techniques in unsupervised learning are used to group data based on similarities in features
- ▶ A4.3.5 Describe how association rule learning techniques are used to uncover relations between different attributes in large data sets
- ▶ A4.3.6 Describe how an agent learns to make decisions by interacting with its environment in reinforcement learning
- ▶ A4.3.7 Describe the application of genetic algorithms in various real-world examples
- ▶ A4.3.8 Outline the structure and function of artificial neural networks (ANNs) and how multi-layer networks are used to model complex patterns in data sets
- ▶ A4.3.9 Describe how convolutional neural networks (CNNs) are designed to adaptively learn spatial hierarchies of features in images
- ▶ A4.3.10 Explain the importance of model selection and comparison in machine learning

Key information

Before proceeding into this chapter, it is important to note that the syllabus content statements above are limited to "Explain", "Describe" and "Outline".

This chapter intentionally contains additional detail that is beyond the syllabus, such as programming code samples demonstrating the use of various algorithms. **You do not need to be able to read or write programming code for the different algorithms presented here in your IB examinations.**

The additional detail has been provided due to machine learning being an extremely popular subset of Computer Science. In discussions with students, many expressed a desire to learn beyond descriptive theory for these topics, and a wish to know how these algorithms work and how to use them. Students also commonly express an intention to experiment with machine learning algorithms within their internal assessments. For these reasons, this introduction is more in-depth than is required solely for the examinations.

A4.3.1 Supervised learning: linear regression

◆ **Linear regression:** a machine learning algorithm that seeks a linear line of best fit for a given data set, from which extrapolations can be made.

Linear regression refers to calculating the correlation and line (or plane) of best fit among the values of a data set, and then using the resulting *equation of the line* to make predictions for new, unseen data.

Linear regression is one of the earliest machine learning algorithms to be developed, and can even be calculated manually for limited data sets as they are purely mathematical constructs.

Linear regression can be used to help answer such questions as:

- Given a person's height, is it possible to predict their weight?
- Given the number of hours a student studies for a test, is it possible to predict their result?
- Given the dollars spent on advertising a product, is it possible to predict the sales volume?
- Given the size of a home in square meters, is it possible to predict its sale price?

As hopefully you can infer from the name, linear regression is only suitable where there is a linear relationship between the independent and dependent variables.

The graph below illustrates a simple form of linear regression with one independent variable (the predictor) and one dependent variable (the response).

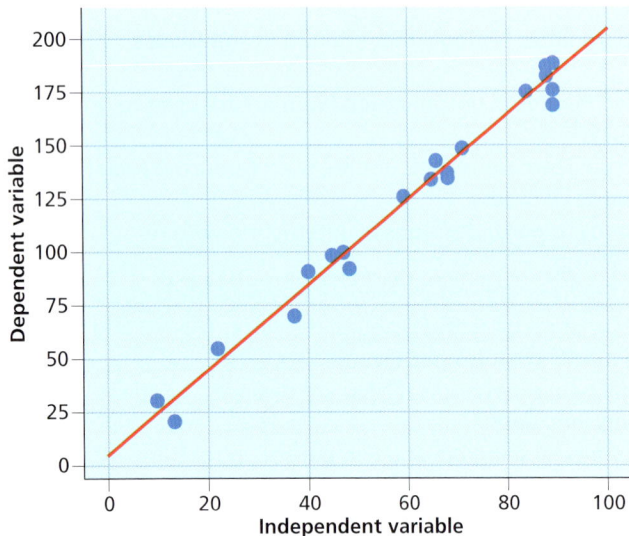

■ Linear regression example

To explore the process involved for linear regression of one independent and one dependent variable, the equation for the line of best fit can be calculated using the *least squares regression* line, which will minimize the distance between the line and individual data points.

By assigning the independent variable to x, and the dependent to y, you can use the standard equation of a line to make predictions.

$$y = a + bx$$

The slope, or gradient, of the line, b, represents the amount that the prediction will change for every increment of one in the independent variable. To calculate b, you find the sum of the difference between each point of the line from the mean:

$$b = \frac{\sum(x_i - \bar{x})(y_i - \bar{y})}{\sum(x_i - \bar{x})^2}$$

The point of intercept, a, is the baseline value for the dependent variable when the independent variable is 0. To calculate a, take the coefficient multiplied by the mean of x and subtract it from the mean of y.

$$a = \bar{y} - b\bar{x}$$

As linear regression is such a common and popular task, both NumPy and scikit-learn libraries have tools built in to perform these calculations for you. The following example uses scikit-learn, as we will use the library a lot for other algorithms coming up.

Python

```python
import numpy as np
import matplotlib.pyplot as plt
from sklearn.linear_model import LinearRegression
# Sample data
x = np.array([45,48,65,68,68,10,84,22,37,88,71,89,89,13,59,66,40,88,47,89])
y = np.array([98,92,134,135,136,30,175,54,70,182,148,169,187,20,126,142,90,186,
99,176])
# Using scikit, calculate the model
# Convert the 1D array of 20 columns, to a 2D array of 20 rows 1 column each
x = x.reshape(-1, 1)
model = LinearRegression()
model.fit(x, y)
```

A4 Machine learning

```
intercept = model.intercept_
slope = model.coef_[0]
# Using scikit, generate a prediction where the independent variable is 70
x_test = np.array([[70]])  # New single data point for prediction
y_test_predict = model.predict(x_test)
print(f"Prediction for independent variable value 70: {y_test_
predict[0]}")
# Using matplotlib, plot the data and the line of best fit
x_line = np.array([[0], [100]])
y_line = np.array([[intercept], [intercept+100*slope]])
plt.scatter(x, y, color="blue")
plt.plot(x_line, y_line, color="red", linewidth=2)
plt.xlabel("Independent variable")
plt.ylabel("Dependent variable")
plt.title("Linear Regression example")
plt.show()
```

● See also

Reference the scikit-learn documentation for supervised linear regression by searching online for scikit-learn's "LinearRegression" (**https://scikit-learn.org/stable/modules/generated/sklearn. linear_model.LinearRegression.html**).

■ Measuring accuracy

◆ **R-squared value (or coefficient of determination):** a statistical measure that indicates how well the linear regression model fits the data points given.

Assessing the accuracy of the model can be performed by calculating the **R-squared value**, also known as the **coefficient of determination**. It is a measure of the proportion of variation in values from the independent variable data, and what the model would have predicted for that point. A value close to 0 indicates the model does a poor job of explaining the relationship of the data, whereas a value close to 1 indicates the model does an excellent job of mapping the relationship of the data.

Why use a measure that relies on squaring? Why not just take the average of the absolute value of the difference between the predicted and actual values? There are a few reasons:

■ Squaring means larger errors will become more pronounced than smaller errors. Absolute differences would treat all variations the same.

■ Squaring results in a function that can be differentiated; a very handy benefit for optimization algorithms that rely on derivatives. Absolute values in a function cannot be differentiated.

■ Squared differences are used within classical statistics with respect to assumptions around normalization, so it is convenient to stick with that approach.

There are approaches, other than R-squared value, that can be used, including:

■ **adjusted R-squared:** modifies the formulae to account for the number of predictors in the model

■ **mean squared error:** the average of the squares of the errors

■ **mean absolute error:** the average of the absolute value of the errors

■ **mean absolute percentage error:** the average of the absolute percentage errors of predictions.

With NumPy, the r-squared value needs to be calculated through each step, whereas scikit-learn has a built-in method for the task.

Python

```python
# Method 1: Using numpy
y_predicted = model.predict(x)
y_residuals = y - y_predicted # Difference between actual and predicted values
ss_res = np.sum(y_residuals**2) # Sum of squares of the residuals
ss_tot = np.sum((y - np.mean(y))**2) # Total sum of squares
r_squared = 1 - (ss_res / ss_tot) # R-squared value
print(f"R-squared: {r_squared:.2f}")
# Method 2: Using scikit-learn
r_squared = model.score(x,y)
print(f"R-squared: {r_squared:.2f}")
```

■ Multidimensionality

The previous example illustrates simple linear regression where there is only one independent variable. In real-world applications, it is highly likely that you will want to model against several independent variables. This is known as "multiple linear regression".

While most humans can mentally visualize data in two, or perhaps three, dimensions, it becomes extremely challenging to visualize beyond that. The good news is our software tools have no problem modelling the relationship across multiple dimensions. Here is an example using scikit for a linear regression model that has four independent variables.

Python

```python
import pandas as pd
from sklearn.model_selection import train_test_split
from sklearn.linear_model import LinearRegression
# Load the data and assign features (independent variables) to x, and the target
# (dependent variable) to y.
df = pd.read_csv("Multidimensional_example.csv")
x = df[["Feature_1", "Feature_2", "Feature_3", "Feature_4"]]
y = df["Target"]
# Train the linear regression model
model = LinearRegression()
model.fit(x, y)
# Generate prediction for new data point
new_point = np.array([[50, -150, 30, 100]])
prediction = model.predict(new_point)
print(f"Predicted target for the new sample: {prediction[0]}")
```

The Multidimensional_example.csv file can be downloaded from **https://github.com/paulbaumgarten/hodder-ibdp-computerscience**

The prediction for the new data point used in the code should be 510.7.

A4 Machine learning

Top tip!

Regression with non-linear data?

If you have a data set you would like to fit to a non-linear function, the `scipy curve _ fit()` function is what you are looking for.

For example, assuming you have NumPy arrays of `x _ data` and `y _ data` that you wish to fit to a quadratic function:

Python

```python
import numpy as np
from scipy.optimize import curve_fit
x_data = [.......your data here.......]
y_data = [.......your data here.......]
def my_quadratic(x, a, b, c):
    return a * x**2 + b * x + c
params, params_covariance = curve_fit(my_quadratic,
x_data, y_data)
a, b, c = params # Extract the fitted coefficients
```

For more information, search online for scipy.optimize.curve_fit (**https://docs.scipy.org/doc/scipy/reference/generated/scipy.optimize.curve_fit.html**).

A4.3.2 Supervised learning: classification techniques

◆ **Classification techniques:** where a machine learning model has been trained to identify, from a predefined list of categories, which category (or class) the input data would most likely be associated with.

One task frequently required of machine learning algorithms is to classify data as belonging to one of a given range of categories. Whereas the output prediction from linear regression is numeric, **classification** algorithms generally produce a non-numeric value to represent a category.

Categorization through machine learning is useful as it facilitates automation of decision-making processes and can be applied to a wide range of practical problems. Examples of everyday classification problems include:

- email spam detection (spam or not spam)
- medical diagnosis (disease or no disease)
- credit score (good credit risk or poor credit risk)
- image recognition (identifying what category of object is in the image)
- natural language processing / sentiment analysis (positive or negative sentiment)
- recommendation engine (what genre of movie to suggest next).

Two popular methods that do not require neural networks are k-nearest neighbours and decision trees.

■ K-nearest neighbours

K-nearest neighbours is a machine learning technique that allows classification of data based on patterns learned from existing labelled data.

◆ **K-nearest neighbours:** where data points are categorized based on the categories of the nearest points around them in the data set; k is a variable representing how many of those nearest points should be used to "vote" and determine what category to assign the new value.

● Top tips!

■ Normalize or standardize data because KNN is sensitive to the magnitude of data points.
■ Choose an odd number for k when the number of classes is even to avoid tie situations.
■ Experiment with different distance metrics (e.g. Euclidean, Manhattan) to see which performs best for your data set.

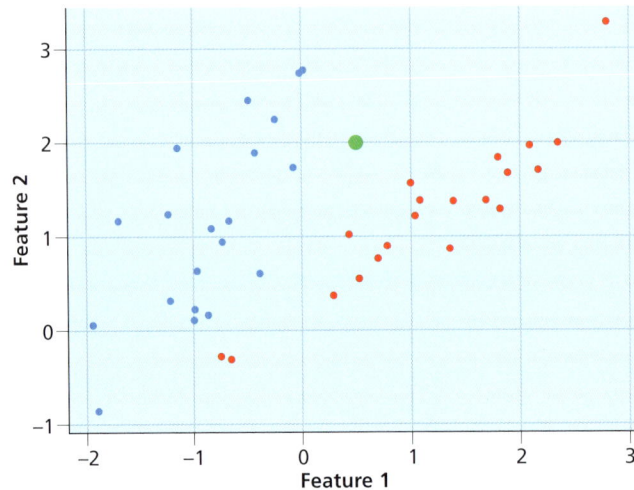

■ K-nearest neighbours

Consider the chart above, in which the data have been classified into either blue dots or red dots. The two axes represent the different features (variables) that have been measured. These can represent anything (such as size, weight, length, time, cost, review rating), provided they can be measured and plotted on a numeric scale.

The green dot represents a new value that the model has not seen before. How can k-nearest neighbours be used to determine whether the green dot should be classed as belonging to the blue group or the red group?

With KNN, a value k is selected to represent how many nearby data points should be used to determine the prediction output. The algorithm will then determine the k-nearest points, and allow each of them to "vote" as to which final category the prediction should award.

The following charts illustrate the decision boundary for different values of k.

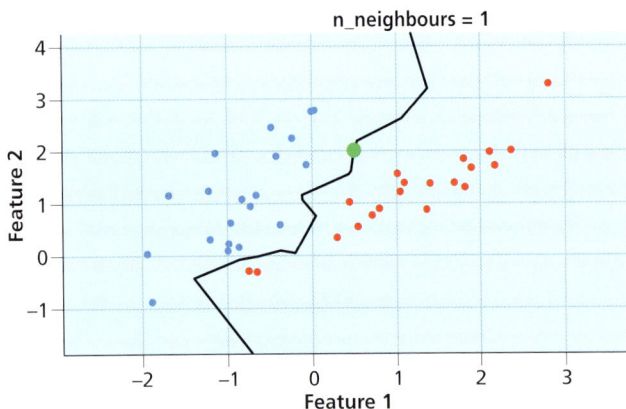

■ KNN where $k = 1$

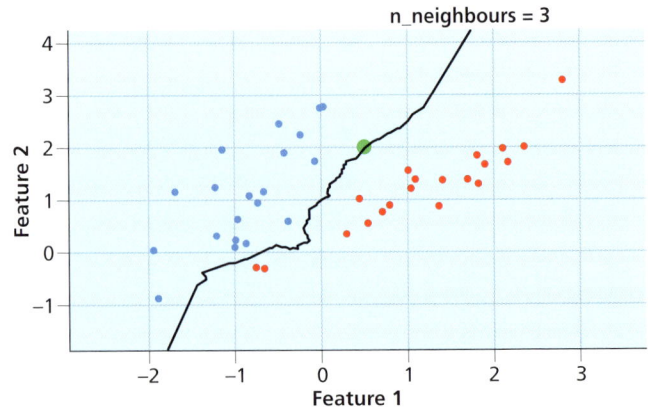

■ KNN where $k = 3$

A4 Machine learning

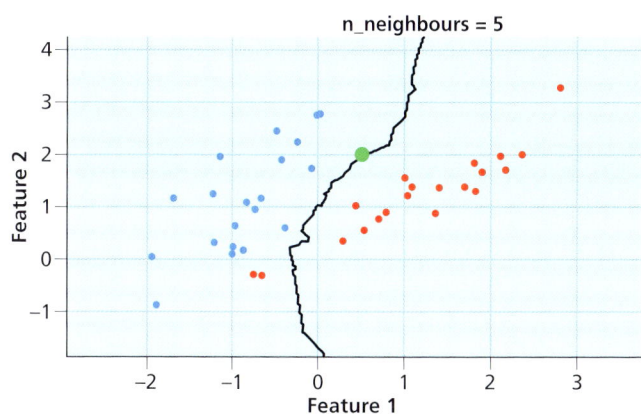

n_neighbours = 5

■ KNN where *k* = 5

In the examples here, values of *k* of 1, 3 and 5 have been used.

When *k* = 1, the line represents the boundary to the nearest single point of either category. Normally, this is susceptible to being influenced by outliers, so a value of *k* = 3 or *k* = 5 is more typical.

It is important when selecting between two categories to ensure that *k* is an odd number to avoid the situation where there could be a tie!

The data set for the charts shown here is the knn_dataset. csv file that can be downloaded from **https://github.com/ paulbaumgarten/hodder-ibdp-computerscience**

Python

```python
import numpy as np
import pandas as pd
import matplotlib.pyplot as plt
from sklearn.neighbors import KNeighborsClassifier
# Load the data
df = pd.read_csv("knn_dataset.csv")
x = df[["Feature_1", "Feature_2"]].values
y = df["Label"].values
# New, unknown point to classify
z = np.array([[0.4, 1.6]])
# Create and fit the KNN classifier with 3 neighbours
knn = KNeighborsClassifier(n_neighbors=3)
knn.fit(x, y)
# Plot the training points
plt.scatter(x[:, 0], x[:, 1], c=y)
plt.scatter(z[:, 0], z[:, 1], color="red", zorder=5)
plt.xlabel("Feature 1")
plt.ylabel("Feature 2")
plt.title("n_neighbors=3")
plt.xlim(xx.min(), xx.max())
plt.ylim(yy.min(), yy.max())
plt.show()
# Make the prediction
predicted_category = knn.predict(z)
print("The predicted category for point z is:",
predicted_category[0])
```

One example application of KNN is in the development of collaborative filtering recommendation systems. Consider a scatter plot for two movies that a wide number of users have reviewed and rated. The *x* axis may represent the ratings by each user for movie A, and the *y* axis may represent the ratings by each user for movie B.

Mark a new point on the plot for the target user, who has viewed movie A but not movie B. By referring to the other points on the scatter, KNN can infer what the target user would rate movie B. If the prediction is for a high rating, the model can recommend the user to watch that movie.

(In reality, rather than performing KNN on pairs of movies at a time, a multidimensional approach would be taken, comparing ratings of many movies at once.)

> ### ● See also
>
> Reference the scikit-learn documentation for supervised k-nearest neighbours classification by searching online for scikit-learn's section 1.6.2 "Nearest Neighbors Classification" (**https://scikit-learn.org/stable/modules/neighbors.html#nearest-neighbors-classification**).

■ Decision trees

◆ Decision tree: a graphical representation of conditions that will result in a classification decision being made; think of it as a decision-making flowchart that the machine learning model creates.

While KNN is considered a lazy learner (it does very little during the training phase and defers most of the computation until prediction), **decision trees** are considered eager learners that build a classification model during training.

Conceptually, you can think of decision trees as a large flowchart or series of nested *if-else* statements that are used to determine classification. Rather than having to manually determine the decision points and write programming code for the *if-else* statements yourself, the algorithm will analyse the training data to automatically determine the cutoff values for each decision point along the way, and how deep to make the nested tree.

Decision trees make for an easy-to-maintain algorithm since the model can be retrained and its decision paths and threshold values subsequently adjusted based on new data. Decision-tree algorithms are a scalable solution that works with large and complex data sets compared to the impracticalities associated with maintaining *if-else* statements yourself that might have hundreds or thousands of decision points and pathways, and therefore also be very much prone to human error.

Iris flower data set

| Setosa | Versicolor | Virginica |

■ Iris flowers

The iris data set is commonly used as an introduction to decision trees. It contains measurements of 150 irises (a type of flower), one-third each of setosa, versicolor and virginica. For each of the 150 measurements, there are four features (variables):

- sepal length in cm
- sepal width in cm
- petal length in cm
- petal width in cm.

One version of the final trained decision tree might look like this:

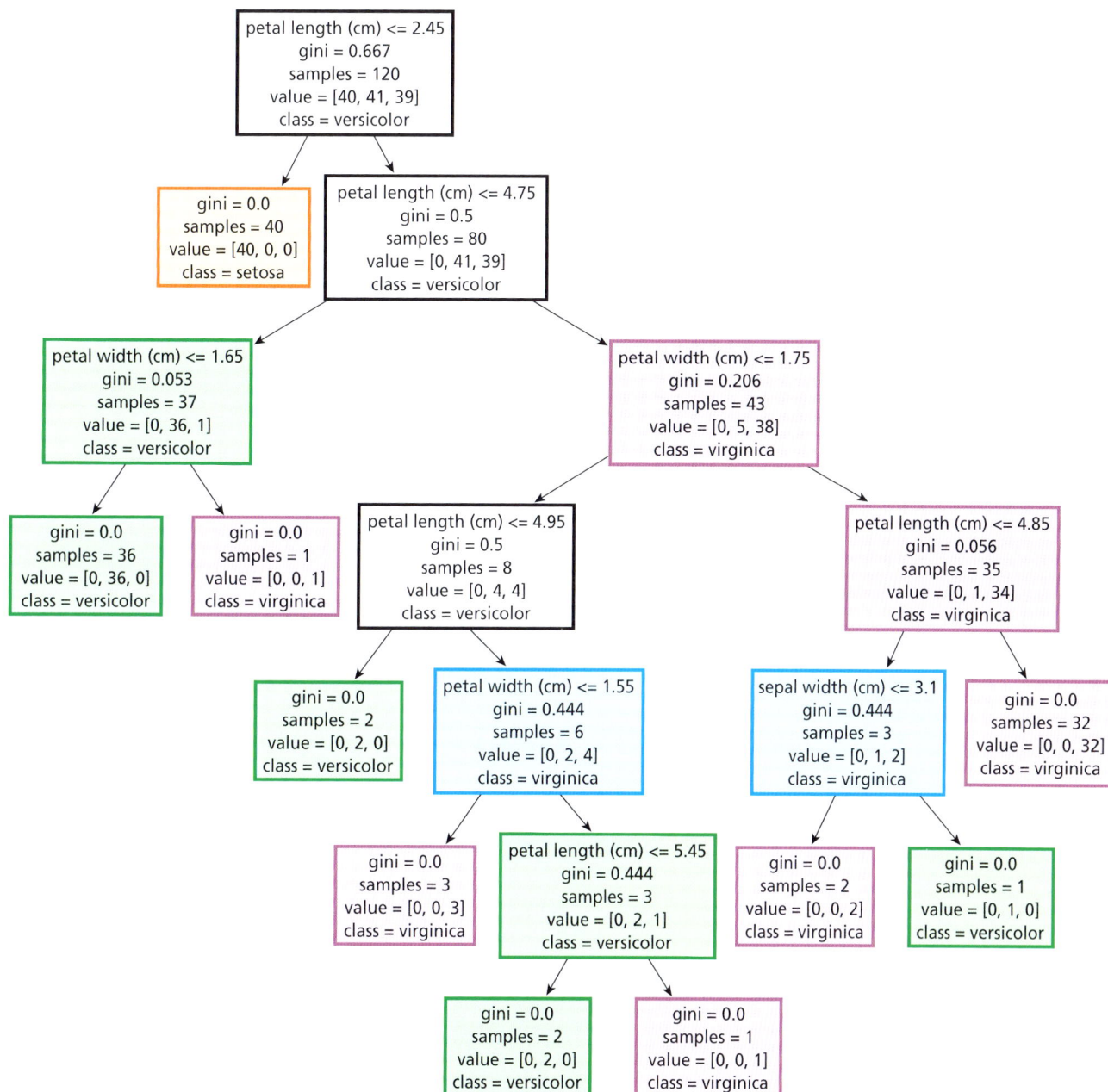

```
petal length (cm) <= 2.45
gini = 0.667
samples = 120
value = [40, 41, 39]
class = versicolor
```

```
gini = 0.0
samples = 40
value = [40, 0, 0]
class = setosa
```

```
petal length (cm) <= 4.75
gini = 0.5
samples = 80
value = [0, 41, 39]
class = versicolor
```

```
petal width (cm) <= 1.65
gini = 0.053
samples = 37
value = [0, 36, 1]
class = versicolor
```

```
petal width (cm) <= 1.75
gini = 0.206
samples = 43
value = [0, 5, 38]
class = virginica
```

```
gini = 0.0
samples = 36
value = [0, 36, 0]
class = versicolor
```

```
gini = 0.0
samples = 1
value = [0, 0, 1]
class = virginica
```

```
petal length (cm) <= 4.95
gini = 0.5
samples = 8
value = [0, 4, 4]
class = versicolor
```

```
petal length (cm) <= 4.85
gini = 0.056
samples = 35
value = [0, 1, 34]
class = virginica
```

```
gini = 0.0
samples = 2
value = [0, 2, 0]
class = versicolor
```

```
petal width (cm) <= 1.55
gini = 0.444
samples = 6
value = [0, 2, 4]
class = virginica
```

```
sepal width (cm) <= 3.1
gini = 0.444
samples = 3
value = [0, 1, 2]
class = virginica
```

```
gini = 0.0
samples = 32
value = [0, 0, 32]
class = virginica
```

```
gini = 0.0
samples = 3
value = [0, 0, 3]
class = virginica
```

```
petal length (cm) <= 5.45
gini = 0.444
samples = 3
value = [0, 2, 1]
class = versicolor
```

```
gini = 0.0
samples = 2
value = [0, 0, 2]
class = virginica
```

```
gini = 0.0
samples = 1
value = [0, 1, 0]
class = versicolor
```

```
gini = 0.0
samples = 2
value = [0, 2, 0]
class = versicolor
```

```
gini = 0.0
samples = 1
value = [0, 0, 1]
class = virginica
```

■ Trained decision tree for the iris data set

Starting at the top of the tree, observe the first decision is whether the petal length is <= 2.45 cm.

The other values printed in the node advise about the model's prediction if there was no further processing beyond this point. The significance of the terms used are:

■ **Gini** indicates the decision tree would be 67 per cent uncertain in the prediction generated (which makes sense as, without taking any branch in the tree, it will effectively be making a 1-in-3 guess).

■ **Samples** indicates that all 120 samples passed through this node (note it is 120 instead of 150 as, when this diagram was produced, 30 samples were retained as unseen for validation testing purposes).

- **Value** indicates the spread of the three classifications at this point (40 setosa, 41 versicolor and 39 virginica).

- **Class** indicates that the prediction at this point would be versicolor (since it had the most samples, with 41).

Based on the measurement of petal length, you either take the branch to the left, if the petal length is <= 2.45 cm, or to the right, if the petal length is > 2.45 cm.

Keep traversing the tree until you reach a termination point, or you have gone as deep into the tree as you would like and wish to terminate, obtaining the model's best prediction at that point. (Keep in mind that, while the model represented here only has a maximum depth of six levels, more complex decision trees can easily have maximum depths of hundreds or thousands of layers, hence the option for stopping once a particular depth is reached.)

The following Python will implement the iris problem.

Python

```python
from sklearn.datasets import load_iris
from sklearn.model_selection import train_test_split
from sklearn.tree import DecisionTreeClassifier
from sklearn import tree
import matplotlib.pyplot as plt
import pandas as pd
import numpy as np
# Load the Iris data set
iris_df = pd.read_csv("iris.csv")
x = iris_df.drop("species", axis=1) # features are all the columns except species
y = iris_df["species"] # target variable
# Split the data set into a training set and a test set
x_train, x_test, y_train, y_test = train_test_split(x, y, test_size=0.2,
random_state=42)
# Create a decision tree and generate predictive data
clf = DecisionTreeClassifier(max_depth=10, random_state=42)
clf.fit(x_train, y_train)
y_pred = clf.predict(x_test)
# Plot the decision tree
plt.figure(figsize=(12, 8))
tree.plot_tree(clf, filled=True, feature_names=iris.feature_names, class_names=
iris.target_names)
plt.show()
# Validate accuracy using the test data
accuracy = clf.score(x_test, y_test)
print(f"Accuracy of the decision tree classifier is: {accuracy:.2f}")
# Generate a prediction for a manual data point
new_flower_measurements = np.array([[5.0, 3.5, 1.5, 0.2]])
predicted_species = clf.predict(new_flower_measurements)
print(f"The predicted species for the new flower is: {predicted_species[0]}")
```

The iris data set csv file can be downloaded from **https://github.com/paulbaumgarten/hodder-ibdp-computerscience**

One real-world application of decision trees is to assist with patient diagnosis. The features (variables) at issue in such a model may include demographic information (age, sex, height, weight); clinical measurements (blood pressure, glucose levels, haemoglobin, cholesterol); lifestyle factors (such as smoking status and alcohol consumption); along with symptoms, conditions, medical history and test results. It is easy to envisage such a model having dozens of features.

ACTIVITY

Thinking skills: Classification with KNN or decision trees?

Select a classification problem and perform a comparison analysis of both KNN and decision trees to solve the problem. Evaluate the trade-offs between the two approaches and create a decision matrix based on criteria such as ease of understanding, computational efficiency, performance on small vs large data sets, and so on.

Top tip!

When choosing between k-nearest neighbours (KNN), decision trees and artificial neural networks for a supervised learning classification scenario, consider the following:

- KNN suits moderate data sizes and low dimensions; decision trees handle mixed data sizes well; neural networks excel with large, complex data sets.
- KNN requires normalization; decision trees need minimal preprocessing; neural networks often require extensive preprocessing.
- KNN and decision trees are highly interpretable; neural networks are less so, and are often considered "black boxes".
- KNN are slow at prediction; decision trees offer fast predictions but can overfit easily; neural networks require significant computational power but handle non-linear data well.
- KNN easily integrate new data; decision trees and neural networks most often require retraining.

A4.3.3 Supervised learning: evaluation and tuning

■ Evaluation metrics

TOK

How can we know that current knowledge is an improvement upon past knowledge?

Machine learning requires evaluating the performance of new algorithms against benchmarks or previous models.

In the context of machine learning, improvement is often quantified in terms of performance on specific tasks. However, Theory of Knowledge invites you to question deeper aspects of this improvement: Does performing better on a task, like object recognition, necessarily mean the algorithm has gained more "knowledge"? Is the understanding deeper or merely more functional?

Additionally, metrics can sometimes be misleading. For example, an algorithm might score very highly on accuracy but fail in particular scenarios that weren't well represented in the training data.

Within supervised learning, there are several important, established metrics that can be used to evaluate the effectiveness of your model.

◆ Confusion matrix: a simple pictorial means of representing how well a machine learning model is performing.

The starting point would typically be to produce a **confusion matrix**. For a binary classification problem, the data forms a two-row, two-column table modelled as follows:

		Predicted	
		Predicted positive	Predicted negative
Actual	Actually positive	True positive	False negative
	Actually negative	False positive	True negative

The number of scores that are *true positive, false negative, false positive* or *true negative* are written into the respective cell (and typically colour coded with dark shading to indicate higher quantities), the idea being that it is a quick visual indicator of the success of your model. If the highest numbers (and dark shading) run down the diagonal of *true positive* and *true negative*, then that is a good sign.

A confusion matrix can also be produced for higher dimensional classification problems. In that instance, each possible classification would be turned into rows and columns. In this case, the diagonal set of cells from top left to bottom right would again represent correct predictions.

Using your confusion matrix, you can proceed to calculate the accuracy, precision, recall and F1 scores.

- **Accuracy**: The fraction or ratio of correct predictions

$$accuracy = \frac{correct\ predictions}{total\ predictions}$$

- **Precision**: The fraction or ratio of correct positive predictions to total positive predictions

    For instance, of all images recognized as being "cats", how many of them were correctly classified? Alternatively, of all the "spam" predictions, how many of those were correctly "spam"? This is important when a false positive may have a significant consequence.

$$precision = \frac{true\ positives}{true\ positives + false\ positives}$$

- **Recall**: The fraction or ratio of correct positive predictions to actual positives

    For instance, this could be number of patients correctly predicted to have diabetes, out of all the patients who truly have diabetes.

$$recall = \frac{true\ positives}{true\ positivies + false\ negatives}$$

- **F1 score**: The harmonic-mean of precision and recall; it is particularly useful where both false positives and false negatives may carry significant consequence

    A harmonic-mean is different from an arithmetic mean in that it will always give a score closer to the smaller of the two numbers. The F1 score will range from 0 to 1, with 1 being the best score.

$$F1\ score = 2 * \frac{precision * recall}{precision + recall}$$

Consider using an F1 score in the criminal justice system, where an algorithm has been devised to predict whether an individual will re-offend if released on parole. (Note that there have been real-world problems in using machine learning modes for this exact scenario; refer to A4.4 Ethical considerations for more.) In this situation, precision measures the correctness of positive predictions. High precision means most individuals predicted to re-offend actually did re-offend. Recall measures how well the model successfully identifies those who will re-offend, so that re-offenders are not being ignored by the system. Both are important for matters of public safety, so combining them through the use of the F1 score is valuable.

Another example scenario is to imagine a school using face recognition to automatically record attendance as students walk through the school gate. In this scenario, high precision implies that when the system identifies a student, it is identifying the correct student (rather than recording the wrong student as present), and high recall suggests the system correctly identifies most or all students who pass through the gate.

Common mistake

It is common for students to over-rely on accuracy and neglect the nuance provided by the other metrics. Have a clear understanding of the distinct roles of precision and recall.

- **Accuracy** is the overall correctness of the model (both true positives and true negatives).
- **Precision** is the proportion of positive identifications that were actually correct (important when the cost of a false positive is high).
- **Recall** is the proportion of actual positives correctly identified (important when the cost of a false negative is high).
- **F1** is the harmonic-mean of precision and recall (useful when a balance between precision and recall is needed).

■ Hyperparameter tuning

Hyperparameters is the technical term for the global variables that affect the entire model. Commonly used hyperparameters include:

- learning rate (neural networks)
- activation function (neural networks)
- number of hidden layers (neural networks)
- maximum depth of tree (decision trees)
- number of neighbours (k-nearest neighbours)
- number of clusters (unsupervised clustering)
- other variables as required by the model.

Hyperparameter tuning is the process of experimentation and adjustment of the combination of parameters that results in optimal performance of a model.

◆ **Hyperparameter:** a parameter (or value assigned to a variable) that is set before the learning process, which guides the algorithm as it learns.

Key information

Hyperparameters exist in all types of machine learning, not just in supervised learning. Take the time to identify the hyperparameters in whatever algorithm you are using and the effect their adjustment will have.

■ Overfitting and underfitting

Overfitting occurs when the model effectively memorizes detail from the training data that is too fine grained for it to make sufficient generalizations for use on unseen data. Reducing the depth of a decision tree, increasing the regularization strength in a linear model or reducing the number of neurons in hidden layers may help with this problem.

Underfitting occurs when the model is too simple and hasn't learned enough detail about the underlying patterns involved, such that the model also performs poorly on unseen data.

Signs of overfitting include:

- the model performs significantly better on the training data compared to the validation data
- a complex architecture is used, with many features

Common mistake

Avoid creating models that are too complex for your data; simpler models are easier to understand and debug, and often perform better on new, unseen data.

- the training error rate decreases, but the testing error rate increases after a given number of epochs

- reducing the model's complexity improves test performance.

Signs of underfitting include:

- the model performs poorly on both the training and test data sets

- a simple model is used, with minimal features

- there are insufficient features to adequately capture the characteristics of the data

- increasing complexity or adding features improves test performance.

A4.3.4 Unsupervised learning: clustering techniques

To review, unsupervised learning is where the data set your model is trained on is unlabelled. That is, you don't supply the *correct* answer that corresponds with each datum you supply. Rather than looking for data that is similar to known answer values, the features of the unlabelled data are compared for similarities among them all, with the goal of identifying naturally forming clusters in the groupings of data.

■ K-means clustering

◆ **Clustering techniques:** where data is grouped into clusters based on similarity or proximity to each other without any labels provided to help indicate the correctness of associating any individual datapoint to the cluster assigned.

K-nearest neighbours is very commonly used for unsupervised **clustering**, in addition to the supervised learning approaches already considered.

With the supervised approach, when a new, unlabelled data point is introduced, the algorithm measures the distance (often Euclidean) from the new point to all those in the training set. From there, it identifies the nearest neighbours to assign a predictive label to the new value. With the unsupervised approach, when a new data point is introduced, the algorithm similarly measures distances to other data points to determine its nearest neighbours but, instead of predicting a label, it uses these relationships to identify the groupings, or clusters, within the entire data set.

The main weakness with a KNN approach is that it assumes clusters are spherical and of similar size, making it sensitive to initial centroids and outliers.

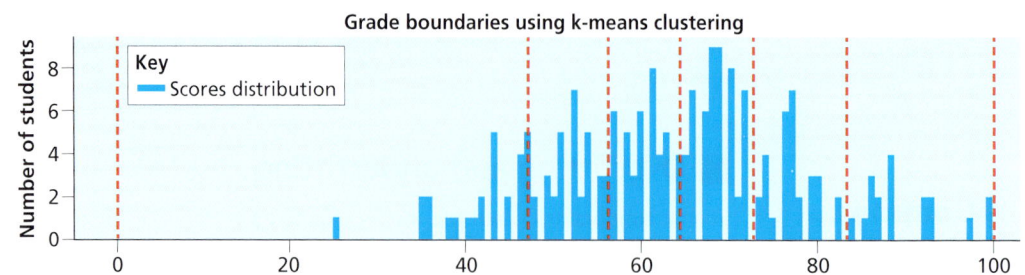

K-means clustering with one dimension

In this example, k-means clustering has been used to determine grade boundaries for a cohort of 200 students. Asked to cluster the grades into six buckets, one for each letter grade, the algorithm determined the following boundaries:

- A: 83.48 to 100
- B: 72.74 to 83.48
- C: 64.45 to 72.74
- D: 56.30 to 64.45
- E: 47.09 to 56.30
- F: 0 to 47.09

Moving from one to two dimensions makes the identification of clusters more accurate. In this instance, k-means could look like the following:

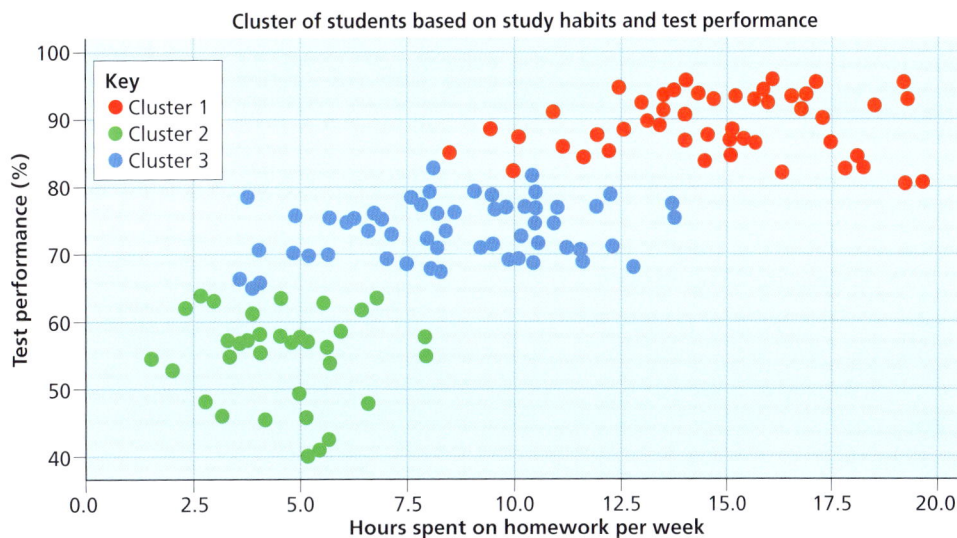

■ K-means clustering with two dimensions

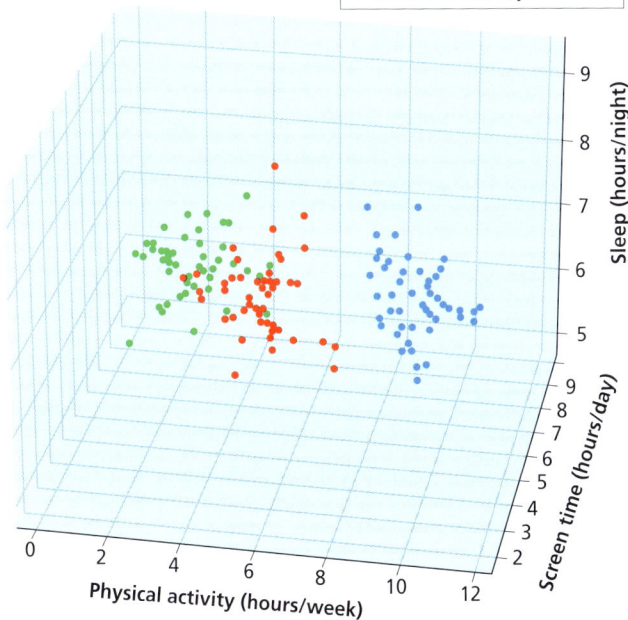

■ K-means clustering with three dimensions

While providing a 3D visualization in the 2D medium of a textbook is problematic, hopefully the point still gets across with the following illustration that, as dimensions go up, so the identification of clusters becomes easier, given the data points become further spread out. This works provided there is still enough data to form actual clusters, otherwise the curse of dimensionality will soon kick in (as can be seen in the illustration; there are many cells with no value).

Python

```
# Example implementation of k-means clustering
import numpy as np
import matplotlib.pyplot as plt
from sklearn.cluster import KMeans
# Generate synthetic data
```

```
np.random.seed(42)
# Students who spend little time but perform variably
group1 = np.random.normal(loc=[5, 60], scale=[2, 10], size=(50, 2))
# Students who spend a moderate amount of time and perform moderately
group2 = np.random.normal(loc=[10, 75], scale=[2, 5], size=(50, 2))
# Students who spend a lot of time and perform well
group3 = np.random.normal(loc=[15, 90], scale=[2, 5], size=(50, 2))
# Combine the groups into a single data set
data = np.vstack([group1, group2, group3])
# Apply k-means clustering
kmeans = KMeans(n_clusters=3, random_state=42)
kmeans.fit(data)
labels = kmeans.labels_
# Plot results
plt.figure(figsize=(10, 6))
colors = ["red", "green", "blue"]
for i in range(3):
    plt.scatter(data[labels == i, 0], data[labels == i, 1], color=colors[i],
    label=f"Cluster {i+1}")
plt.title("Cluster of Students Based on Study Habits and Test Performance")
plt.xlabel("Hours Spent on Homework per Week")
plt.ylabel("Test Performance (%)")
plt.legend()
plt.grid(True)
plt.show()
```

Common mistake

Assuming clusters are globular; k-means does not work well with non-spherical clusters.

See also

Reference the scikit-learn documentation for k-means clustering by searching online for scikit-learn's section 2.3.2 "K-means" (**https://scikit-learn.org/stable/modules/clustering.html#k-means**).

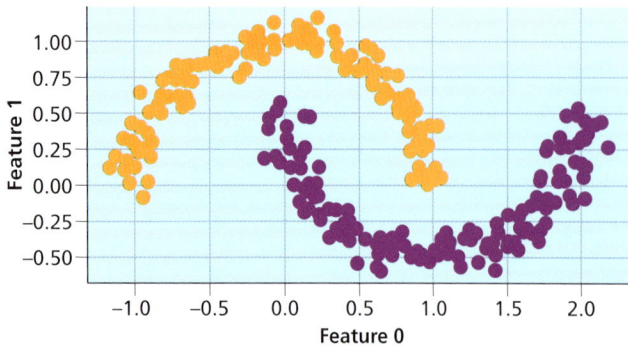

■ Spectral clustering

■ Spectral clustering

Spectral clustering is another technique that is useful where clusters are not linearly separable. To classify any new data point, it will look at where the new point fits best among the groups already made, like finding which circle of friends a new student would fit into at school.

Python

```python
import numpy as np
import matplotlib.pyplot as plt
from sklearn.datasets import make_moons
from sklearn.neighbors import kneighbors_graph
from sklearn.cluster import SpectralClustering
# Generate synthetic data (two interleaving half circles)
x, _ = make_moons(n_samples=300, noise=0.07, random_state=42)
# Create a k-nearest neighbours graph
knn_graph = kneighbors_graph(x, n_neighbors=10, include_self=False,
mode="distance")
# Apply spectral clustering using the KNN graph
spectral = SpectralClustering(n_clusters=2, affinity="precomputed",
assign_labels="kmeans", random_state=42)
labels = spectral.fit_predict(knn_graph)
# Plot the results
plt.figure(figsize=(8, 4))
plt.scatter(x[:, 0], x[:, 1], c=labels, cmap=plt.cm.rainbow, edgecolor="k", s=50)
plt.title("Spectral Clustering results")
plt.xlabel("Feature 0")
plt.ylabel("Feature 1")
plt.show()
```

Social network analysis using spectral clustering

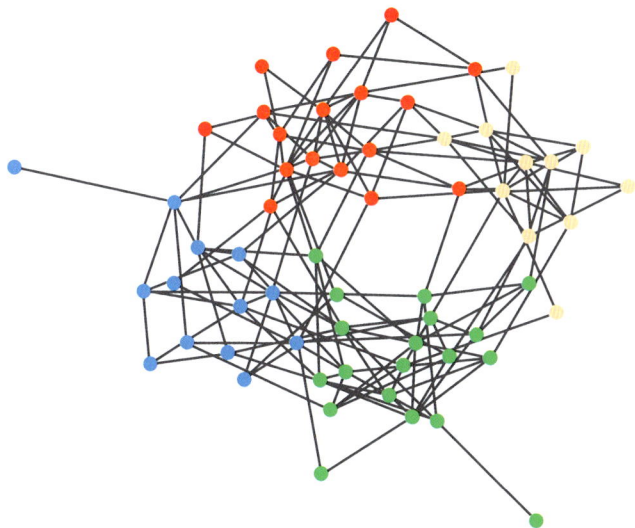

■ Spectral clustering can group people according to social networks

Spectral clustering may be useful in contexts such as social network analysis to identify communities within networks by treating nodes as people and edges as their relationships.

● **See also**

Reference the scikit-learn documentation for spectral clustering by searching online for scikit-learn's section 2.3.5 "Spectral clustering" (**https://scikit-learn.org/stable/modules/clustering.html#spectral-clustering**).

■ Hierarchical clustering

This approach builds a tree of clusters and doesn't require the number of clusters to be specified in advance. It provides a dendrogram (a tree-like diagram) to interpret the data by viewing at different levels of granularity; however, it is computationally intensive for large data sets.

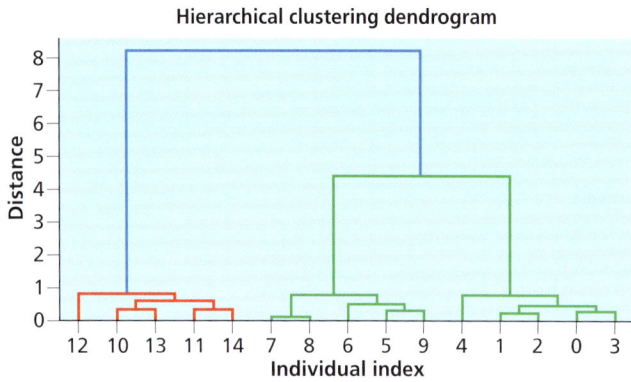

Hierarchical clustering dendrogram

■ Hierarchical clustering tree

Example applications include genealogy research to analyse genetics to understand family relationships, and organizing library resources such as books and journals in a manner that reflects similarity of content based on topics, themes or authors.

In this plot of a family tree, individuals from the same family are grouped closer together first and, as you move up the dendrogram, families start merging based on their similarities (distances).

> ● **See also**
>
> Reference the scikit-learn documentation for hierarchical clustering with a dendrogram by searching online for scikit-learn's "Plot Hierarchical Clustering Dendrogram" (**https://scikit-learn. org/stable/auto_examples/cluster/plot_agglomerative_dendrogram.html**).

■ DBSCAN clustering

◉ Key information

DBSCAN stands for Density-Based Spatial Clustering of Applications with Noise.

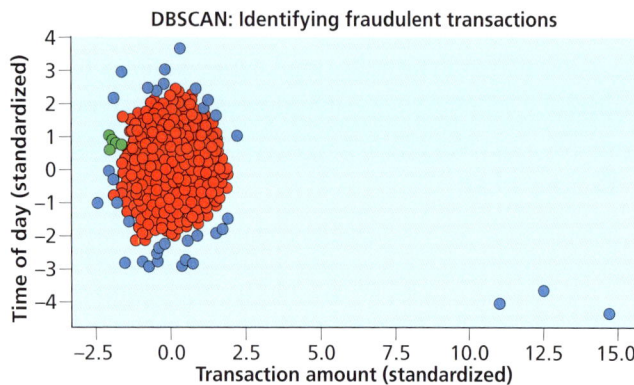

DBSCAN: Identifying fraudulent transactions

■ Density-based spatial clustering

DBSCAN clustering will group together points that are close to each other based on a distance measurement and a minimum number of points. It is very effective for data with clusters of similar density. Unlike k-means, DBSCAN does not require the number of clusters to be specified. It can find arbitrarily shaped clusters and can handle noise and outliers.

An example application might be to detect fraudulent financial transactions by clustering on similarities of amount, location and time. DBSCAN can identify the dense clusters that are "typical" and then separate out unusual transactions for alerts.

> ● **See also**
>
> Reference the scikit-learn documentation for DBSCAN by searching online for scikit-learn's section 2.3.7 "DBSCAN" (**https://scikit-learn.org/stable/modules/clustering.html#dbscan**).

◆ **Association rule:** a process of finding patterns of co-occurrence in data; this means, given the presence of one item in a record, how likely it is that another item will be present.

A4.3.5 Unsupervised learning: association rule

The **association rule** can be understood as a data mining technique that seeks to find co-occurrences within a data set. It is another form of unsupervised learning. The technique is commonly applied for market analysis, as well as crime analysis, healthcare, web / app behaviour tracking, and more.

There are three key metrics associated with association rule learning:

- **Support:** The proportion of transactions that include a particular item or combination of items.
- **Confidence:** The likelihood of occurrence of a particular item (B) when given some other item (A).
- **Lift:** The degree to which two items will appear together in this model, compared to the expected likelihood of them appearing together if the items were statistically independent; a lift value greater than 1 indicates the presence of item A increases the likelihood of B appearing.

The following example uses a data set of transactions from a fresh food market to find the items that are frequently purchased together. You can download the data set from **https://github.com/paulbaumgarten/hodder-ibdp-computerscience**

The first table, *frequent itemsets*, shows the support value for each set of items. In this case, 84 per cent of transactions include the sale of Milk. The *association rules* table illustrates the association between the antecedent (prerequisite) item and the consequent (resulting) item. In this case, the table shows:

- 62 per cent of transactions involve both Milk and Bread
- there is a 73 per cent likelihood that the customer will also purchase Bread if they purchase Milk
- the lift of 1.05 indicates that Bread is 1.05 times more likely to be purchased with Milk than without it.

```
Frequent Itemsets:
            support                                itemsets
0              0.84                                   (Milk)
1              0.70                                  (Bread)
2              0.60                                 (Butter)
3              0.60                                    (Egg)
4              0.54                                 (Cheese)
..              ...                                      ...
244            0.40      (Pasta, Butter, Bacon, Chicken)
245            0.40     (Apple, Banana, Coffee, Chicken)
246            0.40       (Apple, Banana, Bacon, Coffee)
247            0.42     (Banana, Bacon, Coffee, Chicken)
248            0.40      (Pasta, Banana, Bacon, Chicken)
```

```
Association Rules:
          antecedents         consequents   support   confidence       lift
0              (Milk)             (Bread)      0.62     0.738095   1.054422
1             (Bread)              (Milk)      0.62     0.885714   1.054422
2            (Butter)              (Milk)      0.50     0.833333   0.992063
3               (Egg)              (Milk)      0.50     0.833333   0.992063
4            (Cheese)              (Milk)      0.50     0.925926   1.102293
..              ...                  ...       ...          ...        ...
821    (Pasta, Bacon)   (Banana, Chicken)      0.40     0.833333   1.602564
822  (Pasta, Chicken)    (Banana, Bacon)      0.40     0.740741   1.322751
823   (Banana, Bacon)    (Pasta, Chicken)      0.40     0.714286   1.322751
824 (Banana, Chicken)      (Pasta, Bacon)      0.40     0.769231   1.602564
825  (Bacon, Chicken)    (Pasta, Banana)      0.40     0.714286   1.552795
```

Python

```python
import pandas as pd
from mlxtend.preprocessing import TransactionEncoder
from mlxtend.frequent_patterns import apriori, association_rules
# Load data set
df = pd.read_csv("biased_transactions.csv")
# Generate frequent itemsets
frequent_itemsets = apriori(df, min_support=0.4, use_colnames=True)
# Generate association rules
rules = association_rules(frequent_itemsets, metric="confidence", min_threshold=0.7)
# Display the results
print("Frequent Itemsets:")
print(frequent_itemsets)
print("Association Rules:")
print(rules[["antecedents", "consequents", "support", "confidence", "lift"]])
```

This example uses an algorithm called Apriori in the `mlxtend` library for discovering the frequent data sets. Here is a high-level overview of the Apriori algorithm:

- Determine a threshold for the minimum level of support that will be considered (40 per cent in the code example above).
- Identify individual items in the data set that meet the threshold and store their appearance count.
- Progress to identifying pairs of items and larger groupings of items in the data set that also meet the minimum threshold.
- If a set of items does not meet the threshold at a small level, it can be removed from further consideration.
- The result is all combinations of items that appear frequently together at or above the minimum threshold.

> **● See also**
>
> Reference the mlxtend documentation for association rule processing by searching online for mlxtend documentation for association rule processing (**https://rasbt.github.io/mlxtend/user_guide/frequent_patterns/association_rules**).

A4.3.6 Reinforcement learning

Previously, "reinforcement learning" was described as learning from trial and error. In that vein, it can be likened to a toddler learning to walk. Every time the toddler falls over, they learn a little more about how to correctly balance themself next time, until they eventually become a stable and confident walker.

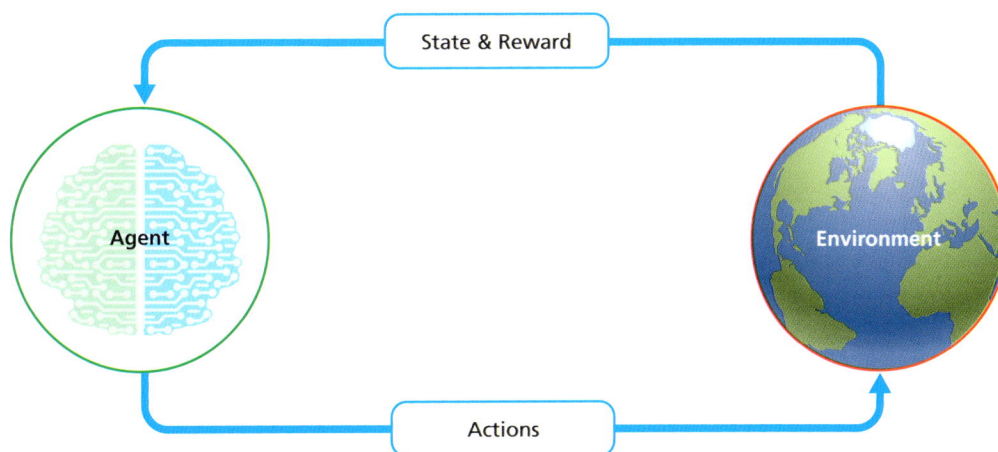

State & Reward

Agent

Environment

Actions

■ Reinforcement learning flowchart

As with most machine learning algorithms, reinforcement learning introduces some new terminology to consider:

- **Agent**: The machine learning model that makes the decisions on what to do.

- **Environment**: The world, as perceived by the agent.

- **State**: A snapshot in time of the world. State is the data that communicates the current situation or the environment. Careful consideration of your state data is critical when developing a reinforcement learning algorithm. What data will you provide to the agent to help it learn the task you have for it? For instance, when training an agent to play a snake game, do you give it values indicating the distance and bearing of the apple, or a pixel map of the entire world?

- **Action**: An operation or behaviour that the agent can perform in the environment (for example walk forward, turn left, turn right).

- **Reward**: An immediate return from the environment in response to the agent's action. Reward may be positive or negative (a punishment).

- **Policies**: The strategies the agent will use to map states to actions. Think of policies as the agent's mental if-this-then-that list.

The general process is as follows:

- The agent will typically begin with a randomized policy, as it has no existing knowledge of the environment.

- The agent observes the environment. Based on what it perceives, and the policy it has recorded so far, the agent chooses an action to perform.

- The agent performs the selected action.

- The environment updates to a new state.

- The environment provides feedback via a reward to the agent.

- The agent updates its policy based on the reward feedback received.

- The process repeats.

Reinforcement learning usually involves a combination of **exploration** and **exploitation**. "Exploration" is when the agent ignores its learned policy and tries something new.

"Exploitation" is when the agent follows the learned policy and behaves according to what it learned. Typically, an algorithm will start with a heavy emphasis on exploration, as the algorithm hasn't had much opportunity to learn anything yet. Over time, the hyperparameter for the exploration / exploitation ratio, known as the "learning rate", should adjust so as to start deferring to the learned data more.

■ Q-learning

The agent's policies are responsible for maintaining what the agent has learned. While there are a few approaches to this, one of the most common is known as "Q-learning".

Q-learning can be thought of as using a 2D array or other data structure to create a giant lookup table for every possible state and action combination. It stores a value for each possible permutation of the two to predict what reward it would receive in each scenario.

	Action 1	Action 2	Action 3	Action 4
State 1	−50	0	10	0
State 2	10	20	0	10
State 3	0	−10	0	50

The table illustrates a simplified version of a Q-learning 2D array. The data would suggest:

- When state 1 is seen, the best thing the agent can do is action 3, and it should avoid doing action 1.

- When state 2 is seen, the agent should do action 2, but action 1 and 4 would also give it a reward.

- When state 3 is seen, the agent should do action 4 for a large reward (possibly winning the game), and avoid action 2.

A Q-learning table can be very large, given the array size is determined by all possible states and all possible resulting actions. When the data requirements are unfeasibly large, an alternative approach is to use an artificial neural network to learn generalizations about the state and resulting output actions. When a neural network is used, it is known as a "Deep Q-Network".

Here is a pseudocode overview of the process:

```
Initialize the Q-table with all zeros (or some initial values)
for each round:
    Initialize the state S to the starting point of the game
    while the episode is not finished:
        Choose action A from state S using a policy derived from Q
        Take action A
        Observe the immediate reward R and the next state S'
        Update the Q-table value for the original state S and action A:
            Q(S, A) <- Q(S, A) + alpha * (R + gamma *
                                          max(Q(S', all_actions)) - Q(S, A))
        S <- S'  # Move to the next state
    end while
end for
```

There are a few comments to note about this pseudocode:

- When choosing action A, take into consideration whether the algorithm should exploit its Q-table or explore other alternatives.

- Alpha here refers to the learning rate. A higher alpha means that newer information has a greater impact on updating the Q-values, allowing the agent to adapt quickly to changes in the environment. A lower alpha will cause slower updates, making the agent more stable but also slower to learn. A starting value between 0.01 and 0.05 would be normal.

- Gamma here refers to the discount factor for how much future anticipated rewards should be considered when making a decision. The ultimate goal of most scenarios is to find an optimal policy that provides the maximum cumulative reward. A gamma value close to 0 makes the agent "myopic" (short-sighted), heavily prioritizing immediate rewards. Conversely, a gamma close to 1 encourages the agent to consider future rewards more strongly, valuing them almost as much as immediate rewards. This makes the agent "far-sighted", planning over a longer horizon.

- This line in the pseudocode is known as the "Bellman equation":

```
Q(S, A) <- Q(S, A) + alpha * (R + gamma * max(Q(S', all_actions))
- Q(S, A))
```

and it states that the Q-value for a state-action is equal to the immediate reward plus the discounted value of the best action to take in the next state, adjusted for the learning rate.

◼ Example: Pong! game

The following example is a Pong!-style paddle-and-bouncing-ball game. It uses the *pygame-ce* library for the graphics, and a *numpy* array for the Q-table. As can be seen in the results chart, this agent requires about 20 minutes of training before it begins showing acceptable results.

◼ Pong! game

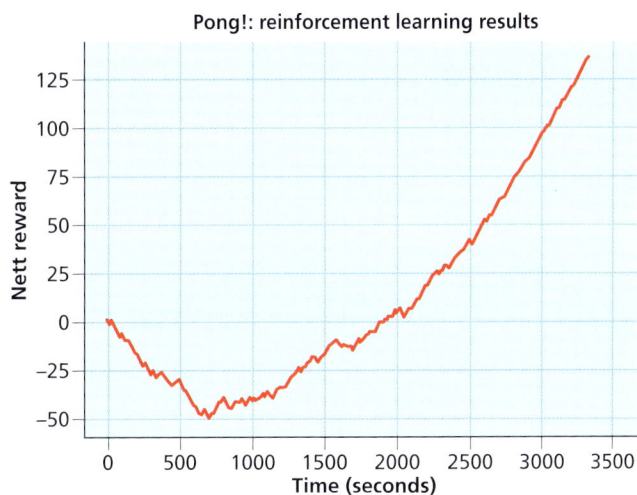

Pong!: reinforcement learning results

◼ Pong! game: nett reward over time

Python

```python
import pygame
import random
import numpy as np
import matplotlib.pyplot as plt
# Constants
```

```python
WIDTH, HEIGHT = 200, 400
FPS = 30
PADDLE_WIDTH, PADDLE_HEIGHT = 30, 15
BALL_RADIUS = 7
BALL_COLOUR = (255, 255, 64)
PADDLE_COLOUR = (255, 64, 255)
BACKGROUND_COLOUR = (64, 64, 128)
# Initialize Pygame
pygame.init()
screen = pygame.display.set_mode((WIDTH, HEIGHT))
clock = pygame.time.Clock()
class Paddle:
    def __init__(self, x, y):
        self.rect = pygame.Rect(x, y, PADDLE_WIDTH, PADDLE_HEIGHT)
    def move(self, x):
        self.rect.x += x
        self.rect.x = max(self.rect.x, 0)
        self.rect.x = min(self.rect.x, WIDTH - PADDLE_WIDTH)
    def draw(self):
        pygame.draw.rect(screen, PADDLE_COLOUR, self.rect)
class Ball:
    def __init__(self, x, y):
        self.rect = pygame.Rect(x, y, BALL_RADIUS*2, BALL_RADIUS*2)
        self.dx = random.choice([-4, 4])
        self.dy = random.choice([-4, 4])
    def move(self):
        self.rect.x += self.dx
        self.rect.y += self.dy
        if self.rect.top <= 0 or self.rect.bottom >= HEIGHT:
            self.dy = -self.dy
        if self.rect.left <= 0 or self.rect.right >= WIDTH:
            self.dx = -self.dx
    def draw(self):
        pygame.draw.ellipse(screen, BALL_COLOUR, self.rect)
# Game objects
paddle = Paddle(WIDTH//2 - PADDLE_WIDTH//2, HEIGHT - PADDLE_HEIGHT)
ball = Ball(WIDTH//2, HEIGHT//2)
# Q-learning parameters
LEARNING_RATE = 0.05
DISCOUNT_FACTOR = 0.99
epsilon = 0.1
# Let state have 10 positions for paddle and ball
# (reduces demands on Q-Table)
def get_state():
    paddle_mid = paddle.rect.x + PADDLE_WIDTH // 2
    ball_mid = ball.rect.x + BALL_RADIUS
    return (paddle_mid//20, ball_mid//20)
```

```python
# Q-table
# 10 possible paddle positions, 10 ball positions, 3 actions
q_table = np.zeros((10, 10, 3))
def update_q_table(state, action, next_state, reward):
    # Bellman's equation
    old_value = q_table[state[0], state[1], action]
    next_max = np.max(q_table[next_state[0], next_state[1]])
    new_value = (1 - LEARNING_RATE) * old_value +
                LEARNING_RATE * (reward + DISCOUNT_FACTOR * next_max)
    q_table[state[0], state[1], action] = new_value
def choose_action(state):
    if random.random() < epsilon:
        # Explore: choose a random action
        return random.randint(0, 2)
    else:
        # Exploit: choose the best action from Q-table
        return np.argmax(q_table[state[0], state[1]])
def get_reward():
    if ball.rect.bottom >= HEIGHT:
        if ball.rect.colliderect(paddle.rect):
            return 1  # Reward for hitting the ball
        else:
            return -1  # Penalty for missing the ball
    return 0  # No reward or penalty
running = True
nett = 0 # nett reward
cumulative = [] # nett reward history for graphing
while running:
    screen.fill(BACKGROUND_COLOUR)
    for event in pygame.event.get():
        # Use the quit icon for game termination
        if event.type == pygame.QUIT:
            running = False
    # Agent decides and acts
    state = get_state()
    action = choose_action(state)
    if action == 1:
        paddle.move(-10)  # Move left
    elif action == 2:
        paddle.move(10)  # Move right
    # Update game state
    ball.move()
    paddle.draw()
    ball.draw()
    # Check reward & state, update Q table
    reward = get_reward()
    next_state = get_state()
```

```
    update_q_table(state, action, next_state, reward)
    if reward > 0:
        PADDLE_COLOUR = (0,255,0)
    elif reward < 0:
        PADDLE_COLOUR = (255,0,0)
    # Update nett reward for graph
    nett += reward
    cumulative.append(nett)
    # Draw the game to screen
    pygame.display.flip()
    clock.tick(FPS)
pygame.quit()
# Graph results
time = [i/FPS for i in range(len(cumulative))]
plt.plot(time, cumulative)
plt.title("Pong: Reinforcement learning results")
plt.xlabel("Time (seconds)")
plt.ylabel("Nett reward")
plt.grid(True)
plt.show()
```

● See also

Gymnasium is a popular library for learning about reinforcement learning. It provides a number of pre-written environments that you can experiment with: **https://gymnasium.farama.org**

A4.3.7 Genetic algorithms

◆ **Genetic algorithm:** imitates the concept of survival of the fittest and evolution by testing a population of possible solutions to a problem, using properties from the best-performing solutions to create a new population of possible solutions, and then repeating the process until a suitably performing solution has been identified.

Genetic algorithms are not normally classified within the traditional categories of "supervised learning", "unsupervised learning" or "reinforcement learning". They are considered an evolutionary algorithm. They learn through a process of optimization inspired by the process of natural selection.

A high-level overview of the algorithmic process is:

■ Start with a *population* of possible solutions to the problem. This may be in the form of an array of strings, for instance, where each string is a randomly generated possible solution.

■ Each item within the population is evaluated through a *fitness function* that returns a metric for how good the possible solution is.

■ Pairs of solutions are *selected* for reproduction. Various algorithms will be discussed that make these selections, but generally the better the fitness function score, the more likely a solution is to be selected.

■ The selected pairs then undergo *reproduction* using a *crossover* algorithm, where part of the genetic code of each parent is selected and then combined together to create a new possible solution.

■ The new offspring may then undergo *mutation*. Random number functions are generally used so that only a small percentage of offspring undergo mutation, and then those selected have parts of their genetic code (their "solution" to the problem) randomly altered.

A4 Machine learning

- Once a new generation of offspring has been generated, they become the current generation, and the process of calculating fitness, selection, reproduction and mutation repeats itself.
- The process repeats until whatever termination criteria you determine is satisfied. This might be to iterate for a given number of generations, or to iterate until a fitness score of a minimum threshold has been reached.

Genetic algorithms are used for problems where it is not essential to identify the most perfect, optimal solution, but where there is a degree of "close enough is good enough" flexibility.

Common example applications of genetic algorithms include:

- **Route planning**, such as the travelling salesperson problem. Consider the scenario of a salesperson who has 50 cities to visit. Rather than crisscrossing the countryside, genetic algorithms can find a *close-to-optimal* route to minimize the distance travelled. In the context of a long journey to 50 cities, it is not necessary to find the most perfect solution, so long as the solution is good enough. Put another way, if the algorithm can find a good solution in a few minutes, is it really worth hours or days of additional processing to find a solution that might be only 1 per cent better? At some point, the route is good enough to use.
- **Timetabling**, such as allocating students to their preferred classes where there are constraints on the number of teachers, rooms and classes available.
- **Civil and mechanical engineering** to help optimize design of structures such as bridges or buildings, and vehicle designs to make choices of materials based on durability, strength and cost.
- **Control systems** and **robotics** use genetic algorithms to optimize the controller for better stability and performance.
- **Finance applications** use genetic algorithms to help optimize a trade-off between risk and reward in selection of an investment portfolio.
- Within machine learning, a genetic algorithm can help select a subset of relevant features from a larger data set to improve model accuracy and reduce overfitting.
- In some types of machine learning problems, it is possible to use genetic algorithms for the training of an artificial neural network as an alternative approach to backpropagation (see later in this section).

■ Selection functions

Selecting pairs of values for reproduction relies on the concept of weighted randomization. It is weighted in the sense that those with higher fitness scores should be more likely to be chosen for reproduction. Randomization is still important, however, to ensure that the algorithm doesn't become trapped in a local maximum.

One of the most commonly used approaches is the concept of a roulette wheel, where the portion of the wheel allocated is determined by the fitness function score.

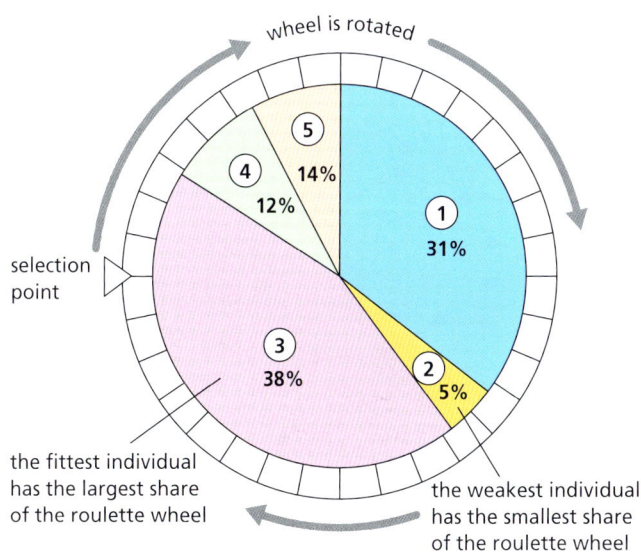

■ Roulette wheel selection

Crossover functions

Crossover functions define the algorithm used for reproduction – taking two input solutions and mixing them in such a way as to produce a "child", representing a new valid solution.

There are a variety of common algorithms to do this, but each needs to be considered in the context of the problem. Any approach will likely need to be tweaked to ensure the "child" created through the process is valid for the scenario.

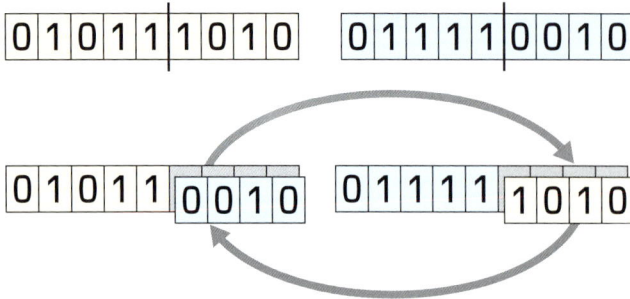

One-point crossover

Two common methods are the one-point crossover and the two-point crossover.

One-point crossover selects a random point in the gene sequence to slice the data. The data from up until the slice point is copied from parent 1 into child 1, and then the rest of child 1's data comes from parent 2. The inverse can also occur at the same time to create a second child.

Two-point crossover works in a similar manner, except two slice points are selected.

There are other commonly used methods as well, but what matters most is that you are using a randomization function to create offspring that are a mix of the data from two parents.

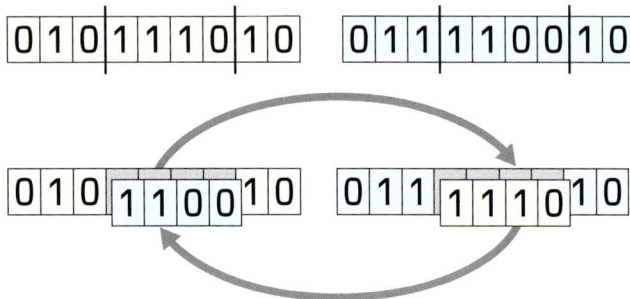

Two-point crossover

Top tip!

Choose appropriate genetic operators (selection, crossover, mutation) for your problem, and ensure diversity within the population to avoid premature convergence.

Example: Travelling salesperson

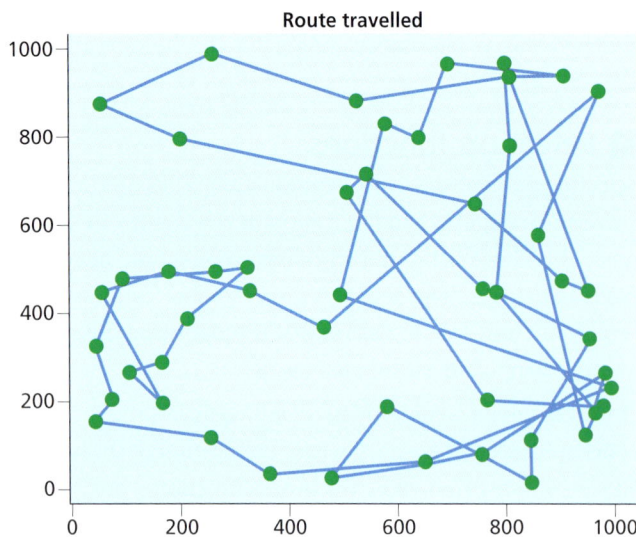

Travelling salesperson – random route

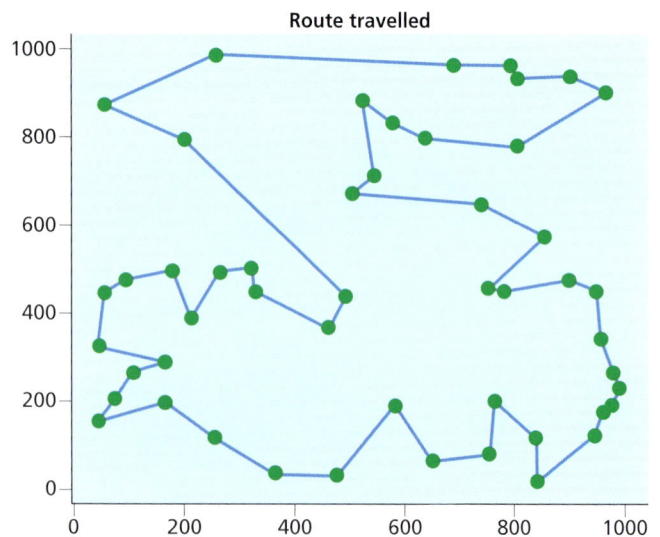

Travelling salesperson – optimized route

Consider the charts to represent a map of 50 cities that a travelling salesperson wishes to visit, with two possible routes for the journey. Clearly, the randomized journey is inefficient, whereas the optimized journey is a lot more efficient.

A4 Machine learning

Two questions to ponder: Is the optimized route perfect? And, does it matter?

To find the absolute most perfect solution would require testing 50! permutations; that is, over 30,000,000,000,000,000,000,000,000,000,000,000,000,000,000,000,000,000,000,000,000,000,000,000 permutations. That is a lot of processing! The reality is, in scenarios such as this, rather than labouring for perfect, good enough will do. In the context of travelling between 50 cities, does it make sense to spend exponential time in calculations to save just a few minutes of travel?

This is an example of the type of problem that genetic algorithms can help solve.

Step 1: Create an initial population

Assign each city a number and use a random number generator to create a randomized route. Do this for an initial population of 500 possible solutions (population size being one of the hyperparameters you may want to tune).

Python

```python
def create_random_route():
    route = [n for n in range(0,50)]
    random.shuffle(route)
    return route
def create_initial_population():
    return [create_random_route() for n in range(0, 500)]
```

Step 2: Create a fitness function to measure the performance of each member of the population

The obvious metric is to use the journey distance of the route; however, given the crossover function will give preference to those with a higher score for reproduction, it is necessary to use a fitness function that gives the highest scores for those routes with lowest distances.

One simple solution might be to calculate the fitness score by setting the distance as a fraction denominator, such as:

$$fitness_i = \frac{1}{distance_i}$$

An alternative approach used in the example code that follows is to use normalization to convert the data into a [0,1] range, where the 0 represents the highest distance and the 1 represents the smallest distance. The resulting normalized values are then used as an exponent to ensure that small differences in the normalized value, especially at the higher end, caused very large differences in fitness.

$$normalized_i = \frac{distance_{max} - distance_i}{distance_{max} - distance_{min}}$$

$$fitness_i = 2^{100*normalized_i}$$

The selection function is yet another hyperparameter for you to tune and experiment with for each given problem. The method outlined here was only selected after experimenting with half a dozen different possible approaches to see which produced the quickest results.

```python
Python
def calc_distance(route):
    dist = 0
    for i in range(1, len(route)):
        # Get the co-ordinates for each pair of cities
        x1,y1 = coords[ route[i-1] ]
        x2,y2 = coords[ route[i] ]
        dist += math.sqrt( abs(x1-x2)**2 + abs(y1-y2)**2 )
    # Don't forget to return home at the end!
    x1,y1 = coords[ route[len(route)-1] ]
    x2,y2 = coords[ route[0] ]
    dist += math.sqrt( abs(x1-x2)**2 + abs(y1-y2)**2 )
    return dist
def calc_fitness(distances):
    max_distance = np.max(distances)
    min_distance = np.min(distances)
    normalized = (max_distance-distances)/(max_distance-min_distance)
    fitness = np.power(2.0, (normalized*100))
    return fitness
```

Step 3: Reproduction using a crossover method

In this case, the code below is using a modified form of one-point crossover. A point in the data is randomly selected, and the genetic data from parent 1 is copied across without change. After that, the remaining cities are copied over from parent 2 in the order in which they appeared in parent 2.

Here is a simple example with six cities:

PARENT 1   = [0, 4, 5, 1, 3, 2]

PARENT 2   = [4, 2, 0, 3, 5, 1]

Randomly decide how many genes to copy from parent 1. In this case, use three.

CHILD   = [0, 4, 5, _, _, _]

Now copy the remaining values from parent 2, skipping the values already present from parent 1.

CHILD   = [0, 4, 5, 2, 3, 1]

```python
Python
def reproduce(parent1, parent2):
    # First set of genes will come from parent 1
    count_of_genes_from_parent1 = random.randint(0, len(parent1))
    child = parent1[0: count_of_genes_from_parent1]
    # Remaining genes will come from parent 2
    for i in range(0, len(parent2)):
        # Only include genes from parent2 not already provided by parent 1
        # (don't want to visit the same city twice)
        if parent2[i] not in child:
            child.append(parent2[i])
    return child
```

A4 Machine learning

Step 4: Mutation

There is no fixed algorithm to use for mutation; it will vary somewhat depending on the context of your problem. In this case, the following code will, in 5 per cent of cases (the mutation rate hyperparameter), randomly pick a pair of cities in the route and swap them.

Python

```python
def mutate(person, mutation_rate):
    if random.random() < mutation_rate:
        a = random.randint(0, len(person)-1)
        b = random.randint(0, len(person)-1)
        person[a], person[b] = person[b], person[a]
    return person
```

Step 5: Promote the children to be the active generation

This will be just a one-line task at the end of the loop to copy the data from the new generation that was being produced, into the array being used for the active generation.

Python

```python
# Move to the next generation
population = next_generation
```

Step 6: Write the main function to bring it all together

Python

```python
import math, random, json
import numpy as np
with open("travelling-salesperson.json","r") as f:
    coords = json.loads(f.read())
def travelling_salesperson(population_size=500, generations=5000):
    # Create randomized population
    population = create_initial_population(population_size)
    minimum = 50000
    generation_number = 0
    while minimum > 5000 and generation_number < generations:
        # Calculate fitness for each person
        generation_number += 1
        distances = np.array([calc_distance(population[n]) for n in range
        (0, population_size)])
        fitness = calc_fitness(distances)
        if generation_number % 25 == 0:
            print(f"Generation {generation_number}: Best {calc_distance
            (population[ np.argmax(fitness) ])} Mean { distances.mean() }")
        # Create the next generation
        next_generation = []
```

```
        for p in range(0, population_size, 2):
            # Select parents
            # Select k=2 items from "population", using the values in "fitness"
            # to determine probability weighting.
            parents = random.choices(population, weights=fitness, k=2)
            # Reproduce
            child1 = reproduce(parents[0], parents[1])
            child2 = reproduce(parents[1], parents[0])
            # Mutate
            child1 = mutate(child1, 0.05)
            child2 = mutate(child2, 0.05)
            next_generation.append(child1)
            next_generation.append(child2)
        # Move to the next generation
        population = next_generation
    # All done. What are the results?
    fitness = np.array([calc_fitness(population[n]) for n in range
    (0, population_size)])
    best = np.argmax(fitness)
    print(f"Best person after {generations} generations is #{best}")
    print(f"Their travel distance: {calc_distance(population[best])}")
print(f"Their route: {population[best]}")
travelling_salesperson()
```

Best route found for travelling salesperson for each generation

As you let that execute, it will print an update every 25 generations with the progress it has made, similar to the following update:

Generation 25: Best 13496.55 Mean 14238.29

Generation 50: Best 11301.76 Mean 11541.97

Generation 75: Best 9265.94 Mean 9365.81

Generation 100: Best 8944.63 Mean 9033.31

Generation 125: Best 8727.39 Mean 8883.68

This chart shows the minimum travel distance calculated after each generation when the algorithm was executed by the author. There are a couple of important aspects to draw your attention to.

Firstly, and most obviously, is that most of the improvement in output occurs very quickly, after which the law of diminishing returns starts to apply.

The second thing to note, though, is that the output will frequently get stuck in a local minimum for several hundred generations before suddenly breaking out of it, so there can be benefits to gain by being patient enough to give that the opportunity to occur.

What is the lowest distance route you can obtain to visit all 50 cities?

Download the data file from **https://github.com/paulbaumgarten/hodder-ibdp-computerscience**

A4 Machine learning

A4.3.8 Artificial neural networks

An artificial neural network (ANN) is an algorithm that learns to make decisions by finding patterns in data using an approach modelled on the biological brain. Just as a biological brain consists of many neurons that are interconnected and send signals to each other via synapses, so too an artificial neural network is an algorithm that defines a series of nodes that transmit data between each other. These nodes are known as **perceptrons**, though they are also very commonly referred to as "neurons".

Input layer   Hidden layer   Output layer

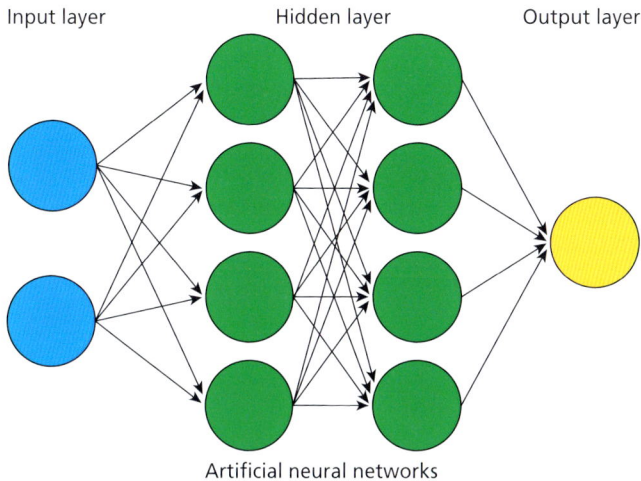

Artificial neural networks

■ Layers in an artificial neural network

The diagram represents a typical structure for an ANN:

■ The input layer receives the input values that the network is being asked to process. Each feature of your model requires its own input perceptron. The value given to each perceptron is numeric (either an integer or float, depending on the problem context).

■ There are usually one or more hidden layers within an ANN. These are layers of perceptrons that identify patterns in the input data to make generalizations useful for the next layer. They receive the values from the previous layer, perform their calculations and then send their respective result to the next layer in the network.

■ The output layer is where the ANN produces a final "answer" value or prediction.

The illustration in this case is also an example of a fully connected network, in that every perceptron from one layer is connected, and sends its output value to, every perceptron in the next layer. Fully connected networks are the norm.

■ A single perceptron

Zooming in on a single perceptron, the following sketch outlines the different elements at work:

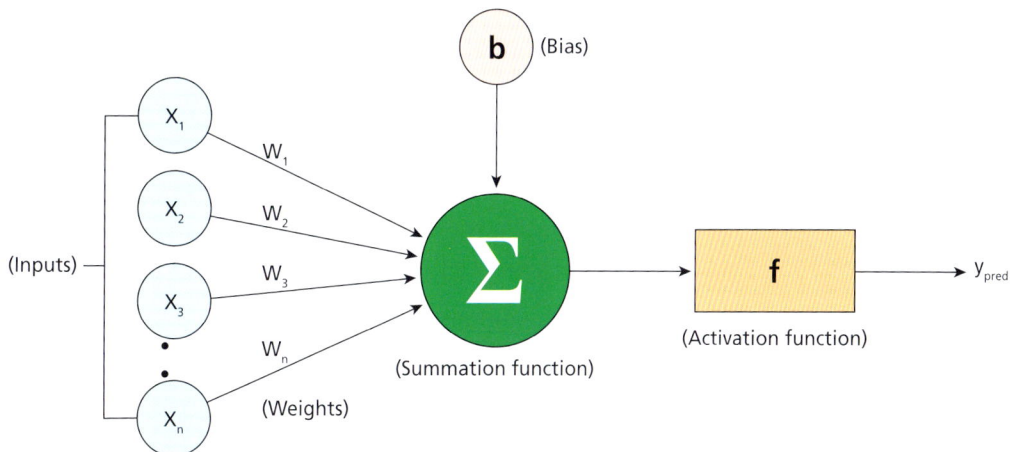

■ A perceptron in an artificial neural network

■ **Input:** The perceptron receives an input value from every perceptron in the layer before.

■ **Weight:** Every input has a weight associated with it. The weight is a value indicating the importance this particular neuron places on the values from the respective input. Weights are usually initialized with a random number between −1.0 and 1.0 and then adjusted by the training process.

- **Summation:** The product of each input value and its respective weight are summed together.
- **Bias:** Supplemental to weights, a typical neuron would also have a value called the "bias". This is added to the value from the summation step, prior to using activation. The bias acts as a way to shift the decision boundary along the curve of the activation function. The bias is usually initialized with a random number between −1.0 and 1.0 and then adjusted by the training process.
- **Activation:** The activation function helps determine whether or not the neuron should be "active" ("inactive" in this case means the neuron would have an output value of 0). The activation function serves to introduce nonlinearity to make neurons more expressive. That is, it helps force the neuron to make a decision. For example, one commonly used activation function is ReLU, which results in a neuron being active for any positive value, and inactive (0) for any negative value. A comparison of common activation functions follows later in this section.
- **Output:** Finally, the resulting value returned from the activation function is sent onward to the neurons in the next layer, or the external system.

The following example is a walkthrough of the calculations for a perceptron:

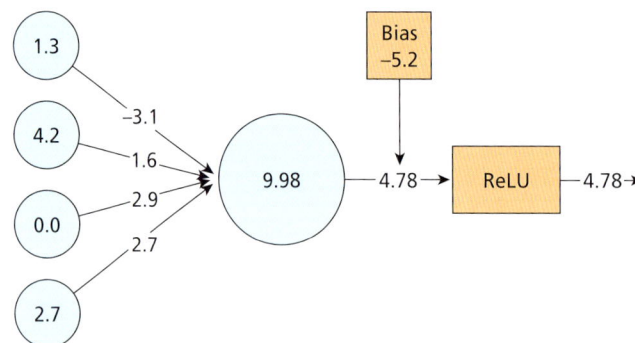

■ Example values in a perceptron

- The perceptron receives input values of 1.3, 4.2, 0.0 and 2.7.
- Each input path has a weight of −3.1, 1.6, 2.9 and 2.7 respectively.
- Each input and its respective weight are multiplied, and the results added together:

  $(1.3 * -3.1) + (4.2 * 1.6) + (0.0 * 2.9) + (2.7 * 2.7) = 9.98$

- The bias value is added, which, for this example, is −5.2:

  $9.98 + (-5.2) = 4.78$

- The resulting value is passed through the activation function, which, in this case, is ReLU:

  $ReLU(4.78) = 4.78$

- The output value 4.78 is passed along to the next layer in the network, or is given as the output value of the network, if it is the output layer.

From a mathematical perspective, up until the activation function, the rest of the perceptron can be considered a linear function, where the weights are the variable coefficients and the bias is the constant:

$y = ReLU(x_1 w_1 + x_2 w_2 + x_3 w_3 + x_4 w_4 + b)$

Or, to express it more generally:

$y = activation\left(\left(\sum_{i=0}^{n} x_i w_i\right) + b\right)$

A4 Machine learning

Given the output of any individual perceptron can be expressed as a function, and that the inputs of perceptrons are either input values or the outputs of other perceptrons, it means that the entire artificial neural network behaves as a function.

◉ Common mistake

Overcomplicating the model architecture can lead to overfitting and high computational costs. Start with a simple architecture and gradually increase complexity, if necessary.

◆ **Activation function:** a mathematical function applied to the output of a neuron that is used to determine whether or not the neuron should be activated (considered to be "on").

■ Activation functions

While there are a large variety of **activation functions** in use, there are four that are more common than all others: **ReLU**, **Sigmoid**, **Softmax** and **tanh**.

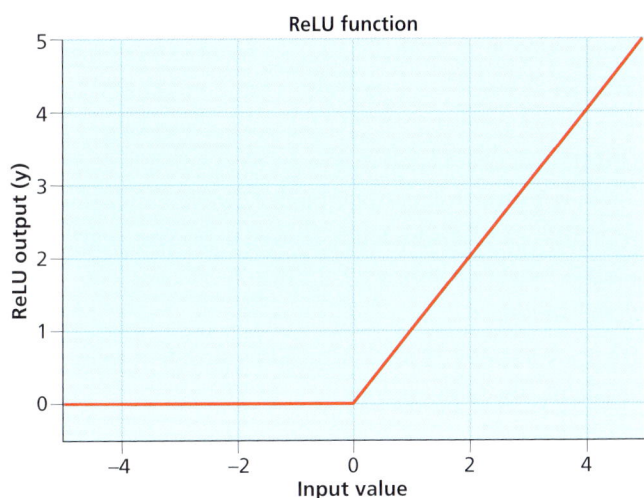

■ The ReLU function

ReLU

ReLU (rectified linear unit) is often the default choice for ANNs. It is computationally efficient and is less likely to have a vanishing (approaching zero) gradient, unlike Sigmoid or tanh. The function for ReLU is:

$$f(x) = \max(0, x)$$

On first impression, it may appear that ReLU is linear; however, it is more accurate to say it is two different lines coming together in the one function, one on the positive side, and another on the negative. The simple act of the zeroing of negative values significantly changes the behaviour within a network as it means that only positive neurons will be activated and any negative-value neurons will be deactivated. This small change makes a big difference when attempting to do classification problems.

Sigmoid

Sigmoid is commonly used in the output layer for binary classification problems since it maps to a distribution between 0 and 1, which is generally what is desired at the output layer. It is used in scenarios like email spam detection (spam or not spam) and medical diagnosis (sick or healthy). It is not usually used in hidden layers in deep networks due to their vanishing gradients. Observe that once the input value is less than −4 or greater than +4, the gradient becomes so insignificant it might as well be zero.

The equation for Sigmoid is:

$$f(x) = \frac{1}{1 + e^{-x}}$$

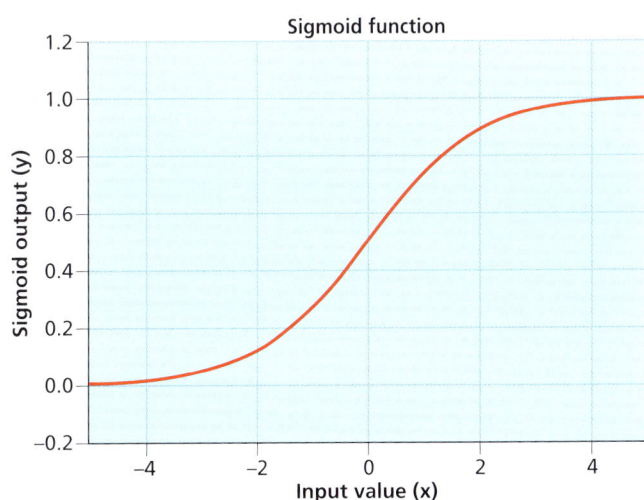

■ The Sigmoid function

Softmax probabilities for varying logits of Class 1

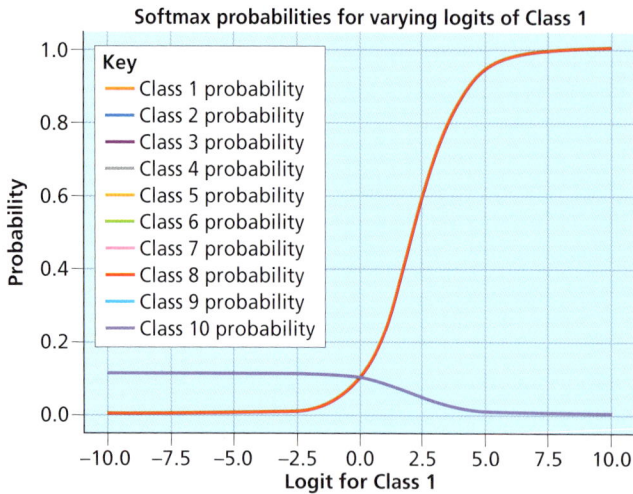

Key
- Class 1 probability
- Class 2 probability
- Class 3 probability
- Class 4 probability
- Class 5 probability
- Class 6 probability
- Class 7 probability
- Class 8 probability
- Class 9 probability
- Class 10 probability

■ The Softmax function

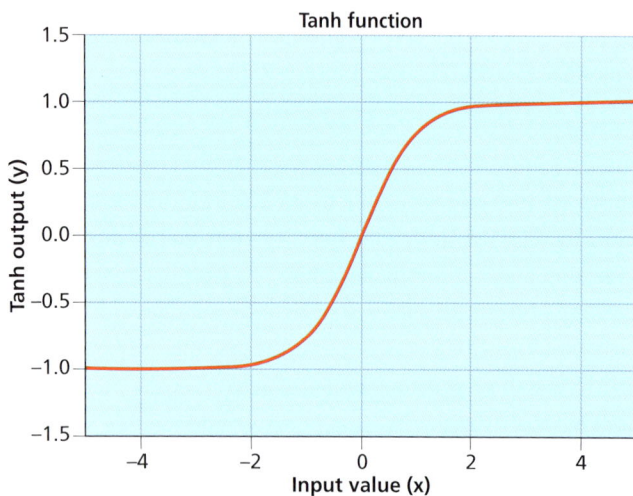

■ The tanh function

Softmax

Softmax produces an output similar to Sigmoid in that both produce values in the range (0,1). Softmax produces a probability distribution for N different outcomes, where N is the number of categories for classification and the probabilities sum to 1. This makes it suitable for distribution across multiple classes, so it is commonly used for the output layer of a multiclass classification problem. (In the chart, the lines for Classes 2 to 10 are aligned and stacked one on the other, which is why it appears as if only two lines are plotted.)

Tanh

Tanh is similar to Sigmoid, but the output values range between −1.0 and 1.0. It is useful when your data is normalized around 0 but, like Sigmoid, it also has vanishing gradients that can be problematic. It is more common to see tanh used for hidden layers than Sigmoid, given its mean distribution is centred on 0. This centring around 0 makes learning for the next layer easier for classification.

There are a couple of mathematically equivalent ways of producing the tanh function:

$$f(x) = \frac{(e^x - e^{-x})}{(e^x + e^{-x})}$$

or

$$f(x) = \frac{2}{(1 + e^{-2x})} - 1$$

■ Generating a prediction

Using an ANN to generate a result is a matter of performing all the calculations on all the perceptrons in one layer, and then feeding forward those results to the next layer. The process continues until the output layer is reached and the process terminates.

While overengineered for the scenario, imagine using a neural network to determine the result of OR and AND logic gates. Consider the following network with two input neurons, four neurons in one hidden layer and two output neurons.

After training (discussed in the next section), the network consists of the following weights and biases. The ReLU activation function is used on the hidden layer and, since the network is seeking to perform a classification task, Sigmoid is used on the output layer.

■ Example values for a logic gate ANN

For those unfamiliar with logic gates, see Section A1.2.3. The network should produce the following results, if behaving correctly:

```
A    B           OR  AND

[0, 0]    ->    [0,  0]

[0, 1]    ->    [1,  0]

[1, 0]    ->    [1,  0]

[1, 1]    ->    [1,  1]
```

Performing the calculations for an input of [1, 0], the following occurs:

```
Hidden1 = ReLU( 1.00 * 0.60 + 0.00 * -1.13 + 0.53 ) = ReLU( 1.13 ) = 1.13

Hidden2 = ReLU( 1.00 * -0.47 + 0.00 * -1.11 + 0.00 ) = ReLU( -0.47 ) = 0.00

Hidden3 = ReLU( 1.00 * 0.70 + 0.00 * 2.10 + 0.00 ) = ReLU( 0.70 ) = 0.70

Hidden4 = ReLU( 1.00 * 2.10 + 0.00 * 0.80 - 0.23 ) = ReLU( 1.87 ) = 1.87
```

Now, use these hidden layer values to generate the output values.

```
Out1 = Sigmoid( 1.13*-0.25 + 0.00*0.94 + 0.70*1.73 + 1.87*0.71 - 0.26 )

     = Sigmoid( 2.00 )

     = 0.88

Out2 = Sigmoid( 1.13*-1.48 + 0.00*-0.69 + 0.70*-0.13 + 1.87*0.77 - 0.84 )

     = Sigmoid( -1.16 )

     = 0.24
```

Since our classification problem is seeking a 0 ("false" or "no") or 1 ("true" or "yes") answer, when 0.88 and 0.24 are rounded, the network has indeed correctly determined that an input of [1,0] into an OR gate results in a 1, and [1,0] into an AND gate results in a 0.

● **See also**

See 3Blue1Brown's YouTube video "But what is a neural network?"

■ Training

While calculating an output result or prediction from a neural network should be a conceptually straightforward mathematical process, the training process is more complex and is far beyond the scope of your course.

The process used is known as **backpropagation**. As a high-level overview, here is what is occurring:

■ We calculate the error in the output values received from the network when compared to the target output values in the training data. A loss function is used for this, such as "mean-squared-error" for regression, or "cross-entropy loss" for classification tasks.

■ We calculate how much each parameter (the weights and biases) in the network contributed to the error. This is done by using the gradient (i.e. the derivative or slope) of the loss function for each parameter.

■ An optimization algorithm such as "gradient-descent" is used to calculate adjustments to the parameters. By knowing the gradient of the error, the parameters can be adjusted in the opposite direction (gradient descent) to reduce the loss (see the videos referenced in the "See also" box).

■ Before applying the adjustment to the weights and biases, we multiply them by the learning rate hyperparameter. This is to ensure we don't overcorrect and solely design the network around any one particular value in the training data set.

■ Once this process has completed for one layer (such as using the output layer to calculate adjustments to the last hidden layer), we repeat the process on the layers before it. This process of moving backwards from the output layer, working through each hidden layer, until finally reaching the input layer, is where the term "backpropagation" comes from.

■ We repeat the entire process a certain number of iterations or until the loss stops decreasing significantly. Each pass over the data set is known as an "epoch".

● See also

See 3Blue1Brown's YouTube videos "Backpropagation, step-by-step | DL3" and "Gradient descent, how neural networks learn".

◆ Backpropagation: backpropagation of errors is the most commonly used technique for training artificial neural networks. The gradient of the loss function is calculated, and used to update parameters such as weights, in the opposite direction of the gradient to reduce the overall error.

■ Example 1: Logic gates

This is the Python code used for the OR and AND logic gates example in the previous walkthroughs.

Python
```
import tensorflow as tf
from tensorflow.keras.models import Sequential
from tensorflow.keras.layers import Dense
import numpy as np
# Inputs: [A, B]
x = np.array([[0, 0], [0, 1], [1, 0], [1, 1]], dtype=float)
# Outputs: [OR, AND]
y = np.array([[0, 0], [1, 0], [1, 0], [1, 1]], dtype=float)
```

A4 Machine learning

```
# Define and compile the model
model = Sequential([
    # Hidden layer with 4 neurons, using ReLU
    Dense(4, input_dim=2, activation="relu"),
    # Output layer with 2 neurons, using Sigmoid
    Dense(2, activation="sigmoid")
])
model.compile(loss="binary_crossentropy", optimizer="adam", metrics=["accuracy"])
model.fit(x, y, epochs=1000, verbose=1)
# Making predictions
predictions = model.predict(x)
print("Predicted outputs:\n", predictions)
# Evaluate the model
loss, accuracy = model.evaluate(x, y)
print("Accuracy: {:.2f}".format(accuracy))
# Print weights and biases for our curiosity
for layer_number, layer in enumerate(model.layers):
    weights, biases = layer.get_weights()
    print(f"Layer {layer_number+1}")
    print("Weights:\n", weights)
    print("Biases:\n", biases)
    print("\n")
```

Common mistake

If you are installing TensorFlow on a computer without a GPU, ensure you install a CPU-only version otherwise you will receive errors that pip is unable to find a version that satisfies the requirements.

That is, from your terminal, run the following:

pip install tensorflow-cpu

For more detailed instructions, refer to the TensorFlow installation guide at **www.tensorflow.org/install/pip**

■ Example 2: ANN for regression

A commonly used example for introducing regression problems with an ANN is the California housing data set. It contains information about various homes in California in the 1990s, including such features as house age, average number of rooms, average number of residents, and latitude and longitude, and is used to predict house prices.

More information on the data set can be found by searching online for Keras California Housing price regression data set (**https://keras.io/api/datasets/california_housing**).

Python

```
import tensorflow as tf
from tensorflow.keras import layers, models
from sklearn.model_selection import train_test_split
import numpy as np
```

```
# Load data set
(x, y), (x_test, y_test) = tf.keras.datasets.california_housing.load_data(
    version="large", path="california_housing.npz", test_split=0.2, seed=113
)
# Split the data into training and validation sets
# x_train is the training data, y_train is the training labels
# x_val is the validation data, y_val is the validation labels
x_train, x_val, y_train, y_val = train_test_split(x, y, test_size=0.2,
random_state=0)
# Define the network, compile, and train it
model = models.Sequential([
    layers.Dense(64, activation="relu", input_shape=(x_train.shape[1],)),
    layers.Dense(64, activation="relu"),
    layers.Dense(1)
])
model.compile(optimizer="adam",
    loss="mse",
    metrics=["mae"])
history = model.fit(x_train, y_train,
    epochs=100,
    validation_data=(x_val, y_val))
# Run the unseen test data through the network to determine success
test_loss, test_mae = model.evaluate(x_test, y_test)
print(f"Test data - mean-absolute-error: {test_mae}")
```

Examples of handwritten digits in the MNIST data set

■ Example 3: ANN for classification

A very common Hello World-style classification problem for ANNs is the MNIST number recognition data set. It comprises 60,000 28×28 grayscale images of the ten digits, along with a test set of 10,000 images.

Python

```
import tensorflow as tf
from tensorflow.keras import layers, models
from tensorflow.keras.utils import to_categorical
import matplotlib.pyplot as plt
import numpy as np
# Load data set
(x_train, y_train), (x_test, y_test) = tf.keras.datasets.mnist.load_data()
```

```
# Convert grayscale pixels into floats with range [0...1]
x_train = x_train/255.0
x_test = x_test/255.0
# Convert the labels into "1 hot encoding" category arrays
# e.g. label of 3 becomes [0,0,0,1,0,0,0,0,0,0]
y_train = to_categorical(y_train)
y_test = to_categorical(y_test)
# Define the network, compile, and train it
model = models.Sequential([
    layers.Flatten(input_shape=(28,28)),
    layers.Dense(64, activation="relu", input_shape=(x_train.shape[1],)),
    layers.Dense(64, activation="relu"),
    layers.Dense(10, activation="sigmoid")
])
model.compile(optimizer="adam",
    loss="binary_crossentropy",
    metrics=["accuracy"])
history = model.fit(x_train, y_train, epochs=5)
# Run the unseen test data through the network to determine success
loss, accuracy = model.evaluate(x_test, y_test)
print(f"Accuracy: {accuracy}")
model.save("mnist-example.keras")
```

One step that may not be intuitively obvious is how to test this with your own data. Suppose you have a 28×28 grayscale PNG file you'd like to test on the ANN. The following is example code to do this task. (*By the way, ensure your image is white text on black background, as that is how the model has been trained.*)

Python

```
import numpy as np
from PIL import Image    # pip install Pillow
import tensorflow as tf
model = tf.keras.models.load_model("mnist-example.keras")
# Load the image file
image = Image.open("your image file.png")
image = image.convert("L") # Grayscale to match the training data
image = image.resize((28, 28)) # Resize to match the training data
# Convert image to numpy array
image_array = np.array(image)
image_array = image_array/255.0 # Normalize to 0..1 scale
# Reshape the array for the model (Add a batch dimension at the beginning)
image_array = image_array.reshape(1, 28, 28)
# Send to the trained ANN
predictions = model.predict(image_array)
predicted_class = np.argmax(predictions, axis=1)
print("Predicted class:", predicted_class)
```

A4.3.9 Convolutional neural networks

A **convolutional neural network** (CNN) extends on the architecture of ANNs by using additional layers of calculations prior to processing the data through a fully connected artificial neural network.

CNNs are ideally suited to processing image data but are also valuable for applications such as video analysis, natural language processing (NLP), audio and speech processing, and recommendation systems.

To explore what makes a CNN different from an ANN, consider the following diagram of a typical convolutional neural network:

■ Structure of a convolutional neural network

■ Input layer

The input layer comprises the raw pixel data of the image being processed. The number of input nodes would be based upon *image width × image height × colour depth*.

It is important to consider that, when dealing with input data such as images, the input data can get very large with relative ease. A small image of only 100 × 100 pixels at full colour resolution (that is, 1 byte each for red, green and blue) would comprise 300,000 values. This is too much to feed directly into an ANN, and so preprocessing through convolution and pooling is used to reduce this to something more manageable.

■ Convolutional layer

The convolutional layers serve as feature extractors that are looking for patterns in the input image.

As the network trains, it develops filters (also known as "kernels") that learn to detect patterns that are important for the individual network at hand. Generally, these patterns are as simple as edge detection or various textures, but they can be used to detect more complex shapes within the image. Other common patterns that may emerge are sharpening filters and blur filters.

Edge detection will typically look for vertical or horizontal edges. For instance, the matrix to find vertical edges may look like this:

$$\begin{bmatrix} -1 & 0 & 1 \\ -1 & 0 & 1 \\ -1 & 0 & 1 \end{bmatrix}$$

Applying an edge detection filter to an image is shown in the following diagram. The first image is the original; the second is the output using vertical edge detection with the matrix above; the third is horizontal edge detection after rotating the matrix clockwise.

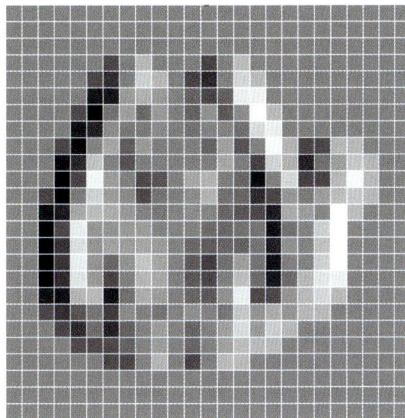

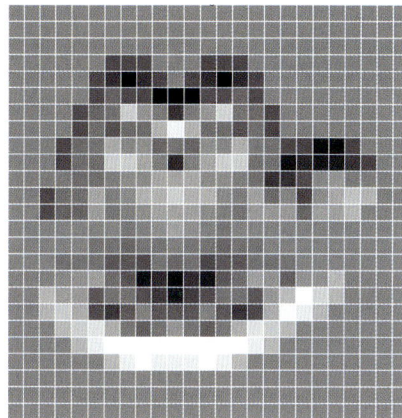

■ Kitten bitmap with its horizontal edges and vertical edges detected

A sharpening filter will emphasize the difference in contrast between adjacent pixel values. This helps make the image look more distinct to later stages of the network. The matrix for a sharpening filter may look like this:

$$\begin{bmatrix} 0 & -1 & 0 \\ -1 & 5 & -1 \\ 0 & -1 & 0 \end{bmatrix}$$

A blur filter will help reduce noise and detail from an image, so the network doesn't focus on minor variations of detail within the image that do not carry significance in meaning. For instance, a gaussian blur may be applied through the following matrix:

$$\begin{bmatrix} 1/16 & 1/8 & 1/16 \\ 1/8 & 1/4 & 1/8 \\ 1/16 & 1/8 & 1/16 \end{bmatrix}$$

The strength of CNNs lies in their ability to learn the most appropriate filters for a given task through backpropagation during the training process. The initial values for these kernels can be set randomly, or by using some heuristic, and then be updated to better suit the specific features of the training data.

The act of iterating over groups of pixels with a filter is known as "sliding" or "striding".

> ● **See also**
>
> See 3Blue1Brown's YouTube video "But what is a convolution?"

■ Activation function

Convolutional operations are linear transformations. Mathematically, they are the dot product between the filter (kernel) values and the pixel values in the image. If you stack multiple convolutional layers, the entire network can still be described as a single linear transformation. No matter how many layers you have, they can still be collapsed into a single layer that performs one linear transformation, because the composition of two linear functions is still a linear function (the function for any one pixel can be reduced to the sum of input values multiplied by various fixed coefficients).

This poses a problem for our network, as a linear system can only perform linear classification. That is, it can only separate data using a straight line (or hyperplane in higher dimensions). While this has its uses, the tasks we generally require of CNNs are too complex for a linear approach to separation.

Therefore, after convolution, the data is run through an activation function to introduce non-linearity to the data.

◼ Pooling layer

The next stage of the process is to pass the data through some down-sampling layers, also known as "pooling layers". The pooling layers serve to reduce the dimensions of the image data.

This serves a couple of important purposes. Firstly, it will reduce the number of parameters that need to be input into a deeply connected network, significantly reducing the computational workload of the network. Secondly, it also assists with network learning, as it will further help negate minor changes in individual pixels (image noise) that are unlikely to be relevant to image classification. This helps to reduce the risk of overfitting.

There are two commonly used methods of pooling:

- **Max pooling**, which takes the maximum value from a set of values.
- **Average pooling**, which takes the average value from the set of values.

◼ Fully connected layer

After pooling, the data is then fed into a fully connected artificial neural network (ANN), which has been previously discussed.

The purpose of the ANN at this point is to take the high-level features learned by the convolutional and pooling layers and use them to perform the final classification or regression task.

Before entering the first fully connected layer, the feature maps will typically be flattened into a one-dimensional vector of values, which will align with the number of input nodes of the ANN.

◼ Output layer

The output layer from the CNN is the output that comes from the fully connected layers of the ANN.

⬤ Top tip!

Don't neglect transfer learning to leverage pre-trained models. This is especially useful if you have limited training data available.

- Explore some of the pre-trained models available through TensorFlow or PyTorch, such as VGG, ResNet and Inception.
- Consider the similarity between the data the model was originally trained on, and your target data.
- Decide whether you will be using transfer learning to assist with feature extraction or fine-tuning. Feature extraction will use the previous network to extract meaningful features from new samples. In this case, freeze the convolutional base and only train a new classifier layer. Fine-tuning doesn't freeze the convolutional base. After adding your new output layer, it will fine-tune the weights of the pre-trained model by continuing the training process, allowing it to learn new task-specific features.
- Remember to preprocess data in the same way the original model was trained, and to use data augmentation techniques (like rotation, scaling, cropping and flipping) to artificially expand the training data set.

◼ Example: CIFAR-10

The CIFAR-10 data set contains 50,000 images of 32×32 pixels in RGB colour, plus another 10,000 test images. The images are labelled over ten categories: airplane, automobile, bird, cat, deer, dog, frog, horse, ship, truck.

The additional complexity of shapes, slightly enlarged size and the inclusion of three colour channels rather than just grayscale make CIFAR a good platform for experimenting with a CNN.

More information about the data set can be found by searching online for Keras CIFAR10 small images classification data set (**https://keras.io/api/datasets/cifar10**).

● TOK

Is it acceptable to benefit from knowledge derived from unethical sources?

CIFAR-10 is a data set that was compiled by Alex Krizhevsky in 2009. It was created as a subset of a larger data set of 80 million images known as Tiny Images.

In June 2020, the decision was made to withdraw the Tiny Images data set and request others to stop using it ,due to "biases, offensive and prejudicial images, and derogatory terminology" within the data set.

CIFAR-10 remains available and is commonly used by many academic institutions. Students use it to learn how to train neural networks for computer vision tasks.

Given its origins from the ethically compromised Tiny Images data set, should CIFAR-10 still be used in scientific research and technological development?

● TOK

Is it ethical to use data scraping for creating data sets without the consent of the content owners?

Web scraping is a prevalent tool used to gather vast amounts of data from across the internet. Typically, this occurs without the explicit consent of the owners or creators of the data.

Web scraping is fundamental to the data sets used for many machine learning models, including computer vision and large language models.

Courts and governments are grappling with the complex ethical issues around this practice, and no clear resolution is in sight. There are vast economic and commercial interests on both sides of the debate.

Some questions include:
- Who owns the information available on the internet, especially on forums such as Reddit, or collaborative efforts such as Wikipedia?
- Is it ethical to use this data for academic purposes? What about for commercial purposes?
- Is it an invasion of privacy to use photos and videos uploaded to social media to form data sets for machine learning purposes?
- Is it too late? Is it time to focus on harm mitigation? Are there ways to share profits, such as through royalty payments?

PYTHON

```python
from tensorflow.keras.datasets import cifar10
from tensorflow.keras import layers, models
import numpy as np
# Load the CIFAR-10 data set
(train_images, train_labels), (test_images, test_labels) = cifar10.load_data()
# Normalize the data to 0-1 ranges
train_images = train_images/255.0
test_images = test_images/255.0
# Define the CNN model
model = models.Sequential([                          # 32 x 32 pixels, 3 colours
    layers.Conv2D(32, (3, 3), activation="relu", input_shape=(32, 32, 3)),
    layers.MaxPooling2D((2, 2)),
    layers.Conv2D(64, (3, 3), activation="relu"),
    layers.MaxPooling2D((2, 2)),
    layers.Conv2D(64, (3, 3), activation="relu"),
    layers.Flatten(),
    layers.Dense(64, activation="relu"),
    layers.Dense(10, activation="softmax")
])
# Compile and train the model
model.compile(optimizer="adam", loss="sparse_categorical_crossentropy",
metrics=["accuracy"])
history = model.fit(train_images, train_labels, epochs=10, validation_split=0.1)
# Evaluate the model
test_loss, test_acc = model.evaluate(test_images, test_labels)
print("Test accuracy:", test_acc)
```

⬤ Top tip!

Start simple! Begin with simple models to establish a baseline, and gradually move to more complex algorithms. Appreciate the power of simple models; sometimes they are all you need.

A4.3.10 Model selection

You have looked at a lot of machine learning algorithms in this chapter. When the time comes to use machine learning to solve your own problems, how do you decide which model to use? Here are some criteria to assist in your decision-making process:

- **Classification or regression?** Does the problem require predicting a continuous output (regression) or categorizing data into predefined classes (classification)?

- **Linear or non-linear relationship?** Linear regression is quick and simple to implement, but will not work with complex non-linear data, in which case a neural network may be required.

- **Low or high dimensionality?** How many features do you need your algorithm to process?

- **Volume of data?** Deep learning requires a large amount of data to work accurately and to avoid overfitting. Decision trees or k-nearest neighbours may be better suited if the data set is small.

- **Feature independence?** If features (variables) interact with each other (such as co-dependency), the complex interplay may be better captured by a decision tree or neural network.

- **Accuracy?** If highly accurate predictions are required, then more complex models may be the better option, but this comes at the cost of requiring more data and computational power.

■ **Training time?** Linear regression and shallow decision trees can be trained very quickly, relative to deep neural networks.

■ **Transparency?** Sometimes the "magic-happens-here" approach of neural networks may be intimidating and undesired by the client. Some domains, such as healthcare or finance, may require models that can be user-interpreted, in which case linear regression or decision trees may be best.

■ **Resources available?** Deep neural networks require significant GPU computational power to train. If all you have is a consumer-grade laptop, a simpler approach may be required.

Key information

Remember that, as far as the syllabus is concerned, Machine Learning is a theory unit rather than a programming one. The following exercises are optional suggestions for students who wish to explore machine learning programming for themselves.

PROGRAMMING EXERCISES

1 **Height and weight (linear regression)**

   Given the height of a person, can you predict their weight?

   Data set @ **www.kaggle.com/datasets/galserge/weight-and-height-from-nhanes**

2 **Vide ogame sales with ratings (linear regression)**

   Given the ratings assigned by critics reviewing a new Video game, can you predict how many millions of units a Video game will sell?

   Data set @ **www.kaggle.com/datasets/rush4ratio/video-game-sales-with-ratings**

3 **Societal impact on education (linear regression)**

   How much is a student's educational outcome influenced by the strength of the economy and health of the society in which they reside?

   Data set @ **www.kaggle.com/datasets/walassetomaz/pisa-results-2000-2022-economics-and-education**

4 **Zoo animal classification (k-nearest neighbours)**

   Classify animals into categories, such as mammal, bird or reptile, based on attributes such as weight, height and type of habitat.

   Data set @ **www.kaggle.com/datasets/uciml/zoo-animal-classification**

5 **Mall customer segmentation (unsupervised k-means clustering)**

   Use k-means clustering to identify distinct customer groups, such as high-income–high-spending vs low-income–high frequency customers.

   Data set @ **www.kaggle.com/datasets/vjchoudhary7/customer-segmentation-tutorial-in-python**

6 **Social network analysis (unsupervised spectral clustering)**

   Discover socially connected communities within the Zachary karate club data set. One challenge often asked with this data set is to find the two groups of people into which the karate club split after an argument between two of the teachers.

   Search "Zachary karate club" to find this data set.

7 **(Unsupervised association rule learning)**

   Analyse the grocery-store data set to discover common product combinations purchased together.

   Data set @ **https://archive.ics.uci.edu/dataset/611**

8   **(Reinforcement learning)**

The previously mentioned Gymnasium has a number of pre-built environments for you to experiment with.

Download @ **https://gymnasium.farama.org**

9   **Optimal stock portfolio (genetic algorithm)**

Use a genetic algorithm to determine what would be the optimal mix of stocks to hold over the duration of a data set to maximize return while minimizing risk. The fitness function could be based on the Sharpe ratio, a measure of return adjusted for risk.

Download historical price data for a set of assets (for example stocks, bonds, ETFs) and calculate returns for each asset to use in the optimization.

Data set @ **www.kaggle.com/datasets/jacksoncrow/stock-market-dataset**

Data set 2 @ **www.nasdaq.com/market-activity/quotes/historical**

10   **Stock-price prediction (artificial neural network)**

Can you create an AI to accurately predict the performance of stock prices? (If you can, don't forget to express your appreciation benevolently to the textbook authors 😊)

Data set @ **www.kaggle.com/datasets/jacksoncrow/stock-market-dataset**

Data set 2 @ **www.nasdaq.com/market-activity/quotes/historical**

11   **Cats and dogs (convolutional neural network)**

Can you tell the difference between a cat and a dog?

Data set @ **www.kaggle.com/datasets/shaunthesheep/microsoft-catsvsdogs-dataset**

12   **Traffic-sign recognition (convolutional neural network)**

Accurately detecting road signs is a core challenge for the development of self-driving cars. The traffic-sign recognition data set contains over 50,000 images across 40 classes of road sign. Should we let you develop the AI for the next breed of self-driving cars?

Data set @ **www.kaggle.com/datasets/meowmeowmeowmeowmeow/gtsrb-german-traffic-sign**

13   **Movie-reviews sentiment analysis (choose between ANN and CNN)**

This exercise will introduce you to natural language processing. Specifically, you will use sentiment analysis to predict positive and negative reviews based on movie reviews on IMDb.

Data set @ **www.kaggle.com/datasets/lakshmi25npathi/imdb-dataset-of-50k-movie-reviews**

Be aware that this exercise will involve learning several additional important concepts to implement. This is because the data set is text, but machine learning models require numeric data to function, so significant preparation and preprocessing of your data is required.

The following tips will guide you:
- ☐ Convert text to lowercase and remove non-alphabetic characters.
- ☐ Tokenize the words, which is the process of splitting the text into individual words or word parts. For instance, the string `"hello world"` would be tokenized into `["hello", "world"]`. Refer to **www.nltk.org/api/nltk.tokenize.html**
- ☐ Remove stop words, which are words that generally don't convey meaning. Examples include "a", "the" and "and". Refer to **https://pythonspot.com/nltk-stop-words**
- ☐ Use a vectorizer such as CountVectorizer or TfidVectorizer to transform your text into numeric vectors. Refer to **https://scikit-learn.org/stable/modules/feature_extraction.html#text-feature-extraction**
- ☐ Convert your vectors into NumPy arrays.
- ☐ Create TensorFlow data sets from the NumPy arrays. Refer to **www.tensorflow.org/api_docs/python/tf/data/Dataset**

Now you can build a neural network model and train it.

REVIEW QUESTIONS

1 An e-commerce company uses linear regression to predict customer spending based on their past purchasing behaviour.

   a State the assumption about the relationship between the dependent and independent variables in linear regression.

   b Describe how outliers could affect the performance of the linear regression model in this scenario.

   c Describe one method to evaluate the accuracy of this linear regression model.

2 A real-estate company uses linear regression to estimate property prices based on features like area, age and number of rooms. One of the technical staff expressed concern that multicollinearity might be a problem with the model. Multicollinearity is when two or more independent variables have a high correlation with one another in a regression.

   a Explain why multicollinearity might be a problem in this linear regression model.

   b Outline a method to handle multicollinearity if it is found in the data set.

3 A college uses linear regression to predict student success based on high-school GPA, standardized test scores and college entrance essays.

   a Outline one reason why it is important to assume linearity in this regression model.

   b Suggest a technique to assess the model's predictive accuracy and explain its importance.

4 A medical research institution develops a decision tree model to classify patients into risk categories for heart disease based on lifestyle and genetic data.

   a Describe one advantage of using decision trees for this type of classification problem.

   b Describe one disadvantage of using decision trees for this type of classification problem.

   c i Identify one critical parameter in decision trees that could impact the model's performance.

      ii Outline its role.

5 An online retailer uses k-nearest neighbours (KNN) to classify customer reviews as positive, neutral or negative.

   a Outline how the choice of k affects the classification accuracy in KNN.

   b Describe one method to determine the optimal k value for this application.

   c Describe how the scales used by features influence the performance of the KNN algorithm.

6 A high school wants to classify students into different learning groups based on their learning styles and previous academic performance.

   a Outline two reasons to select decision trees over KNN for this problem.

   b Outline two reasons to select KNN over decision trees for this problem.

   c The school decided to use a decision tree. Describe one strategy to prevent overfitting in the decision tree model.

7 A maintenance system uses supervised learning to forecast equipment failures in an industrial plant.

   a Define "precision" and "recall" in the context of this predictive system.

   b Explain why the F1 score is a better measure than accuracy in scenarios where false negatives have higher costs.

   c Describe how a confusion matrix can be used to visually illustrate the success of the model.

8 A health diagnostic application uses supervised learning to classify patient results as "normal" or "abnormal".

    a Outline the importance of a high recall rate in this medical classification task.

    b Describe how an imbalanced data set might affect the performance metrics like precision and recall.

    c **i** Identify one method to adjust the classification threshold.

        ii Describe its impact on the F1 score.

9 An online retailer uses k-means clustering to segment customers based on purchasing patterns.

    a Outline the objective of the k-means clustering algorithm.

    b Describe one challenge when using k-means clustering for customer segmentation.

    c Describe how the choice of k affects the outcomes of the k-means algorithm.

10 A telecommunications company uses spectral clustering to segment customers based on usage patterns.

    a Describe the difference between k-means and spectral clustering in handling non-spherical data clusters.

    b Describe one challenge in using spectral clustering for large data sets.

    c Describe how the results of spectral clustering could be used to improve customer satisfaction.

11 A social-media company uses clustering to identify social groups on its network system.

    a Identify which clustering algorithm would allow identification of social groups in this network.

    b Describe one potential challenge in clustering users based on such diverse data.

    c Describe how the choice of the number of clusters can affect the results.

12 Urban planners in a large city are using data collected from traffic sensors at various intersections and highways to identify clusters of intersections and road segments that exhibit similar traffic patterns.

    a Describe a suitable algorithm that the urban planners could use to group sensor data into clusters based on their traffic characteristics. Explain why this algorithm is appropriate for handling data with varying densities and noise.

    b Describe how understanding these traffic clusters could benefit the city's traffic management and infrastructure planning.

13 An e-commerce platform analyses user purchasing data to discover frequent buying patterns.

    a Define "lift" in the context of association rule mining and its importance.

    b Describe how minimum support and confidence levels affect the rules generated in this scenario.

    c Describe the potential impact of these buying patterns on targeted marketing strategies.

14 A library analyses borrowing patterns to find associations between different genres of books borrowed together.

    a Define "confidence" and "support" in association rule mining for this library data.

    b Describe how the library can discover these patterns.

    c Describe one potential limitation of association rule mining in predicting book-borrowing patterns.

15 An engineering firm uses genetic algorithms to optimize the design of a new aerodynamic vehicle model.

    a Outline the role of crossover in genetic algorithms.

    b Outline how mutation affects the evolution process in genetic algorithms.

    c Outline one advantage of using genetic algorithms in complex optimization problems such as vehicle design.

16 A school runs an elective block on the timetable where students can select from a number of creative and optional courses. Students are asked to indicate their preferred courses but are not guaranteed to receive their first preference. The school uses a genetic algorithm to maximize the number of students receiving their first or second preference.

   a   Outline the function of selection in genetic algorithms.

   b   Describe the concept of "fitness function" in genetic algorithms, and how it might be applied in this scenario.

   c   Describe how population size influences the outcome of a genetic algorithm.

   d   Outline two benefits of using genetic algorithms to design a timetable schedule.

   e   Outline two drawbacks of using genetic algorithms to design a timetable schedule.

17 A financial institution employs an artificial neural network to predict loan default risk based on customer profiles.

   a   Identify one type of layer often used in neural networks and its purpose.

   b   Describe why overfitting might be a concern in neural networks.

   c   Describe how a neural network can be trained to minimize prediction error in this financial context.

18 An energy company uses a neural network to forecast electricity demand based on weather conditions and historical usage.

   a   i   Identify whether the neural network in this scenario would be regression or classification based.

       ii   Outline the significance of that on its design.

   b   Outline one type of activation function used in neural networks and its purpose.

   c   Outline which activation function would most likely be suitable for the output layer in this scenario, and why.

   d   Describe why deep neural networks might be more effective than shallow networks for this forecasting task.

   e   Define "backpropagation" and outline its role in learning within a neural network.

   f   Outline two challenges associated with training deep neural networks.

19 A tech company experiments with several machine learning models to predict user engagement on a new app.

   a   Define "model selection" in the context of machine learning.

   b   Identify two metrics that could be used to select the best model for predicting user engagement.

   c   i   Outline the concept of cross-validation.

       ii   Describe one reason why it is important in model selection.

20 A sports analytics company tests multiple models to predict the outcome of basketball games.

   a   Describe the concept of "overfitting" in the context of model selection.

   b   Identify three factors that should be considered in model selection.

Ethical considerations

By the end of this chapter, you should be able to:
▶ A4.4.1 Discuss the ethical implications of machine learning in real-world scenarios
▶ A4.4.2 Discuss ethics as technologies become integrated into daily life

A4.4.1 Ethical implications

> **TOK**
>
> **Does all knowledge impose ethical obligations on those who know it?**
>
> Discuss the ethical use of machine learning, especially in sensitive areas like surveillance or decision-making.
>
> In surveillance (like facial recognition), concerns about privacy, consent and surveillance biases abound. Surveillance systems can be used to monitor, control and sometimes discriminate against populations.
>
> With the involvement of machine learning in decision-making, such as in hiring, lending and law enforcement, these systems can influence people's lives significantly, and have been shown to inherit and amplify biases present in the training data.
>
> Machine learning models – inherently knowledge-driven systems – are based on data that encapsulate various forms of knowledge, from human behaviour to biological patterns. As creators and users of these systems, there is a responsibility to ensure that this knowledge is used ethically.

The world is changing rapidly. Advances in technology, including those in machine learning, pose significant challenges and questions for us as a society. It is important to take some time to weigh these ethical questions and not get caught up by the shiny new tech without taking the time to think through how it will impact us and those around us. The following are some of the ethical issues to consider.

■ **Accountability:** With whom or where does responsibility lie for decisions made by machine learning systems? Is it with the company that produced the AI or the people using it? Is it a blend of both? Is it possible to determine how and why a machine learning system made a particular decision?

One incident that highlights the issue of accountability involved a self-driving car. The driver who was behind the wheel of a self-driving car when it hit and killed a pedestrian in 2018 pleaded guilty to endangerment and was sentenced to three years of supervised probation.

■ **Algorithmic fairness and bias:** Machine learning can perpetuate existing social bias if it is present in the training data, or if the model's design knowingly or unknowingly favours certain groups. Fairness requires actively identifying and mitigating bias in the data set and algorithms.

COMPAS is a recidivism algorithm used by many US court systems. It has been found to have racial bias, predicting higher risk of recidivism for black people and lower risk of recidivism for white people.

Another example is that, in 2018, Amazon scrapped a "secret" AI recruiting tool that was biased against women.

Finally, generative AIs have a constant challenge regarding reinforcing and exacerbating stereotypes and bias.

■ **Consent:** Large data sets used for training regularly contain information collected without explicit consent. Many large companies are now performing machine learning on their customer databases, or selling their customer data to other data-matching companies. How much control should people retain over their personal information?

Google's DeepMind was found to be in breach of UK privacy laws after it failed to adequately inform patients about the use of their personally identifiable health data in developing an app to detect kidney injuries.

■ **Environmental impact:** Machine learning models require enormous computational power, especially in the training phase. This leads to substantial energy consumption and implications for carbon emissions.

Cornell University scientists found that training LLMs (large language models) like GPT-3 consumed an amount of electricity equivalent to 500 metric tons of carbon. In fact, DatacenterDynamics reports global power use by data centres will more than double from 460 TWh in 2022 to over 1000 TWh in 2026.

■ **Privacy:** Machine learning systems can predict or classify personal behaviour in ways that invade personal privacy. The capacity of machine learning systems to apply inference means privacy may be further compromised by systems deducing health conditions not even provided to the model.

In 2018, fitness tracking app Strava released a global heat map of user activities that inadvertently revealed the locations of secret military bases and patrol routes, showcasing a significant privacy leak.

■ **Security:** Machine learning systems can be vulnerable to attack through a variety of means. Three common attacks include:
  □ **data poisoning**, which involves introducing untrue or harmful data into the training data set to manipulate the model for nefarious purposes
  □ **model evasion**, where input (such as prompts) is used to "trick" the model into making incorrect outputs against its training (sometimes known as "jailbreaking", in the context of generative AI)
  □ **model inversion**, referring to gaining access to sensitive data contained within the training data.

Within 24 hours of release, Microsoft's Tay Twitter Bot was manipulated through malicious input data to produce grossly inappropriate and offensive tweets.

When GPT-3 was first released by OpenAI, it lacked many of the filters now present and it was trivially easy to engineer prompts that produced foul, toxic or illegal content.

■ **Societal impact:** Machine learning is increasingly disrupting employment markets, and influencing public opinion. There is a careful balance between technological advancement and maintaining social welfare, which needs to be considered.

Clearview AI, which scrapes billions of photos from the internet for facial recognition, has raised societal concerns about surveillance, consent and civil liberties.

■ **Transparency:** Most engineers cannot explain how their systems generate the outputs they create, especially those that use neural networks. The best that can be done is to point to the training data rather than the algorithm itself. This lack of transparency, or human understandability, of what these algorithms are and how they work poses significant questions.

In 2019, tech entrepreneur David Heinmeier Hansson wrote on X (formerly Twitter) that Apple Card offered him 20 times the credit limit of his wife, although they have shared assets and she has a higher credit score, raising questions about the transparency of the algorithms used for financial decision-making.

- **Bias in training data**: Bias in training data is a core challenge for machine learning. Over- or under-representation of particular demographics will affect the model's predictions and reliability. Rigorous data collection, processing and evaluation methods are required to ensure broad and fair representation.

- **Misinformation**: Machine learning can generate and spread false information with ease, making it very difficult to ensure accurate and reliable communication online. As generative AI, in particular, becomes increasingly realistic and convincing in its outputs, it will become almost impossible to avoid falling victim to fake news, fake images and fake videos.

  It is believed that misinformation on Facebook received six times more clicks than factual news during the 2020 US election, according to a study by NYU.

  As generative AI deep fakes become weapons of the political debate, confusion over what to believe will only pose more complex challenges in the future.

- **Bias in online communication**: Machine learning-based recommendation systems are designed to maximize user engagement on a platform. One method of doing this is by recommending more of the same kinds of content that users have previously engaged with. This can create "echo chambers" that reinforce existing beliefs and minimize alternative viewpoints.

  Facebook newsfeed algorithms and YouTube's recommendation systems have both been criticized for creating filter bubbles and echo chambers, where users are predominantly shown content that aligns with their existing beliefs, potentially polarizing public opinion.

- **Online harassment**: Machine learning can be used to automate harassment on an enormous scale. Bots can troll and target individuals or groups with ease, and can increasingly make it seem like the attacks are coming from people. Generative AI is being used to create deep fakes in hurtful and abusive ways that authorities are struggling to keep up with.

- **Privacy and anonymity in online communications**: Users often are not aware of or do not fully understand how their data are used and processed by machine learning algorithms. Users may think their actions are anonymous, but increasingly machine learning algorithms can perform de-anonymization with a high degree of reliability. There is very little awareness of this in the broader community.

  In 2006, Netflix released a data set containing 100 million movie ratings from 500,000 subscribers, intended for use in a global competition to improve the accuracy of Netflix's recommendation algorithm. The data was supposedly anonymized by removing any personal identifying information. Researchers from the University of Texas at Austin demonstrated that it was possible to re-identify users by comparing the anonymized Netflix data with publicly available movie ratings on the Internet Movie Database (IMDb). Using only a small amount of additional information about an individual's preferences, the researchers were able to identify personal viewing habits and potentially sensitive information.

A4.4.2 Reassessing ethics as technologies become further integrated

As artificial intelligence and other technology continues to advance and evolve over the years ahead, society is going to need to regularly reassess the implications from an ethical viewpoint. There are many challenges that lie ahead; the following list is just a discussion starter.

- **Quantum computing:** Quantum computing could potentially break many of the cryptographic systems that currently secure digital communications and cryptocurrencies. The development of quantum-resistant cryptography is an important area of research that needs to be prioritized.

- **Augmented reality:** AR can collect vast amounts of personal data about users' environments. Additionally, what are the ethics around altering a person's perception of reality? Does this disconnect them from the society of which they are part, resulting in a loss of empathy?

- **Virtual reality:** As VR becomes more realistic, what are the mental-health concerns for those who use the systems excessively or for escapism? What should the limits be when it comes to VR being used to access violent or explicit material?

- **Pervasive AI:** How do we guard against intrusive surveillance and the seemingly never-ending collection of our personal data for use in machine learning data sets?

- **Privacy:** Who owns the data about you? Is it you, or the company that collected it? As data collection becomes more complex, will there be a move towards more transparent and informed consent about what happens with our personal information?

- **Equity:** How can we ensure that advances in technology reduce rather than magnify equitable access to technology across socio-economic, racial, gender, social and geographical groups?

● Top tip!

This section shared real-life case studies on the impact of many of the ethical questions being raised by this topic. Be familiar with case studies that you can refer to in your exam responses. If you can discuss with specificity a relevant situation that occurred, it goes a long way towards demonstrating that you care about the issue.

● Common mistakes

Students make a number of common errors when addressing ethics-related questions, which extends to the discussion of machine learning.

- **Don't oversimplify the issues.** Avoid reducing complex ethical issues to simple right or wrong answers. The ethical implications of machine learning are nuanced and often involve interconnected considerations of accountability, fairness and societal impact.
- **Don't confuse technical bias with ethical bias.** Distinguish between technical bias (deviation in an algorithm that leads to less accurate predictions) and ethical / social bias (prejudices in data that lead to unfair outcomes for certain groups).
- **Don't limit your responses to issues of privacy and security.** Consider a broader range of ethical issues, such as environmental impact, societal changes and the implications for mental health. Show you have a deep understanding of the complexities involved, rather than taking the lazy approach of resorting to an exam response that discusses privacy or security superficially.
- **Don't neglect the importance of reassessment.** Ethics guidelines can never be static, as technology and its impact on society is not static.

Social skills: Set up a class debate or panel discussion where you argue the ethical implications of using machine learning, such as bias, privacy and transparency concerns.

Facilitate peer feedback sessions where you review and provide constructive criticism on each other's machine learning projects or presentations.

Some possible debate prompts include:

- Should health-insurance companies have access to predictions about potential future illnesses to set premiums, even if this could lead to higher costs for those deemed at higher risk?
- Should autonomous vehicles be programmed to prioritize the lives of pedestrians over the life of the vehicle's passenger(s)? How should these ethical decisions be programmed into autonomous systems?
- Is it ethical to use a recruitment tool that shows bias towards certain educational institutions? Should the company stop using it until it can be proven to be unbiased?
- If a city implements widespread facial recognition through CCTV cameras to reduce crime, is this worth the lessening of privacy or the risk of false accusation?
- Should social-media platforms be held responsible for breaking echo chambers and ensuring a balanced exposure to different viewpoints? How can this be balanced with business models that require maximizing engagement to earn revenue?

REVIEW QUESTIONS

1 An AI company develops a facial recognition system used in public surveillance.
   a Outline three ethical implications of using facial recognition technology in public spaces.
   b i Identify two potential biases that could arise in facial recognition systems.
     ii Outline the societal impacts of each.
   c Outline two measures that could be implemented to address these ethical concerns and biases.

2 A social-media company uses algorithms to personalize newsfeeds based on user interactions.
   a Outline two potential ethical issues related to algorithmic bias in personalizing newsfeeds.
   b Outline two strategies the company could implement to ensure the ethical use of personalization algorithms.
   c i Identify two implications of lack of transparency in algorithmic decision-making.
     ii Outline two methods to improve transparency in algorithmic decision-making.

3 A university uses AI to make admissions decisions based on application materials.
   a Outline three potential ethical concerns with using AI in university admissions.
   b i Outline two possible biases that could arise in this AI system.
     ii Outline their impact on students.
   c Describe measures to address these ethical concerns and biases.

Linking questions

1 How can machine learning be applied to optimize network traffic management? (A2)
2 How does database programming in SQL differ from programming computationally in a high-level language? (A3, B2)
3 To what extent are developments in machine learning ethical? (TOK)
4 How can larger models be processed using GPUs and cloud processing? (A1)
5 Can machine learning find and improve network security problems? (A2)

EXAM PRACTICE QUESTIONS

1 **Health monitoring app**
   A tech startup has developed a health monitoring app that uses machine learning to predict potential health issues based on user-inputted symptoms, lifestyle data and historical health data. The app classifies user health into categories such as "low risk", "medium risk" and "high risk".
   a   i   State whether this system should be classified as artificial intelligence or machine learning. [1]
       ii   Outline one reason for your choice. [2]
   b   Describe the potential need for specialized hardware (e.g. GPUs) in deploying this app on mobile devices. [2]
   c   Describe the importance of data cleaning in this scenario, particularly addressing missing values in lifestyle data. [2]
   d   Describe how feature selection could impact the accuracy and efficiency of the predictive model used in the app. [2]
   e   Suggest the type of machine learning algorithm that would be suitable for this classification task. [4]
   f   Outline the implications of choosing a high value of k in a k-nearest neighbours (KNN) algorithm for this application. [2]
   g   Outline three ethical concerns related to privacy and data security in health-related apps. [3]
   h   Describe two measures that could be implemented to address potential biases in the data set, especially relating to underrepresented groups. [2]

2 **Autonomous public transport system**
   A city plans to implement an autonomous bus service that uses machine learning to optimize routes based on traffic patterns, weather conditions and passenger demand.
   a   i   Define "edge computing". [1]
       ii   Describe its relevance in real-time data processing for autonomous vehicles. [2]
   b   Describe whether a deep learning model would be more effective than a traditional machine learning model for processing complex environmental data. [2]
   c   Describe how data normalization affects the performance of machine learning models dealing with varied data types such as weather conditions and traffic density. [2]
   d   i   Identify a common data quality issue that might arise with real-time traffic data. [1]
       ii   Outline a preprocessing step to mitigate these issues. [2]
   e   Describe how reinforcement learning could be applied to optimize bus routes dynamically. [2]
   f   Discuss the potential use of transfer learning from other cities' traffic management systems to improve route optimization. [2]
   g   Describe the ethical implications of using surveillance data (e.g. from traffic cameras) in training machine learning models for public transport systems. [2]
   h   Describe the societal impacts of replacing human-driven buses with autonomous buses, including job displacement and public safety. [2]

3 **AI-powered recruitment tool**
   A multinational corporation implements an AI-powered tool to screen job applications and predict the suitability of candidates based on their résumés and answers to pre-interview questions.
   a   Describe the classification vs regression nature of the predictive model used by the AI tool. [2]
   b   Describe the impact of processing speed and memory requirements on the scalability of the AI tool across the corporation's global offices. [2]
   c   i   Identify potential biases in the training data set. [1]
       ii   Outline how these could be mitigated during data preprocessing. [2]
   d   Describe the importance of feature selection in improving the predictive accuracy of the AI tool. [2]
   e   Describe the use of a decision tree model over a regression-based model for this classification task. [3]

f Outline two ethical concerns related to AI decision-making in recruitment, particularly in terms of fairness and transparency. [2]

g Describe two methods to ensure the ethical use of AI in recruitment with respect to increasing transparency and accountability. [2]

4 Retail customer segmentation

A large retail chain uses machine learning to segment its customer base to personalize marketing strategies and improve customer service.

a Discuss whether supervised or unsupervised learning is more appropriate for customer segmentation. [4]

b Outline the potential benefits of using cloud computing resources over in-house servers for processing large customer data sets. [2]

c Outline the role of outlier detection in customer segmentation. [2]

d i Identify a clustering algorithm suitable for handling large data sets with high dimensionality. [1]

   ii Describe a reason for your choice. [2]

e Describe the potential privacy issues that may arise from the detailed segmentation of customers' buying habits. [3]

f Describe strategies to mitigate the risk of discriminatory marketing practices that could result from biased data in customer segmentation. [2]

5 Natural-disaster prediction and management

A government agency deploys machine learning models to predict natural disasters such as floods and earthquakes, aiming to enhance preparedness and response strategies.

a Describe the application of neural networks in predicting natural disasters and the kind of data they might process. [2]

b Describe the impact of using real-time data processing on system requirements and infrastructure. [2]

c Describe the challenges associated with integrating and cleaning data from multiple sources, such as satellite imagery and geological sensors. [2]

d Describe the role of data augmentation in improving the accuracy of predictions in areas with sparse historical data. [2]

e Describe the use of deep learning over traditional models for predicting complex natural disaster patterns. [2]

f Describe how machine learning models can be trained to adapt to new types of disaster data over time. [2]

g Describe the ethical implications of false positives and false negatives in disaster prediction models. [3]

h Describe protocols for data governance that may ensure sensitive geographical and personal data used in predictions are protected. [2]

6 Automated cyberbullying detection system

A software company is developing an automated system to detect and flag instances of cyberbullying on social-media platforms using natural language processing and machine learning.

a i Define "natural language processing (NLP)". [1]

   ii Describe its relevance in detecting cyberbullying. [2]

b i Describe the computational challenges associated with processing large volumes of social-media data in real time. [2]

   ii Outline appropriate hardware solutions. [2]

c Describe the potential preprocessing steps needed for textual data from social-media posts to prepare it for machine learning models. [2]

d Explain the importance of handling sarcasm and ambiguities in text when setting up preprocessing pipelines for detecting cyberbullying. [2]

e Describe the use of analytical rule-based systems vs machine learning models in the context of cyberbullying detection. [2]

f Outline the ethical considerations of implementing an automated cyberbullying detection system, particularly regarding false positives and false negatives. [3]

g Describe the potential privacy implications of analysing users' social-media content, even for the purpose of detecting cyberbullying. [2]

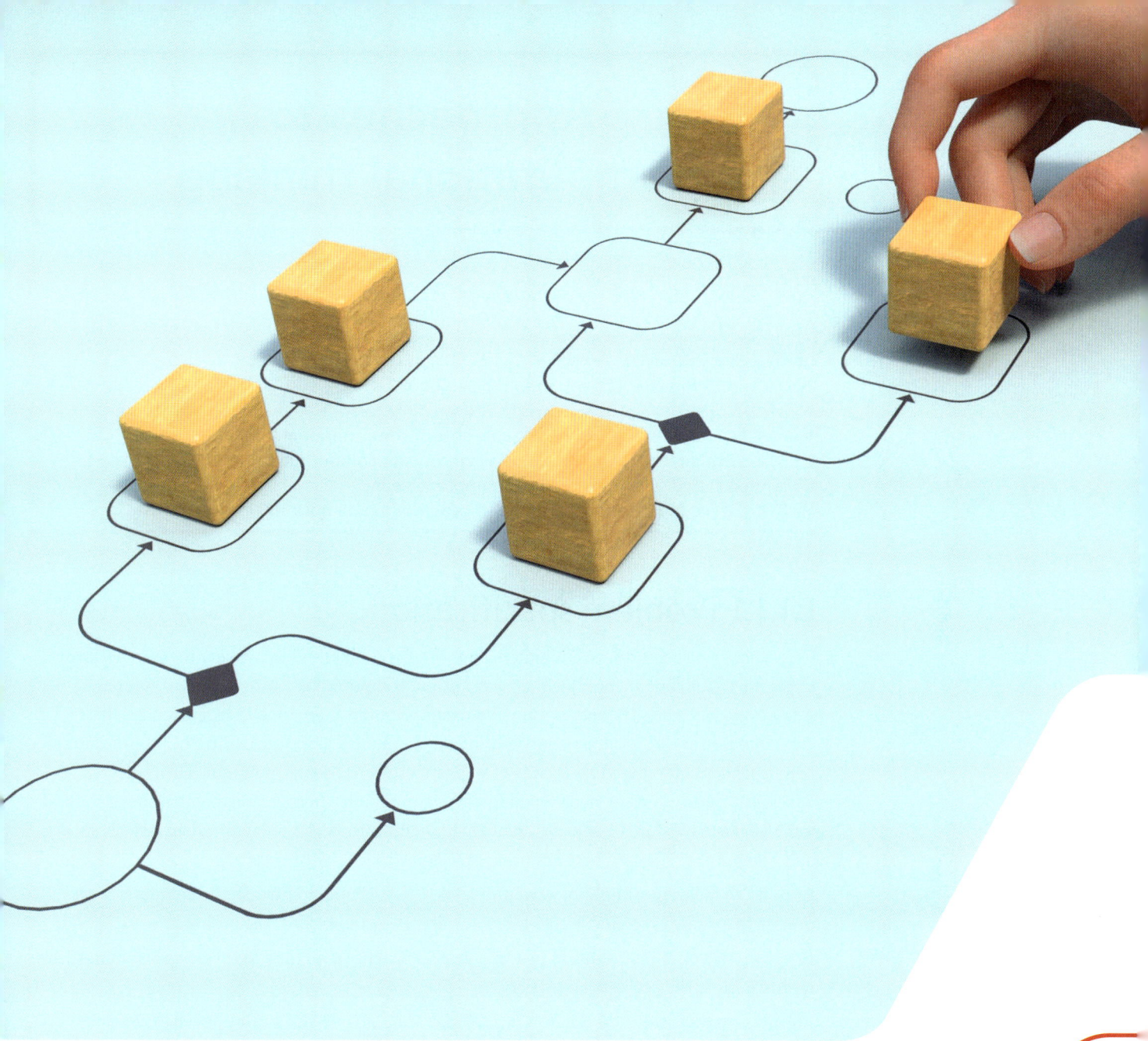

B1 Computational thinking

Approaches to computational thinking

How can we apply a computational solution to a real-world problem?

B1.1.1 Problem specification

Ever since their beginnings, computers have required a method to instruct them to perform a specific task. Now, we provide instructions to a computer via a programming language. Ada Lovelace, Charles Babbage, Alan Turing and Konrad Zuse are all recognized for their contributions to the development of coding and computer languages. Initially, programming languages were developed as a series of steps to wire a particular program. Then, they developed into a series of steps typed into a computer and then executed. Later, they acquired more advanced features, such as iterations; branching and even polymorphism; inheritance; and other object-oriented programming principles.

Even when tackling straightforward problems, it is essential to furnish the computer with precise instructions to enable it to carry out the tasks and resolve the problem.

However, you will not be able to provide clear instructions on how to solve a problem until you clearly outline the problem specifications.

A **problem specification** is a short, clear explanation of an issue, outlining who the **stakeholders** are and why it is important to solve the problem. The problem specification may include a problem statement; constraints and limitations; objectives and goals; input and output specifications; and evaluation criteria.

This is a great opportunity to think of your internal assessment project. When you define the **problem statement**, you need to include a description of the problem itself, who the solution is designed for, the issues encountered and what needs to be solved. To clearly understand the problem, you are encouraged to collect information from existing literature and research, use previous experiences with the problem and discuss it with multiple stakeholders who are impacted by the problem. In this way, you will be able to identify some possible constraints and limitations, for example:

■ Limitations regarding the available technical requirements (hardware or software equipment)

■ Economic aspect (cost of producing the solution)

■ Legislation (regulations regarding the software development; ethical, social and legal aspects)

■ Operational issues (workforce available)

■ Schedule (time required to develop and implement the solution).

◆ **Problem specification:** a short, clear explanation of an issue, which may include: a problem statement; constraints and limitations; objectives and goals; input and output specifications; and evaluation criteria.

◆ **Stakeholder:** an individual or group(s) of people within or outside an organization who are affected or think they are affected by a software development project.

◆ **Problem statement:** a description of the problem itself, identification of who the solution is designed for, the issues encountered and what needs to be solved.

Once those are clearly defined, in collaboration with the main stakeholders you should outline the objectives and goals of the proposed solution, identifying what needs to be solved and what you want to achieve.

Every solution will include some form of input and output. Knowing how the input is being provided, which input is supplied and the expected outcome or output to be produced will help you understand the required process to reach your goal. The input can be in different forms:

- Direct entry (by using barcode scanners; OCR or OMR scanners; or MICR readers)
- Manual entry (keyboard, joystick, touch screen, touch pad or mouse entry, or data manually being entered by human operators)
- Automatic data entry (by using sensors: temperature, light, infrared, pressure, and so on).

Each of those has advantages and disadvantages. For example, manual entry might be cheaper, but it is prone to errors, while automatic entry is clearly more expensive due to the hardware or software involved, but it is more accurate and faster.

When it comes to output, this can be classified as temporary output (displaying the information on a screen), permanent output (printing the data), or electrical or mechanical output (using actuators: switches or relays).

Identifying the input data required and the output expected helps in outlining the data flow and understanding how the data travels through the proposed solution.

Evaluation criteria is the last step in constructing a problem specification. Criteria should be clear, specific, measurable and related to the functionality to be achieved through the proposed solution. This will allow you to use these criteria to evaluate the success of the product at a later stage.

Key information

Problem specification is part of the internal assessment requirements for criterion A. It is considered the starting point of the solution, and it must be used as a basis for the development of the product. The success criteria identified in the problem specification will be used in the planning, development and the evaluation of the product.

REVIEW QUESTIONS

1 Identify three stakeholders in a technical shop selling gaming consoles, games and IT equipment.

2 Define the term "stakeholder".

3 Define the term "problem specification".

4 State three possible constraints and limitations when considering developing a computational solution for a school.

5 In your school, identify those operations that have already been computerized; those that might be computerized soon; and those that are unlikely ever to be computerized.

6 For those activities you have identified as being already computerized at your school (for question 5), identify the inputs and outputs of the system.

7 Identify three reasons why there is a need to formulate a problem statement precisely.

Top tip!

Performance issues related to the lack of identifying limitations and constraints, and inputs and outputs specific to different systems in geographically diverse locations, may hinder end users and reduce compatibility between systems.

Imagine you must design and create an online platform to be used globally.

There are several constraints and limitations to take into consideration to ensure the platform is scalable, user friendly, efficient and accessible across different regions.

Discuss:

- language and regional differences, e.g. currencies, languages supported, date formats, units of measurement
- legal requirements, e.g. GDPR in Europe
- consumer-protection laws / content restrictions
- cultural differences and user behaviours that impact the design of the platform, e.g. meanings of colours for different cultures, sensitivity of specific content, user-interface alignment (left to right or right to left), time zones, scheduling.

How do such constraints support or limit the development of online platforms that can be used worldwide?

Is targeting a local market more advantageous and efficient, rather than targeting a global market?

B1.1.2 Fundamental concepts of computational thinking

■ Abstraction

◆ **Abstraction:** having a higher-level, simplified model to represent a complex system. It allows you to focus on the core ideas or concepts that matter, without being overly concerned about the intricate details of implementation.

Abstraction is the process of extracting essential information, while disregarding irrelevant data, to propose or outline a feasible solution to a given problem. In this way, simplified models can be designed; models that exclude unnecessary details. This plays a crucial role in providing a solution that satisfies the user requirements and needs, as it solves the problem without including unnecessary features, and in a shorter period due to the reduced amount of code written.

Real-world examples of abstraction include designing a map as a representation of a territory; a painting as a representation of a landscape; and a timetable. In programming, abstraction is an important concept in object-oriented programming. It is used to hide complexity from the user by:

- abstracting data entities (by hiding data entities via a data structure, reducing the body of the data to a simplified version of the whole)
- hiding underlying implementation of a process (programmers don't need to know details of how the subroutines are implemented, or what other subroutines they call, but they can simply use them to serve their purpose).

By using abstraction:

- the time required to create a piece of software is reduced
- the program becomes smaller in size, so it requires less space in memory and the download times are reduced
- customer satisfaction increases, as their requirements are met without extra features.

The map as an abstraction of the territory: A map is not the actual territory it represents, but rather a diagrammatical representation of an area, including some features and excluding others. The London Tube map was designed in 1933 as a simplified model of reality, informing the traveller how to navigate between stations, but excluding many other details and not providing an accurate representation of the actual space. Investigate and identify the differences between the London Tube map and other subway maps that you know.

Knowing the map doesn't mean that you know much about the actual territory, just as knowing the names of different items in different languages doesn't reflect your knowledge about the items themselves.

Watch Richard Feynman's "Names Don't Constitute Knowledge", or analyse the following quotation to further explore the concept:

> *Naming things is a human act; it is not an act of nature. We are the ones who, through language, create things out of the phenomena around us. Yet we forget that we control this process and let the process control us. Naming things – using language – is a very high-level abstraction, and when we name something we "freeze" it by placing it in a category and making a "thing" out of it. Language is a map, but three important things to remember about maps are: the map is not the territory; no map can represent all aspects of the territory; and every map reflects the mapmaker's point of view.*

Lutz, Wiliam (1996) The New Doublespeak: Why No One Knows What Anyone is Saying Anymore. HarperCollins, New York, NY.

Investigate how knowing the name of something can positively or negatively influence our life experiences.

■ Algorithmic design

Before starting to write actual code, you should analyse and identify the requirements of the problem and then understand the logical steps required to solve the problem. Once you have a firm grasp of the requirements, the next step involves designing a potential solution. One effective approach for achieving this is to create an algorithm. This involves creating step-by-step solutions with predictable outcomes.

An **algorithm** is a structured set of sequential instructions designed to address and resolve a problem.

> ◆ **Algorithm:** a finite sequence of instructions that needs to be followed step-by-step to solve a problem.

Consider the following problem:

"A user is required to provide two whole numbers. Construct a program that calculates the sum of the two numbers and displays it."

The algorithm corresponding to the problem above is:

- **Step 1**: Ask the user to enter a number.
- **Step 2**: Store this number.
- **Step 3**: Ask the user to enter another number.
- **Step 4**: Store this new value.
- **Step 5**: Add the two numbers together.
- **Step 6**: Store the result.
- **Step 7**: Display the result.

Those steps need to be very specific and in the right order to be able to solve the problem. By applying algorithmic designs, you will develop algorithmic thinking skills that will help you develop efficient problem-solving techniques, by using structured and systematic algorithms.

Top tip!

When outlining algorithms, ensure the instructions are very specific, clear and in the right order. Not following the required order often leads to the wrong solution or different errors. Imagine you need to calculate the average of three numbers. Setting the value of sum to 0 after storing the total of the three values into the variable sum and attempting to divide this by 3 afterwards would produce an error.

Decomposition

Decomposition refers to breaking down complex problems into smaller, more manageable parts. After designing solutions to those smaller problems, they can be put together to build up a final solution to the complex problem. This concept supports modularity, allowing multiple programmers or experts to collaborate and work simultaneously on solving the problem.

In programming, decomposition is often used to structure the solution, by designing several methods or functions.

Common mistake

Students do not always use terminology in an appropriate and competent way, and may approach questions by providing general superficial knowledge, which does not gain full marks.

Students often define "decomposition" as breaking down a program into smaller sub-programs. This isn't accurate as, at the stage decomposition occurs, there is no program created, therefore the problem is the one being broken down into smaller, more manageable parts.

Pattern recognition

Pattern recognition refers to identifying similarities in the details of problems. This simplifies the process of finding a solution by identifying patterns and focusing on reusing solutions proposed to solve those similarities. This means that you will develop reusable code in the form of functions or procedures; reuse existing code that has already been tested; and support the use of modularity, which reduces the development time.

B1.1.3 How fundamental concepts of computational thinking are used to approach and solve problems in Computer Science

Computational thinking is not programming, and it does not make you think like a computer, but rather it makes you think like a computer scientist. It is a toolkit of available techniques for problem-solving. This gives you the skills to efficiently outline a problem specification; to analyse, understand and simplify the problem; and to identify and choose optimal solutions to different problems.

The fundamental concepts of computational thinking, such as abstraction, decomposition, algorithmic thinking and pattern recognition, can be used to solve real-world problems, for example: software development, data analysis, machine learning, database design and network-security problems.

In each of the areas identified above, all the fundamental concepts are equally important:

- **Software development**: You cannot create a program before:
  - □ understanding the problem
  - □ making abstraction of unnecessary details
  - □ finding repeating patterns
  - □ designing efficient algorithms

  Without any of these steps, the software produced might lack accuracy or might not be as efficient as it should be.

- **Games development**: Abstraction is used when the players are provided with a series of clues, some of which are intended to mislead the players. Abstraction refers to disregarding unnecessary details. Players should disregard such clues and focus on the important details.

- **Programming**: Programming languages offer libraries with functions and methods for programmers to use. The programmer makes an abstraction of the way those functions were written, focusing on correctly using them to complete their code.

- **Data analysis**: Computational thinking is used to automate repetitive tasks, predict market trends and improve customer service. Data analysts identify patterns (for example popular products for a category of people, repetitive tasks, frequent customer complaints) and apply algorithmic thinking to propose feasible solutions and break problems into simpler steps, saving hours of extra work on a weekly basis.

- **Machine learning**: Pattern recognition is an important concept, used in classifying data by finding patterns in large amounts of data, for example predicting purchasing behaviour based on buying habits. It can also be used to identify the skills required to be a good football player, by analysing video recordings to automatically find patterns in the behaviour of professional players. The same task might make use of abstraction to exclude irrelevant information provided by the videos and algorithms to promote those skills among new players during their virtual training sessions.

- **Database design**: Abstraction can be used to identify which data sources are relevant and which can be disregarded. Decomposition can be used to design relational databases by breaking down the complex problem into smaller ones. Entities can be represented as tables, and relations shown between them.

- **Database normalization**: Pattern recognition can be used to ensure there are no repeated groups of attributes or algorithmic design in outlining the tables' structures, and identify the logic behind the types of relationships established between tables.

- **Network security**: For solving network-security problems, abstraction enables the generalization of complex security models; decomposition is used to break down cybersecurity ecosystems into models that allow a clear identification of their security roles; pattern recognition is used to outline ways to identify and classify possible threats to the network; and algorithmic design is used to propose clear, step-by-step instructions on how to deal with such risks in similar situations.

REVIEW QUESTIONS

1 Identify three examples of abstraction in Computer Science.

2 Define the term "decomposition".

3 Outline the algorithm for making a cup of tea.

4 Outline an area where computational thinking is used in Computer Science.

5 Define the term "algorithm".

6 Research the bubble sort algorithm. Outline the steps for this algorithm.

7 Research the swap puzzle activity and try to outline an algorithm to solve it in as few steps as possible.

B1.1.4 Flowcharts

Flowcharts are used to design algorithms, and to describe them using diagrams. They can be used to track variable changes, to show execution flow and to determine the expected output of an algorithm.

■ Standard flowchart symbols

Symbol	Name	Description
	Terminator	Start or end of the process
	Input / output	Input or output of data
	Process	Action, such as a calculation or an assignment
	Decision	True / false or yes / no decisions (selection statements)
	Flowline	Direction of data flow between shapes
	Connector	Continuation of a flow through multiple pages or charts

Consider the following problem:

Request the user to input two numbers from the keyboard. Output their average.

To solve the problem, identify the input, processes and output:

■ **Input:** the two numbers (a, b)

■ **Output:** the average of the two numbers (avg)

■ **Processes:** calculate the sum, calculate the average.

The flowchart corresponding to the proposed solution is given below:

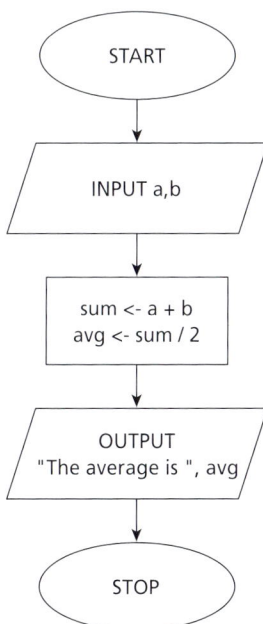

```
        START
          |
          v
      INPUT a,b
          |
          v
      sum <- a + b
      avg <- sum / 2
          |
          v
       OUTPUT
  "The average is ", avg
          |
          v
        STOP
```

Flowcharts can become a little more complex by including selection or iteration. For example, the flowchart corresponding to an algorithm that outputs the larger of two different input numbers requires selection statements:

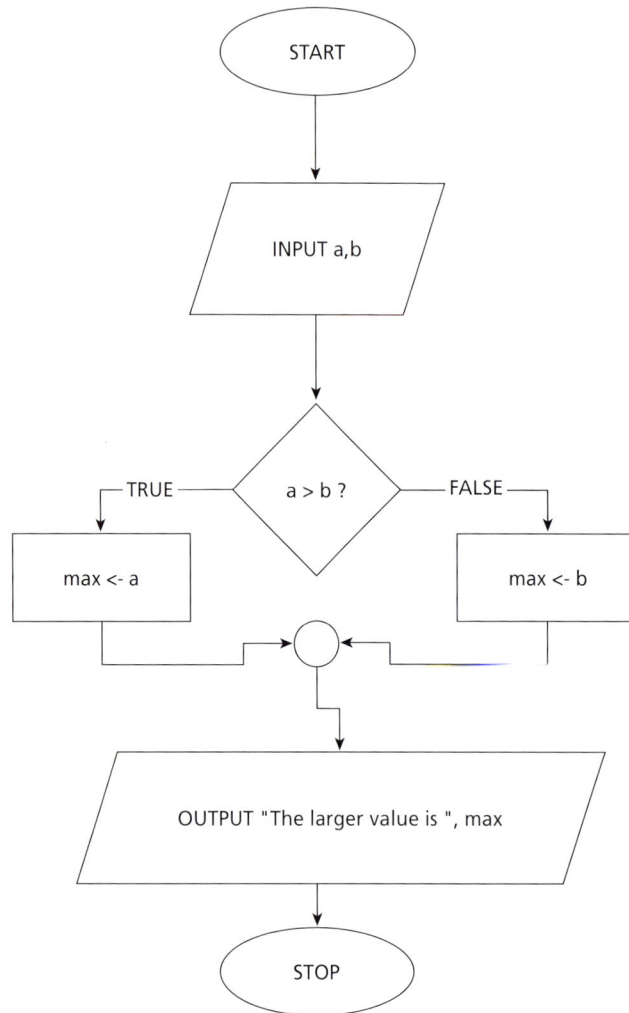

If you wanted to check the algorithm above you could test it with different test data, such as 7 and −3. To find the expected output, a table can be drawn and traced. The table includes the variable changes, decisions and outputs expected.

a	b	max	a>b	output

To trace the table and reach the final output, you need to go through the flowchart and follow the data flow shown by the arrows.

In this case, the first happening in the flowchart is the input. So, as a is the first input it will take the value 7 and b will be set to −3, and the table will look like this:

a	b	max	a>b	output
7	-3			

Students often forget to label the branches of decision boxes when drawing flowcharts. An unlabelled branch would not allow the examiner to identify which process is executed when the condition evaluates to True (Yes) and which executes when the condition evaluates to False (No). Also, make sure the flowlines are connected and none have no connection to a shape.

The next step is to check if the value stored in a is higher than the value stored in b.

a	b	max	a>b	output
7	-3			
			TRUE	
		7		

Finally, the output will be displayed.

a	b	max	a>b	output
7	-3			
			TRUE	
		7		
				The larger value is 7

Please note that you don't have to insert each new value on a new line, but this was done just so you can notice the order of execution of the given operations. Trace tables will be further explored in B2 Programming.

REVIEW QUESTIONS

1 Draw a flowchart that would represent a solution for the following problem:

"Initialize a total to zero. Ask the user to enter 50 integer numbers, add the positive numbers to the total and count how many negative values were entered. Output the total and the count value."

2 Research the insertion sort algorithm. Draw a flowchart for this algorithm.

3 Consider the following flowchart.

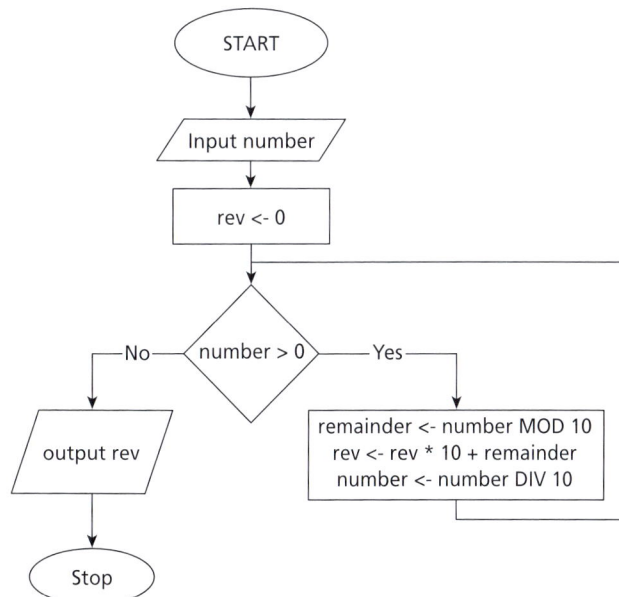

a Research the role of the MOD and DIV functions. Trace the flowchart to find the output for the number 3452 and for the number 1760.

Input: 3452

number	rev	number > 0	remainder	output

Input: 1760

number	rev	number > 0	remainder	output

Top tip!

When filling trace tables, ensure that you write the value a variable takes after an assignment, even if it is a repetition of the previous value. If the variable does not change for a portion of code, you can leave that section blank or rewrite the repeating values.

b Use pattern recognition to predict the output for the number 453453554651.

c Identify the purpose of the algorithm.

d Identify a problem with this algorithm.

ACTIVITY

Thinking skills: Critical and creative thinking: A small family business that delivers goods within its small city is looking to further expand its reach. It is thinking of the following scenarios:

- **Creating brochures, which would include its products and its phone number, and distributing them in the three neighbouring cities.** It would take the orders by phone and deliver them as before, with cash payment on delivery.
- **Creating an online platform that would allow it to promote its products.** Customers would place the orders online and pay for their purchases online, and the company would deliver the goods via available transportation services within the country.
- **Promoting its business via social-media channels.** It would take the orders via instant-messaging services with bank-transfer payments, and deliver the products via transportation services available within the country.

Choose one of the scenarios above. Prepare a presentation that includes a problem specification. Identify the stakeholders; the problem statement; constraints and limitations; objectives and goals; input and output specifications; and evaluation criteria.

Consider the probable cost involved in implementing the scenario you have chosen, the time required to implement it, the hardware and software requirements, and possible effects on the community and staff members.

Deliver your presentation to the class and receive feedback from your peers.

● **Linking questions**

1 How is pattern recognition used to identify different types of traffic flowing across a network? (A2)
2 How are the concepts of computational thinking used in code when designing algorithms? (B2)

EXAM PRACTICE QUESTIONS

Note: All the exam practice questions are representative of those that will be found on Paper 2 for the International Baccalaureate Diploma in Computer Science.

1 Define the term "computational thinking" and outline its role in problem solving. [3]

2 Outline the role computational thinking techniques like decomposition and abstraction play in software development. [4]

3 Identify three items that should be included in the problem specification and define one of them. [4]

4 Explain how pattern recognition can be used in data analysis, machine learning and database design. [6]

5 A teacher is asking 30 students how long they spend each day reading. The students will specify this duration in minutes and hours, for example 1 hour and 20 minutes. The teacher wants to write an algorithm that will output their input in minutes only.

    a Identify the input, process and output required for this algorithm. [3]

    b The teacher wants to create a ranking and send to parents the list of students in descending order based on their time spent reading books. Outline the steps required (the algorithm) to complete this task. [3]

    c Identify two stakeholders involved in this process. [2]

    d To keep their personal details anonymous, the teacher decides to create a username for each student. The username is made of the last two characters of their first name and the first three characters of their last name.

        i The first student's name is Sam Sung. State the corresponding username. [1]

        ii Draw a flowchart to outline the creation of usernames for the 30 students. [4]

        iii Explain one limitation of this algorithm and propose a better one. [3]

B2 Programming

Programming fundamentals (part 1)

How can we apply programming to solve problems?

SYLLABUS CONTENT

By the end of this chapter, you should be able to:
▶ B2.1.1 Construct and trace programs using a range of global and local variables of various data types
▶ B2.1.2 Construct programs that can extract and manipulate substrings

B2.1.1 Variables

◆ **Variable:** a designated memory location that stores a value that can change during the execution of a program.

◆ **Loop / iteration:** a repetition.

◆ **Selection:** a conditional statement or decision statement, e.g. IF, CASE statements.

◆ **Data storage:** storage of data within primary or secondary memory.

◆ **Operator:** a character that represents a mathematical, arithmetic or logical operation.

◆ **Identifier:** a lexical token that names the language's entities.

◆ **Declaration:** a language construct specifying the properties of an identifier.

◆ **Initialization:** assigning an initial value to a data structure.

Converting an algorithm into code involves using **variables** to store and manipulate data, **loops** to repeat instructions, and **selection** structures to make decisions on a path to follow to complete a task. Important constructs to understand when developing a program are:

■ **data storage:** the use of variables and constants

■ **operators:** used to manipulate and compare data (mathematical and logical operators)

■ selection/branching structures: used to construct decision statements

■ iteration: loops to repeat blocks of code: counter-based and conditional looping structures.

■ Data storage – use of variables

Consider a sales representative receiving a fixed-base salary, supplemented by a bonus that is tied to monthly sales performance. This bonus fluctuates from month to month; hence it can be characterized as variable over time. In fields like Mathematics and Computer Science, the term "variable" is used to encapsulate such dynamic values.

A variable has an **identifier** (name) and a current value. Each variable can only hold one value at a time. Before being used, a variable must be declared and initialized.

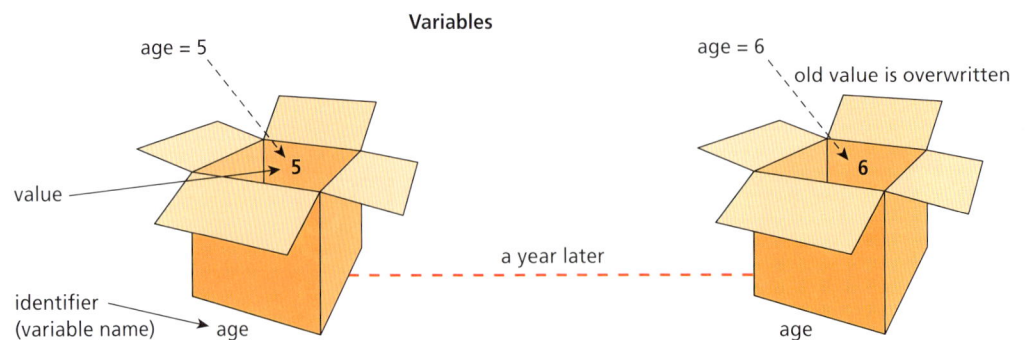

Variables

Variable **declaration** refers to specifying the data type of the variable, while **initialization** refers to providing it with an initial value.

🟢 Top tip!

In Python, there is no need to declare the variables used. Therefore, for assessment purposes, they can be mentioned via a **comment** (a comment is used to provide explanations of code, or notes, to the developer, but it is removed at lexical analysis stage – it is not necessary during the compilation of the program, so it will be ignored).

ACTIVITY

Inquirer: Nurture your curiosity, developing skills for inquiry and research.

Research skills: Research the term "constant" and understand the difference between constants and variables. Outline those differences and specify when each of them could be used.

■ Data types

The **data type** tells you what type of value a variable will store and what kind of operations are allowed on that specific value.

Is the variable going to store a whole number or a decimal number; is it a piece of text or just a true / false value; or one single character? Every programming language has its own way of declaring variables.

String

String is used to store a sequence of characters, digits and / or symbols (a text). The text is written in double quotation marks in Java, while Python can use single or double quotation marks.

Java
```
String password="Bob@123";
```

Python
```
password ='Bob@123'
password ="Bob@123"
```

In this example, the password is **assigned** (becomes) the value Bob@123.

The primitive data types considered for the curriculum are: `int`, `double`, `char` and `Boolean`.

Integer

Integer (int) is used to store whole numbers (positive or negative integers).

Java
```
int age=54;
```

Python
```
age = 54
```

Decimal

The **float** and **double** data types are used to store decimal numbers (double precision). As double has a higher precision than float, it is safer to use double in your exercises.

Java
```
double salary=5998.96;
```

Python
```
elevation = -3.1
```

Char

Char is used to store a single character, digit or symbol.

Java	Python
`char at= '@';`	`at = '@'`

Boolean

Boolean is used to store one of the two possible values: true or false. So, a Boolean variable could be used to store such data as whether or not a product is still in stock; whether or not a person is a male; whether or not a trip has been paid for, and so on.

Java	Python
`boolean a = false;`	`a = False`

Boolean variables are often used to evaluate logic expressions. In code, conditions often need to be added and, if the condition would evaluate to true, some statements would be executed; otherwise, different statements would be executed.

Another example of the need for a Boolean variable would be to continue repeating a piece of code as long as an expression evaluates to true or false, based on the requirements.

Consider the following variables: `a = 7` and `b = 54`

`((a<9) and (b>30))` evaluates to true: if both conditions evaluate to true, the result is true. 7 is smaller than 9 and 54 is greater than 30 (both conditions are met).

`((a>3) or (b<3))` evaluates to true: if either condition is true, the result is true. (The first condition is true; the second is false.)

REVIEW QUESTIONS

1. Define the term "variable".
2. Explain why variables are used in programming.
3. State three data types used in programming.
4. Suggest a way to declare a variable in the programming language you are currently studying.
5. Identify rules and conventions that you could follow when naming variables.
6. Explain why it is important to choose an appropriate data type for a variable.
7. Identify a situation where you need to change the data type of a variable during the execution of a program.
8. Identify an example of a common error when using variables and explain how you would fix it.
9. Explain how the choice of data type affects memory usage and performance in a program.

10 Evaluate the following Boolean expressions if a = 8 and b = 3:

   a   E = (a<b) or (a>5)

   b   E =! (a>=b)

   c   E = (a<8) and (b>3)

   d   E = (a==8)

   e   E =! (a==b) or (a>b)

11 Identify the most appropriate data type to store:

   a   your name

   b   your age

   c   your phone number

   d   whether an item is out of stock

   e   the price of a flight ticket.

12 Identify three legal and three illegal identifier names in the programming language you study.

PROGRAMMING EXERCISES

1   Construct code to output a joke on the screen.

2   Construct code to ask the user to enter their name, store it in a variable and display it on the screen, together with a welcome message.

3   Copy the following expressions and display the value of E after each one of them. Check whether your answers to review question 10 above are correct.

```
a = 8
b = 3
E = (a<b) or (a>5)
E =! (a>=b)
E = (a<8) and (b>3)
E = (a==8)
E =! (a==b) or (a>b)
```

ACTIVITY

Use your answers to the programming exercises above to answer the following questions.
1   Did you follow variable naming conventions to solve questions 1 and 2?
2   Were the variable names meaningful and descriptive?

ACTIVITY

Self-management skills: Set goals that are challenging and realistic: Practise five coding challenges of your choice per week. This will greatly improve your coding skills, and it will increase your self-confidence.

Communicators: Express yourself confidently and creatively in many ways. Collaborate effectively with and listen carefully to the perspectives of other class members.

Communication skills: Use appropriate forms of writing for different purposes and audiences. Explore and create a table to present to the class the different ranges available for the data types you have studied.

◼ Assignments

Assignment refers to setting a value to a variable; this operation is typically carried out using the equals sign (=). The value on the right of the equals sign is assigned to the variable on the left side of the equals sign; it can never be done the other way around.

```
count = 1
```

This statement assigns the value of 1 to the variable count. In other words, count is now 1.

But you will often see statements like this: count = count + 1. This statement means that the variable count is incremented (or increased) by one, or its new value is one greater than it was. **Incrementing** a variable by one is a special case, and you can also write it as count++. If ++ means the variable is incremented by one, **decrementing** a variable by one becomes count-- or count = count - 1.

> ◆ **Increment:** to increase a value by another value (usually by one).
>
> ◆ **Decrement:** to decrease a value by another value (usually by one).

Another example is when you decrease the variable by a value other than one, such as:

```
price = 5000
```

```
price = price - 100
```

Here, the variable price becomes 100 lower than it was. So, it was initially 5000, and after the second line of code is executed the new price is 4900. When assigning new values to variables, the previous value is overwritten, so the variable occupies the same memory location. Therefore, in this case, after the two lines of code are executed, the value of 5000 is completely lost.

As such, a challenging question would be: how do you swap the contents of two variables? Imagine that you have two variables, a and b, storing the values 5 and 7 in this exact order. How could you swap their contents, and end up with a storing the value of 7 and b storing the value of 5?

One attempt to solve the problem might be the following:

```
a = 5
b = 7
a = b
b = a
```

If you have been tempted to do this, what happens is that you end up with two variables storing the same value; in this case, 7. On line 3, the variable a becomes 7, and on line 4, the variable b becomes a, which means b becomes 7 as well.

Therefore, to solve such a problem, you need to imagine that, instead of numbers, you are dealing with liquids. Imagine that the variable a is a cup that is filled with water, and the variable b is a cup filled with tea. What you want is to swap the contents of your cups: the water to get into cup b and the tea into cup a. You cannot mix those contents, so what is the solution? A third cup! The solution is to bring in a third cup, which will temporarily hold the content of one of your cups. So, you pour the water into cup c. Cup a is now available to store the content of cup b, which is the tea. After this step, you can pour the water from cup c into cup b. By doing this, your contents are swapped successfully. The example below shows you how this works with numbers:

```
a = 5
b = 7
temp = a     // 5 is saved into the temporary variable temp
a = b        // 7 is stored into a
b = temp     // 5 (from temporary variable) is stored into b
```

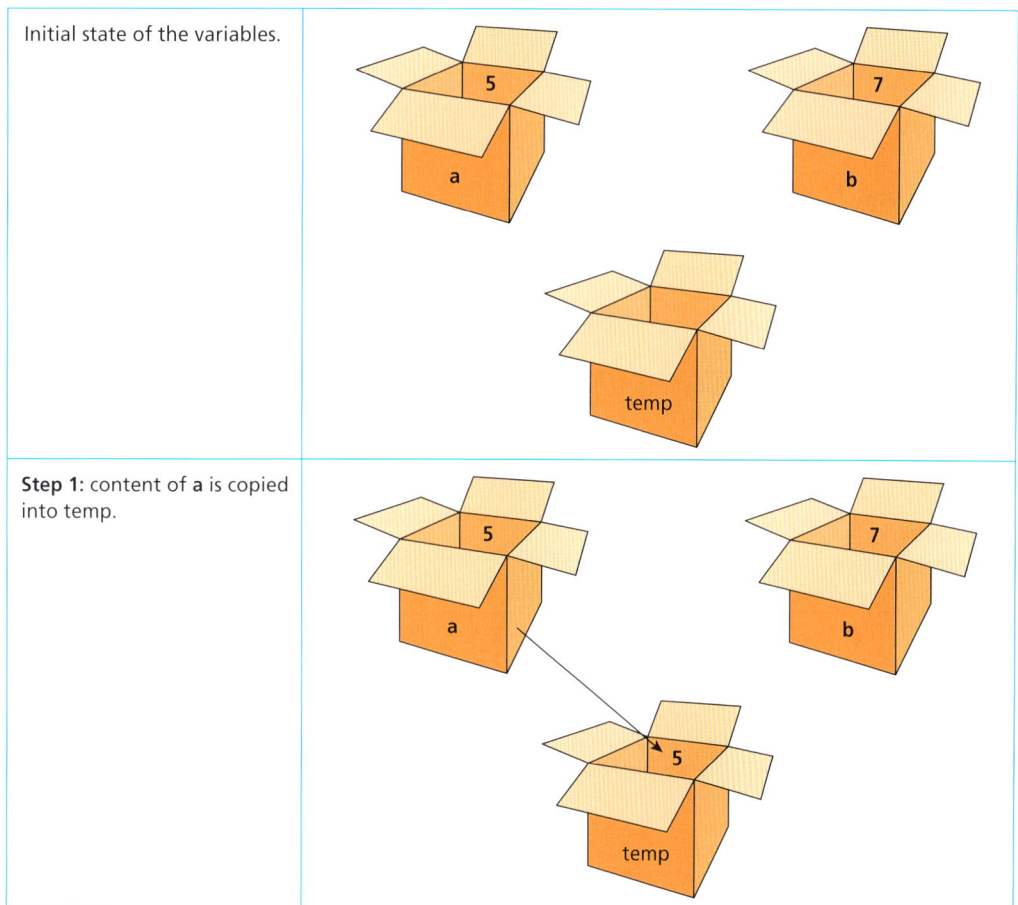

Initial state of the variables.	
Step 1: content of **a** is copied into temp.	

Step 2: content of the variable **b** is copied into **a**.	
	The content of **a** is overwritten.
Step 3: content of the variable temp is copied into **b**.	
	Now the content of the two variables **a** and **b** is swapped.

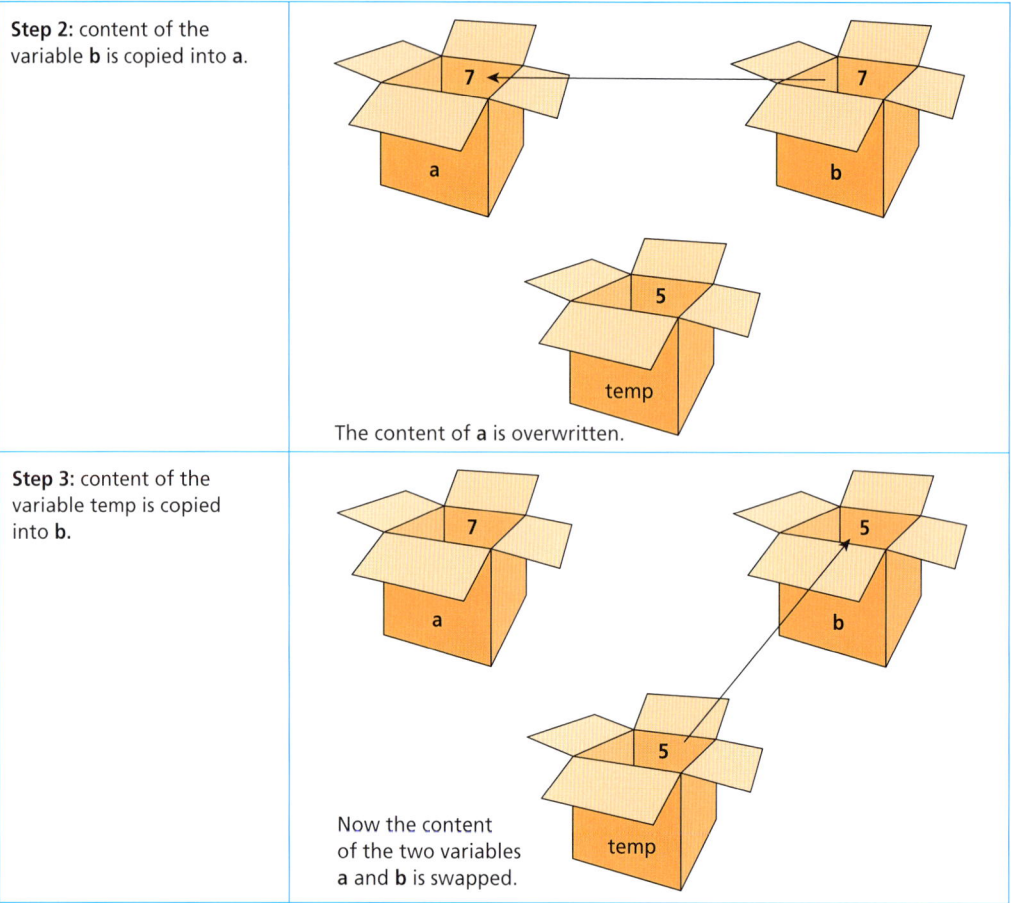

Although this might seem an irrelevant challenge right now, this swapping method is part of several sorting routines that you will study later.

■ Operators

Operators are used to perform calculations, comparisons and other logical operations. Operators can be **arithmetic operators**, such as +, -, /, *, %; or **Boolean operators**, such as !, &&, | |; or **relational operators**, such as <=, <, >, >=, ==, != .

◆ **Arithmetic operator:** a character that is used to perform a calculation.

◆ **Boolean operator:** a character that represents a specific logical operation that is used to produce a true or false outcome.

◆ **Relational operator:** an operator used to compare values or expressions.

Operator in Java	Operator in Python	Meaning
+	+	addition
-	-	subtraction
*	*	multiplication
/	/	division
%	%	modulus (returns the remainder)
<	<	smaller than
<=	<=	smaller than or equals to
>	>	greater than
>=	>=	greater than or equals to
==	==	equals to
!=	!=	not equals to
&&	and	and
||	or	or

Arithmetic operators are used to perform calculations such as addition, multiplication, subtraction, and so on. The arithmetic operators presented so far are **binary operators**, meaning they require two **operands** (two values) to apply the calculation on. There are also **unary operators** (that require only one operand), such as:

Unary operator	Meaning
-	negative numbers
++	incrementing the value by 1
--	decrementing the value by 1

While it is quite straightforward to understand when you would use the addition, subtraction or multiplication operators, it might be a bit trickier to understand what the *div* and *mod* operators are.

Div: division operator

In Java and Python, there are two types of division: **integer division** and **floating-point division**.

Both types use the same symbol (forward slash) in Java. However, when dividing two integer values, the result will be an integer (integer division); when dividing two floating-point number numbers or a decimal and an integer, the result will be a decimal number (floating-point division).

Java
```
int no1 = 7;
int no2 = 2;
System.out.println(no1/no2);
```

In the example above, even if the result would be 3.5, the answer displayed would be 3, as the two numbers are whole numbers (integers).

Java
```
double no1 = 7.0;
double no2 = 2.0;
System.out.println(no1/no2);
```

However, in this example, as both variables store decimal numbers, the result displayed is a decimal number as well (3.5).

Java
```
float no1 = 7.0;
int no2 = 2;
System.out.println(no1/no2);
```

In the example above, the values stored are numbers of mixed data types, and the result will be a decimal number: 3.5.

In Python, as the type of variables is not specified, there are different operators to represent the different types of divisions. Floating-point division is performed by the / (forward slash) operator, so the result will be a decimal number. However, integer division uses the // (double slash) operator. // will return the floor division (this means that, no matter the result, it will always round it down – what happens is that the decimal part is truncated or, in simpler words, it is ignored or deleted.

Python
```
no1 = 7
#no1 = 7.0
no2 = 2
print(no1/no2)
```

In this example, the output will be 3.5, no matter the data type of the two numbers.

Python
```
no1 = 7
#no1 = 7.0
no2 = 2
print(no1//no2)
```

However, this time the output will be 3, as the result is truncated, without taking into consideration the data type of the variables.

PROGRAMMING EXERCISES

Construct code in the language of your choice to solve the following problems.

1. Ask the user to enter three numbers. Output their average. For example, if the input is: 3, 4 and 5, the output is 4.

2. Ask the user to enter their name and age. Output a message that includes the name and the age that the user will be in 10 years. For example, if the input is Bob, 15, the output should be [Bob, in ten years you'll be 25 years old].

3. Ask the user to enter a three-digit number. Output the sum of all three digits. For example, if the input is 125, the output should be 8.

Common mistake

Algorithms written to solve a problem need to be specific and accurate. Many students lose marks for missing small details, like forgetting to initialize a variable such as a counter or a total.

ACTIVITY

Use your solutions to the programming exercises above to answer the following questions.
1. Did the correct mathematical operations occur for question 1?
2. How did you concatenate the name and the age to display the output for question 2?
3. Was the expected result displayed for question 3?

ACTIVITY

Communication skills: Give and receive meaningful feedback – work in pairs to exchange solutions to the programming exercises and give each other feedback on what could have been done to improve or optimize the proposed solutions.

B2.1.2 String manipulation

In coding, there is often a need to manipulate text. You might want to display some special characters, such as double quotations " ", single quotations ' ' or a backslash \.

As those characters are already used for a specific purpose in most programming languages, displaying them might be challenging. At the same time, programmers might want to extract parts of text belonging to a string, join them together, alter or delete them. How is all this possible?

Including an escape character (backslash) supports typing special characters that are usually used for specific purposes in the language. For example, single quotations are used for storing a character in Java or even a string in Python; the same happens with double quotations. Therefore, when wanting to include single or double quotations in the text, you must use the backslash:

Character	Java and Python
"	\"
'	\'
\	\\

■ Text blocks

In Java, multiple line strings can be written like this:

```java
Java
System.out.println("Write multiple\n"
+ "Lines like this");
```

Text on different lines is joined together via the + operator. \n represents the new line character, denoting that the new line of text will be displayed on the next line.

In Python, multiple line strings can be written by using triple double quotation marks:

```python
Python
print(""" Write multiple
Lines like this
""")
```

The programming language offers several built-in functions that can be used to manipulate strings.

In the examples below, `text` is a variable that stores a piece of text, such as: "Computer Science is fun!"

■ Length

The length function returns the length (number of characters, spaces included) of the value stored in the string `text`. In this situation, the value stored in x is 24.

```java
Java
x = text.length()
```

```python
Python
x = len(text)
```

■ Concatenation

Concatenation refers to joining two or more string values together.

Both Java and Python allow several ways to achieve concatenation. One of them is with the +
operator, which will join the two strings together.

Java

```java
String part1 = "Computer Science is fun";
String part2 = ", isn't it?";
String text = part1 + part2;
System.out.println(text);
```

Python

```python
part1 = "Computer Science is fun"
part2 = ", isn't it?"
text = part1 + part2
print(text)
```

Another function that can be used in Java to concatenate two strings is the function `concat`:

Java

```java
String part1 = "Computer Science is fun";
String part2 = ", isn't it?";
String text = part1.concat(part2);
System.out.println(text);
```

Note that concatenation is a technique that is applied to a series of string variables, rather than a
combination of strings and integers or decimals. If there is a need to concatenate a combination
of strings and integers, the + operator can be used in Java, or the integer or decimal value can
be converted to a string prior to the concatenation taking place. In Python, the interpolation
operator (%), the `str` function, `str.format` or f-strings can be used for this purpose.

Java

```java
String exam = "Computer Science";
int grade = 9;
System.out.println("Your "+ exam + " exam score is " + grade);
```

Python: Use of interpolation operator

```python
exam = "Computer Science"
grade = 9
print("%s%s%s%s" % ("Your " , exam, " exam score is ", grade))
```

Python: Use of str function

```python
exam = "Computer Science"
grade = 9
print("Your " + exam + " exam score is " + str(grade))
```

Python: Use of str.format

```python
exam = "Computer Science"
grade = 9
print("{}{}{}{}".format("Your " , exam, " exam score is ",
grade))
```

Python: Use of f-strings

```python
exam = "Computer Science"
grade = 9
print(f'{"Your "}{exam}{" exam score is "}{grade}')
```

● Top tip!

In Python, if you want to display the content of the two variables without saving it into another variable, you can simply use the `print` function, which accepts several parameters separated by a comma:

Python

```python
part1 = "Computer Science is fun"
part2 = ", isn't it?"
print(part1, part2)
```

■ Substring

`substring` is the function that is used to retrieve part of the string, for example if you want to extract the first word or letter in a string, or the text between specific positions in the string.

Note that the first position in a string is 0.

In Java, the function used for this purpose is called `substring`:

Java

```java
String text = "Computer Science is fun";
String part = text.substring(8);
System.out.println(part);
```

By providing one argument to the `substring` function, it indicates the starting index of the text to be extracted. In this example, the output would be "Science is fun" as the variable `part` will be assigned the value from the string, starting with position 8 until the end of the string.

Java

```java
String text = "Computer Science is fun";
String part = text.substring(8,16);
System.out.println(part);
```

In the example above, the call of the substring function is passed two arguments. The first one (8) indicates the starting index (position in string) and the second one (16) indicates the ending index. The substring produced will be from starting index until the ending index –1. Therefore, the text produced in this example will be "Science". This is the case because "S" is the letter at index 8 and "e" is the letter at index 15. The letter at index 16, which is a space character, is not included.

In Python, the substring function is often referred to as slicing.

Python

```python
text = "Computer Science is fun"
part = text[0:1]
print(part)
```

The code above extracts the first character of the text variable: "C".

Python

```python
text = "Computer Science is fun"
part = text[:5]
print(part)
```

In this case, the part will include the first five characters from the text: "Compu", as "C" is in position 0 and "u" in position 4.

Python

```python
text = "Computer Science is fun"
part = text[-1]
print(part)
```

Because the index is –1, this piece of code will store the last character into the string part; in this case, the letter "n".

Python

```python
text = "Computer Science is fun"
part = text[-6:]
print(part)
```

In this example, the last six characters in the string will be assigned to the variable part: "is fun".

```python
Python
text = "Computer Science is fun"
part = text[1:-4]
print(part)
```

Above, the extracted text will start at index 1 and will end at the last index −4. So, the value stored in the variable part is "omputer Science is".

Replace

The replace method searches a string for a character or set of characters and replaces it or them with another character or with other characters.

```java
Java
String text = "Computer Science is fun";
text = text.replace('e', '@');
System.out.println(text);
```

In Java, the replace method will replace one single character, so the text now becomes "Comput@r Sci@nc@ is fun". To replace several characters, the replaceAll method should be used.

```java
Java
String text = "Computer Science is fun";
text = text.replaceAll("is", "will be");
System.out.println(text);
```

In Python, the replace method is used for replacing both one single character and more characters.

```python
Python
text = "Computer Science is fun"
text = text.replace("e", "@")
print(text)
```

```python
Python
text = "Computer Science is fun"
text = text.replace("is", "will be")
print(text)
```

Strip

Sometimes, when reading values from a text file or any permanent storage, you might want to remove the trailing white spaces. This can be achieved by using the strip method.

Some versions of Java accept `trim` instead of `strip` for the same purpose:

```Java
String text = "   Computer Science is fun   !   ";
text = text.trim();
System.out.println(text);
```

The leading and trailing spaces will be removed, therefore the new text that will be output is: "Computer Science is fun !"

To achieve the same output in Python, you can use the `strip` function:

```Python
text = "    Computer Science is fun    !    "
text = text.strip()
print(text)
```

TOK

How does knowledge in Computer Science develop?

Knowledge in Computer Science develops through a dynamic interplay of various Ways of Knowing and Areas of Knowledge. Logical reasoning and empirical evidence form the backbone of technical advancements, while intuition, creativity and ethical considerations shape the broader impact and direction of the field. The interdisciplinary nature of Computer Science ensures that it continually evolves, influenced by and influencing other domains of knowledge. This multifaceted development makes Computer Science a rich field for TOK debates, highlighting the complexity and depth of how knowledge grows and transforms within it.

Is Computer Science knowledge primarily objective, grounded in mathematical truths and empirical data, or does it also encompass subjective elements, such as user experience and ethical considerations? How significant is intuition in developing new algorithms or systems? Can purely logical and empirical approaches lead to all breakthroughs, or is there a place for creative intuition?

PROGRAMMING EXERCISES

1 Construct code that asks the user to provide their name, house / flat number and their street number or name.. Concatenate this information to display a message such as the following. (Attempt to write the message by using one single line of code, and ensure it is displayed on two separate lines, as shown.)

From: Name

Address: Full Address

Message:

Why was there a bug in the computer?

Because it was looking for a "byte" to eat!

2 Construct code that allows the user to enter their first and last names. Concatenate the two values, add a space in between and display the full name together with its length without the space.

3 Construct code that allows the user to enter a noun and a letter. Replace all occurrences of that letter with the @ symbol.

Programming constructs

SYLLABUS CONTENT

By the end of this chapter, you should be able to:
▶ B2.3.1 Construct programs that implement the correct sequence of code instructions to meet program objectives
▶ B2.3.2 Construct programs utilizing appropriate selection structures
▶ B2.3.3 Construct programs that utilize looping structures to perform repeated actions
▶ B2.3.4 Construct functions and modularization

B2.3.1 Sequencing

When solving problems, the order in which the statements are executed matters. Taking the swapping example in section B2.1, if you were to change the order of the instructions it would produce an incorrect output:

```
a = 5
b = 7
a = b       // 7 is stored into a
temp = a    // 7 is saved into the temporary variable temp
b = temp    // 7 (from temporary variable) is stored into b
```

Here, even if they are the same statements, the result will be incorrect just because they are not in the right order. In this example, in the end both variables, a and b, will store the value 7. As such, no swapping occurred, even if a temporary variable was introduced exactly as was done in the correct algorithm.

◆ **Sequence:** to execute instructions one after another in the given order.

Sequence refers to the instructions being executed once and in the exact order they are written.

Following the right order of the instructions is important in programming, as this impacts the outcome, which could lead to incorrect functionality (as demonstrated above), logic errors or infinite loops.

B2.3.2 Selection structures

■ Selection or branching structures

Selection is a programming construct used to decide what statement(s), if any, are to be executed based on one or more given conditions.

Conditions are usually built using logic operators. IF statements are an example of selection or branching structures. The condition in the IF statement is evaluated: if it evaluates to true, specific statements are executed; otherwise, nothing happens, or other statements are executed.

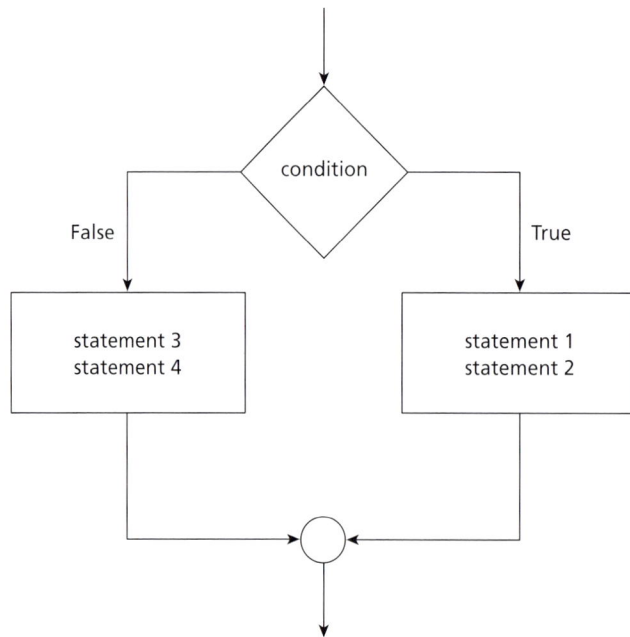

■ IF statements flowchart

In this flowchart, if the condition is met, statements 1 and 2 will be executed; otherwise, statements 3 and 4.

```
IF condition THEN
.........
END IF
```

■ General structure

■ Selection statement flowchart

In this case, nothing happens if the condition is not met. As an example, this structure could be used in a situation where a buyer receives a discount of 20 per cent if their purchase value is 100 or more. As such, if their purchase value is below 100, nothing happens.

B2 Programming

Java

```java
private static Scanner read;
public static void main(String[] args) {
    read = new Scanner(System.in);
    double purchaseValue, discount;
    discount=0;
    System.out.println("enter value of goods purchased: ");
    purchaseValue = read.nextDouble();
    if (purchaseValue>=100)
        discount = purchaseValue * 0.2;
    System.out.println("Your discount is: " + discount);
}
```

In this example, the `purchaseValue` and `discount` variables have been declared as `double` because they are meant to store an amount of money, which could be a decimal value.

As the discount is only calculated if the condition is met, we had to initialize it to 0 in the beginning, so there is a value to display if no calculation occurs. The indentation inside the IF statement in the Python below shows what instruction is going to be executed when the condition is met. In Java, the indentation is replaced by curly brackets and, if those are missing, then the next line will be interpreted as belonging to the selection statement. Therefore, the output statement will be run independently of the given condition, as it is not included in the IF statement.

Python

```python
discount = 0
purchaseValue= float(input("Enter the value of your goods:"))
if purchaseValue>=100:
    discount = purchaseValue * 0.2
print("Your discount is ", discount)
```

In Python, there is no need to declare the variables, so only the `discount` variable is initialized to 0. However, the input value is converted to `float`, to ensure the user will enter a decimal number (integers are included into the range of decimal values). If the float conversion did not happen, the user's input value would be a text, and this would throw an error when attempting to use it in calculations.

You can further expand this code and include a variable to store and display the due amount:

Java

```java
double purchaseValue,toPay, discount;
toPay=0;
System.out.println("enter the value of your goods: ");
purchaseValue = read.nextDouble();
if (purchaseValue>=100) {
    discount = purchaseValue * 0.2;
    toPay = purchaseValue - discount;
}
System.out.println("You need to pay: " + toPay);
```

In the example above, you need the brackets to indicate that both calculations will happen only if the condition is met.

Python
```python
toPay = 0
purchaseValue= float(input("Enter the value of your goods:"))
if purchaseValue>=100:
    discount = purchaseValue * 0.2
    toPay = purchaseValue - discount
print("You need to pay: ", toPay)
```

In Python, the indentation replaces the brackets, so they are not included.

The IF statement can be further expanded to include an ELSE. The statements corresponding to the ELSE are the statements that will be executed if the condition evaluates to false instead.

```
IF condition THEN
.........
ELSE
.........
END IF
```

■ General structure

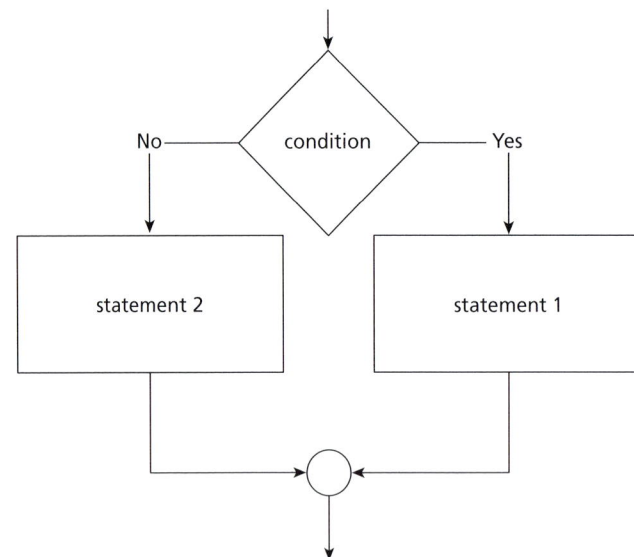

■ Selection statement flowchart

Java
```java
if (purchaseValue>=100) {
    toPay= purchaseValue * 0.8;
} else {
    toPay = purchaseValue;
}
System.out.println("You need to pay: " + toPay);
```

Note that the brackets can still be used even if only a single instruction is included in the IF or ELSE part.

```python
Python
toPay = 0
purchaseValue= float(input("Enter the value of your goods:"))
if purchaseValue>=100:
    discount = purchaseValue * 0.2
    toPay = purchaseValue - discount
else:
    toPay = purchaseValue
print("You need to pay: ", toPay)
```

As you may have realized, the block of code can even be further expanded to include another IF statement inside the current one. (One IF statement inside another is called a "nested IF".)

```
IF condition THEN
        IF condition 2 THEN
.........
        ELSE
.........
        ENDIF
ELSE
.........
END IF
```

■ General structure

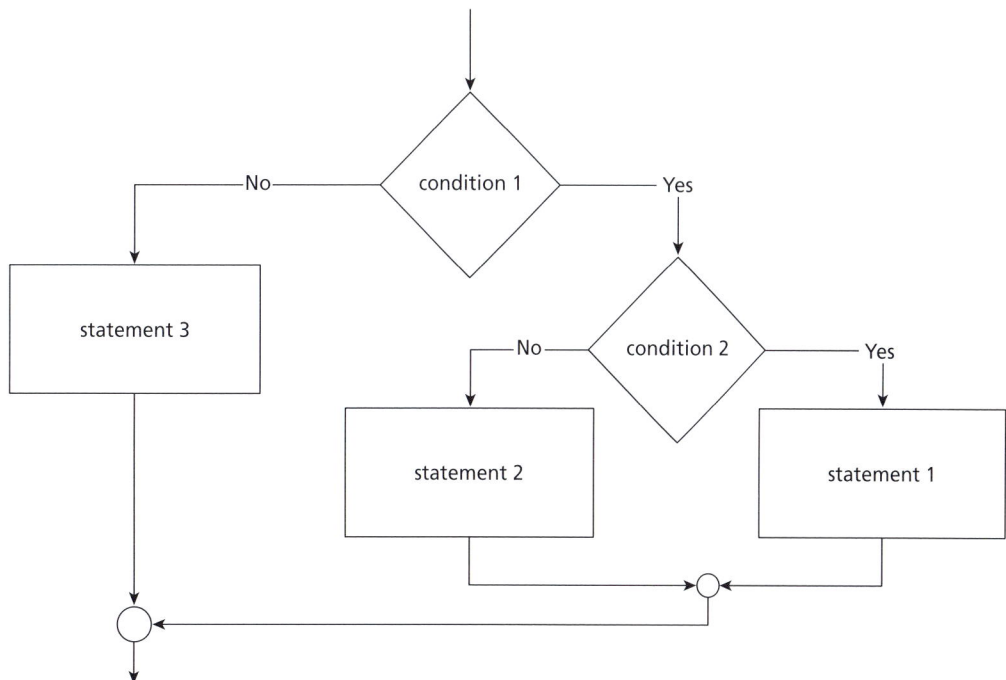

■ Nested IF flowchart

Java

```java
boolean member = false;
toPay=0;
System.out.println("do you have a membership card(true/
false): ");
member = read.nextBoolean();
if (purchaseValue>=100) {
    if(member == true) {
        discount = purchaseValue * 0.2;
        toPay = purchaseValue-discount;
    } else {
        toPay = purchaseValue*0.9;
    }
} else {
    toPay = purchaseValue;
}
System.out.println("You should pay: " + toPay);
```

In this case, a new variable was included that will decide whether the discount is 20 per cent or 10 per cent, depending on whether or not the buyer is a member. Also, observe that, as there is no requirement to display the discount value, you could have calculated the due amount by simply multiplying the purchase price by 0.9, thus applying the discount of 10 per cent.

Python

```python
toPay = 0
purchaseValue= float(input("Enter the value of your goods:"))
member = input("Do you have a membership card (true/false)?")
member = eval(member)
if purchaseValue>=100:
    if member == True:
        discount = purchaseValue * 0.2
        toPay = purchaseValue - discount
    else:
        toPay = purchaseValue * 0.9
else:
    toPay = purchaseValue
print("You need to pay: ", toPay)
```

The value input and stored into the member variable should be a Boolean value. However, if there is an attempt to check whether the value entered is True or False by using the bool keyword instead of eval, it will not return the right answer: bool checks whether or not the string entered is empty and, as the user will write True or False, the value of the variable member will always be True as the string is not empty. Therefore, the eval function is used in this situation, to ensure the value entered is evaluated to True or False and then stored into the member variable.

However, there is another way of solving this problem, by using the `and` logic operator in the condition.

```java
Java
if (purchaseValue>=100 && member==true) {
    discount = purchaseValue * 0.2;
    toPay = purchaseValue-discount;
} else if (purchaseValue>=100 && member==false) {
    toPay = purchaseValue*0.9;
} else {
    toPay = purchaseValue;
}
System.out.println("You should pay: " + toPay);
```

In the example above, both conditions should be met (to be a member and purchase value to be 100 or above) for the discount of 20 per cent to be applied. The second condition is checking whether both conditions are met again, but this time they should have a purchase value of 100 or above, but not be a member. The statement executed on the `else` branch is the statement happening if the purchase is not 100 or above.

```python
Python
toPay = 0
purchaseValue= float(input("Enter the value of your goods:"))
member = input("Do you have a membership card (True/False)?")
member = eval(member)
if purchaseValue>=100 and member==True:
    discount = purchaseValue * 0.2
    toPay = purchaseValue - discount
elif purchaseValue>=100 and member == False:
    toPay = purchaseValue * 0.9
else:
    toPay = purchaseValue
print("You need to pay: ", toPay)
```

In Python, `else if` is replaced by the keyword `elif`.

Conditions can use other logic operators, such as OR and NOT.

In case you wanted the discount to be applied if the purchase value was 100 or above or the buyer owned a membership card, the OR operator would replace the AND operator in the condition above, for example:

```java
Java
if (purchaseValue>=100 || member)
```

```python
Python
if purchaseValue>=100 or member:
```

As in the example above, a comparison with a true value can be written by using the conditional statement if, followed by the variable that needs to be evaluated to true:

if (member)

This will evaluate to TRUE if the member stores the value true, and to FALSE otherwise.

Therefore, the expression if (! member) in Java or if not member: in Python would return TRUE if the member variable stores a value of false, and it would return FALSE if the variable stores true; this expression being read as if not member.

Other relational operators can be part of the comparison, such as: ==, !=, <, >, <=.

Because = is used in assignments, == is used in comparisons to check for equality.

PROGRAMMING EXERCISES

1   Construct code to let the user input their favourite food. If the user enters pasta, PASTA or Pasta, output the message "Go to Italy". Otherwise, output the message "[favouriteFood] will never replace pasta!"

2   Construct code that requires the user to input a number and a Boolean variable flag. If the flag is true, output double the number. Otherwise, output the squared number.

3   Retirement ages differ for men and women. In some countries, women can retire at the age of 62 and men at 65. Construct a program that asks the user to enter their name, gender and age. Calculate and output whether the user is eligible for retirement, or how many years they need to wait to get their pension.

4   Construct a program that requires the user to enter the measurements of the sides of a right-angled triangle. Calculate and display its area.

5   Construct code to create a calculator that converts temperatures between Celsius and Fahrenheit.

6   Construct code to create a quiz that asks the user to guess the capital city of five different countries of your choice. Add a score to your quiz. At the end, display the right answers for the missed questions and the score.

7   Construct a program that asks the user to enter their favourite colour and their lucky number. If their favourite colour is green and their lucky number is between 4 and 7, output the message "In [LuckyNumber] years, you'll buy a [colour] bicycle". Otherwise, if the lucky number is below 4 and above 1, output the message "I suppose you wanted a [colour] ball [LuckyNumber] years ago". Otherwise, display the message "[LuckyNumber] is not so lucky!"

8   Construct code that requires the user to input two numbers. Compare the two numbers and output the larger one. If the two numbers are the same, output an appropriate message instead.

B2.3.3 Loops and iteration

Consider a scenario where you need to display your name multiple times. Initially, you might achieve this by writing individual print statements for each repetition. However, this approach quickly becomes cumbersome when dealing with a larger number of repetitions, such as 100 times. Moreover, if you want to repeat the actions based on user input or until a certain condition is met, manually writing each repetition becomes impractical. To handle such situations efficiently, loops come into play.

Loops provide a way to execute a block of code repeatedly, either for a predetermined number of iterations or until a specific condition is satisfied. Whether you know the exact number of repetitions in advance, or need to iterate dynamically based on runtime conditions, loops offer a flexible and concise solution.

Loops are used to repeat different instructions or blocks of code. One loop refers to one repetition. There are several types of loops, such as count-controlled loops (FOR loops) and conditional loops. Conditional loops can be pre-condition loops (WHILE loops) or post-condition loops (REPEAT–UNTIL loops).

■ Count-controlled loop

A count-controlled loop (FOR loop) is used when the number of repetitions is known in advance, prior to the execution of the code. For example, if you need to write all the numbers between 1 and 100, before writing any code it can be said that the program will repeat 100 times.

```
loop i from 0 to n
......
end loop
```

■ General structure

■ Count-controlled loop flowchart

If `n` is the number of repetitions required, a FOR loop would look like this:

Java
```java
for(int i = 0; i<n; i++) {
//code to be repeated
}
```

Python
```python
for i in range (0,n):
#code to be repeated
```

In Java, `i = 0` is the starting point of the repetition, so `i` is initialized to 0. `i<n` is the condition to be met so, when `i` is no longer smaller than `n`, the repetition will stop. As the variable `i` was initially 0 to avoid running the code to infinite, the value of `i` needs to be changed with every repetition. In this case, `i` is incremented (`i++`).

In Python, the range indicates the initial value of `i` (in this case, 0) and the ending value of `i` (in this case, `n`). Note here that the code will stop when `i` becomes `n-1`. For example, if `n = 5`, `i` will take the values of 0, 1, 2, 3, 4. There are five repetitions in total; when `i` reaches the value of 5, the repetition will stop and so the value won't be displayed.

In the example above, because the starting point is 0, which is the default value, the statement could have been written as `for i in range (n):` and it would have had the same effect.

In both Java and Python, the starting point can be changed. Consider that you must display all the numbers between 1 and 100. To solve this problem, you can set the starting point to 1 and the ending point to 101, ensuring 100 is also included.

Java
```java
for(int i = 1; i<101; i++) {
    System.out.println(i);
}
```

Python
```python
for i in range (1,101):
    print(i)
```

The Java example could have used the less-than-or-equal-to sign in the condition to ensure the upper bound of 100 is included. Alternatively, the loop could have been maintained to iterate from 0 to 100, with the printing statement adjusted to display the value of `i+1` instead.

Java
```java
for(int i = 1; i<=100; i++) {
    System.out.println(i);
}
```

Python
```python
for i in range (100):
    print(i+1)
```

Imagine wanting to display all the odd numbers between 1 and 100. A solution would be to keep the same structure as before, but to check whether or not the number is odd.

Java
```java
for(int i = 1; i<=100; i++) {
    if (i%2 == 1) {
        System.out.println(i);
    }
}
```

Python
```python
for i in range (1,100):
    if (i%2 == 1):
        print(i)
```

`i%2==1` checks whether the remainder of division by 2 of the variable `i` is 1. In other words, if there is a remainder, the number is odd; if there is no remainder, the number is even.

The same problem can be solved without the need to use an IF statement. A step can be included to change the incrementation so, instead of incrementing the value of i by 1, which is the default value, it increments it by a different value.

Java
```java
for(int i = 1; i<=100; i=i+2) {
    System.out.println(i);
}
```

Python
```python
for i in range (1,100,2):
    print(i)
```

In this situation, in Java, the increment was changed, so the value of i is increased by 2, and in Python a step was included: 2, to specify the same thing. So, the variable `i` will take the values: 1, 3, 5, ... 99.

But what if you are requested to display the numbers from 100 to 1 instead?

Java
```java
for(int i = 100; i>0; i=i-1) {
    System.out.println(i);
}
```

Python
```python
for i in range (100,0,-1):
    print(i)
```

In Java, the starting point is set to 100, so that value is displayed first. The condition is changed, as you want to repeat as long as the value is greater than 0, and also the step is changed to decrement the value instead of incrementing it. `i=i-1` could be written as `i--`.

In Python, the range is changed to start at 100. It should stop when it reaches 1 (0 is not touched) and the step is set to −1, so the number is decremented by 1.

■ Pre-condition loop

```
i = 0
loop while
        ......
        i = i + 1
end loop
```

■ General structure

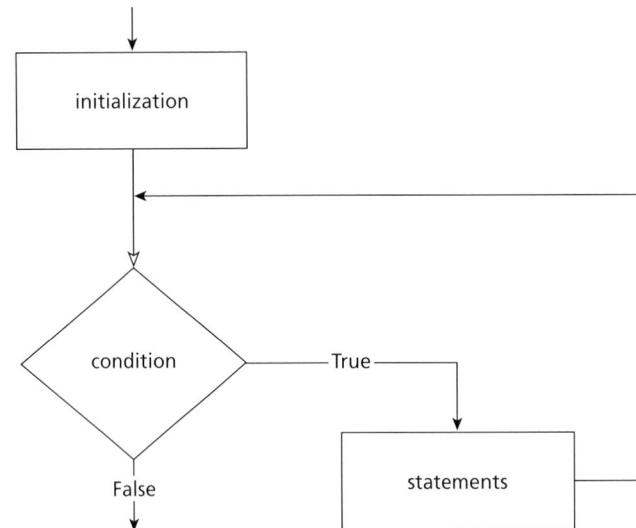

■ Pre-condition loop flowchart

◆ **Termination condition:** a condition in a loop that interrupts or stops the repetition.

◆ **Validation:** a process to ensure input data is sensible or reasonable.

◆ **Verification:** a process to ensure input data is accurately copied from one source to another.

A pre-condition (WHILE) loop is used when the number of repetitions is not known prior to the execution of the code. The code is expected to be repeated as long as a condition is met, or it evaluates to true.

When the condition is no longer met, called **termination condition**, the loop execution will stop. In a WHILE loop, the repetition might not run at all; this happens when the condition is never met. WHILE loops are loops that are often used for **validation** or **verification** purposes. For example, when the user is asked to enter a password twice, the computer will compare the two entries to check if they match (double entry verification). In this case, a loop would be used to repeat entering the password until the two inputs match.

B2 Programming

```java
Java
String password, pass;
password = "apple";
System.out.println("Re-enter the password:");
pass = read.nextLine();
while (! password.equals(pass)) {
    System.out.println("Re-enter the password:");
    pass = read.nextLine();
}
System.out.println("The two passwords matched");
```

In this case, `.equals` is used to compare the value stored in `password` with the one stored in `pass`, as those two values are of type string. If the two values were numbers, then `==` would be used for comparison. The `!` is a negation, therefore, in this case, it is checking if the two values are not the same, and the user is asked to re-enter the password until the two values match. The output at the end will be displayed only after the loop is exited. If the second password never matches the first, the code inside the loop will continuously repeat.

Any FOR loop can be rewritten as a WHILE loop. Considering our example that displays all the numbers between 1 and 100, using a WHILE loop the code would look like this:

```java
Java
int i = 1;
while(i<101) {
    System.out.println(i);
    i = i+1;
}
```

```python
Python
i = 1
while(i<101):
        print(i)
        i=i+1
```

In the example above, the loop will repeat as long as i is smaller than 101. The termination condition will be that `i>=101`. The role of the incrementation is to change the value of i, so the loop will stop at one moment. Otherwise, without that statement, the loop would run to infinite.

■ Post-condition loop

```
i = 0
repeat
        ......
        i = i + 1
until i >= n
```

■ General structure

■ Post-condition loop flowchart

In the post-condition (REPEAT–UNTIL) loop, the condition is checked at the end. In this case, the code inside the loop will execute at least once.

Both in Java and Python, post-condition loop structures are written using WHILE loops.

Java
```java
int i = 1;
do {
    System.out.println(i);
    i = i+1;
} while(i<=100);
```

Python
```python
i = 1
while(True):
    print(i)
    i=i+1
    if i>100:
        break
```

In the example above, the variable i is initially set to 1. This value is displayed and then incremented. This happens no matter what the condition evaluates to. If the condition evaluates to true, the loop is repeated; if the condition evaluates to false, the repetition stops.

REVIEW QUESTIONS

1 Define the term "loop".

2 Explain why it is useful to use loops in coding.

3 Explain the difference between a pre-condition and a post-condition loop.

4 Identify a situation when you would use a count-controlled loop.

5 Define the term "termination condition".

6 Explain why it is important to avoid infinite loops.

7 Identify a situation where an infinite loop could occur.

PROGRAMMING EXERCISES

1 Construct a program that allows the user to enter a number. Output all numbers between 1 and that number.

2 Construct code that requires the user to enter a number and a word. Display each letter in the word on a separate line. Repeat the process the user's number of times.

3 Construct code that asks the user to input ten numbers. Calculate and display the sum of all even numbers entered.

4 Construct a program that creates a variable and initializes it to the value 7. Ask the user to guess a number between 1 and 20. If the user guesses the value 7, output the number of attempts. Do not allow the user to try to guess the number more than three times. If the user doesn't guess the number after three attempts, output the message: "The game is locked. Try again later!"

5 Construct a program that asks the user whether they want an apple. Repeat the question until their answer is yes. At the end, output the message: "Apples are delicious, aren't they? Let's have one!"

ACTIVITY

Use your answers to the programming exercises above to answer the following questions.

1 What loop did you use to solve question 1? Could you replace that loop with another one? How would you do that?

2 Did the program you constructed to solve question 2 handle user input correctly? Can you think of an easier way to extract each letter from a given word?

3 Did your program for question 3 extract the even numbers correctly? What change would calculate the sum of all the odd numbers instead?

4 Why do you think a FOR loop is not appropriate for solving question 4?

5 What termination condition did you use for question 5?

Key information

FOR loops are called "count-controlled" loops, WHILE loops are called "pre-condition" loops and REPEAT-UNTIL loops are called "post-condition" loops.

Count-controlled loops are used when the number of repetitions is known prior to the execution of the code. Pre-condition loops might not be executed at all (if the condition is not met). Post-condition loops will execute at least once, even if the condition is never met.

Top tip!

When you are asked to identify the type of loop exemplified in a piece of code, refer to them as count-controlled, pre-condition or post-condition loops. For example, saying it is a FOR loop instead of a "count-controlled" loop is not enough, as it is not clear that you know what type of loop a FOR loop is.

B2.3.4 Functions and modularization

Functions represent blocks of code that can be reused in various parts of the program and include a return value. Using functions makes the code look neater, and it saves development time as they can be reused as needed. At the same time, they allow for modularity, meaning multiple programmers can work together, each developing a function and then those functions can be put together to build up a more complex program. Once a function has been written and tested, the programmer can reuse it without worrying about its functionality.

Writing **maintainable code** is an important skill for any programmer. Maintainable code refers to code that is clear; easy to read and modify; and can be reused by the programmer themself or by other programmers. Using functions aids in the creation of maintainable code.

Such a reusable block of code is called a **procedure** or a **function**; the difference between the two being the returned value(s). A procedure can take several parameters or none and it has no return value, so it could update a variable or output a message or a value. However, a function will return a value. This returned value can further be used in a mathematical expression, or it can simply be displayed.

Consider the following problem: A user is required to provide two whole numbers. Construct a program that calculates the sum of the two numbers and displays it.

A simple solution would be to ask the user to enter the two numbers, add them together and display the result, such as:

```java
Java
read = new Scanner(System.in);
int no1, no2, sum;
System.out.println("enter no1:");
no1 = read.nextInt();
System.out.println("enter no2:");
no2 = read.nextInt();
sum = no1+no2;
System.out.println("The result is "+ sum);
```

```python
Python
no1 = int(input("enter no1:"))
no2 = int(input("enter no2:"))
sum = no1 + no2
print("The result is ", sum)
```

■ Solution 1

But if you needed to perform the same operation again, with different values, you would have to rewrite the code, which is not very time or memory efficient. Therefore, to complete such tasks, a procedure is required.

◆ **Maintainable code:** clear, easy-to-read and modify code that can be reused within the same program or in other programs, by the same or other programmers.

◆ **Procedure:** a set of statements that can be grouped together and called in a program as needed; they don't return a value.

◆ **Function:** a set of statements that can be grouped together and called in a program as needed; they always return at least one value.

Java

```java
private static Scanner read;
public static void add() {
    int no1, no2, sum;
    System.out.println("enter the first number:");
    no1 = read.nextInt();
    System.out.println("enter the second number:");
    no2 = read.nextInt();
    sum = no1+no2;
    System.out.println("The result is "+ sum);
}
public static void main(String[] args) {
    read = new Scanner(System.in);
    add();
}
```

Python

```python
def add():
    no1 = int(input("enter no1:"))
    no2 = int(input("enter no2:"))
    sum = no1 + no2
    print("The result is ", sum)
add()
```

■ Solution 2

Because this does not return the sum, but only prints it, it is a procedure.

Java

```java
private static Scanner read;
public static void add(int no1, int no2) {
    int sum;
    sum = no1+no2;
    System.out.println("The result is "+ sum);
}
public static void main(String[] args) {
    read = new Scanner(System.in);
    int value1, value2;
    System.out.println("enter the first number:");
    value1 = read.nextInt();
    System.out.println("enter the second number:");
    value2 = read.nextInt()
    add(value1, value2);
}
```

Python

```python
def add(no1,no2):
    sum = no1 + no2
    print("The result is ", sum)
value1 = int(input("enter no1:"))
value2 = int(input("enter no2:"))
add(value1, value2)
```

■ Solution 3

In the code above, the same procedure is created, but two parameters are passed to it (no1 and no2). When the procedure is called in the main program, the values being passed to it are called "arguments" (value1 and value2).

When a return is added to the block of code, the procedure becomes a function. The returned value can be displayed on the screen or used in other mathematical expressions. The number of parameters also differs when it comes to functions: one, none or more parameters can be passed to a function.

When implementing functions in Java, the void keyword from the method signature is replaced by the data type of the value being returned.

Java

```java
private static Scanner read;
public static int add(int no1, int no2) {
    int sum;
    sum = no1+no2;
    return sum;
}
public static void main(String[] args) {
    read = new Scanner(System.in);
    int value1, value2;
    System.out.println("enter the first number:");
    value1 = read.nextInt();
    System.out.println("enter the second number:");
    value2 = read.nextInt();
    System.out.println("The result is "+ add(value1, value2));
    int newVal = 3;
    newVal = newVal + add();
    System.out.println("The new value is "+newVal);
}
```

Python

```python
def add(no1,no2):
    sum = no1 + no2
    return sum
value1 = int(input("enter no1:"))
value2 = int(input("enter no2:"))
print("The result is ", add(value1, value2))
newVal = 3
newVal = newVal + add(value1, value2)
print("The new value is ", newVal)
```

In the example above, the function add will return a value of data type integer.
The function is called once to be displayed and the other time to increase the value of the variable newVal.

REVIEW QUESTIONS

1 Compare functions and procedures.
2 Identify three things you can do to keep a maintainable code.
3 Outline the difference between validation and verification. Provide an example where a selection can be used for validation checks.
4 Differentiate between pre- and post-condition loops.

PROGRAMMING EXERCISES

1 Construct code to let the user create a function called factorial that takes a natural number (n) as a parameter. The function should return the factorial value of that number (n!).

2 Construct a program that consists of a procedure called odds that takes a natural number (n) as a parameter. The procedure should display all the odd numbers from 1 to that number (n).

3 Construct code that creates a function called perfect that takes n (a natural number) as a parameter. The function should return true/false if n is a perfect number.

   A perfect number is a positive integer that is equal to the sum of its positive proper divisors, excluding the number itself. For example, 28 is a perfect number as its proper divisors are: 1, 2, 4, 7, 14. Adding those values together we get 28, and this result is equal to the initial number.

4 Construct a function called palindrome that takes a word as a parameter. The function should return true/false if the given word is a palindrome.

   A palindrome is a word that reads the same forwards or backwards. For example, kayak, racecar, level and civic are all palindromes.

Reflect on the errors you encountered when constructing your code, and how you resolved them.
■ How did you go about debugging the issues?
■ Did you notice any patterns in the errors you encountered?
■ What can you do to avoid such errors in the future?

■ Scope of variables

Based on their scope, variables can be classified into various categories, such as **local** or **global** variables.

The **scope of the variable** defines its lifetime in the program, meaning the block of code where it has been declared, where it can be used and modified. How and where the variables are declared defines the scope.

Local variables

Local variables are variables that have their scope limited to the block of code within which they are declared and used.

Once that block of code is executed, the variable is automatically removed from the memory. It is recommended to use local variables as often as possible. An example of a local variable is when using a counter in a FOR loop. That counter is required only within the body of the loop for storing temporary data but, once the loop is finished, you do not need that counter any longer.

Java: `i` is a local variable

```java
for(int i=0; i<3;i++) {
    System.out.println("hello world");
}
```

As `i` is a local variable, it exists within the loop, and it will take values from 0 to 3. When it reaches 3, the variable is no longer smaller than 3 and the repetition will stop. After this loop, the variable `i` does not exist any longer.

Python: `text` is a local variable

```python
def hello():
    # text is the local variable
    text = "hello world"
    print(text)
# code to text
hello()
# the print below will throw an error as text does not exist
# outside the procedure
print(text)
```

In this example, `text` is the local variable. When printing the variable `text` inside the subprocedure, the message "hello world" will be displayed. However, when attempting to print the `text` again, after the call of the method, an error will be thrown as `text` is used without having an initial value.

Global variables

Global variables are variables that are visible and accessible throughout the program.

In Python, the global variables are initialized at the top of the code or module and, whenever they are used within a function or procedure, they are declared as global. As Java is an object-oriented programming language, it does not use the concept of global variables. However, by using the `static` or `static final` keywords, the variables can have all the properties of global variables.

Python

```python
text = "hello "
def hello():
    # text is a global variable
        global text
    # text is concatenated with a new text value
        text = text + "world"
# Driver code
hello()
print(text)
```

In this example, the `text` is a global variable, which means that, by calling the `hello` procedure, the content of the variable text is changed and, once it is printed, even if it is printed outside the procedure, it will display the updated content: `hello world`.

Top tip!

When writing code, aim to preponderantly use local variables rather than global variables. Local variables are confined to the function or block in which they are declared, promoting encapsulation and modularity. This makes functions self-contained and easier to understand, test and debug. Global variables can be modified by any part of the code, leading to unintended side effects that can make the program behaviour difficult to predict and debug. Local variables prevent such side effects by limiting the scope of variable modifications.

REVIEW QUESTIONS

1 Trace the following program to determine its output.

Java

```java
static String student = "Bob";
public static void changeOfName(String st) {
    st = "Jim";
    System.out.println("Student inside the method: "+st);
}
public static void main(String[] args) {
    changeOfName(student);
    System.out.println("Student outside the method: " +
    student);}
```

Python

```python
student = "Bob"
def changeOfName(st):
    st = "Bobby"
    print("Student inside the method: ", st)
changeOfName(student)
print("Student outside the method: ", student)
```

2 Identify a local variable in the code above. Explain why the chosen variable is not a global variable.

3 Construct a program that changes the code above so that, after the method is executed, both outputs display the name Jim, without changing the first line of code.

4 Construct code to update the method above to include a validation check: the new name should be input from the keyboard and the change should occur only if the new name is different from the previous name. Display a message if the new name is not different and display the current name.

5 Identify the scope and data type of the variable you have created to validate the name change.

How can we apply programming to solve problems?

B2.1.3 Exception handling

When a computer program is run, different reasons or events might cause the program to halt or produce an unexpected outcome. These reasons could include logical errors in the code, unexpected user inputs or resource unavailability.

Logic errors refer to incorrect sequences in the logic of the program, incorrect choices of condition or incorrect calculations. For example, when attempting to calculate the average of three numbers, dividing the sum of the three numbers by 2 instead of dividing it by 3 would produce an incorrect outcome.

Such errors can only be detected through testing, as they would pass the compilation stage.

Runtime errors could cause the program to crash. These errors refer to problems occurring as the program runs, such as division by 0; a file not being found; truncation; overflow or underflow errors; a hardware device not being available, such as a printer not being ready; or a class file not being found.

Also, a user can enter unexpected inputs, such as entering text instead of a number or entering values that would lead to an attempt to divide by 0, or entering the wrong file location to read data from or write data to.

Resource unavailability refers to hardware and software equipment not being available for the operation, such as a file not being found or a printer not being ready for the operation.

All those events can be dealt with, so the program does not crash, using **exception handling**. Even if the desired operation would not be achieved, the user can get an idea of what went wrong, and they can continue attempting other features of the program.

The role of exception handling techniques is to maintain the normal flow of the program, by catching and throwing **exceptions** that cannot be handled locally. In Java, this takes the form of `try/catch` blocks, while in Python they are found as `try/except` blocks. The code that might throw an error is written within the `try` block and the exception is caught and displayed, if needed, in the `catch/except` block. Both languages allow for a `finally` block that is found at the end of the `try/catch` or `try/except` block and this includes code that will always execute after leaving the try statement, regardless of the `try` block outcome: whether or not it raises an error.

◆ **Logic error:** an error in a program that makes it operate incorrectly; it will not crash the program.

◆ **Runtime error:** an error that occurs when executing a program; the program might stop unexpectedly.

◆ **Exception handling:** a process of responding to an exception, so the system does not halt unexpectedly.

◆ **Exception:** an unexpected event that stops the execution of a program, e.g. division by 0.

Java

```java
read = new Scanner(System.in);
System.out.println("Enter a number: ");
int number = read.nextInt();
int result;
try {
    result = 10/number;
    System.out.println(result);
}
catch(Exception e){
    System.out.println(e.toString());                }
finally {
    System.out.println("This would be printed anyway");
}
```

Python

```python
number = int(input("Enter a number: "))
try:
    result = 10/number
    print(result)
except ZeroDivisionError:
    print("You can't divide by zero")
finally:
    print("This would be printed anyway")
```

In the example above, the user is requested to enter a number. If the number entered is 0, then this would be caught in the exception; otherwise, the calculation will be performed and the result displayed. Independent of the action completed, the message included in the `finally` block will be displayed.

Java

```java
read = new Scanner(System.in);
System.out.println("Enter a number: ");
int number = read.nextInt();
int result;
try {
    result = 10/number;
    System.out.println(result);
}
catch(Exception e){
    System.out.println(e.toString());
}
```

```Python
Python
number = int(input("Enter a number: "))
try:
    result = 10/number
    print(result)
except:
    print("There was a problem!")
```

The exception handling construct can include only a `try/catch` block in Java, or just a `try/except` block in Python. There is no need to specifically indicate the type of error that might have caused the program to crash, but this is useful to help the programmer debug the code and fix issues that might be solved or to let the user understand the problem if the wrong input is provided.

Key information

"Exception" refers to the event that interrupts the execution of a program, while "exception handling" refers to the actions taken to deal with an exception or how the system is prevented from halting unexpectedly. For example, a division by 0 is an exception; using a `try/catch` or `try/except` block is the exception handling technique.

REVIEW QUESTIONS

1 Explain how exceptions differ from errors.
2 Explain why it is important to handle exceptions in your code.
3 Identify some common types of exceptions.
4 Explain a scenario when a runtime error could occur.
5 Explain the risks of showing detailed exception messages to end users.

B2.1.4 Debugging techniques

◆ **Debugging:** finding and fixing errors in a program.

◆ **Trace table:** a technique used to test an algorithm, and to predict how it will be run and how values of variables will change.

◆ **Breakpoint:** a marker to interrupt the execution of code for debugging purposes.

Debugging refers to finding and fixing errors in code. Common debugging techniques include **trace tables**, **breakpoint** debugging, print statements and step-by-step code execution.

■ Trace tables

Trace tables represent a technique usually used at design stage to test an algorithm and predict step by step how it will run. They can be used to demonstrate the outcome of an algorithm or to identify logic errors.

A trace table is a table in which the columns represent variables, conditions or an output in the algorithm. However, not all variables, conditions or outputs are always needed; this depends on the purpose of the trace table.

Its role is to identify how variables change, what conditions evaluate to and what are the produced outcomes. By producing a trace table, the purpose of the algorithm can be determined or any flaws in the algorithm can be detected.

For example, consider the following problem: Students taking a language course will pass their final examination if their score is 80 or above. As the students register for the course every term, the number of students is unknown. Therefore, the teacher will enter 999 to terminate the program. The teacher is required to identify the number of students passing the assessment.

The following flowchart has been designed to suggest a possible solution to the problem:

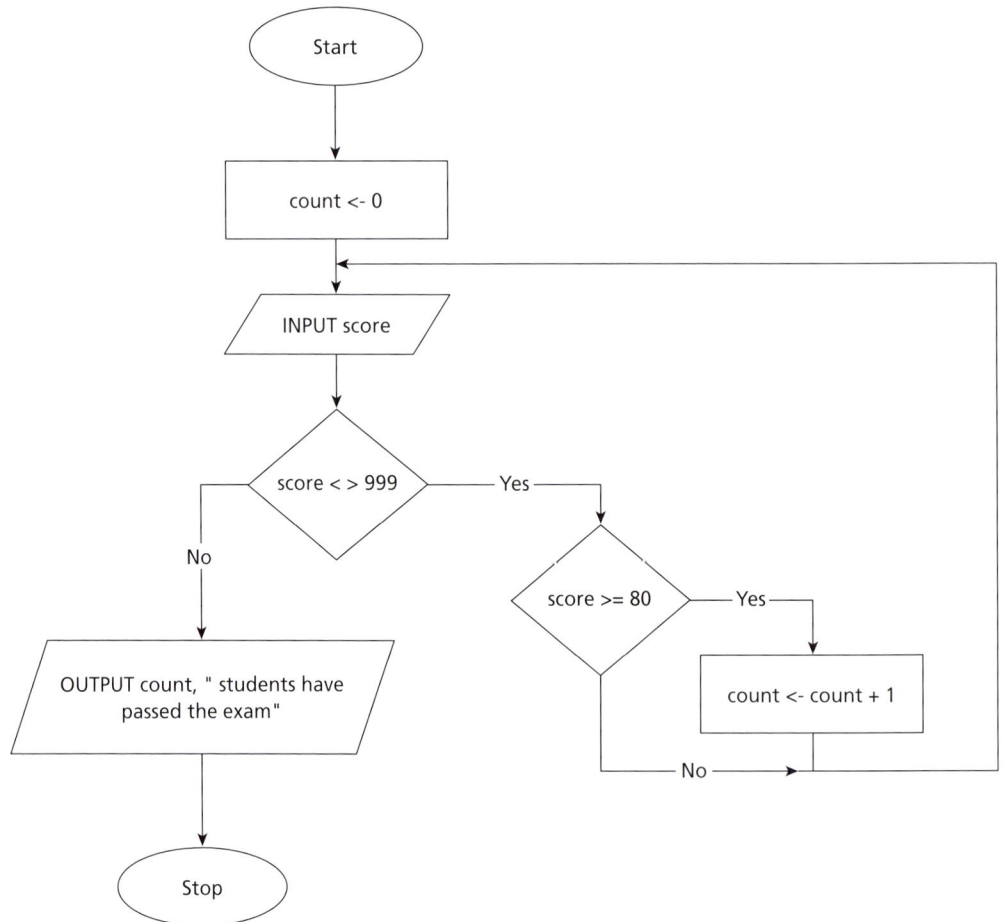

The trace table for the input data would look like this:

23, 98, 33, 45, 78, 80, 81, 84, 34, 999

count	score	output
0	23	
	98	
1	33	
	45	
	78	
	80	
2	81	
3	84	
4	34	
	999	4 students have passed the exam

When the value 98 is entered, the count is incremented. 33, 45, 78 will not affect the count, so its value stays the same. You might choose to repeat the previous value for the count variable, or just leave it blank as there is no change. Be aware if there is a statement reassigning the value of the variable to something, then even if the value is the same as the previous one, it should appear within the count column, as that is a change to the variable. When value 80 is entered, the count is incremented again, and the procedure repeats for the values 81 and 84, but nothing happens to the count when 34 is entered. 999 is the value that will terminate the program, and so the output will be displayed, as the output is displayed only after 999 is entered, in this example.

REVIEW QUESTIONS

The following flowchart represents an algorithm.

```
                    ( START )
                        |
                        v
                 / INPUT num /
                        |
                        v
              +-------------------+
              |   temp <- 0       |
              |   value <- num    |
              +-------------------+
                        |
                        v
              +----------------------------+
    +-------->| reminder <- value MOD 10   |
    |         | value <- value DIV 10      |
    |         | temp <- temp*10 + reminder |
    |         +----------------------------+
    |                   |
    |                   v
    |              < value > 0 >----- Yes ----+
    |  No ---------/   (diamond)              |
    |  |                                      +
    +--+                                   (loop back)
       v
   < temp = num >----- Yes -----+
    (diamond)                   |
       |                        v
       | No               / OUTPUT true /
       v                        |
 / OUTPUT false /               v
       |                       ( o )------>( STOP )
       +----------------------->
```

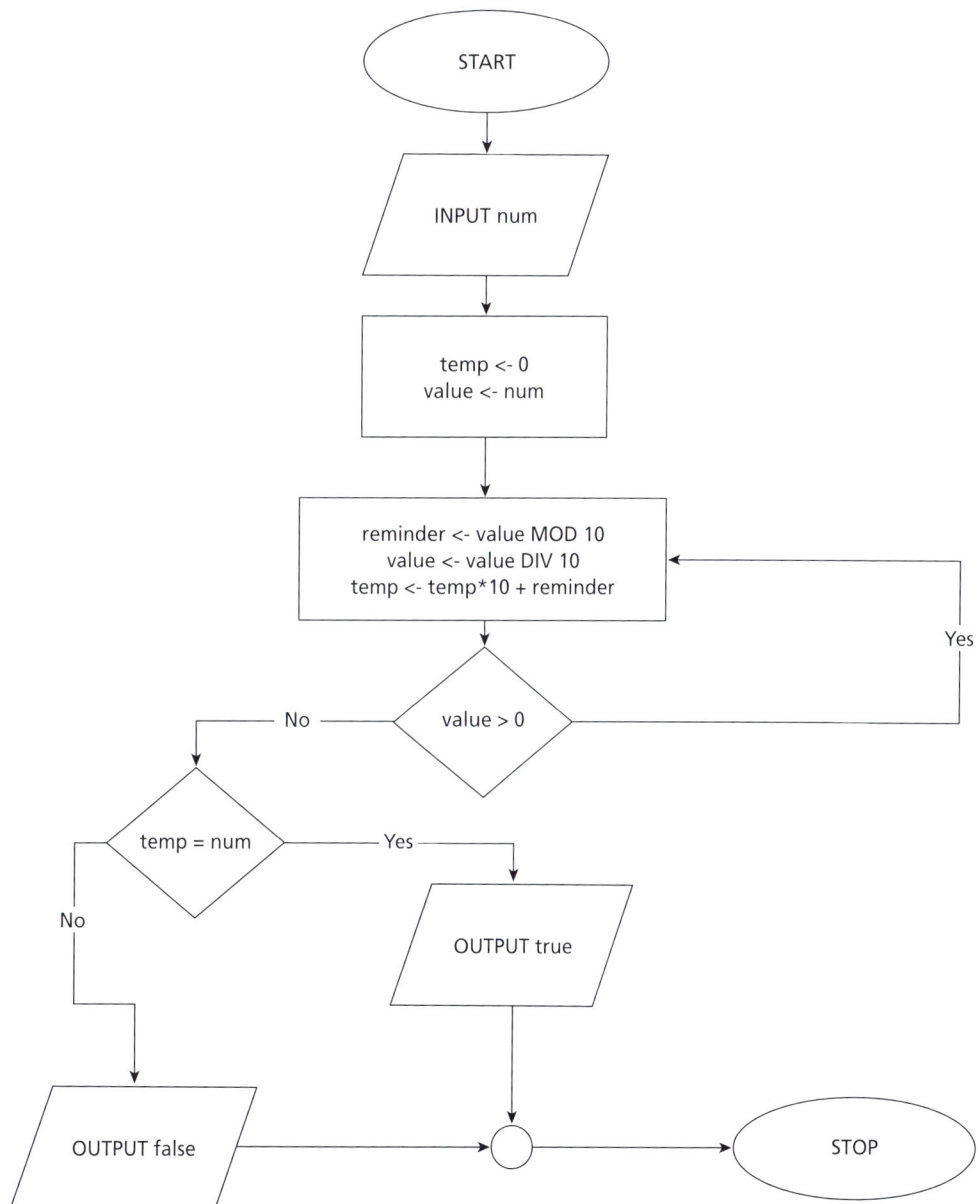

1 Copy and complete the trace table below for the value: 1221.

num	temp	value	reminder	value > 0	temp = num	output

2 Copy and complete the trace table below for the value: 1231.

num	temp	value	reminder	value > 0	temp = num	output

3 Identify the purpose of the algorithm represented by the flowchart above.

■ Breakpoint debugging

Breakpoints are special markers that interrupt the execution of the code for debugging purposes. To set a breakpoint in Eclipse IDE, it is sufficient to right-click on the blue section beside the line number and toggle a breakpoint as shown in the screenshot below (this differs from IDE to IDE).

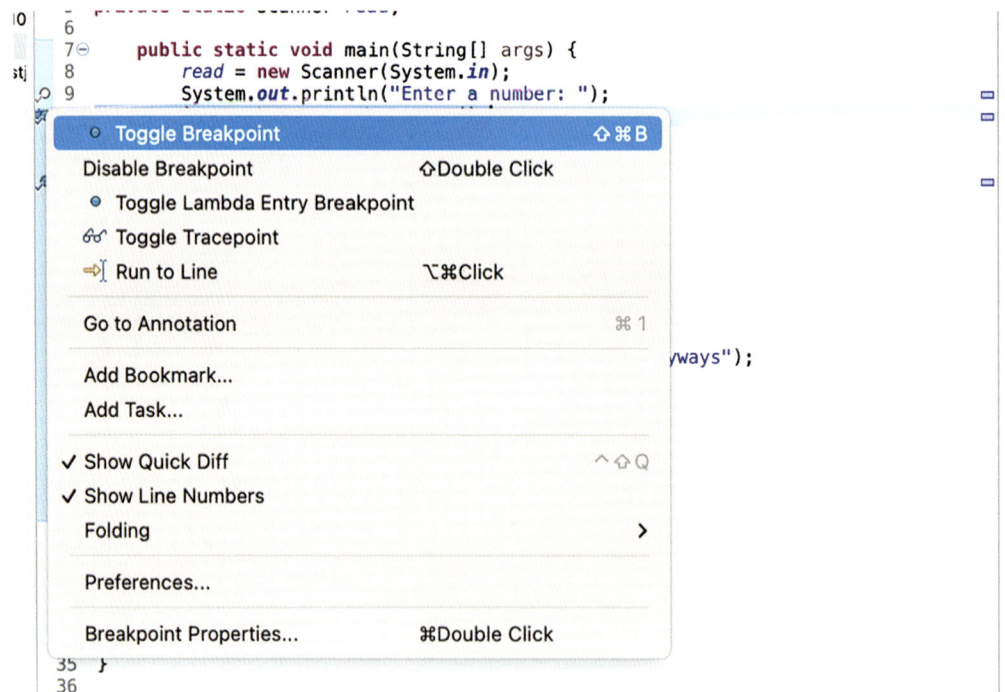

```
6
7⊖    public static void main(String[] args) {
8         read = new Scanner(System.in);
9         System.out.println("Enter a number: ");
```

○ Toggle Breakpoint	⇧⌘B
Disable Breakpoint	⇧Double Click
● Toggle Lambda Entry Breakpoint	
👓 Toggle Tracepoint	
⇒ Run to Line	⌥⌘Click
Go to Annotation	⌘1
Add Bookmark...	
Add Task...	
✓ Show Quick Diff	^⇧Q
✓ Show Line Numbers	
Folding	>
Preferences...	
Breakpoint Properties...	⌘Double Click

```
35 }
36
```

■ Breakpoint debugging in Eclipse

After setting up the breakpoints, the next step is to run the program in debugging mode. This is done by clicking on the Debug button (the one next to the Run button), which looks like a little bug, as shown in the image below.

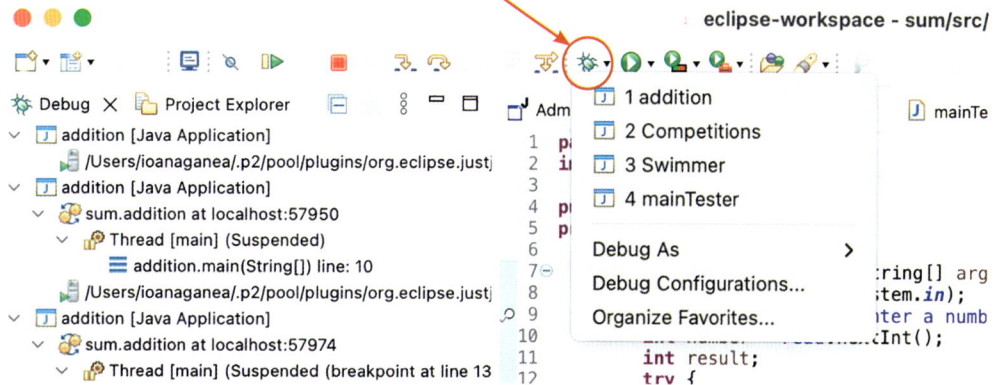

■ Running the program in debugging mode in Eclipse

Next, you can see the Breakpoint window that shows the variables, breakpoints and expressions, as here:

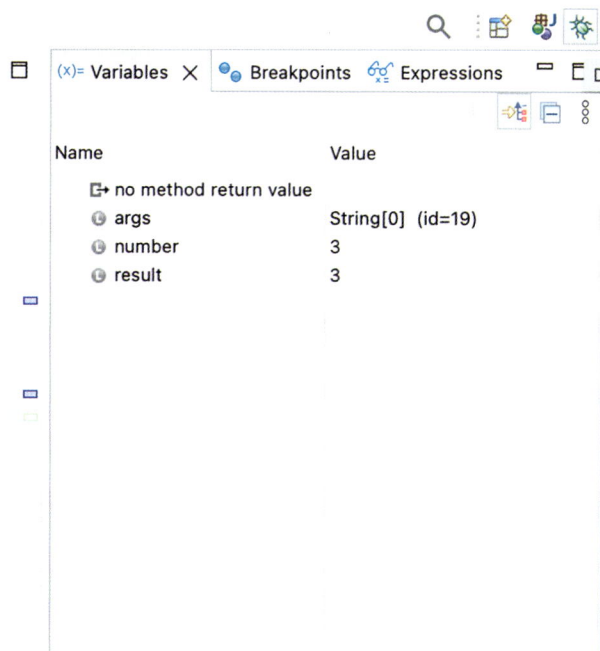

■ Breakpoint window in Eclipse

The code will execute as normal, but it will interrupt its execution the moment it reaches the set breakpoint.

In IDLE (Python), there is only a need to right-click on the line where you want the breakpoint to be set and choose the option Set Breakpoint.

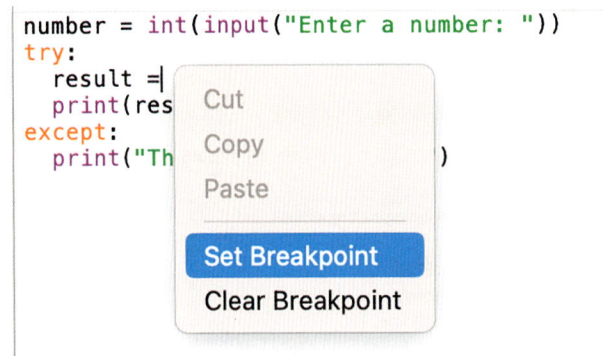

■ Breakpoint debugging in IDLE

After that, you can simply run the script (F5). Once this has happened, you can press Debug on the menu and the debugger window will appear.

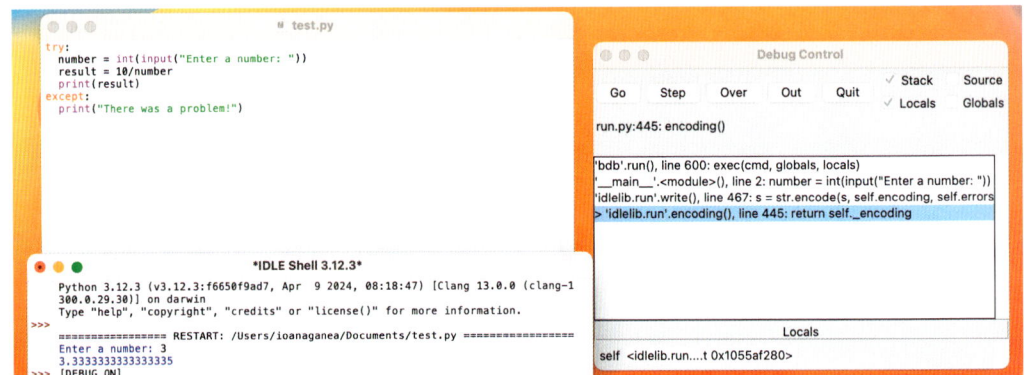

■ Debugger window in IDLE

■ Step-by-step code execution

To monitor and see what happens with the variables, you have to press Step into / Step over or use Step filters buttons. If you want to check what happens at the breakpoint line then you would choose the Step into button, but if you want to skip that line and execute the following one you would choose the Step over button. In Eclipse, those buttons are the arrows shown in the following screenshot:

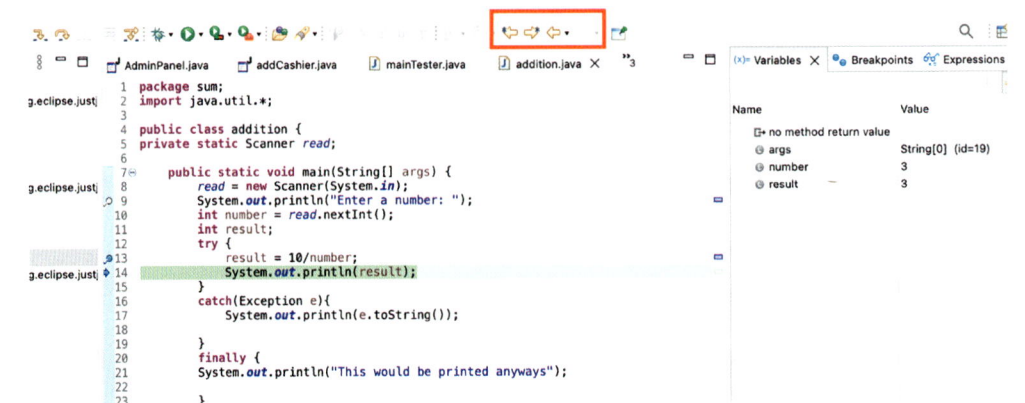

■ Step-by-step execution in Eclipse

Print statements

When testing your code, you might ask yourself whether the execution of the program has reached a specific line of code, whether a variable changed its value as expected or whether a decision statement has been evaluated to true or false. Including print statements into your code to trace such changes is a useful method that would help you identify when exactly your code stopped running as expected and give you an idea of what went wrong. The only impediment might be that, once the debugging has occurred and the errors are fixed, you will have to delete those print statements.

REVIEW QUESTIONS

1 Define the terms "exception" and "exception handling".
2 Identify three possible causes of an exception.
3 Outline three features that support the debugging of the code in an IDE.

ACTIVITY

Affective skills: Demonstrate persistence and perseverance. Don't give up when you realize that coding becomes challenging – use debugging techniques to identify the errors, focus on understanding the errors report and try different approaches to solving problems.

TOK

Language and meaning

We use different programming languages to code, each with its own syntax and grammar rules. English is not suitable to be used as a programming language because it is ambiguous and many expressions can be interpreted differently based on the context in which they are used.

Analyse the following statements and identify the possible meanings of each of them:

- Peter and Anna are married.
- A salesman visited every house in the area.
- Look at that dog with one eye.

What are the essential features of a computer language? Why is there a need for a fixed vocabulary, unambiguous meaning and consistent grammar and syntax?

SYLLABUS CONTENT

By the end of this chapter, you should be able to:
▶ B2.2.1 Compare static and dynamic data structures
▶ B2.2.2 Construct programs that apply arrays and lists
▶ B2.2.3 Explain the concept of a stack as a Last In First Out (LIFO) data structure
▶ B2.2.4 Explain the concept of a queue as a First In First Out (FIFO) data structure

B2.2.1 Static vs dynamic data structures

A data structure is a way of storing and organizing data, so it allows for its manipulation in an efficient way and attempts to reduce the time and space complexity. Arrays, lists, stacks, queues, binary trees and hash tables are all examples of data structures. Data structures can be **static** or **dynamic**, the two differing in terms of storage and access to their elements.

A static data structure has a predefined fixed size, a specific memory space being allocated to it, that will not change when running the program, and elements that are stored in contiguous memory locations. Elements in a static data structure can be either **directly accessed** or **sequentially accessed**.

A dynamic data structure has no predefined fixed size, it can grow or decrease at runtime and its elements are stored in memory locations that are chained together but are not necessarily contiguous. Elements in a dynamic data structure cannot be directly accessed.

◆ **Static data structure:** a data structure with predefined fixed size and elements stored in contiguous memory locations.

◆ **Dynamic data structure:** a data structure that can grow or decrease at runtime, with elements stored in memory locations that are chained together, but not necessarily contiguous.

◆ **Direct access:** a method of access where elements are directly retrieved by using their index (position).

◆ **Sequential access:** a method of access where elements are checked one after another, from the beginning to the end of the data structure.

Static data structure	
Advantages	**Disadvantages**
• Fast access time, as elements can be directly accessed via the index (position of the element in the data structure) • No need to deal with possible overflow or underflow errors when adding or deleting elements as the size is fixed • Easier to program; there is no need to check on its size at any time	• Inefficient use of memory, as there is a need to know in advance the likely size of the structure to allocate sufficient memory • Memory is allocated, regardless or whether or not it is needed • Does not allow for flexibility, as its size is fixed • Deletion of an element might create a vacant slot between two other elements, and changing the code to reuse this space might take time • Insertion of elements between two other elements if there isn't a vacant space is time-consuming

Dynamic data structure	
Advantages	**Disadvantages**
• Allows for flexibility – it can shrink or grow as needed at runtime (suitable when the size of data is not known in advance or may change in time) • Efficient use of memory; as it can resize itself, there is no memory waste • Insertion and deletion operations are optimal concerning time and space complexity	• The programmer needs to deal with overflow (the structure might exceed the memory limit) and underflow (it might attempt to delete an item from an already empty structure) situations when inserting or deleting elements • Harder to program, as the programmer is required always to keep track of its size and data allocations

B2.2.2 Arrays and lists

◼ One-dimensional arrays (Java) and one-dimensional lists (Python)

Suppose your teacher wants to store the grades of 100 students. One way to complete this task is to use 100 variables, but this means lots of memory waste, many lines of code and a lot of effort. And what if this teacher needs to store 1000 grades?

A better solution is to store all those 100 or 1000 elements under a single name or a single identifier. The array data structure allows you to do this.

A 1D array (Java) or a 1D list (Python) is a data structure that stores elements of the same data type, under one single identifier (name). Those elements can be directly accessed by using an index (plural *indices*), where the index indicates the position in the array. Some languages indicate the first index as being the 0 element, and others allow the programmer to indicate how the items will be addressed.

For example, an array of five integers storing students' grades out of 100 is called `grades`.

Graphically, arrays can be represented horizontally or vertically.

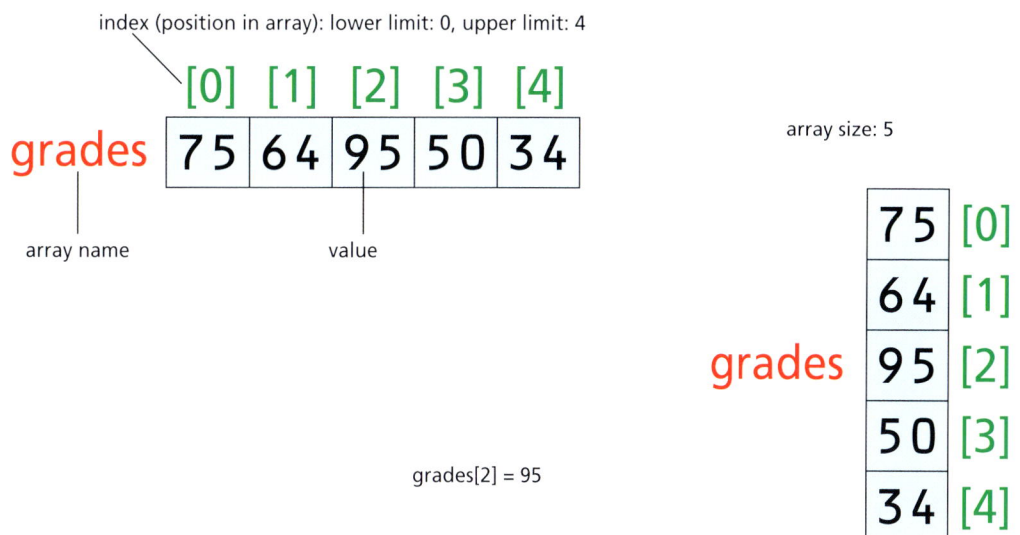

index (position in array): lower limit: 0, upper limit: 4

grades `[0] [1] [2] [3] [4]` : 75 64 95 50 34

array name   value

array size: 5

grades[2] = 95

grades (vertical): 75 [0], 64 [1], 95 [2], 50 [3], 34 [4]

◼ 1D array (list)

The array element at index 2 (the 3rd element, when counting from 0) can be directly accessed by using the name of the array followed by the index: `grades[2]`. Keep in mind that, if the first element has index 0, the last element is at index 4 (in this case, the grades array has only five items).

To process arrays, loops are used. Loops can be used to traverse the array; therefore, any time you perform calculations on all elements of an array, find an element, sort them, and so on, you will use loops.

One-dimensional arrays (Java)

Array declaration and initialization:

To use arrays in Java, they must be declared, and the language allows for different ways to do this. First, square brackets `[]` are used to differentiate between a variable and an array. They can appear before or after the array name:

```java
int grades []; //an array called grades of integers
int [] grades; //grades array of integers
```

After deciding where you want to place the square brackets (most often, the first example is used), you need to specify the size of the array, as it is a static data structure.

Declaration:

```java
int grades[]=new int[5]; //grades array can store maximum 5
//elements
```

If the array is of integer or double or float type, and there is no further initialization of the array elements, Java automatically initializes all its elements to 0.

Initialization:

```java
grades[0]=75;
grades[1]=64;
grades[2]=95;
grades[3]=50;
grades[4]=34;
```

At this point, the elements of the array are given specific values, the value 0 being overwritten. Another way to declare and initialize the array is like this:

```java
int grades[]= new int[]{75,64,95,50,34};
```

But this can also be rewritten in a simpler way, like this:

```java
int grades[]={75,64,95,50,34};
```

Sometimes, the developer will have to allow the user to initialize the array. In such cases, you can simply declare the array and use a loop to allow the user to populate the array.

```java
read = new Scanner(System.in);
int grades[]=new int[5];
    for(int i=0;i<5;i++) {
System.out.println("Enter a number: ");
int value = read.nextInt();
grades[i]=value;
}
```

The loop repeats five times, and it requires the user to enter an integer value that will be stored into the array indicated by index i (from 0 to 4).

If the array is of type string, it would look like this:

```
String pilots[] = {"Bob", "John", "Elvis"};
```

An array of Boolean data type can look like this:

```
Boolean passedExam[ ] = {true, false, true};
```

One-dimensional lists (Python)

Python replaces arrays with lists, but you can manipulate those lists to behave like arrays.

In Python, data structures don't need to be declared. Square brackets are still used to specify that the data structure used is a 1D list.

For example, the grades array will look like this:

```
grades = [75,64,95,50,34]
```

If the user wants to initialize a 1D list by using a FOR loop, then the code would look like this:

```
grades = [0]*5 #creates an array of 5 zeros
    for i in range(5): #repeats 5 times
    #stores value entered at given index
    grades[i] = int(input("enter a value: "))
```

The first line in the code above specifies the initial value each element in the list will take (in this case, 0). After the *, it is the size of the list (meaning there are five 0s in this list at first).

If you were to write this line of code as `grades = [ ]`, when trying the FOR loop an error would be thrown (index out of range), as the size of the list would be none or zero, so there would not be a way to add any new elements to it. However, the following statement is completely valid:

```
grades = []
grades = [0 for i in range(5)]
```

And this is possible because the `grades` list is overwritten. But this could have been just like this:

```
grades = [0 for i in range(5)]
```

The purpose of the line above is to initialize the `grades` list to 0 for all its five elements.

The following two lists are examples of a 1D list of type string and a 1D list of type Boolean:

```
pilots = ["Bob", "John", "Elvis"]
passedExam = [True, False, True]
```

Parallel arrays represent two or more arrays of the same size, such that the nth element of the first array is related to the nth element of the second array, and so on. The values stored on those arrays at a given index will be related in some form, for example defining a record data structure to store details about students. So, the first array will store the students' names, the second array their ages, the third array their addresses. When retrieving the element of position 3 from each of those arrays, you'll be able to identify the name, age and address of the third student.

PROGRAMMING EXERCISES

1   Construct a program that creates a 1D array or list that stores six integer values. Output true if the first element in the array is the same as the last element in the array.

2   Construct code that requires the user to enter a number. Use that number as the size of an array or list of integers to be inputted from the keyboard. Calculate the sum of all even numbers in the array or list; calculate the average of all its elements; and count how many of those elements are odd numbers. Display those values.

3   Construct a program that creates an array or list that stores five names. Copy those elements in a second array or list in reverse order. Display the second array or list.

ACTIVITY

Use your answers to the programming exercises above to answer the following questions.

1   What data type was your output for question 1? Was it a Boolean or a string variable? Which one do you think is more appropriate?

2   What was the initial value of the count variable you used for question 2 to count how many array elements were odd? Why was it important to set an initial value for this variable?

3   Did the results for question 3 display accurately? What loops did you use to traverse the arrays? Could those loops have been replaced by other types of loops? Which are those?

● Common mistake

Algorithms written to solve a problem should function correctly. When asked to construct an algorithm that finds the smallest value in a 1D array or 1D list, many candidates initialize a variable called min to 0 and then compare each element in the array with that one to find a smaller value.

The data structure could store only positive numbers; therefore, you will not find a value smaller than 0.

Remember to initialize that variable to the first element in the array. In this case, if no other element is smaller, you have already stored the smallest one.

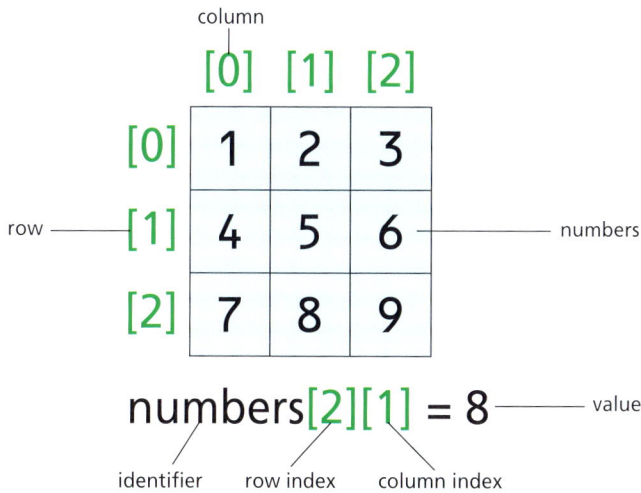

column

	[0]	[1]	[2]
[0]	1	2	3
[1]	4	5	6
[2]	7	8	9

row ——— numbers

numbers[2][1] = 8 ——— value

identifier   row index   column index

■ 2D array (list)

■ Two-dimensional arrays / lists

A two-dimensional array can be seen as a table, with rows and columns. To manipulate and traverse a 2D array, two indices are used: one for the rows and one for the columns. When writing code, rows are always first and columns second.

Look at the figure for storing numbers from 1 to 9 in a table with three rows and three columns. You will create a 2D array or a 2D list for this purpose.

Each element in a 2D array (Java) or 2D list (Python) can be directly accessed by specifying its indices (row index and column index).

Declaration

Java
```
int numbers[ ] [ ] = new int [3] [3];
```

Python
```
numbers = [[0 for i in range(3)] for j in range(3)]
```

The first value of 3 indicates the number of rows, and the second one the number of columns. The value of 0 in the Python example refers to the initial value this list will be set to.

In Python, the 2D list will appear as a table with three rows and three columns, all filled with zeros, as shown in the diagram below:

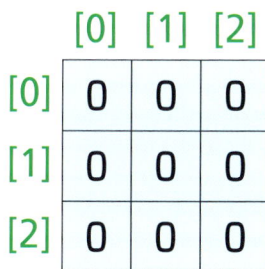

In Java, the 2D array will only include the structure of the table, as there are no initial values provided:

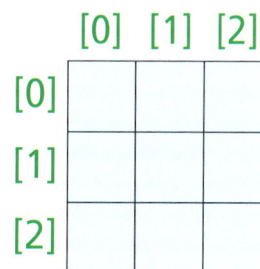

	[0]	[1]	[2]
[0]	0	0	0
[1]	0	0	0
[2]	0	0	0

■ 2D array (list) filled with zeros

	[0]	[1]	[2]
[0]			
[1]			
[2]			

■ Empty 2D array

Manipulating 2D arrays or lists requires the use of two loops: the first one for the rows and the second one for the columns. When addressing one specific item in the array or list, this is done by using the name of the array or list followed by square brackets that include the row and column indices.

numbers[0][2] refers to the element in the array numbers, located at the intersection of the first row with the third column.

Java

```java
Scanner reader = new Scanner(System.in);
int numbers[][]= new int[3][3];
for(int i = 0; i<3;i++) {
    for(int j=0; j<3;j++) {
        System.out.println("enter a number: ");
        int value = reader.nextInt();
        numbers[i][j]=value;
    }
}
for(int i = 0; i<3;i++) {
    for(int j=0; j<3;j++) {
        System.out.print(numbers[i][j]+ " ");
    }
    System.out.print("\n");
}
```

Python

```python
numbers = [[0 for i in range(3)]for j in range(3)]
for i in range (0,3):
    for j in range(3):
        value = int(input("enter a number: "))
        numbers[i][j]=value
for i in range(3):
    for j in range(3):
        print(numbers[i][j], " ", end ="")
    print("\n")
```

The first two count-controlled loops are used to traverse the array (i for the rows and j for the columns). Then the user is asked to enter a number that is stored in the variable value, which is then assigned to the array or list numbers.

The last two loops are used to traverse the array or list, so the values stored in the array are displayed on the screen.

A 2D array can also have a different number of rows and columns.

Java

```java
int numbers[ ] [ ] = new int [2] [3];
```

Python

```python
numbers = [[0 for i in range(2)] for j in range(3)]
```

In the example above, the array numbers will be constructed with two rows and three columns.

To fill the array with values, the following code can be used:

Java
```java
int numbers[ ] [ ] = new int [2] [3];
```

Python
```python
numbers = [[0 for i in range(2)] for j in range(3)]
```

PROGRAMMING EXERCISES

1   Construct code that creates a two-dimensional array or list with three rows and three columns. Fill it with values read from the keyboard. Calculate the sum of all values and their average, and display the results.

2   Construct a program that creates a two-dimensional array or list with three rows and three columns. Display the sum of all elements per column. Display the average of all elements per row.

3   Construct code that creates a two-dimensional array or list with three rows and three columns that stores random numbers. Display the array and output the sum of all the elements on the principal diagonal. Calculate the sum of the elements on the secondary diagonal and display this value as well.

4   Matrix calculations are used extensively in machine learning within Computer Science. The following constraints exist to calculate a dot product: width of matrix A must match height of matrix B. Given two 2D arrays (lists) of integers that represent matrices, construct a program to calculate and solve the dot product of those two matrices.

"Dot product"

$$\begin{bmatrix} 1 & 2 & 3 \\ 4 & 5 & 6 \end{bmatrix} \times \begin{bmatrix} 7 & 8 \\ 9 & 10 \\ 11 & 12 \end{bmatrix} = \begin{bmatrix} 58 & \\ & \end{bmatrix}$$

$$\begin{bmatrix} 1 & 2 & 3 \\ 4 & 5 & 6 \end{bmatrix} \times \begin{bmatrix} 7 & 8 \\ 9 & 10 \\ 11 & 12 \end{bmatrix} = \begin{bmatrix} 58 & 64 \\ 139 & 154 \end{bmatrix} \checkmark$$

Reflect on the most challenging parts of the programming exercises. How did you approach them? Did you seek support, did you research or did you apply any other strategies? What did you learn from this experience that you can apply to solve future problems?

Common mistake

Algorithms written to solve a problem should function correctly. Many students lose marks for incorrect use of indices in 2D arrays or incorrectly looping through 2D arrays, such as overlooking boundaries or not using two indices to traverse the array. Remember that you always use rows first and columns second.

ArrayLists in Java

An ArrayList in Java is a class that allows the use of a dynamic array to store elements, this time without a pre-defined size. ArrayLists can hold duplicate elements, they allow for random access and they maintain the insertion order.

To be able to use an ArrayList, you need to import the `java.util` package:

```java
import java.util.*;
```

This will import the entire package, or you can specifically choose to import just the required class:

```java
import java.util.ArrayList;
```

After this step is completed, an ArrayList can be declared, as follows:

```java
ArrayList<Integer> grades = new ArrayList<Integer>();
```

Keep in mind that, when working with ArrayLists, the data type integer appears as `Integer` instead of `int`.

If the ArrayList will store text, then it would look like this:

```java
ArrayList<String> pilots= new ArrayList<String>();
```

To be able to manipulate elements in an ArrayList, there are specific methods that can be used:

Method	Explanation	Code example
add()	Add a new element passed as an argument	grades.add(75);
get()	Access an element at a given position (specified in the brackets)	grades.get(2);
set()	Update an element at a given index (first argument is the index; the second one is the value)	grades.set(2, 64);
remove()	Delete an item at a specific index	grades.remove(2);
size()	Returns the number of elements in the ArrayList	grades.size();
clear()	Delete all elements in the ArrayList	grades.clear();

To traverse an ArrayList, you can use a FOR loop:

```java
ArrayList<Integer> grades = new ArrayList<Integer>();
grades.add(75);
grades.add(64);
grades.add(95);
grades.add(50);
grades.add(34);
    for(int i=0;i<grades.size();i++) {
        System.out.println(grades.get(i));
}
```

In the code above, the grades ArrayList of type integer is declared. Five elements are added to the ArrayList. A loop is used to traverse it (the `size()` method will return the number of items in the ArrayList to specify how many repetitions will occur), and each element is retrieved using the `get()` function and passing the corresponding index of the element that is then displayed on the screen.

Another example of traversing the ArrayList is by using a FOR-EACH loop instead:

```java
ArrayList<Integer> grades = new ArrayList<Integer>();
grades.add(75);
grades.add(64);
grades.add(95);
grades.add(50);
grades.add(34);
    for (int i: grades) {
        System.out.println(i);
}
```

In this example, the variable `i` is not an index, but it is an element in the `grades` ArrayList instead.

■ Dynamic lists in Python

A dynamic list in Python is a dynamic data structure, meaning it does not have a fixed size. Dynamic lists can store duplicate values. When creating a dynamic list, you can simply declare it as an empty list: `grades = []`

However, when wanting to insert a new element, attempting to write something like this: `grades[0] = 75` will throw an error.

To manipulate dynamic lists, specific methods can be used:

Method	Explanation	Code example
append()	Add a new element passed as an argument at the end of the list	grades.append(75)
insert()	Insert a new element at a given index (first argument is the index, the second is the value to be inserted)	grades.insert(0,64)
remove()	Delete the first occurrence of a given item passed as an argument	grades.remove(75)
pop()	Delete the element at the specified index	grades.pop(0)
pop()	Delete the last element if no index is given	grades.pop()
clear()	Empty the entire list	grades.clear()
len()	Return the size of the list	len(grades)

To loop through a dynamic list, a FOR loop can be used:

```python
grades=[]
grades.append(75)
grades.append(64)
grades.append(95)
grades.append(50)
grades.append(34)
    for i in range (len(grades)):
        print(grades[i])
```

Another way to achieve the same is:

```
grades=[]
grades.append(75)
grades.append(64)
grades.append(95)
grades.append(50)
grades.append(34)
    for i in grades:
        print(i)
```

In this case, i is not the index, but an element in the dynamic list.

PROGRAMMING EXERCISES

1 Construct programming code to create an ArrayList in Java or a dynamic list in Python that stores five colours.

   a Construct code to insert a sixth colour after the third.

   b Change the element at the second position to a different colour.

   c Delete the last element.

   d Display the new data structure.

2 Construct a program that creates an ArrayList in Java or a dynamic list in Python that stores three numbers.

   a Append three more values to the end of the data structure.

   b Display the size of the data structure.

   c Display the first element.

   d Store the first element into a variable.

   e Replace all the other elements with this value.

   f Display the new values.

3 Construct a program that creates an ArrayList in Java or a dynamic list in Python that stores three different numbers.

   a Store the second value into a variable and insert it into the data structure at the end.

   b Display the index of the first occurrence of that value.

4 Construct programming code that creates an ArrayList in Java or a dynamic list in Python that stores four different values.

   a Display all the elements.

   b Swap the values of the second and third elements.

   c Display the new data structure.

B2.2.3 Stacks

If you were a bank cashier, you would deal with lots of coins. To easily manipulate those, the coins are categorized based on their values and stored in piles, for example a pile of 10p coins, a stack of 20p coins, another stack of 50p coins, and so on. When the cashier needs one of these coins, they would get it from the top of the pile containing the required coin value, so the stack remains intact. When the cashier needs to add a new coin to one of the piles, they would add the new coin to the pile; again, on top of it.

Another example would be a stack of plates: a new plate is added to the top of the stack and a plate is removed from the top of the stack, otherwise plates can break.

In Computer Science, when performing actions that work on the same principle, a specific abstract data structure called **stack** can be used. The stack works on the principle of **Last In First Out** (LIFO) or **First In Last Out** (FILO), meaning that only the top element is accessed. The operation of removing an item from the stack is called **pop**, which means taking off the top element, while the operation of adding an item to the stack is called **push**, meaning adding an item to the top of the stack.

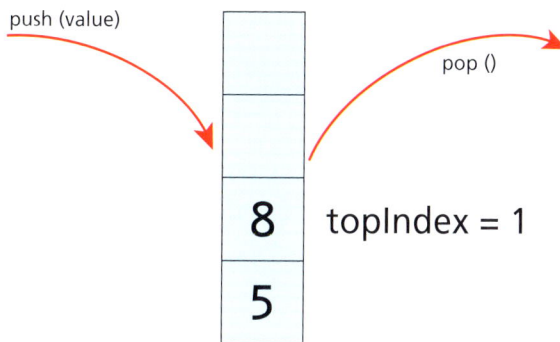

■ Stacks of coins

◆ **Stack:** an abstract data structure that works on the LIFO principle.

◆ **Last In First Out** or **First In Last Out** **principle:** the last element inserted is the first element removed.

◆ **Pop:** a method for deleting the element from the top of a stack.

◆ **Push:** a method for inserting an element at the top of a stack.

◆ **Stack pointer:** a register used to store the memory address of the last added data in a stack, or sometimes the first available address in a stack.

push (value)

pop ()

8   topIndex = 1

5

■ Stack

A stack could use a **stack pointer** variable to indicate the next free available slot in the stack.

A stack can be implemented as a static data structure using arrays (it would have a fixed size) or as a dynamic data structure using a linked list (which would not have a fixed size).

■ Stack operations

Operations performed on a stack are:

■ isEmpty: to check whether the stack is empty; attempting to pop an item from an empty stack would throw an underflow error

```
public static boolean isEmpty() {
    if(topIndex == -1)
        return true;
    else
        return false;
    }
```

```
topIndex = -1
def IsEmpty():
    if topIndex == -1:
        return True
    else
        return False
```

topIndex = −1

stack is empty

■ Stack operation: isEmpty

■ `isFull`: to check whether the stack is full; attempting to push an item into a full stack would throw an overflow error

```
public static boolean isFull() {
    if(topIndex == StackSize -1)
        return true;
    else
        return false;
    }
```
```
def IsFull():
    if topIndex == StackSize -1:
        return True
    else:
```

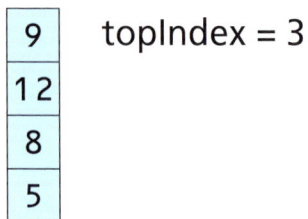

| 9 |
| 12 |
| 8 |
| 5 |

topIndex = 3

StackSize = 4

■ Stack operation: isFull

■ `push`: to add an item to the top of the stack

```
public static void push(int value) {
    if(isFull())
    System.out.println("Stack
overflow!");
    else {
    topIndex++;
    stack[topIndex]=value;
    }
```
```
def push(value):
    global topIndex
    if IsFull():
        print("Stack overflow")
    else:
        topIndex += 1
        Stack[topIndex] = value
```

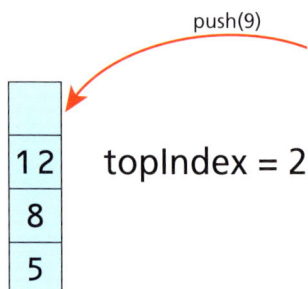

push(9)

| |
| 12 |
| 8 |
| 5 |

topIndex = 2

■ Stack operation: push

■ `pop`: to delete an item from the top of the stack

```
public static void pop() {
    if(isEmpty())
    System.out.println("Stack underflow");
    else
    topIndex--;
    }
```
```
def pop():
    global topIndex
    if isEmpty():
        print("Stack underflow")
    else:
        topIndex -= 1
```

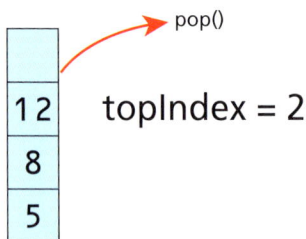

pop()

| |
| 12 |
| 8 |
| 5 |

topIndex = 2

■ Stack operation: pop

■ `peek`: to return the top element

```
public static int peek() {
    return stack[topIndex];
    }
```
```
def peek():
    return Stack[topIndex]
```

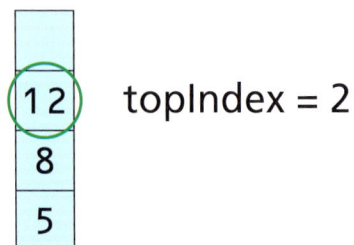

| |
| 12 |
| 8 |
| 5 |

topIndex = 2

■ Stack operation: peek

■ Uses of stacks

Stacks are used when storing data in the order they occurred and when it might be necessary to track back to a certain point or action in the past, as they respect the LIFO principle of operation.

Stacks can be used:

- to **create an UNDO feature in games:** actions are pushed into the stack; when undoing, actions are popped

- to **allow backwards navigation on a web browser:** pressing the back button performs a pop operation; opening a new website performs a push operation

- for **interrupt handling:** when the current activity of the CPU is interrupted, the content of variables and return addresses are stored in a stack; after the **interrupt** is dealt with, those are popped from the stack to restore its activity

- to **evaluate arithmetic expressions:** when evaluating RPN (reverse polish notation) expressions, the operands are pushed on to the stack; when an operator is met, if it is a binary operator (requires two operands) two more pop operations will occur, the calculation is performed and the result is pushed back into the stack – the process will continue until the result is reached

- for **recursion:** return addresses and values of parameters are stored into a stack to help with the unwinding process.

◆ **Interrupt handling:** handling interrupt requests.

◆ **Interrupt:** a signal sent from a device or software to request the processor's attention; the processor will stop its current activity until the interrupt has been serviced.

◆ **Recursion:** a process that uses a function or procedure that is defined in terms of itself and calls itself.

◆ **Queue:** an abstract data structure that works on the FIFO principle.

◆ **First In First Out principle:** when the first element inserted is the first element removed.

B2.2.4 Queues

A **queue** is a data structure that functions on the FIFO (**First In First Out**) **principle**. An example of a queue is a line of people waiting to check out at a grocery store. The first to join the queue is the first to leave. A new person who joins the line will enter at the end of the queue.

A queue uses a front pointer to show where elements will be removed from and a rear pointer to show where elements will be added to.

A queue can be implemented as a static data structure using arrays (it will have a fixed size, and it is possible to become full as this fixed size cannot be exceeded). Or, a queue can be implemented as a dynamic data structure, using a linked list (which would not have a fixed size).

When a queue is implemented as an array, it can often be seen and managed as a circular queue. This is in case there are elements removed from the queue, so that there is still a way to add new elements, even if the last index has been reached, as the queue will not actually be full. In a circular queue, if the rear pointer becomes equal to the front pointer after an item is added, the queue becomes full; if they become equal after an item is removed, the queue becomes empty.

■ Queue

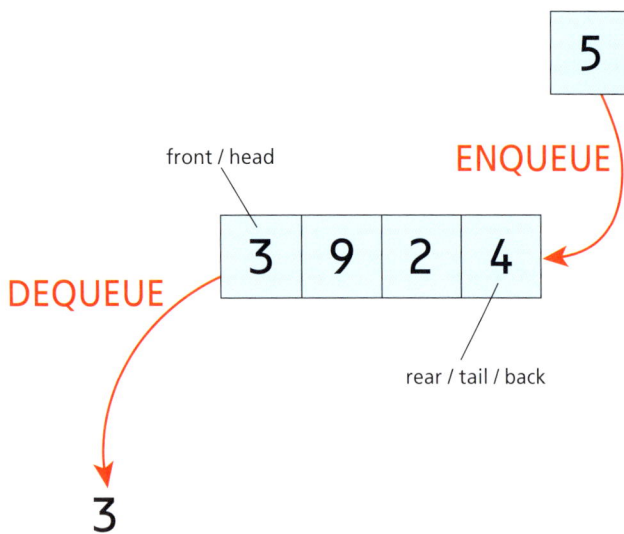

5

front / head

ENQUEUE

DEQUEUE

| 3 | 9 | 2 | 4 |

rear / tail / back

3

■ Queue pointers

◆ **Enqueue:** a method of inserting an element at the rear of a queue.

◆ **Dequeue:** a method of deleting an element from the front of a queue.

■ Queue operations

Operations performed on a queue are:

■ isFull: checking whether the queue is full; trying to **enqueue** an item into a full queue would throw an overflow error

■ isEmpty: checking whether the queue is empty; trying to **dequeue** an item from an empty queue would throw an underflow error

■ enqueue: adding an item to the rear of the queue

■ dequeue: removing an item from the front of the queue

■ front: displaying the element stored at the front of the queue.

■ Uses of queues

Queues are used when dealing with simulations or situations that require the first item entered to be the first item dealt with. Applications of queues include:

■ **Printer queues:** Printing jobs are stored in a queue. The first printing job sent is the first to be dealt with. New printing jobs join the queue at the rear of the queue. As such, all printing jobs are dealt with on a first come first served basis.

■ **Keyboard queues:** The keyboard buffer (which stores characters as they are typed) operates as a queue. As such, the first letter to be shown on the screen is the first letter typed. New characters are added to the end of the queue.

■ **Simulations of real-life situations:** Checkout queues, car-washing queues, carpark-exiting queues, and so on, are all situations that require a queue. People or cars enter the queue on one side and exit it on the other side.

REVIEW QUESTIONS

1 Define the term "stack".

2 Define the term "queue".

3 Identify the main operations of a stack.

4 Identify the main operations of a queue.

5 Explain the FIFO and the LIFO principles and how they apply to stacks and queues.

6 Identify a real-life scenario where you could use a stack.

7 Identify a real-life scenario where you could use a queue.

8 Outline a situation where the use of a stack might be more efficient than the use of a queue.

9 Outline a situation where the use of a queue might be more efficient than the use of a stack.

10 Identify a scenario where you might combine a stack and a queue within the same program.

11 You must store a list of numbers in a particular sequence and then retrieve them in reverse order. Identify the data structure that is most suitable for this task and explain your reasoning.

12 Outline three uses of a stack.

13 Outline three uses of a queue.

14 Describe two characteristics of a stack.

B2 Programming

15 Describe two characteristics of a queue.

16 Compare the use of a stack with arrays or lists.

17 Compare static and dynamic data structures in terms of data storage and data access.

18 Explain the meaning of stack overflow and stack underflow and describe when they occur.

19 Use a stack to evaluate the following arithmetic expression: 5 2 * 3 2+ -

PROGRAMMING EXERCISES

1 Construct a program that creates a stack that has a maximum size of seven elements. Push five words into the stack. Display the top element. Pop two words from the stack and display the top element.

2 Construct a program to reverse the elements from a given queue using a stack.

ACTIVITY

Use your solutions to the programming exercises above to answer the following questions.

1 Why is the maximum size of the stack important? What happens if this maximum size is exceeded?

2 How would you change the solution to Exercise 2 if you were asked to reverse the elements of a stack using a queue structure instead?

●Common mistake

Students often lose marks by not giving responses appropriate to the keywords used in the question. For example, "compare static and dynamic data structures" is expecting you to provide both similarities and differences between the two types of data structures, rather than just differences.

●Common mistake

When required to state applications of a data structure, such as a queue or stack, students often lose marks for not being clear enough to gain the marks. For example, saying that stacks are used to undo would not be enough to gain any marks.

Be specific and explain a clear situation where an undo feature is needed, such as implementing an undo feature in games: actions are pushed on to the stack and, when the previous action is needed, the undo feature is used to pop the top action from the stack.

Programming algorithms

By the end of this chapter, you should be able to:
▶ B2.4.1 Describe the efficiency of specific algorithms by calculating their Big O notation to analyse their scalability
▶ B2.4.2 Construct and trace algorithms to implement a linear search and a binary search for data retrieval
▶ B2.4.3 Construct and trace algorithms to implement bubble sort and selection sort, evaluating their time and space complexities
▶ B2.4.4 Explain the fundamental concept of recursion and its applications in programming (HL)
▶ B2.4.5 Construct and trace recursive algorithms in a programming language (HL)

B2.4.1 Big O notation

Complexity analysis of algorithms includes time and space analysis. Time complexity analysis refers to how long an algorithm will take to run or how many steps an algorithm will take to run, while space analysis refers to how much memory space it takes to run the algorithm.

■ Time complexity

Consider the following algorithm:

Java
```java
for(int i = 0; i<5;i++) {
    System.out.println("hello");
}
```

Python
```python
for i in range (0,5):
    print("hello")
```

How many times will this loop repeat? The variable i will take values from 0 to 4 included; therefore, it is simple to say that the algorithm will repeat five times. If we are to replace the 5 with n, the algorithm will repeat n times and the time complexity will be of the order of n. This is written as $O(n)$, which is known as **Big O notation**. The time it takes to run the algorithm is approximately proportional to n. The larger the n, the more accurate the approximation; therefore, when calculating the Big O notation, the worst-case analysis is considered (the larger the n, the better).

◆ **Big O notation:** used to find the upper bound (worst-case scenario or the highest possible amount) of the growth of a function; the longest time or space required to turn the input into output.

Java
```java
for(int i = 0; i<n; i++) {
    System.out.println("hello");
}
```

Python
```python
for i in range (0,n):
    print("hello")
```

Consider the following example:

Java
```java
for(int i = 0; i<n; i++) {
    for(int j = 0; j<n; j++) {
        System.out.println("hello");
    }
}
```

Python
```python
for i in range (0,n):
    for j in range (0,n):
        print("hello")
```

In the example above, the algorithm will repeat n times for the outer loop and n times for the inner loop, so a total of n*n times, which means time complexity becomes $O(n^2)$.

Let's look at another example:

Java
```java
for(int i = 0; i<n; i++) {
    for(int j = 0; j<n+3; j++) {
        System.out.println("hello");
    }
}
```

Python
```python
for i in range (0,n):
    for j in range (0,n+3):
        print("hello")
```

In the example above, the number of repetitions is $n^2 + 3n$. As time complexity becomes more accurate for larger numbers, when n takes a very high value, the addition of 3n is not even taken into consideration. As such, constants are ignored (the rate of growth is what matters) and the lower-order terms are ignored (as n grows larger, the larger term dominates all other terms). Therefore, the Big O notation is still $O(n^2)$. In the same way, if the number of repetitions is $25n^3$, $n^3 + 25n^2 + \frac{1}{2}n$, the coefficients will be ignored and only the term with the highest exponent will be used, and so the Big O notation will be $O(n^3)$.

The final example is a simple statement, without any loops:

Java
```java
System.out.println("enter a number: ");
int value = reader.nextInt();
sum = 50 + value;
```

Python
```python
value = int(input("enter a number: "))
sum = 50 + value
```

In this case, Big O notation is constant; no matter how large the input value, the algorithm will take the exact same time to run, so we can say the time complexity is $O(1)$.

The common time complexities expressed using Big O notation are:

- $O(1)$ – **constant time**: The algorithm performs a fixed number of operations; the time taken to run the algorithm does not depend on the size of the input. Such algorithms are ideal for operations where you need consistent performance regardless of input size, such as basic operations in data structures like hash tables.

- $O(n)$ – **linear time**: The algorithm scales linearly with the size of the input. Such algorithms are appropriate for simple searches where each element must be considered.

- $O(n^2)$ – **quadratic time:** The time taken to run the algorithm is directly proportional to the square of the input size. Such algorithms are often used when dealing with small data sets; they are inefficient for large data sets.

- $O(2^n)$ – **exponential time:** The algorithm's running time doubles with every increase in the input size. Such algorithms are generally impractical for large inputs due to rapid growth in execution time.

- $O(\log n)$ – **logarithmic time:** The algorithm's running time scales logarithmically with the increase in the input size. Such algorithms are suitable for searching and some divide-and-conquer algorithms. They are ideal for cases where you can efficiently reduce the problem size.

■ Space complexity

Space complexity analyses the amount of memory used by an algorithm with respect to its input size.

Common space complexities expressed using Big O notation are:

- $O(1)$ – **constant space:** The space used by the algorithm is not dependent on the size of the input. The algorithm uses a fixed amount of memory, no matter the input size.

- $O(n)$ – **linear space:** The memory usage scales linearly with the input size.

- $O(n^2)$ – **quadratic space:** The space taken to run the algorithm is directly proportional to the square of the input size.

Consider the following example:

Java
```java
int sum = 0;
for(int i = 0; i<n; i++) {
    sum = sum + i;
}
System.out.println(sum);
```

Python
```python
sum = 0
for i in range (0,n):
    sum = sum + i
print(sum)
```

In the example above, no matter how many repetitions there are, the space taken to store the `sum` and `i` variables in memory is always the same. The `sum` and `i` will be overwritten with every repetition, so the space complexity stays constant: $O(1)$.

As memory is not a real issue these days, it is often the case when writing an algorithm to aim for reducing the time complexity, even if that means trading off more space.

To calculate the space complexity of an algorithm, you need to look at:

- **Variables and constants:** As variables are overwritten and constants don't change their value during the execution of the program, they will always take up the same amount of space, so they don't need to be recalculated after the execution of the program.

- **Inputs:** Inputs are important for space complexity. If the inputs are variables, arrays or other data structures, their space complexity differs.

- **Execution:** Based on how the algorithm is written, the space complexity can be constant (when a fixed number of simple operations are performed) or differ (when, for example, a function calls itself several times, and so extra space is needed to store the return values and values of the parameters that will be used in unwinding to provide a solution).

In the example above, the sum will include each value stored in the array, so the space required to run the algorithm is linear to the number of elements in the array: **O(n)**.

■ Choosing algorithms based on scalability and efficiency

- **Small data sets:** Simpler algorithms with higher time complexity (for example $O(n^2)$ or $O(n^3)$) can be acceptable.
- **Large data sets:** Algorithms with lower time complexity (for example O(n log n) or O(log n)) are preferred, for better scalability.
- **Real-time requirements:** Algorithms with constant time complexity (O(1)) or logarithmic complexity (O(log n)) are considered, where possible.
- **Complex problems:** Dynamic programming or divide-and-conquer approaches with manageable time complexity are used.

Selecting the right algorithm depends on the problem constraints, input size and performance requirements. Analysing time complexity helps ensure that the chosen algorithm will perform efficiently as the input size grows.

REVIEW QUESTIONS

1 Explain what Big O notation is and why it is used in Computer Science.
2 Define the terms "time complexity" and "space complexity".
3 Outline the difference between O(n) and $O(n^2)$. Identify two algorithms that present these complexities.
4 Explain why you think it is important to consider the worst-case space complexity of an algorithm.
5 Sketch a graph to compare the time complexity of O(n) and O(log n). What differences do you notice?
6 Consider the following statement: "An algorithm with a Big O value of O(n) will always be slower than one with a value of O(log n)". Evaluate this statement to true or false and explain your reasons.
7 Outline the two types of complexity analysis.
8 Identify which is generally faster for a very large n: O(log n) or $O(2^n)$.

B2.4.2 Linear search and binary search

Search algorithms are used to find a specific item in a data structure. Such algorithms can be used to find an item in a list or in a database; to search for an item (word or phrase) in a document; to find a relevant webpage based on a keyword typed in a search engine; or to find a location on a map.

Step 1

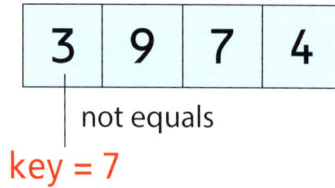

not equals

key = 7

Step 2

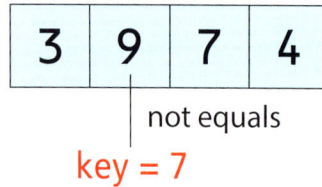

not equals

key = 7

Step 3

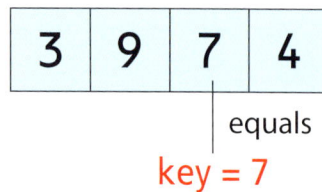

equals

key = 7

■ 1D array (list) – linear search

♦ **Linear search:** a method of searching, in which each element is checked in sequential order.

■ Linear search

A **linear search** is also called a "sequential search" as it traverses a data structure from the beginning to the end when looking for a specific item. In the best-case scenario, the item is found in the first position, but in the worst-case scenario the item is the last item in the list and so the entire list is traversed.

Consider an array (list) of integers with ten elements and a key, being the element you are searching for.

To find the key, you will use a loop to traverse the array (list).

Starting at the first index, the element stored at position 0 will be compared with the key. If they are the same, the element is found; otherwise, the process repeats until the element is found or until the end of the array (list) is reached.

If a conditional loop is used, the algorithm can be stopped once the element is found. But if a count-controlled loop is used, the algorithm will traverse the entire list (array), even if the searched element has been found.

Java

```java
int numbers= {3,9,7,4};
int key = 7;
int position = -1;
for(int i = 0; i<numbers.length; i++) {
    if(key==numbers[i]){
        position = i;
    }
}
if(position != -1){
    System.out.println("element found on position "+
position);
}
else{
    System.out.println("element was not found!");
}
```

```
Python
numbers = [3,9,7,4]
key = 7
position = -1
for i in range (0,len(numbers)):
    if key == numbers[i]:
        position = i
if position != -1:
    print("element found on position ", position)
else:
    print("element was not found")
```

This algorithm can be improved, so it stops when the element is found by using a conditional loop.

When you think of Big O notation, linear search has a time complexity of O(n), as in the worst-case scenario every single element in the array (list) will be traversed in the attempt to find the searched key. At the same time, the space complexity is O(1), as the space required to run the algorithm is constant.

■ Binary search

Linear search is not a very efficient algorithm, especially when the size of the array (list) is considerably high.

Binary search is a more efficient searching algorithm as it reduces the number of searches to half with every comparison performed, so the time complexity is logarithmic O(log n). However, to be able to perform a binary search on an array (list), the data structure *must be sorted* (it must be in order). This is because the algorithm works as follows:

◆ **Binary search:** a method of searching an ordered array (list) by repeatedly checking the value of the middle element and disregarding the half of the data structure that does not contain the searched element.

- Set a variable (lower) to store the lower bound index.
- Set a variable (upper) to store the upper bound index.
- Calculate the middle index (mid) by using the formula mid = (lower+upper)/2
- Compare the value in the middle index with the search key (if numbers[mid]==key).
- If they are the same, the value is found and the algorithm can stop.
- If the value in the middle position is smaller than the key, you can disregard the left side of the array (if the array is sorted in ascending order) by setting the lower variable to the middle index + 1: lower = mid + 1
- If the value in the middle position is greater than the key, you can disregard the right side of the array (if the array is sorted in ascending order) by setting the upper variable to the middle index – 1: upper = mid - 1
- Repeat the entire process, starting from the third point until the value is found or the end of the array (list) is reached.

key = 7

new lower

mid

[0] ([1]) [2] [3]

| 3 | 4 | 7 | 9 |

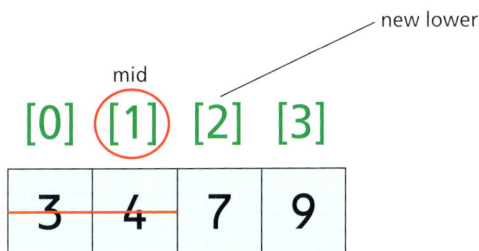

lower = 0
upper = 3
mid = (lower + upper)/2 = 1
7 > 4, so
lower = mid + 1 = 2
mid = (lower + upper)/2 = 2
7 = 7, so the element is found

■ 1D array (list) – binary search

Java

```java
int numbers[] = {3,4,5,7,9,11,13};
int key = 11;
boolean found = false;
int lower = 0;
int mid = 0;
int upper = numbers.length;
while((lower<=upper) && !found ) {
    mid = (lower+upper)/2;
    if (numbers[mid]==key) {
        found = true;
    } else if(numbers[mid]<key) {
        lower = mid+1;
    } else {
        upper = mid-1;
    }
}
if (found) {
    System.out.println("the value was found on position " + mid);
} else {
    System.out.println("the value was not found" );
}
```

Python

```python
numbers= [3,4,5,7,9,11,13]
key =11
found = False
lower = 0
upper = len(numbers)
mid = 0
while lower<=upper and not found:
    mid = int((lower + upper)/2)
    if numbers[mid]==key:
        found = True
    elif numbers[mid]<key:
        lower = mid + 1
    else:
        upper = mid - 1
if found:
    print("the value was found on position ", mid)
else:
    print("the value was not found")
```

Each algorithm is more appropriate in different scenarios. For example, if the list (array) needs to be searched once for a given element, such as the ID of a worker, and the organization has fewer than 50 employees, it would be faster to simply use a linear search, rather than having to sort the data structure and then apply a binary search on it. However, if there is a need to search for the home address of a student based on their school ID, in a data structure already ordered based on the students' IDs, and the school has 1500 students, it would be much more appropriate to use a binary search to retrieve the student's details.

B2.4.3 Bubble sort and selection sort

Sorting refers to arranging the elements in an array (list) into ascending or descending order. You already practised a swapping technique at the beginning of the unit. This technique is used in sorting routines.

◆ **Bubble sort:** a sorting algorithm that compares adjacent values and swaps them if they are in an incorrect order.

■ Bubble sort

Bubble sort is a sorting algorithm that uses an incremental approach, and it works by repeatedly swapping the adjacent elements if they are not in the right order. If the array (list) was traversed only once, there might still be elements in the array (list) that are not yet sorted.

Bubble sort algorithms work as follows:

- Start at the beginning of the array (list).
- Compare the current element with the next one.
- If the two values are not in order, swap their contents.
- Move to the next element in the array (list).
- Repeat the process until all the elements have been sorted.

As shown in the diagram, once the array (list) has been traversed once, the last element is surely in the right position. Therefore, to optimize the algorithm, the number of repetitions can be reduced by 1.

Unsorted array (list)

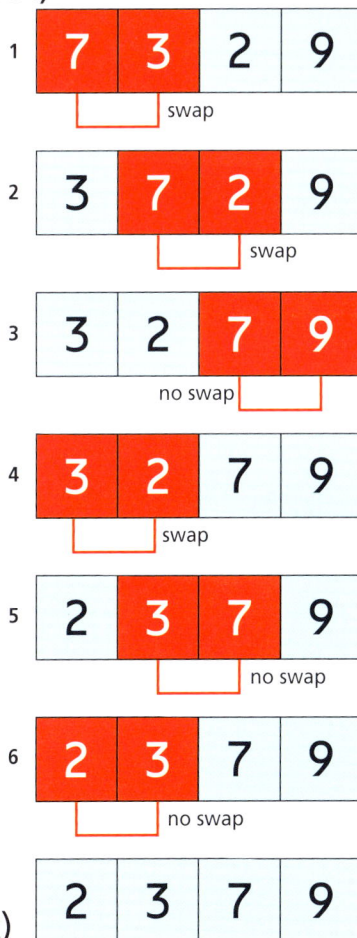

Sorted array (list)

■ Bubble sort

Java

```java
int numbers[] = {7,3,2,9};
for (int i = 0; i <numbers.length; i++) {
    for (int j = 0; j<numbers.length-1-i; j++) {
        if(numbers[j]>numbers[j+1]) {
            int temp = numbers[j];
            numbers[j] = numbers[j+1];
            numbers[j+1]=temp;
        }
    }
}
for (int i=0;i<numbers.length; i++) {
    System.out.print(numbers[i]+" ");
}
```

Python

```python
numbers = [7,3,2,9]
for i in range(len(numbers)):
    for j in range(0, len(numbers)-1-i):
        if numbers[j]>numbers[j+1]:
            temp = numbers[j]
            numbers[j]=numbers[j+1]
            numbers[j+1]=temp
for i in range(len(numbers)):
    print(numbers[i], " ", end="")
```

The inner loop repeats from 0 to the size of the array (list) −1, because you compare one element with an adjacent one and, when the current element is the second last to be compared with the last element, that should be the last comparison that takes place.

The same repetition is reduced by i every time. This ensures that, when the array (list) is traversed the first time, it will repeat to its size −1, as i is initially 0, but with the next traversal it will repeat to size −2, and the next pass it will be size −3, and so on. This is happens because, with the first pass of the array (list), the last element moves to the correct position; with the second pass, the last and the second last are in the correct position, and so on.

Another way to implement a bubble sort is by using a conditional loop:

Java
```java
int numbers[] = {7,3,2,9};
boolean swapped = true;
int n = numbers.length;
while (n>0 && swapped) {
    swapped = false;
    n = n-1;
    for (int i = 0; i<n-1; i++) {
        if(numbers[i]>numbers[i+1]) {
            int temp = numbers[i];
            numbers[i] = numbers[i+1];
            numbers[i+1]=temp;
            swapped = true;
        }
    }
}
for (int i=0;i<numbers.length; i++) {
    System.out.print(numbers[i]+" ");
}
```

Python
```python
numbers = [7,3,2,9]
swapped = True
n = len(numbers)
while(n>0 and swapped):
    swapped = False
    n=n-1
    for i in range(0, n-1):
        if numbers[i]>numbers[i+1]:
            temp = numbers[i]
            numbers[i]=numbers[i+1]
            numbers[i+1]=temp
            swapped = True
for i in range(len(numbers)):
    print(numbers[i], " ", end="")
```

Although it is quite simple to understand the algorithm and to implement it, the bubble sort has a time complexity of $O(n^2)$, which means it is a very inefficient algorithm, especially when it comes to large sets of data. In terms of space complexity, the bubble sort algorithm is very efficient $O(1)$, requiring a constant memory space to store the variables read from the array, the indices and the temporary variable. This required space would not depend on the size of the input; it would not require additional space proportional to the size of the input array.

Unsorted array (list)

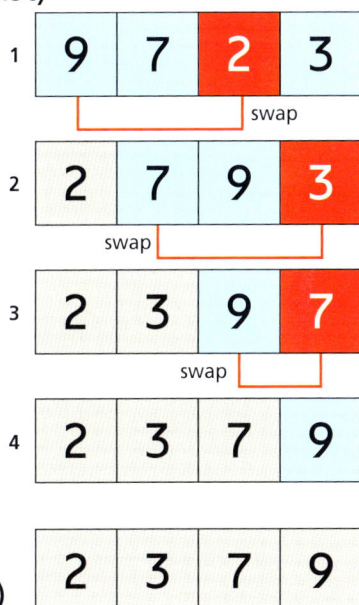

Sorted array (list)

■ Selection sort

■ Selection sort

To easily understand the algorithm, imagine you split the original array (list) into two parts. The first part is the sorted part, which is initially empty, and the second part is the unsorted part, which initially contains the entire array (list). With the first part, the smallest element in the unsorted part is selected and swapped with the first element in the array. This smallest element now becomes the sorted part of the array. In the second pass, you now search for the smallest element in the unsorted part and swap it with the second element. The sorted part now includes the first and second element. The process repeats until all the elements are sorted, the sorted part includes the entire array and the unsorted part is empty.

Java

```java
int numbers[] = {9,7,2,3};
int min, minIndex;
for(int i = 0; i<numbers.length; i++) {
    min = numbers[i];
    minIndex = i;
    for(int j = i+1; j<numbers.length; j++) {
        if(numbers[j]<min) {
            min = numbers[j];
            minIndex=j;
        }
    }
    numbers[minIndex] = numbers[i];
    numbers[i] = min;
}
for(int i = 0; i<numbers.length; i++) {
    System.out.print(numbers[i] + " ");
}
```

Python

```python
numbers = [9,7,2,3]
for i in range(len(numbers)):
    min = numbers[i]
    minIndex = i
    for j in range(i+1, len(numbers)):
        if numbers[j] < min:
            min = numbers[j]
            minIndex = j
    numbers[minIndex] = numbers[i]
    numbers[i] = min
for i in range(len(numbers)):
    print(numbers[i], " ", end="")
```

The same algorithm can be implemented by using just the index of the smallest element, instead of retrieving the smallest element and its index to swap:

Java

```java
int numbers[] = {9,7,2,3};
int min;
for(int i = 0; i<numbers.length-1; i++) {
    min =i;
    for(int j = i+1; j<numbers.length; j++) {
        if(numbers[j]<numbers[min]) {
            min=j;
        }
    }
    int temp = numbers[i];
    numbers[i]=numbers[min];
    numbers[min]=temp;
    for(int i = 0; i<numbers.length; i++) {
        System.out.print(numbers[i] + " ");
    }
}
```

Python

```python
numbers = [9,7,2,3]
for i in range(len(numbers)-1):
    min = i
    for j in range(i+1, len(numbers)):
        if numbers[j] < numbers[min]:
            min = j
    temp = numbers[i]
    numbers[i] = numbers[min]
    numbers[min] = temp
for i in range(len(numbers)):
    print(numbers[i], " ", end="")
```

◆ **Selection sort**: a sorting algorithm that repeatedly selects the smallest or largest element (ascending or descending order) from the unsorted part of the data structure and moves it to the sorted part.

The limitation of the **selection sort** is that it doesn't allow for an early exit if the array (list) is ordered at an earlier point. The time complexity of the selection sort is $O(n^2)$ and the space complexity is $O(1)$. Selection sort performs a smaller number of swaps; therefore, it is said to be a more efficient algorithm than the bubble sort algorithm. However, it is possible to stop the algorithm if all elements are sorted during an early pass in a bubble sort by using the flag in a conditional statement, which is not possible in a selection sort.

ACTIVITY

Research skills: Present information in a variety of formats and platforms – find an ingenious way to explain one of the programming algorithms you have studied. For example, use labelled cups to explain a sorting algorithm, create an animation, a video, and so on.

B2.4.4 Recursion (HL)

Recursion represents a technique that involves the use of functions, procedures or algorithms calling themselves one or more times until one or more specific conditions are met, at which point the process unwinds itself to produce a solution, by processing the last call to the first.

Characteristics of a recursive algorithm include:

- a method or function that calls itself
- a termination condition or a **base case** – a termination solution that is not recursive; without a base case, the algorithm will run to infinite
- a **general case** that calls itself recursively or is defined in terms of itself, and moves towards the base case by changing its state (**winding**)
- **unwinding**, which occurs when the algorithm reaches the base case (cascades up until the original problem is solved or, in other words, is processing the results, starting at the last call and building up towards the base case).

Recursive algorithms provide elegant solutions to complex problems, by often using less code and fewer variables than iterative approaches. They allow the programmer to divide complex problems into smaller sub-problems that are more readable and easier to solve. However, if many recursive calls are made, there is a heavy use of the stack, a process that is memory intensive and could potentially lead to stack overflow, and the computer running out of memory. If the termination condition is not set correctly, the algorithm might run to infinite, or the system might crash or freeze due to the high number of recursive calls.

Recursion might take longer to execute than other techniques or iterative approaches, as each call takes a specific amount of time, in addition to the time required to build up the final solution.

Recursion can also be challenging to follow sometimes, which can make it difficult for other programmers to maintain, document or modify it.

Recursion can be used:

- to implement sorting algorithms, such as quick sort
- for fractal image creation
- for traversing binary trees or graphs
- for solving mathematical problems, such as factorial functions and towers of Hanoi.

When choosing whether to solve a problem by using a recursive algorithm, ask yourself the following questions:

- Is it possible to identify a base case?
- Is it possible to solve the problem by calling itself or splitting it into smaller instances of the same problem?
- Does it require data structures like graphs, trees or linked lists – data structures that can be seen as repetitive instances of itself?
- Does it require backtracking?
- Is there a mathematical expression that can be translated into a recursive algorithm?
- Are you solving the problem in a more elegant, simpler and logical way by using recursion, without sacrificing too much memory or performance?

◆ **Base case:** a terminating solution (that is not recursive) to a process.

◆ **General case:** a process where the recursive call takes place.

◆ **Winding:** a process occurring when recursive calls are made until the base case is reached.

◆ **Unwinding:** a process occurring when the base case is reached, and the values are returned to build a solution.

B2.4.5 Recursive algorithms (HL)

■ Factorial of a number

One of the exercises in Section B2.3.4 required you to find the factorial of a number. You were able to solve this problem by using a loop. However, now you understand the concept of recursion, you can easily establish that this problem can be solved by using a recursive algorithm. Starting from the mathematical formula that defines the factorial of n: n! = n * (n-1)!, you can identify that 5! can be defined as 5 *4! and 4! can be defined as 4*3!, and so on, until n = 1, which will return 1. The base case is when n = 1, as 1 will be returned, and the recursive call is when the method calls itself with n - 1 as a parameter. Therefore, the solution to this problem is:

Java
```java
public static int factorial(int n) {
    if (n==1) {
        return 1;
    }
    else {
        return n * factorial(n-1);
    }
}
public static void main(String[] args) {
    int fact = factorial(5);
    System.out.println(fact);
}
```

Python
```python
def factorial(n):
    if(n==1):
        return 1
    else:
        return n * factorial(n-1)
fact = factorial(5)
print(fact)
```

■ Fibonacci sequence

Another application of a recursive method is in solving the Fibonacci sequence.

The Fibonacci sequence looks like this:

0, 1, 1, 2, 3, 5, 8, 13, 21, 34…

THE FIBONACCI SEQUENCE

Each number is the sum of the two that precede it.

0 1 1 2 3 5 8 13 21

$0 + 1 = 1$
$1 + 1 = 2$
$1 + 2 = 3$
$2 + 3 = 5$
$3 + 5 = 8$
$5 + 8 = 13$
$8 + 13 = 21$

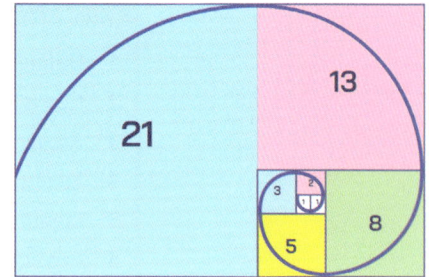

■ Fibonacci sequence

■ $F_0 = 0$

■ $F_1 = 1$

■ $F_2 = F_1 + F_0$

■ …

■ $F_n = F_{n-1} + F_{n-2}$

To find the sequence for the first n terms, the base cases are identified as being F_0 and F_1, where the returned values would be 0 and 1 and the recursive call: $F_{n-1} + F_{n-2}$.

Java

```java
public static int fib(int n) {
    if (n==0) {
        return 0;
    } else if (n==1) {
        return 1;
    } else {
        return fib(n-1) + fib(n-2);
    }
}
public static void main(String[] args) {
    Scanner read = new Scanner(System.in);
    System.out.println("Enter a number: ");
    int n = read.nextInt();
    for(int i = 0; i<n; i++) {
        System.out.print(fib(i) + " ");
    }
}
```

Python

```python
def fib(n):
    if n==0:
        return 0
    elif n==1:
        return 1
    else:
        return fib(n-1) +
        fib(n-2)
n = int(input("enter a number: "))
for i in range(n):
    print(fib(i), " ", end="")
```

■ Quicksort

♦ **Quicksort:** a sorting algorithm that repeatedly selects an element as a pivot and partitions the other elements into two sub-arrays (lists): one that includes elements that are smaller than the pivot and the other one that includes elements that are larger than the pivot.

If the bubble sort and selection sort discussed earlier use an incremental approach, the **quicksort** is an efficient sorting routine that uses the divide-and-conquer algorithm. The divide-and-conquer principle refers to dividing the problem into two or more identical, smaller sub-problems that can be solved individually, and their solutions combined to produce the solution to the larger problem.

The quicksort algorithm makes use of a pivot element from the data set, against which the other elements are compared, to identify their correct position. The pivot element can be the first element, the last element, a random element or the middle element in the data set. Imagine that the data structure is broken into two partitions (sections): one that contains elements smaller than the pivot and one that contains elements larger than the pivot.

A way to construct the quicksort algorithm is by implementing the following logic:

- Set the pivot as the middle element.
- Start at each end of the list by using a left pointer and a right pointer.
- Move the values smaller than the pivot to the left partition.
- Move the values larger than the pivot to the right partition.
- Recursively apply the same principle for the left partition until all elements are sorted.
- Recursively apply the same principle for the right partition until all elements are sorted.

Java

```java
public static void quickSort(int start, int finish, int[]numbers) {
    if(start>=finish) {
        return;
    }
    int left = start;
    int right = finish;
    int pivot = numbers[(start+finish)/2];
    System.out.print("start:" + start + " finish: " + finish + " left: " + left
    + " right: " + right + " pivot: " + pivot );
    while(left<right) {
        while(numbers[left]<pivot) {
            left = left+1;
            System.out.println("left: " + left);
        }
        while(numbers[right]>pivot) {
            right = right-1;
            System.out.println("right: " + right);
        }
        if(left<=right) {
            int temp = numbers[left];
            numbers[left] = numbers[right];
            numbers[right] = temp;
            left = left+1;
            right = right-1;
            System.out.println();
```

```
                for(int i = 0; i<numbers.length; i++) {
                    System.out.print(numbers[i] + " ");
                }
                System.out.println();
                System.out.println("left: " + left);
                System.out.println("right: " + right);
            }
        }
        System.out.println("quickSort from start: " + start + " right: " + right);
        quickSort(start, right, numbers);
        System.out.println("quickSort from left: " + left + " finish: " + finish);
        quickSort(left, finish, numbers);
    }
    public static void main(String[] args) {
        int numbers[] = {16,13,4,6,22,1,9,5};
        quickSort(0,numbers.length-1, numbers);
        for(int i = 0; i<numbers.length; i++) {
            System.out.print(numbers[i]+ " ");
        }
    }
}
```

Python

```python
def quickSort(start, finish, numbers):
    if(start>=finish):
        return
    left = start
    right = finish
    pivot = numbers[int((start+finish)/2)]
    print("start: ", start, "finish: ", finish, "left: ", left, "right: ",
    right, "pivot: ", pivot)
    while left<right:
        while numbers[left]<pivot:
            left = left + 1
            print("left: ", left)
    while numbers[right]>pivot:
        right = right - 1
        print("right: ", right)
    if left<=right:
        temp = numbers[left]
        numbers[left] = numbers[right]
        numbers[right]= temp
        left = left + 1
        right = right - 1
        print()
```

```
        for i in range (len(numbers)):
            print(numbers[i], " ", end="")
        print()
        print("left: ", left)
        print("right: ", right)
    print("quickSort from start: ", start, " to right: ", right)
    quickSort(start, right, numbers)
    print("quickSort from left: ", left, " to finish: ", finish)
    quickSort(left, finish, numbers)
numbers = [16,13,4,6,22,1,9,5]
quickSort(0, len(numbers)-1, numbers)
for i in range(len(numbers)):
    print(numbers[i], " ", end="")
```

Common mistake

Always pay attention to the logic behind the algorithms you write. Many students implement sorting algorithms incorrectly or they confuse the algorithms in between. For example, when the question is requiring the sorting of an array in ascending order by using the selection sort, a common mistake is to implement an incorrect bubble sort, or an algorithm that outputs the values in descending order instead of ascending, as required.

Pay attention to the features of each of the sorting algorithms and understand the logic behind them.

[0] [1] [2] [3] [4] [5] [6] [7]

1 | 16 | 13 | 4 | 6 | 22 | 1 | 9 | 5 | swap 16 and 5

start: 0 finish: 7
left: 0 right: 7 pivot 6

[0] [1] [2] [3] [4] [5] [6] [7]

2 | 5 | 13 | 4 | 6 | 22 | 1 | 9 | 16 | swap 13 and 1

left: 1 right: 6
right: 5

[0] [1] [2] [3] [4] [5] [6] [7]

3 | 5 | 1 | 4 | 6 | 22 | 13 | 9 | 16 | swap 6 and 6

quickSort start: 0 right: 2

left: 2 right: 4
left: 3 right: 3

left: 4 right: 2
start: 0 finish: 2
left: 0 right: 2 pivot 1
right: 1

[0] [1] [2] [3] [4] [5] [6] [7]

4 | 5 | 1 | 4 | 6 | 22 | 13 | 9 | 16 | swap 5 and 1

quickSort start: 0 right: 0
quickSort left: 1 finish: 2

left: 1 right: 0
start: 1 finish: 2
left: 1 right: 2 pivot 5

[0] [1] [2] [3] [4] [5] [6] [7]

5 | 1 | 5 | 4 | 6 | 22 | 13 | 9 | 16 | swap 5 and 4

quickSort start: 1 right: 1
quickSort left: 2 finish: 2
quickSort left: 4 finish: 7

left: 2 right: 1
start: 4 finish: 7
left: 4 right: 7 pivot 13
right: 6

[0] [1] [2] [3] [4] [5] [6] [7]

6 | 1 | 4 | 5 | 6 | 22 | 13 | 9 | 16 | swap 22 and 9

quickSort start: 4 right: 3
quickSort left: 5 finish: 5
quickSort left: 5 finish: 7

left: 5 right: 3
start: 5 finish: 7
left: 5 right: 7 pivot 22
left: 6

[0] [1] [2] [3] [4] [5] [6] [7]

7 | 1 | 4 | 5 | 6 | 9 | 13 | 22 | 16 | swap 22 and 16

quickSort start: 5 right: 6
start: 5 finish: 6
left: 5 right: 6 pivot 13
right: 5

left: 7 right: 6
left: 6 right: 4

quickSort start: 5 right: 4
quickSort left: 6 finish: 6
quickSort left: 7 finish: 7

[0] [1] [2] [3] [4] [5] [6] [7]

8 | 1 | 4 | 5 | 6 | 9 | 13 | 16 | 22 |

■ Quicksort

REVIEW QUESTIONS

1 Complete a trace table for a bubble sort algorithm to sort the numbers: 16, 13, 4, 6, 22, 1, 9, 5.

2 Complete a trace table for a selection sort algorithm to sort the numbers: 16, 13, 4, 6, 22, 1, 9, 5.

3 Complete a trace table for a quicksort algorithm to sort the numbers: 16, 13, 4, 6, 22, 1, 9, 5.

4 Create a table outlining the Big O value for both time and space complexities for all the searching and sorting algorithms you have studied.

5 Outline the principles of working of a selection sort and a quicksort algorithm.

■ Traversal of binary trees

At this point, you will need to review the binary trees concepts in Section B4.1.4. If you have not covered this topic yet, take the time to do it now.

Binary trees can be traversed by using a recursive algorithm as well. The logic behind this is the following:

- ■ Visit a node or display its content.
- ■ Traverse the left subtree.
- ■ Traverse the right subtree.

The order of those three operations depends on the type of traversal used. For example, in an in-order traversal you need to follow the left, root, right pattern, as shown in the algorithm below; as such you will go to the leftmost node and visit it, then the data in the node above, and then the right node. Once this is done, you move one level up and repeat the process, so the left subtree will be first traversed, then the root and then the right subtree. In a post-order traversal you need to follow the left, right, root pattern, and in a pre-order traversal you need to follow the root, left, right traversal.

Java

```java
class Node
{
    int data;
    Node left;
    Node right;
    Node(int value){
        data = value;
        left=right=null;
    }
}
class testTraversal {
    void inorder(Node root)
    {
        if (root == null) {
            return;
        }
        inorder(root.left);
        System.out.println(root.data);
        inorder(root.right);
    }
    public static void main(String[] args) {
        Node root = new Node(5);
        root.left = new Node(3);
        root.right = new Node(8);
        root.left.left = new Node(2);
        root.left.right = new Node(4);
        root.right.left = new Node(6);
        root.right.right = new Node(9);
        inorder(root);
    }
}
```

Python

```python
class Node:
    def __init__(self, value):
        self.data = value
        self.left = None
        self.right = None
def inorder(root):
    if root is None:
        return
    inorder(root.left)
    print(root.data, " ", end="")
    inorder(root.right)
root = Node(5)
root.left = Node(3)
root.right = Node(8)
root.left.left = Node(2)
root.left.right = Node(4)
root.right.left = Node(6)
root.right.right = Node(9)
inorder(root)
```

PROGRAMMING EXERCISE

Implement the post-order and pre-order traversals of a binary tree using recursion.

ACTIVITY

Thinking skills:
Create novel solutions to problems – choose an iterative program you have created before, and attempt to rewrite it using a recursive approach.

ACTIVITY

Use your answer to the programming exercise above to answer the following questions.

1 Did you use two different functions to solve the exercise? Did the functions work as expected?

2 Did you use any local or global variables? Why did you need any local variables, if you used any?

●Common mistake

Practical questions requiring algorithms to be described often lack clarity. Ensure steps are clearly outlined. You can support explanations by adding code or pseudocode statements, but those should be clearly explained to gain marks.

B2.5 File processing

SYLLABUS CONTENT

By the end of this chapter, you should be able to:
▶ B2.5.1 Construct code to perform file-processing operations

When creating a program, you might want to store data permanently so that, once you close your program or switch off the computer and you turn it on again, the data can still be retrieved and manipulated. One way to achieve this is to store the data in a file. The program will be able to manipulate the data stored in several types of files, such as text files (.txt), comma-separated value files (.csv), binary files (.dat), and so on.

To avoid having to use the **absolute path** of your file (to specify the entire location), save the file within the same folder as your program. This will allow you to access the file by simply using its file name, also called the **relative path** of the file.

A text file is a sequential file, meaning that data in the file can be accessed sequentially (line by line) and new records will be added to the end of the file.

A file can be opened in several modes: write, read and append. When opening a file in **write** mode, new data inserted into the file will overwrite the existing content in the file. **Read** mode is used to allow you to access the data from the file to read it, and **append** mode allows you to insert new records at the end of the file without erasing previous content.

The process to **write** text to a text file is as follows:

- Open the file for write or append, as needed.
- Prepare the line of text to be written.
- Write the line to the file.
- Close the file.

The process to **read** text from a text file is as follows:

- Open the file for read.
- Read the content from the file:
  - ☐ Read a single line from the file.
  - ☐ Use a loop to repeat for all the lines in the file and read them line by line.
  - ☐ Read the entire file into a data structure.
- Close the file.

> ◆ **Absolute path:** the location of a file specified from the root directory (the full path).
>
> ◆ **Relative path:** the location of a file relative to the current folder.

File processing in Java

To process files in Java, you can use:

- the Scanner class
- the FileWriter class
- the BufferedReader class.

■ Scanner class

The Java package `java.io` includes the `Files` class that allows you to manipulate files, so this package needs to be imported first.

To create a file, follow the procedure of creating an object of type `File` and pass the file name as a parameter to the constructor.

```
File f = new File ("fileName.txt");
```

There are specific methods that can be used on the newly created file:

Method	Explanation
`exists( )`	Returns true if the file exists on the disk
`delete( )`	Deletes the file
`getName( )`	Returns the name of the file
`length( )`	Returns the number of characters in the file
`renameTo( )`	Receives a parameter to specify the new name of the file
`canRead( )`	Returns true if the file can be read

You have already used the `Scanner` class several times by now to read input from the keyboard. You can use the same class to read a file, by passing a file object as a parameter.

```
Scanner nameOfScanner = new Scanner (f);
```

In the line of code above, the `nameOfScanner` variable is an identifier, chosen to label the scanner for future use, and the f variable passed to the `Scanner` constructor is the file object created above.

The same purpose can be achieved by using:

```
Scanner nameOfScanner = new Scanner (new File ("fileName.txt"));
```

The `Scanner` uses tokens. When you use a function like `nextLine()`, the `Scanner` will split the input into tokens (units of user input, separated by whitespaces).

For example, if the text file contains the following two lines of text:

```
"Bobby Bob"
```

```
3 75.5
```

the `Scanner` will split this into tokens, as follows:

Token	Possible data types
`"Bobby`	string
`Bob"`	string
`3`	int, double, string
`75.5`	double, string

Each call to the functions `next( )`, `nextInt( )`, `nextDouble( )`, and so on, will consume a token, meaning it will read the token and advance the cursor to the next one.

Consider the following exercise: Construct a program that will read five numbers from the text file called "numbers" and will output their average.

Consider that the text file includes the following numbers on five different lines:

3

3.4

4

4.6

5

```java
Java
import java.util.*;
import java.io.*;
    public static void main(String[] args) {
        try {
            Scanner read = new Scanner(new File("numbers.txt"));
            double sum = 0.0;
            double average = 0.0;
            for (int i = 0; i<5; i++) {
                double value = read.nextDouble();
                sum = sum + value;
            }
            average = sum/5;
            System.out.println("average is: " + average);
        } catch (FileNotFoundException e) {
            e.printStackTrace();
        }
    }
}
```

In the code above, the function `nextDouble( )` is used to read the next token in the file, as the problem already described the data type of the values stored in the file. But in case you don't know what type of data is stored, the scanner has functions that will return true or false when checking whether the next token is of a specific data type. As such, the function `hasNextInt( )` will return true if there is a next token in the file of data type integer. Similarly, you can use `hasNextDouble( )` or `hasNextLine( )`.

Another structure used above is a FOR loop that repeats five times. This is possible as the number of lines in the text file is known. In case that is unknown information, a conditional loop can be used to repeat, as long as there is a next token in the file. The condition would include the function `hasNext( )`.

To read a file line by line, the function `nextLine( )` can be used.

```java
Java
import java.util.*;
import java.io.*;
    public static void main(String[] args) {
        try {
            Scanner read = new Scanner(new File("numbers.txt"));
            while(read.hasNext()) {
                String line = read.nextLine();
                System.out.println(line );
            }
        } catch (FileNotFoundException e) {
            e.printStackTrace();
        }
    }
}
```

Even if the values stored in the file are of decimal numbers, they can be read with `nextLine( )`, which interprets them as being of string data type. This is because, as described above, the values stored in a file can have more possible data types. If a conversion is possible to one of the required data types, there will be no error thrown.

In both examples, a `try/catch` block is used for exception handling. This is because the text file might not exist, or any other error might occur when reading the data and performing the required operations. By using exception handling techniques, the code will not crash.

The `java.io` package is used for both input and output. Therefore, it also includes the `PrintStream`, which allows you to write output to the text file.

```java
Java
import java.util.*;
import java.io.*;
    public static void main(String[] args) {
        try {
            PrintStream out = new PrintStream(new File
            ("numbers.txt"));
            out.println("Hello world!");
            out.println("I added content to the text file!");
        } catch (FileNotFoundException e) {
            e.printStackTrace();
        }
    }
}
```

When creating the `PrintStream`, the `out` variable has been used as an identifier. The file passed as a parameter is generated by calling the constructor called `File`. In case this file already exists, it will be overwritten. Otherwise, a new file called `numbers.txt` will be created.

It is important to keep in mind that you should not open a file for both reading and writing at the same time (`Scanner` and `PrintStream`).

If you want to append data to the file so the new text will be added at the end of the file, rather than overwriting its contents, you can replace the `File` constructor with `FileOutputStream` and pass the parameter true together with the file name to it. By setting the second parameter to true, it sets the file to append mode.

```java
Java
import java.util.*;
import java.io.*;
    public static void main(String[] args) {
        try {
            PrintStream out = new PrintStream(new
            FileOutputStream("numbers.txt", true));
            out.println("A new line appended!");
            out.close();
        }
        catch (FileNotFoundException e) {
            e.printStackTrace();
        }
    }
}
```

The `PrintStream` can be closed at the end, by simply using the `close( )` function: `out.close()`.

■ FileWriter class

The `FileWriter` class is also part of the `java.io` package, and it is used to write data in character form to the file (streams of characters). To create a `FileWriter`, simply create a `FileWriter` object that will pass the file name as a parameter to the constructor.

`FileWriter out = new FileWriter("numbers.txt");`

Again, if the file does not exist, a new one will be created, but if it exists it will be overwritten.

To write data to the file, the `write( )` function is used and the writer can be closed by using the `close( )` function.

```java
Java
import java.util.*;
import java.io.*;
    public static void main(String[] args) {
        try {
            FileWriter out = new FileWriter("numbers.txt");
            out.write("This is the first line!");
            out.close();
        } catch (IOException e) {
            e.printStackTrace();
        }
    }
}
```

The code above will overwrite the existing text in the file. To open the file in append mode, just set the append mode to true, by adding a second parameter to the `FileWriter` constructor.

```java
Java
import java.util.*;
import java.io.*;
    public static void main(String[] args) {
        try {
            FileWriter out = new FileWriter("numbers.txt", true);
            out.write("This is the second line!");
            out.close();
        } catch (IOException e) {
            e.printStackTrace();
        }
    }
}
```

To read data from a file in character format, `FileReader` can be used.

`FileReader read = new FileReader("numbers.txt");`

This allows you to read a single character from the file with the `read( )` method, to read the characters from the file and store them into a named array with the `read(char[ ] arrayName)`, or to read a given number of characters from the file starting at a specific index and store them into a named array with `read(char[ ] arrayName, int startIndex, int length)`.

```java
Java
import java.util.*;
import java.io.*;
    public static void main(String[] args) {
        char[] text = new char[100];
        try {
            FileReader reader = new FileReader("numbers.txt");
            reader.read(text);
            System.out.println(text);
            reader.close();
        } catch (IOException e) {
            e.printStackTrace();
        }
    }
}
```

■ BufferedReader class

`BufferedReader` class is used to read data from a character-based file. It can read a single character by using the `read( )` function or read an entire line of text by using the `readLine( )` function. To use the `BufferedReader`, there is a need to instantiate a `FileReader` object as well.

Java

```java
import java.util.*;
import java.io.*;
    public static void main(String[] args) {
        char[] text = new char[100];
        try {
            FileReader reader = new FileReader("numbers.txt");
            BufferedReader br = new BufferedReader(reader);
            int singleChar = br.read();
            while(singleChar!=-1) {
                System.out.print((char)singleChar + " ");
                singleChar = br.read();
            }
            br.close();
            reader.close();
        } catch (IOException e) {
            e.printStackTrace();
        }
    }
}
```

Before printing the character, it is converted to a `char`, as the values read from the `BufferedReader` are integer values representing the given character. If the method returns −1, it means there are no more characters in the file; therefore, this condition is included in the conditional loop.

Java

```java
import java.util.*;
import java.io.*;
    public static void main(String[] args) {
        char[] text = new char[100];
        try {
            FileReader reader = new FileReader("numbers.txt");
            BufferedReader br = new BufferedReader(reader);
            String line = br.readLine();
            while(line!=null) {
                System.out.println(line);
                line = br.readLine();
            }
            br.close();
            reader.close();
        } catch (IOException e) {
            e.printStackTrace();
        }
    }
}
```

File processing in Python

To process files in Python, use the following functions:

- `open( )`
- `read( )`
- `readline( )`
- `write( )`
- `close( )`

The `open( )` function takes two parameters: the name of the file and the mode the file should open in. There are several modes available in Python:

- `"w"` – write mode: The file is opened for writing text to it:
  - ☐ If the file does not exist, it creates a new file with the given name.
  - ☐ When adding text in write mode, the new text added will overwrite the previous text.
- `"a"` – append mode: The file is opened for adding text at the end of the file:
  - ☐ If the file does not exist, it creates a new file with the given name.
  - ☐ When adding text in append mode, the new text is added at the end of the file, so the previous text is not overwritten.
- `"r"` – read mode: The file is opened for reading data from it:
  - ☐ If the file does not exist, it will throw an error.

The default mode is the read mode. Therefore, writing `f = open("numbers.txt")` is the same as writing `f = open("numbers.txt", "r")`.

Python

```python
f = open("numbers.txt", "w")
f.write("First line")
f.close()
```

The code above will create a file called `numbers.txt` in case it does not exist on the disk, and it will write the given text to it. Once this is done, the file is closed. If the program is run again with a different line of text, the existing text in the file will be overwritten.

Python

```python
f = open("numbers.txt", "w")
f.write("First line")
f.close()
f = open("numbers.txt", "r")
print(f.read())
f.close()
```

The code above opens the file, writes the given text to the file and closes it. Afterwards, the file is open in read mode, the line is read and displayed, and then the file is closed.

`read( )` will read the entire content of the file so, if the file contains several lines, as shown below, they will all be displayed. Although this might seem an inefficient method, it can be used to read the entire content of the file into a data structure, such as a list, and then to manipulate the data stored in the respective data structure.

```python
f = open("numbers.txt", "w")
f.write("First line\n")
f.write("Second line\n")
f.close()
f = open("numbers.txt", "r")
print(f.read())
f.close()
```

The \n will move the cursor on to the next line after a line of text has been written. To read a single line of text, the readLine( ) function can be used.

```python
f = open("numbers.txt", "w")
f.write("First line\n")
f.write("Second line\n")
f.close()
f = open("numbers.txt", "r")
print(f.readline())
f.close()
```

In the code above, although the file contains two lines of text, only the first one will be displayed.

To display every line of text in the file, a conditional loop can be used.

```python
try:
    f = open("numbers.txt", "w")
    f.write("First line\n")
    f.write("Second line\n")
    f.close()
    f = open("numbers.txt", "r")
    text = f.readline()
    while text!="":
        print(text)
        text = f.readline()
except:
    print("There was a problem")
```

In the code above, a new line of text is read until the retrieved line is blank. As manipulating files might produce several errors, such as the file not being found on the disk, or an operation on the file being impossible to be completed, it is always a good idea to use exception handling via try/except blocks.

Python

```python
try:
    f = open("numbers.txt", "w")
    f.write("First line\n")
    f.write("Second line\n")
    f.close()
    f = open("numbers.txt", "r")
    text = f.readline()
    while len(text)!=0:
        print(text)
        text = f.readline()
except:
    print("There was a problem")
```

The same result can be achieved by changing the condition of the loop to check whether the retrieved line of text has a length different from 0.

Another way to do this is to use the following loop:

Python

```python
try:
    f = open("numbers.txt", "w")
    f.write("First line\n")
    f.write("Second line\n")
    f.close()
    f = open("numbers.txt", "r")
    for line in f:
        print(line)
except:
    print("There was a problem")
```

This would repeat for each line in the file and display it accordingly.

Sometimes, you might want to check whether the file exists before attempting to perform an operation on it. This can be done by importing the os library and using the os.path.exists command:

Python

```python
import os
if os.path.exists("numbers.txt"):
    print("the file exists")
else:
    print("the file does not exist")
```

It is very important to close the file once it has been manipulated for a given mode.

⬤ Top tip!

When creating programs that manipulate files, if you are using a relative path in your program, ensure that both the text file (.txt) and the coding file (.py or .exe) are within the same folder. If they are not within the same folder, the program won't be able to access that file unless the absolute path is provided.

PROGRAMMING EXERCISES

1. Construct a program that checks whether a given file exists (called `name.txt`). If the file does not exist, the program asks the user what their name is, prints a personalized greeting message to them and saves the person's name into `name.txt`. If the file does exist, instead of prompting for their name, it loads the name from the file and prints the personalized greeting immediately.

2. Construct a program that uses a file to store a number to represent the number of times the program has run. Every time the program runs, it should increase the number by one and save the new value.

3. Construct programming code that generates 100 random numbers with values between 1 and 70. Store those numbers into a text file, one number per line. Call the file `numb.txt`.

4. Construct code that uses the `numb.txt` file to read the numbers, identify the number of duplicate values and delete those duplicate values from the file. Output how many numbers were deleted.

5. Construct code to append to the same file the exact number of elements that were deleted in question 4, including values from 71 to 150.

6. Construct programming code to read the text file and sort the values in ascending order using an efficient bubble sort algorithm.

7. Construct a program to read the values from the text file and identify the odd numbers. Store those numbers into a new text file.

Linking questions

1. Does database programming in SQL require computational thinking? (A3)
2. Why is an understanding of variables and their scope important for effective memory management in computer systems? (A1)
3. Is algorithmic efficiency relevant to machine learning, where large data sets are processed, and computational cost can be significant? (A4)
4. Are data structures, such as stacks and queues, applicable in networking algorithms for packet routing and load balancing? (A2)
5. How can graph theory be applied to packet distribution in networks? (Mathematics A&I HL)
6. How do graph algorithms and terminologies, such as vertices and edges, impact machine learning algorithms like network analysis? (A4, Mathematics A&I HL)
7. How can network traffic be used as an example or connection to programming algorithms? (A2)
8. How can programming algorithms be used to develop machine learning methods? (A4)

1 Consider the following code that processes an input string:

Java

```java
public static void content(String text) {
    String value = "";
    int pos = 0;
    while (pos < text.length()) {
        String letter = text.substring(pos, pos + 1);
        if (letter.equals(",")) {
            System.out.println(value);
            value = "";
        } else {
            value += letter;
        }
        pos++;
    }
    if (!value.isEmpty()) {
        System.out.println(value);
    }
}
```

Python

```python
def content(text):
    value = ""
    pos = 0
    while pos<len(text):
        letter = text[pos:pos+1]
        if letter==",":
            print(value)
            value=""
        else:
            value = value + letter
        pos = pos + 1
    if value:
        print(value)
```

a Trace the algorithm for the input value of: "car,boat,ball" by copying and completing the following table, up to the variable pos becoming 7. [4]

VALUE	POS	LETTER	LETTER = ","	OUTPUT

b Deduce the purpose of the algorithm. [3]

c The output is dependent on the exact format of the input. Identify two strings that would not generate the desired output. [2]

2　A group of friends play a round-robin tournament game of table tennis, where each person plays against each other player for 5 minutes at a time. The information from the tournament is recorded in parallel arrays (lists), NAMES and SCORES, examples of which are shown below.

When two people have their round against each other, each player records the points they win in their assigned row, in the column for the person they are playing against. For example, in the data set below, when Annabelle played against Jack, SCORES[0][3] shows that Annabelle scored 4 points, and SCORES[3][0] shows that Jack scored 8 points.

NAMES

0	Annabelle
1	Benjamin
2	Claire
3	Jack
4	Fran
5	Mark

SCORES

	0	1	2	3	4	5
0	0	3	4	4	3	5
1	5	0	3	5	3	3
2	7	5	0	4	3	5
3	8	6	4	0	5	4
4	2	1	4	5	0	2
5	2	3	2	5	4	0

a　Construct an algorithm that will declare and populate the NAMES array (list), based on the example data above. [2]

b　Identify the data type of the elements in the SCORES array (list). [1]

c　Identify the winning player in the game between Claire and Benjamin. [1]

d　Construct an algorithm that will print the names of players for every round, each player's respective scores and who the winner was. If the game was a tie, output an appropriate message. For example:

Annabelle scored 3 vs Benjamin scored 5: Benjamin won

Annabelle scored 4 vs Claire scored 7: Claire won

…
[6]

e　Construct an algorithm that will declare two new parallel arrays (lists) to keep track of a leaderboard based on net points each player has won. Perform the calculations necessary to populate these arrays. The two parallel arrays should be LeaderName and LeaderPoints. Each player's element in the LeaderPoints array should be the total of points they won minus the total of points they conceded.

For example, the first two rows using the data above would be:

LeaderName　　　　LeaderPoints

Annabelle　　　　　−5　　　　　　　(Annabelle won 19 points but conceded 24)

Benjamin　　　　　　1　　　　　　　(Benjamin won 19 points and conceded 18) [8]

f　Construct an algorithm that will sort the parallel arrays (lists) of LeaderName and LeaderPoints in descending order of LeaderPoints. [6]

g　Construct an algorithm that will save the parallel arrays (lists) of NAMES and SCORES to names.txt and scores.txt text files. [4]

3　A company has exported its sales data from a spreadsheet to a couple of text files. NAMES.txt contains a list of the names of its salespeople and SALES.txt contains a list of the total sales made by each person in the last month.

For example, the first few lines of each file may resemble the following:

NAMES.txt　　　　　SALES.txt

Amina　　　　　　　23424

Carlos　　　　　　　42549

Emily　　　　　　　52488

Hao　　　　　　　　37562

Isabella　　　　　　44770

a　Construct an algorithm that will declare two parallel arrays or lists, NAMES and SALES, open the files and load their content into the respective array or list. You may assume there is a maximum of 1000 entries in the file. [4]

b　Construct an algorithm that will use a recursive quicksort to sort the two parallel arrays or lists by SALES in descending order. [8]

c　The content of the NAMES array (list) was iterated over with a loop, and its elements added into an empty stack (element 0 was the first to be added to the stack). What can be said about the order of the NAMES that will be popped off the stack in respect to their sales? [3]

4   **a**   Define the term "queue". [2]
    b   Describe an application that uses a queue in a computer system. [2]
5   State the efficiency of the quicksort algorithm in Big O notation. [1]
6   Outline two uses of a stack in a computer system. [4]
7   Outline the differences between storing a queue in a linear form as opposed to a circular form. [4]
8   State which data type is best for storing a telephone number (e.g. 00352 661 008 990) and give two reasons. [3]
9   Arrays or linked lists can be used to implement stacks and queues.
    a   Describe the advantage of using an array to implement a stack or a queue. [1]
    b   Describe the advantage of using a linked list to implement a stack or a queue. [1]
10 The following list of numbers needs to be put into ascending order:
    3, 11, 7, 2, 4, 1, 6
    State the list that would be obtained after two iterations of a selection sort. [1]
11 Define the term "recursion". [1]
12 Construct a program to calculate the sum of numbers from 1 to n using recursion. [4]
13 State one advantage and one disadvantage of recursion vs iteration. [2]
14 Consider the code shown below.

Java
```java
public static void manipulate(int n, int[] a) {
    a[0] = 15;
}
public static void main(String[] args) {
    int[] a = {0, 1};
    manipulate(3, a);
    for(int i = 0; i<a.length; i++) {
        System.out.println(a[i]);
    }
}
```

Python
```python
def manipulate(n, a):
    a[0]= 15
a= [0,1]
manipulate(3,a)
print(a)
```

    a   State the scope of the variable n. [1]
    b   An integer array (list) called b is initialized with the values {11,12,13,14}. The procedure manipulate is called again with the parameters 14 and b. Explain why the assignment a[0]=15 in the body of the procedure changes the values stored in the array (list) b. [3]
15 Consider the following data structure:

Java
```java
int a = {1,2,3,4,5};
```

Python
```python
a = [1,2,3,4,5]
```

    a   State the name of the data structure. [1]
    b   Outline how the data value 3 can be directly accessed. [1]

B3 Object-oriented programming (OOP)

Fundamentals of OOP for a single class

Is OOP an appropriate paradigm for solving complex problems?

SYLLABUS CONTENT

By the end of this chapter, you should be able to:
- ▶ B3.1.1 Evaluate the fundamentals of OOP
- ▶ B3.1.2 Construct a design of classes, their methods and behaviour
- ▶ B3.1.4 Construct code to define classes and instantiate objects
- ▶ B3.1.5 Explain and apply the concepts of encapsulation and information hiding in OOP
- ▶ B3.1.3 Distinguish between static and non-static variables and methods

B3.1.1 Fundamentals of OOP

◆ **Object-oriented programming:** a form of programming that involves creating code for classes of objects, allowing many such objects to be created from a single code base, achieving a more modular and extensible software development process. It is like the idea of producing architectural blueprints, from which many similar houses can be constructed.

Object-oriented programming (OOP) is a paradigm in Computer Science that increases modularity by providing a new type of abstraction.

Just as you have experienced the benefits of modularity through writing functions that allow you to standardize behaviour for a given combination of input parameters, OOP lets you take this even further. It allows you not only to standardize behaviour, but also to standardize the structure of the data within your code.

OOP achieves this level of modularity by empowering you to define custom data types, known as "classes". You are no longer constrained to basic data types like integers, floats and strings; you can now craft custom variables of types such as `Person`, `Book`, `BankAccount` or `ShoppingBasket`. Similar to creating various instances of integers or strings, you can instantiate numerous instances of your classes.

When you manage existing data types like strings and integers, they come with standardized methods for setting their values and for manipulation. For example, with strings, you don't need to program custom functions to extract substrings, locate the first occurrence of a character or convert to uppercase or lowercase. These capabilities are inherent to the data type. With OOP, you tailor functionality specifically for your class, creating methods that align with the nature of the data it represents. Furthermore, similarly to using strings and integers without knowledge of their internal storage mechanisms, the internal data structure of your classes remains encapsulated, hidden behind the interface you provide as the creator of the class.

TOK

Are some types of knowledge less open to interpretation than others?

The structured nature of OOP, with its defined classes and behaviours, might suggest it is less open to interpretation than more flexible paradigms like procedural programming.

■ The advantages and disadvantages of using OOP in various programming scenarios

There are numerous advantages to using OOP in your programming, including:

- **Increased modularity:** Designing programming code around data and the functions that manipulate it can make it easier to manage large code bases. Objects can be created and modified independently of each other.

- **Code reusability:** A class, once written, can be imported into other projects and reused many times.

- **Encapsulation:** Hiding the internal mechanisms through which a class manages its internal data means that programmers only interact with the class through its well-defined interfaces, such as publicly exposed functions, and don't attempt to access the internal data directly. Programmers trust the class to know how to update its own internal data. This helps prevent unintended consequences resulting from managing data directly.

- **Scale:** By allowing increased modularity and reusability, OOP allows projects to scale in size yet remain maintainable.

- **Collaboration:** Increased modularity also increases the ease for delegating different parts of the project to different team members, allowing more people to work on the same project with ease.

It is worth acknowledging that OOP is not a perfect solution to all programming problems. There are some potential drawbacks to be aware of, including:

- **Learning curve:** OOP-related concepts, such as classes, objects and inheritance, can be difficult to understand for beginner programmers.

- **Increased complexity:** Small problems where a procedural approach would suffice can become unnecessarily complex to implement in a purely OOP approach. This complexity can also make projects more challenging to debug and maintain.

- **Overuse:** OOP is good at solving certain types of problems, but it is not a one-size-fits-all solution. Attempting to force everything to be viewed as an object of a class can result in deep inheritance hierarchies, leading to code that can be difficult to understand and maintain.

- **Overhead:** OOP will typically introduce additional overhead in time and space requirements compared to using paradigms with less abstraction.

- **Lack of optimization:** The focus of OOP is on providing abstractions to improve modularity. That comes at a cost in terms of organizing code into constructs that are more efficient for the CPU. In performance-critical applications, lower-level paradigms may be more suitable.

- **Object-centric design limitations:** OOP's focus on objects can sometimes lead to design limitations when dealing with certain problem domains. Some problems may be better modelled using alternative paradigms, such as functional programming or procedural programming.

So, while an important and valuable tool for any programmer, OOP is not a magic solution to all programming needs.

●**Common mistake**

Not thinking in objects: OOP requires a mental shift in how to approach your programming problems compared to procedural programming. It is very easy to fall back into old habits. Try to practise abstract thinking and simplify complex real-world items into classes. It can be hard to figure out what should be an object, a class or a method at times, and it will take practice to get right.

● Linking question

Is OOP necessary for all programming or just in the modelling of complex situations? (B2)

Bank accounts

To begin, study an example of how code that uses OOP may look. The following code is based on a scenario of Bank Accounts. The process of creating variables (known within OOP as "objects"), and then performing simple tasks with them, could be enacted through the following code.

Python

```python
amy = BankAccount("Amy")
brian = BankAccount("Brian")
clare = BankAccount("Clare")
# Do some transactions
amy.deposit(100)
brian.deposit(200)
clare.deposit(150)
amy.withdraw(75)
brian.deposit(75)
brian.transfer(250,clare)
# Print account info
print(amy)
print(brian)
print(clare)
```

Java

```java
class Main {
    public static void main(String[] args) {
        BankAccount amy = new BankAccount("Amy");
        BankAccount brian = new BankAccount("Brian");
        BankAccount clare = new BankAccount("Clare");
        // Do some transactions
        amy.deposit(100);
        brian.deposit(200);
        clare.deposit(150);
        amy.withdraw(75);
        brian.deposit(75);
        brian.transfer(250, clare);
        // Print account info
        System.out.println(amy);
        System.out.println(brian);
        System.out.println(clare);
    }
}
```

B3 Object-oriented programming (OOP)

Notice that, without having to know anything about how these objects manage their internal variables, you can understand the expected behaviour and reasonably estimate the output, which may resemble the following:

Account "Amy" has balance $25
Account "Brian" has balance $25
Account "Clare" has balance $400

This is OOP at work. It allows you to create data types and write functions that are attached to, and have access to, the information stored within.

B3.1.2 Designing classes, their methods and behaviour

Before writing code, it is important to introduce the idea of the UML Class diagram. "UML" (Unified Modelling Language) is the umbrella term for a series of standardized diagrams used within Computer Science. These have been established to provide consistency in the design of computing projects. One diagram within UML, the Class diagram, is used for articulating the design of an OOP Class.

A UML Class diagram looks like a table in three rows.

- **Row 1**: The Class name is specified in the top row for identification purposes.
- **Row 2**: The variables within each instance are listed in the second row, along with their data type.
- **Row 3**: The methods associated with the Class are listed in the third row, including their parameter signatures and return data type.

Compare the following tables to clarify. The left example provides a generic outline of the Class diagram, whereas the example on the right could be an implementation of the BankAccount Class.

Classname
+ field: type
+ field: type
+ field: type
+ method(type): type
+ method(type): type
+ method(type): type

BankAccount
– name: string
– balance: float
+ BankAccount(name)
+ deposit(float): void
+ withdraw(float): void
+ transfer(float, BankAccount): void

■ Template and example of a UML Class diagram

Within UML Class diagrams, a final important element to note is with respect to visibility. Notice that each element is preceded by a plus or minus sign. This indicates whether the element should be set to public (plus sign) or private (minus sign). This will be discussed further as part of B3.1.5 in the topic of encapsulation.

UML Class diagrams can also be used to depict relationships when classes are dependent on one another. This is discussed further in B3.2.4.

You are expected to be able to create UML Class diagrams for classes from code, and construct code for a Class from its UML. There are practice exercises for you to complete at the end of this chapter.

Top tip!

Use your UML diagrams. UML diagrams are your blueprints. Sketch out your Classes and their relationships before writing code. This may seem unnecessary at the start, but it is a useful habit to form early that will pay dividends when you are devising increasingly large and complex projects. As you do, start with the basic classes that form the core of your project and then expand as needed. Don't try to add everything at once as you will overcomplicate it.

B3.1.4 Coding classes and instantiating objects

■ Creating the class

Instantiation is the process of creating a specific instance of a class, which is called an "object". There are two key tasks performed as part of the instantiation process: the allocation of memory for the new object, and the execution of the constructor method.

The **constructor** is a special method whose role is to initialize a new object, with a specific focus on any instance variables within the object. In Java, the constructor is identified by a method having the same name as the class. In Python, the constructor is identified by the name `__init__()`. The constructor doesn't have a return type (technically, it is returning the initialized object).

In Java, the `this` keyword is used to refer to the current object instance of the class. It can be used to prefix any instance variable or method. It is particularly useful as a way of differentiating between instance variables and local variables that may have the same name. The `this` keyword is optional unless ambiguity exists, such as needing to differentiate between an instance variable and a parameter variable.

In Python, the `self` keyword performs the task of referring to the current object instance of the class. The `self` keyword is mandatory to prefix an instance variable or method. Additionally, `self` must be listed as the first parameter for all methods belonging to the class. When calling these methods in your code, you do not need to pass anything for that value; Python will do it for you.

To illustrate the syntax of constructing classes in Java and Python, the following will serve initially to construct the BankAccount example.

> ◆ **Instantiation:**
> the line of code that declares a new object variable based on the template code provided by a class, which then executes the constructor to initialize the object.
>
> ◆ **Constructor:**
> a special method within a class that is automatically executed during instantiation; its main task is to initialize any instance variables required before an instance of the object can be used by other code.

● Top tip!

When naming your classes, it is standard practice to use a singular noun that represents the entity the template represents. The methods (or functions) within that class should then be named as verbs, indicating the action they will perform on the objects of the class.

In addition, the naming convention dictates the following for upper- and lower-casing of names:
- **Class names:** Capitalize all words (e.g. MyClass, BankAccount)
- **Object instances:** Camel case in Java (e.g. myObject) and snake case in Python (e.g. my_object)
- **Method names:** Camel case in Java (e.g. calculateTotal) and snake case in Python (e.g. calculate_total)
- **Instance variables:** Camel case in Java and snake case in Python.

Python

```python
class BankAccount:
    def __init__(self, name):
        self.name = name # Create an instance variable "name"
        # and set it to value parameter variable "name".
        self.balance = 0.0 # Set instance variable "balance" to 0.0.
    def deposit(self, amount):
        self.balance = self.balance + amount
    def withdraw(self, amount):
        self.balance = self.balance - amount
```

```python
    def transfer(self, amount, recipient):
        self.withdraw(amount)
        recipient.deposit(amount)
    def __str__(self):
        return f"Account {self.name} has balance ${self.balance}"
```

Java

```java
public class BankAccount {
    private String name; // Create an instance variable
    private double balance; // Create an instance variable
    public BankAccount(String name) {
        this.name = name // Set instance 'name' to value of parameter 'name'
        this.balance = 0.0;
    }
    public void deposit(double amount) {
        balance = balance + amount;
    }
    public void withdraw(double amount) {
        balance = balance - amount;
    }
    public void transfer(double amount, BankAccount recipient) {
        this.withdraw(amount);
        recipient.deposit(amount);
    }
    public String toString() {
        return "Account " = this.name + " has balance $" + this.balance;
    }
}
```

■ Creating an object

Creating an array is the process of declaring and instantiating an object variable based on the class type. It is at this point that you pass any parameters required by the constructor.

The following example creates an instance of an object using the identifier name `acc`, of the type `BankAccount`. You can treat `acc` just like any other variable from that point onward.

Python

```python
# Python
acc = BankAccount("Neo")
print(acc)
```

Java

```java
public class Main {
    public static void main(String[] args) {
        BankAccount acc = new BankAccount("Neo");
        System.out.println(acc);
    }
}
```

■ Creating an array of objects

When initializing an array of objects, it is important to note that each individual object still requires its constructor function to be executed. This may require iterating over the entire array to explicitly execute the constructor on each element. Some examples based on the BankAccount scenario follow.

● Top tip!

Because arrays contain multiple objects, their names should always be a plural of the object contained within. In this case, it could be `bankAccounts` (Java's camelCase) or `bank_accounts` (Python's snake_case).

Python

```python
# Python - example 1
accounts = [
    BankAccount("Amy"),
    BankAccount("Brian"),
    BankAccount("Clare")
]
# Python - example 2
accounts = []
for i in range(0, 3):
    name = input("Name for new bank account:")
    accounts.append( BankAccount( name ) )
```

Java

```java
// Java - example using static array
BankAccount[] accounts = new BankAccount[3];
accounts[0] = new BankAccount("Amy");
accounts[1] = new BankAccount("Brian");
accounts[2] = new BankAccount("Clare");
// Java - example iterating over static array
String[] names = {"Amy", "Brian", "Clare"};
BankAccount[] accounts = new BankAccounts[3];
for (int i=0; i<accounts.length; i++) {
    accounts[i] = new BankAccount( names[i] );
}
// Java - example using ArrayList
// Remember to import java.util.ArrayList
ArrayList<BankAccount> accounts = new
ArrayList<BankAccount>();
accounts.add(new BankAccount("Amy"));
accounts.add(new BankAccount("Brian"));
accounts.add(new BankAccount("Clare"));
```

B3 Object-oriented programming (OOP)

B3.1.5 Encapsulation and information hiding in OOP

Encapsulation is the idea that programming code outside of the class should not have direct access to the data within the class. You can visualize the data as being protected by a capsule wrapped around it! The only way to permeate the capsule is through the methods the class allows.

By controlling access, encapsulation ensures that variables are only used in the manner in which they were intended, helping protect your code from invalid, error-inducing values. It also means that you can write code that uses encapsulated classes without needing to know or care how the class manages its internal state.

Successful encapsulation of your classes is fundamental to facilitating modularity in object-oriented programming.

● Linking question

How can the principles of encapsulation and information hiding (B2.5) be applied to secure network communication? (A3)

■ Access modifiers

Encapsulation is achieved through using **access modifiers**. The structure of access modifiers is different between Java and Python.

In Java, the access modifier is specified by supplying the relevant keyword in front of the variable or method definition. There are four access modifiers to know:

- **Private:** Indicates it should only be accessible by the current object.
- **Protected:** Indicates that it may be accessed by the current object, and any objects that inherit it (more on that in B3.2.1).
- **Public:** Indicates it may be accessible to any code within your program.
- **Default:** When no modifier is provided, it allows access for any object within the same Java package (as denoted by the package statement at the top of your Java file); Python does not have an equivalent of this.

In Python, access modifiers work slightly differently. They are specified through a naming convention for your variables and methods. They can be bypassed. In this sense, they are more guidelines than rules. That said, for the purposes of your course, you should avoid bypassing them.

- **Public:** The default behaviour is that variables and methods are treated as public.
- **Internal use:** The single underscore prefix (e.g. `_variable`) is used to indicate it is only for internal use within the class. While this is purely a convention, and the Python interpreter does not enforce it, most Python editors strongly hint at not using these variables by hiding them or making them less visible.
- **Name mangled:** The double underscore prefix (e.g. `__variable`) is used to instruct the Python interpreter to rename the variable or method at runtime. The name is mangled to include the class name, which makes it harder (but not impossible) to access from outside the class. For example, `__variable` in a class named `MyClass` would be mangled to `_MyClass__variable`.

This might seem like it makes a variable private, but Python doesn't have truly private variables. Name mangling was created to avoid naming conflicts, rather than to enforce strict access control. The mangled name can still be accessed from outside the class; it just requires knowledge of the name-mangling pattern Python uses.

For the purposes of your course, you can treat either the single or double underscore prefix as denoting private, but ensure you are aware of the technical subtleties involved.

■ Accessors and mutators

By setting your variables to private, the inevitable consequence is you will need to create a number of public methods through which code outside your class can interact with those variables, query their value or request they be updated.

Methods that perform these tasks are formally known as **accessors** and **mutators**. They are also often referred to as getters and setters.

For instance, if a `Person` class has variables for `name` and `age`, then there may be accessor methods `getName()` and `getAge()`, as well as mutator methods `setName()` and `setAge()`.

Crucially, the example above serves to reinforce the important role that encapsulation can play in protecting your data. You may not want it to be so easy to update a person's name in your application, and the person's age may be calculated behind the scenes using the current date and a stored date of birth, rather than just being stored as an integer that will soon drift to being out of date.

Requiring accessor and mutator methods, rather than giving external code free access to your variables, allows separation of responsibilities and keeps the class in control of what happens to its data.

> ◆ **Accessor:** a public method that allows external code to "access" the value of a private instance variable within an object; also known as "getter method" as it "gets" the value.
>
> ◆ **Mutator:** a public method that allows external code to update or mutate the value of a private instance variable within an object; also known as "setter method" as it "sets" the value.

● Top tip!

For beginner programmers, the following is recommended good practice:
- Set variables to **private** where possible. Create accessor and mutator methods for any attribute you want external code to have access to.
- Methods (or functions) should be **public** if you want external code to have access to them. If the method is an internal helper function, set it to **private**.

Study the updated code for the Bank Account scenario in Section B3.1 to see inclusion of access modifiers.

ACTIVITY

Research skills and thinking skills: Code analysis

Operation sabotage! Take a piece of OOP programming code and insert some deliberate errors into it that break the principle of encapsulation. Swap with a classmate, and refactor the code you are given to ensure proper use of encapsulation again. Discuss and compare changes with your classmate afterwards. Did you both spot all the errors and apply appropriate corrections?

> ◆ **Static:** methods and variables that belong to the class, not the individual objects. Only one copy is created that is shared with all instances in common.

B3.1.3 Static and non-static variables and methods

The term **static** is used to represent variables and methods that are associated with the class itself rather than any individual object instances.

Static variables and methods don't require an instance to be created for them to exist. They are created by the interpreter / compiler at runtime when the class is defined. This is why the `main` function in Java is defined as static, as it needs to exist and be executed before any objects have been created by the code itself.

Because statics do not depend on an object having been instantiated, it does mean that no static method may access instance variables within an object. It also means that any time an instantiated object makes use of a static variable or method, the objects are all accessing the same shared variable or method instead of their own instance of it. Consequently, should an object change the value of a static variable, that change will be visible to all other objects. You can think of a static variable as a global variable that is shared in common with all the objects of that class. Static variables come in useful when something needs to be shared across all objects within a class, or when the particular variable does not depend on an instance existing.

The term "non-static", therefore, refers to the normal instance variables you have been defining within objects up until this point. Each object creates its own unique instance of these variables so, when used by one object, it does not affect the value stored in the matching variable of another object.

When referring to static variables and methods in code, it is best practice to prefix it with the class name, for example `ClassName.variableName` (see the examples in BankAccount below).

Using a static variable to track ID values

One common scenario for using a static variable is to ensure each object of a class has a unique ID number. An example might be product numbers for a supermarket application.

```python
class Product:
    next_product_id = 0 # define a static variable
    def __init__(self, name):
        self.name = name
        self.product_id = Product.next_product_id
        Product.next_product_id += 1
    def __str__(self):
        return "Product "+str(self.product_id)+": "+self.name
if __name__ == "__main__":
    products = [
        Product("Bread"),
        Product("Milk"),
        Product("Apples"),
        Product("Icecream")
    ]
    for i in range(0, len(products)):
        print(products[i])
```

Java

```java
class Product {
    private static int nextProductID = 0; // define a static
    // variable
    private String name;
    private int productid;
    Product(String name) {
        this.name = name;
        this.productID = Product.nextProductID;
        Product.nextProductID++;
    }
    public String toString() {
        return "Product "+Integer.toString(this.productID)+":
        "+this.name;
    }
}
class Main {
    public static void main(String[] args) {
        Product[] products = new Product[4];
        products[0] = new Product("Bread");
        products[1] = new Product("Milk");
        products[2] = new Product("Apples");
        products[3] = new Product("Icecream");
        for (int i=0; i<products.length; i++) {
            System.out.println( products[i] );
        }
    }
}
```

Using a static variable to track number of items in array (Java only)

In Java, another common usage of static variables is to keep track of the number of items populated within an array. Given arrays are fixed in size, the static variable can be used to ensure you place the next item at the next empty location. This is less of an issue in Python since static arrays are not really a thing, and the list construct is dynamic in size.

Alternative approaches to this would be:

- having an `if` statement testing for null inside a loop
- using an `ArrayList`, since it is dynamically resizable.

Here is an example:

Java

```java
class Thing {
    private string name;
    Thing(String name) {
        this.name = name;
    }
    public String toString() {
        return this.name;
    }
}
class CollectionOfThings {
    private static int nextThing = 0; // static variable
    private Thing[] things;
    CollectionOfThings() {
        things = new Thing[100]; // Create an array of 100
        // null Things
        CollectionOfThings.nextThing = 0;
    }
    public void add(Thing t) {
        things[Collection.nextThing] = t;
        CollectionOfThings.nextThing++;
    }
    public void remove(Thing t) {
        boolean found = false;
        for (int i=0; i<CollectionOfThings.nextThing-1; i++) {
            if (things[i].equals(t)) {
                found = true;
            }
            if (found) {
                things[i] = things[i+1];
            }
        }
        if (found) {
            CollectionOfThings.nextThing--;
        }
    }
    public void printAll() {
        for (int i=0; i<CollectionOfThings.nextThing; i++) {
            System.out.println(things[i]);
        }
    }
}
```

Top tip!

Remember that static means one shared item for the class, not individual instances. Only use static for things that are common to all objects (like a company name), and use normal, non-static for properties specific to an instance (like an employee number). Experiment with writing code snippets to see the effect of changing members from static to non-static, and vice versa.

Linking question

In what ways can OOP (B1) be applied to database (A3) development?

B3.1 End-of-section examples

■ Bank accounts

See below for the full code for the Bank Accounts scenario, updated to illustrate initialization of an array, use of access modifiers and static with non-static variables and methods.

Notice two static variables and one static method have been implemented:

- `interest_rate`: As all bank accounts will have the same interest rate, it makes sense for this to be static. That way, it only needs updating once, and all bank accounts will automatically apply the change.

- `next_account_number`: By checking and incrementing this value every time an object is created, it can ensure that no two bank accounts have the same account number.

- `find()`: Provides functionality to search an array of BankAccounts to find one of the requested name (supplied through the parameters).

Python

```python
class BankAccount:
    interest_rate = 5.00 # Static variable
    next_account_number = 1001 # Static variable
    def __init__(self, name):
        self._name = name
        self._balance = 0
        # Use the class name as a prefix to access the static variables
        self._account_number = BankAccount.next_account_number
        BankAccount.next_account_number += 1
    def deposit(self, amount):
        self._balance += amount
    def withdraw(self, amount):
        if self._balance < amount:
            return False
        self._balance -= amount
        return True
    def transfer(self, amount, recipient):
        if self.withdraw(amount):
            recipient.deposit(amount)
            return True
        else:
            return False
```

```python
    def apply_interest(self):
        self._balance += self._balance * (BankAccount.interest_rate / 100)
    def get_balance(self):
        return self._balance
    def get_name(self):
        return self._name
    def __str__(self):
        return f"Account {self._account_number}: {self._name} has balance
${self._balance}"
    @staticmethod
    def find(accounts, name):
        for acc in accounts:
            if acc.get_name() == name:
                return acc
        return None  # No matching account found
# Example usage:
if __name__ == "__main__":
    # Initialize a list with 3 accounts
    accounts = [BankAccount("Amy"), BankAccount("Brian"), BankAccount("Clare")]
    # Perform some transactions
    accounts[0].deposit(500)
    accounts[1].deposit(500)
    accounts[2].deposit(500)
    accounts[0].transfer(150, accounts[2])
    # Apply interest to all account balances
    for acc in accounts:
        acc.apply_interest()
    # Perform transaction using a static method to search the list
    amy = BankAccount.find(accounts, "Amy")
    if amy:
        amy.deposit(42)
    # Print balances using the __str__ method
    for acc in accounts:
        print(acc)
```

Java

```java
public class BankAccount {
    private static double interestRate = 5.00; // static variable
    private static int nextAccountNumber = 1001; // static variable
    private String name;
    private double balance;
    private int accountNumber;
```

```java
    public BankAccount(String name) {
        this.name = name;
        this.balance = 0;
        // Use the class name as a prefix to access the static variables
        this.accountNumber = BankAccount.nextAccountNumber;
        BankAccount.nextAccountNumber++;
    }
    public void deposit(double amount) {
        balance += amount;
    }
    public boolean withdraw(double amount) {
        if (balance < amount) {
            return false;
        }
        balance -= amount;
        return true;
    }
    public boolean transfer(double amount, BankAccount recipient) {
        if (withdraw(amount)) {
            recipient.deposit(amount);
            return true;
        } else {
            return false;
        }
    }
    public void applyInterest() {
        // balance is instance variable, interestRate is static variable
        balance += balance * (BankAccount.interestRate/100);
    }
    public double getBalance() {
        // Since balance is private, this public function will allow external
        // code to check the balance
        return balance;
    }
    public String getName() {
        // Since name is private, this public function will allow external code
        // to get the name
        return name;
    }
    public String toString() {
        return "Account "+accountNumber+": "+name+" has balance $"+balance;
    }
    public static BankAccount find(BankAccount[] accounts, String name) {
        for (BankAccount acc : accounts) {
            if (acc.getName().equals(name)) {
                return acc;
            }
```

```
        }
        return null; // No matching account found;
    }
    public static void main(String[] args) {
        // Initialize an array with 3 accounts
        BankAccount[] accounts = new BankAccount[10];
        accounts[0] = new BankAccount("Amy");
        accounts[1] = new BankAccount("Brian");
        accounts[2] = new BankAccount("Clare");
        // Perform some transactions using array index
        accounts[0].deposit(500);
        accounts[1].deposit(500);
        accounts[2].deposit(500);
        accounts[0].transfer(150, accounts[2]);
        // Apply interest to all account balances
        for (int i=0; i<3; i++) {
            accounts[i].applyInterest();
        }
        // Perform transaction using a static function to search the array
        BankAccount amy = BankAccount.find(accounts, "Amy");
        if (amy != null) {
            amy.deposit(42);
        }
        // Print balances using the toString() function
        for (int i=0; i<3; i++) {
            System.out.println(accounts[i]);
        }
    }
}
```

■ Students and grades

Here is another complete example, this time also showing the use of objects as instance variables within other objects. In this case, each Student object contains an array of Grade objects. Study the example and identify the use of access modifiers, static and non-static variables.

Student
– gradeBoundaries : int[]
– grades : char[]
– studentName : String
– assessments : ArrayList<Assessment>
– currentGrade : char
+ Student(String)
+ addAssessment(Assessment) : void
+ getAverageScore() : double
+ toString : String

Assessment
– assessmentName : String
– score : double
+ Assessment(String, double)
+ getScore() : double
+ toString() : String

■ UML diagram of Student and Assessment Classes

Python

```python
class Assessment:
    def __init__(self, assessment_name, score):
        self._assessment_name = assessment_name
        self._score = score
    def get_score(self):
        return self._score
    def __str__(self):
        return f"{self._assessment_name}: {self._score}%"
class Student:
    _grade_boundaries = [80, 65, 50, 35, 20]
    _grades = ["A","B","C","D","E"]
    def __init__(self, student_name):
        self.student_name = student_name
        self._assessments = []
        self.current_grade = "N"  # Default to N before any grades are added
    def add_assessment(self, assessment):
        self._assessments.append(assessment)
        # Calculate new average
        average = self._get_average_score()
        # Update current grade
        self.current_grade = "N" # Start with the default
        for i in range(0, len(Student._grade_boundaries)):
            if average >= Student._grade_boundaries[i]:
                self.current_grade = Student._grades[i]
                break
    def _get_average_score(self):
        if not self._assessments:
            return 0
        total = 0
        for assessment in self._assessments:
            total += assessment.get_score()
        return total / len(self._assessments)
    def __str__(self):
        return f"Student {self.student_name} has grade {self.current_grade}"
if __name__ == "__main__":
    student = Student("Doris")
    student.add_assessment(Assessment("Test 1", 75))
    student.add_assessment(Assessment("Homework", 85))
    student.add_assessment(Assessment("Exam", 65))
    print(student)
```

Java

```java
import java.util.ArrayList;
class Assessment {
    private String assessmentName;
    private double score; // Score as a percentage
    public Assessment(String assessmentName, double score) {
        this.assessmentName = assessmentName;
        this.score = score;
    }
    public double getScore() {
        return score;
    }
    public String toString() {
        return assessmentName + ": " + score;
    }
}
class Student {
    private static final int[] gradeBoundaries = { 80, 65, 50, 35, 20 };
    // Represents A, B, C, D, E
    private static final char[] grades = { 'A', 'B', 'C', 'D', 'E' };
    private String studentName;
    private ArrayList<Assessment> assessments;
    private char currentGrade;
    public Student(String studentName) {
        this.studentName = studentName;
        this.assessments = new ArrayList<>();
        this.currentGrade = 'N'; // Default to N before any grades are added
    }
    public void addAssessment(Assessment assessment) {
        assessments.add(assessment);
        // Calculate new average
        double average = getAverageScore();
        // Update current grade
        currentGrade = 'N'; // Start with the default
        for (int i = 0; i < Student.gradeBoundaries.length; i++) {
            if (average >= Student.gradeBoundaries[i]) {
                currentGrade = Student.grades[i];
                break;
            }
        }
    }

    private double getAverageScore() {
        if (assessments.isEmpty()) {
            return 0;
        }
        double sum = 0;
```

```
        for (Assessment assessment : assessments) {
            sum += assessment.getScore();
        }
        return sum / assessments.size();
    }
    @Override
    public String toString() {
        return "Student " + studentName + " has grade " + currentGrade;
    }
}
public class Main {
    public static void main(String[] args) {
        Student student = new Student("Doris");
        student.addAssessment(new Assessment("Test 1", 75));
        student.addAssessment(new Assessment("Homework", 85));
        student.addAssessment(new Assessment("Exam", 65));
        System.out.println(student);
    }
}
```

ACTIVITY

Self-management skills and thinking skills: Extend one of these sample projects

Using one of the sample projects provided as a starting point, add methods and variables to provide supplemental functionality to the project. Create a checklist of skills you want to add to the project, perhaps including the following suggestions:

- Reading and writing data to files so data is not lost between program execution.
- Adding a console user interface to provide interactivity and the capacity to use the program to perform different tasks.
- Using a combination of static arrays and dynamic lists, as well as static and non-static OOP methods and variables.

REVIEW QUESTIONS

1 Which of the following is NOT an advantage of using OOP?

   a Reusability of code

   b Easy to debug

   c Improved performance in all scenarios

   d Encapsulation of data

2 What does abstraction in OOP help with?

   a Removing all bugs from an application

   b Hiding complex implementations behind simpler interfaces

   c Decreasing the use of memory

   d Making code public to all classes

3   In UML Class diagrams, there is a three-row box used to represent a Class. What does the second row contain?

  a   Class name

  b   Methods

  c   Properties

  d   Statics

4   Which of the following is true about methods in a Class diagram?

  a   They are depicted with a minus sign (–) for private methods

  b   They cannot accept parameters

  c   They must be static

  d   They are optional

5   Which statement is true about static methods in Java?

  a   They can be called on instances of a Class

  b   They are called on the Class itself, not the instance

  c   They can directly access and modify instance variables

  d   They must return a value

6   What is a non-static variable also known as?

  a   Class variable

  b   Local variable

  c   Global variable

  d   Instance variable

7   What is the purpose of a constructor in a Class?

  a   To declare variables

  b   To initialize an object

  c   To clean up resources

  d   To return data

8   Which of the following declarations correctly creates an array of objects in Java?

  a   `ClassName[] arrayName = new ClassName[5];`

  b   `ClassName arrayName[] = new ClassName(5);`

  c   `ClassName arrayName = new ClassName[5];`

  d   `ClassName[] arrayName = new ClassName();`

9   Which of the following best describes encapsulation?

  a   Storing data in public fields

  b   Combining data and methods that operate on the data into a single unit or Class

  c   Dividing code into various functions

  d   Making all methods static

10   What are access modifiers used in OOP for?

  a   To define how variables can be modified

  b   To name methods and variables

  c   To indicate static methods only

  d   To control the visibility of Class members

11   Describe one disadvantage of using OOP.

12   Explain how encapsulation can benefit a software project.

13   Explain why a static method cannot access non-static fields or methods.

14   Explain the role of the new keyword in object creation.

15   Describe an example of how private access modifiers contribute to information hiding.

1 Library system

Create a simple library system where each book can be either available or borrowed. Implement methods to manage the state of each book and track the total count of books in the library.

Java

```java
class Book {
    private static int bookCount = 0;
    private String title;
    private boolean isBorrowed;
    public Book(String title) {
        this.title = title;
        this.isBorrowed = false;
        bookCount++;
    }
    public void borrow() {
        if (!isBorrowed) {
            isBorrowed = true;
            System.out.println(title + " has been borrowed.");
        } else {
            System.out.println(title + " is already borrowed.");
        }
    }
    public void returnBook() {
        // Implement logic to mark the book as not borrowed
    }
    public static int getBookCount() {
        return bookCount;
    }
    public String toString() {
        return title + " - " + (isBorrowed ? "Borrowed" : "Available");
    }
}
public class Library {
    public static void main(String[] args) {
        Book[] books = new Book[5];
        books[0] = new Book("Java Fundamentals");
        books[1] = new Book("The Art of Computer Programming");
        // Add more books and implement borrowing logic
    }
}
```

a Complete the returnBook method.

b Instantiate more books and simulate borrowing and returning books.

c Print the status of all books and the total book count.

2 Simple inventory system

Create a basic inventory management system for a store. Each product has an ID, name, price and quantity. Implement functionality to add products, update inventory quantity and list all products.

Java

```java
class Product {
    private static int nextProductId = 100;
    private int productId;
    private String name;
    private double price;
    private int quantity;
    public Product(String name, double price, int quantity) {
        this.productId = nextProductId++;
        this.name = name;
        this.price = price;
        this.quantity = quantity;
    }
    public void updateQuantity(int amount) {
        // Implement logic to update product quantity
    }
    @Override
    public String toString() {
        return "Product{" +
                "productId=" + productId +
                ", name='" + name + '\'' +
                ", price=" + price +
                ", quantity=" + quantity +
                "}";
    }
}
class Inventory {
    private Product[] products;
    private int size;
    public Inventory(int capacity) {
        products = new Product[capacity];
        size = 0;
    }
    public boolean addProduct(Product product) {
        if (size < products.length) {
            products[size] = product;
            size++;
            return true;
        }
        return false;
    }
```

```
    public void listProducts() {
        for (Product product : products) {
            if (product != null) {
                System.out.println(product);
            }
        }
    }
}
public class Main {
    public static void main(String[] args) {
        Inventory inventory = new Inventory(100);
        inventory.addProduct(new Product("Laptop", 999.99, 10));
        inventory.addProduct(new Product("Smartphone", 499.99, 20));
        // Update quantities and list inventory

    }
}
```

a   Implement the updateQuantity method in the Product class to adjust the stock of a product.

b   Test adding products, updating quantities and listing all products to ensure the inventory displays correctly.

B3.2 Fundamentals of OOP for multiple classes (HL)

By the end of this chapter, you should be able to:
▶ B3.2.1 Explain and apply the concept of inheritance in OOP to promote code reusability
▶ B3.2.2 Construct code to model polymorphism and its various forms, such as method overriding
▶ B3.2.3 Explain the concept of abstraction in OOP
▶ B3.2.4 Explain the role of composition and aggregation in class relationships
▶ B3.2.5 Explain commonly used design patterns in OOP

B3.2.1 Inheritance and code reusability

TOK

How does the way that we organize or classify knowledge affect what we know?
The classification of knowledge into objects, classes and inheritance in OOP affects how problems are approached and solved.

◆ **Inheritance:** where a class takes a copy of an existing class as the starting point for all its internal methods and variables. These can then be overridden and extended upon to provide additional functionality, as required.

Drawing from biology, **inheritance** is a concept that aims to ease code reuse in complex projects. It does this by allowing construction of a class that derives (inherits) existing functionality and properties from another, existing class. Once derived, you need only apply whatever custom modifications are required. The derived class is known as a "child class" or "subclass", whereas the origin class is known as the "parent class" or "superclass".

Consider writing an OOP application for a coffee shop. The business might have a loyalty scheme requiring the storing of customer details in the system. It would likely also need to store employee information to be able to pay them. While customers and employees would have very different functions within the program, there would be some commonalities as well, such as name and contact details. Inheritance allows the programmer to put these commonalities into a parent class called `Person`, while putting the specialist functionality into the `Customer` and `Employee` classes. The common code contained within `Person` does not need to be reproduced; it is automatically available for any subclass that derives from it.

In this scenario, the `Person` class would contain the programming code responsible for any person's name, phone number, email and address. The `Customer` class inherits these basic properties and functions from `Person` and then extends upon them by adding a membership number, the points the customer has accrued and their

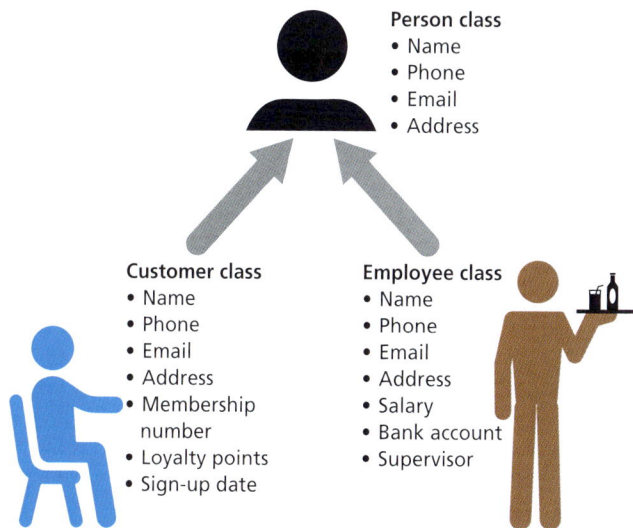

Person class
• Name
• Phone
• Email
• Address

Customer class
• Name
• Phone
• Email
• Address
• Membership number
• Loyalty points
• Sign-up date

Employee class
• Name
• Phone
• Email
• Address
• Salary
• Bank account
• Supervisor

■ Inheritance

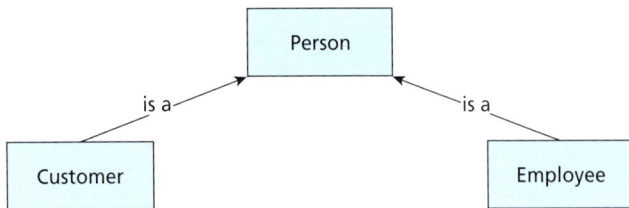

■ Inheritance using UML

sign-up date. The `Employee` class likewise inherits the basic properties and functions of `Person` and extends them by adding salary and bank-account details, along with information about an individual employee's supervisor.

Drawn using UML, this inheritance relationship is denoted via an "is-a" arrow pointing from the derived class to the parent class.

The following code blocks illustrate how to create these three classes in code. Note particularly that:

■ in Python:

  □ the invoking of the inheritance relationship occurs through the use of parenthesis in the class definition, e.g. `class Customer(Person)` creates a class Customer, inheriting from Person

  □ the constructor of the superclass must still be called; this must be the first line in the subclass constructor, achieved through `super().__init__()`

■ in Java:

  □ the invoking of the inheritance relationship occurs through the use of the `extends` keyword in the class definition, e.g. `class Customer extends Person` creates a class Customer, inheriting from Person

  □ the constructor of the superclass must still be called; this must be the first line in the subclass constructor, achieved through `super()`

  □ the protected access modifier will allow the subclasses to directly access the instance variables that have been defined within the superclass.

Python

```python
class Person:
    def __init__(self, name, phone, email, address):
        self.name = name
        self.phone = phone
        self.email = email
        self.address = address
    def __str__(self):
        return "Person: "+self.name
class Customer(Person): # The parenthesis indicates Customer inherits Person
    def __init__(self, name, phone, email, address, membership, points, signup):
        # Call the constructor of the parent class
        super().__init__(name, phone, email, address)
        # Define other instance variables specific to this child class
        self.membership = membership
        self.points = points
        self.signup = signup
    def __str__(self):
        return "Customer: "+self.name+" has "+str(self.points)+" points."
```

B3 Object-oriented programming (OOP)

```
class Employee(Person): # The parenthesis indicates Employee inherits Person
    def __init__(self, name, phone, email, address, salary, bankaccount, supervisor):
        # Call the constructor of the parent class
        super().__init__(name, phone, email, address)
        # Define other instance variables specific to this child class
        self.salary = salary
        self.bankaccount = bankaccount
        self.supervisor = supervisor
    def __str__(self):
        return "Employee: "+self.name+" earns $"+str(self.salary)
```

Top tip!

When first learning how to use dates and times in Java, you will discover a multitude of different options. New approaches have evolved as the language has matured, while the old approaches had to be retained for the language to be backwards-compatible for older projects. Since Java 8, the java.time package is the recommended best practice approach for managing dates and times.

Java

```java
import java.time.LocalDate;
class Person {
    // By using protected instead of private, these variables will be accessible
    // by classes that inherit Person. Refer to the section on access modifiers
    // for more.
    protected String name;
    protected String phone;
    protected String email;
    protected String address;
    Person(String name, String phone, String email, String address) {
        this.name = name;
        this.phone = phone;
        this.email = email;
        this.address = address;
    }
    public String toString() {
        return "Person: "+this.name;
    }
}
class Customer extends Person { // The "extends" keyword indicates inheritance
    private long membership;
    private long points;
    private LocalDate signup;
    Customer(String name, String phone, String email, String address, long
    membership, long points, LocalDate signup) {
        // Call the constructor of the parent class
```

```
        super(name, phone, email, address);
        // Initialize other instance variables
        this.membership = membership;
        this.points = points;
        this.signup = signup;
    }
    @Override
    public String toString() {
        return "Customer: "+super.name+" has "+Long.toString(this.points)+" points";
    }
}
class Employee extends Person { // The "extends" keyword indicates inheritance
    private long salary;
    private String bankaccount;
    private Person supervisor;
    Employee(String name, String phone, String email, String address, long
salary, String bankaccount, Person supervisor) {
        // Call the constructor of the parent class
        super(name, phone, email, address);
        // Initialize other instance variables
        this.salary = salary;
        this.bankaccount = bankaccount;
        this.supervisor = supervisor;
    }
    @Override
    public String toString() {
        return "Employee: "+super.name+" earns $"+Long.toString(this.salary);
    }
}
```

●Common mistake

Overusing inheritance can lead to tightly coupled code that is difficult to modify. Use inheritance sparingly – only when classes share a logical and robust "is-a" relationship. If two classes do not share enough functionality, consider alternatives such as composition.

ACTIVITY

Research skills and thinking skills: Organize a class debate around the value of inheritance. Does inheritance in object-oriented programming lead to better designed and more efficient code, or does it overly restrict and limit flexibility?

B3 Object-oriented programming (OOP)

B3.2.2 Polymorphism and method overriding

◆ **Polymorphism:**
meaning "many forms", it allows objects to exhibit different behaviours based on their specific class implementation while still adhering to a shared interface or contract.

Polymorphism refers to how related objects can perform the same task or interaction in a different way. "Polymorphism" is another term that Computer Science has taken from biology; it refers to something that can take many forms (*poly* means many and *morph* means change form).

Overriding occurs when a child class creates a property or method of the same name as the parent class, thereby overriding it.

You can see an example of polymorphism occurring in the example above. The Python `__str__()` functions and the Java `toString()` functions are overridden in the child classes of Customer and Employee. Creating main code of what follows will demonstrate that it is, in fact, the `__str__()` and `toString()` functions of the child classes that execute, rather than those in the parent classes.

If `__str__()`/`toString()` was not defined in the subclass, then the version that exists in the superclass is what would be executed.

Python

```python
from datetime import datetime
if __name__ == "__main__":
    p = Person("Jordan McFly", "555 1234", "jordan@example.com", "1885 Brown
    Estate")
    c = Customer("Skyler Serenity", "555 2345", "skyler@example.com", "1701
    Asimov Plaza", 1, 0, datetime.now())
    e = Employee("Avery Shephard", "555 3456", "avery@example.com", "1955 Lone
    Pine Mall", 75000, "123-456-888", p)
    print(p)
    print(c)
    print(e)
```

Java

```java
import java.time.LocalDate;
class Main {
    public static void main(String[] args) {
        Person p = new Person("Jordan McFly", "555 1234", "jordan@example.com",
        "1885 Brown Estate");
        Customer c = new Customer("Skyler Serenity", "555 2345", "skyler@
        example.com", "1701 Asimov Plaza", 1, 0, LocalDate.now());
        Employee e = new Employee("Avery Shephard", "555 3456",
        "avery@example.com", "1955 Lone Pine Mall", 75000, "123-456-888", p);
        System.out.println(p);
        System.out.println(c);
        System.out.println(e);
    }
}
```

These should render the following output, demonstrating the different versions of the `toString()` function are executing.

> Person: Jordan McFly
>
> Customer: Skyler Serenity has 0 points
>
> Employee: Avery Shephard earns $75000

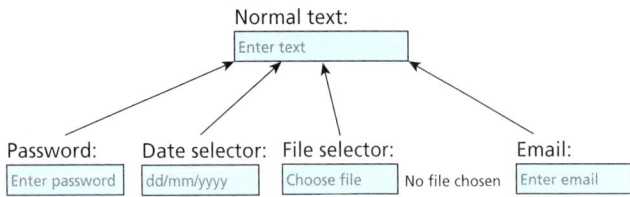

Normal text:

`Enter text`

Password: Date selector: File selector: Email:

`Enter password`   `dd/mm/yyyy`   `Choose file` `No file chosen`   `Enter email`

■ Inheritance in graphical user interfaces

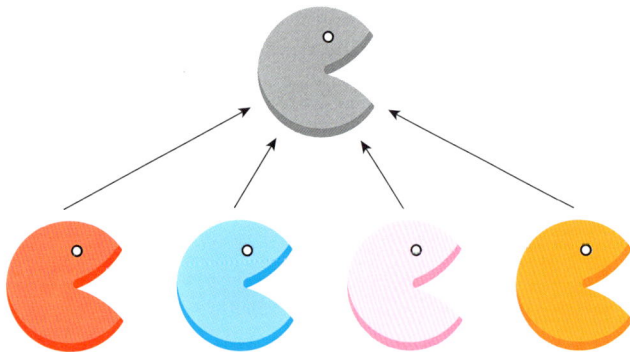

■ Inheritance in game design

Example uses

Two examples that illustrate the benefit of inheritance combined with polymorphic overriding are:

■ Consider the variety in input boxes available for graphical user interfaces. The core functionality of a text input box can be written once, and then inheritance can be used to use that functionality as the basis for more specialized input types, such as *PasswordInput*, *DateInput*, *FileInput* or *EmailInput*, where some of the original code is overridden to provide the new, specialized experience.

■ A second example is in the area of game design. A game that possesses multiple bots to play against could have one generic bot with a random move strategy. Specialized bots could then inherit this basic code and override the strategy function, or the abilities function.

Overriding default methods

◆ **Overriding:** the process of providing a different implementation of a method in a subclass, which replaces the original implementation inherited from the superclass.

Earlier in this section, you **overrode** the `toString()` / `__str__()` functions in Java and Python respectively. These are automatically called whenever the context calls for a string value from the object, such as being used by a `print()` method.

There are other default method names that are handy to know about so you can override their behaviour when appropriate. Some of these are:

■ in Java:
  □ `equals(Object obj)`: checks whether another object passed to it is "equal to" the current instance; the default implementation checks for reference equality (i.e. whether they point to the same object in memory) – overriding this method allows you to compare the contents of two objects for logical equality
  □ `hashCode()`: returns an integer hash code value for the object, which is used by hash-based collections like `HashMap` and `HashSet`; when you override `equals()`, you must also override `hashCode()` to maintain the general contract for the `hashCode()` method, which states that equal objects must have equal hash codes – see Section B4.1.6 for an explanation of what this means

■ in Python:
  □ `__eq__(self, other)`: called when the equality operator `==` is used to compare two objects; overriding it allows for custom comparison logic

B3 Object-oriented programming (OOP)

- `__hash__(self)`: returns an integer hash value for the object, and is used in hashable collections such as sets and dictionaries; if you override `__eq__`, you should also override `__hash__`, ensuring that objects that are considered equal have the same hash value – see Section B4.1.6 for an explanation of what this means

- `__lt__(self, other)`, `__le__(self, other)`, `__gt__(self, other)`, `__ge__(self, other)`: used for comparison operators <, <=, > and >= respectively; they are used by the `sorted()` function and other areas where there is a concept of an ordering of objects

- `__getitem__(self, key)`, `__setitem__(self, key, value)`, `__delitem__(self, key)`: called to retrieve, set or delete an item using the indexing syntax `obj[key]`

- `__iter__(self)` and `__next__(self)`: used to make an object iterable (usable in a FOR loop, for example); `__iter__` should return an iterator object, which is typically the object itself, and `__next__` should return the next item or raise StopIteration to end the iteration.

Refer to the Java and Python documentation for examples of implementing each of the methods above, as relevant.

B3.2.3 Abstraction and abstract classes

One common way of making use of inheritance and polymorphism is through the use of abstract classes. Abstract classes can be thought of as generic templates without any executable code of their own. They are classes that cannot be instantiated. They are designed to be extended by other classes.

You use abstract classes when you know that all your subclasses should have certain methods or fields, but the implementation of these methods is inherently specific to each subclass, such that it doesn't make logical sense to provide a default implementation.

While it doesn't provide any functionality, the abstract class provides standardization and consistency in the implementation of subclasses; the benefit being that anyone using your class hierarchy will know that certain methods are always available, and any new derived classes need to adhere to the defined contract.

As an example, consider an application that needs objects to manage the properties of various 2D geometric shapes, such as a possible computer game. It makes sense to require that all classes that implement a 2D shape have a function that returns its surface area, and another that returns its perimeter. An abstract class of Shape can be defined that stipulates these requirements, as the following example demonstrates.

Notice that, because Python and Java can rely upon the contract associated with Shape, there is no problem creating code that executes `getPerimenter()` and `getArea()` on an array containing a mix of `Rectangle` and `Circle` objects.

Java

```java
abstract class Shape{
    public abstract double getArea();
    public abstract double getPerimeter();
}
class Rectangle extends Shape {
    protected double width;
    protected double height;
    Rectangle(double width, double height) {
        this.width = width;
        this.height = height;
    }
    @Override  // Specify we are overriding the abstract method
    public double getArea() {
        return this.width * this.height;
    }
    @Override // Specify we are overriding the abstract method
    public double getPerimeter() {
        return 2 * (this.width + this.height);
    }
}
class Circle extends Shape {
    protected double radius;
    Circle(double radius) {
        this.radius = radius;
    }
    @Override
    public double getArea() {
        return Math.PI*this.radius*this.radius;
    }
    @Override
    public double getPerimeter() {
        return 2*Math.PI*this.radius;
    }
}
class Main {
    public static void main(String[] args) {
        Shape[] shapes = new Shape[4];
        shapes[0] = new Rectangle(10.0, 4.0);
        shapes[1] = new Rectangle(36.0, 7.0);
        shapes[2] = new Circle(42.0);
        shapes[3] = new Circle(10.0);
        for (int i=0; i<shapes.length; i++) {
            System.out.println( shapes[i].getArea() );
            System.out.println( shapes[i].getPerimeter() );
        }
    }
}
```

B3 Object-oriented programming (OOP)

Python

```python
from abc import ABC, abstractmethod
import math
# Shape: Abstract class in Python, inherits from ABC (Abstract Base Class)
class Shape(ABC):
    @abstractmethod
    def get_area(self):
        pass
    @abstractmethod
    def get_perimeter(self):
        pass
# Rectangle class, inherits from Shape
class Rectangle(Shape):
    def __init__(self, width, height):
        self.width = width
        self.height = height
    def get_area(self):
        return self.width * self.height
    def get_perimeter(self):
        return 2 * (self.width + self.height)
# Circle class, inherits from Shape
class Circle(Shape):
    def __init__(self, radius):
        self.radius = radius
    def get_area(self):
        return math.pi * self.radius ** 2
    def get_perimeter(self):
        return 2 * math.pi * self.radius
# Main section
if __name__ == "__main__":
    shapes = [
        Rectangle(10.0, 4.0),
        Rectangle(36.0, 7.0),
        Circle(42.0),
        Circle(10.0)
    ]
    for i in range(len(shapes)):
        print(shapes[i].get_area())
        print(shapes[i].get_perimeter())
```

● Common mistake

Confusing the role of abstract classes

It is common to misunderstand the purpose of abstraction, and to use it where a simple base class with inheritance might suffice. Use abstract classes when you have a base class that should not be instantiated itself, but has common code to share with the subclasses that are instantiated. Make sure any subclass implements all the abstract methods from the abstract superclass.

B3.2.4 Composition and aggregation

Because a class is analogous to a data type, and an object is analogous to a variable, you can quickly end up with programs where an object contains many other objects of different classes as variables within it, and this process can repeat itself into multiple layers of depth. When this occurs, these different objects are said to be related to each other and dependent on each other.

There are different ways of defining these dependent relationships. Inheritance, for example, is a type of dependent relationship where the child class requires the parent class to exist as its original source of properties and methods.

There are two other means of defining dependent relationships that we will look at now: composition and aggregation.

■ Composition

Composition is where one object is composed of one or more objects, and the composed objects cannot exist without the containing object. This creates a strong "one is part of the other" relationship, where the lifetime of the composed objects is managed by the container. This can even be referred to as a "death relationship", meaning if the whole is destroyed, its parts are destroyed as well.

Some examples of composition relationships include:

- **Car and Engine:** A Car object is composed of an Engine object. The engine is an integral part of the car. Outside of the car, it does not serve the purpose it was designed for. If the car is destroyed, the engine is as well.

- **House and Room:** A House object is composed of multiple Room objects. Rooms are part of a house; if the house is demolished, the rooms also cease to exist as functional units.

- **Computer and Components:** A Computer object is composed of CPU, Motherboard, Memory, and so on. These components are parts of a computer and do not function independently if separated.

- **Human and Organs:** A Human object is composed of a Heart, a Brain and Lungs. These organs are essential parts of a human body, and they do not function outside the body.

■ Aggregation

Aggregation is where one object contains one or more objects, but the contained objects can exist independently without the "container". Should the containing object cease to exist, the previously contained objects may still exist in their own right. In this way, the lifecycle of the contained objects is not managed by the containing object.

Some examples of aggregation relationships include:

- **University and Student:** A University contains many Student objects. If the university was to close (or once a student completes their studies), the student continues to exist even when no longer attached to the university.

- **Library and Books:** A Library contains many Book objects. The library has books, but the books can exist outside of the library as well.

- **Shopping Cart and Products:** A Shopping Cart object contains multiple Product objects. The shopping cart has products, but products are not dependent on the shopping cart for their existence.

◆ **Composition:** where objects are composed of other objects, forming a "has-a" style of relationship. The objects that comprise the internal objects cannot exist independently of the containing object.

◆ **Aggregation:** where one object "has" another object as part of it, but the two objects can exist independently of each other.

B3 Object-oriented programming (OOP)

- **Computer System and Peripheral Devices:** A Computer System object can have references to Keyboard, Monitor, Mouse, and so on. The computer system has these peripheral devices, but these devices can be used with other computer systems.
- **Airline and Airplanes:** An Airline has a fleet of Airplane objects. The airline owns airplanes, but airplanes can be sold or transferred to other airlines and continue to operate.

Sometimes the distinction between composition and aggregation can seem arbitrary and open for debate. Consider, for instance, the example of Car and Engine. In some contexts, such as at a mechanic's garage, it could be argued the engine can be configured to function outside of the car for testing purposes. This subtlety is where your understanding of the context of the problem at hand is important: what might be correct for one question or scenario may be different for another. (Note that, even in the mechanic's shop, you could argue an Engine lacks autonomy or control over its own lifecycle; it is the containing object – the mechanic's garage – that has that role in that edge case.)

■ Relationships in UML

Composition and aggregation relationships can be depicted in UML diagrams using a diamond-pointed arrow that is filled for composition, and hollow for aggregation.

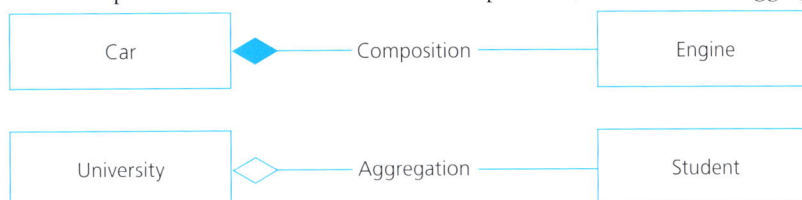

■ UML styling of composition and aggregation

Example

Consider the following scenario, where a `Person` object has an `Address` object as an instance variable.

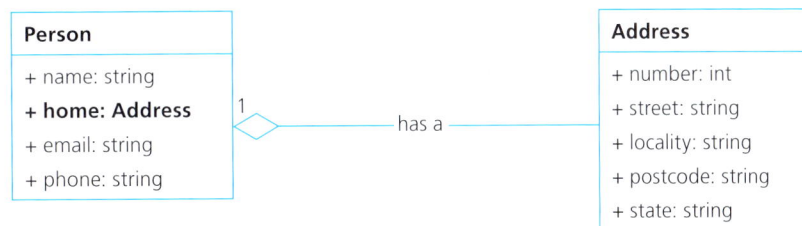

■ UML Person has an Address (aggregation)

Is this an example of composition or aggregation? Take a moment to consider before reading on.

The appropriate guiding question is: Can each exist independently of the other? While ambiguity exists here and a case could be made either way, the situation would most likely favour that of aggregation. The `Person` object, as the owning class, doesn't have control over the lifecycle of the `Address`. If a `Person` moves house, or is deleted from the application, that `Address` may continue to exist. In this scenario, an `Address` may, in fact, be used by multiple `Person` objects at once, so one `Person` ceasing to use it wouldn't have much bearing on it at all.

B3.2.5 Design patterns in OOP

● TOK

What are the implications of having, or not having, knowledge?

In OOP, knowledge of design patterns, best practices and anti-patterns significantly impacts the quality and maintainability of software.

Design patterns are common approaches to solving problems that are seen time and time again in software design. They are best practices formulated by experienced object-oriented software developers. Design patterns are useful because they provide tested, proven development paradigms, thereby improving code readability, reusability and reliability.

Some of the most commonly used design patterns that are relevant for beginners in object-oriented programming are the *singleton pattern*, the *factory pattern* and the *observer pattern*.

● Linking question

How can design patterns in OOP facilitate the architecture of scalable and maintainable machine learning models? (A4)

◼ Singleton pattern

♦ **Singleton pattern:** a class that is designed only ever to have one instance instantiated throughout the lifecycle of the program.

When using a **singleton pattern**, there will only ever be one instance of the class. That one instance will be made available globally throughout the project. It is often used for resource management, such as maintaining an open connection to a database or network location, or for settings management. In these scenarios, there is no need for more than one instance to do the job.

◼ Factory pattern

♦ **Factory pattern:** a design pattern that provides an alternative interface for creating objects in contrast to normal constructor-based instantiation.

The **factory pattern** is used for providing a *factory* that can be used for creating a range of similar objects that will adhere to a common interface.

A graphical user interface toolkit might use a factory method to create windows, buttons or other UI elements. For instance, a button factory can return buttons of different styles using a *Primary*, *Secondary* or *Alert* colour scheme, or perhaps completely different looks, such as classic vs modern.

■ Observer pattern

The **observer pattern** is used to maintain a list of dependent objects that have subscribed to it so that they receive notifications when an event occurs. The observer pattern allows the observing object to communicate changes to other objects that are interested in those changes.

This pattern is widely used in implementing distributed event handling systems such as in web pages, where you might add event listeners to handle user input (clicks, keyboard events, and so on).

■ Interface

Before looking at how to apply each pattern, it is worth noting Java examples that demonstrate the use of an interface. The interface is not in your syllabus, but a quick introduction is merited as it is the right tool for the job to demonstrate these patterns.

An interface is a construct that defines a set of methods that implementing classes must provide, without specifying *how* these methods should be implemented. It allows different classes to interact with each other through a common set of behaviours, ensuring consistency and interoperability. Interfaces are similar to, but not quite the same as, abstract classes. They differ in the following ways:

- Interfaces do not store state (no instance variables). They simply define methods that need to be implemented.

- A class can implement multiple interfaces, whereas using normal inheritance is limited to only one parent class.

- Interfaces do not have constructors as they are not concerned with the logic of implementation (no variables, remember). They are just focused on providing a list of methods that require implementation.

An example might be an interface called `School`. This interface defines methods `attendClass()`, `doHomework()`, `takeExam()`. Different students might implement these methods differently, but they must implement all of them in one form or another.

Java

```java
/* The interface designs a contract specifying methods that must be provided by
/* those classes that implement it. */
interface School {
    void attendClass();
    void doHomework();
    void takeExam();
}
class StudentA implements School {
    public void attendClass() {
        System.out.println("Student A attends class online via Zoom.");
    }
    public void doHomework() {
        System.out.println("Student A does homework in the early morning with a
        quiet background.");
    }
```

```java
    public void takeExam() {
        System.out.println("Student A prefers taking exams in a quiet
classroom.");
    }
}
class StudentB implements School {
    public void attendClass() {
        System.out.println("Student B attends class in person at the school.");
    }
    public void doHomework() {
        System.out.println("Student B does homework late at night with music
        playing.");
    }
    public void takeExam() {
        System.out.println("Student B takes exams online with open book
        resources.");
    }
}
public class Main {
    public static void main(String[] args) {
        StudentA studentA = new StudentA();
        StudentB studentB = new StudentB();
        studentA.attendClass();
        studentA.doHomework();
        studentA.takeExam();
        studentB.attendClass();
        studentB.doHomework();
        studentB.takeExam();
    }
}
```

■ Application of design patterns

Singleton example

The following code is an example of a singleton pattern that can be used to provide access to application settings that have been stored into a settings.json file. The example content of such a file follows:

```
{
    "databaseUrl": "postgresql://user:password@host:port/database",
    "timeout": 10
}
```

Note: Java users, if you plan to implement this, you will need to add the `org.json` library. Your IDE should allow you to easily add dependencies to other libraries.

Python

```python
import json
class ConfigManager:
    _instance = None
    def __new__(cls):
        if cls._instance is None:
            cls._instance = super(ConfigManager, cls).__new__(cls)
            cls._instance.load_settings()
        return cls._instance
    def load_settings(self):
        try:
            with open("settings.json", "r") as f:
                self.settings = json.load(f)
        except FileNotFoundError:
            print("Error: The settings file was not found.")
            self.settings = {}
        except json.JSONDecodeError:
            print("Error: JSON decode error in settings file.")
            self.settings = {}
    def get_setting(self, key):
        return self.settings.get(key)
if __name__ == "__main__":
    config_manager = ConfigManager() # Initialize the singleton
    database_url = config_manager.get_setting("databaseUrl")
    timeout = config_manager.get_setting("timeout")
    print(f"Database URL: {database_url}")
    print(f"Timeout: {timeout}")
```

Java

```java
import org.json.JSONObject;
import org.json.JSONTokener;
import java.io.FileInputStream;
import java.io.IOException;
import java.util.HashMap;
import java.util.Map;
public class ConfigManager {
    private static ConfigManager instance;
    private Map<String, Object> settings;
    // Private constructor to prevent instantiation
    private ConfigManager() {
        loadSettings();
    }
    // Public method to get the instance
```

```java
    public static synchronized ConfigManager getInstance() {
        if (instance == null) {
            instance = new ConfigManager();
        }
        return instance;
    }
    // Load settings from file
    private void loadSettings() {
        try (FileInputStream inputStream = new FileInputStream("settings.json")) {
            JSONTokener tokener = new JSONTokener(inputStream);
            JSONObject jsonObject = new JSONObject(tokener);
            settings = toMap(jsonObject);
        } catch (IOException e) {
            e.printStackTrace();
            settings = new HashMap<>(); // Fallback to an empty map
        }
    }
    // Helper method to convert JSONObject to Map
    private Map<String, Object> toMap(JSONObject jsonObject) {
        Map<String, Object> map = new HashMap<>();
        jsonObject.keys().forEachRemaining(key -> map.put(key, jsonObject.get
        (key)));
        return map;
    }
    // Get a setting value by key
    public Object getSetting(String key) {
        return settings.get(key);
    }
}
public class Application {
    public static void main(String[] args) {
        ConfigManager configManager = ConfigManager.getInstance(); // Initialize
        // the Singleton
        String databaseUrl = (String) configManager.getSetting("databaseUrl");
        Integer timeout = (Integer) configManager.getSetting("timeout");
        System.out.println("Database URL: " + databaseUrl);
        System.out.println("Timeout: " + timeout);
    }
}
```

B3 Object-oriented programming (OOP)

Factory example

The following code is an example of the factory pattern.

Python

```python
class Dog:
    def speak(self):
        return "Woof!"
class Cat:
    def speak(self):
        return "Meow!"
class AnimalFactory:
    @staticmethod
    def get_animal(animal_type):
        if animal_type == "dog":
            return Dog()
        elif animal_type == "cat":
            return Cat()
        return None
# Usage
if __name__ == "__main__":
    factory = AnimalFactory()
    dog = factory.get_animal("dog")
    cat = factory.get_animal("cat")
    print(dog.speak())  # Output: Woof!
    print(cat.speak())  # Output: Meow!
```

Java

```java
// Factory pattern example - Produce dogs and cats
interface Animal {
    String speak();
}
class Dog implements Animal {
    public String speak() {
        return "Woof!";
    }
}
class Cat implements Animal {
    public String speak() {
        return "Meow!";
    }
}
```

```java
class AnimalFactory {
    public static Animal getAnimal(String animalType) {
        if ("dog".equalsIgnoreCase(animalType)) {
            return new Dog();
        } else if ("cat".equalsIgnoreCase(animalType)) {
            return new Cat();
        }
        return null;  // or throw an exception
    }
}
public class Main {
    public static void main(String[] args) {
        Animal dog = AnimalFactory.getAnimal("dog");
        Animal cat = AnimalFactory.getAnimal("cat");
        System.out.println(dog.speak());  // Output: Woof!
        System.out.println(cat.speak());  // Output: Meow!
    }
}
```

Observer example

Finally, here is an example of the observer pattern at work:

Python

```python
class NotificationService:
    def __init__(self):
        self._observers = []
    def attach(self, observer):
        self._observers.append(observer)
    def detach(self, observer):
        self._observers.remove(observer)
    def notify(self, message):
        for observer in self._observers:
            observer.update(message)
class Observer:
    def update(self, message):
        print(f"Received: {message}")
# Usage
notifier = NotificationService()
observer_a = Observer()
observer_b = Observer()
notifier.attach(observer_a)
notifier.attach(observer_b)
notifier.notify("Hello World!")  # Output: Received: Hello World! from both
```

B3 Object-oriented programming (OOP)

Java

```java
// Observer pattern example - notification service
interface Observer {
    void update(String message);
}
class NotificationService {
    private List<Observer> observers = new ArrayList<>();
    public void attach(Observer observer) {
        observers.add(observer);
    }
    public void detach(Observer observer) {
        observers.remove(observer);
    }
    public void notifyObservers(String message) {
        for (Observer observer : observers) {
            observer.update(message);
        }
    }
}
class ConcreteObserver implements Observer {
    public void update(String message) {
        System.out.println("Received: " + message);
    }
}
// Usage
public class Main {
    public static void main(String[] args) {
        NotificationService notifier = new NotificationService();
        Observer observerA = new ConcreteObserver();
        Observer observerB = new ConcreteObserver();
        notifier.attach(observerA);
        notifier.attach(observerB);
        notifier.notifyObservers("Hello World!");  // Output: Received: Hello
        // World! from both
    }
}
```

REVIEW QUESTIONS

1 In UML diagrams, which symbol is used to represent inheritance between two classes?

    a A dashed line with an arrow

    b A solid line with a hollow arrow

    c A solid line with a filled arrow

    d A dashed line without any arrows

2   What keyword is used in Java to inherit a class?

   a   Implements

   b   Extends

   c   Inherits

   d   Superclass

3   Which principle of OOP is primarily used to enhance code flexibility and maintainability through interfaces?

   a   Encapsulation

   b   Inheritance

   c   Polymorphism

   d   Abstraction

4   What is required for method overriding to occur in object-oriented programming?

   a   The method must have the same name and different parameters in the subclass

   b   The method must have the same name and parameter list in the subclass, and be marked with final

   c   The method must have the same name and parameter list in the subclass

   d   The method must have a different name but the same parameters in the subclass

5   Which statement is true about abstract classes?

   a   Abstract classes can be instantiated

   b   Abstract classes cannot have any method implementations

   c   Abstract classes can contain both abstract and implemented methods

   d   All methods in an abstract class must be abstract

6   What is the purpose of declaring a class as abstract?

   a   To force a class to provide implementations of all its methods

   b   To prevent the class from being instantiated directly

   c   To ensure that the class can only contain static methods

   d   To make the class available only to other classes in the same package

7   Which of the following best describes aggregation?

   a   A strong "has-a" relationship where the lifetime of the contained objects depends on the lifetime of the container

   b   A weak "has-a" relationship where the contained objects can exist independently of the container

   c   An "is-a" relationship between two entities

   d   None of the above

8   Which scenario is an example of composition?

   a   A library owns books

   b   A university has students

   c   An apartment building includes apartments

   d   A shopping cart contains products

9   Which design pattern ensures that a class has only one instance and provides a global point of access to it?

   a   Factory pattern

   b   Singleton pattern

   c   Observer pattern

   d   Builder pattern

B3 Object-oriented programming (OOP)

10 In the observer design pattern, what is the role of the "Subject"?

    a To notify all observers about any changes

    b To keep track of all dependencies

    c To update the state of various subjects

    d To request updates from observers

11 Describe why inheritance is considered a powerful feature of OOP.

12 Discuss how polymorphism enhances software maintainability.

13 Discuss two benefits that abstract classes provide over using normal inheritance.

14 Outline an example, not based on any given in this book, that illustrates the difference between composition and aggregation.

15 Describe the factory design pattern and give an example of its use.

PROGRAMMING EXERCISES

Some exercises require you to download files for processing or performing calculations. Those files can be downloaded from:
https://github.com/paulbaumgarten/hodder-ibdp-computerscience

1 **Extend bank accounts**

Implement the bank account example provided at the end of Section B3.1, and debug any transcription errors to ensure it behaves as expected before continuing.

☐ Download the following files from the B3 folder in the Github repository:
- names.txt
- bank-transactions.txt

☐ Use the file reading techniques from B2.5 to read each file into an array of strings (one string per line of the file).

☐ Create an array of bank accounts, one for each person in your array, from the names.txt file.

☐ Process the list of transactions in bank-transactions.txt.

☐ Apply interest calculations on all accounts.

☐ Print all accounts' final balances.

Do you get the correct final balances for your account holders, as shown below?

Account 1001: Eustolia has balance $5571.3

Account 1002: Nathan has balance $9515.1

Account 1003: Milissa has balance $61.95

Account 1004: Willie has balance $1912.05

Account 1005: Hoyt has balance $4697.7

Account 1006: Alexandria has balance $2461.2

Account 1007: Clelia has balance $3311.7

Account 1008: Alpha has balance $1942.5

Account 1009: Delbert has balance $4670.4

Account 1010: Boyd has balance $547.05

Account 1011: Milton has balance $2331.0

Account 1012: Vivan has balance $1275.75

Account 1013: Constance has balance $2983.05

Account 1014: Hilma has balance $258.3

Account 1015: Irving has balance $76.65

Account 1016: Carie has balance $2654.4

Account 1017: Nicky has balance $297.15

Account 1018: Adele has balance $3287.55

Account 1019: Carlene has balance $882.0

Account 1020: Hermina has balance $2.1

Account 1021: Ayana has balance $586.95

Account 1022: Frederica has balance $261.45

Account 1023: Arianna has balance $541.8

Account 1024: Zandra has balance $725.55

Account 1025: Vina has balance $2553.6

2 Flight reservation system

You are constructing a ticket reservation system for a budget airline. This airline doesn't have seating classes (no first class or business class – everyone sits in economy), and doesn't accept seat reservations. The only thing the airline is interested in is ensuring enough seats are available on each flight for the tickets it sells.

You are taking over from another programmer who started designing your classes for you. The following is the UML they created.

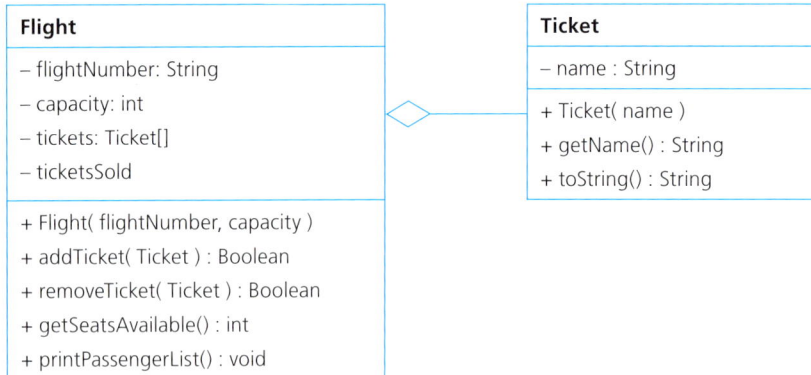

Flight
– flightNumber: String
– capacity: int
– tickets: Ticket[]
– ticketsSold
+ Flight(flightNumber, capacity)
+ addTicket(Ticket) : Boolean
+ removeTicket(Ticket) : Boolean
+ getSeatsAvailable() : int
+ printPassengerList() : void

Ticket
– name : String
+ Ticket(name)
+ getName() : String
+ toString() : String

■ UML Flight and Ticket

Create the Ticket class and Flight class in code, to adhere to the following rules:

☐ The `capacity` variable in the Flight constructor indicates the number of seats available on a given flight. Use this variable to determine the size of your tickets array.

☐ Implement `addTicket()` and `removeTicket()` to add or remove a ticket from the tickets array. `ticketsSold` should increment whenever a new ticket is added, and decrement whenever a ticket is removed. Refer to the CollectionOfThings example in Section B3.1.3 for hints on how to implement this.

☐ `getSeatsAvailable()` should just be the result of `capacity` minus `ticketsSold`.

☐ `printPassengerList()` should print a list of all the names of `tickets` for a given flight.

The following code is example main code for testing the result, and an indication of what the output should resemble.

Python

```python
if __name__ == "__main__":
    cx619 = Flight("CX 619", 280) # Cathay – HKG-SIN
    aa6914 = Flight("AA 6914", 266) # American – JFK-LHR
    ek89 = Flight("EK 89", 354) # Emirates – DBX-GVA
    jordan = Ticket("Jordan Deckard")
    cx619.addTicket(Ticket("Taylor Ripley"))
    cx619.addTicket(jordan)
    cx619.addTicket(Ticket("Casey Neo"))
    aa6914.addTicket(Ticket("Cameron Quaid"))
    aa6914.addTicket(Ticket("Phoenix Andor"))
    cx619.printPassengerList()
    print(cx619.getSeatsAvailable())
    cx619.removeTicket(jordan)
    cx619.printPassengerList()
```

Java

```java
class Main {
    public static void main(String[] args) {
        Flight cx619 = new Flight("CX 619", 280); // Cathay – HKG-SIN
        Flight aa6914 = new Flight("AA 6914", 266);
        // American – JFK-LHR
        Flight ek89 = new Flight("EK 89", 354); // Emirates – DBX-GVA
        Ticket jordan = Ticket("Jordan Deckard");
        cx619.addTicket(new Ticket("Taylor Ripley"));
        cx619.addTicket(jordan);
        cx619.addTicket(new Ticket("Casey Neo"));
        aa6914.addTicket(new Ticket("Cameron Quaid"));
        aa6914.addTicket(new Ticket("Phoenix Andor"));
        cx619.printPassengerList();
        System.out.println(cx619.getSeatsAvailable());
        cx619.removeTicket(jordan);
        cx619.printPassengerList();
        System.out.println(cx619.getSeatsAvailable());
    }
}
```

Anticipated output:

```
Flight CX 619 has passengers:
Taylor Ripley
Jordan Deckard
Casey Neo
277
Flight CX 619 has passengers:
Taylor Ripley
Casey Neo
278
```

3   **School enrolments and grade book**

Implement the students and grades example as provided in the end of Section B3.1, and debug any transcription errors to ensure it behaves as expected before continuing.

Extend the scenario to include a new class called "Course" that contains an array of students who are enrolled in it.

☐ Course should contain an `addStudent()` and `removeStudent()` method.
☐ Course should have the following additional functions:
  • `printClassList()` generates a list of all student names (in name sort order)
  • `getClassAverage()` returns the average of all student scores.

4 Library system

Create a system to manage book loans for a library.

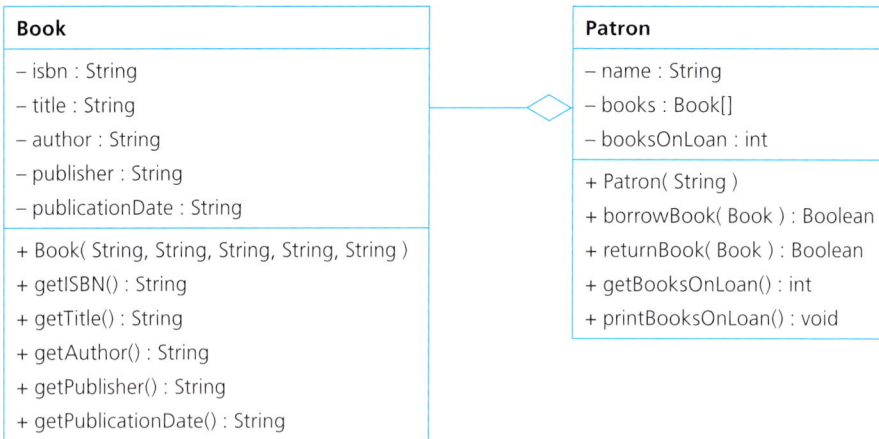

Book
– isbn : String
– title : String
– author : String
– publisher : String
– publicationDate : String
+ Book(String, String, String, String, String)
+ getISBN() : String
+ getTitle() : String
+ getAuthor() : String
+ getPublisher() : String
+ getPublicationDate() : String

Patron
– name : String
– books : Book[]
– booksOnLoan : int
+ Patron(String)
+ borrowBook(Book) : Boolean
+ returnBook(Book) : Boolean
+ getBooksOnLoan() : int
+ printBooksOnLoan() : void

■ UML Book and Patron

- ☐ Create a Book class and Patron class, as per the UML diagram.
- ☐ Download the following files from the B3 folder in the Github repository:
  - names.txt
  - books.txt or books.csv
  - library-transactions.txt
- ☐ Use the file reading techniques from Section B2.5 to read each file into an array of strings.
- ☐ Create an array of patrons, one for each name in your array from the names.txt file, and create an array of books based on the data in books.txt.
- ☐ Process the list of transactions in library-transactions.txt, subject to the following:
  - Each patron can only have a maximum of three books on loan at a time.
  - If a patron attempts to borrow a fourth book, it should be denied.
  - A book can be borrowed more than once at a time (imagine there are unlimited copies of each book).

At the end, print a summary of each patron's current books. The final list starts with:

Person Eustolia has these books:
- ■ 9780141030142 Memory Keeper's Daughter,The
- ■ 9780099387916 Birdsong
- ■ 9780006498407 Angela's Ashes:A Memoir of a Childhood

Person Nathan has these books:
- ■ 9780099419785 To Kill a Mockingbird
- ■ 9781904994497 Guinness World Records 2010
- ■ 9780140237504 Catcher in the Rye,The

Person Milissa has these books:
- ■ 9780701181840 Nigella Express
- ■ 9780099450252 Curious Incident of the Dog in the Night-time,The

Person Willie has these books:
- ■ 9780563384304 Delia's How to Cook:(Bk.1)
- ■ 9780590112895 Subtle Knife,The:His Dark Materials
- ■ 9780747581109 Harry Potter and the Half-Blood Prince

How many times did someone attempt to borrow a book over their limit? You should get 1125.

How many books are on loan at the end of the sequence? You should get 51.

5 Social-media platform (HL)

Use the following UML as the basis for creating an OOP application for a social-media platform.

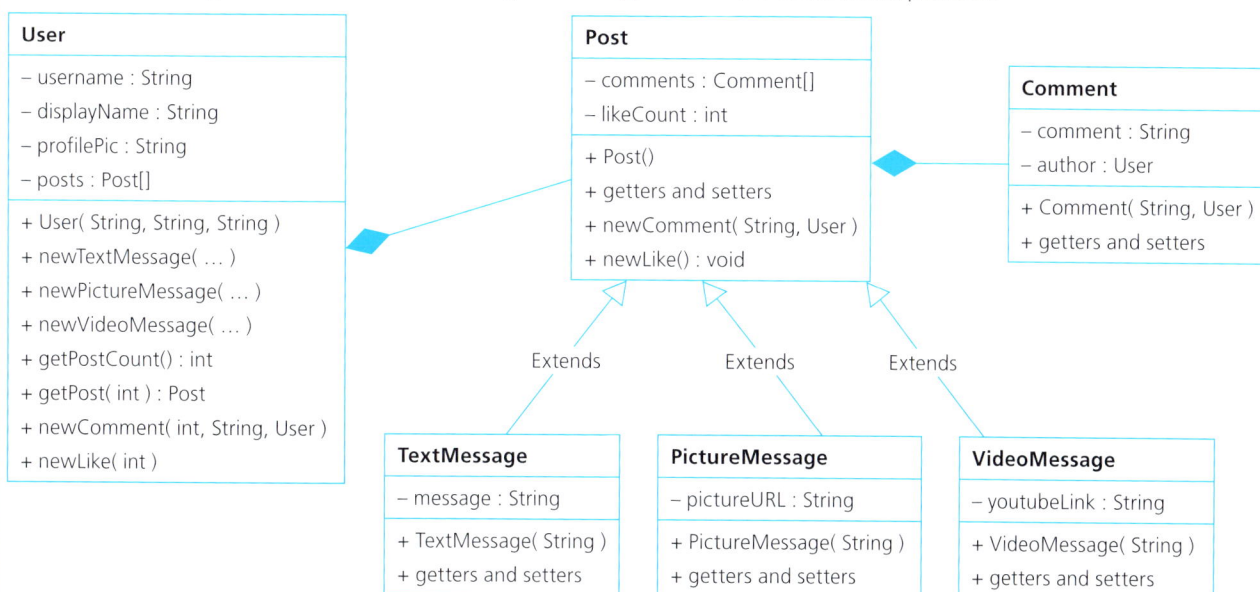

User

– username : String
– displayName : String
– profilePic : String
– posts : Post[]

+ User(String, String, String)
+ newTextMessage(…)
+ newPictureMessage(…)
+ newVideoMessage(…)
+ getPostCount() : int
+ getPost(int) : Post
+ newComment(int, String, User)
+ newLike(int)

Post

– comments : Comment[]
– likeCount : int

+ Post()
+ getters and setters
+ newComment(String, User)
+ newLike() : void

Comment

– comment : String
– author : User

+ Comment(String, User)
+ getters and setters

Extends   Extends   Extends

TextMessage

– message : String

+ TextMessage(String)
+ getters and setters

PictureMessage

– pictureURL : String

+ PictureMessage(String)
+ getters and setters

VideoMessage

– youtubeLink : String

+ VideoMessage(String)
+ getters and setters

■ UML social-media platform

For a Java implementation, you may assume the maximum number of posts per user is ten, and the maximum number of comments per post is ten.

Your final program should be able to:

☐ create a new user
☐ allow a user to create a post, via their user object's `.newTextMessage()`, `.newPictureMessage()` or `.newVideoMessage()` function
☐ allow a comment to be added to any post via the user object's `.newComment()` function, where the integer value represents the index of the relevant item in the posts array, and the `String`, `User` parameters are then passed to the `posts[i].newComment(String, User)` function.
The user object's `.newLike()` works similarly, using the integer as the index of the post, to then call the `.newLike()` on the relevant item in the posts array.

The following code is test code for your main function:

```python
Python
import random
if __name__ == "__main__":
    frodo = User("frodo", "Frodo Baggins", "frodo.png")
    gandalf = User("gandalf", "Gandalf the Grey", "gandalf.png")
    samwise = User("samwise", "Samwise Gamgee", "samwise.png")
    aragorn = User("aragorn", "Aragorn", "aragorn.png")
    # Create posts
    frodo.new_text_message("Just finished my quest to destroy the One Ring.
    What an adventure! #MissionAccomplished #RingBearer")
    frodo.new_picture_message("Pic of me after the quest! #MountDoom #Mordor")
    aragorn.new_text_message("Reunited with my love, Arwen. Forever grateful
    for her love and support. ♥ #Elessar #LoveAndDestiny")
```

```python
gandalf.new_video_message("Just having some fun with my staff and
showing off a little wizardry on the dance floor! 💃✨ #GandalfTheDancer
#WizardGrooves")
# Create comments
frodo.new_comment(0, "Mr. Frodo! I'm so proud of you! You're the bravest
hobbit I know. #TrueFriendship #HobbitHeroes", samwise)
frodo.new_comment(0, "Frodo, you have my gratitude and respect. Your
sacrifice has saved Middle-earth. #KingOfGondor #HeroicDeeds", aragorn)
frodo.new_comment(0, "Well done, Frodo! You've shown incredible strength
and determination. The world is safer because of you. #RingDestroyer
#WizardPride", gandalf)
frodo.new_comment(1, "Who's that great looking bloke next to you?",
samwise)
frodo.new_comment(1, "Amazing!", aragorn)
aragorn.new_comment(0, "Aragorn, may your love with Arwen be as enduring
as the light of the Silmarils. #LoveAndHope #FellowshipForever", frodo)
aragorn.new_comment(0, "Aragorn, you have found true love. Cherish it
always. #Shieldmaiden #HappilyEverAfter", gandalf)
gandalf.new_comment(0, "Love it! #WizardsCanDance", frodo)
gandalf.new_comment(0, "rofl", samwise)
# Create likes
frodo.new_like(1)
frodo.new_like(1)
aragorn.new_like(0)
r = random.randint(1001, 2000)
for i in range(r):
    gandalf.new_like(0)
```

Java

```java
import java.util.Random;
class Main {
    public static void main(String[] args) {
        User frodo = new User("frodo", "Frodo Baggins", "frodo.png");
        User gandalf = new User("gandalf", "Gandalf the Grey", "gandalf.png");
        User samwise = new User("samwise", "Samwise Gamgee", "samwise.png");
        User aragorn = new User("aragorn", "Aragorn", "aragorn.png");
        // Create posts
        frodo.newTextMessage("Just finished my quest to destroy the One Ring.
        What an adventure! #MissionAccomplished #RingBearer");
        frodo.newPictureMessage("Pic of me after the quest! #MountDoom
        #Mordor");
        aragorn.newTextMessage("Reunited with my love, Arwen. Forever grateful
        for her love and support. ❤ #Elessar #LoveAndDestiny");
        gandalf.newVideoMessage("Just having some fun with my staff
        and showing off a little wizardry on the dance floor! 💃✨
        #GandalfTheDancer #WizardGrooves");
```

B3 Object-oriented programming (OOP)

```
        // Create comments
        frodo.newComment(0, "Mr. Frodo! I'm so proud of you! You're the
        bravest hobbit I know. #TrueFriendship #HobbitHeroes", samwise);
        frodo.newComment(0, "Frodo, you have my gratitude and respect. Your
        sacrifice has saved Middle-earth. #KingOfGondor #HeroicDeeds", aragorn);
        frodo.newComment(0, "Well done, Frodo! You've shown incredible
        strength and determination. The world is safer because of you.
        #RingDestroyer #WizardPride", gandalf);
        frodo.newComment(1, "Who's that great looking bloke next to you?",
        samwise);
        frodo.newComment(1, "Amazing!", aragorn);
        aragorn.newComment(0, "Aragorn, may your love with Arwen
        be as enduring as the light of the Silmarils. #LoveAndHope
        #FellowshipForever", frodo);
        aragorn.newComment(0, "Aragorn, you have found true love. Cherish it
        always. #Shieldmaiden #HappilyEverAfter", gandalf);
        gandalf.newComment(0, "Love it! #WizardsCanDance", frodo);
        gandalf.newComment(0, "rofl", samwise);
        // Create likes
        frodo.newLike(1);
        frodo.newLike(1);
        aragorn.newLike(0);
        Random random = new Random();
        int randomNumber = random.nextInt(1001) + 1000;
        for (int i=0; i<randomNumber; i++) {
            gandalf.newLike(0);
        }
    }
}
```

EXAM PRACTICE QUESTIONS

1   Customer loyalty system

A chain of stores has launched a new customer loyalty program, where each dollar customers spend accrues loyalty points that can be exchanged for discounts on future purchases. An object-oriented program has been created to manage the loyalty program.

The following classes exist in the system:

☐ Customer: Represents customer information, including a list of all their purchase history items

☐ Transaction: Represents the purchase of a single item by a customer.

The UML diagram for the Customer class is provided below:

Customer	
– int	id
– String	name
– long	balance
– Transaction[]	history
– long	historyItemCount
+ Customer (int id, String name)	addTransaction(Transaction item)
+ void	spendPoints(String description, int points)
+ Boolean	getTransactionByID(int id)
+ Transaction	getTransactionByDesc (String description)
+ Transaction	getBalance()
+ long	getName()
+ String	

(Up to 10,000 items)

■ UML Customer class

    a State the relationship between Customer and Transaction.   [1]
    b Construct a simplified UML diagram showing the relationships between Customer and Transaction.   [2]
    c Outline the significance of the minus sign in front of `long balance` in the UML diagram.   [2]
    d Construct the code for the constructor of Customer.   [3]

A Transaction object has two properties: a string containing a description of the item purchased and a long integer containing the cost / value of the item in dollars (you can assume cents are not used). The following code forms the basis of the Transaction class:

Python

```python
class Transaction:
    def __init__(self, description, points):
        self.description = description
        self.points = points
    # Getters and setters for description and points
```

Java

```java
public class Transaction {
    private String description;
    private int points;
    public Transaction(String description; int points) {
        this.description = description;
        this.points = points;
    }
    // Getters and setters for description and points
}
```

Additionally, the following code describes the functionality of the `addItem(Transaction item)` function in the Customer class:

B3 Object-oriented programming (OOP)

Python

```python
def add_item(item):
    history[ self.history_item_count ] = item
    self.history_item_count += 1
    self.balance += item.get_points()
```

Java

```java
public void addItem(Transaction item) {
    history[ historyItemCount++ ] = item;
    balance += item.getPoints();
}
```

e Describe the purpose of the `historyItemCount` property. [2]

f Construct the code for the `getTransactionByDesc(String description)` function using a linear search. [4]

g To improve the efficiency of searching for transactions within each customer object, it has been decided to create a `sort()` function within Customer that will sort the transactions alphabetically by description. This algorithm will use a selection sort for the task. Construct the code for the new `sort()` function to be added to the Customer class. [6]

h Now that the history array is sorted, construct new code for `getTransactionByDesc(String description)` that will implement a binary search algorithm. [5]

i The `spendPoints()` function should first check whether the customer has enough points for the transaction and return false if not. Assuming enough points exist, it should create a new Transaction object that is added to the history, and deduct the points spent from the balance. Construct the code for the `spendPoints()` function. [6]

j The `getBalance()` function should iterate over all items in the history to calculate the correct balance, then update the value stored in the balance property appropriately, and finally return that value. Construct the code for the `getBalance()` function. [6]

k The `main()` of the program contains the following test code. State the output from this block of code. [4]

Python

```python
if __name__ == "__main__":
    t - new Transaction(250, "Special deal")
    # Create list of 10 None items to replicate an empty array
    customers = [ None for _ in range(10) ]
    customers[0] = Customer(0, "Ava")
    customers[1] = Customer(1, "Brian")
    customers[2] = Customer(2, "Cherry")
    customers[0].add_item(50, "Burger meal deal")
    customers[0].add_item(Transaction(100, "Birthday bonus"))
    customers[1].add_item(200, "Bluetooth earphones")
    customers[1].spend_points(50, "Discount for shopping")
    customers[2].spend_points(80, "Discount for shopping")
    customers[2].add_item(t)
    print( customers[0].get_balance() )
    print( customers[1].get_balance() )
    print( customers[2].get_balance() )
    print( customers[3].get_balance() )
```

Java

```java
public static void main(String[] args) {
    Transaction[] t = new Transaction(250, "Special deal");
    Customer[] customers = new Customer[10];
    customers[0] = new Customer(0, "Ava");
    customers[1] = new Customer(1, "Brian");
    customers[2] = new Customer(2, "Cherry");
    customers[0].addItem(50, "Burger meal deal");
    customers[0].addItem(new Transaction(100, "Birthday bonus"));
    customers[1].addItem(200, "Bluetooth earphones");
    customers[1].spendPoints(50, "Discount for shopping");
    customers[2].spendPoints(80, "Discount for shopping");
    customers[2].addItem(t);
    System.out.println(customers[0].getBalance());
    System.out.println(customers[1].getBalance());
    System.out.println(customers[2].getBalance());
    System.out.println(customers[3].getBalance());
}
```

2 **Animal shelter**

An animal rescue shelter requires a computer system to manage the animals under its care and the adoption process. When an animal is brought to the shelter, it is given an ID, and its species, age, health status and other relevant details are recorded in the system. When an animal is adopted, its record is updated to reflect the change in status.

Animals are identified by a unique ID, which is a combination of letters and numbers (e.g. C4T00123). This is used to track their information in the system.

A programmer created the classes AnimalShelter and Animal to model the situation above.

Python

```python
class AnimalShelter:
    def __init__(self, location, capacity):
        self.location = location
        self.animals = [ None for _ in range(capacity) ]
    def get_location(self):
        return self.location
    def get_capacity(self):
        return len(animals)
    def find_animal(self, id:str):
        # Method to find an animal by an ID in the list and return the index
class Animal:
    def __init__(self, id, species):
        # Missing code to initialize _id, _species, _age, _is_healthy
    def set_age(self, age):
        self._age = age
    def set_health_status(self, is_healthy):
        self._is_healthy = is_healthy
```

```python
    def get_id(self):
        return self._id
    def get_species(self):
        return self._species
    def get_health_status(self):
        return self._is_healthy
    def get_age(self):
        return self._age
```

Java

```java
public class AnimalShelter {
    private Animal animals[];
    private String location;
    AnimalShelter(String location, int capacity) {
        this.location = location;
        this.animals = new Animal[capacity];
    }
    String getLocation() {
        return location;
    }
    public int getCapacity() {
        return animals.length;
    }
    public int findAnimal(String id) {
        // Method to find an animal by ID in the array and return the index
    }
}
public class Animal {
    private String id;
    private String species;
    private int age;
    private boolean isHealthy;
    public Animal(String id, String species) {
        // Missing code
    }
    public void setAge(int age) {
        this.age = age;
    }
    public void setHealthStatus(boolean isHealthy) {
        this.isHealthy = isHealthy;
    }
    public String getId() {
        return id;
    }
```

```java
    public String getSpecies() {
        return species;
    }
    public boolean getHealthStatus() {
        return isHealthy;
    }
    public int getAge() {
        return age;
    }
}
```

a Explain the purpose of encapsulation in object-oriented programming and how it is applied in the classes above. [2]
b Construct the missing code for the constructor of the Animal class. [3]
c Explain the use of the keyword `this` in the `setAge` method of the Animal class. [2]
d Construct code to create an instance of the Animal class with the ID "C4T00123" and species "Cat". [2]
e Construct code to set the age of the object created above to 3 years. [2]
f Construct the method `addAnimal(Animal a)` that will add an Animal to the first empty position of the array `animals[]` in the AnimalShelter class and return the position at which it has added the animal. If the array is full and the animal cannot be added, the method should return –1. [5]

HL extension
Two subclasses, Dog and Cat, are created.

Python
```python
class Dog(Animal):
    def __init__(self, id, is_vaccinated):
        super().__init__(id, "Dog")
        self._is_vaccinated = is_vaccinated
    def get_vaccination_status(self):
        return self._is_vaccinated
class Cat(Animal):
    def __init__(self, id, is_neutered):
        super().__init__(id, "Cat")
        self._is_neutered = is_neutered
    def get_neutered_status(self):
        return self._is_neutered
```

Java
```java
public class Dog extends Animal {
    private boolean isVaccinated;
    public Dog(String id, boolean isVaccinated) {
        super(id, "Dog");
        this.isVaccinated = isVaccinated;
    }
}
```

```java
        public boolean getVaccinationStatus() {
            return isVaccinated;
        }
    }
    public class Cat extends Animal {
        private boolean isNeutered;
        public Cat(String id, boolean isNeutered) {
            super(id, "Cat");
            this.isNeutered = isNeutered;
        }

        public boolean getNeuteredStatus() {
            return isNeutered;
        }
    }
```

g Construct a UML diagram that shows the relationships between the AnimalShelter, Animal, Dog and Cat classes. Include only the class names and relationships. [3]

The Animal class needs a method that returns a description of the animal, including its ID and species.

h Construct a method `getDescription()` in the Animal class that returns a string describing the animal. [2]

The array `animals[]` in the AnimalShelter class is used to store instances of any kind of animal, including Dog and Cat.

i Justify why Animal is a suitable type for this array. [2]

The shelter has a program that recognizes the loyalty of volunteers by rewarding every tenth time someone donates time to work at the shelter with a free pet-food voucher. The method to print this voucher has been implemented in the static method `Rewards.printPetFoodVoucher()`.

(Note for clarity that the system is not keeping track of how many times each individual person volunteers; just the raw count for every tenth person who shows up – so one individual may get the voucher the first time they volunteer, or may attend for weeks without receiving a voucher!)

A `getVolunteerCount()` method has been added to the AnimalShelter class, which returns the current count of volunteers.

j Describe the necessary changes to the AnimalShelter class and any other methods to integrate the volunteer reward program into the system. [5]

The method `removeAnimal()` in the AnimalShelter class searches the array for an Animal object with a specified ID and removes it by setting that index to null. The method returns a reference to the Animal object that has been removed. You may assume that an Animal with the ID exists in the array.

k Construct the `removeAnimal(String ID)` method. [5]

3 Streamify music service

An online music and multimedia platform, Streamify, provides users with access to millions of tracks, podcasts and videos. To manage the vast collection, Streamify uses a computer system to keep track of the digital media, user preferences and playlists.

Each track is identified by a unique identifier, and contains metadata including the title, artist, duration and genre. Users can create their own playlists by adding tracks to a personalized list.

A programmer created the classes MediaLibrary and Track to model this situation.

Python

```python
class MediaLibrary:
    def __init__(self, name, capacity):
        self._name = name
        self._tracks = []
```

```python
    def get_name(self):
        return self._name
    def get_size(self):
        return len(self._tracks)
    def find_track(self, id):
        # Method to locate a track in the list by its ID
        # Not yet implemented
class Track:
    def __init__(self, id, title, artist, duration, genre):
        self._id = id
        self._title = title
        self._artist = artist
        self._duration = duration
        self._genre = genre
    # Accessor methods for each attribute
```

Java

```java
public class MediaLibrary {
    private ArrayList<Track> tracks;
    private String name;
    MediaLibrary(String name) {
        this.name = name;
        this.tracks = new ArrayList<>();
    }
    String getName() {
        return name;
    }
    public int getSize() {
        return tracks.size();
    }
    public int findTrack(String id) {
        // Method to locate a track in the array by its ID
        // Not yet implemented
    }
}
public class Track {
    private String id;
    private String title;
    private String artist;
    private int duration; // in seconds
    private String genre;
```

B3 Object-oriented programming (OOP)

```
    public Track(String id, String title, String artist, int duration, String
    genre) {
        this.id = id;
        this.title = title;
        this.artist = artist;
        this.duration = duration;
        this.genre = genre;
    }
    // Accessor methods for each attribute
}
```

a Outline why the programmer may have decided to use a list instead of an array to store the tracks within the MediaLibrary class. [2]

b Describe the relationship between the classes Track and MediaLibrary. [3]

c Discuss the importance of using the keyword `this` in the constructor of the Track class. [2]

d Construct code to create an instance of the Track class with the following details:
  – ID: TRK12345
  – Title: Oceans
  – Artist: Dive Deep
  – Duration: 215 seconds
  – Genre: Ambient [2]

e Construct a method in the MediaLibrary class that allows a user to add a Track to the library. [2]

Streamify allows users to search for media based on genre or artist.

f Construct a method `searchByGenre(String genre)` in the MediaLibrary class that returns an array of Track objects that match the genre. [4]

g Discuss the process of overriding methods of the Track class if it were to be extended by Podcast and Video classes. [4]

Two classes, Playlist and User, are now introduced.

Python

```python
class Playlist:
    def __init__(self, name):
        self.name = name
        self.track_list = []
    # Methods to add and remove tracks from the playlist
class User:
    def __init__(self, username):
        self.username = username
        self.playlists = []
    # Methods to create and manage playlists
```

Java

```java
public class Playlist {
    private String name;
    private ArrayList<Track> trackList;
    public Playlist(String name) {
        this.name = name;
        this.trackList = new ArrayList<Track>();
    }
    // Methods to add and remove tracks from the playlist
}
public class User {
    private String username;
    private ArrayList<Playlist> playlists;
    public User(String username) {
        this.username = username;
        this.playlists = new ArrayList<Playlist>();
    }
    // Methods to create and manage playlists
}
```

h   Construct a UML diagram that shows the relationships between the MediaLibrary, Track, Playlist and User classes. Include only the relationships without the attributes or methods of each class.   [4]

Streamify calculates the total duration of a playlist by summing the duration of each track in the playlist.

i   Construct a method in the Playlist class that returns the total duration of the playlist.   [2]

j   Explain why the Playlist class uses a list to store tracks instead of an array.   [2]

The User class can have multiple playlists, and the Playlist class contains multiple tracks.

k   Discuss why composition is used between the User and Playlist classes, and between the Playlist and Track classes.   [2]

To enhance user engagement, Streamify introduces a feature that rewards users with a free month of premium subscription for every 100 tracks they add to their playlists.

The method rewardUser has been added to the User class, which checks the total number of tracks across all playlists and rewards the user if they meet the criteria.

l   Without writing code, describe any changes required to the addTrack method in the Playlist class and the User class to make the new reward system work.   [5]

The removeTrack method of the Playlist class allows users to remove a track from their playlist by specifying the track's unique ID.

m   Construct the removeTrack() method for the Playlist class.   [4]

B4 Abstract data types (ADTs) (HL)

B4.1 Fundamentals of abstract data types

Which ADTs are most appropriate for different situations?

By the end of this chapter, you should be able to:
▶ B4.1.1 Explain the properties and purpose of abstract data types (ADTs) in programming
▶ B4.1.2 Evaluate linked lists
▶ B4.1.3 Construct and apply linked lists (singly, doubly and circular)
▶ B4.1.4 Explain the structures and properties of binary search trees (BST)
▶ B4.1.5 Construct and apply sets as an abstract data type (ADT)
▶ B4.1.6 Explain the core principles of abstract data types (ADTs)

B4.1.1 Properties and purposes of abstract data types

◆ **Interface:** a contract that specifies a set of methods a class must implement, without defining how these methods are implemented, serving as a blueprint that promotes modularity, flexibility and abstraction in software development. This structure allows different classes to implement the same interface in diverse ways, while ensuring they provide the functionalities declared by the interface.

◆ **Modularity:** a design principle that involves dividing a system into distinct and manageable sections or modules, each with its own specific responsibilities, which can be developed, tested and maintained independently, but function cohesively when combined.

Abstract data types (ADTs) are fundamental constructs in programming that provide a theoretical framework for data manipulation through a clearly defined **interface**. ADTs embody the concept of abstraction by hiding the complexity of their operations from the user. Users interact with an ADT through a set of well-defined operations without needing to understand the underlying implementation details. This separation of interface from implementation allows programmers to focus on the "what" of the operations rather than the "how", enhancing readability and maintainability.

Furthermore, encapsulation is integral to ADTs, safeguarding the data's integrity by restricting direct access to the underlying data structure. The internal state of an ADT is accessed and modified solely through its methods, preventing unauthorized or harmful modifications to the data structure. This protective barrier ensures that the ADT operates reliably and as expected, regardless of the external use-case scenarios.

ADTs are defined by their behaviour rather than their physical implementation, allowing them to be applied universally across different programs and systems without modification. This property makes ADTs highly reusable and adaptable to various applications, promoting code reusability and reducing development time.

ADTs also exemplify the principle of **modularity**: the practice of decomposing complex systems into discrete, manageable components. This modularity facilitates debugging and testing, by isolating issues within discrete units without affecting the entire system. It also enhances the system's scalability and understandability, making ADTs invaluable for building complex, robust applications.

● Common mistake

It is easy to get confused about the difference between interface and implementation. The interface is what operations are available, whereas the implementation is how these operations are carried out.

TOK

Areas of Knowledge (AOKs) and ADTs: Guiding questions
- How does abstraction in ADTs mirror abstraction in other disciplines?
- To what extent is modularity essential for organizing and simplifying complex systems?

ACTIVITY

Abstraction and modularity are key concepts in ADTs. In groups, investigate how abstraction and modularity are applied in their assigned AOK, such as natural sciences, arts and mathematics. Consider:
- How is abstraction used to simplify complex ideas?
- Are there risks or benefits to simplifying reality through abstraction?
- How does modularity help organize knowledge or creativity in these fields?

Present your findings and discuss as a class.

B4.1.2 Linked lists

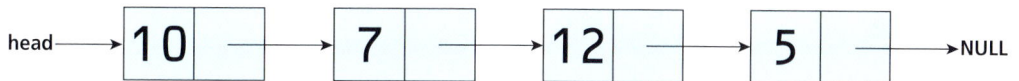

■ Linked list structure

A linked list consists of two main elements: nodes and pointers.

Nodes are the data element of the list. This could be a single piece of data, or it may be an object containing multiple data. There are two particularly important nodes: the *head* and the *tail*. The head is the first node in the linked list and the tail is the last. These help us navigate through the linked list.

Pointers are contained within the node. These point to the next node in the list (and sometimes the previous). A pointer may also be referred to as a *reference*, as it refers to the memory address of where the next node resides.

◆ **Node:** a basic unit of a data structure, e.g. a linked list or tree, which contains data and typically links to or references other nodes.

◆ **Pointer:** a variable that stores the memory address of another variable, typically used in programming to reference, or access, the location of data stored in memory.

Top tip!

■ A trail of elephants (nodes), linked by their tails and trunks (pointers)

To visualize a linked list, you might imagine it as a chain of elephants, where each elephant represents a node. The trunk of one elephant extends to the tail of the next, similar to how pointers connect one node to another in a linked list.

■ Advantages and disadvantages of linked lists

Advantages

- **Dynamic data structures:** Due to their implementation, linked lists are dynamic data structures. This means that they can grow and shrink in size as we add and remove nodes. This is unlike an array, which is a static data structure.

- **Memory utilization:** Linked lists can be more efficient with memory usage, as they do not create a reserved space in memory like an array does when it is declared.
- **Efficient insertion and deletion:** Linked lists generally outperform arrays when inserting or deleting data due to their dynamic nature.

Disadvantages

- **Sequential access:** As linked lists cannot be accessed via an index like arrays, searching a linked list requires a linear search algorithm, where you start at the head node and continue traversing until you find what you are looking for. This means that using a binary search algorithm, for example, is not possible on a linked list. For large data structures, this restriction when searching can be very time consuming when compared to accessing an array.
- **Memory utilization:** Each node requires a reference to the next (and possibly the previous) node, as well as storing the data within it. This takes up system resources in the primary memory. As linked lists can grow, they potentially can go beyond the system resources that are available, causing a heap exhaustion as the system will run out of **heap space**.

◆ **Heap space:** a region of dynamically allocated memory managed by the operating system where programs store variables and data structures that require memory allocation during runtime, allowing for flexible memory usage that can grow and shrink as needed by the application.

■ Types of linked lists

Singly linked lists

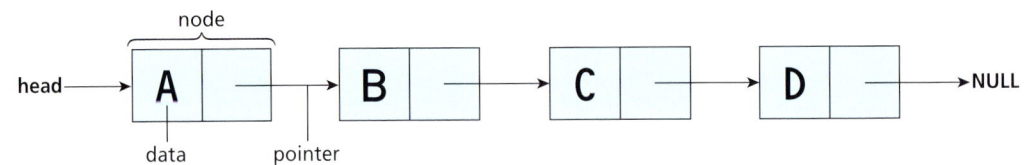

■ Singly linked list

This is the simplest of the three types. Each node contains a single pointer pointing to the next node in the list. The tail nodes contain a pointer that points to null (or none). This can be used to recognize the end of the list when traversing it.

Doubly linked lists

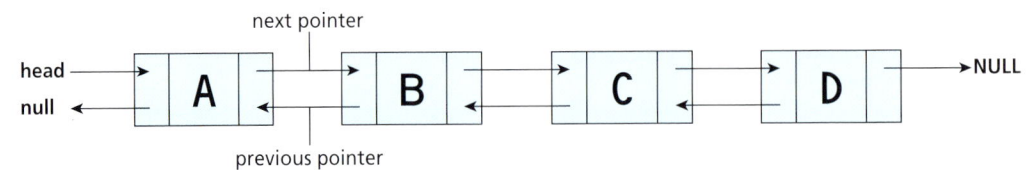

■ Doubly linked list

These differ from singly linked lists because the nodes have two pointers – one reference to the next node in the list and one to the previous. This allows for easier traversing of the list, as you can move forward and backward with ease.

Circular linked lists

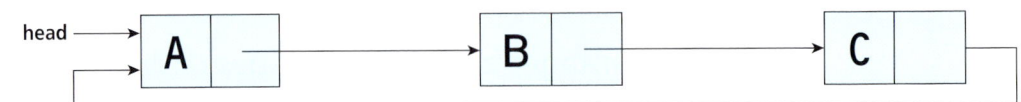

■ Circular linked list

These are similar to singly linked lists, but with one major difference: the tail node, instead of pointing to null, points back to the head node. This allows for circular, continuous traversal of the list. Doubly linked lists can also be implemented in this manner.

REVIEW QUESTIONS

1 Sketch out a singly linked list containing the numbers 1 to 5.
2 Sketch out a doubly linked list containing the names of five of your classmates.
3 Sketch out a circular linked list containing the names of five of your idols.

●Common mistake

Do not forget to label the head and to point the tail node to null (or to the head node in a circular linked list).

●Top tip!

Remember to clearly show the node, as illustrated above. It should be represented as a box, divided into either two or three sections. The pointers should be arrows clearly indicating the node they are referring to.

B4.1.3 Linked lists

■ Linked list operations

These steps all refer to the operations based on a singly linked list.

Traversal / search

This is essentially a linear traversal / search, where you start at the beginning of the linked list and move along the list, following the pointers to the nodes.

1 Start with the head pointer to find the first node in the linked list.
2 From this node, follow the pointer within the node to the next node.
3 Repeat step 2 until you find the node you are searching for or until the pointer points to null / none, which means you have reached the end of the list.

Insertion

There are three methods for inserting into a linked list. Which one you use depends on where you need to insert the node.

Inserting at the beginning:

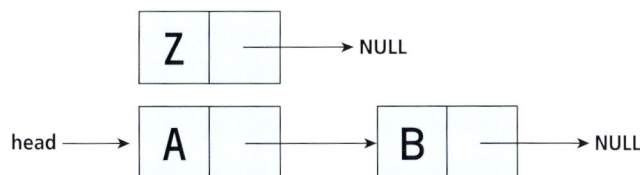

1 Create a new node.

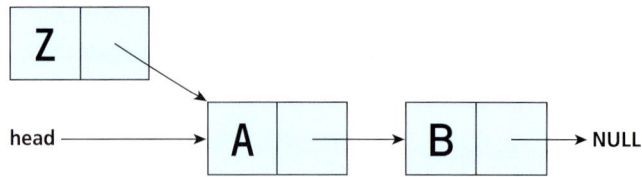

2 Point the new node to the current head node.

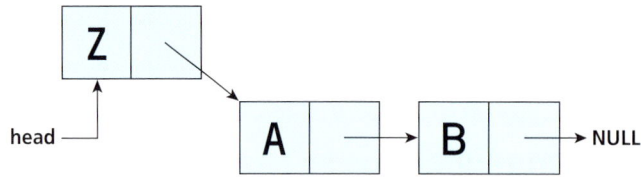

3 Update the head pointer of the linked list to the new node.

Inserting at the end:

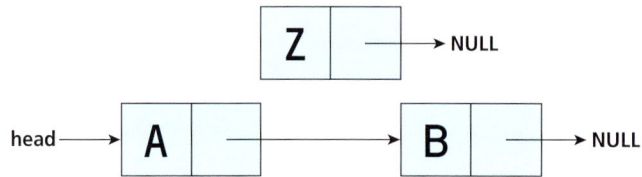

1 Create a new node.

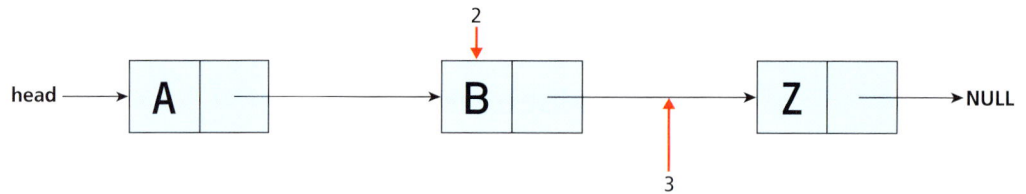

2 Find the last node by traversing the list until you find the tail node that points to null.
3 Point the current tail node to the new node (the new node pointer has not been set, so it will point to null).

Inserting in the middle:

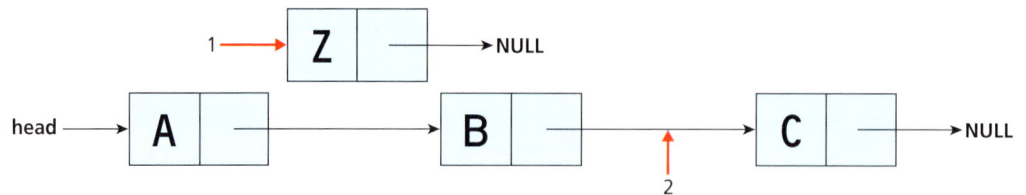

1 Create a new node.
2 Traverse the list to find the node after which you want to insert the new node.

B4 Abstract data types (ADTs) (HL)

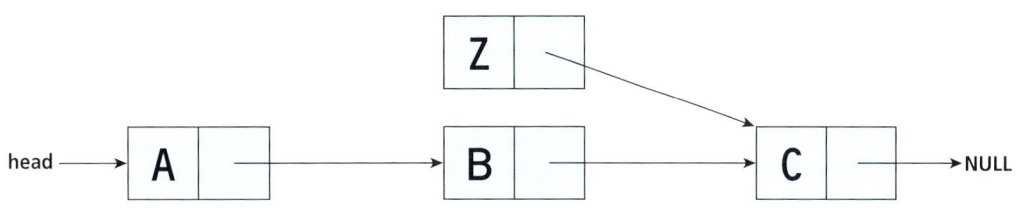

3 Set the new node's pointer to point to the newly found node's pointer (at this point, both nodes will be pointing to the next node in the list).

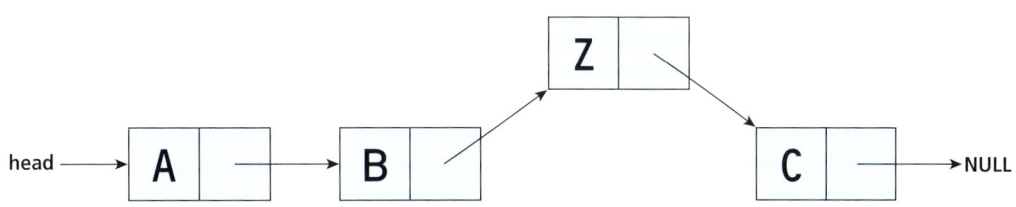

4 Set the newly found node's pointer to the new node.

⬤ Common mistake

Be careful not to complete action 4 before action 3 when inserting into the middle of the linked list. If you do this, you will lose any pointers to the second part of the list, and every node beyond the point of the insertion will be lost.

Deletion

There are also three methods for deleting from a linked list. Which one you use depends on where you need to delete the node.

Deleting the first node:

1 Check whether the list is empty. (If the head pointer is already null, the list is empty.)

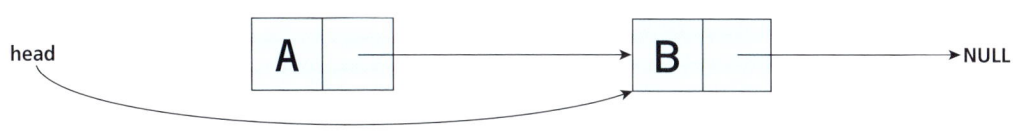

2 Set the head pointer to the new first node's pointer. (Now nothing is pointing to the original first node, which eliminates it from the list. Most high-level languages have garbage collection to realize this and clear it up without you having to delete it.)

Deleting a middle node:

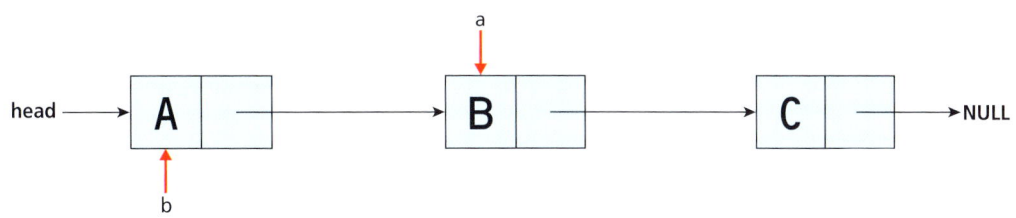

1 a Traverse the list, starting from the head, to find the node you want to delete.

b While doing this, you will need to manually keep a pointer / reference to the previously visited node.

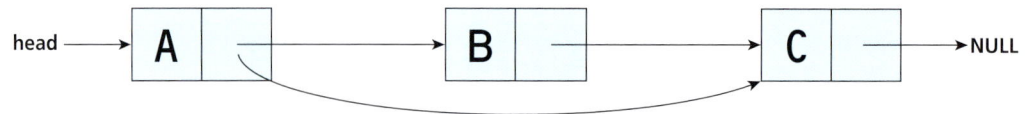

2 If you find the node you want to delete, use the previously visited node's pointer and adjust it to point to the found node's pointer. (Now nothing is pointing to the found node, which eliminates it from the list.)

Deleting the end node:

1 a This process is similar to the deletion from a middle node. Traverse the list, starting from the head, until you find the tail node pointing to null.

b While doing this, you will need to manually keep a pointer / reference to the previously visited node.

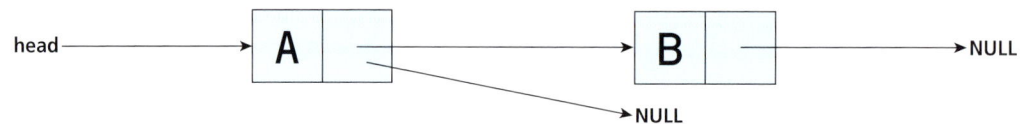

2 Adjust the previously visited node's pointer to point to null (or none).

REVIEW QUESTIONS

Draw a singly linked list with the following names: Aarav, Yuki, Sofia, Jamal and Elena.

With the aid of diagrams:

1 Show the steps to insert Nia after Sofia.

2 Show the steps to delete Elena.

3 Show the steps to add Liam at the head.

■ Construct linked lists

Initial set-up and traversal

Each linked list has a class that is the starting point when creating a linked list. This often just includes a single instance variable: the pointer to the first node (the head).

We will also create a method that traverses the list to output the contents. Take note of how the loop works. We initially get access to the first node through the head pointer, and then we traverse through the nodes until we come to the tail node that points to null or none.

B4 Abstract data types (ADTs) (HL)

Python

```python
class LinkedList:
    """ Constructor """
    def __init__(self):
        self.head = None  # Initialize the head pointer
    """Function to print the linked list"""
    def print_list(self):
        current = self.head # Set to first node
        while current != None: # Loop until no further nodes
            print(current.data, end=" -> ") # Output node data
            current = current.next # Move pointer to next node
        print("None")
```

Java

```java
public class LinkedList {
    ListNode head; // Head of the list
    // Method to print the LinkedList
    public void printList() {
        ListNode n = head; // Set to first node
        while (n != null) { // Loop until no further nodes
            System.out.print(n.data + " -> "); // Output node
            // data
            n = n.next; // Move pointer to next node
        }
        System.out.println("NULL");
    }
}
```

We then create a node class that contains data and at least one pointer. If we were creating a doubly linked list, we would have a second variable (`self.previous` for Python, or `ListNode previous` in Java).

Python

```python
class ListNode:
""" Constructor (1 parameter data with a default value of 0) """
def __init__(self, data=0):
    self.data = data
    self.next = None
```

Java

```java
class ListNode {
    int data; // This example will create a node with data of type int, but you
    // may use any type here depending on your needs
    ListNode next;
    // Constructor to create a new node
    ListNode(int d) {
        data = d;
        next = null; // Set to null
    }
}
```

Insertion

The insertion method should be created inside the LinkedList class. This should have a parameter to receive the data passed to it. From there, it should create a new node with that data and insert it into the correct position in the list. Remember that there are three different insertion methods: at the beginning, in the middle or at the end.

The insert_after_value method assumes we want to insert after a found value. This could be implemented in different ways. It could be inserted in a certain position or after a node that has already been identified and passed as a parameter.

Python

```python
def insert_at_beginning(self, data):
    new_node = ListNode(data) # Create the new node with the data given
    new_node.next = self.head # Set new node pointer to current head node
    self.head = new_node # Set head pointer to new node
        """
        Inserts a new node with 'data' after the first node found with 'target_
        value'.
        If 'target_value' is not found, does not insert the new node.
        """
def insert_after_value(self, target_value, data):
    current = self.head
    while current is not None:
        if current.data == target_value: # If we find the node to insert after
            new_node = ListNode(data) # Create a new node with provided data
            new_node.next = current.next # Set new node pointer to the same
            # pointer as the found node
            current.next = new_node # Set the found node pointer to the new
            # node
            return # We can now end the method early
        current = current.next # Otherwise move to the next node
    print(f"Node with data {target_value} not found.") # If loop ends we did
    # not find our target
```

B4 Abstract data types (ADTs) (HL)

```python
def insert_at_end(self, data):
    new_node = ListNode(data) # Create new node
    if self.head is None: # Check if list is empty
        self.head = new_node # Insert new node as head of list
    else:
        current = self.head # Get a link to the first node in the list
        while current.next != None: # Keep moving down the list
            current = current.next
    # When the above loop ends, the next pointer must be None, indicating we
    # have reached the last node
    current.next = new_node # Set pointer on current last node to the new node
```

Java

```java
public void insertAtBeginning(int data) {
    ListNode newNode = new ListNode(data); // Create a new node with the data given
    newNode.next = head; // Set new node pointer to current head node
    head = newNode; // Set head pointer to new node
}
public void insertAfter(int targetValue, int data) {
    ListNode current = head;
    // Traverse the list to find the target value
    while (current != null && current.data != targetValue) {
        current = current.next;
    }
    // At this point current will either be null (not found) or our target node
    // If the target node is found, insert the new node after it
    if (current != null) {
        ListNode newNode = new ListNode(data); // Create new node with data
        // provided
        newNode.next = current.next; // Set new node pointer to the same pointer
        // as the found node
        current.next = newNode; // Set the found node pointer to the new node
    } else {
        // If the target value is not found in the list
        System.out.println("Node with value " + targetValue + " not found.");
    }
}
public void insertAtEnd(int data) {
    ListNode newNode = new ListNode(data); // Create a new node
    if (head == null) { // Check if list is empty
        head = newNode; // Insert new node as head of list
    } else {
        ListNode last = head; // Get link to the first node in the list
        while (last.next != null) { // Keep moving down the list
            last = last.next;
        }
```

```
        // When the above loop ends, the next pointer must be null, indicating
        // we have reached the last node
        last.next = newNode; // Set pointer on current last node to the new node
    }
}
```

Deletion

Like the insertion methods, the deletion method will also reside in the LinkedList class. We assume here that all items in our list are unique. If this were not the case, these methods would delete the first occurrence. Our method has one parameter: the data we are looking for.

Our delete method must be prepared for three possible outcomes:

1 We are deleting the head node
2 We are deleting a middle node or the tail node
3 The node may not be found.

Python

```python
def delete_node(self, data):
    current = self.head # Get the head node
    prev = None
    # Case 1: If the node to be deleted is the head of the list
    if current != None and current.data == data:
        self.head = current.next  # Change head to the current head's pointer
        current = None  # Free the old head
        return
    # Search for the node to be deleted, remembering to keep track of the
    # previous node
    while current != None and current.data != data:
        prev = current
        current = current.next
    # Case 3: If the node is not found
    if current == None:
        print(f"Node with data {data} not found.")
        return
    # Case 2: Unlink the node from the list
    prev.next = current.next
    current = None
```

B4 Abstract data types (ADTs) (HL)

Java

```java
public void deleteNode(int data) {
    ListNode current = head
    prev = null;
    // Case 1: If the head node is to be deleted
    if (current != null && current.data == data) {
        head = current.next; // Changed head
        return;
    }
    // Case 2: If the node to be deleted is somewhere other than at the head
    while (current != null && current.data != key) {
        prev = current;
        current = current.next;
    }
    // Case 3: If the key is not present in the list
    if (current == null) {
        System.out.println("Node with value " + key + " not found.");
        return;
    }
    // Unlink the node from the linked list
    prev.next = current.next;
}
```

Search

The search method also resides in the LinkedList class. This is a relatively straightforward method that combines some of the techniques we have already used. The method needs a single parameter to look for and, in these examples, will return true or false, depending on whether the item was found. This could be modified to return the position in the list of the node itself, if needed.

Python

```python
def search(self, key):
    current = self.head # Get the head node
    while current != None: # Keep looping until we have run out of nodes
        if current.data == key: # If we find the node we are looking for
            return True
        current = current.next # Move to the next node
    return False  # Value not found in the list
```

Java

```java
public boolean search(int key) {
    ListNode current = head; // Get the head node
    while (current != null) { // Keep looping until we have run out of nodes
        if (current.data == key) { // If we find the node we are looking for
            return true;
        }
        current = current.next; // Move to the next node
    }
    return false; // Value not found in the list
}
```

REVIEW QUESTION

Create the LinkedList class and ListNode class. Using a test table, plan out the actions you will take to ensure that these list methods are working correctly. When you have done that, carry out the tests.

B4.1.4 Structures and properties of binary search trees

■ How binary search trees are used for data organization

A tree structure in Computer Science is used to hold data in order and is usually drawn upside down, with the root at the top and the leaves at the bottom.

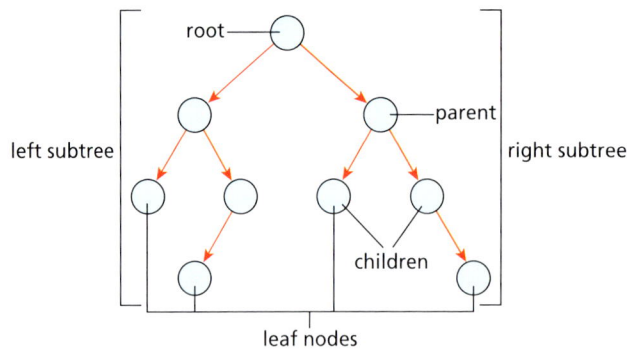

■ Tree structure and its parts

In this section, we will be focusing on a tree that follows some strict rules, which allow us to optimize search, insertion and deletion operations.

However, before we discuss the rules of binary search trees (BST), it is important to understand the terminology. The node at the top of the tree is known as the **root** node. If a node has a node attached below it, it is known as a **parent** node, with the one below being the **child** node. Each parent node can have one or two child nodes. The child node that is less than the parent goes on the left; the child node that is greater than the parent, on the right.

◆ **Root:** the topmost node from which all other nodes descend, serving as the starting point for any traversal or operation within a binary search tree.

◆ **Parent:** a node that has one or more nodes directly beneath it, connected by edges, and it directly controls these subsequent child nodes.

◆ **Child:** any node that has a direct link from a parent node positioned above it, potentially having further child nodes of its own.

◆ **Subtree:** any node, along with its descendants, functioning as a standalone binary search tree, with its node acting as the root.

◆ **Leaf:** a node that does not have any children, representing the endpoints of a binary search tree's branches.

The sub-section to the right of a node is known as the right **subtree** and to the left, the left subtree. All nodes at the bottom of the tree, without children, are known as **leaves**.

We can assume that all items within the BST are unique (there are no duplicates).

● Common mistake

Make sure you move in the correct direction when navigating through the tree:
- Move **left** if the item is smaller than the node.
- Move **right** if the item is larger than the node.

■ Tree structure and node insertion

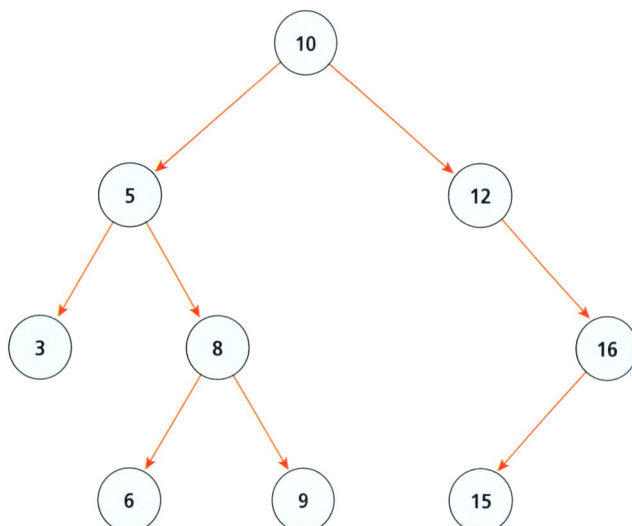

Here, you can see these two rules in place. In this example, 10 was the first node entered into the BST and set as the root. Each new node works its way through the tree until it finds a space where it can join. We cannot be completely sure what was entered next, but let us assume that it was node 5:

- Node 5: This would be compared to node 10; as it is smaller than node 10, it would join to the left of that node. This is now a child of node 10, which is the parent node of node 5. At this point, node 5 is also a leaf, but this will change as more nodes are added later.

- Node 12: This would be compared with 10 and, as it is greater, it would join to the right. This is now a child of node 10, which is the parent node of nodes 5 and 12.

- Node 3: This would be compared to node 10; as it is smaller, it would move to the left. It would then be compared with node 5 and, as it is smaller, it would be moved to the left again, where it would join the tree. This is now a child of node 5, and node 5 is the parent of node 3.

- Node 8: This is smaller than node 10, so it moves to the left; it is greater than node 5, so it moves to the right. This is now a child of node 5, and node 5 is the parent of nodes 3 and 8.

REVIEW QUESTIONS

1 Write the statements for how nodes 6, 9, 16 and 15 join the tree.

2 Sketch the resulting binary tree when the following items are entered:

    10, 15, 3, 12, 7, 1, 22, 18, 5

3 Which nodes are:

    a parents?

    b children?

    c leaves?

    d right subtree?

    e left subtree?

    f root?

■ Node search

To find a node in a BST, we follow these steps, looking for the key we are searching for:

1 **Start at the root node:** Begin your search from the root of the BST.

2 **Check for null / none:** If the current node is null (or none in Python), the search concludes without finding the key. The key is not present in the BST.

3 **Compare the node value with the key:**

    a If the current node's value matches the key, the search is successful. The key is found in the BST.

    b If the key is smaller than the current node's value, proceed to the left child of the current node.

    c If the key is larger than the current node's value, move to the right child of the current node.

4 **Repeat the process:** Continue the process from step 2 with the new current node.

■ Node traversal

Depending on the requirements, there are different ways to traverse the BST and return the data within. These are:

■ in-order traversal

■ pre-order traversal

■ post-order traversal.

To perform these operations, it is important to remember the order of actions as you move through the BST. The easiest way to do this is to remember that you *always* move left before right. After that, you just need to remember when you output the node data.

● Top tip!

The traversal name gives you a clue to where the node check is:
■ Pre-order: check before left and right (NLR)
■ Post-order: check after left and right (LRN)
■ In-order: goes in the middle (LNR).

Let us look again at the BST illustrated above.

In-order traversal (left, node, right)

We start at the root (10) and need to perform all three operations on this node. We start with the first, **left**. This takes us to node 5 with the same situation, **left** and we move to node 3. Here, we move **left** (no further node), **node** so we output 3, and then move **right** (no further node). We have now completed all three actions on this node. So, we move back to node 5. Here we have already gone left, so now we output **node**, which would be 5, and then we move **right**. We continue with these operations until all three have been completed on every node.

The final output would be:

3, 5, 6, 8, 9, 10, 12, 15, 16

You will notice the numbers are output in order. This is the main purpose of an in-order traversal – to output the nodes, sorted, in ascending order.

Pre-order traversal (node, left, right)

We carry out the same operations here, but in a different order. We start again at the root (10), but this time we output **node** value first. We then move **left** to node 5, where we output the **node** value there. We move **left** again and output **node** 3. We move **left** and **right** on node 3, completing the operations, and then move back to node 5, where we move **right** to node 8. We then continue in this manner until all three operations have been completed on every node.

The final output would be:

10, 5, 3, 8, 6, 9, 12, 16, 15

This method is useful for creating a copy of the tree or for exploring paths, as it visits the parent prior to the children.

Post-order traversal (left, right, node)

Once you have understood the first two methods, this third should not cause any problems. It follows the same idea again, but this time we visit the node last. We start at the root (10), and we go **left** to node 5. We then go **left** again to node 3, where we complete all three operations, **left**, **right** and then finally **node**, where 3 is output. We then go back to node 5 and move **right** to node 8, where we go **left** to node 6 and complete all three actions, with 6 being output. We then move back to node 8 and move **right** to node 9. We then continue in this manner until all three operations have been completed on every node.

The final output would be:

3, 6, 9, 8, 5, 15, 16, 12, 10

This method is often used for deleting nodes within the tree as it visits children before their respective parent nodes.

REVIEW QUESTIONS

1. On the BST you drew for the previous review questions, carry out the following and show the output:

   a In-order traversal

   b Pre-order traversal

   c Post-order traversal

2. What would happen if non-numerical data were input into a BST? Sketch the following BST when the data is input in this order:

   Ava, Alex, Bella, Catherine, Carlos, Brian, Aaron, Chloe

■ Node deletion

To delete a node in a BST, we take the following steps, looking for the **key** to delete and then carrying out the action based on the situation we find ourselves in:

1 **Start at the root node:** Begin the deletion process from the root of the BST.

2 **Search for the key:** Follow the algorithm from the node search.

3 **Once the node is found, determine its type:**

   a **Leaf node (no children):** if the node has no left or right child

   b **One child:** if the node has exactly one child (either left or right)

   c **Two children:** if the node has both a left and a right child.

4 **Delete the node based on its type:**

   a **Leaf node:** Simply remove the node from the tree by setting its parent's appropriate (left or right) child pointer to null.

   b **One child:** Bypass the node by linking its parent directly to its child. If the node is a left child, update the parent's left pointer; if a right child, update the parent's right pointer.

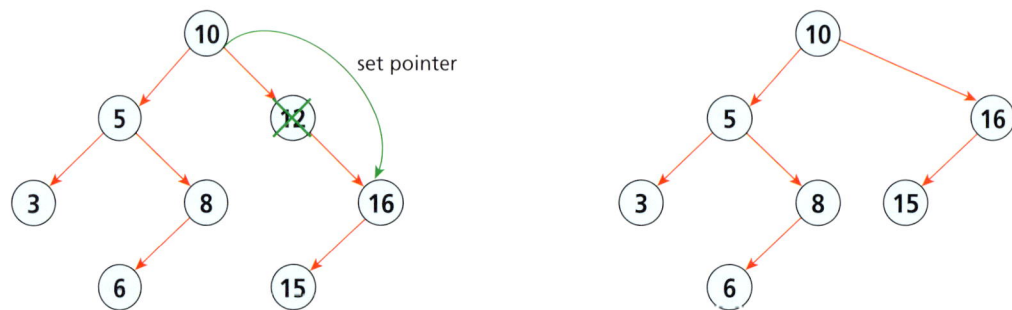

■ Deletion of node with one child

   c **Two children:**

   i Find the in-order successor (smallest value in the right subtree) or the in-order predecessor (largest value in the left subtree).

   ii Replace the value of the node to be deleted with the in-order successor's (or predecessor's) value.

   iii Delete the in-order successor (or predecessor) by repeating step 4, which now becomes a case of deleting a node with at most one child.

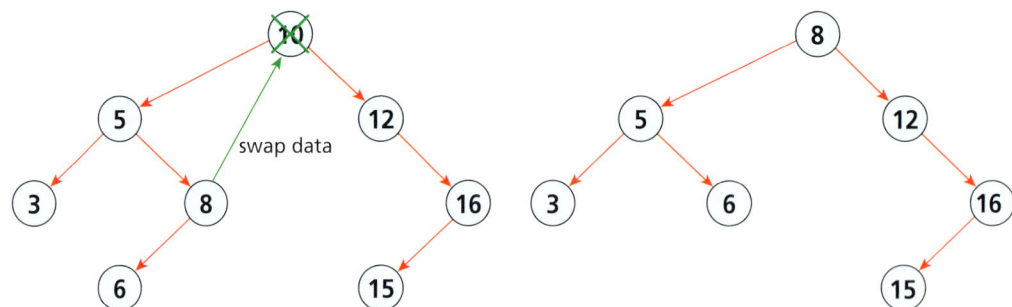

■ Deletion of node with two children

5 **Repeat the process as needed:**

   If you had to delete the in-order successor or predecessor (step 4c), repeat the deletion process for that node.

B4.1.5 Sets as an abstract data type

◆ **Unordered set:** a collection of unique elements where the elements do not have a specific order or sequence and their arrangement can vary each time they are accessed.

◆ **Mutable:** a set whose state or content can be changed after it has been created, allowing for modifications, e.g. adding, removing or altering elements within the object.

Like lists and arrays, sets can be used to store multiple values in a single variable. Sets are **unordered**, meaning that they cannot be accessed via index or key, but they are **mutable**, allowing the addition and removal of items. However, the individual items cannot be updated or change values. Sets contain only unique elements.

They are a powerful data structure when unique elements and efficient operations are crucial. They are extremely useful when you want to ensure a collection consists of only unique elements, such as when working with usernames where duplicates are not allowed. They are also extremely fast when needing to check whether an item is already part of a collection. When needing to perform mathematical set operations, such as union, intersection and difference, which are commonly used with database queries, search algorithms and data analysis, sets perform very well.

Key characteristics of sets are that:

- they are unordered
- they are mutable
- they contain unchangeable values
- they contain only unique elements.

■ Creating sets

There are two ways of creating a set in Python:

```python
# Using curly brackets
my_set = {1, 2, 3, 4, 5}
# Using the set() constructor
my_set2 = set([1, 2, 2, 3, 4, 5]) # Duplicate entries will
# automatically be removed
```

In Java, there are a number of classes that implement the Set interface. For our example purposes, we will use the HashSet. The other possibilities are LinkedHashSet and TreeSet, which will not be covered here. Using HashSet requires the import of two libraries:

```java
import java.util.HashSet;
import java.util.Set;
// Creating a HashSet of type Integer
Set<Integer> mySet = new HashSet<>();
```

■ Set methods

To add and remove elements:

Python
```python
my_set = {1, 2, 3, 4, 5}
my_set.add(6) # Add 6 to the set
my_set.remove(1) # Remove 1 from the set
```

Java
```java
Set<Integer> mySet = new HashSet<>();
my_set.add(6); // Add 6 to the set
my_set.remove(1) // Remove 1 from the set
```

To check whether elements are present in the set:

Python
```python
if 2 in my_set:
    print("2 is in the set")
else:
    print("2 is not in the set")
```

Java
```java
if (my_set.contains(2)) {
    System.out.println("2 is in the set.");
} else {
    System.out.println("2 is not in the set.");
}
```

■ Set operations

There are three main operations that are used to manipulate and compare sets. These are **union**, **intersection** and **difference**. We will show their differences using the set created below.

◆ **Set union:** the union of two sets is a new set containing all the elements that are in either of the original sets, effectively combining them without any duplicate elements.

◆ **Set intersection:** the intersection of two sets is a new set containing only the elements that are present in both of the original sets, identifying their common elements.

◆ **Set difference:** the difference between two sets is a new set containing elements that are in the first set but not in the second set, effectively subtracting the elements of the second set from the first.

Python
```python
# Define two sets
A = {1, 2, 3, 4}
B = {3, 4, 5, 6}
```

Java
```java
// Define two sets
Set<Integer> A = new HashSet<>();
A.add(1);
A.add(2);
A.add(3);
A.add(4);
Set<Integer> B = new HashSet<>();
B.add(3);
B.add(4);
B.add(5);
B.add(6);
```

B4 Abstract data types (ADTs) (HL)

Union

A union joins two sets to create one that contains all the elements from both, without any duplicates.

Python
```python
# Union
union_set = A | B   # or A.union(B)
print("Union:", union_set)
# Output
# Union: {1, 2, 3, 4, 5, 6}
```

Java
```java
// Union
Set<Integer> unionSet = new HashSet<>(A); // Creates a new
// set containing all elements from A
unionSet.addAll(B); // Performs a union join with B
System.out.println("Union: " + unionSet); // Output set contents
// Output
// Union: [1, 2, 3, 4, 5, 6]
```

Intersection

An intersection of two sets creates a new set that contains only the elements that are present in both.

Python
```python
# Intersection
intersection_set = A & B   # or A.intersection(B)
print("Intersection:", intersection_set)
# Output
# Intersection: [3, 4]
```

Java
```java
// Intersection
Set<Integer> intersectionSet = new HashSet<>(A);
intersectionSet.retainAll(B);
System.out.println("Intersection: " + intersectionSet);
// Output
// Intersection: [3, 4]
```

Difference

The difference between two sets is a set containing elements that are in the first set but not in the second.

Python

```python
# Difference
difference_set = A - B  # or A.difference(B)
print("Difference:", difference_set)
# Output
# Difference: [1, 2]
```

Java

```java
// Difference
Set<Integer> differenceSet = new HashSet<>(A);
differenceSet.removeAll(B);
System.out.println("Difference: " + differenceSet);
// Output
// Difference: [1, 2]
```

REVIEW QUESTIONS

Set A: {4, 8, 15, 16, 23}

Set B: {42, 8, 16, 60, 7}

1 Show the output if a union operation is performed.

2 Show the output if an intersection operation is performed.

3 Show the output if a difference operation is performed.

ACTIVITY

Social Skills: Collaborative group work

Social-media friend recommendation

With a partner, working in your chosen language, create two sets consisting of the following names:

A: Carlos Gomez, Yuna Kim, Dmitri Ivanov

B: Yuna Kim, Dmitri Ivanov, Leila Al-Farsi, Sean O'Brien

A and B represent two users on a social-media network. A and B are friends with each other.

1 Using set operations, identify the users' common friends.

2 Using set operations, identify friends of B that are not friends with A, so the platform can recommend new connections.

B4 Abstract data types (ADTs) (HL)

■ Check whether subset or superset

A **subset** or superset describes the relationship between two sets.

Set A is considered a **subset** of B if all of A's elements are present in B – which would be considered the **superset**. All elements of the subset can be found in the superset.

To check whether set A is a subset of set B, or whether B is a superset of A:

Python

```python
# Define two new sets
A = {1, 4, 7}
B = {1, 2, 3, 4, 5, 6, 7}
# Check if A is a subset of B
# Both of these methods are acceptable
print(A.issubset(B)) # True
print(A <= B) # True
# Check if B is a superset of A
# Both of these methods are acceptable
print(B.issuperset(A)) # True
print(B >= A) # True
```

Java

```java
// Define two new sets
Set<Integer> A = new HashSet<>();
A.add(1);
A.add(4);
A.add(7);
Set<Integer> B = new HashSet<>();
B.add(1);
B.add(2);
B.add(3);
B.add(4);
B.add(5);
B.add(6);
B.add(7);
// Check if A is a subset of B
System.out.println(B.containsAll(A)); // True
// Check if B is a superset of A by checking if A is contained within B, but B
// is not contained within A
System.out.println(B.containsAll(A) && !A.containsAll(B)); // False
```

B4.1.6 Core principles of abstract data types

■ Hash tables

Hash tables are a particularly important data structure in Computer Science. They offer rapid retrieval and insertion capabilities into an array-like structure. However, rather than an abstract integer being used by the programmer for the index, a key can be provided instead.

This key is then processed through a **hashing algorithm** to find which array index to store the data in. This allows the data to be stored in an array-like structure that provides an **O(1) average-time complexity** for search, insert and delete operations under ideal conditions.

For example, "name" could be used as the key by the developer. A hashing algorithm then processes this with the aim of producing an integer so that where the data this key is linked to can be stored in the array. One example method where this could be achieved is by adding up the **ASCII** values of all the letters and then using modulus and the size of the table to determine the index.

```
# Hash table size
table _ size = 10
# ASCII values for letters
'n' = 110
'a' = 97
'm' = 109
'e' = 101
110 + 97 + 109 + 101 = 417
417 % table _ size = 7
```

This data would then be stored at index 7.

Hash tables: Creating, inserting and retrieving data

This is how we can create a hash table, as well as insert, delete and retrieve items:

Python

```python
# Creating a hash table as a Python dictionary
hash_table = {}
# Inserting two items
hash_table["key1"] = "value1"
hash_table["key2"] = "value2"
# Retrieving and printing one item
value = hash_table["key1"]
print("The value for 'key1' is:", value)
# Deleting an item
del hash_table["key2"]
```

Java

```java
import java.util.HashMap;
public class Main {
    public static void main(String[] args) {
        // Creating a hash table using HashMap
        // The first data type is for the key, the second is for the data
        HashMap<String, String> hashTable = new HashMap<>();
        // Inserting two items
        hashTable.put("key1", "value1");
        hashTable.put("key2", "value2");
```

```
      // Retrieving and printing one item
      String value = hashTable.get("key1");
      System.out.println("The value for 'key1' is: " + value);
      // Deleting an item by key
      String removedValue = hashTable.remove("key2");  // Returns the value
      // associated with the key
   }
}
```

Collision factors

As you may have already guessed, the hashing algorithm demonstrated above is not foolproof. There could be other example keys that also generate the number 7 for the index – when this happens it is called a "collision". Ideally, our hashing algorithm should generate a unique index for each key and, while there are some more complex algorithms than the one we looked at that are better at doing this, there is no complete solution available. We cannot store two data items in an array at the same index, so how do we get around this problem? There are two main methods used: "chaining" and "open addressing". Before we look at these methods, it is important to understand the impact of the number of items we are trying to store in the hash table. This is called the "load factor".

Load factors

The load factor is a measure that indicates how full the hash table is. The load factor is defined as the ratio of the number of elements currently stored in the table to the total number of slots available. The formula for load factor is:

$$Load\ factor = \frac{number\ of\ entries\ in\ the\ table}{total\ number\ of\ slots}$$

The load factor can heavily affect the performance of the hash table. A hash table with a high load factor will have more collisions, which will impact performance when performing operations on the table.

Rehashing

When the load factor exceeds a certain threshold, **rehashing** is necessary to maintain efficient performance. Rehashing involves creating a new, larger array and redistributing the existing elements using a new hash function or the same hash function applied to the new array size. This process reduces the load factor and minimizes collisions, ensuring that the hash table operations remain efficient.

Steps involved in rehashing:

1 Monitor the load factor of the hash table and, when this exceeds 0.7 (70 per cent), trigger rehashing.
2 Prepare a new array that is at least double the size of the current array. Ideally, the new size should be a prime number to help reduce collisions.
3 For each element already in the hash table, all new hash values need to be computed based on the new array size.
4 Insert the elements into the new, larger array, ensuring that any collisions are handled appropriately.

♦ **Rehashing:** a process in hash tables where the data is redistributed into a new, larger array to reduce the load factor and minimize collisions, maintaining efficient performance.

●Common mistake

Do not overlook the impact of a high load factor on hash-table performance. Keeping the load factor low is incredibly important for efficiency.

Chaining

Chaining utilizes linked lists (or a similar structure) to be able to store more than one item of data at a single index. When a collision occurs, and two keys hash to the same index, the new key-value pair is added to the end of the list at that index.

Let us consider a simple hash function as "key mod 6" and a sequence of keys as 35, 800, 82, 92, 122 and 94.

■ **Empty table**

0	
1	
2	
3	
4	
5	

■ **Insert 35**

0	
1	
2	
3	
4	
5	35

■ **Insert 800 and 82**

0	
1	
2	800
3	
4	82
5	35

■ **Insert 122: Collision, so it is added to a chain**

0			
1			
2	800	92	122
3			
4	82		
5	35		

■ **Insert 94: Collision, so it is added to a chain**

0			
1			
2	800	92	122
3			
4	82	94	
5	35		

Advantages:

■ **Simplicity:** It is relatively easy to implement.

■ **Handles high load factors well:** If the number of items you are inserting is greater than the amount of spaces in the table, it will still operate efficiently. However, lookup times may become slower when having to access a linked list.

■ **Good for unknown data sizes** (connected to the point above): If you do not know in advance how many items you will be inserting into the table, chaining will have an advantage as you will not need to rehash the table to resize it.

Disadvantages:

■ **Memory overhead:** As it is utilizing a linked list, the more items there are in the chain, the more memory it will require.

■ **Complexity for deletion:** If the deletion is within a linked list, performance will degrade due to the need to adjust pointers.

■ **Variable performance:** When accessing an index with a linked list, this will perform worse than one without, which can impact search and delete actions.

Open addressing

Open addressing only stores data within the hash table itself. When a collision occurs, it will find another empty slot in the hash table, according to a predefined sequence, and store the data there.

Several methods can be used to achieve this:

■ **Linear probing** sequentially checks the next spot until a space is found. However, this can lead to clustering, where a group of adjacent slots get filled, increasing the search time for these elements in particular.

- **Quadratic probing** searches in a more spaced-out manner for an available slot using the original hash value and a quadratic function. If the next space is also full, it increments the value of the quadratic function and searches again until it finds an available slot.
- **Double hashing** uses a second hash function to determine the probe step. The first hash function is performed first, and then a second one to give an offset from the original index. This offers better distribution and minimizes clustering compared to linear and quadratic probing, but requires more computational overhead.

Advantages:

- **Space efficient:** Stores all elements directly within the hash table array, eliminating the need for extra data structures, such as linked lists.
- **More memory efficient:** No pointers are required.
- **Simpler to serialize:** As it is a simpler data structure with contiguous memory allocation, converting the structure to a format to be stored or transmitted is simpler than a hash table using chaining.

Disadvantages:

- **Increased computational overhead:** If there are high load factors, performance may decrease due to the probing methods required.
- **Clustering:** This can be an issue especially when using linear probing, where consecutive slots are filled, which increases the average time for insertions, deletions and searches that do not find the element they are searching for.
- **Complex deletion:** Deleting an element is a complex process as you may break probe sequences.

PROGRAMMING EXERCISE 1

Using a hash table, create a simple voting system. The system should have the ability to add and remove candidates. Use the name input by the user as the key in the hash table. Once the candidates have been input, it should allow voters to cast votes for the candidates in the system and allow the current totals to be viewed. There should be an option to end the election when the voting is over, and the winner should be output to the user.

PROGRAMMING EXERCISE 2

Working in a team, conduct a small experiment by implementing two different ADTs to solve the same problem and compare the performance. You could consider execution time and memory usage, for example.

Collaborate on this project by assigning roles, managing your time and co-operating to achieve your goal. You could create a shared code repository to help you work together.

When you have finished, prepare a presentation summarizing your project. Include the problem definition, implementation details, test results, analysis and conclusions.

An example project:

Spell checker

Implement a spell checker using a hash table and a binary search tree. Compare the performance for the following operations:

- Inserting words into the dictionary.
- Checking whether a word is in the dictionary.
- Suggesting corrections for a misspelled word (finding the nearest match).

EXAM PRACTICE QUESTIONS

1 Construct a diagram to represent a double-linked list that holds the following sequence of names:

Kaja, Aiko, Carlos, Fatima [4]

2 The names of a group of people attending a conference were recorded in a stack data structure. The first name stored in the stack was "Sofia".

...
Tariq
Maya
Jasper
Rina
Rafael
Aisha
Zara
Sofia

Note that "Tariq" is currently in position 0 in the stack.

a Compare and contrast the use of a binary search tree and a stack when searching for a specific item. [2]

b The tree is populated with the data from the stack. By considering only the data visible in the stack above, sketch the binary search tree that has been created from the items removed from the stack. [2]

3 Sketch a binary search tree that would allow the following output when traversed using an in-order traversal:

Zebu, Tapir, Hedgehog, Falcon, Dugong, Bison, Armadillo [2]

4 A hash table has been used to store a company's current stock. The hashing algorithm used is:

stock number MOD 100.

a Determine the value returned by the hashing function when it is applied to stock number 1021. [1]

b Explain how a value is stored in a hash table. [1]

c Describe the steps involved in rehashing. [2]

5 Given two sets, A = {1, 2, 3, 4} and B = {3, 4, 5, 6}, perform the following operations and provide the resulting set:

a Union [2]

b Intersection [2]

c Difference. [2]

Case study

Case study

The computer science case study provides the stimulus to investigate a scenario involving current developments, emerging technologies and ethical issues in computer science.

The case study for SL is a scenario that includes two challenge questions that stimulate the required research. The information obtained will prepare students to answer the questions in this section of the examination.

HL students conduct deeper research into the case study which is reflected in the extra two challenge questions in the case study for HL, additional recommended teaching hours and time during paper one.

Adapted from the *IBDP Computer science guide*

The case study is assessed in section B of Paper 1, as shown in the table below. There is a mix of short-answer questions and one essay question.

The short-answer questions typically focus on your understanding of the main ideas of the case study, along with the terminology contained within. The command terms for these questions are words such as **define**, **identify**, **outline** and **describe**. The last page of the case study contains a list of terminology that is specific to the case study, over and above the terminology of the course, which the IB will expect you to be familiar with in your exam responses.

The essay question is where you demonstrate the depth of research-based understanding you have gained about the topics presented within the case study. The essay question is worth half the marks of section B of Paper 1. The marking criteria for the essay question are fixed and are provided later in this chapter.

■ Case study key information

	Standard Level students	**Higher Level students**
Recommended teaching time allocation	15 hours	30 hours
Proportion of Paper 1 exam	12 of 50 marks (24%)	24 of 80 marks (30%)
Marks for the essay question	6 marks	12 marks
"Challenges faced" research prompts that form the basis of the essay question	2	4
Approximate working time for the essay question in the examination	18 minutes	36 minutes

Responding to the case study

Here is a suggested approach to understanding and researching the issues surrounding the case study, and preparing for exam questions on it. Use this as a starting point and then modify it to your personal approach to learning.

■ Step 1: Understand the text of the case study

- ■ Read the case study. Highlight and identify key points.

- ■ Prepare definitions for the terminology list provided at the end of the case study.

- ■ Quiz and test yourself and your peers on terminology definitions and introductory concepts.

■ Step 2: Understand the technology in the case study

The case study will involve field(s) of emerging technology not otherwise covered by the course syllabus.

- ■ Identify resources such as video lectures and technical articles that provide an overview and introduction to the technologies present in the case study.

- ■ Prepare notes based on those technologies from the resources you found. Ensure you have a good understanding of how the relevant technologies work. You will not have to include any programming code as part of a case study examination question, but you should have a good working technical understanding of the issues.

■ Step 3: Consider the scenario of the case study in its proper context

Now, with your renewed understanding of the technologies within the case study, give the complete scenario another careful read.

- ■ What is the case study really about?

- ■ Identify the big issues of the case study.

- ■ What is interesting about the case study?

- ■ What is confusing?

■ Step 4: Consider the challenges of the case study

For each of the challenges identified within the case study:

- ■ Research any background information on the challenge so you have an appreciation of its relevance.

- ■ Why is this a challenge in the scenario presented?

- ■ What are the implications of not being able to meet this challenge?

- ■ What are some potential solutions to the challenge?

It is recommended to produce a revision document that contains a summary of the issues and technology pertinent to each of the challenges.

■ Step 5: Consider the relevance of the challenges beyond the case study

Research and identify real-world examples of the challenges. Add these examples to your revision document from the previous step. This step is crucial as it will empower you to refer to other, real-life examples relevant to the case study when writing your exam responses, thereby helping you demonstrate meaningful research.

■ Step 6: Review for exam questions

- The essay question will be based on one or more of the challenges that are identified at the end of the case study document.

- Brainstorm potential examination questions that focus on the challenges.

- Write practice essays for each of the challenges faced. Prepare a bullet-point list of key points to convert into revision index cards in the lead-up to the examinations.

- Swap practice essays with a friend and provide feedback based on the essay question marking criteria provided below.

Suggested strategies for case-study research

1 Use generative AI to read the case study and have it prepare a summary of issues for each of the challenges. An example prompt might be: "Given the case study on the theme of [CASE STUDY THEME], prepare explanatory bullet points on [CHALLENGE FACED]." Then, perform a literature review to determine the accuracy of each of the assertions made by the AI. (Do not accept the responses of the AI at face value!)

2 Arrange with your classmates to present to or peer-teach each other about the various challenges, and then take questions from your class. Your confidence when answering those questions will help identify areas you need to research further.

3 Read major research papers and publications relevant to the case study so you can speak about developments in the field with authority. Refer to the papers that discuss those developments as you speak.

   Cornell University runs the arXiv.org service, which is an excellent starting point: "arXiv is a free distribution service and an open-access archive for nearly 2.4 million scholarly articles in the fields of physics, mathematics, computer science, quantitative biology, quantitative finance, statistics, electrical engineering and systems science, and economics. Materials on this site are not peer-reviewed by arXiv" (arxiv.org).

   As the chief examiner notes: "Students who read journal articles and complete video courses on the case study topic have a broader understanding of the concepts. This additional reading allows students to employ references to real-world examples or research in the extended response question" (*IBDP Computer science subject report*, May 2024).

4 Watch interviews or lectures given by technologists who are working with, or helped develop, the technology. For example, for the 2023 case study on recommendation systems, there are many excellent lectures available on YouTube by engineers from Netflix and Spotify, who discuss in great technical detail how their algorithms work.

5 Ask your teacher to arrange a class visit to a company or organization that is working with the technology. Meet with their team and interview them.

   Consider, for example, the 2019 case study on computer-aided dispatch systems for emergency-service vehicles. The author arranged a class visit to a nearby app-development company that was creating an emergency-services app for the local government. This gave the students a firsthand account they could reference in their exam response.

6 Contact your local universities and ask to speak with professors or research thesis students who are conducting research in fields of Computer Science that are relevant to the case study. Most universities have PhD and Masters students conducting research in the fields of emerging technology that case studies tend to draw upon.

7   Find relevant connections with real-world usage of the technologies.

For example, for the 2024 case study on rescue robotics, several students discussed the use of rescue robots in the 9/11 disaster and compared it to the use of rescue robots to search buildings damaged in the Ukraine conflict. Students were able to evaluate how the technology had changed in the intervening 20 years.

⬤ Top tips!

- Know what to expect before walking into the exam. Be sure you understand the structure of the paper, including the command terms and requirements of each question, particularly the extended response.
- Depending on the topic, see whether you and your classmates can organize a field trip or a relevant guest speaker. It would be great if you could refer to some primary research in your answers ("the time I visited the …").
- Take five minutes in the exam to plan your extended response before you start writing. Any extended writing is vastly improved by spending just a few minutes planning.
- Ensure that any assertions you make are fully substantiated and underpinned by balanced analysis.
- Use appropriate Computer Science terminology throughout your response.
- Arrange with your classmates to present to or peer-teach each other about the various challenges, and then take questions from your classmates. Your confidence when answering those questions will help identify areas you need to research further.
- Use generative AI to read the case study and have it prepare a summary of issues for each of the challenges. Use the generated output to perform a literature review of the summary to determine the accuracy of assertions it makes. Due to the well-known and documented issues of hallucinations, do not rely on generative AI outputs without performing an independent review!

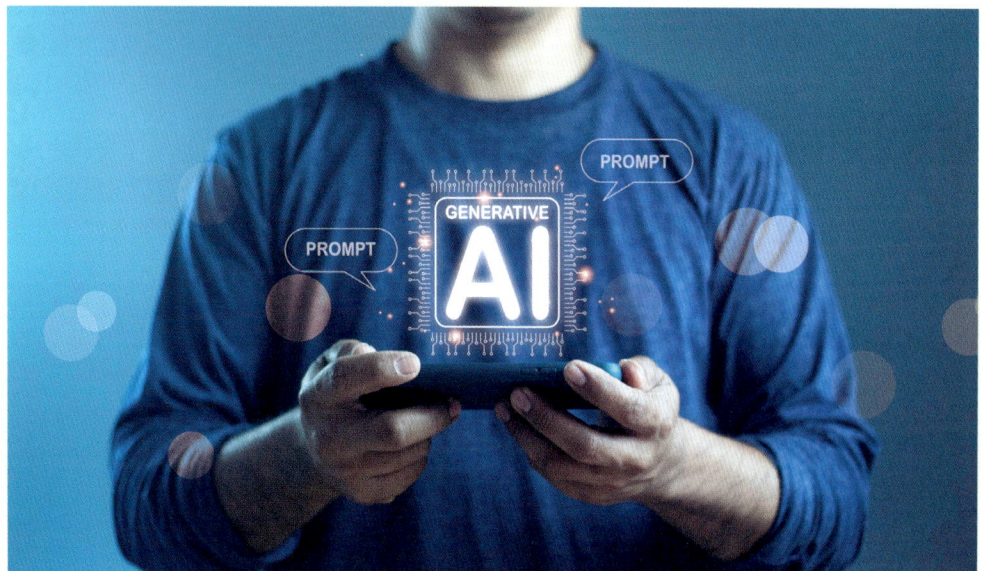

Common mistakes

- It is very easy to tell when a student doesn't know the terminology and is making it up. Incorrect use of terminology implies poor understanding of the issues, so will considerably limit the marks you can earn. Do not neglect to have a thorough understanding of the terminology list provided.
- If you are going to provide a citation in an examination response, don't make it up! As indicated, the examiners will be broadly familiar with the major papers and publications relevant to the case study.
- Many low-performing essays only regurgitate the content given in the case study itself. The exam marker already knows what is in the case-study document; they want to see what additional insights you can provide from your research beyond the case study.
- Another common error is not to provide a balanced analysis. For a top-band response, you must be nuanced enough to present multiple perspectives from which you draw a conclusion.
- Pay close attention to the wording of the questions and, in particular, their command terms. The type of response depends upon the command term, and merely writing down everything you know is not an effective strategy.
- "Several unofficial online forums have provided questionable information and guidance. You should research broadly and cross-check information found" (*IBDP Computer science subject report*, May 2024).

Essay question marking criteria

■ Essay question marking criteria for Standard Level students

Marks	Description
0	No knowledge or understanding of the relevant issues and concepts.
	No use of appropriate terminology.
1–2 Basic	Minimal knowledge and understanding of the relevant issues.
	Minimal use of appropriate terminology.
	The answer may be little more than a list.
	No reference is made to the case study or independent research.
3–4 Adequate	A descriptive response with limited knowledge and / or understanding.
	A limited use of appropriate terminology.
	There is some analysis.
	There is evidence of some research.
5–6 Competent	Knowledge and understanding of the related issues and / or concepts.
	Uses terminology appropriately in places.
	There is evidence of analysis.
	There is evidence of research.
	There is a conclusion.

SL Paper 1 markscheme, page 8

Marks	Description
0	No knowledge or understanding of the relevant issues and concepts. No use of appropriate terminology.
1–3 Basic	Minimal knowledge and understanding of the relevant issues or concepts. Minimal use of appropriate terminology. The answer may be little more than a list. No reference is made to the information in the case study or independent research.
4–6 Adequate	A descriptive response with limited knowledge and / or understanding of the relevant issues or concepts. A limited use of appropriate terminology. There is limited evidence of analysis. There is evidence that limited research has been undertaken.
7–9 Competent	A response with knowledge and understanding of the related issues and / or concepts. A response that uses terminology appropriately in places. There is some evidence of analysis. There is evidence that research has been undertaken.
10–12 Proficient	A response with a detailed knowledge and clear understanding of computer science. A response that uses terminology appropriately throughout. There is competent and balanced analysis. Conclusions are drawn that are linked to the analysis. There is clear evidence that extensive research has been undertaken.

HL Paper 1 markscheme, pages 13–14

Analysing past case studies

This section provides a high-level overview of some recent case studies to illustrate the typical style in which they are presented and the essay questions that may appear as a result.

Additionally, chief examiner feedback on the quality of the essay responses is provided to help highlight common weaknesses in responses given by students to these questions. You will quickly notice common themes that echo throughout the examination seasons as you read those comments. Take the time to learn from the mistakes of those who have gone before you.

■ Blockchain (May & November 2020, May 2021)

- **Scenario:** Based on the mayor of Santa Monica, Pablo, who wants to establish a local currency, called MONS, that uses blockchain technologies.

- **Technologies:** Technologies referred to include:
  - ☐ digital ledgers
  - ☐ digital signatures
  - ☐ proof of work (mining)
  - ☐ structure of a blockchain
  - ☐ Merkle trees
  - ☐ SHA256.

- **Challenges:** There are a number of challenges that are linked to the introduction of MONS; these include:
  - ☐ understanding how new blocks are added to the ledger and how the proof of work prevents malicious nodes from taking over the MONS network

☐ understanding how the MONS architecture is scalable and can remain efficient as the number of users increases

☐ understanding the use of cryptographic techniques in the MONS project

☐ explaining to the Santa Monica citizens how their MONS balance is calculated from transaction data securely stored in a publicly accessible blockchain ledger

☐ investigating how the distributed nature of a blockchain cryptocurrency and the confirmation process may have disadvantages for the citizens of Santa Monica.

■ **Questions:** Essay questions asked include:

☐ Pablo states: "In a traditional banking system, users trust the banks to keep everyone's money safe; but with MONS, the whole blockchain, right from the very first transaction, would be visible to all MONS users, so it is important to be able to explain to citizens how their money is guaranteed to be safe" (lines 109–112).

With reference to the key technologies, to what extent do you believe the MONS project will ensure the safety of the residents' money? (November 2020)

☐ Pablo has claimed that the use of blockchain technology for the MONS cryptocurrency will mean the cryptocurrency is both secure and scalable.

To what extent do you agree with Pablo? (May 2021)

■ **Feedback:** The chief examiner, summarizing the quality of responses to this question, stated:

The majority of responses covered immutability, distributed consensus, cryptographic hashes, digital signatures, and the 51% attack. **Better candidates were able to reference real-world situations**, but most candidates did not. Candidates tended to identify increasing the blocksize and adjusting the nonce difficulty. Very few candidates had understood how sharding and layer 2 protocols could assist with scalability.

Many candidates discussed economic and environmental issues with blockchain, rather than the Computer Science aspects of security and scalability. **This approach lacks focus and detracts from the overall response.**

IBDP Computer science subject report, May 2021

■ Genetic algorithms (May & November 2022)

■ **Scenario:** Based on the travelling salesperson problem.

■ **Technologies:** Technologies referred to include:

☐ genetic algorithms:
  – population
  – selection algorithms
  – crossover
  – mutation.

■ **Challenges:** There are a number of challenges associated with genetic algorithms; these include:

☐ understanding the role of convergence in genetic algorithms and the factors affecting convergence

☐ evaluating the use and implementation of roulette-wheel selection, tournament selection and truncation selection strategies used within genetic algorithms

☐ discussing the different solutions for addressing the failure of simple crossover strategies for the travelling salesperson problem; in particular:
  – why they are necessary
  – how they are applied

- how they preserve the parental traits
- what other possible methods are available
☐ understanding the advantages and disadvantages of genetic algorithms with respect to other approaches to the travelling salesperson problem, and to combinatorial optimization problems in general.

■ **Question:** Essay questions asked include:
☐ To what extent do the characteristics of genetic algorithms make them an appropriate approach to solving the route optimization problems? (May 2022)

■ **Feedback:** The chief examiner, summarizing the quality of responses to this question, stated:

The challenge was to understand the advantages and disadvantages of genetic algorithms with respect to other approaches to the travelling salesperson problem and combinatorial optimization problems in general.

The broadness of the question meant that candidates could incorporate information from the other three challenges. Perhaps, for this reason, many candidates failed to demonstrate more than adequate understanding of how genetic algorithms can arrive at a successful solution and this approach's main weaknesses.

The majority of responses were descriptive rather than evaluative. Many candidates wrote incorrect statements or did not understand how the different characteristics affect each other. There were very few proficient responses, and **it was rare to see journal articles referenced**.

IBDP Computer science subject report, May 2022

■ **Quotation:** The case study states:
☐ Successful implementations of genetic algorithms strike a natural balance between exploration and exploitation, and techniques such as simulated annealing can fine-tune that balance as the algorithm progresses towards convergence (page 7, Discussion).

■ **Question:**
☐ Discuss the role of convergence in genetic algorithms and how exploration and exploitation can affect its success. (November 2022)

■ **Feedback:** The chief examiner, summarizing the quality of responses to this question, stated:

Some candidates produced excellent answers demonstrating an understanding of how initial routes, population size, selection method, crossover method and mutation affect convergence. Proficient answers critically analysed the interplay between these choices and how they affected exploration and exploitation. Unlike previous case studies, there was no opportunity to reference real-world situations.

Many candidates only talked about exploration and exploitation in the broadest sense, failing to identify how they could be manipulated. Some students tried to involve details from earlier questions, stating the same content without a consistent structure.

Even though there was little opportunity to reference real-world scenarios in this case study, **some candidates referenced research papers** when they defined critical terms. **A reference to a relevant, newsworthy article or research paper is recommended for Question 4.** Schools that approach the case study from a research perspective provide context for students. For example, researching practical applications of genetic algorithms will increase students' conceptual understanding and make the topic more engaging.

IBDP Computer science subject report, November 2022

■ Recommendation systems (May & November 2023)

- **Scenario:** Based on a new application that allows users to view the work of artists who have yet to be discovered. Artists may include actors, singers, screenwriters, comedians, painters, sculptors and filmmakers. In fact, any artist who wants to demonstrate a talent will be able to upload files to the application. The uploaded content can be rated by all users. Based on their ratings, the application recommends new content to each user.

- **Technologies:** Technologies referred to include:
  - ☐ cloud computing
  - ☐ machine learning
  - ☐ recommender systems:
    - – content-based filtering and collaborative filtering
    - – k-nearest neighbours
    - – matrix factorization
    - – training of recommender systems
    - – evaluating recommender systems.

- **Challenges:** To help with this new business venture, called NextStar, there are a number of challenges that you need to research:
  - ☐ understanding the similarities and differences between supervised learning, unsupervised learning and reinforcement learning
  - ☐ understanding how the k-NN algorithm and matrix factorization can be used within recommender systems
  - ☐ understanding how to train, test and evaluate a recommender system
  - ☐ comparing content-based filtering and collaborative filtering recommender systems
  - ☐ understanding the ethical concerns linked to the collection, storage and use of users' behavioural data.

- **Question:** Essay questions asked include:
  - ☐ "Recommender systems can use content-based filtering, collaborative filtering, or a combination of both. Hybrid recommender systems combine several machine learning algorithms." (lines 43–44)

    Discuss the advantages and disadvantages of these different approaches for building a recommendation system. (May 2023 TZ1)

- **Feedback:** The chief examiner, summarizing the quality of responses to this question, stated:

  Most candidates focused on content-based and collaborative filtering, **describing their process with little evaluation**. Some candidates stated challenges such as popularity bias, overfitting and cold start but failed to explain strategies to deal with these issues.

  The majority of candidates wrote an adequate response. **Few referenced the case study**, and their analysis was on generic movie-recommendations systems. Often the examples were YouTube-related rather than NextStar. There were very few proficient responses, and **it was rare to see journal articles referenced**.

  IBDP Computer science subject report, May 2023 TZ1

- **Question:**
  - ☐ Discuss whether the challenges associated with the development of an effective recommender system can be overcome through the choice of algorithm, training data and methods of evaluation. (May 2023 TZ2)

- **Feedback:** The chief examiner, summarizing the quality of responses to this question, stated:

  The majority of candidates wrote an adequate response. While many referenced NextStar, often their analysis was on a generic movie-recommender system.

  The **better responses honed in on the challenges and built their essay around them**, offering ways to address them. These candidates understood that the type of recommender system might start off simple and evolve over time.

  There were few proficient responses. **Most candidates failed to structure their essays** to focus on the challenges while explaining the computer science relating to recommender systems. **Very few candidates referenced journals** or other sources, and although some included real-world recommender systems, **it was rarely as a comparative analysis**.

  The broadness of the question troubled some students who tried to include all three areas and **ended up with no depth** whatsoever. Their responses were usually **descriptive and lacked any analysis or evaluation**.

  IBDP Computer science subject report, May 2023 TZ2

- **Question:**
  - A recommender system that uses a supervised learning K-nearest neighbour (k-NN) algorithm is selected. Supervised learning algorithms require several decisions to be made, including setting any hyperparameters, choosing data sets, training and testing procedures, and evaluation strategies.
    Discuss whether the selection and implementation of a k-NN algorithm in the development of a recommender system will give precise and accurate recommendations. (November 2023)

- **Feedback:** The chief examiner, summarizing the quality of responses to this question, stated:

  Many students had not researched this topic and wrote basic responses, often copying several lines from the case study. Even those students who wrote adequate responses often failed to explore the algorithm beyond describing its operation. Technical terminology tended to be used appropriately but not expanded upon.

  The better responses explored supervised learning, analysed the k-NN algorithms, and discussed how the recommender system could be evaluated. Weaknesses such as the cold start problem, popularity bias, and overfitting were considered. Very few responses considered strategies for overcoming these problems.

  There were few proficient responses. However, those were analytical and considered the question from a broad perspective, even considering data sets and preprocessing strategies. **One or two students referenced journals or other sources.**

  IBDP Computer science subject report, November 2023

■ Rescue robots (May & November 2024)

- **Scenario:** Based around rescue robots, which are designed to help with the search and rescue of humans after a disaster, such as an earthquake or tsunami. These robots may assist the efforts of rescue teams by searching and mapping areas, assessing damage, removing debris, delivering supplies and evacuating casualties.

- **Technologies:** Technologies referred to include:
  - computer vision
  - visual simultaneous localization and mapping (vSLAM)
  - pose estimation.

- **Challenges:** In the development of the new rescue robot, the design team at BotPro face a number of challenges:
  - understanding how vSLAM navigates an environment with unknown obstacles and contours
  - minimizing the time rescue robots spend scanning and learning an environment
  - estimating the pose of people despite varying light and environmental conditions and body-part or multiple-object occlusion
  - updating existing maps in a dynamically changing environment, such as an earthquake where rubble is still shifting
  - developing an understanding of the ethical considerations of using autonomous robots in life-and-death situations.

- **Question:** Essay questions asked include:
  - A governmental department of disaster management is considering deploying rescue robots made by BotPro that use computer vision technologies for rescue operations in closed spaces, such as buildings and factories.
    Discuss the benefits and costs of deploying rescue robots that use the vSLAM process and pose estimation techniques to carry out rescue operations in closed spaces.
    (May 2024 TZ1)

- **Feedback:** The chief examiner, summarizing the quality of responses to this question, stated:

  The extended response challenge was to discuss the benefits and costs of deploying rescue robots that use the vSLAM process and pose estimation techniques to carry out rescue operations in closed spaces.

  Most students **focused excessively on ethical points**, such as the safety of deploying robots rather than human rescue teams. When technical concepts were mentioned, this was done **without any depth. Few students referenced information beyond the case study**, giving the impression that little research had been conducted.

  IBDP Computer science subject report, May 2024 TZ1

- **Question:**
  - vSLAM algorithms are designed to operate in GPS-denied or GPS-degraded environments. Rescue teams in these environments cannot rely on GPS tracking. BotPro wants your opinion on whether rescue robots installed with vSLAM algorithms will be effective when looking for injured or unconscious people in an emergency situation, such as a factory fire. Such emergencies are time critical.
    Evaluate the effectiveness of robots that use vSLAM algorithms to find casualties in an appropriate timeframe. (May 2024 TZ2)

- **Feedback:** The chief examiner, summarizing the quality of responses to this question, stated:

  The better responses provided a balanced account, displaying that the effectiveness of rescue robots can vary depending on several factors, including the environment, resources available, computational complexity, the quality of the sensor data and the complexity of the search area. Moreover, they demonstrated an awareness of factors such as battery life, availability of factory blueprints and operational time. **Proficient responses provided real-world examples of situations where rescue robots had been deployed and referenced research papers.**

  Weaker responses either focused on the ethics of deploying rescue robots or merely listed the technologies without describing or evaluating them

  IBDP Computer science subject report, May 2024 TZ2

Internal assessment

Internal assessment

The internal assessment is a summative task for you to showcase your Computer Science skills and prowess. It is marked by your school teacher and moderated by the IB, prior to contributing to your final grade for the course. The *IBDP Computer science guide* provides these details on the internal assessment:

> *The internal assessment requires the student to identify a problem of their own choice and develop a software solution using the computational thinking process.*
>
> Adapted from the *IBDP Computer science guide*

◆ **Solution:** the documentation and video submitted by the student for the internal assessment.

For Standard Level students the internal assessment is worth 30 per cent of your final grade, and for Higher Level students it is worth 20 per cent of your final grade.

For all students, it is recommended that 35 hours of teaching time is allocated to work on the internal assessment. According to the *IBDP guide*, this time includes:

- time for the teacher to explain the requirements of the internal assessment
- class time for students to work on the internal assessment component and ask questions
- time for consultation between the teacher and each student
- time to review and monitor progress, and to check authenticity.

> *IBDP Computer science guide*

■ The internal assessment can earn up to 30 marks, spread over five criteria

Criteria	Title	Marks	Recommended word count	Extras
A	Problem specification	4	300	
B	Planning	4	150	Diagrams
C	System overview	6	150	Diagrams
D	Development	12	1000	Video (max 5 minutes in length; format: MP4, AVI, WMV
E	Evaluation	4	400	

Choice of problem

Making a wise choice of the problem you will tackle is critical, as the rest of the internal assessment flows from that. Don't rush into a decision without consulting closely with your Computer Science teacher. The *IBDP guide* states:

> *In identifying a problem, the student can select to apply to the problem any topic in computer science that interests them. It does not have to be directly related to the specified themes in the syllabus.*
>
> *The problem chosen should require a software solution with sufficient complexity to be commensurate with the level of the DP Computer Science course. It should also require sufficient innovation for the student to demonstrate their organizational skills, algorithmic thinking and ability to code their algorithms.*
>
> *IBDP Computer science guide*

◆ **Product:** the completed software only (in the internal assessment).

The programming language and choice of technologies you use in preparing your **product** are not constrained to either Python or Java. You may use whichever language and technologies you deem to be the best fit for your product. Also, you may choose to develop a new computational solution: a standalone application; a computer or mobile game; an interactive website with a connection to a database; a mobile application; or even add functionality to an existing product. You should demonstrate problem-solving techniques combined with the use of data structures, logic conditions and data manipulation (via file processing or databases) using either a procedural or OOP approach.

Some examples of inappropriate products, from the *IBDP guide*, are:

- the development of a programming product using only copied code
- the development of a website (product) using a web-based template that determines its structure and layout
- the use of exemplar products or templates provided with software such as the Northwind database in MS Access
- a copied computer game without major modifications to the code that have been properly documented
- a product that does not meet the ethical requirements outlined in the 'Requirements and recommendations' section of the *IBDP guide*
- a computer / mobile application created using a builder / wizard / drag and drop tool without the need for code development.

IBDP Computer science guide

Additionally, examples of weaker products identified by IB moderators in the annual subject report for the previous version of the syllabus, which are still relevant to this version of the IA, include:

- Java programs that mainly focus on GUI and not on actual functionality
- Java programs that consist of one class only
- Java programs consisting of a Greenfoot template with only two methods overwritten
- Rudimentary versions of freely available games (like Sudoku)
- Websites that are template-based (Wordpress, Wix or Weebly) or that have minimal content.

IBDP Computer science subject report, May 2016, page 2

● Top tips!

Choice of problem

Some general advice from the authors:

- Choose a problem that you are 80 per cent confident about being able to solve. This allows a good mix of confidently being able to deliver on what you set out to achieve, with a little bit of a stretch for you to challenge yourself with and learn something new through your IA.
  - ☐ A problem you are 100 per cent confident about from the start is probably too simple to allow for high grades.
  - ☐ A problem you are only 50 per cent confident about means you are trying to do more than is realistically feasible for your current skill set and available time. There are likely too many unknowns that could trip you up.

- Do not confuse a "large" project with a "complex" one. An example of this going wrong is creating a project that requires 10+ different GUI screens. One or two screens is enough to demonstrate you have the skill to create it; the rest is repetitious and wasted effort (from the perspective of the marking criteria).
- While on the subject of GUI screens, user interfaces generally do not require much algorithmic skill, so don't focus too much on the user interface itself beyond proper use of input validation techniques. Similarly, writing HTML or CSS does not, by itself, demonstrate algorithmic thinking.

■ When selecting a problem, ask yourself where you will have the opportunity to showcase your understanding of both algorithmic thinking and data structures. When you consider the criterion D marking criteria, you will observe it is largely driven by algorithms, and by extension data structures. That said, your use of various algorithms and data structures must make sense in the context of your project – artificially forcing an algorithm into a project in a manner that appears contrived will not satisfy the criteria.

■ Higher achieving products will typically have some technical complexity (being demonstrated through algorithms or data structures) beyond that learned through the course syllabus. Remember: the course guide allocates 35 hours of class time to this IA and, while it is an assessment, all assessments are also learning experiences. The IB does not intend for you to go through 35 hours of class time without learning anything. Seek out new skills to learn and implement in your IA.

■ To contrast the previous statement, however, do not attempt a scenario that requires technical abilities beyond your capabilities. You should not introduce unnecessary complexity if a simpler solution is at hand. Simple code is elegant code.

■ Do not neglect the importance of the documentation and video. Under the previous syllabus, it was very achievable for a product of moderate complexity to achieve a 7 overall on the basis of excellent, thorough, detailed documentation. Likewise, too many technically outstanding and brilliant products have ended up with low grades because students spent all their time programming and neglected the written work. As the *IBDP Computer science guide* states:
"Whichever problem and form of solution a student chooses, it is essential that the student explicitly demonstrates and documents their algorithmic thinking skills."

■ You are not constrained to the content of the syllabus in selecting a problem. In fact, the *Guide* specifically states: "the student can select to apply to the problem any topic in computer science that interests them. It does not have to be directly related to the specified themes in the syllabus."

Project ideas and inspiration

The following overviews are projects that the authors' students have had success with. All of these projects received a post-moderation grade of 7 (27+ points). While aspects of the projects would need to be adapted for the updated syllabus, they are still instructive and valuable for illustrating the variety of projects with which students can find success.

The authors wish to express their appreciation to these former students for their willingness to have their projects shared in this book. Several of the example diagrams that appear in later sections of this chapter are also from these former students' IA projects.

■ Mushroom: Friend or foe?

by H Ng, used with permission

This project aims to develop a mobile application to assist users in identifying mushrooms. The app will utilize a machine learning model trained on a North American data set to determine whether a mushroom is edible, based on its features. The app will also provide educational resources to help users learn more about mushrooms. The goal is to create a user-friendly and informative tool for mushroom foragers.

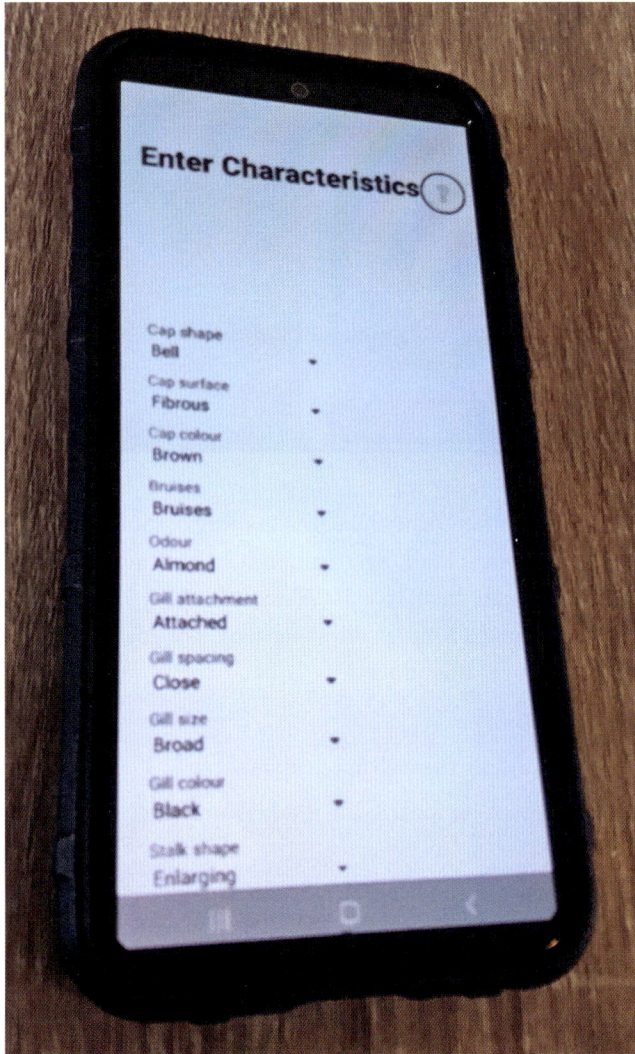

■ Mushroom: Friend or foe?

Key technologies and techniques

- **Machine learning**: Classification models (e.g. logistic regression, decision trees) for mushroom-edibility prediction

- **Python**: Programming language for machine learning model development

- **Java**: Programming language for Android app development

- **Graphical user interface (GUI)**: For user interaction and data input

- **Server–client architecture**: To separate the machine learning model and the mobile app

- **Data structures**: JSON to represent mushroom features and model predictions

- **Error handling**: To handle unexpected inputs or errors gracefully

- **Web development**: Flask framework for building the web API

- **Mobile app development**: Techniques for creating Android apps, including layout design, resource management and testing

■ Automated grading tool

by a former student, used with permission

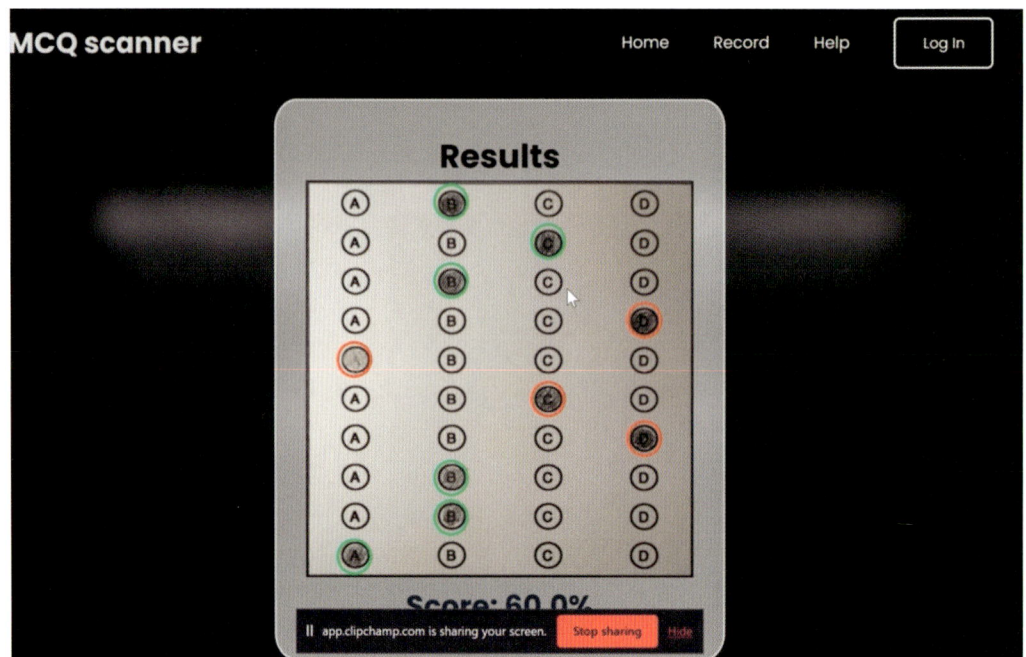

■ Automated grading tool

This project aims to develop a web-based application to automate the grading of multiple-choice assessments. The application will use Optical Mark Recognition (OMR) to identify student answers from scanned images and compare them to a model answer sheet. Key features include automatic scoring, test saving and a user-friendly interface. The goal is to save teachers time and improve the efficiency of the grading process.

Key technologies and techniques

- **Web development**: Flask framework for building the web application
- **Optical Mark Recognition (OMR)**: Techniques for identifying marked areas on scanned images
- **Computer vision**: OpenCV library for image processing and analysis
- **Python**: Programming language for overall implementation
- **SQLite database**: For storing user data and test results
- **User interface design**: Creating a user-friendly interface for uploading images, viewing results and managing tests
- **Error handling**: Implementing mechanisms to handle potential errors during image processing or data storage
- **Data structures**: Using appropriate data structures to represent test data, scores and user information
- **Image processing**: Techniques for preprocessing images, such as thresholding and noise reduction
- **Server-side scripting**: Handling user interactions, processing image data and updating the database

■ ASL (American Sign Language) interpreter

by Jared Xin, used with permission

Live Streaming - e to append, backspace to delete and f to add space

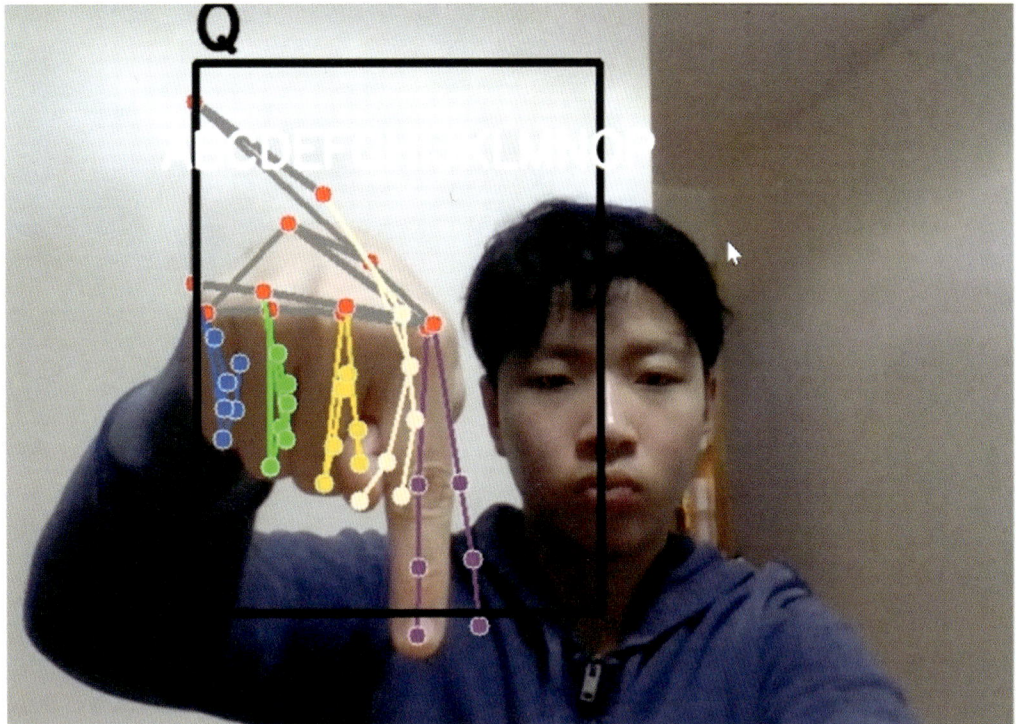

■ ASL (American Sign Language) interpreter

This project aims to develop a web-based application to facilitate communication between hearing and deaf individuals by providing real-time translation of American Sign Language (ASL) into text. The application will use machine learning and computer vision techniques to analyse hand gestures and predict the corresponding ASL letters. Key features include a user-friendly interface, live video-streaming and accurate translation. The goal is to improve accessibility and communication for the deaf community.

Key technologies and techniques

- **Web development**: Flask framework for building the web application

- **Machine learning**: Algorithms for predicting ASL letters from hand gestures

- **Computer vision**: OpenCV library for image processing and hand detection

- **Python**: Programming language for overall implementation

- **Webcam integration**: Techniques for accessing and using the user's webcam

- **User interface design**: Creating a visually appealing and user-friendly interface

- **Real-time processing**: Ensuring efficient processing of video frames for real-time translation

- **Data structures**: Representing hand shapes and predicted letters

- **Error handling**: Implementing mechanisms to handle potential errors during image processing or model prediction

- **Model training**: Training the machine learning model on a data set of ASL signs

- **Accuracy evaluation**: Evaluating the model's performance and making improvements

■ Vacation route planner

by Edward Zhang, used with permission

Bath, United Kingdom `Delete`

Southampton, United Kingdom `Delete`

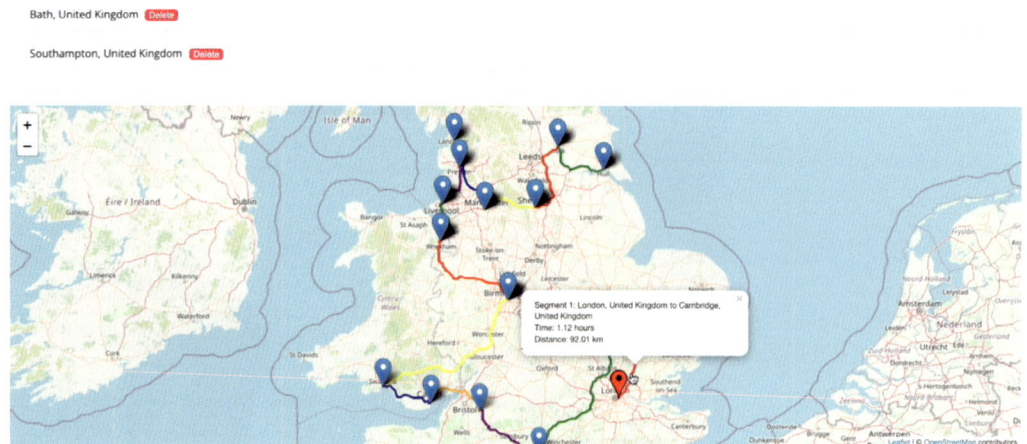

Segment 1: London, United Kingdom to Cambridge, United Kingdom
Time: 1.12 hours
Distance: 92.01 km

Route: London, United Kingdom -> Cambridge, United Kingdom -> Southampton, United Kingdom -> Bath, United Kingdom -> Cardiff, United Kingdom -> Swansea, United Kingdom -> Birmingham, United Kingdom -> Wrexham, United Kingdom -> Liverpool, United Kingdom -> Preston, United Kingdom -> Lancaster, United Kingdom -> Manchester, United Kingdom -> Sheffield, United Kingdom -> York, United Kingdom -> Hull, United Kingdom

Total drive time: 15.5 hours.

Time taken to calculate route: 5.50 seconds.

■ Vacation route planner

This project aims to develop a web-based application to assist users in planning multi-destination vacations. The application will allow users to input locations, generate optimized routes and view detailed information about each location. Key features include efficient route planning, location suggestions and mobile compatibility. The goal is to simplify the vacation planning process and provide users with personalized recommendations.

Key technologies and techniques

- **Web development**: Flask framework for building the web application
- **Mapping**: Leaflet.js library for interactive maps
- **Routing algorithms**: Travelling salesperson algorithm to calculate the most efficient routes between locations
- **Location data**: APIs to access and process location data using OpenStreetMap API
- **User interface design**: Creating a user-friendly interface for inputting locations, viewing routes and interacting with the map
- **Error handling**: Implementing mechanisms to handle potential errors during data processing or API requests
- **Data structures**: Representing locations, routes and other relevant data
- **Mobile optimization**: Ensuring the application is compatible with mobile devices
- **Deployment**: Using PythonAnywhere for deployment and hosting
- **Server-side scripting**: Handling user interactions, processing location data and generating routes

■ IBDP subject recommender

by Sofia Cornu, used with permission

■ IBDP subject recommender

This project aims to develop a desktop application that will allow students to input information such as their subject interests, career aspirations and recent grades to receive a recommendation of which subjects they should choose for their IB diploma. The solution will take into account IB subject requirements and the school's timetable scheduling.

Key technologies and techniques

- Java programming language
- JavaFX GUI
- MySQL database to hold the school's timetable
- Excel file containing IB subjects that are recommended for different career paths, converted to JSON for easier use
- **Unique algorithm:** Developed to give students suggestions for their IBDP choices based on the data input

■ Stock-trading predictor

by a former student, used with permission

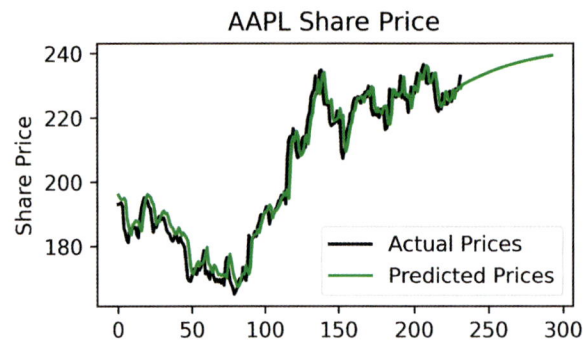

AAPL Share Price

■ Stock-trading predictor

This project aims to develop an AI-powered tool to assist in making more informed stock-trading decisions. The tool will use a long short-term memory neural network to predict stock prices based on historical data. The AI models will be trained individually for each stock and saved to the user's computer. The program will feature a simple GUI with minimal UI elements and will provide error handling for invalid inputs. The tool will also allow users to retrain existing AI models.

Key technologies and techniques

■ **AI**: Long short-term memory neural networks for stock-price prediction

■ **Python**: Programming language for implementation

■ **yFinance API**: For accessing stock data

■ **Tkinter**: For creating the GUI

■ **matplotlib**: For displaying graphs

■ **Machine learning libraries, e.g. TensorFlow or PyTorch**: For neural network training and implementation

■ D&D battle map generator

by Tom Chan, used with permission

■ D&D battle map generator

This project aims to create a desktop application that generates custom battle maps for Dungeons & Dragons. The application will feature a user-friendly interface, allowing users to customize maps easily with various textures and elements. The goal is to provide a quick and efficient solution for creating unique battle maps. Key features include procedural map generation, texture import, and easy saving and exporting.

Key technologies and techniques

- **Python**: Programming language for implementation
- **PySimpleGUI**: Front-end framework for creating the user interface
- **PIL (Pillow)**: For image processing and rendering
- **Procedural generation algorithms**: To generate structures, paths and hazards
- **Algorithms**: Breadth first search, A* path finding, recursive back-tracking
- **Data structures**: OOP to represent the map, rooms and paths
- **Texture mapping**: To apply textures to the generated map
- **File I/O**: For saving and loading maps
- **Image export**: For exporting maps as png, jpeg or pdf

Music art creator (Visuca)

by Anjali Bhimani, used with permission

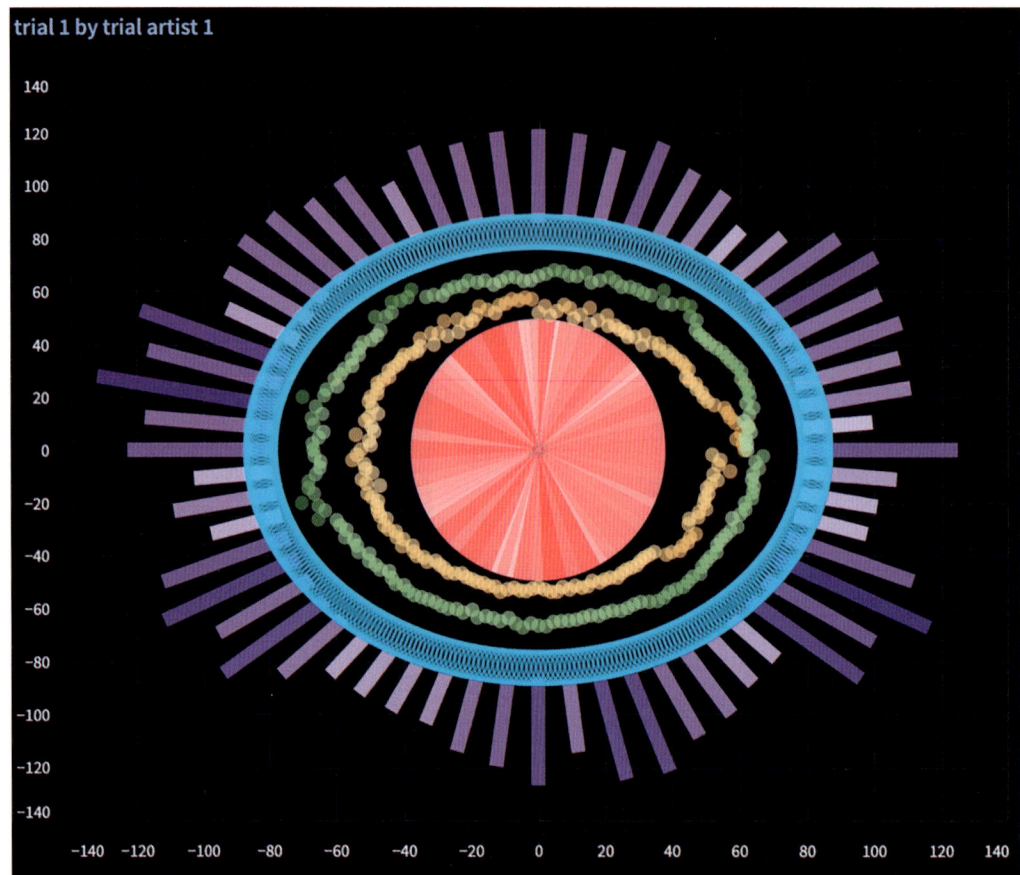

■ Example Visuca output

This project aims to create a desktop application that will generate a poster based on the musical elements of a song. The application will request the upload of a csv file with the musical element details and will have instructions for the user to convert their song of choice into a csv file. The application will then take into consideration the musical elements to create different posters that vary based on shape, pattern and colour intensity. The poster designs will change based on the client's song choice, so the deconstructed musical elements are represented as a 'visual display'.

Key technologies and techniques

- **Python**: Programming language for implementation
- **Streamlit**: Front-end framework for creating a user interface
- **Librosa**: Python library for extracting music data from MP3s
- **Vega-Altair**: Python library to create visual output
- **Algorithms**: Unique algorithm to display the music data visually
- **Data structures**: OOP to hold music data for individual tracks, lists and Panda data frames
- **File I/O**: Text files and Pickle library to import and export data

■ Network airlines (file transfer system)

by Eladio Hosseinpour, used with permission

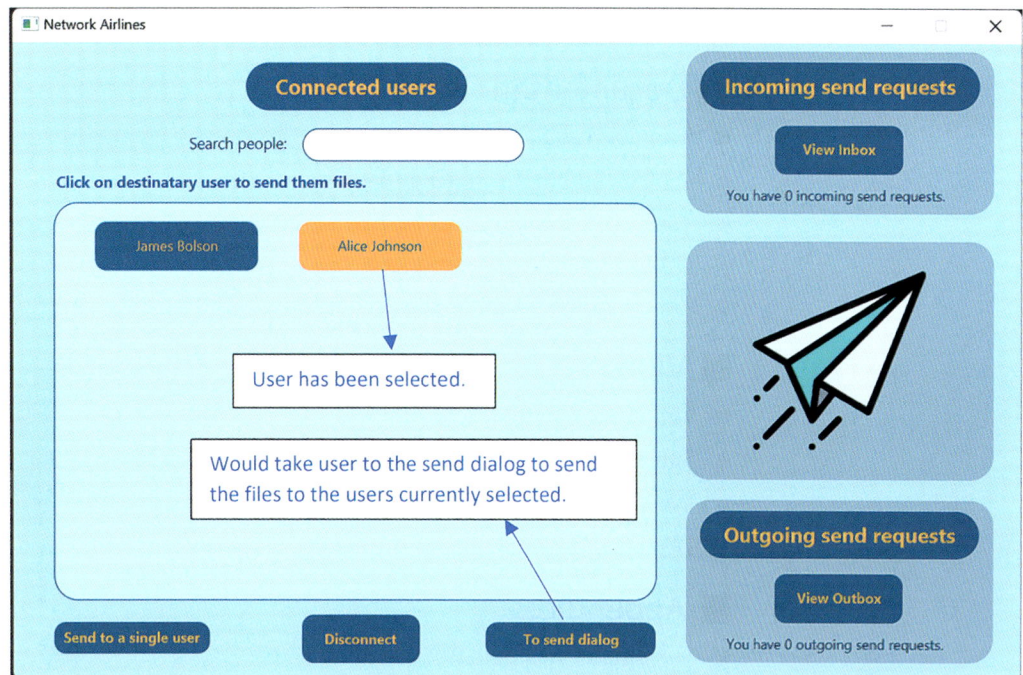

■ Network airlines (file transfer system)

This project aims to create a file transfer system that downloads files from one computer to another on the same network, through the ethernet – which connects devices on the local network – rather than the internet, so the data can travel directly between computers on the same network rather than having to be uploaded and downloaded, which is inefficient.

Key technologies and techniques

- **Java**: Programming language for implementation
- **JavaFX**: Front-end framework for creating a user interface
- **Multi-threading**: To boost the efficiency of the application
- **Asymmetric encryption**: Ensuring transmission security
- **Recursion**: Used for searching directories and sorting data
- **Algorithms**: Network scanning
- **Data structures**: OOP to hold file data and user information

Submission requirements

There are three files that will be submitted at the conclusion of your internal assessment: the documentation, the video and the appendices. Briefly, the role of each is as follows:

■ Documentation

- Submitted as a single PDF file
- Should contain five separate sections, one for each criterion
- Total word count must not exceed 2000 words (not including code excerpts, comments or diagrams)
- The overall word count should be clearly written on the cover page.

■ Video

- Maximum length of five minutes
- Submitted in a commonly used file format such as MP4, AVI or WMV
- Demonstrates the full functionality of the product
- Demonstrates examples of the testing strategy used in the development of the product.

■ Appendices

- Submitted as a single PDF file
- Must include the full source code and other resources developed that are referred to in the documentation
- While appendices are not used as evidence for the awarding of marks, and examiners are not required to read them, solutions that do not include an appendix with full source code cannot be awarded full marks for techniques demonstrated in criterion D.

Criterion A: Problem specification

The *Guide* provides the following information on criterion A:

> *The problem specification is the starting point of the solution and must be used as a basis for the development of the product.*
>
> *The student should have the necessary technical skills, access to appropriate hardware and software and the availability of relevant data to address the problem.*

- The success criteria identified in the problem specification (assessed by criterion A) will be used in the planning (assessed by criterion B), in the development (assessed by criterion D) and in the evaluation (assessed by criterion E).
- The recommended word count for this criterion is 300 words.

■ Criterion A assesses the problem specification (4 marks)

Marks	Description
0	The response does not reach a standard described by the descriptors below.
1–2	Outlines a problem scenario. States limited success criteria. Outlines the nature of the solution in a computational context.
3–4	Describes the problem scenario in terms of its measurable solution requirements. States appropriate success criteria. Explains the choice of computational context for the solution.

Clarifications:

- **Problem scenario:** The problem scenario is a clear description of the problem, including its measurable solution requirements. The description should relate directly to the problem, whether this be in the world around us, in other fields of knowledge or a current issue in computing.

- **Success criteria:** These are measurable outcomes derived from the solution requirements that indicate the successful development of the product.

- **Computation contexts:** The computational context is the specific area of computing that is selected to be used in the solution.

IBDP Computer science guide

Top tips!

Criterion A

1 Use the SMART technique to be as specific as possible with your success criteria (Specific, Measurable, Achievable, Relevant, Time-bound).

2 Use technical language in your success criteria (in the correct context). Vague, generic success criteria are unlikely to score marks.

3 Ensure you are not just recreating a clone of an existing app, such as a game. There must be an original idea, with an element of innovation, to your project. Be sure to articulate what sets your project apart from all the others. The IB provides some questions that may help:
   - ☐ What is the current situation?
   - ☐ Who is affected by the problem?
   - ☐ What causes the problem?
   - ☐ What are the objectives or general requirements for the computational solution?
   - ☐ Are there any constraints associated with the problem?

☐ Are there existing computational solutions and, if so, why are they not effective? What are their shortcomings?

☐ Why is it valuable or significant to construct a computational solution for the problem?

☐ Are there any time or resource limitations or specific conditions?

IBDP Computer science teacher support material

4 Examples of good success criteria include:
   - ☐ The solution will be able to input, edit and delete customer records from the customer database.
   - ☐ The solution will give appropriate warning messages to the user in case of extreme or invalid input.
   - ☐ The solution will be menu-driven with eight menu choices (including an indication of the choices).

5 Examples of inadequate success criteria include:
   - ☐ The code will compile.
   - ☐ The code will run without crashing.
   - ☐ The code will use loops.
   - ☐ The program will be aesthetically pleasing.

Common mistakes

Criterion A

1 **Criteria for success that do not actually make reference to the core functions of the proposed solution** (for example, creating a task manager without any mention of the core functions associated with being a task manager): This will always imply there are key criteria absent from this list. If you are designing a game, include some aspects of the game-play in your CfS – it will make your testing far easier.

2 **Make sure your success criteria are testable and not subjective:** A success criterion such as "The UI should look good" is not suitable, as it is vague and subjective and people may disagree on the outcome.

3 **Your success criteria have a key role in later assessment criteria:** You will design tests for them, and evaluate your project based on them, so ensure your success criteria meaningfully summarize the core functional requirements for your project.

■ Checklist for criterion A

- ■ Problem scenario:
  - ☐ The purpose, or idea, inspiring your problem solution has been clearly identified and described.
  - ☐ Explicitly relates to one of: the world around us; another field of knowledge; or a current issue in computing.
  - ☐ Measurable solution requirement(s). What is the essence or core functionality for your project? Summarize the purpose of your project here in a way that can be objectively measured, and then expand on it in the success criteria.

- ■ Computational context:
  - ☐ Clearly identify your choice(s) of computational context. This may include:
    - – Language environment – which programming language will you use and why? What are any potential flaws or weaknesses with this choice and how are they not a factor, or how have they been mitigated?
    - – Software environment – specific operating systems, libraries, frameworks to be used. Justify your choice.
    - – Hardware environment – specific components or computing infrastructure to be used/required. Justify your choice.
    - – Data environment – format, structure, size and source of the data you will be using or generating; any database engine you may use.
    - – Implementation environment – system configuration, network conditions, security constraints, resource availability and compatibility requirements.
  - ☐ Explain and justify why you have chosen these computational context(s).
  - ☐ If you have not yet finalized your choices, you can identify the options you are evaluating and what your guiding concern may be in making a choice. Be sure to identify this as a research task in your criterion B planning.
  - ☐ You may consider using a table such as the one below to help structure your computational context.

■ Table to help structure your computational context

Context	Chosen	Alternatives considered	Justification
Main language	Java	Python	Because …
Hardware environment			
Libraries / frameworks			
OS			
Data environment			

- ■ Success criteria:
  - ☐ Related to the problem scenario previously described
  - ☐ Clearly measurable, with precise language
  - ☐ Testable
  - ☐ Achievable and feasible within the constraints of your skills and time available
  - ☐ The sum of the success criteria will indicate successful development of the product
  - ☐ 8 to 10 in number
  - ☐ Should be application-feature focused rather than what programming techniques will be used.

- ■ 300 words.

■ Examples for criterion A

These are based on two of the projects outlined in the 'Project ideas and inspiration' section, reworked for the updated assessment criteria.

Vacation route planner

Based on the project by Edward Zhang

Problem scenario:

As a frequent traveller, I've struggled with planning multi-destination vacations, particularly across different countries. Existing tools like Google Maps and Tripadvisor lack the functionality to effectively sequence travel routes and offer limited customization, presenting a significant challenge in the travel and tourism sector. This problem highlights a gap in **current computing** solutions concerning data handling and real-time optimization for personalized travel planning. My project shall consist of a web-based application that allows users to select different cities and landmarks they wish to visit, creating a "tour" as a list of destinations. The application shall use route optimization and personalization features (such as travel method) to generate recommended itineraries.

Computational contexts:

The proposed solution is a web-based travel-planning application using **Flask** for back end operations due to its simplicity and effectiveness in managing routes and endpoint setups, and the ease with which it allows use of Python for back end functionality while using web technologies for a modern, stylish front end. The front end will utilize **HTML** for structure, **CSS** for styling and **JavaScript** for functionality, while incorporating the **Leaflet.js** library for advanced interactive mapping capabilities. This stack was chosen to ensure broad compatibility across devices, essential for real-time travel use. The combination of HTML/CSS/JS is industry standard for UI and there is plenty of documentation available to assist in creating the front end with these tools. The application will be hosted on **PythonAnywhere** due to its tooling being specifically designed for hosting Python projects with ease, in contrast with setting up a VPS with AWS or similar. This setup provides the flexibility needed for a personalized, dynamic travel-planning tool that meets the needs of myself and my friends.

Word count: 257

Success criteria:

The project will be considered successful if it meets the following criteria:

1 Generates a near optimal route (with respect to estimated travel time) connecting user-selected locations, starting and ending at user-specified points, using the travelling salesperson algorithm.
2 Displays the calculated route within 10 seconds for up to 15 locations.
3 Accurately recognizes and suggests locations based on partial or non-English inputs.
4 Provides interactive map functionalities with detailed markers and route segments.
5 Integrates with APIs to ensure accurate and current routing and location data.
6 Displays clear error messages for unreachable locations or invalid inputs.
7 Alerts users to input locations before attempting route planning.
8 Manages user inputs effectively, preventing entry of more locations than supported and prompting corrections.
9 User interface designed for mobile phone browsers, specifically the current version of iPhone Safari.

IBDP subject recommender

Based on the project by Sofia Cornu

Problem scenario:

As students entering the International Baccalaureate (IB) Diploma Programme, my friends and I are challenged by selecting subjects that align with our interests, career goals and IB requirements, while avoiding timetable conflicts. This relates to the **world around me** as it directly affects the planning of my future education through the ability to combine personal preferences with logistical constraints. The current manual approach, reliant on individual counselling, is inefficient and inadequate. Highlighting problems in educational logistics and computing, such as data integration and user personalization, there's a clear need for a digital solution that systematically addresses these challenges, enhancing educational planning through advanced computational techniques.

As such, I will create a solution that allows aspiring IB students to enter previous report grades, and personal preference data, from which the solution will generate a proposed subject enrolment that is personalized for the student. The solution will also ensure the proposed subject enrolment is compatible with the school's IB timetable offerings and blocking structure.

Computational contexts:

The application will be developed using **Java** due to its robust **static typing** system, which reduces bugs and enhances performance. Java's compatibility with **JavaFX** makes it ideal for creating a user-friendly **desktop environment** that operates seamlessly across **multiple operating systems**. Data management will be handled using a **MySQL server**, facilitating real-time updates and secure storage of timetable and student information. This approach leverages Java's capabilities for complex data structures and secure, scalable application development, addressing the specific needs of educational administration and compliance with educational standards.

Word count: 248

Success criteria:

The application must meet the following criteria to be considered successful:

1 **Personalization:** Users can input personal interests, career goals and academic performance. The application will recommend subjects based on these inputs.

2 **Scheduling integration:** It accesses the school's timetable data to ensure recommended subjects do not clash.

3 **Compliance with IB requirements:** Ensures the proposed subject combination is valid for the IB Diploma, including the correct level distribution (three Higher Level and three Standard Level subjects).

4 **User interface:** Features a graphical user interface (GUI) that allows for easy input of personal information using text boxes, check boxes and drop-down menus.

5 **Flexibility:** Includes a feature for selecting optional group 6 subjects and considers 'Environmental and Social Sciences' as applicable to multiple groups.

6 **Security:** Only authorized personnel (e.g. the IB coordinator) can alter timetable settings, secured via password protection.

7 **Cross-platform compatibility:** Functions on both Windows 10 and MacOS, aligning with the technology available to the students.

Criterion B: Planning

The *Guide* provides the following information on criterion B:

The planning of the product must be consistent with the problem specification in criterion A.

- This criterion assesses how the problem scenario has been decomposed into component parts.

- The plan should address the requirements of the solution, in terms of the success criteria, and include a proposed chronology for the steps involved in planning, designing, developing, testing and evaluating the solution.

- A plan can be presented in different forms, but diagrams such as Gantt and Agile charts can effectively support the planning process.

- The plan may include the allocation of time toward conducting research into code libraries, frameworks or other tools that may be suitable for the project.

The recommended word count for this criterion is 150 words.

- Criterion B assesses the planning (4 marks)

Marks	Description
0	The response does not reach a standard described by the descriptors below.
1–2	Constructs a **partial** decomposition of the problem scenario. Constructs a plan that addresses **some** of the success criteria of the solution.
3–4	Constructs a **reasonable** decomposition of the problem scenario. Constructs a plan that addresses the success criteria of the solution.

Clarification of planning:

- **Decomposition** is the breaking down of the problem scenario identified in criterion A into smaller, more manageable sub-problems or components. The decomposition can be effectively constructed using diagrams.

- A **reasonable decomposition** breaks the problem down into essential components that support the construction of a plan.

IBDP Computer science guide

Common mistakes

Criterion B

1 **Producing diagrams that are not technically accurate:** For any diagram you produce, make sure it complies with the standard for that type of diagram.

2 **Plans that are later contradicted by the solution submitted,** for example if the plan states you will use Microsoft SQL but you then end up using SQLite.

3 **Missing areas of the design cycle,** for example not showing any evidence of testing being carried out on a component.

Top tips!

Criterion B

1 Show you have carried out the design cycle for each sub-problem / component (planning, designing, developing, testing and evaluating).

2 There are multiple tools to facilitate decomposition, for example:
   □ The general solution can be documented by a use case diagram together with flowcharts, dataflow diagrams or equivalent.
   □ For procedural coding, it may be good to use a flowcharting tool to break down a complex task into modules.
   □ For object-oriented coding, it is important to identify and describe the objects in the problem scenario.
   □ A database project would require the identification and description of the data and processing required.

IBDP teacher support material, page 76

3 The plan should take into account the order of tasks, the timeline for their completion and the resources needed to complete the individual tasks. This is also a time when any research that is required can be planned for.

■ Checklist for criterion B

Decomposition

- Each of the success criteria from criterion A has been identified within the decomposition process.

- You may use a table or bullet point format. Alternatively, a structure chart with short comments underneath can be a useful means to articulate the different sub-parts of your problem (see example).

- Optionally you may also include a high-level overview of some key logic (such as a flowchart) or your data structures (such as an OOP relationship diagram). If included, these are "big picture" only as detailed design diagrams occur in criterion C.

Planning

- The plan should address all five stages:
  - ☐ Planning
    - – May include relevant research required for completion of the product (e.g. code libraries, frameworks, algorithms)
  - ☐ Designing
  - ☐ Developing
  - ☐ Testing
  - ☐ Evaluating

- Each of the sub-parts identified in the decomposition should be shown to have time allocated within your plan for designing, developing, testing and evaluating.

- Time limits and resources are considered to assign realistic timeframes and needs.

- You may, optionally, use planning diagrams such as a Gantt chart to present your planning (see the example).

- 150 words.

The IB offers this useful reminder:

> *Note that the plan is not a process journal. While an Agile approach is encouraged, the planning stage of the documentation should not be written after the computational solution is completed.*

■ Example for criterion B

The following example has been constructed for a hypothetical, personalizable Pacman clone game. Remember that, at this stage, you are only decomposing and planning your problem. These diagrams will not necessarily reflect the final version of your solution.

Project: Pacman clone

Decomposition

For my Pacman clone project, I have decomposed the problem into five main objects of Game, Map, Entity, Player and Ghost, as modelled in the UML relationship diagram that follows. Additionally I have decomposed the core functionality of the project according to the structure chart that follows (brief descriptions of each category follow the structure chart).

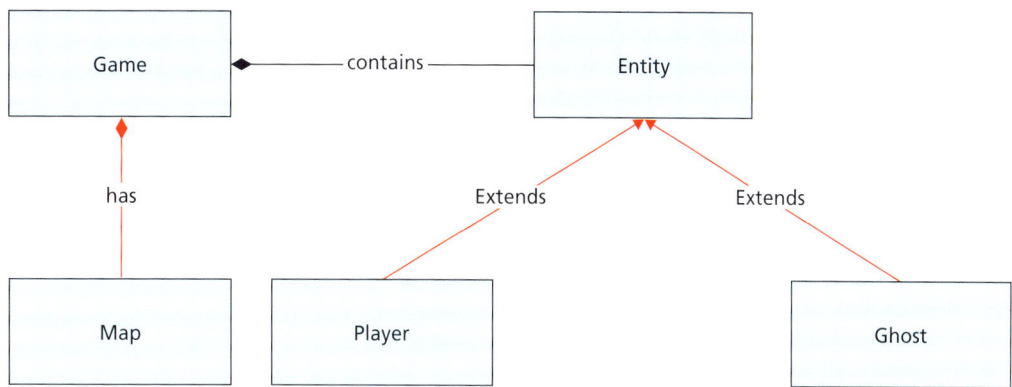

■ Class relationships UML

Structure chart identifying the key components of the decomposed project:

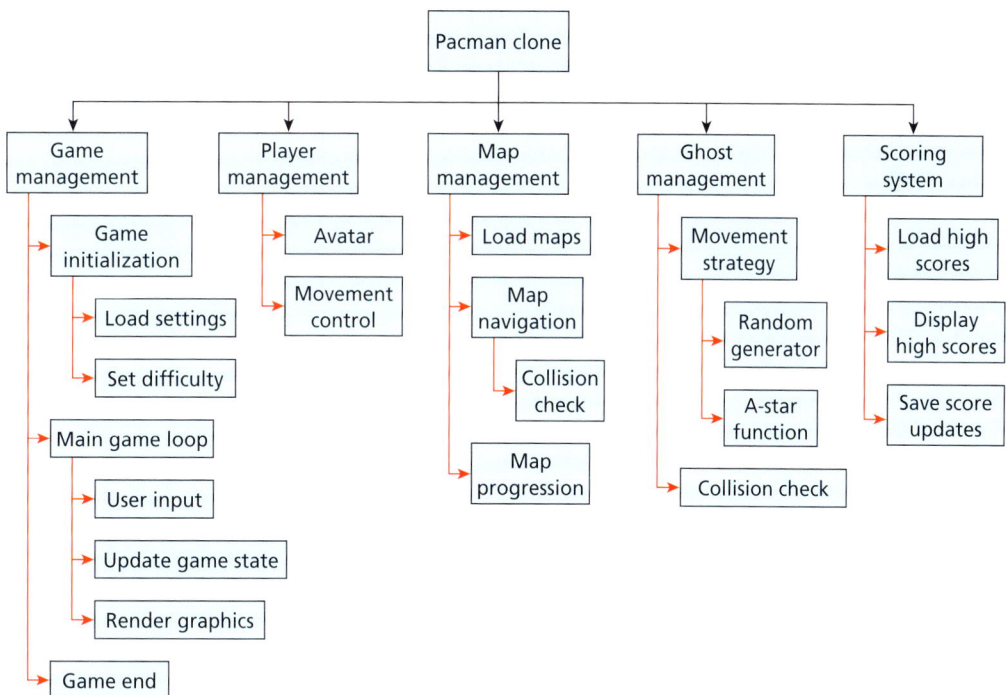

■ Structure chart

Further descriptions of the key components in the structure chart:

- **Game management**: This module handles the core loop and initialization, making sure the game starts and ends appropriately.

- **Player management**: Manages everything related to the player character, from avatar customization to handling movements based on keyboard inputs.

- **Map management**: Responsible for loading different maps and managing elements within them, including transitioning between different difficulty levels.

- **Ghost management**: Controls the ghosts' behaviour, utilizing an A-star algorithm for pathfinding and deciding their movement strategy based on the current difficulty level.

- **Scoring system**: Manages the scoring, including calculating scores based on game events (e.g. eating fruits) and handling high scores' storage and retrieval.

Gantt chart:

ID	Task Name
45	Initial planning
46	Initial design
1	▼ Game management
2	Plan
3	Design
4	Develop - Game initialisation
33	Develop - Main game loop
34	Develop - Game end
5	Test
12	Evaluate
7	▼ Map management
18	Plan
19	Design
20	Develop - Load maps
36	Develop - Man navigation
37	Develop - Map progresion
38	Develop - Collision detection
21	Test
22	Evaluate
11	▼ Player management
13	Plan
14	Design
15	Develop - Avatar
35	Develop - Movement control
16	Test
17	Evaluate
8	▼ Ghost management
23	Plan
24	Design
25	Develop - Movement
41	Develop - Random generator
42	Develop - A-star function
26	Test
27	Evaluate
9	▼ Scoring system
28	Plan
29	Design
30	Develop - Load high scores
39	Develop - Display high scores
40	Develop - Update scores
31	Test
32	Evaluate
43	Integration testing
44	Project evaluation

Timeline columns: 2024-09 (16, 22), 2024-10 (29, 06, 13, 20, 27), 2024-11 (03, 10, 17)

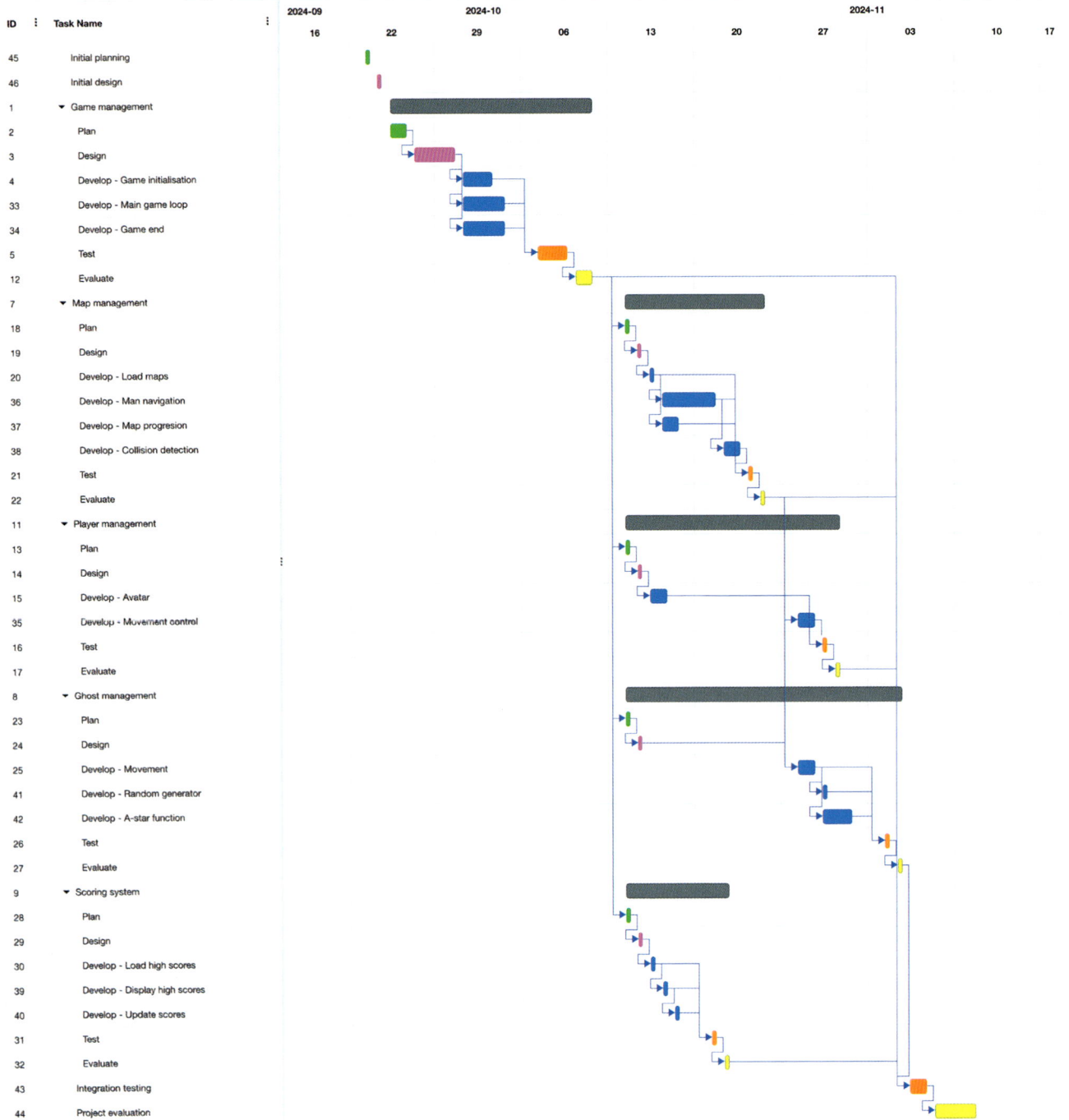

■ Gantt chart, illustrating the planning, designing, developing, testing and evaluation of each of the key components identified in the decomposition process and shown in the structure

Criterion C: System overview

The *Guide* provides the following information on criterion C:

The system overview of the product must be consistent with the problem specification in criterion A, and the planning in criterion B.

- The system overview should include a system model with the key components; their relationships; the rules governing their interaction; and the algorithms required by these components and the user interface.

- The system overview should have the clarity to enable a third party to re-create the product.

- The system model should provide the information for a viable testing strategy.

The recommended word count for this criterion is 150 words.

■ Criterion C assesses the system overview (6 marks)

Marks	Description
0	The response does not reach a standard described by the descriptors below.
1–2	Outlines a **limited** system model.
	Identifies algorithms for the components of the system model.
	Identifies a testing strategy for **at least one** success criterion.
3–4	Constructs a system model that is **not complete**.
	Constructs algorithms for the components of the model that lead to **partial functionality** of the product.
	Outlines a testing strategy that aligns with **at least three** success criteria.
5–6	Constructs a **complete** system model.
	Constructs algorithms for the components of the system model that enable the product to **perform**.
	Describes a testing strategy that aligns with the success criteria.

System overview clarifications:

- A **system model** consists of diagrams that include the components of the system and how they are connected. The system model will include the design of the User Interface. A **complete system model** does not include the algorithms for each of the components.

- **Algorithms** can be presented in different forms, including natural language, flowcharts or pseudocode, and should address the individual components of the system model.

- The **testing strategy** refers to a systematic approach for evaluating whether the computational solution works as intended. The testing strategy should ensure that code functions correctly and handles unexpected or incorrect inputs. This can be represented effectively in a table with proposed test data and expected outcomes.

IBDP Computer science guide

Criterion C

1 Testing strategies should be explicitly identified for each of your criteria for success. Functionally test and verify that your software functions according to requirements. Test that the range of inputs and outputs aligns with expected behaviour.

2 Never trust the user! As discussed in A2.4.3, user inputs should always be validated before being used for any calculations or algorithms. Common validation methods for user inputs include:

☐ **Presence check:** Has a value been input?

☐ **Length check:** Is the input an acceptable length (minimum or maximum length)?

☐ **Type check:** Does the input correspond to the correct data types: integer, float, absence of illegal characters?

☐ **Format check:** Have any complex formatting rules been correctly applied (such as dates, times or currency)?

3 Validate your inputs by supplying expected and unexpected input values to test how your software responds. Normal data, boundary data and erroneous data inputs should all be tested. Remember that the guiding principle for this assessment criteria in the *Guide* is:

the system overview should have the clarity to enable a third party to re-create the product

Does your response provide that level of clarity?

4 Recommended diagrams:

☐ UI – mandatory

☐ ERD (normalized) – if you have a database

☐ Data dictionary – if you have a database or persistent file storage

☐ UML diagram – if you are using OOP anywhere

☐ Component design diagram – if you have any physical hardware components

☐ Rules of engagement, attack surface mapping – if you have networking involved

☐ Flowcharting – for procedural code.

Criterion C

1 **A lack of design thinking being applied to your solution:** If you have genuinely decomposed your problem scenario, there really shouldn't be blocks of code hundreds of lines long (in criterion C, this could present as pseudocode that is overly long). This could be interpreted as a lack of effort to adequately think through and decompose your problem into abstractions such as classes or functions. The presence of variable names such as `person1`, `person2`, `person3` may be interpreted as something that could have been better designed with an array.

2 **Avoid any technical errors in your diagrams** (for example flowchart diagrams that have two arrows coming out of a non-decision element).

3 **Tests not actually relevant to achieving the proposed solution** (likely linked to poorly devised success criteria): Things like "starts up within 10 seconds" or "does not crash", instead of genuinely testing functionality, such as "successfully adds record to the XXX table of the database when a message is received".

◼ Checklist for criterion C

◆ **Functional testing:**
testing concerned with the behaviour of the application – specifically, whether it meets the requirements specified. This type of testing evaluates the software by providing inputs and examining the outputs, without considering how internal systems work. You are testing each of the success criteria on the whole application from the user's point of view.

◆ **Structural testing:**
testing concerned with the internal workings of the application – based on the code structure and internal pathways. This type of testing requires an understanding of the codebase and is used to ensure that all aspects of the code are properly tested. You are testing that all conditional branches execute correctly, and all error-handling code triggers when needed and responds appropriately.

◼ **System model – holistic overview:**

A system overview presents key components, their relationships and the rules governing their interaction. Some appropriate tools to facilitate this are:

☐ **Procedural coding:** Flowcharting to break down modules or a bulleted list with indentations.

☐ **OOP:** UML diagrams that show dependencies between classes.

☐ **Database project:** Table designs with normalization and a description of data dictionaries.

◼ **System model – for each component:**

Students are expected to show algorithms for key components only. There is no need to design all components of the system.

☐ Diagrams for each component, including the design of the user interface.

☐ Algorithms are not required for all components, but should be provided for those that lead to the functionality of the product. These algorithms may be presented using either natural language, flowcharts or pseudocode.

◼ **Testing strategies:**

Your document should contain two test tables:

1 **Functional testing table:** This table should evaluate the application against all success criteria, ensuring that the functionality meets user expectations and requirements.

2 **Structural testing table (white box testing):** This table should rigorously test major algorithms, using valid, extreme and invalid data to ensure the application performs correctly under all possible conditions.

◼ **Functional testing:**

Address all elements of the success criteria.

◼ **Structural testing:**

☐ Verify the major algorithms function correctly.

☐ Verify the solution handles unexpected or incorrect inputs and that you have tested the acceptable boundaries (valid, extreme and invalid data).

Examples for criterion C

The following tables provide a suggested format for documenting your testing strategy:

◼ Functional testing

Success criteria	Test number	Test	Expected outcome
1	1	Upload files of different types and sizes	All files upload correctly and are resized to a resolution of 300×300
2	2		
3	3	Load the game with a single ghost and observe its movement	Ghost should move to Pacman using a sensible path
4	4		
5	5	Run the game, and use the WSAD keys to observe Pacman movement	Movements should be: W = up S = down A = left D = right

■ Structural testing

Algorithm / structure	Test	Test type	Test data	Expected outcome
Uploading avatars	Upload files of different types and sizes	Valid	A mix of PNG and JPG files of resolutions: 100×100 500×500 1000×1000 2000×2000	Image file is correctly uploaded. Post-upload, the code resizes to a 300×300 avatar, and saves to internal memory for use within the game.
		Invalid	Non-image files uploaded, e.g. docx, xlsx, pdf	Error message displayed to the user with instructions about permitted image sizes and types.
		Extreme	File over 5MB in size, and / or dimensions over 2000×2000	Error message displayed to the user with instructions about permitted image sizes and types.
A-star algorithm	Unit testing on the A_Star() function	Valid	A range of source and target coordinates that are valid locations in the maps	Unit testing should pass these tests when expecting the correct next closest coordinate to be returned.
		Invalid	A range of source and target coordinates that are out of bounds / located in a wall / otherwise not valid locations in the maps	Unit testing should fail these checks.
		Extreme	Test on: map with no pathway from source to target; also test with source and target being at the same location	Unit testing should fail these checks.
User input controls	Use unittest. mock to simulate a range of keyboard inputs and combinations	Valid	A mix of W, A, S, D keyboard inputs	Game should correctly process the input.
		Invalid	Inputs of other keys	Game should ignore the input.
		Extreme	Rapid repeated key presses or simultaneous key presses	Game should ignore the input.

■ Example diagrams for criterion C

The following are exemplar diagrams of the type that may be commonly included for this criterion (depending on your project choice).

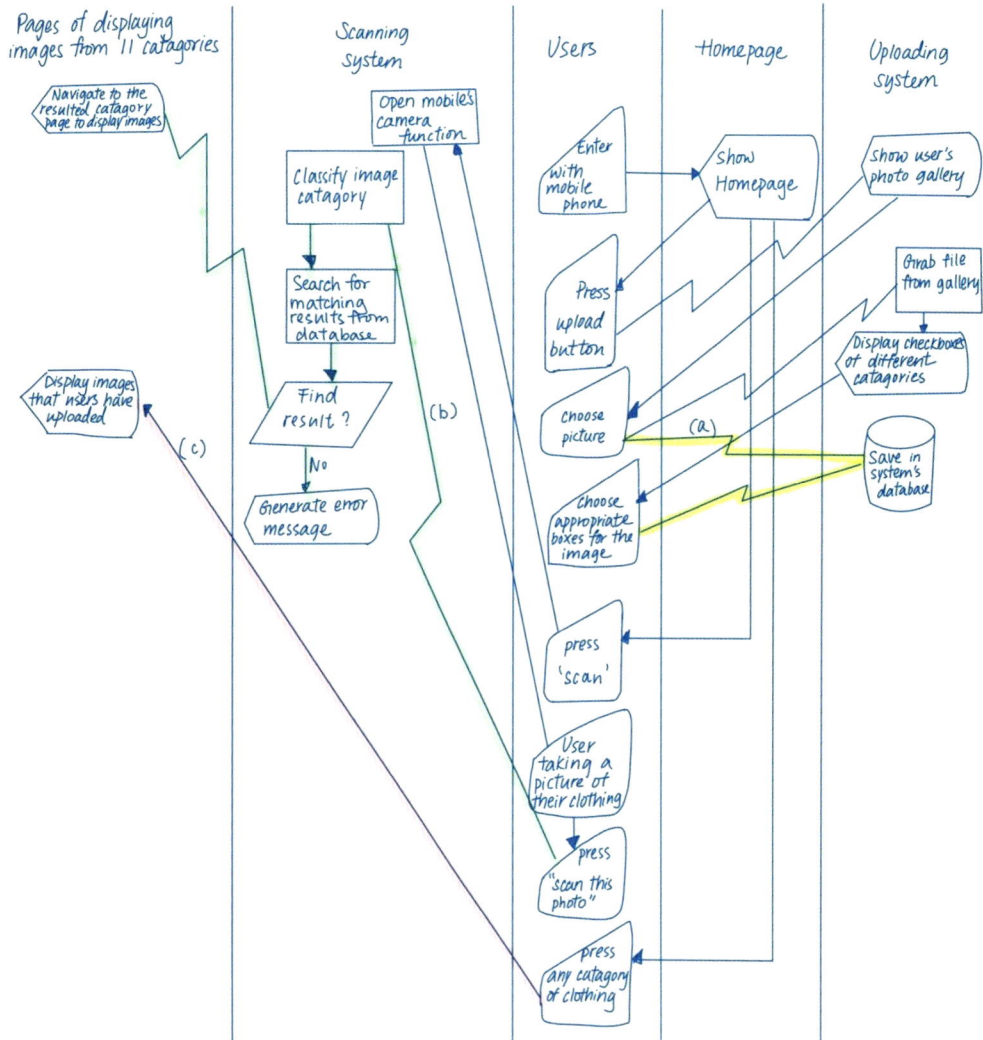

■ System flow diagram (credit: Hailey Annabelle Loh)

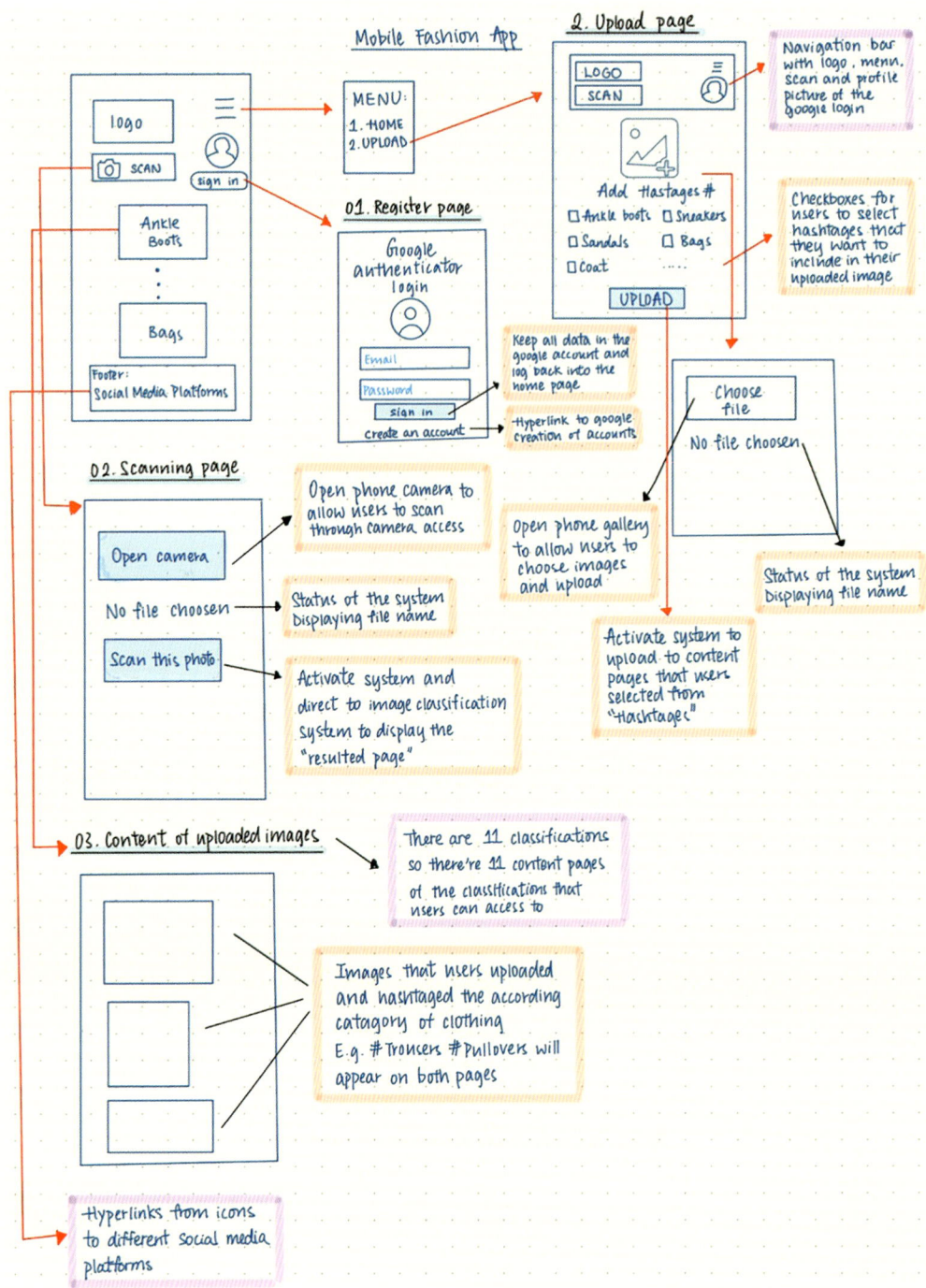

Mobile Fashion App

2. Upload page

MENU:
1. HOME
2. UPLOAD

Navigation bar with logo, menn, scan and profile picture of the google login

Add Hashtages #
☐ Ankle boots ☐ Sneakers
☐ Sandals ☐ Bags
☐ Coat ....

UPLOAD

Checkboxes for users to select hashtages that they want to include in their uploaded image

logo

SCAN

sign in

Ankle Boots
⋮
Bags

Footer:
Social Media Platforms

01. Register page

Google authenticator login

Email
Password
sign in
create an account

Keep all data in the google account and log back into the home page

Hyperlink to google creation of accounts

Choose file

No file chosen.

Open phone gallery to allow users to choose images and upload

Status of the system Displaying file name

02. Scanning page

Open camera

No file choosen

Scan this photo

Open phone camera to allow users to scan through camera access

Status of the system Displaying file name

Activate system and direct to image classification system to display the "resulted page"

Activate system to upload to content pages that users selected from "Hashtages"

03. Content of uploaded images

There are 11 classifications so there're 11 content pages of the classifications that users can access to

Images that users uploaded and hashtaged the according catagory of clothing
E.g. #Trousers #Pullovers will appear on both pages

Hyperlinks from icons to different social media platforms

■ User interface mock-up 1 (credit: Hailey Annabelle Loh)

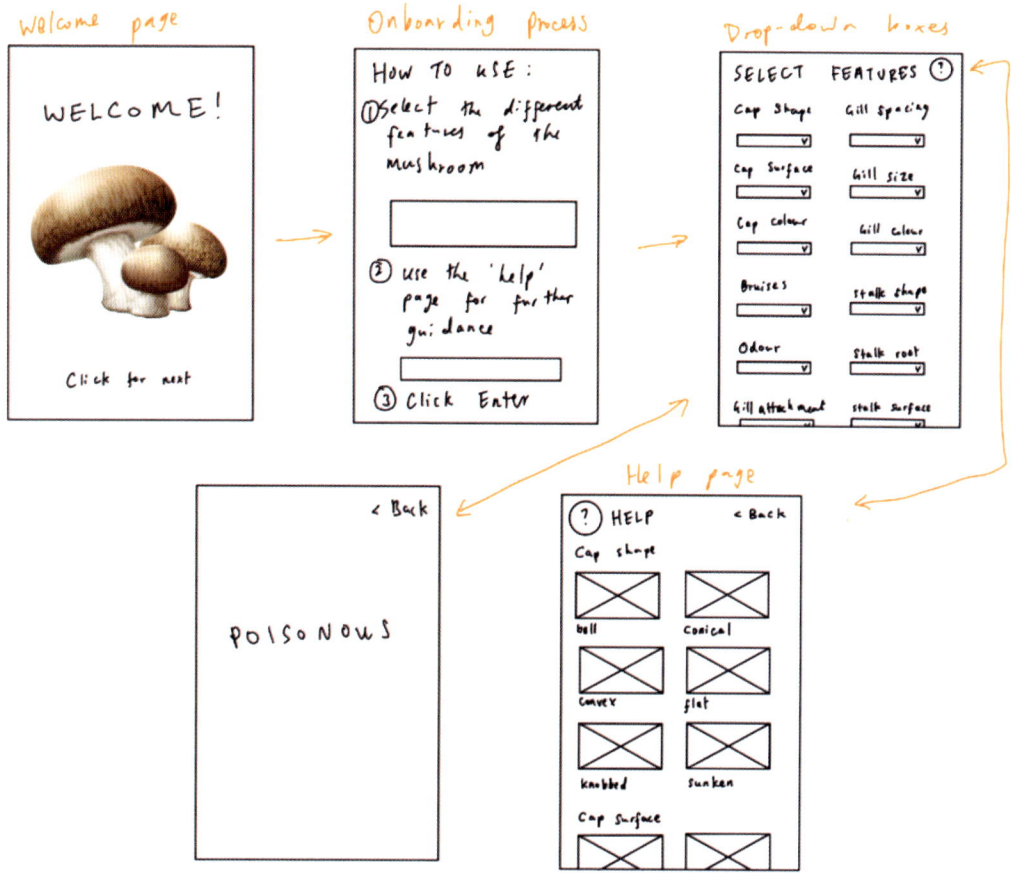

Welcome page

WELCOME!

Click for next

Onboarding Process

HOW TO USE:
① Select the different features of the mushroom

② Use the 'help' page for further guidance

③ Click Enter

Drop-down boxes

SELECT FEATURES ⑦

Cap Shape   Gill spacing

Cap Surface   Gill size

Cap colour   Gill colour

Bruises   Stalk shape

Odour   Stalk root

Gill attachment   Stalk surface

< Back

POISONOUS

Help page

⑦ HELP   < Back
Cap shape

bell   conical

convex   flat

knobbed   sunken

Cap Surface

■ User interface mock-up 2 (credit: H Ng)

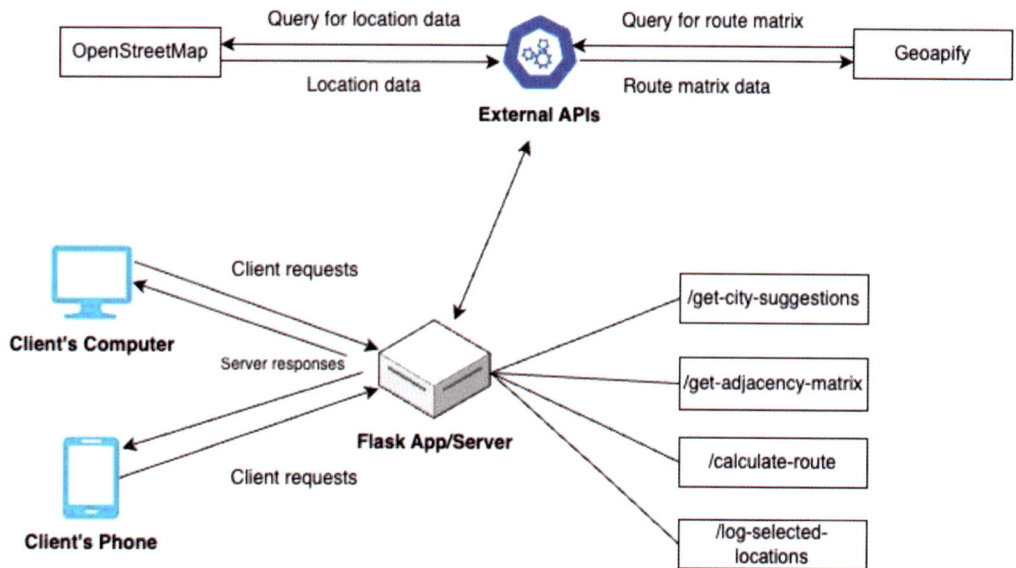

Query for location data

OpenStreetMap

Location data

External APIs

Query for route matrix

Route matrix data

Geoapify

Client requests

Client's Computer

Server responses

Flask App/Server

Client requests

Client's Phone

/get-city-suggestions

/get-adjacency-matrix

/calculate-route

/log-selected-locations

■ Network architecture diagram (credit: Edward Zhang)

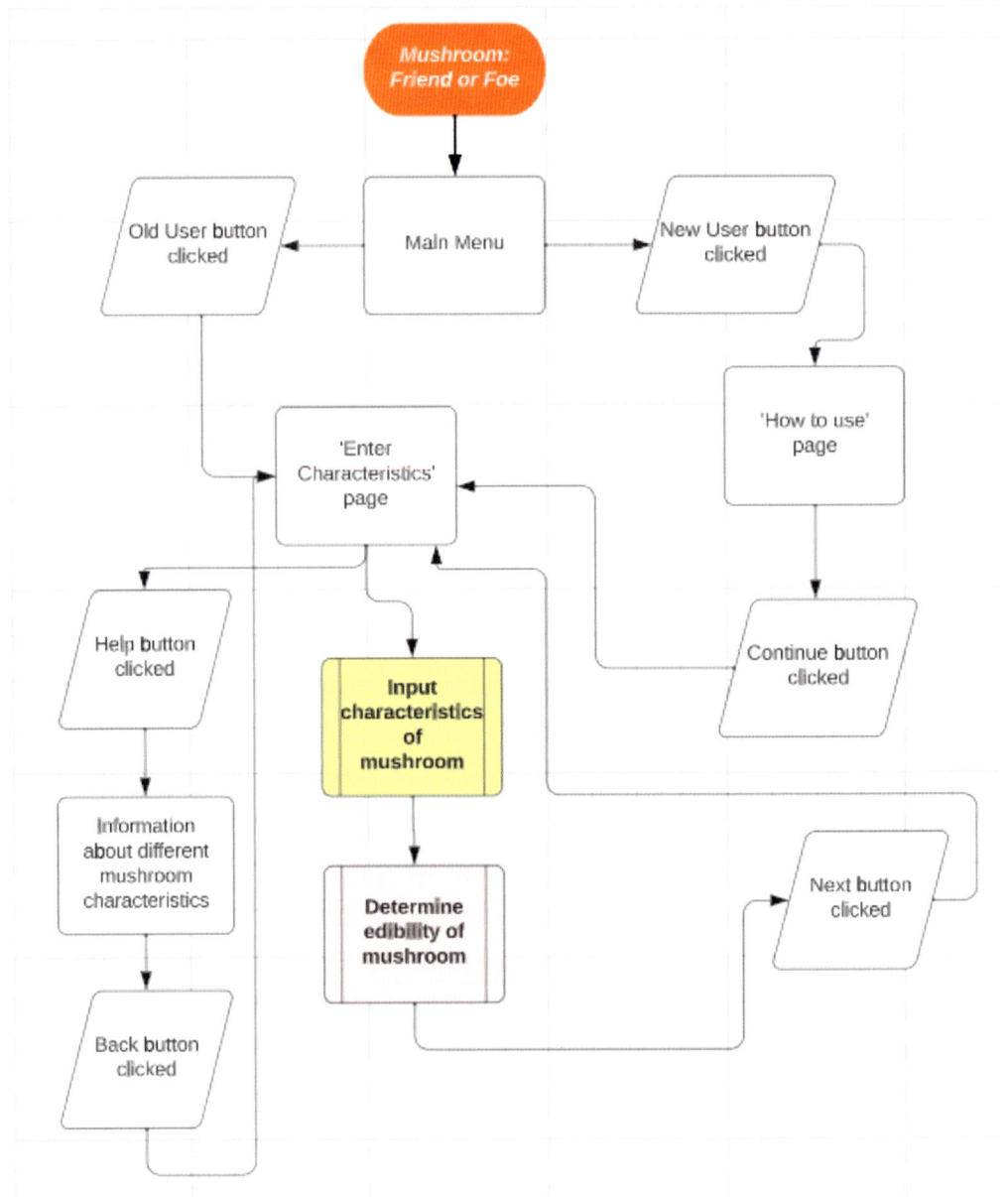

■ High-level overview flowchart (credit: H Ng)

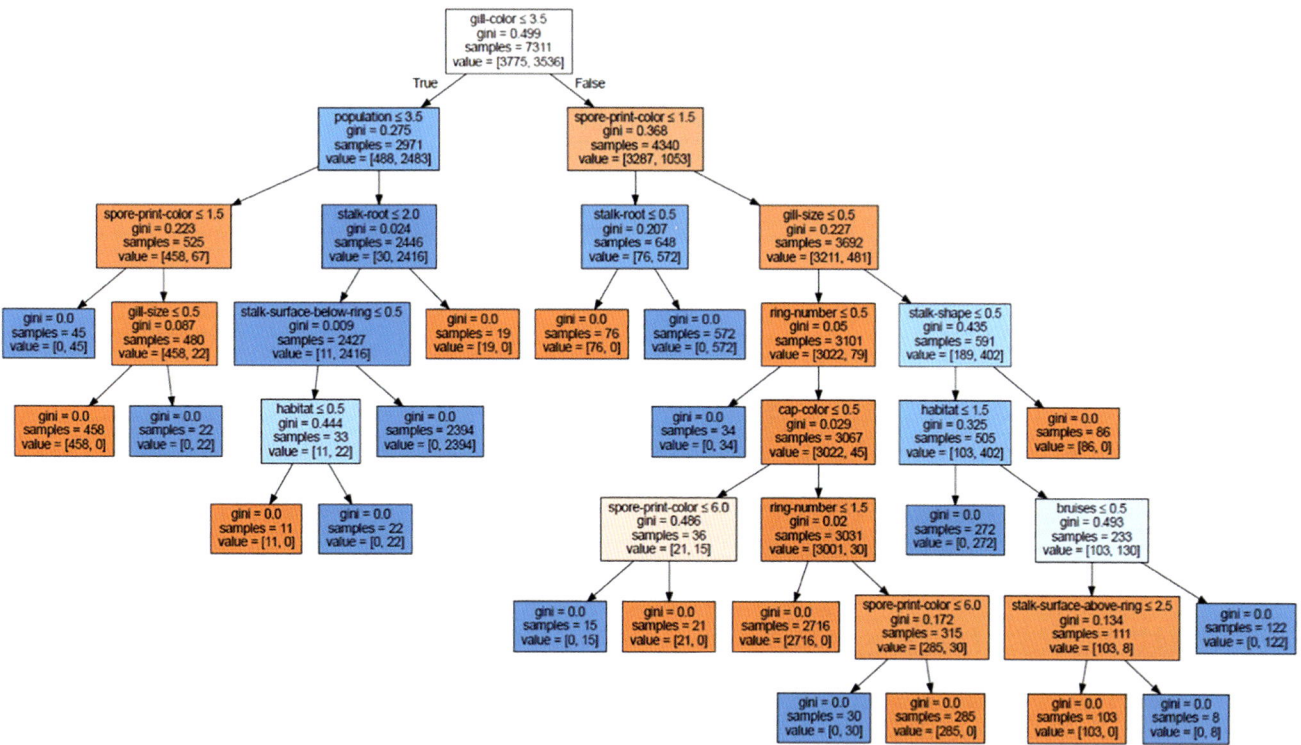

■ Decision tree ML model (credit: H Ng)

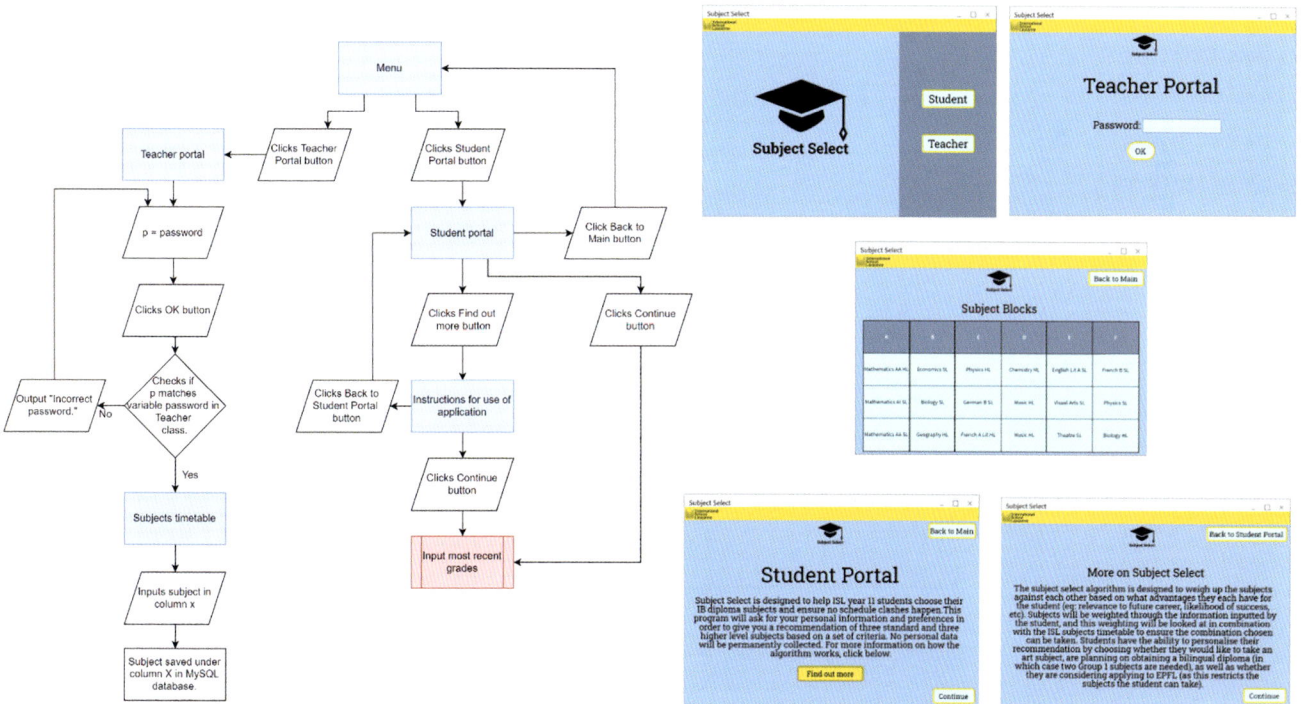

■ User interface with relevant logic side by side (credit: Sofia Cornu)

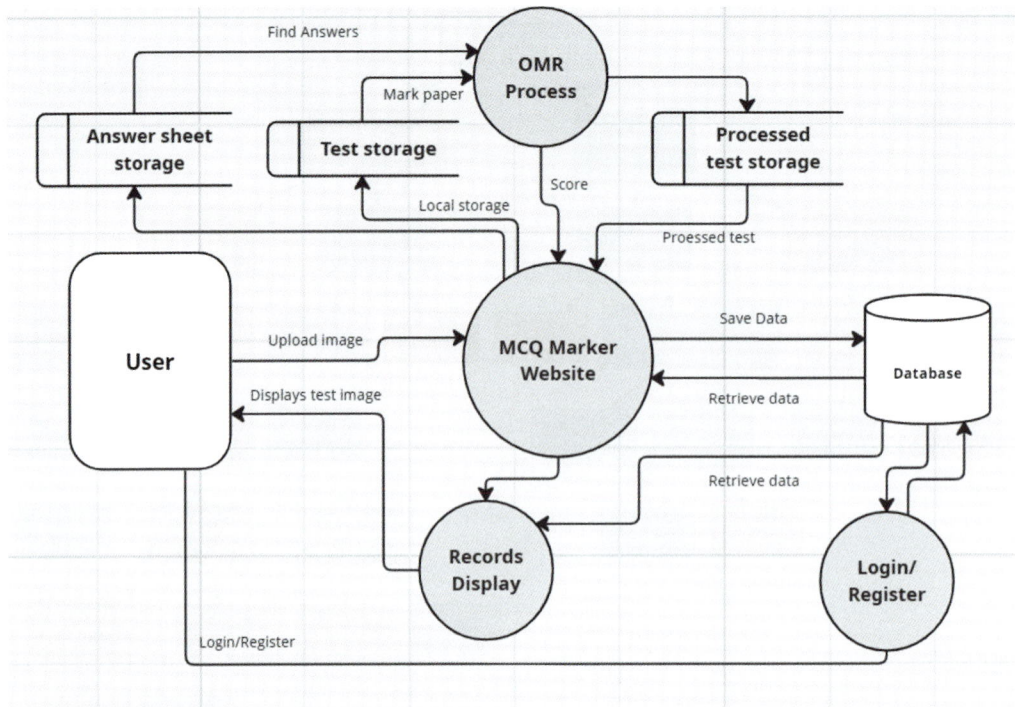

■ Data flow diagram (credit: former student)

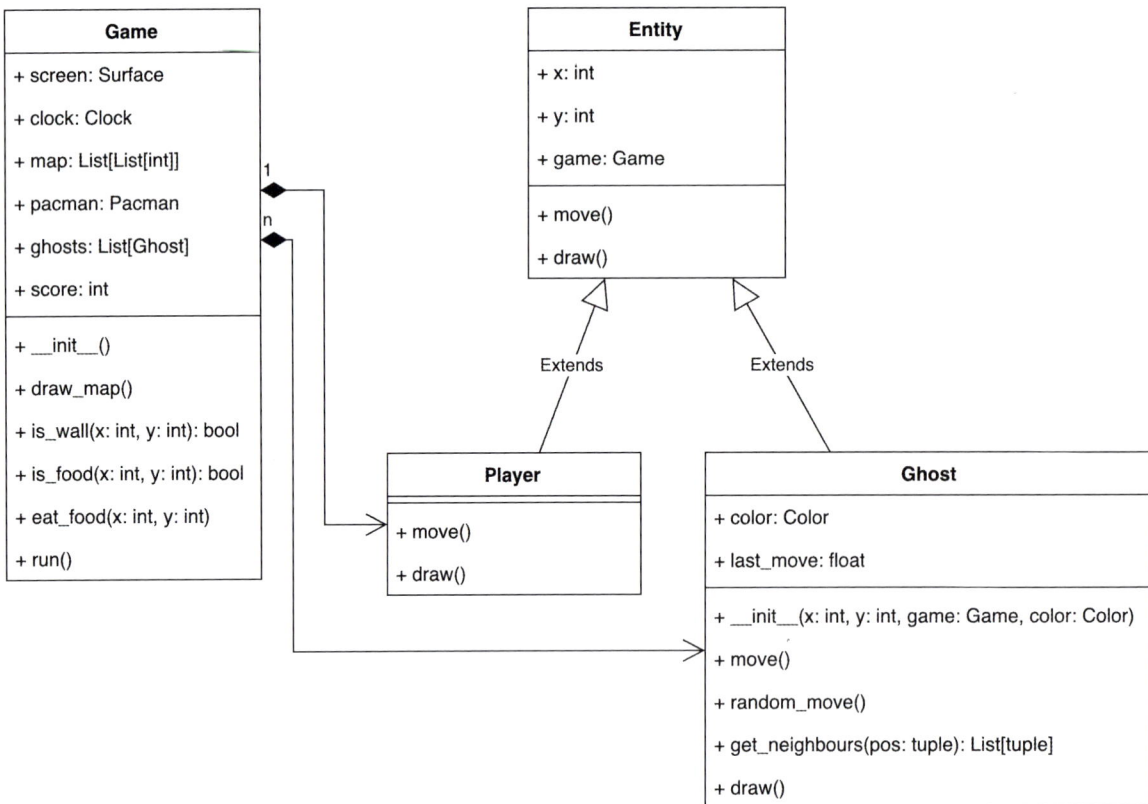

■ Entity relationship diagram

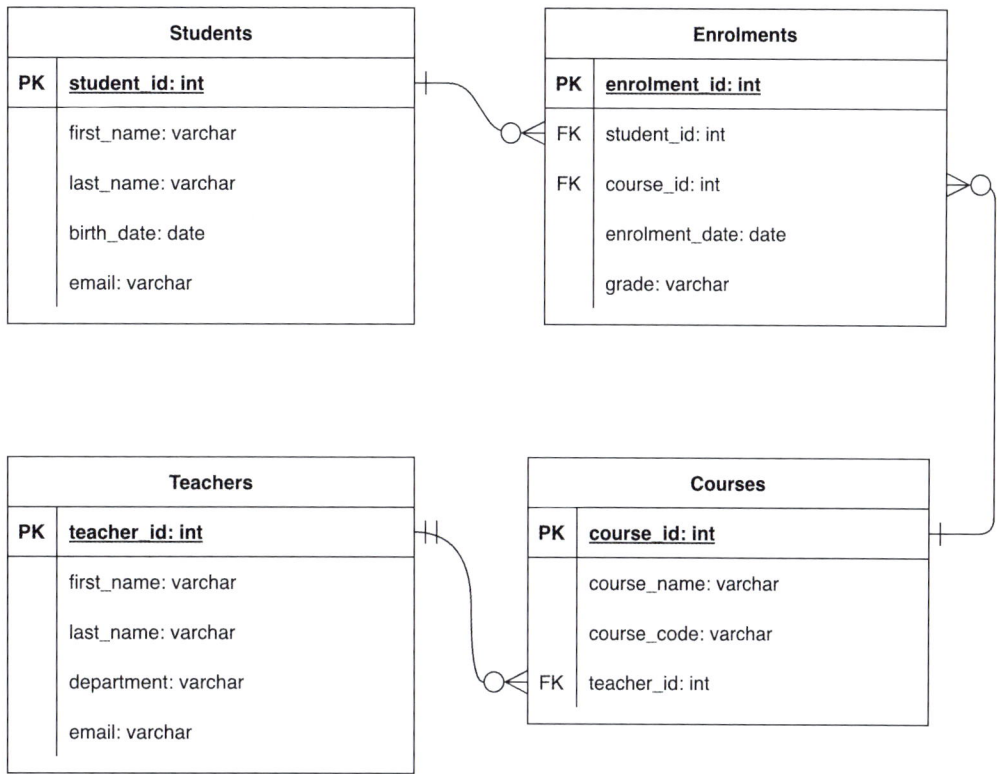

■ UML class diagram with relationships

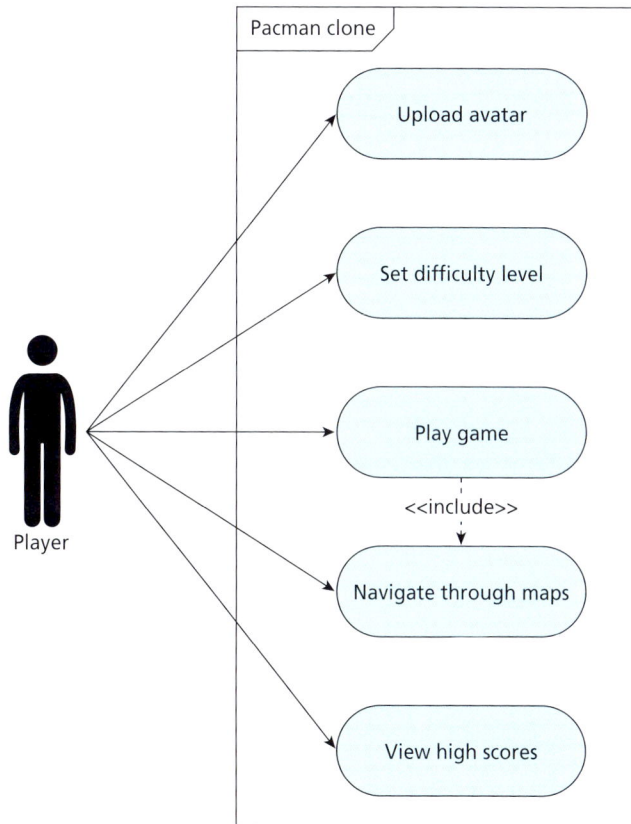

■ Use case UML

SETTINGS.JSON

```json
{
    "language": "en",
    "timezone": "Asia/Bangkok",
    "dateFormat": "dd/mm/yyyy",
    "server": {
        "ipAddress": "192.168.1.100",
        "apiPort": 8080,
        "apiKey": "a1b2c3d4e5f6g7h8i9j0"
    }
}
```

■ Configuration file example

PSEUDOCODE FOR MAIN GAME LOOP IN PACMAN

```
METHOD run()
    Set game_running to True
    WHILE game_running is True
        Process events:
            If a quit event is detected, exit the game
        Clear the screen to the background color
        Draw the map with walls and food
        Move and draw Pacman
        Check and handle food consumption at Pacman's position
        For each ghost in ghosts array:
            Move and draw the ghost
            Check collision between the ghost and Pacman:
                If collision, print "Game over" with the score,
                set game_running to False
        Update the display to reflect any changes
        Control the frame rate with the clock
    END WHILE
END METHOD
```

■ Pseudocode example

Criterion D: Development

The development of the product must be consistent with the problem specification in criterion A, the planning in criterion B and the system overview developed in criterion C.

■ The video should provide evidence of the functionality and give examples of the testing of the product.

■ The development of the solution should justify the structure of the product and why it is appropriate, and demonstrate the techniques used to develop the product based on the algorithms constructed in criterion C. These techniques may include loops, data structures, existing libraries and the integration of software tools.

■ The testing strategy should include testing for correctness, reliability and efficiency. The testing should be described and justified in the documentation, with supporting examples seen in the video.

The recommended word count for this criterion is 1000 words.

■ Criterion D assesses the development of the product (12 marks)

Marks	Description
0	The response does not reach a standard described by the descriptors below.
1–3	Constructs a product with **very limited** functionality. Constructs a product using **no appropriate techniques** to implement the algorithms. **States** the choices made to implement the algorithm. **States** the testing strategy used.
4–6	Constructs a product that has **limited** functionality. Constructs a product using **at least one appropriate technique** to implement the algorithms. **Outlines** the choices made to implement the algorithm. States the **effectiveness** of the testing strategy used.
7–9	Constructs a product that has **partial** functionality. Constructs a product that uses **some appropriate techniques** to implement the algorithms. **Explains** the choices made to implement the algorithm. **Describes** the effectiveness of the testing strategy used.
10–12	Constructs a **fully functional** product. Constructs a product that uses **appropriate techniques** to implement the algorithms. **Evaluates** the choices made to implement the algorithm. **Justifies** the effectiveness of the testing strategy used.

Clarification of development:

■ **The implementation and coding of the algorithms:** Techniques in the criteria refer to the process of programming algorithms using code. The documentation should highlight key elements of code that are important for the efficient functioning of the algorithms. Any code presented in the solution should include relevant comments, be consistent and be readable. Code excerpts included in the documentation should be referenced to the full source code submitted as an appendix.

■ **Functionality and testing:** The **video** should demonstrate the functionality of the product. The deployment of the testing strategy and its effectiveness should be described in the documentation with examples of the testing seen in the video.

IBDP Computer science guide

Top tips!

Criterion D

1 The top band for this criterion shifts the focus from *explanation* and *description* to that of *evaluation* and *justification*. Why were the techniques you used appropriate? Why did you make the choices you did when implementing your algorithm(s)?

2 Why was your method of testing the solution optimal for the context? Show at least three of the outcomes of your test cases against this area of your application, covering both functional and structural testing.

3 Structure your criterion D with subheadings based on the success criteria, rather than as a narrative telling the history of the development of the solution. For each of your success criteria, present the case for the most appropriate techniques for completing it and your testing strategy used for it.

4 Ensure your video demonstrates testing of your product – not just for expected, but for unexpected, inputs. The video should also show that the software correctly processes the inputs, not just by showing the output produced, but by also showing that any internal state changes of the software have correctly occurred (for example demonstrate that a "save" function does produce a resulting change in the database).

5 When taking screenshots of your code to use in your documentation, include the line numbers. This makes it easier for you to refer to sections of your code in your writing.

6 The IB states that it is acceptable to improve code with GPT, but any use of GPT needs to be explicitly documented and the improvements need to be properly discussed and justified. Techniques must be recognized to receive marks for development and the choices made must be discussed.

Common mistakes

Criterion D

1 **A very common issue is having limited discussion that explains why the approach was selected.** Justify why you programmed using the approach taken. There are several ways to do this, but the best is to contrast against alternative valid approaches and then explain the rationale of your decision.

2 **Remember your code that is submitted within the appendix forms part of criterion D.** Ensure your code is meaningfully stylized, structured and designed in accordance with the plans articulated in criteria B and C. One long file with thousands of lines in it, with functions and mainline code inter-mixed, no use of classes or meaningful modularization, will not likely score in the top band.

3 **The video is not for showing or explaining your code**, but for demonstrating the functionality of your application based on the success criteria. You only have five minutes; use them wisely.

4 **Videos longer than five minutes will not score more marks** as the moderator will likely stop watching at the five-minute mark. Anything beyond this will not be considered for your grade.

■ Checklist for criterion D

■ Video:

1 Your video addresses the problem described in criterion A.

2 A single test-run of the product is often sufficient to demonstrate the functionality, and then some examples of the testing strategy.

3 Ensure you showcase you have met every success criteria in your video (although full functionality can be achieved if your product is a working solution to an adequate problem specification, even if the success criteria have not been fully met).

- **Development document:**

    4 Identify and address five to seven of your most advanced techniques / algorithms / data structures:

    – Discuss the techniques used to complete them.

    – Use screenshot excerpts of your code. Comments should be provided with code to explain their purpose.

    – Discuss alternative solutions you considered, where appropriate. Evaluate your choices.

    5 Evidence of testing:

    – Functional testing

    – Structural testing

    – At least three separate test cases included (e.g. valid, extreme, invalid input data)

    – Evaluate the comprehensiveness of the testing

    – Justify your testing strategy.

For the evidence of testing, it is suggested you reproduce areas of the table from criterion C, with an additional column for 'results obtained'. If word count is a problem, you could simplify the table by numbering the tests in the criterion C table, and then referring to tests by their number when providing the results here in criterion D.

◼ Examples for criterion D

Multithreading

```
// create instance of TalkToServer class and submit it to the executor. multithreading.
ExecutorService executor = Executors.newSingleThreadExecutor();
Future<JSONObject> future = executor.submit(new TalkToServer(jsonObject));
// wait for task to finish executing
while (! future.isDone()) {
    Thread.sleep( millis: 100);
    System.out.println("waiting....");
}
JSONObject jsonResponse = future.get();
// go to results page
Intent intent = new Intent( packageContext: this, results.class);
intent.putExtra( name: "jsonResponse", jsonResponse.getString( name: "RESULT"));
startActivity(intent);
```

Create an ExecutorService with a thread

Submit the TalkToServer task (JSON request and response) to the executor

Retrieve the response

◼ Multithreading in "Mushroom: Friend or foe?" (credit: H Ng)

Explanation
In the Android application, multithreading is used to perform network operations, like fetching data from an API, without blocking the main UI thread. This approach keeps the UI responsive as network requests are handled in the background.
Justification
The advantage of this approach is that using separate threads to execute communication with the server ensures that the task can be completed concurrently in the main thread. As a result, the application stays responsive even if the request and response process takes a long time. An alternative approach could have been to use AsyncTask, however this is prone to memory leaks for beginner programmers. Kotlin Coroutines are a new feature designed to be a simple alternative to thread management, however these are not available for Java.
Testing
Structural tests (unit testing) and functional tests were conducted to ensure thread safety and correct data fetching. Tests under simulated slow network conditions confirmed the UI remains responsive.
Links to: success criterion 5

Calculating optimal route - Bitmasks Dynamic Programming and 2D array processing

Transition: Iterate over all possible masks, which represent all subsets of nodes

- Consider all other nodes "v" that haven't been visited yet

This is the base case, all other elements in the array are set to infinity

```python
108  def find_min_cost_path(cost):
109      n = len(cost)
110      MAX_INT = 1 << n
111      dp = [[float('inf')] * n for _ in range(MAX_INT)]
112      dp[1][0] = 0
113
114      for mask in range(1, MAX_INT):
115          for u in range(n):
116              if mask & (1 << u):
117                  for v in range(n):
118                      if mask & (1 << v) and u != v:
119                          dp[mask][u] = min(dp[mask][u], dp[mask ^ (1 << u)][v] + cost[v][u])
120
121      min_cost = min(dp[MAX_INT - 1])
122      end_node = dp[MAX_INT - 1].index(min_cost)
```

mask XOR (1 << u): Removes node u from the set of visited nodes in mask

dp[mask XOR (1 << u)][v]: Gives the minimum cost of reaching node v from the start, having visited the set of nodes in mask minus node u

dp[mask XOR (1 << u)][v] + cost[v][u]: Total cost of reaching node u from the start, having first reached node v and then traveling from v to u

The minimum of these two values is then set as the new cost to reach u.

min_cost is the minimum value from the last row of the DP array, which contains the minimum costs of reaching the final node from all other nodes.
end_node is the index of the minimum cost, which is the last node in the optimal path.

Set the initial bitmask to all 1s to represent that all nodes have been visited in the final state of the path.

```python
121      min_cost = min(dp[MAX_INT - 1])
122      end_node = dp[MAX_INT - 1].index(min_cost)
123
124      mask = MAX_INT - 1
125      path = [end_node]
126
127      while mask and end_node != 0:
128          for v in range(n):
129              if mask & (1 << v) and dp[mask][end_node] == dp[mask ^ (1 << end_node)][v] + cost[v][end_node]:
130                  path.append(v)
131                  mask ^= (1 << end_node)
132                  end_node = v
133                  break
134
135      return min_cost, list(reversed(path))
```

Check if 'v' is part of the current mask (subset) and leads to the optimal path for 'end_node'. If yes, then it's part of the optimal route.

Update the mask by removing 'end_node' from the current subset, preparing for the next iteration of backtracking.

Set the current 'end_node' to 'v' as we move backwards through the path.

■ Calculating optimal route in "Vacation route planner" (credit: Edward Zhang)

Explanation
The 2D array `dp` is used to represent the states of the solution. Each state has a bitmask `mask` and a position `u`. The bitmask represents the subset of nodes visited so far, and the position represents the current node being processed. `dp[mask][u]` stores the minimum cost to reach node `u` after visiting the set of nodes represented by the bitmask `mask` (Datta, Subham). Refer to the screenshots above for a detailed explanation.

Justification
By using bitmask dynamic programming, the algorithm transforms the problem from a brute-force search of $O(N!)$ time complexity to $O(N^2 \times 2^N)$, which is feasible for N up to 15 to 20 (Kaçar, Kaan). Compared to more efficient heuristics such as Christofides' algorithm or the nearest-neighbour heuristic, dynamic programming always guarantees the optimal solution, while heuristics only provide an approximation (GeeksForGeeks).
An iterative approach was adopted because recursion could lead to stack overflow and increase computational complexity. The bottom-up dynamic programming approach builds up the solution from smaller subproblems to obtaining the final answer, which optimizes performance and memory usage.

Testing
Structural testing (with unittest) targeted the correctness of the bitmask operations and the 2D array update process. Tests showed that all possible states (mask combinations) correctly influence subsequent states.
Functional tests simulated different node arrangements to ensure the algorithm consistently finds the optimal path.

Links to: success criterion 1

Criterion E: Evaluation

The evaluation of the product must be consistent with the problem specification and success criteria in criterion A.

The recommended word count for this criterion is 400 words.

■ Criterion E assesses the evaluation of the product

Marks	Description
0	The response does not reach a standard described by the descriptors below.
1–2	**States** the extent to which the success criteria were met. **Describes** improvements to the product.
3–4	**Evaluates** the extent to which the success criteria were met. **Justifies** improvements to the product.

IBDP Computer science guide

●Top tips!

Criterion E
1   The IB suggests that you may wish to include a table that lists all the success criteria together with an in-depth evaluation that addresses to what extent each criterion has been achieved by the solution.
2   Ensure you evaluate all of your success criteria individually and specifically.
3   When evaluating your success criteria and justifying the outcome, it is a good idea to refer back to the tests you carried out as evidence for this outcome.
4   Think of the improvements you would introduce if you were to develop a 2.0 version of your application. What features would you add?

● Common mistakes

Criterion E

1   A common mistake with evaluation is overly simplistic and repetitive comments (e.g. "haven't run into bugs or errors"). The top band requires you to evaluate, not just state whether each of the success criteria is met. The *Guide* defines "evaluate" as "make an appraisal by weighing up the strengths and limitations".

2   Examples of inadequate improvements include:

   a   To include more colour / more data / more calculations / more functionality (unless very specifically justified).

   b   To add more functionality for success criteria that have not been met.

   c   To add a GUI interface for a solution that was developed as a CLI.

   d   To add functionality that is an essential (but missing) component of a fully functional solution (e.g. adding payment functionality to a web shop, or permanent storage for a database).

■ Checklist for criterion E

■ **Evaluation:**

   1   Evaluate the success of **every** success criterion.

   2   Come to a conclusion: Were the success criteria met, partially met or not met? Justify your reason for this conclusion, using the results of your tests to help evaluate this.

■ **Improvements:**

   1   Improvements should be justified with reference to how they will address the specific issues.

   2   Adequate improvement suggestions should be specific and actionable.

■ Examples for criterion E

Keep in mind that these examples are from the previous syllabus that required a client. The updated IA does not require a client. Rather than referring to your client feedback to evaluate each of your success criteria, you should refer back to your testing process as much as possible.

■ Evaluating success criteria in "Mushroom: Friend or foe?" (credit: H Ng)

Success criteria	Visuals	Evaluation
The program makes use of a graphical user interface to facilitate the input of mushroom features using drop-down boxes.	**Enter Characteristics** ⓘ Bell ▾ Cap surface **Fibrous** ▾ Cap colour **Brown** ▾ Bruises **Bruises** ▾ Odour **Almond** ▾ Gill attachment **Attached** ▾ Gill spacing **Close** ▾ Gill size **Broad** ▾ Gill colour **Black** ▾ Stalk shape **Enlarging** ▾ Stalk surface above ring **Fibrous** ▾	The client was able to enter mushroom features using drop-down boxes. The inputs that could be made through the drop-down boxes were all valid and were correctly saved in JSON string format. When asked if this criterion was satisfied, my client replied "absolutely" (Appendix 4).

■ Evaluating success criteria in "Automated grading tool" (credit: former student)

The program can automatically mark a multiple-choice paper with above 99% accuracy by comparing it to the mark scheme.	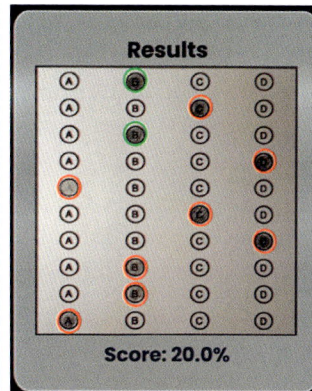	The program marked 30 out of 30 sample tests correctly. The client has confirmed that "Under good lighting conditions, this seems to work very well" (Appendix A.3).

■ Evaluating success criteria in "IBDP subject recommender" (credit: Sofia Cornu)

Application makes use of a graphical user interface to facilitate the inputting of personal information (the user can input this information through textboxes, checkboxes and choice boxes / drop-down select).	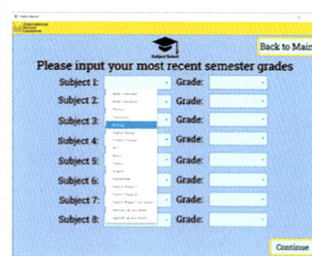	All of the data is either input by selecting from a drop-down select menu or by ticking checkboxes (as shown in visuals). My client stated that he thought the students found the inputting process "intuitive" and "quite self-explanatory" (Appendix E.1).

One of the improvements that my client and I discussed was the ability of the application to save features that had been input into the drop-down boxes, "even if the user were to go to a different page" (Appendix 4). As of now, the characteristics that have been entered disappear when the user clicks on the help page. To address this, an array can be made. When the help button is clicked, the chosen characteristics can be immediately saved to the array. Then, when the user returns to the "enter characteristics" page, they can seamlessly continue inputting additional characteristics that will be saved in the same array. The contents can then be sent to the neural network for processing.

Secondly, my client disliked that the application was "reliant on WiFi" to function. To fix this issue, the machine learning algorithm could be configured to run independently on the local system. The appropriate libraries (for example scikit-learn and NumPy) would have to be set up, and the h5 file containing the machine learning model would be downloaded on to my client's phone.

Thirdly, my client suggested that entering 21 characteristics for each mushroom was "tedious". To fix this, the importance of each feature could be calculated. A method to approach this is detailed by Fisher et al. Essentially, the value of a feature should be randomized and the accuracy of the model computed. This process can be repeated for each feature, and the ones with the lowest importance can be removed.

Finally, to enhance the educational aspect of the app, functionality can be added to provide guesses about the mushroom species. This can be achieved by creating a database that contains the characteristics of 50 common mushroom species. Each mushroom in the database would initially have a score of 0. When the user inputs characteristics, the app can compare them with the characteristics in the database. For each matching characteristic, the score of the corresponding mushrooms in the database can be incremented. The mushrooms with the highest scores can then be presented as guesses for the species of mushroom the user is trying to identify.

■ Suggested improvements in "Mushroom: Friend or foe?" (credit: H Ng)

Firstly, one of the improvements that my client and I discussed in our final interview was that of taking into account the possibility of "start[ing] the diploma with four higher levels", which my client has said is "a conversation that [he has] often". This could simply be done by adding another checkbox with this option, which would change the number of HLs SubjectSelect would pick.

Secondly, as my school has recently created a webpage with "details as to what are the assessments, what's the difference between Higher and Standard Level" for each subject, my client suggested that having a link to this website from my SubjectSelect information page would be "something that could be really nice".

Thirdly, another area for extension would be to break down some of the career field options I give (e.g. Physics, or anything related) into smaller more specific sub-sections, like "architecture, engineering and medicine", and "work with people like Mr McArthur and Ms Edmunds" (my school's counsellors) to implement the subject requirements for these careers in Switzerland, as these are, according to my client, the ones "that give (them) the most problems during the options process".

Finally, another improvement to the project that I believe would add to its usefulness for students would be to include a screen that displays the weighting that each subject obtained (a simple change, as these weights are already all held in an arraylist). This would allow students to better understand why SubjectSelect chose the subjects it did.

■ Suggested improvements in "IBDP subject recommender" (credit: Sofia Cornu)

Frequently asked questions

■ Academic integrity

The IB provides the following guidance for your teachers when they are supporting you with this course:

> *The most important responsibility of all students is that the work they submit is their own. Students must understand and actively apply concepts related to academic integrity, such as authenticity, respect for intellectual property, and citing and referencing according to accepted systems. This includes instances where AI tools were used, such as to refine code. If students researched an existing solution then this must be clearly referenced and cited in a bibliography. Students must include the full source code of their solution in an appendix. Excerpts of code in the documentation should be referenced to the appended full source code.*
>
> *IBDP Computer science teacher support material*

The *Guide* also states that:

> *All work submitted to the IB for moderation or assessment must be authenticated by a teacher, and must not include any known instances of suspected or confirmed malpractice. Each student must confirm that the work is their authentic work and constitutes the final version of that work.*
>
> *IBDP Computer science guide*

Each school has its own academic integrity policy, which takes precedence over the generalized advice offered here. That said, advice follows below.

◼ Using programming code from other sources

The use of programming code found through online sources is common in the Computer Science internal assessment. Sources of code may come from tutorials, example projects on Github, bug fixes found on Stack Overflow, generative AI, or any number of other sources.

When using code that has come from, or is adapted from, another source, then the equivalent to an 'in text' citation should be provided through the use of an in-code comment. The full bibliographical reference can then be included in the appendix to your written submission.

Consider the following Javascript example:

Java

```java
// Adapted from "Arrow function expressions" (Mozilla)
// https://developer.mozilla.org/en-US/docs/Web/JavaScript/
Reference/Functions/Arrow_functions
document.querySelector("[name='go']").
addEventListener("click", e=>{
    console.log("You clicked on ${e.target.name}");
});
```

◼ Using generative AI

The IB has updated its academic integrity policy with respect to its views on the use of generative artificial intelligence tools. It is appendix 6 of the Academic Integrity Policy document available on the IB's website.

The overarching ethos comes from this statement:

> The IB will not ban the use of AI software. The simplest reason is that it is the wrong way to deal with innovation. Over the next few years, the use of this kind of software will become as routine as calculators and translation programs. It is more sensible to adapt and teach students how to use these new tools ethically.

IB Academic integrity policy, 2023, page 53

From the perspective of how to apply the principle of ethical use of AI in your assessments, such as the internal assessment, the key statement is:

> Students need to be aware that the IB does not regard any work produced – even only in part – by such tools to be their own. Therefore, as with any quotation or material from another source, it must be clear that any AI-generated text, image or graph included in a piece of work has been copied from such software. The software must be credited in the body of the text and appropriately referenced in the bibliography. If this is not done, the student would be misrepresenting content – as it was not originally written by them – which is a form of academic misconduct.

IB Academic integrity policy, 2023, page 54

As an IB student, you will need to keep in mind these points when using AI software:

- If you use the text (or any other product) produced by an AI tool – be that by copying or paraphrasing that text or modifying an image – you must clearly reference the AI tool in the body of your work and add it to the bibliography.

- The in-text citation should contain quotation marks, using the referencing style already in use by the school, and the citation should also contain the prompt given to the AI tool and the date the AI generated the text.

IB Academic integrity policy, 2023, page 54

■ Standard Level vs Higher Level

The IA is graded the same regardless of whether a student is at Standard Level or Higher Level, and both levels are graded against the same assessment criteria.

In fact, when IB moderators grade student IAs, they are not aware of whether a student is an SL or HL student.

■ Ethical guidelines

The *Guide* provides the following ethical guidelines for students completing the IA:

> *Given the nature of the internal assessment, students must take into account ethical problems and implications for undertaking research and developing the solution, for example ensuring the confidentiality and security of data. Wherever possible, original data should be used or collected by the student.*

The following guidelines must be applied:

- Consent must be obtained from people who will be involved in the development of the computational solution before any investigation is begun.

- Written consent must be obtained from the owner of any existing system that is to be used as part of the internal assessment, for example when implementing a security analysis protocol on an existing system.

- All data collected must be stored securely in order to maintain confidentiality.

- Data collected can only be used for the computational solution. It must not be used for any other purpose without explicit permission.

IBDP Computer science guide

Acknowledgements

The Publishers would like to thank the following for permission to reproduce copyright material.

p. 1 © Eric d'Ario/stock.adobe.com; **p. 2** © Oleksandr Delyk/stock.adobe.com; **p.5** *t* © Ahmed Shaffik/stock.adobe.com, *m* © Gorodenkoff/stock.adobe.com; **p. 6** © Chinnapong/stock.adobe.com; **p. 9** *t* © Siiixth/stock.adobe.com, *m* © Fdsmsoft/stock.adobe.com; **p. 14** © Ssstocker/stock.adobe.com; **p. 16** *l* © BillionPhotos.com/stock.adobe.com, *r* © Sved Oliver/stock.adobe.com; **p. 17** *m* © A_A88/stock.adobe.com, *b* © Capix Denan/Shutterstock.com; **p. 18** *t* © Dmytro/stock.adobe.com, *m* © AjayTvm/Shutterstock.com; **p. 19** *l* © Insideportugal/stock.adobe.com, *r* © Blickpixel/stock.adobe.com; **p. 24** *t* © GRANGER - Historical Picture Archive/Alamy Stock Photo, *b* © Semenov/Sputnik/Sipa; **p. 37** © Photo Researchers/Science History Images/Alamy Stock Photo; **p. 46** © Sueddeutsche Zeitung Photo/Alamy Stock Photo; **p. 51** © The History Collection/Alamy Stock Photo; **p. 69** *r* © Aminul/stock.adobe.com; **p. 79** © Syda Productions/stock.adobe.com; **p. 80** © Cherezoff/stock.adobe.com; **p. 81** © Lito_lakwatsero/Shutterstock.com; **p. 93** *tl* © Pixel/stock.adobe.com, *tm* © AlexR/stock.adobe.com, *tr* © D'Mhnd/stock.adobe.com, *bl* © Vlabo/stock.adobe.com, *bm* © Oleksandr/stock.adobe.com, *br* © LuchschenF/stock.adobe.com; **p. 95** © Monicaodo/stock.adobe.com; **p. 111** © Peterschreiber.mediaF/stock.adobe.com; **p. 116** *b* © Steve/stock.adobe.com; **p. 151** © Diki/stock.adobe.com; **p. 167** © Phonlamaiphoto/stock.adobe.com; **p. 205** © Alexandr Vasilyev/stock.adobe.com; **p. 216** *both* Chart by Tyler Vigen/https://tylervigen.com/spurious-correlations/ https://creativecommons.org/licenses/by/4.0/; **p. 230** *l* © JT Fisherman/stock.adobe.com, *m* © Jim/stock.adobe.com, *r* © Barry/stock.adobe.com; **p. 265** *l* © SickleMoon/stock.adobe.com; **p. 281** © Maximilian/stock.adobe.com; **p. 295** © Markus Spiske/stock.adobe.com; **p. 372** © Anshuman Rath/stock.adobe.com; **p. 393** © Teeranon/stock.adobe.com; **p. 453** © Yellowj/stock.adobe.com; **p. 481** © Mykhailo/stock.adobe.com; **p. 485** © Naret/stock.adobe.com; **p. 493** © Tierney/stock.adobe.com

Glossary

Absolute path: the location of a file specified from the root directory (the full path).

Abstraction: having a higher-level, simplified model to represent a complex system. It allows you to focus on the core ideas or concepts that matter, without being overly concerned about the intricate details of implementation.

Access modifiers: the mechanisms provided by the programming language to control visibility of methods and variables within an object.

Accessor: a public method that allows external code to "access" the value of a private instance variable within an object; also known as "getter method" as it "gets" the value.

Activation function: a mathematical function applied to the output of a neuron that is used to determine whether or not the neuron should be activated (considered to be "on").

Aggregate functions: functions used to perform calculations on multiple records based on a given field, e.g. AVERAGE, COUNT, MAX, MIN, SUM.

Aggregation: where one object "has" another object as part of it, but the two objects can exist independently of each other.

Algorithm: a finite sequence of instructions that needs to be followed step-by-step to solve a problem.

Amplitude: the magnitude of change in a sound wave, representing the loudness or intensity of the sound.

Analogue: a continuous signal that represents varying physical quantities, such as sound waves, which varies smoothly over a range; digital represents data in discrete binary values (0s and 1s), enabling precise and error-resistant processing.

Arithmetic operator: a character that is used to perform a calculation.

Artificial intelligence: computer technology able to perform tasks and make decisions in a manner that imitates human intelligence. There are two main forms of AI: narrow (or weak) AI is designed to perform specific tasks or solve specific types of problems; general (or strong) AI processes human-level intelligence and can operate across a range of domains. While speculation persists that general AI is "close", at this time only narrow AI technology is available.

ASCII (American Standard Code for Information Interchange): a character-encoding standard used to represent text in computers and other devices, defining a numerical value for each symbol and character commonly used in the English language.

Assignment: to set, reset or copy a value into a variable.

Association rule: a process of finding patterns of co-occurrence in data; this means, given the presence of one item in a record, how likely it is that another item will be present.

Atomic: each attribute in a table containing indivisible values (values that cannot be broken down into more detailed sub-values).

Attribute: a data item or a characteristic of an entity; a column in a table.

Backpropagation: backpropagation of errors is the most commonly used technique for training artificial neural networks. The gradient of the loss function is calculated, and used to update parameters such as weights, in the opposite direction of the gradient to reduce the overall error.

Base case: a terminating solution (that is not recursive) to a process.

Basic Multilingual Plane (BMP): the most commonly used characters and symbols for almost all modern languages.

Bidirectional bus: a bus that can transfer data in both directions.

Big O notation: used to find the upper bound (worst-case scenario or the highest possible amount) of the growth of a function; the longest time or space required to turn the input into output.

Binary operator: an operator that requires two operands (values).

Binary search: a method of searching an ordered array (list) by repeatedly checking the value of the middle element and disregarding the half of the data structure that does not contain the searched element.

Bit: binary digit; a single digit, either 1 or 0.

Bitmap: a type of digital image composed of a grid of pixels, each holding a specific colour value, representing the image in a rasterized format.

Boolean: a data type to represent one of the two possible values: true or false.

Boolean operator: a character that represents a specific logical operation that is used to produce a true or false outcome.

Breakpoint: a marker to interrupt the execution of code for debugging purposes.

Brute force: a method of breaking a cipher by systematically trying every possible key until the correct one is found.

Bubble sort: a sorting algorithm that compares adjacent values and swaps them if they are in an incorrect order.

Buffering: the process of temporarily storing data in a memory area (buffer) while it is being transferred between two devices or processes, helping to manage differences in data-flow rates and ensuring smooth, uninterrupted operation.

Business intelligence: technologies, applications and practices for collecting, integrating, analysing and presenting business information.

Byte: 8 bits.

Cache hit: when the CPU requests data and it is found in the cache memory.

Cache miss: when the CPU requests data and it is not found in the cache memory, necessitating retrieval from slower main memory or storage.

Caching: the process of temporarily storing frequently accessed data in a high-speed storage area (cache) to reduce access time and improve system performance by enabling quicker retrieval of the data.

Cardinality: the maximum number of times an instance in one entity can be associated with instances in the related entity.

Char: a data type used to represent one single character, digit or symbol.

Child: any node that has a direct link from a parent node positioned above it, potentially having further child nodes of its own.

Classification: machine learning where the output generated should be a category, chosen from among a discrete set of categories available.

Classification techniques: where a machine learning model has been trained to identify, from a predefined list of categories, which category (or class) the input data would most likely be associated with.

Cloud database: a database that runs on cloud computing platforms, providing scalability, high availability and flexible resource management.

Clustering techniques: where data is grouped into clusters based on similarity or proximity to each other without any labels provided to help indicate the correctness of associating any individual datapoint to the cluster assigned.

Colour depth: also known as "bit depth"; the number of bits used to represent the colour of each pixel in a digital image, determining the range and precision of colours that can be displayed.

Comment: a note that explains some code, which will be ignored at compilation stage.

Composite key: a set of attributes that form a primary key.

Composition: where objects are composed of other objects, forming a "has-a" style of relationship. The objects that comprise the internal objects cannot exist independently of the containing object.

Computational thinking: a toolkit of available techniques for problem-solving; its fundamental concepts are abstraction, decomposition, algorithmic thinking and pattern recognition.

Computer network: a system that connects computers and other devices to share resources (digital or physical) and information.

Concatenation: joining strings together.

Conceptual schema: an abstract model describing the structure of the data without considering how it will physically be implemented.

Confusion matrix: a simple pictorial means of representing how well a machine learning model is performing.

Constructor: a special method within a class that is automatically executed during instantiation; its main task is to initialize any instance variables required before an instance of the object can be used by other code.

Convolution: a mathematical operation that combines two functions to produce a third function. In the context of a convolutional neural network being used for image processing, convolution applies filtering functions to the pixels in an input image to compute distinctive features from the data.

Curse of dimensionality: each feature in a machine learning model adds another dimension to the overall model the algorithm is attempting to map and create generalizations about; the curse of dimensionality refers to the problem that occurs when there are too many dimensions relative to the quantity of data available, so that patterns cannot be meaningfully observed.

Data definition language: language that is used to create, modify and remove data structures from a relational database.

Data manipulation language: language that is used to add, modify, delete and retrieve data stored in relational databases.

Data mining: the process of sorting through large data sets to identify patterns and relationships that can help solve business problems through data analysis.

Data sparsity: how "spread out" data points are from each other in a model.

Data storage: storage of data within primary or secondary memory.

Data type: defines the type of value a variable or data structure has and what type of mathematical, relational or logical operations can be applied without causing an error.

Data warehouse: a specialized type of database designed for analytical purposes rather than transactional processing.

Database: an organized collection of structured information or data that can be accessed in different ways.

Database schema: an architecture showing how data is organized and how the relationship between data is managed.

Debugging: finding and fixing errors in a program.

Debugging tools: software applications or utilities used by developers to identify, analyse and fix bugs or issues within a program by inspecting code, variables and execution flow.

Decision tree: a graphical representation of conditions that will result in a classification decision being made; think of it as a decision-making flowchart that the machine learning model creates.

Declaration: a language construct specifying the properties of an identifier.

Decomposition: breaking down complex problems into smaller, more manageable parts.

Decrement: to decrease a value by another value (usually by one).

Deep learning: a subset of machine learning that uses an artificial neural network to imitate the design of the human brain to find generalizations in complex data that can be used for decision-making.

Defragmentation: the process of reorganizing the data on a hard drive so that files are stored in contiguous blocks, reducing fragmentation and improving access speed and overall system performance.

Denormalization: deliberately allowing for data redundancy in a database design to improve the performance of queries.

Dequeue: a method of deleting an element from the front of a queue.

Device drivers: specialized software programs that allow the operating system to communicate with and control hardware devices, e.g. printers, graphics cards or network adapters, by providing the necessary instructions and protocols.

Direct access: a method of access where elements are directly retrieved by using their index (position).

Distributed database: a database made of two or more files located on different sites on the same network or on completely different networks.

Domain name: a human-readable name assigned to a specific IP address on the internet, e.g. www.example.com.

Double: a data type used to represent a decimal number.

Dynamic data structure: a data structure that can grow or decrease at runtime, with elements stored in memory locations that are chained together, but not necessarily contiguous.

Encapsulation: bundles data and the methods that manipulate that data together into a single object. It serves to hide the implementation details of the object from outside code.

Encryption: the conversion of information or data into a mathematically secure format that cannot be easily understood by unauthorized people.

Encryption key: a string of characters or numbers used by an encryption algorithm to encode or decode data. It is the values that are input into the mathematical functions responsible for scrambling or descrambling the data.

Enqueue: a method of inserting an element at the rear of a queue.

Entity: a living or non-living thing that can have data stored about it that can be described, e.g. a person, a chair or an aeroplane.

Entity-relationship diagram: a visual representation of the entities in a database and the relationship between them.

Exception: an unexpected event that stops the execution of a program, e.g. division by 0.

Exception handling: a process of responding to an exception, so the system does not halt unexpectedly.

Extract: to gather data from various operational databases, flat files, APIs, etc.

Factory pattern: a design pattern that provides an alternative interface for creating objects in contrast to normal constructor-based instantiation.

Feature: a numeric property that can be used to contribute a data point for a machine learning algorithm to train on. Think of it as a variable in your data set.

File extension: a suffix at the end of a filename that indicates the file type and the program associated with opening or processing that file (e.g. .docx for Word documents, .jpg for images).

Firewall: a security system (hardware or software) that monitors and controls incoming and outgoing network traffic based on a set of security rules.

First In First Out principle: when the first element inserted is the first element removed.

First normal form: the status of a relational database in which entities do not contain repeating groups of attributes.

Float: a data type used to represent a decimal number.

Floating-point division: division in which the fractional part is kept.

Foreign key: an attribute in a table that refers to the primary key in another table.

Frame: a single image in a sequence of images that makes up a video or animation.

Full functional dependency: where dependent attributes are determined by the determinant attributes.

Function: a set of statements that can be grouped together and called in a program as needed; they always return at least one value.

Functional dependency: a relationship that exists between attributes, where one set of attributes (the determinant) determines the value of the other set (the dependent).

Functional testing: testing concerned with the behaviour of the application – specifically, whether it meets the requirements specified. This type of testing evaluates the software by providing inputs and examining the outputs, without considering how internal systems work. You are testing each of the success criteria on the whole application from the user's point of view.

Gateway: a device that connects different networks together and manages the traffic flow between them; often used to connect a local network to the internet.

General case: a process where the recursive call takes place.

Generative AI: a form of artificial intelligence capable of generating text, images, audio, video and other digital artefacts, usually in response to a prompt. It is a form experiencing rapid advances at the time of writing.

Genetic algorithm: imitates the concept of survival of the fittest and evolution by testing a population of possible solutions to a problem, using properties from the best-performing solutions to create a new population of possible solutions, and then repeating the process until a suitably performing solution has been identified.

Global variable: a variable that exists throughout a program.

Hash table chaining: a collision-resolution technique in hash tables where each bucket or index in the array can store multiple elements in the form of a linked list, allowing more than one entry to be stored at the same index.

Hashing algorithm: a function that converts input data of any size into a fixed-size string of characters, which typically represents the data in a compressed and seemingly random format and is used primarily for indexing and retrieving items in databases more efficiently.

Heap space: a region of dynamically allocated memory managed by the operating system where programs store variables and data structures that require memory allocation during runtime, allowing for flexible memory usage that can grow and shrink as needed by the application.

High load factors (hash tables): a condition where a sizeable portion of the hash table's slots are filled, leading to increased collisions and potentially degraded performance, due to more frequent need for collision resolution mechanisms.

High-frequency data: correspond to rapid changes in pixel values, representing fine details, edges and textures.

Hyperparameter: a parameter (or value assigned to a variable) that is set before the learning process, which guides the algorithm as it learns.

Hypervisor: software that creates and manages virtual machines by allowing multiple operating systems to run simultaneously on a single physical machine, sharing the underlying hardware resources.

Identifier: a lexical token that names the language's entities.

Image resolution: the number of pixels contained within a digital image, typically expressed as the dimensions (width × height) in pixels, and sometimes as the pixel density (PPI / DPI) for print quality.

Increment: to increase a value by another value (usually by one).

Inheritance: where a class takes a copy of an existing class as the starting point for all its internal methods and variables. These can then be overridden and extended upon to provide additional functionality, as required.

Initialization: assigning an initial value to a data structure.

In-memory database: a database that stores data entirely in the main memory (RAM) rather than on disk, providing extremely fast read and write operations.

Instantiation: the line of code that declares a new object variable based on the template code provided by a class, which then executes the constructor to initialize the object.

Integer: a data type used to represent a whole number.

Integer division: division in which the fractional part is discarded.

Interface: a contract that specifies a set of methods a class must implement, without defining how these methods are implemented, serving as a blueprint that promotes modularity, flexibility and abstraction in software development. This structure allows different classes to implement the same interface in diverse ways, while ensuring they provide the functionalities declared by the interface.

Internet: a global network of computer networks that are interconnected with each other and communicate through standardized protocols.

Interrupt: a signal sent from a device or software to request the processor's attention; the processor will stop its current activity until the interrupt has been serviced.

Interrupt handling: handling interrupt requests.

Interrupt service routine (ISR): a special function in a computer system that automatically executes in response to an interrupt signal, handling specific tasks, e.g. processing input from hardware devices or managing system events, before returning control to the main program.

IP address: a set of numbers that uniquely identifies each computer based on the Internet Protocol (either version 4 or version 6).

kHz (kilohertz): a unit of frequency equal to 1000 cycles per second, commonly used to measure the sampling rate of audio signals.

K-nearest neighbours: where data points are categorized based on the categories of the nearest points around them in the data set; *k* is a variable representing how many of those nearest points should be used to "vote" and determine what category to assign the new value.

Last In First Out or First In Last Out principle: the last element inserted is the first element removed.

Latency: the delay between the initiation of an action and the corresponding response, often referring to the time it takes for data to travel from its source to its destination in a network or system.

Leaf: a node that does not have any children, representing the endpoints of a binary search tree's branches.

Least significant bit (LSB): the rightmost bit in a binary number, representing the smallest value position (20 or 1).

Linear regression: a machine learning algorithm that seeks a linear line of best fit for a given data set, from which extrapolations can be made.

Linear search: a method of searching, in which each element is checked in sequential order.

Load: to load transformed data into a data warehouse.

Load balancing: the process of distributing network or application traffic across multiple servers or resources to ensure optimal performance, reliability and availability, preventing any single server from becoming overwhelmed.

Local area network: a system that connects computers and other devices within a small geographical area, such as an office or home.

Local variable: a variable that exists only within the block of code where it is defined.

Logic error: an error in a program that makes it operate incorrectly; it will not crash the program.

Logical schema: a detailed design of the structure of tables (fields and data types), relationships between tables and constraints.

Loop / iteration: a repetition.

Low-frequency data: correspond to slow changes in pixel values, such as broad areas.

Machine learning: a branch of AI where computers learn from data and experiences to perform specific tasks or solve specific problems, without being explicitly programmed to do so.

Maintainable code: clear, easy-to-read and modify code that can be reused within the same program or in other programs, by the same or other programmers.

Malware: a general term for any software designed with malicious intent, e.g. viruses, worms, trojans, spyware and ransomware, which can damage systems, steal data or disrupt operations.

Matrix and vector multiplications: fundamental operations in machine learning and graphics that involve complex mathematical calculations.

Memory dump: a process where the contents of a computer's memory are captured and saved, typically for the purpose of diagnosing and debugging software issues.

Metadata: information that describes other data, providing context and details about the data's content, structure and attributes. In the context of digital images, metadata includes such information as the image's dimensions, colour depth, creation date, author, camera settings and other properties that help with managing, understanding and using the image effectively.

Middleware: software that connects different applications, allowing them to communicate and share data. It helps different parts of a computer system work together smoothly.

Modality: the minimum number of instances of one entity that can be associated with an instance of another entity.

Modularity: a design principle that involves dividing a system into distinct and manageable sections or modules, each with its own specific responsibilities, which can be developed, tested and maintained independently, but function cohesively when combined.

Monopolize resources: the control or domination of the use of system resources (e.g. CPU, memory or network bandwidth) by a single process or user, often to the detriment of other processes or users, leading to inefficiency or system slowdowns.

Multi-core architectures: systems with multiple CPU cores on a single chip, allowing parallel execution of instructions and tasks.

Mutable: a set whose state or content can be changed after it has been created, allowing for modifications, e.g. adding, removing or altering elements within the object.

Mutator: a public method that allows external code to update or mutate the value of a private instance variable within an object; also known as "setter method" as it "sets" the value.

Network address translation: modifies the IP addresses of data packets as they pass through a router or firewall; this helps improve security and manages the limited number of IP addresses available through IPv4 by allowing multiple devices to share a single global IP address.

Network segmentation: dividing a computer network into smaller, distinct subnetworks to improve performance, security and management.

Network switch: a device that connects multiple other devices within a single segment of a computer network, only forwarding data to the specific device it is intended for.

Neural network: a computer algorithm that imitates the design of the human brain by using a set of interconnected nodes for the processing and analysing of data.

Nibble: 4 bits.

Node: a basic unit of a data structure, e.g. a linked list or tree, which contains data and typically links to or references other nodes.

Noise: unwanted electrical disturbances that can affect the integrity of signals being processed by a computer; this noise is not related to sound, but to variations in voltage or current that can disrupt the accurate transmission and processing of digital data.

Normalization: the process of organizing data in a relational database in a way to reduce data redundancy and to improve data integrity.

NoSQL database: a database designed to handle large volumes of data and diverse data types, structured differently from relational databases.

O(1) time complexity: describes an algorithm that takes the same amount of time to execute regardless of the size of the input data set.

Object-oriented programming: a form of programming that involves creating code for classes of objects, allowing many such objects to be created from a single code base, achieving a more modular and extensible software development process. It is like the idea of producing architectural blueprints, from which many similar houses can be constructed.

Observer pattern: provides a one-to-many link between objects to notify objects of changes in state via a subscription-style service.

Online analytical processing: the software technology you can use to analyse business data from different points of view.

Open addressing: a collision resolution method in hash tables where, instead of using structures like linked lists to store multiple items at the same index, any colliding item is placed into the next available open slot in the hash table itself, according to a probing sequence.

Operand: a value used in a mathematical expression.

Operator: a character that represents a mathematical, arithmetic or logical operation.

Outlier: a data point that deviates from the typical pattern of values in a data set, indicating a possible unusual or erroneous value that should be discounted.

Overriding: the process of providing a different implementation of a method in a subclass, which replaces the original implementation inherited from the superclass.

Packet switching: a method of sending data in small blocks, known as "packets", across a network. Each packet can take a different path to reach its destination.

Parallel arrays: a group of arrays of the same size, where the element at a given index in one of the arrays corresponds to another element at the same index in another array, like descriptions of a single entity.

Parallel processing: the ability of the GPU to perform many calculations simultaneously due to its highly parallel structure.

Parent: a node that has one or more nodes directly beneath it, connected by edges, and it directly controls these subsequent child nodes.

Partial functional dependency: when dependent attributes are partially determined by the determinant attributes.

Pattern recognition: identifying similarities in the details of problems.

Perceptron: the data structure at the heart of an artificial neural network; it represents a single artificial neuron that takes in multiple inputs and weights, and generates an output value.

Personal area network: a network for personal devices within the range of an individual person, usually connected with Bluetooth.

Physical schema: an implementation of logical schema into a specific DBMS (database management system), showing how data is stored, indexed or accessed.

Pixel: short for "picture element"; the smallest unit of a digital image or display, representing a single point in the image with a specific colour and intensity.

Plug and Play (PnP): a technology that allows the operating system to detect, configure and install drivers automatically for new hardware devices when they are connected to the computer, enabling them to work without requiring manual set-up by the user.

Pointer: a variable that stores the memory address of another variable, typically used in programming to reference, or access, the location of data stored in memory.

Polymorphism: meaning "many forms", it allows objects to exhibit different behaviours based on their specific class implementation while still adhering to a shared interface or contract.

Pop: a method for deleting the element from the top of a stack.

Primary key: a field that uniquely identifies a record in a table.

Problem specification: a short, clear explanation of an issue, which may include: a problem statement; constraints and limitations; objectives and goals; input and output specifications; and evaluation criteria.

Problem statement: a description of the problem itself, identification of who the solution is designed for, the issues encountered and what needs to be solved.

Procedure: a set of statements that can be grouped together and called in a program as needed; they don't return a value.

Product: the completed software only (in the internal assessment).

Proof of work: a consensus mechanism requiring cryptominers to solve complex problems to add a new block to the blockchain.

Protocol: a set of rules and standards that define how data is transmitted and received across a network for a given application.

Push: a method for inserting an element at the top of a stack.

Queue: an abstract data structure that works on the FIFO principle.

Quicksort: a sorting algorithm that repeatedly selects an element as a pivot and partitions the other elements into two sub-arrays (lists): one that includes elements that are smaller than the pivot and the other one that includes elements that are larger than the pivot.

Quotient: the result obtained when one number is divided by another, e.g. in the division of 15 by 3, the quotient is 5.

RAID (Redundant Array of Independent Disks): a data storage technology that combines multiple physical drives into a single logical unit to improve performance, provide redundancy and ensure data protection.

Record: one instance of an entity; a row in a table.

Recursion: a process that uses a function or procedure that is defined in terms of itself and calls itself.

Regression: machine learning where the output generated should be a numerical value.

Rehashing: a process in hash tables where the data is redistributed into a new, larger array to reduce the load factor and minimize collisions, maintaining efficient performance.

Reinforcement learning: machine learning by trial and error. Based on what it has learned at any moment in time, the algorithm selects an action to take in a given environment. The environment provides feedback (called a "reward"), which the algorithm will use to learn from and refine its decision-making process moving forward.

Relational operator: an operator used to compare values or expressions.

Relationship: a relation established between different tables, where the foreign key in one table refers to the primary key in another table.

Relative path: the location of a file relative to the current folder.

Rendering: the process of generating an image from a model by means of computer programs.

Root: the topmost node from which all other nodes descend, serving as the starting point for any traversal or operation within a binary search tree.

Router: a device that forwards data packets between computer networks, routing the traffic along the most efficient path.

Routing: the process of selecting paths along a computer network to send network traffic, based on the routing table, network performance and protocols.

R-squared value (or coefficient of determination): a statistical measure that indicates how well the linear regression model fits the data points given.

Runtime error: an error that occurs when executing a program; the program might stop unexpectedly.

Sampling: the process of converting a continuous analogue signal into a series of discrete digital values by measuring the signal's amplitude at regular intervals.

Second normal form: status of a relational database in which entities are in 1NF and any non-key attributes depend upon the primary key.

Security tokens: physical or digital devices that generate or store authentication credentials, such as one-time passwords or cryptographic keys, used to verify a user's identity and secure access to systems, networks or online services.

Selection: a conditional statement or decision statement, e.g. IF, CASE statements.

Selection sort: a sorting algorithm that repeatedly selects the smallest or largest element (ascending or descending order) from the unsorted part of the data structure and moves it to the sorted part.

Sequence: to execute instructions one after another in the given order.

Sequential access: a method of access where elements are checked one after another, from the beginning to the end of the data structure.

Server: a computer or device on a network that manages and provides various network resources on behalf of other computers (clients) on the network.

Set difference: the difference between two sets is a new set containing elements that are in the first set but not in the second set, effectively subtracting the elements of the second set from the first.

Set intersection: the intersection of two sets is a new set containing only the elements that are present in both of the original sets, identifying their common elements.

Set subset: a set where all elements of this set are also elements of another set, indicating that the first set is entirely contained within the second set.

Set union: the union of two sets is a new set containing all the elements that are in either of the original sets, effectively combining them without any duplicate elements.

Shaders and textures: techniques used in 3D rendering to apply effects, lighting and details to models.

Shift cipher: a type of substitution cipher, where each letter in the plaintext is shifted a certain number of positions down or up the alphabet.

Singleton pattern: a class that is designed only ever to have one instance instantiated throughout the lifecycle of the program.

Solution: the documentation and video submitted by the student for the internal assessment.

Spatial database: a database optimized to store and query data related to objects in space, including points, lines and polygons.

Spooling: the process of queuing data or tasks in a buffer, typically for input / output devices such as printers, so that they can be processed sequentially and at their own pace, allowing the system to continue working on other tasks in the meantime.

Stack: an abstract data structure that works on the LIFO principle.

Stack pointer: a register used to store the memory address of the last added data in a stack, or sometimes the first available address in a stack.

Stakeholder: an individual or groups of people within or outside an organization who are affected or think they are affected by a software development project.

Static: methods and variables that belong to the class, not the individual objects. Only one copy is created that is shared with all instances in common.

Static data structure: a data structure with predefined fixed size and elements stored in contiguous memory locations.

Statistical redundancy: the repetition of information within a data set that does not contribute to its uniqueness.

Stereo: a method of sound reproduction that uses two or more audio channels to create the perception of sound coming from different directions, enhancing the sense of spatial depth and dimension.

String: a data type used to represent a sequence of characters, digits and / or symbols.

Structural testing: testing concerned with the internal workings of the application – based on the code structure and internal pathways. This type of testing requires an understanding of the codebase and is used to ensure that all aspects of the code are properly tested. You are testing that all conditional branches execute correctly, and all error-handling code triggers when needed and responds appropriately.

Subtree: any node, along with its descendants, functioning as a standalone binary search tree, with its node acting as the root.

Supervised learning: when a machine learning algorithm is provided a data set of pairs of items, where the pair comprises a value and what response the network should provide if it sees that value. By learning the answers to the values given, the network will make generalizations to be able to estimate the answer when given a previously unseen value.

Table: a structure of rows and columns for storing a group of similar data.

Tensor: a mathematical term for an array with three or more dimensions. A single number (no dimensions) is known as a "scalar". A one-dimensional array of numbers is known as a "vector". A two-dimensional array of numbers is known as a "matrix". Three or more dimensions is known as a "tensor".

Termination condition: a condition in a loop that interrupts or stops the repetition.

Third normal form: status of a relational database in which entities are in 2NF and all non-key attributes are independent.

Trace table: a technique used to test an algorithm, and to predict how it will be run and how values of variables will change.

Transfer learning: when a previously trained machine learning model is applied to a similar yet new situation, context or problem. The goal is to speed up the training process by using an already trained model, even if the problem is slightly different.

Transform: to aggregate and transform data into a consistent format suitable for analysis.

Transitive dependency: a type of functional dependency that occurs when a non-prime attribute is dependent on another non-prime attribute, rather than on the primary key.

Trojans: deceptive programs that appear legitimate but carry hidden malicious code, which can create backdoors, steal data or cause harm once executed by the user.

Tuple: one instance of an entity; a row in a table.

Unary operator: an operator that requires one single operand.

Unordered set: a collection of unique elements where the elements do not have a specific order or sequence and their arrangement can vary each time they are accessed.

Unsupervised learning: a method of machine learning where the data set does not include the "answers" or expected outputs for the data provided. The algorithm will attempt to discover the patterns on its own.

Unwinding: a process occurring when the base case is reached, and the values are returned to build a solution.

Validation: a process to ensure input data is sensible or reasonable.

Variable: a designated memory location that stores a value that can change during the execution of a program.

Variable scope: the lifetime of a variable within a program; it determines whether you can access and modify the variable within a specific block of code.

Verification: a process to ensure input data is accurately copied from one source to another.

Vertex and pixel data: data used by the GPU to render 3D objects and images.

View: a virtual table based on the result set of a SELECT query. They do not store data themselves but provide a way to present the data from one or more tables in a customized manner.

Virtual memory: a memory-management technique that allows a computer to use more memory than is physically available by temporarily transferring data from RAM to disk storage, enabling the execution of larger programs and multitasking.

Virtual private network: a secure connection that runs across the internet to provide private communication between your network and a remote server.

Viruses: malicious software programs that attach themselves to legitimate files or programs and spread to other files or systems, often causing damage or disruption.

Volatile: a type of memory or storage that loses its data when the power is turned off.

Wide area network: a system that connects computers and other devices across a large geographic area, usually connecting multiple LANs together.

Winding: process occurring when recursive calls are made until the base case is reached.

Worms: self-replicating malware that spreads across networks without needing to attach to other programs, exploiting vulnerabilities to infect multiple systems.

Index

absolute path 378
abstract classes 423–5
abstract data types (ADTs) 453–80
abstraction 284–5, 287, 394, 423–5, 454–5
access modifiers 401–2
accessibility 74, 78
accessors 402
accountability 274
accounting 72
accumulators (ACs) 3
accuracy 225–6, 234–5, 268, 499
ACID (atomicity, consistency, isolation and durability) 193, 200
activation functions 256–9, 265–6
actuators 93
aggregation 426–8
algebraic simplification 60–5
algorithms 285–6, 499–501, 503–5, 515, 517–18, 527
    control 94
    design 285–6
    fairness/bias 274–5
    genetic 248–54, 270, 488–9
    programming 358–77
    scheduling 79–80, 82–4
American Sign Language (ASL) 499
amplitude 44, 45
analogue 37
analogue-to-digital conversion (ADC) 44
Analytical Engine 24
analytics 184
anomaly detection 200
anonymity 276
append 198, 378, 385
application management 74
Application-Specific Integrated Circuits (ASICs) 6, 213
Apriori algorithm 242
architecture
    network 127–35
    see also database schema; multi-core architectures
Arduino 97, 100, 101
arguments 328
arithmetic expressions 355
arithmetic logic units (ALUs) 2
ArrayLists 350–1
arrays 213, 343–52
    creation 399, 400
    one-dimensional 343–5
    parallel 346
    quicksort 373–5

    searches 362–3, 365
    sorting 365–7, 369
    tracking item numbers 404–5
    two-dimensional 347–9, 530–1
    see also lists
artificial intelligence (AI) 5–6, 206–7, 279–80, 288, 502
see also generative AI; pervasive AI
ASCII (American Standard Code for Information Interchange) 31–2, 476
assignment 297, 300–2
association rule 199, 240–2, 269
atomic 179–80
attributes 168
audio 44–6
Audio Interchange File Format (AIFF) 44–5
auditing 71, 73
augmented reality 277
authentication 124, 148
automated grading tool 498, 533
autonomous vehicles 95
backpropagation 260
backups, secure 152–3
bandwidth 112, 116, 128, 138–9
banking 133, 396–400, 406–9, 437
base case 370
Basic Multilingual Plane (BMP) 34
Bellman equation 245
bias 156, 274–7
Big O notation 358–61, 363
billing 73
binary 24–8
    conversions 26–30
    and data storage 31–51
    fractions 50
    gray code 49
    representation of integers 25–8
    signed 47–8
    unsigned 47
binary search 363–5
binary search tree (BST) 376, 466–70
binary semaphore 89–90
binary-coded decimal (BCD) 48–9
BIOS (basic input/output system) 9
bitcoin 6, 134
bitmap 37–40
bitmasks dynamic programming 530–1
bits 25–7, 29, 37–40, 44
BitTorrent 134
blockchain 6, 134, 157, 487–8
Boolean algebra 25, 51, 53–6, 60–6
Boolean data types 298, 302, 316, 345

breakpoint debugging 335, 338–40
brute force 36
bubble sort 365–7, 369
buffering 70
BufferReader class 383–4
buses 3
business intelligence 198
bytes 25–6
C++ 99–100, 101–2
cache memory 9–10, 70
Caesar ciphers 35–6
California housing data set 261–2
cardinality 177
case studies 481–92
central processing unit (CPU) 2–16, 67, 70, 72, 79–89, 210–13
chaining 477–8
char 298
characters, storage 31–6
chargeback 73
chatbots, customized 210
child (node) 267, 466, 470
CIFAR-10 data set 267
classes 397–405, 417–52, 423–5
classification 199, 208, 227–33, 262–3, 268–9
client–server models 132–3
closed-loop systems 92, 94–7
cloud computing 21–2, 115, 197, 211
clustering techniques 199, 236–40, 479
code reusability 395, 417–20
coefficient of determination 225
collaboration 395
collision factors 477
colour depth 37, 38–9
comments 297
compilers 103–9
    just-in-time (JIT) 105–9
composite key 169–70
composition 426–8
compression 19–21, 44–5, 47
computational thinking and problem solving 281–480
computer fundamentals 1–110
computer hardware 2–23, 210–13
computer logic 51–66
computer operation 2–23
computer vision 498, 499
computing platforms 210–12
concatenation 306–7
conceptual schema 174–5
concurrency control 171, 200–1

configuration files 526
confusion matrix 234
consent 275
constants 360
constructors 398
control algorithms 94
control systems 67–102, 249
control units (CUs) 2
controllers 92–3
convolutional neural network (CNN) 264–8, 270
cores 4, 7, 14–16
cost allocation 72
cross site scripting (XSS) 148
cross-platform development 109, 510
crossover functions 250–4
curse of dimensionality 219
customer loyalty system 443–6
customization 75
cyberbullying detection 280
data 8
    and binary search trees 466–7
    dimensional 219–21
    ethics 267
    filtering irrelevant 216, 221
    grouped 191
    high-frequency 21
    identifying incorrect 216
    improperly formatted 216
    integrated 198
    location 500
    low-frequency 21
    metadata 37, 38
    missing 216, 221
    normalization 216–17, 221
    ordering 190
    security 201
    standardization 216–17, 221
    volume of 268
data analysis 287
data cleaning 215–17
data consistency 171, 178, 184, 191, 193, 200–1
data definition language (DDL) 186–7
data duplication 171, 181, 216, 221
data entry 283
data flow diagrams 524
data handling 172, 173
data integrity 124, 171, 174, 179, 183, 193–4
data language types 186–8
data manipulation language (DML) 186, 187–8
data mining 198, 199–200
data normalization 179–83
data partitioning 201
data poisoning 275
data preprocessing 215–22
data redundancy 172, 179, 183–4

data representation 24–51
data retrieval 171, 184
data scraping 267
data sets 220, 261–2, 267, 361, 471
data sparsity 219
data storage 31–51, 67, 296–7
data structures 217, 342–57, 471, 497–500, 503–5
    dynamic 342, 351–2, 455
    hash tables 475–9
    static 342, 355
data transmission 136–43
data types 178, 297–9, 453–80
data warehouses 184–5, 197–202
database schema 172, 174–6, 183
database views 191–2
databases 167–203, 517
    alternative 195–202
    cloud 197
    denormalizing 183–5
    design 172, 174–85, 287
    distributed 200–1
    document 195
    fundamentals 168–73
    graph 196
    in-memory 197
    key-value 196
    managed/self-managed 197
    normalized 181–3, 187
    NoSQL 195–6, 197
    programming 186–94
    relational 168–73, 178–81
    scalability 172, 174, 183–4, 201
    spatial 197
    wide-column store 196
DBSCAN clustering 240
deadlocks 90–1
debugging 29, 335–41
decimal numbers 26–8, 30–1, 48–9, 297
decision trees 227, 230–3, 268–9, 523
decision-making 319
declaration 296
decomposition 286, 287, 511–13
decompress 20
decrement 300
deep learning 6, 207–8
defragmentation 69
deletion 456, 459–60, 464–5, 470, 478, 479
dendograms 239–40
deployment 500
dequeue 356
design patterns 428–35
design philosophies 7
device drivers 70
device management 67, 70
Diffie Hellman key exchange 157–8
digital certificates 152–3, 155–8
digital infrastructures 114–16

digital signatures 153
dimensionality 219, 219–21, 268
direct access 342
disk input/output operations 87
DISTINCT in a SELECT statement 188
distributed denial of service (DDos) 146, 150
distributed systems 115
distribution transparency 201
divide-and-conquer principle 373
documentation 506
domain name servers (DNS) 129–30, 163
double (data type) 297
dynamic data structures 342, 351–2, 455
Dynamic Host Configuration Protocol (DHCP) 75, 124–5, 130, 162
Eclipse IDE 338–9
edge computing 116, 211
efficiency 361
elevator control system 94–5
ELSE 314–17
emails 133, 150
embedded methods 87, 218, 221
Embedded MultiMediaCard (eMMC) 17
encapsulation 395, 401–2
encryption 71, 124, 149, 153–8, 505
    asymmetric 154–5, 157
    encrypted protocols 150
    symmetric 153–4, 157
encryption key 154
endpoint-protection 151
engineering 249
enqueue 356
entities 168
entity-relationship diagrams (ERDs) 174–7, 524
environmental impact 275
equity 277
errors 29, 106–7, 225, 333, 335–41, 497–500
ethical issues 267, 274–80, 536
evaluation metrics 233–5
exceptions 333–5, 386
excess-N (biased representation) 49–50
execution 11–13, 15–16, 360
extract, transform, load (ETL) 198
F1 score 234, 235
factorials 371
factory pattern 428, 433–4
fault tolerance 201
feature selection 217–18, 268
feedback mechanisms 92, 94–7
fetch–decode–execute cycle 11–13, 15
Fibonacci sequence 371–2
fibre-optic cabling 138
field-programmable gate arrays (FPGAs) 213
file extension 69
file management 69, 74, 78
file processing 378–91
file server 130–1

file transfer protocol (FTP) 130
file transfer system 505
FileReader class 383
FileWriter class 382–3
FILTERING 189
filters 218, 221, 264–5
finance 133, 209, 249, 396–400, 406–9, 437
firewalls 118, 144–5, 161
first come first served (FCFS) 79–82
First in First Out (FIFO) 355
First in Last Out (FILO) 353
first normal form (1NF) 179–80, 182
fixed-point representation 50
flight reservation systems 438–9
float 297
floating-point division 303–4
floating-point representation 50–1
flowcharts 288–93, 312, 314–15, 522
FOR loop 330, 345, 350–2, 380
foreign key 169, 171
frames 8, 46
Free Lossless Audio Codec (FLAC) 44–5
functional dependency 180
functionality 527
functions 326–32
gaming 209, 245–8, 269, 287, 355, 422, 512–14, 517–18, 524–6
Gantt charts 514
gateways 117
general case 370
generative AI 206, 484–5, 535–6
genetic algorithms 248–54, 270, 488–9
Gini 231
global query processing 201
graphical user interface (GUI) 73–5, 497
graphics processing unit (GPU) 5–8, 210–13
gray code (reflected binary code) 49, 62–4
grayscale 42–3, 262–3
hard disk drive (HDD) 16–17, 18, 69
hash table chaining 477–8
hash tables 475–9
hashing algorithm 476, 479
HAVING clause vs WHERE clause 188
health monitoring apps 279
heap space 456
Hello World classification 262–3
hexadecimal numbers 29–31
hierarchical clustering 239–40
high-frequency data 21
high-performance computing (HPC) 212
home-security systems 96
hyperparameter 235
Hypertext Transfer Protocol Secure (HTTPS) 120, 122–3, 132
hypervisor 75
ID values 403–4
identification apps 497, 521–3, 529, 532
identifiers 296

IDLE (Python) 340
if (member) 318
IF statements 311–18
    nested 315–16
image generators, customized 210
image recognition 210
image resolution 37
images, storage 37–43
in-memory databases 197
increment 300
information hiding 401–2
Infrastructure as a Service (Iaas) 22
inheritance 417–20, 422–3
initialization 296
input validation 150–1
inputs 91–2, 255–6, 264, 283, 289–90, 360, 389
insertion 456–9, 462–4, 467–8, 476–7
instantiation 398–400
instruction register 3
integer division 303–4
integers 25–31, 47–51, 297, 394
interface 429–30, 454
internal assessment 493–536
internet 114, 125
interpreters 103–9
    bytecode 105–9
interrupt 355
interrupt handling 85–8, 355
interrupt service routine (ISR) 85, 86
intrusion detection system (IDS) 151
intrusion prevention system (IPS) 151
inventory systems 415–16
IP addresses 136–8, 144–5
irrigation control systems 96
Java
    and abstract data types 461–6, 471–5, 476–7
    and binary data storage 33, 36, 41, 43
    and data structures 347–9, 350–1
    and data types 297–8
    and error detection 106–7
    and file processing 378–84, 389, 391
    and the internal assessment 495, 497, 501, 505, 509–10, 535
    and object-oriented programming 396, 398–401, 403–5, 407–9, 411–12, 414–16, 418–22, 424, 429–30, 431–5, 439, 442–52
    and operators 302, 303
    and programming algorithms 358–62, 364, 366–9, 371, 372, 373–4, 376
    and programming constructs 313, 314, 316–18, 320–4, 326–8, 330–1
    and programming fundamentals 333–5, 343–5
    and string manipulation 305–6, 307–10
JOIN in a SELECT statement 188
k-nearest neighbours 227–30, 233, 236–8, 269, 490–1

Karnaugh maps (K-maps) 60–5
kernels 264–5
keyboards 86–7, 356
keys 154, 169–71, 468
kilohertz (kHz) 44
knowledge 288
laptops 210
Last in First Out (LIFO) 353, 355
latency 85, 86
leaf (node) 467, 470
learning curves 395
least significant bit 27, 48
length function 305
library systems 414, 440
line of best fit 223–4
linear discriminant analysis (LDA) 220
linear probing 478
linear regression 223–7, 268–9
    multiple 226
linear search 362–3, 365
linear space 360
linear transformation 265–6
lists 343–52
    dynamic 351–2
    linked 455–66
    one-dimensional 232, 345–6
    quicksort 373–5
    searches 362–3, 365
    sorting 365–7, 369
    two-dimensional 347–9
Little Man Computer 11–12
load 198
load balancing 75
load factors 477, 478
local area networks (LAN) 112–13, 134, 141–2
location data 500
location transparency 201
locks 90
logic 51–66
logic circuits 56–9, 65–6
logic errors 333
logic gates 51–66
    AND gates 53, 59–60, 65–6, 258–61, 317
    and ANNs 258–61
    basic 52–4
    Buffer gates 52
    derived (complex) 54–6
    history of 51
    NAN gates (NOT AND) 54
    NOR gates (NOT OR) 55
    NOT gates 52, 54, 60, 66
    OR gates 52–3, 59–62, 64, 66, 258–61
    XNOR gates (exclusive NOT OR) 55–6
    XOR gates (exclusive OR) 55
logical expressions 60–5
logical schema 175
loops/iterations 296, 319–24, 366

Index

conditional 319, 322–4, 362–3, 380, 384, 386
  count-controlled (FOR) 319–23, 325, 348, 362
  post-condition (REPEAT–UNTIL) 319, 323–5
  pre-condition (WHILE) 319, 322–5
low-frequency data 21
machine learning 5–6, 205–80, 287–8, 497, 499, 502
mail servers 131
maintainable code 326
malware 72, 146, 149
man-in-the-middle (MitM) 147
mapping 500, 503
matrix and vector multiplications 5
mean absolute/squared error 225
media access control (MAC) 152
memory 7–11, 67–8, 72, 456, 478–9
  primary 8–11
  secondary 16–19
  virtual 68
memory address/data register 3
memory cards 18–19
memory dump 29
Memory Hog program 77
metadata 37, 38
method overriding 421–3
middleware 72
misinformation 276
mobile networks 116
mobile optimization 500
modality 177
model evasion/inversion 275
model training 499
modems 118
modularity 326–32, 394–5, 454–5
monitoring 71
monitors 90
monopolize resources 79
motor control system 100–2
mouse 86–7
movie-review sentiment analysis 270
MPEG Audio Layer III (MP3) 44–5
multi-core architectures 4, 14–16
multi-valued dependency 181
multidimensionality 226–7
multifactor authentication (MFA) 151
multitasking 89–91, 91
multithreading 529
music art creator (Visuca) 504
mutable 471
mutation 248, 253
mutators 402
mutual exclusion 89
network address translation (NAT) 137–8, 145
network architecture diagrams 521
Network Attached Storage (NAS) 18–19

network communications 87
network devices 117–19
network interface cards 118
network protocols 119–25, 146
network security 131–2, 138–40, 144–65, 287
network segmentation 134–5
network switches 118–19
network topologies 127–9
networking 75–6, 132–4
networks 111–65
neural networks 207–8, 244
  artificial (ANNs) 5–6, 255–64, 266, 270
  convolutional 264–8, 270
  training 260, 269, 276
neural processing unit (NPU) 212–13
nibbles 29
nodes 455–70
  deletion 470
  insertion 467–8
  search 468
  traversal 468–9
noise 25
non-volatile 198
normalization 179–83, 187, 216–17, 221, 287
NoSQL database 195–6, 197
O(1) time complexity 476
object-oriented programming (OOP) 393–452, 505, 517
object-relational impedance mismatch 173
objects, creation 399
observer pattern 429, 434–5
one's complement 48
online analytical processing (OLAP) 198–9
online harassment 276
open addressing 477, 478–9
open-loop systems 92
operands 303
operating systems (OS) 67–102
operators 296, 302–4
optical discs/drives 18
Optical Mark Recognition (OMR) 498
outliers 215, 221
outputs 255–6, 266, 283, 289–91
overfitting 235–6
packet switching 140–1
parallel processing 5
parent (node) 466, 467
partial functional dependency 180
passkeys 150
passwords 149–50
pattern matching 189
pattern recognition 286, 287
peer-to-peer model 133–4
perceptrons 255–7, 258
performance monitoring 72
performance-critical applications 109
personal area network (PAN) 113

personalization 75
pervasive AI 277
phishing 147
physical schemas 176
pipelining 14–16
pivot elements 373
pixels 8, 37–9, 42
Platform as a Service (Paas) 22
plug and play (PnP) 70
pointers 455–64
polling 85–8
polymorphism 421–3
Pong! (game) 245–8
pooling layers 266
pop 353
portability 107–8
positional notation method 26
power efficiency 7
precision 234, 235
predictions 258–9
primary key 169, 179, 180–1
principal component analysis (PCA) 220
print statements 341
printer queues 356
privacy 274, 275, 276, 277
problem description 59–60
problem specification 282–4
problem statement 282
problem-solving 286–8, 470
procedure 326–8
process 289
process accounting 72
processors 212–13
product 495
program counter 3
programming 287, 295–391
  algorithms 358–77
  constructs 311–32
  data structures 342–57
  database 186–94
  file processing 378–91
  fundamentals 296–310, 333–41
  see also C++; Java; object-oriented programming; Python
proof of work 6
proxy servers 131–2, 162
pseudocode 244–5, 526
push 353
Python 83
  and abstract data types 461–5, 471–5, 476
  and binary data storage 33, 42, 45–6
  and data preprocessing 215, 217, 221
  and data structures 345–6, 347–9, 351–2
  and data types 297–8
  and error detection 106–7
  and file processing 385–8, 389, 391

and the internal assessment 495, 497–9, 502–4, 509

and machine learning 224–7, 229, 232, 237–9, 242, 245–8, 252–4, 260–3, 268

and network protocols 121

and object-oriented programming 396, 398–404, 406–7, 410, 418–19, 421–4, 431, 433–4, 438, 441–2, 444–51

and operating systems 77

and operators 302, 303–4

and programming algorithms 358–61, 363–4, 366–9, 371, 372, 374–6

and programming constructs 313–18, 320–4, 326–9, 330–2

and programming fundamentals 333–5, 343

and scheduling algorithms 83–4

and servers 130

and string manipulation 305–10

Q-learning 244–5

quadratic probing 479

quadratic space 360

quantum computing 277

queues 355–7

quicksort 373–5

quota management 72

quotients 27

R-squared value 225–6

RAID (Redundant Array of Independent Disks) 18, 131

RAM (random access memory) 8–9, 10, 68

randomization, weighted 249

rapid development/testing 109

Raspberry Pi 160–3

read mode 378, 385

read-intensive apps 184

read-only views 191

real-time systems 88, 361, 499

real-world apps 86–8, 133–4, 233, 284, 356

reasoning 319

recall 234, 235

recommendation systems 209, 229–30, 276, 490–1

records 168–9

recruitment tools, AI-powered 279–80

recursion 355, 370–7, 505

registers 3

regression 199, 208, 261–2, 268

rehashing 477

reinforcement learning 209, 242–8, 270

RELATIONAL operators 189

relationship 170–1, 175

relative path 378

ReLU 257, 258–9

rendering 7, 8

replace method 309

replication 201

reporting 73, 184

reproduction 248–54

resolution 38, 39

resource allocation 89–91

resource contention 89–90

resource management 73

resource usage tracking 72

RGB values 41–2

robotics 209, 249, 491–2

ROM (read-only memory) 8–9

root (node) 466, 469, 470

round robin (RR) 80, 82

route planning 249–51, 254, 500, 509, 530–1

routers 118, 161

routing, static/dynamic 141–2

run-length encoding (RLE) 20

runtime errors 106, 333

sampling 44

scalability 172, 174, 183–4, 201, 361, 395

scanner class 379–82

scheduling 70–1, 79–84, 89

schema, database 172, 174–6

scikit 217–18, 220–2, 224–6, 230, 233, 238–40

searches 361–5

second normal form (2NF) 180, 182

secure file transfer protocol (SFTP) 130

secure socket layer (SSL) certificate 152

security 71–2, 73, 86, 201, 510

   and data transmissions 138–40

   database 172, 174, 192

   and machine learning 275, 277

   network 131–2, 138–40, 144–65, 287

   server 131, 132

security tokens 71

selection 249, 296

selection sort 367–9

selection structure 311–19

semaphores 89–90

sensors 93, 94–7

sequencing 311

sequential access 342, 456

sequential pattern discovery 199

server–client architecture 497

server-side scripting 498, 500

servers 129–33, 162

set difference 472, 474

set intersection 472, 473

set methods 472

set operations 472–4

set union 472, 473

sets 471–5

   subsets/supersets 475

shaders and textures 5

shift cipher 35–6

Sigmoid 257, 258–9

sign-magnitude 48

singleton pattern 428, 430–2

social media platform 441–3

societal impact 275

Softmax 258

software development 287

Software as a Solution (SaaS) 22

software updates 152

solid state drive (SSD) 16–17, 18

solution 494

sorting 365–9

space analysis 358

space complexity 360–1, 367

spatial databases 197

spectral clustering 238–9, 269

speech recognition 210

spell checkers 479

spooling 70

SQL 186–91, 193–4, 197

SQL injection 147–8

SQLite database 498

stack 352–5

stack operation 353–4

stack pointer 353

stakeholders 282–3

static variables and methods 402–5

statistical redundancy 19

step-by-step code execution 340

stereo 44, 45

stock-trading 270, 502

Streamify music 449–52

string 31–6, 297, 305–10, 394

strip method 309–10

structure charts 512–13

student apps 409–12, 439, 498, 501, 533–4

subject-oriented 198

subnetting 134

substrings 307–9

subtree (node) 467

summation 256

supervised learning 208, 223–36, 248

surveillance 274

system flow diagrams 519

system management 74

system models 515, 517

tables

   database 168–70, 178–9, 188–90

   hash tables 475–9

   Q-learning 244, 245

   see also trace tables; truth tables

tanh 258

TCP/IP (Transmission Control Protocol/Internet Protocol) model 75, 117–20, 125–6, 136–7

Tensor Processing Unit (TPU) 211, 212–13

TensorFlow 260–1

termination condition 322

testing 152, 341

   functional 517, 531

   strategies 515, 517–18, 527, 529

   structural 517, 531

text blocks 305

third normal form (3NF) 180–3

time complexity analysis 358–60

time-variant 198

timetabling 249

Tinkercad 97–9, 100–1

trace tables 335–8

traffic control 96–100, 270

training 152, 260, 269, 276, 499

transaction control language (TCL) 193–4

transaction processing 172

transducers 93

transfer learning 210

transform 21, 198

transistors 51–4

transitive dependency 180, 181

translation 103–10

transmission control protocol (TCP) 119–21

transparency 269, 275–6

transport layer security (TLS) certificate 152

traversal/search 376, 457, 460–2, 468–9

trojans 72

truth tables 52–65

tuning, hyperparameter 235

tuples 168

twisted-pair cabling 139

two's complement 47

UML (Unified Modelling Language) Class diagrams 397, 427–8, 512–13, 525

underfitting 235–6

UNDO feature 355

Unicode encoding 31, 32–5

unordered sets 471

unpatched software 148

unsupervised learning 209, 236–42, 248, 269

unwinding 370

user accounting 72

user authentication 71

User Datagram Protocol (UDP) 119–21, 125

user interface 73, 498–500, 510, 520, 523

utilitarianism 185

validation 322

variables 296–304, 360, 401–2

    global/local 330–2

    static/non-static 402–5

verification 322

vertex and pixel data 8

video 5, 46–7, 506, 527–8

view 191–2

virtual local area network (VLAN) 134

virtual memory 68

virtual private network (VPN) 114, 152

virtual reality 277

virtualization 75

viruses 72

visual feedback 75

visual simultaneous localization and mapping (vSLAM) 491–2

Voice over IP 134

volatility 9

VRAM (video RAM) 7

Waveform Audio File Format (WAV) 44, 45

web browsing 133, 355

web development 497–500

web scraping 267

web servers 123, 132, 162

webcam integration 499

weight (neural networks) 255–6

wide area network (WAN) 113

winding 370

wireless access point 119, 161–2

wireless transmission 139–40, 152

workstations, dedicated 211

worms 72

wrapper methods 218, 221

write mode 378, 385

zero-day exploits 148–9

Computer Science for the IB Diploma